MASTERPLOTS II

SHORT STORY SERIES
REVISED EDITION

MASTERPLOTS II

SHORT STORY SERIES
REVISED EDITION

Volume 1
A–Chi

Editor, Revised Edition
CHARLES MAY
California State University, Long Beach

Editor, First Edition
FRANK N. MAGILL

SALEM PRESS
Pasadena, California   Hackensack, New Jersey

Editor in Chief: Dawn P. Dawson

Editorial Director: Christina J. Moose   *Assistant Editor:* Andrea E. Miller

Project Editor: R. Kent Rasmussen   *Research Supervisor:* Jeffry Jensen

Production Editor: Cynthia Beres   *Acquisitions Editor:* Mark Rehn

Copy Editor: Rowena Wildin   *Layout:* Eddie Murillo

Some of the essays in this work originally appeared in *Masterplots II, Short Story Series*, edited by Frank N. Magill (Pasadena, Calif.: Salem Press, Inc., 1986), and in *Masterplots II, Short Story Series Supplement*, edited by Frank N. Magill and Charles E. May (Pasadena, Calif.: Salem Press, Inc., 1996).

∞ The paper used in these volumes conforms to the American National Standard for Permanence of Paper for Printed Library Materials, Z39.48-1992 (R1997).

Library of Congress Cataloging-in-Publication Data

Masterplots II : Short story series / editor Charles May. — Rev. ed.
     p. cm.
     Includes bibliographical references and index.
     ISBN 1-58765-140-8 (set : alk. paper) — ISBN 1-58765-141-6 (vol. 1 : alk. paper) —
     1. Fiction—19th century—Stories, plots, etc. 2. Fiction—19th century—History and criticism. 3. Fiction—20th century—Stories, plots, etc. 4. Fiction—20th century—History and criticism. 5. Short story. I. Title: Masterplots 2. II. Title: Masterplots two. III. May, Charles E. (Charles Edward), 1941-
PN3326 .M27 2004
809.3′1—dc22

2003018256

First Printing

TABLE OF CONTENTS

MASTERPLOTS II

TABLE OF CONTENTS

TABLE OF CONTENTS

PUBLISHER'S NOTE

Masterplots II: Short Stories Series, Revised is one of seventeen members of Salem Press's Masterplots family of literary reference works. Salem's other literary reference works include twelve members of the Critical Survey of Literature family and three miscellaneous sets. In contrast to the Critical Survey sets, which are organized around individual authors, the Masterplots sets are organized around the titles of individual works of literature. The Masterplots sets fall into two complementary groups. The original, or "core," series is the twelve-volume *Masterplots, Revised Second Edition* (1996). It covers more than 1,800 individual works of literature, from the ancient classics to great works of modern world fiction, drama, poetry, and nonfiction. Salem's "Masterplots II" series are designed as companions to the original *Masterplots*. Each Masterplots II set is organized around one of two principles: either a broad literary genre, such as novels, drama, poetry, short stories, nonfiction, and juvenile and young-adult literature, or a category of writers, such as women, African Americans, and American novelists. A representative of the first type, *Masterplots II: Short Story Series, Revised* covers 1,490 short stories by more than 590 different authors. While dividing lines between short stories and "novellas" are not always precisely defined, it should be understood that the goal of this set is to focus on short stories, not novellas or longer forms.

This New Edition

The present eight-volume set is the first true revision of *Masterplots II: Short Story Series*, which was first published in six volumes in 1986. That set covered 729 short stories. In 1996, four supplement volumes covering an additional 511 stories were appended to that set, bringing to ten the total of sequentially numbered volumes. The indexes in the fourth volume of the supplement covered the authors and story titles in all ten volumes; however, no changes were made within the original six volumes themselves. *Masterplots II: Short Story Series, Revised* incorporates all the short-story articles in the earlier ten volumes and adds 250 new articles—for a total of more than 20 percent of entirely new material. None of the stories that are subjects of new articles in this set is covered in any other Masterplots set.

In contrast to Salem's other recently revised Masterplots II sets, *Masterplots II: Short Story Series, Revised* duplicates some of the coverage of the core *Masterplots*. However, this duplication is minor, as *Masterplots* has articles on only five works that are classified as short stories: O. Henry's "The Gift of the Magi," Edgar Allan Poe's "The Gold-Bug" and "Ligeia," Franz Kafka's "The Metamorphosis," and Nikolai Gogol's "The Overcoat." The Editors decided that omitting those classic stories from this set would be a disservice to readers. *Masterplots II: Short Story Series, Revised* is thus the only Masterplots set that readers need consult for critical reviews of short stories. A complete title index appears at the back of every volume.

Content

Readers of *Masterplots II: Short Story Series* will find in its articles penetrating discussions of the content, themes, structure, and techniques of 1,490 stories from every region in the world. While the majority of the stories are by North American writers, 38 stories are by Africans, 56 are by Asians, 60 by West Indians and Latin Americans, 20 by Australians and New Zealanders, 207 by British writers, and 395 by other Europeans. A complete breakdown of story titles by countries and regions is given in the Geographical Index in volume 8.

The chronological range of the stories is also broad. Although the modern short story form is largely a mid-nineteenth century creation, the earliest story covered in this set is Daniel Defoe's "A True Relation of the Apparition of One Mrs. Veal," which was originally published in 1706. The next-earliest story, however, was published nearly a century later: Charles Brockden Brown's "Somnambulism" (1805). The set covers a total of 60 stories from the early nineteenth century and 141 from the late nineteenth century. Most of the 476 stories from the early twentieth century that are covered were published in the 1920's, 1930's, and 1940's. The 812 stories from the second half of the century are more evenly distributed, with the largest share coming from the 1980's. The Chronological List of Titles at the back of volume 8 lists every story in the set in order of its original publication.

Of the 593 different authors whose stories are covered, slightly more than half are represented by at least two stories each in these volumes, and 75 are represented by at least five stories. Nineteen authors are represented by at least ten stories each: Donald Barthelme (12 stories), Ann Beattie (10), Jorge Luis Borges (13), John Cheever (10), Anton Chekhov (18), Nathaniel Hawthorne (11), Ernest Hemingway (15), Henry James (12), James Joyce (12), Franz Kafka (10), D. H. Lawrence (11), Bernard Malamud (10), Katherine Mansfield (11), Alice Munro (11), Flannery O'Connor (11), Joyce Carol Oates (13), Edgar Allan Poe (13), Katherine Anne Porter (11), and Eudora Welty (13). For a complete list of the authors and their covered works, see the Author Index in volume 8. The Bibliography in volume 8 includes a special section on every author represented by at least 5 stories.

The range of genres is also large, encompassing everything from absurdist plots to witty stories. A complete list of stories, arranged by types of plots is one of the indexes in volume 8.

Format of Articles

Arranged alphabetically by story titles, articles average about 1,500 words each in length. Every article is divided into identically headed sections in a format that allows easy access to text discussions:

• *Title:* Title by which the story is best known to English-speaking audiences (any alternative titles are given in the "First published" line below)

• *Author:* Name by which the writer is best known, followed in parentheses by alternative names, if any, and the writer's years of birth and death

• *Type of plot:* Genre, or genres, to which the story belongs

- *Time of plot:* Date or period in which the story is primarily set
- *Locale:* Physical setting of the majority of the story's action
- *First published:* Year in which the story was first published and, as applicable, the story's original English or foreign-language title and the date of its translation into English
- *Principal characters:* Names and brief descriptors of the most important characters in the story, generally arranged in approximately descending order of importance
- *The Story:* Detailed synopsis of the story
- *Themes and Meanings:* Critical discussion of the most important issues that the story raises
- *Style and Technique:* Analysis of such features as plot devices, imagery, and characterizations

Appendices

Three appendices may be found at the back of volume 8:
- *Glossary:* Definitions, many with specific examples, of 135 terms in short-fiction criticism, ranging from *allegory* to *yarn*
- *Bibliography:* Completely updated and annotated entries on more than 50 important studies of the short-story form, followed by unannotated bibliographies on the 75 writers who are the most frequently represented authors covered in this set
- *Chronological List of Titles:* Lists all the stories covered in this set in the order of the earliest dates when they were published

Indexes

Four indexes follow the appendices in volume 8:
- *Title Index* lists all the stories by their best-known titles and includes cross-references from other titles by which they are known, including original foreign-language titles; this index also appears at the back of the other volumes
- *Author Index* lists all the stories under their authors' names and includes cross-references from other names by which the authors are known
- *Geographical Index* lists authors by the countries and world regions from which they come or with which they are associated; many authors are listed under more than one country
- *Type of Plot Index* lists stories by genre categories, such as coming-of-age stories, domestic realism, and mystery and detective

Other Salem Reference Sources on Short Fiction

A collateral member of the Masterplots family, the five-volume *Cyclopedia of World Authors, Fourth Revised Edition* (2004) contains articles on more than 2,200 authors, including many whose works are covered in *Masterplots II: Short Story Series*. Each article lists all the author's major works, presents a short biography, and offers an up-to-date annotated bibliography of studies of the author.

Salem's seven-volume *Critical Survey of Short Fiction, Revised Edition* (2001) contains profiles of 480 short-story writers , as well as 29 broad essays on the history and techniques of short-fiction, writing techniques, and writers of all the world's regions. Its many appendices include lists of major awards. Author profiles in *Critical Survey* differ from the primarily biographical articles in *Cyclopedia of World Authors* in being substantially longer and analyzing each writer's works in depth. These profiles complement articles in *Masterplots II: Short Story Series* by offering focused discussions of about 2,000 individual stories. Like all of Salem's Critical Survey sets, *Critical Survey of Short Fiction* is thoroughly indexed, making it easy to find references to individual story titles.

Acknowledgments

The articles in *Masterplots II: Short Story Series* were written by more than five hundred scholars, whom the editors of Salem Press wish to thank for helping to make this work possible. An alphabetical list of their names, with their affiliations, follows this note. We are also grateful to Dr. Charles E. May, California State University, Long Beach, who served as Editor of both this revised edition and the earlier supplement to *Masterplots II: Short Story Series*. Professor May's expertise in the field of short fiction has enhanced every aspect of this project.

EDITOR'S INTRODUCTION

One of the most curious inconsistencies between literary education and academic research is that while the short story is the most frequently taught literary form in high school and college classrooms, it is also the literary form most ignored and neglected by academic critics and scholars. There are many reasons for this schism: the "bigger-is-better" attitude that prejudices critics in favor of the novel, the old-fashioned notion that the short story is gimmicky and popular instead of serious, and the unquestioned assumption that complex emotions and ideas cannot be treated in the short narrative form.

After having taught and written about the short story form for the past thirty-five years, I am happy to be associated with such rare reference works as Salem Press's *Critical Survey of Short Fiction* and the present *Masterplots II: Short Story Series, Revised*. I greatly value these works for the role they play in healing the rupture between what goes on in the classroom and what transpires on the pages of America's august—but often unreadable—literary journals.

Because so few academic critics take the short-story form seriously, I am pleased to join scholars in *Masterplots II: Short Story Series* who agree with me that the short story *is* important. Their articles provide students with helpful practical criticism about the form and about the writers who find it demanding and satisfying in spite of the odds against it in the publishing world.

The pressure on writers by literary agents, editors, and critics to abandon the short story as soon as possible and do something "serious" with their writing careers—such as writing a novel—is unrelenting. This bias that bigger is better persists in spite of the fact that the faithful few who have ignored it are among the most critically acclaimed writers of the twentieth century: Anton Chekhov, Jorge Luis Borges, Flannery O'Connor, Peter Taylor, Alice Munro, Grace Paley, and Raymond Carver.

The most obvious fact about the short story is that agents and book editors are seldom enthusiastic about taking on collections of short stories—unless their authors are "names" with novels on their résumés or unless they promise to deliver novels in the near future. The fact is that most people prefer not to read short stories. As the popularity of so-called "reality" television makes clear, many people prefer the real to the fictional, especially if the real is highly fictionalized. Only a half dozen or so large-circulation magazines still publish fiction now. *The New Yorker* is at the top of the list, with at least one short story a week. It is followed by *The Atlantic, Harper's, Esquire, Playboy*, and *GQ*, all of which publish perhaps one story a month. Their combined output adds up to only slightly more than one hundred new stories a year that appear in widely circulated publications.

In addition to the stories that appear in wide-circulation magazines, hundreds more appear in such reviews and journals as *Agni, Cimarron, Descant, Gulf Stream, Kalliope, Nimrod, River Styx, Rosebud, Salmagundi*, and *ZYZZYVA*. However, the subscription lists of these so-called "little magazines" are limited mostly to university and college libraries, and their stories are not widely read.

Another problem with short fiction is that most people who do read fiction would rather read novels than short stories. One reason is that most readers want to believe that the characters they read about have lives of their own and must live with the characters long enough to believe that is true. Once readers get started with novels, they become friends, get familiar, and take up residence. By contrast, with a short story, the reader no sooner is introduced to the story than it ends, leaving the reader a bit dazed. A person reading a collection of stories must do this over and over again. Unlike chapters in a novel that tease readers with the illusion of continuity, short stories are constantly and quickly ending. Moreover, the endings of stories—one of the form's most important aspects—are often frustrating in their inconclusiveness. A reader finishing a novel typically closes the book with a satisfied thump and a sense of a big job well done. By contrast, a reader finishing a short story often reacts with a puzzled "Huh?"

Despite the short story's struggle in modern publishing, many teachers continue to find it a most useful form with which to introduce students to the conventions and techniques of prose fiction. However, students searching for guidance in their study of the short story are often frustrated by the lack of good criticism of the form. They find it especially difficult to locate helpful discussions of important recent short stories. For that reason, this revised edition of *Masterplots II: Short Story Series* makes a conscientious effort to cover stories that are reprinted in current high school and college textbooks, even though the stories may have yet to be recognized by academic criticism.

What students will find in *Masterplots II: Short Story Series* is not a substitute for reading an original short story but rather an overview, a context, and a perspective that will make the reading of the story more rewarding. The short story is a deceptively difficult form. Merely because it is small in size does not make it simple to understand. In fact, the contrary is usually true. Short stories often involve a more scrupulous use of language than novels, and they are often more like poetry than prose. In truth, the short story is not a form that comes naturally but one that must be learned in order to be read intelligently. The essays in *Masterplots II: Short Story Series* with their summary overviews of stories, their compact discussions of themes and meanings, and their commentaries on style and technique will not make the reading of the short stories they treat unnecessary. Rather, they will make that reading a genuine interaction with literature's most demanding fictional form.

Charles E. May

CONTRIBUTING REVIEWERS

Brenda B. Adams
Syracuse University

McCrea Adams
Independent Scholar

Michael Adams
*City University of New
York Graduate Center*

Amy Adelstein
Independent Scholar

Kerry Ahearn
Oregon State University

Yasuko Akiyama
University of Iowa

Betty Alldredge
Angelo State University

Candace E. Andrews
*San Joaquin Delta
College*

P. Angelo
*Edinboro University of
Pennsylvania*

Stanley Archer
Texas A&M University

Gerald S. Argetsinger
*Rochester Institute of
Technology*

Edwin T. Arnold
*Appalachian State
University*

Dorothy B. Aspinwall
*University of Hawaii at
Manoa*

Bryan Aubrey
Independent Scholar

S. Badrich
Independent Scholar

Joachim T. Baer
*University of North
Carolina at Greensboro*

Charles F. Bahmueller
*Center for Civic
Education*

Louise S. Bailey
Marshall University

Barbara J. Bair
Library of Congress

James Baird
University of North Texas

Dean Baldwin
*Pennsylvania State
University—Behrend
College*

Jane Lee Ball
Independent Scholar

Thomas Banks
Ohio Northern University

Carl L. Bankston, III
Tulane University

Donna J. Barbie
*Embry-Riddle
Aeronautical University*

James Barbour
Oregon State University

Dan Barnett
Butte College

Henry J. Baron
Calvin College

David Barratt
Independent Scholar

Harold Barratt
*University College of
Cape Breton*

Jane M. Barstow
University of Hartford

Melissa E. Barth
*Appalachian State
University*

Miriam Bat-Ami
*Southwest Missouri State
University*

E. Beatrice Batson
Wheaton College

Margaret D. Bauer
Independent Scholar

L. Elisabeth Beattie
Elizabethtown Community College

Cynthia S. Becerra
Humphreys College

Thomas Becknell
Bethel College

Carol F. Bender
Alma College

Joseph Benevento
Northeast Missouri State University

Robert Bensen
Hartwick College

Chris Benson
Independent Scholar

Joe Benson
North Carolina A&T State University

Mary G. Berg
Harvard University

Anthony J. Bernardo, Jr.
Cecil Community College

Robert L. Berner
University of Wisconsin— Oshkosh

Jerry M. Bernhard
Emmanuel College

Dorothy M. Betz
Georgetown University

Dale B. Billingsley
University of Louisville

Cynthia A. Bily
Adrian College

Margaret Boe Birns
New York University

Nicholas Birns
New School University

Robert G. Blake
Elon University

Pegge Bochynski
Salem State College

Rochelle Bogartz
Independent Scholar

Brinda Bose
Hindu College, Delhi University

J. H. Bowden
Indiana University, Southeast

Robert L. Bowie
Miami University

Kevin Boyle
Elon University

Harold Branam
Savannah State University

Gerhard Brand
California State University, Los Angeles

Jean R. Brink
Huntington Library

J. R. Broadus
University of North Carolina at Chapel Hill

Lawrence Broer
University of South Florida

Keith H. Brower
Salisbury State University

James S. Brown
Charleston Southern University

Stephen G. Brown
University of South Florida

Faith Hickman Brynie
Independent Scholar

Jeffrey L. Buller
Mary Baldwin College

Susan Butterworth
Salem State College

Judith Callarman
Cisco Junior College

Edmund J. Campion
University of Tennessee

Krista Ratkowski
Carmona
*University of California at
Los Angeles*

David A. Carpenter
Eastern Illinois University

John R. Carpenter
University of Michigan

Warren J. Carson
*University of South
Carolina, Spartanburg*

Jerome Cartwright
Utica College

Jocelyn Creigh Cass
Fraser Valley College

Mary LeDonne Cassidy
*South Carolina State
University*

Thomas Cassidy
*South Carolina State
University*

Cida S. Chase
*Oklahoma State
University*

Allan Chavkin
Yale University

Laura Chavkin
Yale University

Dennis C. Chowenhill
*Chabot Community
College*

C. L. Chua
*California State
University, Fresno*

John R. Clark
*University of South
Florida*

Bruce Clarke
Texas Tech University

Julian W. Connolly
University of Georgia

Elizabeth Cook-Lynn
*Eastern Washington
University*

Janice B. Cope
U. S. Air Force Academy

F. A. Couch, Jr.
University of Calgary

Chella Courington
Huntingdon College

Catherine Cox
University of Florida

Don Richard Cox
University of Tennessee

Virginia M. Crane
*California State
University, Los Angeles*

Lee B. Croft
Arizona State University

Marsha Daigle-
Williamson
Spring Arbor University

Donald A. Daiker
Miami University

Richard Damashek
*Calumet College of
St. Joseph*

J. D. Daubs
Independent Scholar

Susan Jaye Dauer
Baylor University

Jo Culbertson Davis
Williams Baptist College

Paul B. Davis
*Truckee Meadows
Community College*

Susan Davis
Measurement, Inc.

Frank Day
Clemson University

A. Bruce Dean
*University of Maine at
Farmington*

Bill Delaney
Independent Scholar

Ann Marie Depas
*Auburn University,
Montgomery*

A. A. DeVitis
Purdue University

James E. Devlin
*State University of New
York at Oneonta*

M. Casey Diana
*University of Illinois at
    Urbana-Champaign*

Carolyn F. Dickinson
Columbia College

Margaret A. Dodson
Independent Scholar

Rosanne Fraine Donahue
*University of
    Massachusetts at
    Boston*

Margaret Hawthorne Doty
Independent Scholar

Sally V. Doud
*Virginia Commonwealth
    University*

Leon V. Driskell
University of Louisville

Sarah Smith Ducksworth
Kean University

Margaret Duggan
*South Dakota State
    University*

Charles Duncan
Clark-Atlanta University

Joyce Duncan
*East Tennessee State
    University*

Gweneth A. Dunleavy
University of Louisville

Ann Edward
Chestnut Hill College

Bruce L. Edwards, Jr.
*Bowling Green State
    University*

Margaret V. Ekstrom
St. John Fisher College

Janet M. Ellerby
*University of North
    Carolina at Wilmington*

Robert P. Ellis
Independent Scholar

Darryl Erlandson
Portland State University

Thomas L. Erskine
Salisbury University

James Feast
*Baruch College, City
    University of New York*

Donald M. Fiene
University of Tennessee

John W. Fiero
*University of Louisiana at
    Lafayette*

Patricia A. Finch
Independent Scholar

Beverly A. Findley
Troy State University

Edward Fiorelli
St. John's University

Gustavo Pérez Firmat
Duke University

Bonnie Flaig
*Kalamazoo Valley
    Community College*

Robert J. Forman
St. John's University

Leslie D. Foster
*Northern Michigan
    University*

Thomas C. Foster
*University of Michigan,
    Flint*

Robert J. Frail
Centenary College

Carol Franks
Portland State University

Thomas B. Frazier
Cumberland College

Edgar Frost
University of Alabama

Mary Pierce Frost
Santa Rosa Junior College

Patricia H. Fulbright
Clark College

Kelly Fuller
*Claremont Graduate
    University*

Constance M. Fulmer
Pepperdine University

CONTRIBUTING REVIEWERS

Frank Gado
Union College

Robert L. Gale
University of Pittsburgh

Ann D. Garbett
Averett University

Greg T. Garrett
Baylor University

Helen S. Garson
George Mason University

Charles J. Gaspar
U. S. Air Force Academy

Betty G. Gawthrop
*Purdue University,
Calumet*

Roger Geimer
*Purdue University,
Calumet*

Marshall Bruce Gentry
University of Indianapolis

Jill B. Gidmark
University of Minnesota

Howard Giskin
*Appalachian State
University*

Jonathan A. Glenn
*University of Central
Arkansas*

Beaird Glover
Independent Scholar

Joseph Gold
University of Waterloo

Marc Goldstein
Independent Scholar

Linda Silverstein Gordon
Worcester State College

Sidney Gottlieb
Sacred Heart University

William E. Grant
*Bowling Green State
University*

James Green
Arizona State University

Gerald R. Griffin
Northeastern University

John L. Grigsby
*Appalachian Research &
Defense Fund of
Kentucky, Inc.*

L. M. Grow
*Broward Community
College*

M. A. Grubbs
University of Kentucky

Drewey Wayne Gunn
*Texas A&M University—
Kingsville*

Charles Hackenberry
*Pennsylvania State
University—Altoona*

Kenneth Hada
East Central University

Angela Hague
*Middle Tennessee State
University*

Donna B. Haisty
Clemson University

Elsie Galbreath Haley
*Metropolitan State
College of Denver*

Cynthia Whitney Hallett
St. Mary's University

Barbara J. Hampton
Independent Scholar

Cathryn Hankla
Hollins College

Natalie Harper
*Simon's Rock College of
Bard*

Gregory Harris
Independent Scholar

Sandra Hanby Harris
*Tidewater Community
College*

Stephen M. Hart
*University College
London*

John C. Hawley
Santa Clara University

David M. Heaton
Ohio University

Peter B. Heller
Manhattan College

Terry Heller
Coe College

Walter Herrscher
*University of Wisconsin—
Green Bay*

Erwin Hester
East Carolina University

Nina Hibbin
Independent Scholar

Roseanne L. Hoefel
Alma College

Dennis Hoilman
Ball State University

W. Kenneth Holditch
University of New Orleans

Hal Holladay
*Simon's Rock College of
Bard*

John R. Holmes
*Franciscan University of
Steubenville*

Joan Hope
Independent Scholar

Glenn Hopp
Howard Payne University

Gregory D. Horn
*Southwest Virginia
Community College*

Eric Howard
Independent Scholar

Ronald W. Howard
Mississippi College

William L. Howard
Chicago State University

Randall Huff
Iowa State University

Linda Humphrey
Citrus College

Theodore C. Humphrey
*California State
Polytechnic University,
Pomona*

Mary Hurd
*East Tennessee State
University*

Susan Hwang
Independent Scholar

Rebecca Dunn Jaroff
Ursinus College

Helen Jaskoski
*California State
University, Fullerton*

Jeffry Jensen
Independent Scholar

D. Barton Johnson
*University of California at
Santa Barbara*

Jeff Johnson
*Brevard Community
College*

Ronald L. Johnson
Independent Scholar

Sheila Golburgh Johnson
Independent Scholar

Michelle Jones
Muskingum College

Myra H. Jones
*Manatee Community
College*

Michael Scott Joseph
*Rutgers University
Libraries*

Albert E. Kalson
Purdue University

Tina Kane
Independent Scholar

Sita Kapadia
*College of Staten Island,
City University of New
York*

Carola M. Kaplan
*California State
Polytechnic University,
Pomona*

Ludmila
Kapschutschenko-
Schmitt
Rider University

CONTRIBUTING REVIEWERS

Cynthia Lee Katona
Ohlone College

Stephen Katz
State Technical Institute at Memphis

Susan E. Keegan
Mendocino Community College

William P. Keen
Washington and Jefferson College

Richard Keenan
University of Maryland, Eastern Shore

Steven G. Kellman
University of Texas at San Antonio

Richard Kelly
University of Tennessee at Knoxville

W. P. Kenney
Manhattan College

Paul Kindlon
University of Illinois at Chicago

Cassie Kircher
Elon University

Susan S. Kissel
Northern Kentucky University

Wm. Laird Kleine-Ahlbrandt
Purdue University

Edgar C. Knowlton, Jr.
University of Hawaii at Manoa

Grove Koger
Boise Public Library

Stephen W. Kohl
University of Oregon

Tom Koontz
Ball State University

James Kurtzleben
University of Northern Iowa

Linda L. Labin
Husson College

Marvin Lachman
Independent Scholar

James B. Lane
Indiana University, Northwest

Michael J. Larsen
Saint Mary's University

Eugene Larson
Pierce College

Donald F. Larsson
Mankato State University

William Laskowski
Jamestown College

Jon Lavieri
Independent Scholar

William T. Lawlor
University of Wisconsin— Stevens Point

Linda Ledford-Miller
University of Scranton

Anne Thompson Lee
Bates College

L. L. Lee
Independent Scholar

Leon Lewis
Appalachian State University

Merrill Lewis
Western Washington University

Anna Lillios
University of Central Florida

Paul R. Lilly, Jr.
State University of New York at Oneonta

Laurie Lisa
Arizona State University

James L. Livingston
Northern Michigan University

Eileen Lothamer
California State University, Long Beach

Michael Loudon
Eastern Illinois University

R. C. Lutz
University of the Pacific

Janet McCann
Texas A&M University

Joanne McCarthy
Independent Scholar

Barbara A. McCaskill
University of Georgia

Mark McCloskey
Independent Scholar

Mary Davidson
McConahay
University of Colorado

Dennis McCormick
University of Montana

Andrew Macdonald
Loyola University, New Orleans

Gina Macdonald
Nicholls State University

William J. McDonald
Baylor University

Ron McFarland
University of Idaho

Edythe M. McGovern
West Los Angeles College

S. Thomas Mack
University of South Carolina, Aiken

Joseph McLaren
Hofstra University

John L. McLean
Missouri Valley College

A. L. McLeod
Rider University

Marian B. McLeod
Trenton State College

Jim McWilliams
Southern Illinois University at Carbondale

David Madden
Louisiana State University

David W. Madden
California State University, Sacramento

Paul D. Mageli
Independent Scholar

Maria Theresa Maggi
University of Idaho

Annette M. Magid
Erie Community College

Edward A. Malone
Missouri Western State College

Philip Maloney
University of Montana

Martha Manheim
Siena Heights College

Lois A. Marchino
University of Texas at El Paso

Peter Markus
Independent Scholar

S. Elaine Marshall
Atlantic Christian College

William Matta
University of Guam

Anne Laura Mattrella
Southeastern University

Charles E. May
California State University, Long Beach

Laurence W. Mazzeno
Alvernia College

Patrick Meanor
State University of New York at Oneonta

Jeffrey Meyers
University of Colorado at Boulder

Walter E. Meyers
North Carolina State University

Vasa D. Mihailovich
University of North Carolina

CONTRIBUTING REVIEWERS

Jane Ann Miller
Dartmouth College

Paula M. Miller
Biola University

Leslie B. Mittleman
*California State
University, Long Beach*

Peter Monaghan
Independent Scholar

Robert A. Morace
Daeman College

Bernard E. Morris
Independent Scholar

Gregory L. Morris
*Pennsylvania State
University—Behrend
College*

Toni J. Morris
University of Indianapolis

William E. Morris
*University of South
Florida*

Robert E. Morsberger
*California State
Polytechnic University,
Pomona*

Sherry Morton-Mollo
*California State
University, Fullerton*

Charmaine Allmon
Mosby
*Western Kentucky
University*

Edwin Moses
Bloomsburg University

James V. Muhleman
Hawaii Loa College

Roark Mulligan
*Christopher Newport
University*

C. Lynn Munro
*University of Missouri—
Kansas City*

Eunice Myers
Wichita State University

D. G. Nakeeb
Pace University

William Nelles
*University of
Massachusetts at
Dartmouth*

Anna B. Nelson
St. Peter's College

Hanh Nguyen
*University of California at
Riverside*

Terry Nienhuis
*Western Carolina
University*

John Nizalowski
Mesa State College

Gisela Norat
Agnes Scott College

Emma Coburn Norris
Troy State University

George T. Novotny
*University of South
Florida*

Peter West Nutting
Colby College

George O'Brien
Georgetown University

Rafael Ocasio
Agnes Scott College

J. D. O'Hara
University of Connecticut

I. T. Olken
University of Michigan

Bruce Olsen
Alabama State University

Brian L. Olson
*Kalamazoo Valley
Community College*

William O'Rourke
University of Notre Dame

Sylvia G. O'Sullivan
University of Maryland

Coilin Owens
George Mason University

Robert J. Paradowski
*Rochester Institute of
Technology*

Joyce M. Parks
Independent Scholar

David B. Parsell
Furman University

Jay Paul
*Christopher Newport
University*

D. G. Paz
University of North Texas

Thomas R. Peake
King College

David Peck
*California State
University, Long Beach*

William E. Pemberton
*University of Wisconsin—
La Crosse*

Leslie Maile Pendleton
Independent Scholar

Robert C. Petersen
*Middle Tennessee State
University*

Marion Boyle Petrillo
Bloomsburg University

Lela Phillips
Andrew College

Karen A. Pinter
*Sauk Valley Community
College*

Marjorie Podolsky
*Pennsylvania State
University—Behrend
College*

Leonard Polakiewicz
University of Minnesota

Patricia A. Posluszny
Francis Marion College

David Powell
*Western New Mexico
University*

Verbie Lovorn Prevost
*University of Tennessee at
Chattanooga*

Cliff Prewencki
Independent Scholar

Victoria Price
Lamar University

Norman Prinsky
Augusta State University

Charles H. Pullen
Queen's University

Rosamond Putzel
Temple University Library

David J. Quinn
University of Hawaii

Josephine Raburn
Cameron University

Sanford Radner
Montclair State College

Tony Rafalowski
*Western Kentucky
University*

Victor J. Ramraj
University of Calgary

K. S. Narayana Rao
*University of Wisconsin—
Oshkosh*

R. Kent Rasmussen
Independent Scholar

Abe C. Ravitz
*California State
University, Dominguez
Hills*

John D. Raymer
Holy Cross College

Bette Adams Reagan
*Kutztown University of
Pennsylvania*

Michael D. Reed
Pan American University

Rosemary M. Canfield
Reisman
*Charleston Southern
University*

Ann E. Reynolds
Independent Scholar

Richard Rice
*University of Tennessee at
Chattanooga*

Constance Sherak
Connecticut College

Nancy E. Sherrod
*Georgia Southern
University*

Agnes A. Shields
Chestnut Hill College

Thelma J. Shinn
Arizona State University

T. A. Shippey
St. Louis University

Wilma J. Shires
Cisco Junior College

R. Baird Shuman
*University of Illinois at
Urbana-Champaign*

Anne W. Sienkewicz
Independent Scholar

Charles L. P. Silet
Iowa State University

Karin A. Silet
*University of California at
Berkeley*

Rennie Simson
Syracuse University

Armand E. Singer
West Virginia University

Carl Singleton
Fort Hays State University

Silvio Sirias
*Appalachian State
University*

Jan Sjåvik
University of Washington

Genevieve Slomski
Independent Scholar

Nick David Smart
College of New Rochelle

Marjorie Smelstor
*University of Missouri—
Kansas City*

Gilbert Smith
*North Carolina State
University*

Pamela J. Olubunmi
Smith
*University of Nebraska at
Omaha*

Ira Smolensky
Monmouth College

James Smythe
Pepperdine University

Katherine Snipes
Independent Scholar

Jean M. Snook
*Memorial University of
Newfoundland*

Stephen Soitos
*University of
Massachusetts*

Nancy Sorkin
*Philadelphia College of
Textiles*

George Soule
Carleton College

Scott M. Sprenger
Brigham Young University

Michael Sprinker
*State University of New
York at Stony Brook*

Brian Stableford
King Alfred's College

James A. Stanger
*University of California at
Riverside*

Isabel B. Stanley
*East Tennessee State
University*

Joshua Stein
Los Medanos College

Judith L. Steininger
*Milwaukee School of
Engineering*

Larry L. Stewart
The College of Wooster

Ingo R. Stoehr
Kilgore College

Louise M. Stone
Bloomsburg University

Gerald H. Strauss
Bloomsburg University

CONTRIBUTING REVIEWERS

Mary J. Sturm
Independent Scholar

James Sullivan
*California State
 University, Los Angeles*

David Sundstrand
*Association of Literary
 Scholars & Critics*

Roy Arthur Swanson
*University of Wisconsin—
 Milwaukee*

Susan Elizabeth Sweeney
Holy Cross College

Sheila Ortiz Taylor
Florida State University

Terry Theodore
*University of North
 Carolina at Wilmington*

Julie Thompson
Independent Scholar

Lou Thompson
Texas Woman's University

Traci S. Thompson
*Hardin-Simmons
 University*

Jonathan L. Thorndike
Belmont University

Tiffany Elizabeth Thraves
*Randolph-Macon
 Woman's College*

Zacharias P. Thundy
*Northern Michigan
 University*

Jonathan Tittler
Cornell University

Michael Trussler
University of Regina

Richard Tuerk
*Texas A&M University—
 Commerce*

Lewis W. Tusken
*University of Wisconsin—
 Oshkosh*

Shelly Usen
Independent Scholar

George W. Van Devender
*Hardin-Simmons
 University*

Dennis Vannatta
*University of Arkansas at
 Little Rock*

A. M. Vazquez-Bigi
University of Tennessee

Michael Verdon
Independent Scholar

Constance Vidor
Cathedral School

Jon S. Vincent
University of Kansas

Jennifer Vinsky
*California State
 University, Chico*

Mary E. Virginia
Independent Scholar

Ka Ying Vu
*California State
 University, Fresno*

Albert Wachtel
Pitzer College

J. M. Walker
*State University of New
 York at Geneseo*

Kathryn A. Walterscheid
*University of Missouri—
 St. Louis*

Qun Wang
*California State
 University, Monterey
 Bay*

Gladys J. Washington
Texas Southern University

Jane B. Weedman
Texas Tech University

Manfred Weidhorn
Yeshiva University

James M. Welsh
Salisbury State University

Thomas Whissen
Wright State University

Terry White
Salem College

Bruce Wiebe
Independent Scholar

Barbara Wiedemann
*Auburn University,
Montgomery*

Albert E. Wilhelm
*Tennessee Technological
University*

Thomas Willard
University of Arizona

Donna Glee Williams
*North Carolina Center for
the Advancement of
Teaching*

Ora Williams
*California State
University, Long Beach*

Tyrone Williams
Xavier University

Judith Barton Williamson
*Sauk Valley Community
College*

Resa Willis
Drury College

Jerry W. Wilson
Mount Marty College

John Wilson
Independent Scholar

Michael Witkoski
*University of South
Carolina*

Susan Wladaver-Morgan
Independent Scholar

Pat M. Wong
Binghamton University

Philip Woodard
National University

Robert E. Yahnke
University of Minnesota

Scott Yarbrough
*Charleston Southern
University*

Clifton K. Yearley
*State University of New
York at Buffalo*

Mary Young
The College of Wooster

Rhona E. Zaid
Independent Scholar

Laura M. Zaidman
*University of South
Carolina, Sumter*

Weihua Zhang
*Savannah College of Art
and Design*

Gay Pitman Zieger
*Santa Fe Community
College*

Laura Weiss Zlogar
*University of Wisconsin—
River Falls*

MASTERPLOTS II

SHORT STORY SERIES
REVISED EDITION

A & P

Author: John Updike (1932-   )
Type of plot: Coming of age
Time of plot: The 1950's
Locale: A small coastal town near Boston
First published: 1961

> *Principal characters:*
> SAMMY, a nineteen-year-old checker at the A & P
> LENGEL, the middle-aged manager of the supermarket
> THREE GIRLS, unnamed teenagers from the nearby summer beach
>   colony

The Story

"A & P" is a short initiation story in which the young protagonist, in a gesture of empty heroism, quits his job at the supermarket because the manager has embarrassed three girls—and learns just "how hard the world was going to be to him hereafter."

Most of the action in the story takes place in the short time Sammy stands at his cash register on a summer afternoon watching three girls from the nearby beach colony, dressed in "nothing but bathing suits," wander the store in search of a jar of "Fancy Herring Snacks in Pure Sour Cream." By the time the three reach his checkout stand, Sammy is halfway in love with their leader, a girl he nicknames "Queenie," who has "nothing between the top of the suit and the top of her head except just her." Sammy is attracted to the girl not only by her physical beauty but also by her regal bearing and by her clear disdain for small-town mores. Sammy is highly sensitive to the class differences between "the Point," where the three are apparently vacationing ("a place from which the crowd that runs the A & P must look pretty crummy"), and the supermarket where he works (where "houseslaves in pin curlers" push shopping carts up and down the aisles, followed by squalling children).

Sammy's fantasies are rudely interrupted when Lengel, the officious supermarket manager (and Sunday school teacher), notices and reprimands the girls for their dress: "We want you decently dressed when you come in here." Queenie blushes, and Sammy jumps to their defense in the only way he can: "I say 'I quit' to Lengel quick enough for them to hear, hoping they'll stop and watch me, their unsuspected hero." They do not, and Sammy is left to confront Lengel. "You didn't have to embarrass them," he says. Lengel explains, in defense of the town's provincial mores, "It was they who were embarrassing us." Lengel reminds Sammy that his impulsive action will hurt his parents and that he will "feel this" for the rest of his life, but Sammy is trapped by his own chivalric gesture, and by the romantic code of which it is a part and by which he swears: "It seems to me that once you begin a gesture it's fatal not to go through with it." Remembering how Lengel "made that pretty girl blush," Sammy punches "the No Sale tab" on his register and walks out into the hot and empty parking lot.

Themes and Meanings

On its simplest level, "A & P" is a humorous adventure story, in which a young protagonist acts in the name of romantic love—and pays the price. The optimistic reader may feel that a sensitive hero has been freed from a dead-end job and a restrictive moral code, but a more realistic response will also recognize that Sammy's act has left him in a kind of limbo: He now belongs neither to the world of Lengel and his parents (because he has quit the job they hoped he would keep) nor to the world the girls represent and to which, through his romantic gesture, he aspires. Like Sarty in William Faulkner's "Barn Burning" (another story about a young boy acting against his parents), Sammy's act takes him, not from one world to another but to a place in between—and nowhere.

Like so many short stories, both European and American, "A & P" is primarily a story of initiation, as a young boy moves from innocence (and ignorance) to experience (and knowledge). Like the young boy in James Joyce's "Araby," perhaps the quintessential initiation story, Sammy has gained some knowledge (through what Joyce called an "epiphany" or revelation) both of himself and of adulthood, but he has also discovered "how hard the world was going to be" to those who cling to their romantic notions about life. Lacking as yet the maturity to accept compromise or to live with the world's injustices, this noble and still uncorrupted youth has acted rashly and lost everything, except perhaps himself. The reader implicitly feels that Sammy's initiation into the adult world will continue long after this short story is over.

Short as it is, the story has a number of classical overtones. Like the hero in an Arthurian legend, Sammy is on a romantic quest: In the name of chivalry, he acts to save the "queen" (and her two consorts) from the ogre Lengel. At the same time, Sammy is tempted by the three Sirens from "the Point" and rejects his mentor (or older guide), Lengel, to follow them; from this perspective, Sammy's initiation comes when he recognizes the futility of this quest and returns to Lengel, who presents him with the truth. Such mythical possibilities point up the richness of John Updike's prose.

There are also sociopsychological implications in this initiation story. Although Sammy defends the three girls against the provincial morality of Lengel and the town ("Poor kids, I began to feel sorry for them, they couldn't help it"), it is only Sammy who holds to the outmoded romantic code; the three girls ignore him. Sammy, in other words, is a working-class "hero" defending a privileged upper class that does not even acknowledge his existence. In the medieval romance, all the characters were aristocratic. Here Sammy loses his job because of romantic notions to which only working-class characters, apparently, still subscribe.

Style and Technique

Style is meaning in "A & P." The story opens abruptly—"In walks these three girls"—and maintains that vernacular, conversational, ungrammatical voice throughout its 250 lines. The point of view is strictly Sammy's and, although tense shifts occasionally from past to historical present (as it would in such a retelling), Sammy's voice has an authenticity and immediacy that is matched in very few twentieth century stories. That voice can be both pedestrian ("I thought that was so cute") and poetic (as when Sammy describes Queenie's bare upper chest as "a dented sheet of metal tilted in the light").

Sammy's voice is also explicitly humorous. When he first sees the girls, he cannot remember whether he has rung up the box of HiHo crackers under his hand.

> I ring it up again and the customer starts giving me hell. She's one of these cash-register watchers, a witch about fifty with rouge on her cheekbones and no eyebrows, and I know it made her day to trip me up. She's been watching cash registers for fifty years and probably never seen a mistake before.

When Lengel tells the girls, "this isn't the beach," it strikes Sammy as humorous, as if the thought had just occurred to Lengel, "and he had been thinking all these years the A & P was a great big dune and he was the head lifeguard."

All the characters, in Sammy's language, become animals: Lengel is about to "scuttle" crablike into his office when he first sees the girls; the other customers group like "sheep" and "pigs in a chute" when they see the trouble at the front register; the three girls "buzz" to one another, like a queen bee and her two drones. Sammy's voice, his humor, and his detailed descriptions of the supermarket setting undercut the implicitly romantic and sentimental situation of the story.

What Updike has achieved in "A & P" is a story of richness and ambiguity. The girls and Lengel argue the meaning of "decent," for example, and the word reverberates with socioeconomic import; Sammy jumps to the defense of the girls, but he has earlier shown that his attitude toward the dress code is similar to Lengel's ("You know, it's one thing to have a girl in a bathing suit down on the beach").

"A & P" works well as a story because the tone, the language, and the point of view are so appropriate to and consistent with the subject. Updike, in writing a seriocomic story on the common theme of initiation, has achieved a small masterpiece through a rich, supple prose that conveys the story's comic tragedy through its very language and imagery.

David Peck

ABLE, BAKER, CHARLIE, DOG

Author: Stephanie Vaughn (1943-   )
Type of plot: Domestic realism
Time of plot: The 1950's to 1960's
Locale: New York, Ohio, and the Philippines
First published: 1978

> *Principal characters:*
> GEMMA JACKSON, the narrator
> ZACHARY JACKSON, her father, a military officer and later a
>   hardware salesperson
> HER MOTHER
> HER GRANDMOTHER

The Story

Gemma Jackson describes her relationship with her father, Zachary, a military man who after being forced to leave the service started a career in the hardware business. The story is a collection of scenes from Gemma's childhood that explain how her alcoholic father dealt with her and other members of the family.

The opening vignette takes place at Fort Niagara, a military post to which Gemma's father, an air defense officer, is assigned. The twelve-year-old Gemma sits at home with her mother and grandmother, who have prepared lunch only to watch it spoil because her father is late. The conversation between the older women makes it clear to the reader, if not to Gemma, that tension exists between the adults in the house. After her father arrives, lunch is like many other meals in the Jackson home: Over his wife's protests, Zachary uses the time to teach his daughter lessons he believes she will need as an adult. On this day, he lectures Gemma on proper speaking etiquette.

Gemma then recounts how her father taught her another lesson when she was only five and the family was living in Manila. Ignoring an approaching typhoon, the elder Jackson drilled his daughter on the military system for reciting the alphabet, which designates letters with words, beginning with "Able," "Baker," "Charlie," and "Dog." Again, the tension between her mother and father is evident in a conversation that Gemma relates without authorial commentary.

A year later, after the family's return to the United States, Gemma's lessons continued. Her father spoke to her about a variety of topics that she did not then comprehend, but in retrospect, she remembers that they demonstrated her father's wide-ranging interests. Ironically, when he was assigned to remote areas without his family, Gemma found herself unable to write to him; in retrospect, she realizes how much his physical presence meant to her.

Returning to the time when she was twelve, Gemma recounts additional details about the family's life at Fort Niagara. The installation has a stately beauty that even the grandmother, no admirer of her son-in-law, found breathtaking. Gemma's father teaches her the history of the region and the significance of the fort in U.S. history. The highlight of his assignment, however, is a trip to Niagara Falls. Gemma is mesmerized by the falls, and her father enhances the experience by relating stories of several men who had attempted to travel over the falls in various contraptions.

Shifting the focus from her relationship with her father, Gemma relates her own fear and embarrassment at going through puberty. The development of her breasts has come unexpectedly to her, and she becomes convinced she had cancer. Her mother intervenes to save her from further angst, however, by explaining that the pain she feels is normal. Relieved, Gemma goes to bed, only to wake up in the middle of the night and overhear an argument between her parents. She hears her grandmother encouraging her mother to leave her father, who had become belligerent. Gemma vaguely realizes that her parents are fighting over a bottle of scotch. The girl's presence has a calming effect on the adults, and the fight dissipates. Later that evening, however, Gemma hears her father going out, and she follows him to the edge of the Niagara River. Although she pleads with him not to go any farther, he descends the bank and walks onto the ice.

In the next vignette, however, it becomes apparent that Zachary returned from his trek unharmed, and Gemma relates the cause of the next family problem. Zachary is passed over for promotion and is forced to resign from the military service and seek another position. The family moves to Ohio, where Zachary invests in a chain of hardware stores. His penchant for learning new things makes him successful in this business, but the family tensions continue all through Gemma's high-school years. The lessons continue, and even when she goes away to college, her father calls to share his wisdom with her.

While Gemma is away pursuing her master's degree, she is called home to be with her dying father. Standing beside his grave, Gemma realizes that she will have to carry on with the wisdom he has already imparted to her.

Themes and Meanings

As a story of parental love for a child, "Able, Baker, Charlie, Dog" ranks among some of the finest tales in American literature. The bond between the rigid, dogmatic polymath Zachary Jackson and his daughter Gemma is genuine: He is concerned about her welfare and her future, and she is devoted to him and appreciative of his interest in her. Even in the vignettes relating her experiences as a teenager, she grudgingly accepts the tutelage he offers because she somehow senses its importance not only to her but also to him.

Gemma's relationship with her father stands in stark contrast to that between Zachary and the adult women in the household. Because she is a child, Gemma seldom realizes the extent to which tension is building in the Jackson home. She is aware that her grandmother does not respect her father, and that her mother is frequently protective of him. Not until she is twelve, however, does she realize that alcoholism is at the root of the family's discord. Only obliquely do readers come to realize that the father's dependence on alcohol costs him his military career and creates constant strain within the family. Also, because Gemma brings only a child's perspective to her observations of family relationships, readers are left to imagine how her mother manages to stay with a man gradually consumed by the disease of alcoholism.

What is especially noteworthy is that Stephanie Vaughn does not paint Zachary Jackson as a bad man. Rather, readers are given a portrait of a genuinely good man, intensely devoted to his work and to his family, intent on seeing his daughter succeed in life. It is almost impossible to judge him a failure, even though his constant drinking causes him and his family tremendous pain. Through her portrait of Gemma's father, Vaughn demonstrates how individuals can be good people although they are alcoholics.

Style and Technique

Vaughn tells her story through a series of discrete vignettes, focusing more on the creation of mood and the study of character than on the development of plot. As a consequence, readers will find that they are required to piece together portraits of the Jackson family from the episodes related through the eyes of the narrator. Furthermore, because Vaughn has Gemma relate the events as she witnessed them as a child, readers must imagine many of the emotions being felt by the adults in these scenes.

By using first-person narration, Vaughn powerfully conveys the strong bond between Gemma Jackson and her father. Employing reminiscences, she has Gemma relate key childhood events that reveal how important her father was to her as she was growing up. One might wonder, however, why Vaughn inserts the story of Gemma's distress over her development of breasts; the segment reminds readers that the story is really about Gemma, not Zachary, and this is one event in her life for which she had to turn to her mother for help. Whether this suggests that Gemma was oblivious to her mother's influence throughout her life is left to speculation.

What is clear is that the narrator has learned her lessons well, because the story she tells of her relationship with her father is related with precision and insight, two of the qualities Zachary wished his daughter to develop. Vaughn herself reflects exceptional ability to reflect on childhood experiences and to provide readers insight into the world of a child caught in a web of complex relationships with people who, despite their weaknesses, are admirable role models because they are complex human beings.

Laurence W. Mazzeno

ABSOLUTION

Author: F. Scott Fitzgerald (1896-1940)
Type of plot: Realism
Time of plot: The early twentieth century
Locale: A small town in the Dakotas
First published: 1926

Principal characters:
RUDOLPH MILLER, the protagonist, a boy of eleven
CARL MILLER, his father, a freight agent
FATHER ADOLPHUS SCHWARTZ, a priest of Rudolph's parish

The Story

"Absolution" begins with Rudolph Miller's visit to Father Schwartz's room to reveal to the priest a terrible sin that Rudolph has committed and that is retold along with the events following it in a flashback. One Saturday afternoon Rudolph's father, a devout Catholic, orders him to go to confession. In the confessional, Rudolph recites to Father Schwartz a list of minor sins, reflecting his romantic, imaginative nature as when he says that he believed he was too good to be the real son of his parents. He also tells the priest that he never lies, which is itself a lie. Rudolph does not realize this until his confession is nearly over and he is unable to confess this sin before the priest closes the confessional slat. Rather than feeling guilty, Ralph takes refuge, as at other times, in daydreams in which he is the debonair Blatchford Sarnemington.

With such a sin on his conscience, Rudolph must avoid going to communion the next day, so he resolves to drink a glass of water "accidentally" before going to church because, under the Catholic law of the time, this prevents him from going to communion. Thus, early Sunday morning he sneaks into his kitchen to drink a glass of water and lend his story verisimilitude, when he is surprised by his father, Carl, just before he can put the glass to his lips. Seeing Rudolph about to disregard a religious injunction for no apparent reason, Carl verbally abuses his son and then beats him as punishment for defiantly throwing the glass into the sink. This is not an uncommon occurrence between the frustrated Carl and his willful son.

As they enter the church, Carl forces Rudolph to go to confession for his offense that morning, thus providing Rudolph with the opportunity to confess to lying so that he can go to communion with an easy conscience. Instead, Rudolph enters the confessional and lies a second time. This deliberate violation of religious practice marks a turning point in Rudolph's life: "The pressure of his environment had driven him into the lonely secret road of adolescence." A greater self-confidence enters him and he begins to recognize his own daydreams and ambitions. Ironically, Carl, seeing his son come back from confession, begins to regret his anger toward the boy. Rudolph receives communion with great trepidation and afterward believes that he is damned.

Whereas the rest of the communicants are alone with God, Rudolph is alone with himself. He resolves to confess his sins to Father Schwartz the next day.

This brings the story back to its beginning: The reader now knows the events that Rudolph has been telling the priest. Father Schwartz, instead of giving conventional comfort or admonishing the boy, begins to speak in a strange fashion about parties and amusement parks and how "when a whole lot of people get together in the best places things go glimmering all the time." At first the priest's chaotic mumblings frighten Rudolph, but then he realizes that Father Schwartz is simply expressing his own romantic, imaginative longings. However, Father Schwartz also warns Rudolph not to become too closely involved with these beautiful things, "because if you do you'll only feel the heat and the sweat and the life." Father Schwartz collapses under the strain of releasing his own feelings to the boy. Rudolph, terrified, runs out of the rectory with his sins absolved in a strange fashion.

Themes and Meanings

The principal theme of "Absolution" is the conflict between the conventional world and the romantic imagination, a conflict that runs throughout F. Scott Fitzgerald's fiction. Indeed, this story was originally written as the prologue to *The Great Gatsby* (1925), with the young Gatsby as the central character; this plan was discarded, and the story was altered and published separately. Thus, the novel informs the story, adding an extra dimension to this tale of a young boy's coming to terms with his fantasies.

Rudolph Miller is a romantic dreamer of the type often found in Fitzgerald's fiction. He creates for himself a daydream existence in which he is Blatchford Sarnemington and not the son of a frustrated, ineffectual railroad clerk, living in a small Midwestern town. This is a form of escape, of avoiding responsibility, or so Rudolph originally believes, for his religious tradition and his father have told him that these fictions are lies. However, the events of the story lead him to a kind of "absolution" for his sins.

Lying plays an integral part in this story. Rudolph's first sin is to lie to his confessor about never telling lies. Next he lies to his father about drinking water, and finally he lies a second time in the confessional. Lying is conventionally seen as evil, but Fitzgerald treats it paradoxically, saying that Rudolph is a habitual liar with a great respect for the truth. Fitzgerald sees lying as part of the romantic imagination, the ability to see things greater than the common and everyday. Rudolph realizes that his lies in the confessional were a way of making life seem grander. When Father Schwartz tells him about the glories of an amusement park, this affirms that there does exist a world outside Catholic theology and Midwestern small-town life. Father Schwartz himself has great longings, but they have been sublimated to his duties as a priest. Rudolph's confession, however, raises his feelings to an uncontrollable level, and he has a nervous breakdown—the fate of a romantic nature that has denied itself. Carl Miller has also suppressed his romantic dreams into an intense Catholicism, as well as hero-worship of railroad magnate James J. Hill, so that he must take out his frustrations on his son. Rudolph comes to believe that his "unrealistic" ideals are not unattainable or evil and that they may eventually be realized.

Fitzgerald, however, does not suggest that the conflict between imagination and reality can be resolved simply by the former's unwillingness to conform to the latter. If Rudolph's romanticism is not foolishness, neither is it a substitute for knowledge of the real world. Rudolph is said to have entered the state of adolescence, not adulthood, and there is no guarantee that as he gets older his confidence in his dreams will not fade away. Moreover, Father Schwartz, while telling Rudolph about the glimmering world, warns him about giving himself wholly over to it because such a world cannot be concrete without coming to terms with "the heat and the sweat and the life." This double vision of involvement in and detachment from romantic idealism is one of the central themes of Fitzgerald's fiction.

Style and Technique

The style of "Absolution" makes great use of detailed descriptions of states of mind, as its central theme is a young boy's entrance into adolescence, a time when the imagination sometimes dominates one's perception of the real world. Rudolph's fear of having offended God for his childish offenses is described as if it were the fear of eternal damnation, for so it seems to Rudolph; similarly, when Father Schwartz's raving confirms Rudolph's faith in imaginative reality, it is presented as an entrance into a world of chivalric glory. These devices provide a sympathetic but detached view of Rudolph's consciousness. Father Schwartz's own consciousness is also dwelt on as an example of the romantic nature that suppresses itself and is continually assaulted by the sensuous world. The story begins, "There was once a priest with cold watery eyes, who, in the still of the night, wept cold tears." The fairy-tale-like opening and lyric, evocative quality of the prose establish the pervasiveness of the romantic imagination in the world of "Absolution."

Fitzgerald also weaves elements of Catholicism throughout the story to suggest that Rudolph, in abandoning his old religion, is entering a new religion of the imagination. The story's title is the formal term for the remission of sins in the sacrament of penance, but here it refers to Rudolph's absolution for the "sin" of romantic idealism. Rudolph's statement that he never lies is seen as an affirmation of "immaculate honor." Thus, the story also suggests the power of Catholicism on the imagination, stylistically presenting unrestrained romanticism and the discipline of organized religion as the two polarities of "Absolution."

Anthony J. Bernardo, Jr.

ACCEPTANCE OF THEIR WAYS

Author: Mavis Gallant (1922-   )
Type of plot: Domestic realism
Time of plot: The late 1950's
Locale: Italian Riviera
First published: 1960

> *Principal characters:*
> LILY LITTEL, a middle-aged English woman living abroad
> VANESSA FREEPORT, her landlady, a widow
> EDITH GARNETT, Freeport's relative and guest, also a widow

The Story

Lily Littel is a rather wilted "Lily-girl" from London, with champagne taste on a ginger-ale budget. Although her name and accent betray humble social origins, she aspires to live like the aristocracy. She lost her working-class husband, Cliff, during World War II, or perhaps simply lost interest in him, and began calling herself "Miss" Littel. She served for eight years as the paid companion of an elderly lady and received a modest bequest in the lady's will. She now spends most of the year in a pensione on the Italian Riviera, which is all that her ginger-ale budget will allow. When her quarterly dividend arrives, however, she goes to Nice on the more fashionable French Riviera to indulge her taste for champagne—indeed any sort of alcohol— because she is a binge drinker. As the story begins, her latest check is in the mail and she looks forward to another getaway. She will pretend to lavish her time and money on a poor sister and will enjoy being missed for a few days.

Mrs. Freeport has been running the small pensione for thirteen years, perhaps to be near the cemetery where her husband is buried. Among her annual paying guests is Mrs. Garnett, a cousin's widow, who is the oldest and wealthiest of the three characters. When Mrs. Garnett requests an Italian meal for the last night of her stay, Mrs. Freeport grudgingly sets the Christmas leftovers to one side. She even serves the wine undiluted. She orders Lily about like a serving girl, and Lily complies. The dinner is a disaster, nevertheless. Mrs. Garnett nibbles at her food and declines the main course. Mrs. Freeport takes offense and accuses her guest of secret eating, which is as bad in their book as secret drinking. She keeps up the insults until Mrs. Garnett faints and must be carried to bed.

After Mrs. Garnett leaves the next morning, Mrs. Freeport breaks into tears, lamenting that she will never see her dear old friend again. Lily replies, quite sensibly, that this sort of behavior has never kept Mrs. Garnett away in the past. Reassured, Mrs. Freeport begins to plan for the next tourist season, when she will make better provisions for her friend. Lily announces her plan to visit her sister and Mrs. Freeport responds politely, but both are too shaken by the day's events to speak more.

Themes and Meanings

Like most British citizens of the period in which this story is set, the three characters are intensely conscious of their social status. The seasonal guest, Mrs. Garnett, gives orders to the landlady, Mrs. Freeport, who in turn gives orders to her regular lodger, Lily. Each follows orders from another but only grudgingly. Mrs. Freeport thinks her late cousin was crazy to indulge his wife, Mrs. Garnett, even to take her for a wife. Lily, meanwhile, thinks that the aristocratic life is her future; she no more wants to go back to work than she wants to go back to Mr. Littel. She is a shrewd observer of the upper class, well aware of its moral shortcomings but not about to let moral shortcomings get in her way. She is learning how to be a subtle cheapskate, just like the other characters.

It is Lily, above all, who makes the "Acceptance of Their Ways" in watching the richer widows and seeing through their ruses but still wanting to share their way of life. Each woman seems to realize that she needs the others: Lily cannot afford Nice for more than a few days each year; Mrs. Freeport cannot afford a servant; and Mrs. Garnett does not have better prospects for the next Christmas season. Each woman also has her secrets. Lily has her diary and her drinking habit; Mrs. Freeport has the gravesite to visit; and Mrs. Garnett has a book on optimism to which she turns when others would engage in conversation. However, they need one another in subtle ways, and so must be accepting.

What these women cannot accept are the ways of the Italian people among whom they live at the moment. Mrs. Garnett is regularly offended by bus drivers and others who try to serve her, and she is constantly offensive in turn. She wants new travel options and is annoyed that the Suez Crisis of 1956 has made travel to Egypt out of the question. Mrs. Freeport hates Italian cuisine, and Lily is more comfortable with the English way of life. Their expatriate world is a narrow world, but as narrow worlds go, it seems a pleasant enough place in which to exist.

Style and Technique

The story begins and ends with Lily, and although narrated in the third person, is told from her point of view. Lily is a shrewd woman, easily the most interesting. Her observations of the others range from envy to scorn and say as much about her as about them. When she forgets about the dinner arrangements for a moment and imagines how much she will be missed when she goes away to Nice, she thinks about the dresses that her landlady will fondly examine in her room and the diary that will be discreetly removed, so that her landlady cannot read its pointed remarks. Mavis Gallant says much about both characters in this brief scene, and more about their relationship; it is typical of her economy with words that all these nuances of character description and dialogue are contained in such a brief story. Like many of Gallant's stories, "Acceptance of Their Ways" first appeared in *The New Yorker*, where it covered four pages with room left for cartoons; it was reprinted in Gallant's collection *An Unmarried Man's Summer: Eight Stories and a Short Novel* (1965).

With her ironic outlook and terse style, Gallant is especially attracted to the oxymoron or contradiction in terms. Lily's past as a paid companion and her present position as a paying guest cast doubt on the companionship and hospitality by placing them within the cash nexus. Lily's manner is characterized at once by bullying and servility, showing her ambivalence toward the other characters. Her eyes look kind when she is plotting mischief. She is generous by nature, but her generosity is overshadowed by an envious admiration for superior women. The very name she goes by, "Miss Littel," reveals some duplicity, for it combines her married surname and her claim to be a spinster, not a widow.

Meanwhile, Mrs. Freeport's pensione smells of "regularly aired decay." The very name "Freeport" is contradictory because her port is not free. Indeed, her name recalls that of Sir Andrew Freeport, the archetypal capitalist in Joseph Addison and Richard Steele's *Spectator* (1711-1712). The ugly evening gets reduced, the next day, to the yogurt affair because Mrs. Garnett prefers fresh yogurt to the old cheese that Lily passes, and because Mrs. Freeport is such a stingy hostess that she quickly takes offense. In her nasty fit, she accuses her guest of making a mess on her plate and leaving a wreck of lettuce.

Along with the economy of phrase, there is an economy of scene and action. The story's first half takes place as a series of thoughts occurring to Lily in the time that it takes her to follow Mrs. Freeport's opening request and serve the cheese. The rest is a consequence. When Mrs. Garnett prefers yogurt to the moldy cheese, Mrs. Freeport takes offense.

As an expatriate writing about expatriates, Gallant describes a provisional life, defined in many ways by absent men: Cliff Littel, Mr. Freeport, and William Henry Garnett. In the brief ending, on the morning of Mrs. Garnett's departure, the remaining characters think for a moment about a world that is not a repetition of the same things. Mrs. Garnett, who looks skeletal when tears wash away her makeup, will die. Miss Littel will move to Nice in order to care for her "sister." Although Lily relished the thought of being missed in this way, she cannot bear the prospect now. She now does the most familiar of tasks to reassert her old position in the house: She straightens the lily on Mrs. Freeport's hat.

Thomas Willard

ACE IN THE HOLE

Author: John Updike (1932-   )
Type of plot: Psychological
Time of plot: The 1950's
Locale: Olinger, Pennsylvania
First published: 1955

Principal characters:
FRED "ACE" ANDERSON, a twenty-six-year-old who prefers to
   relive his high school days rather than to face the present
MOM, his mother, who defends her son against Evey
EVEY, his wife, who is upset about Ace losing another job
BONNIE, their baby daughter

The Story

Ace Anderson is a former star high school basketball player. As the story opens, he is driving home after being fired. Fearing the wrath of Evey, his wife, he finds some consolation in listening to "Blueberry Hill" on the car radio, while he sucks power-fully on a cigarette. Reverting to adolescence, Ace challenges the teenager in the fat car in the next lane, emerging triumphant when his opponent's vehicle stalls. He then decides to stop at his mother's house to pick up Bonnie, the baby. His mother offers him the consolation that he was probably seeking by welcoming his dismissal from a job that had no future. She also states that he and Bonnie are welcome in her house if Evey is too angry. Evey, she suggests, is a wonderful girl, but she is a Catholic and should have married one of her own kind.

When Ace declines his mother's offer, she changes the subject by informing him that his name is in the newspaper. Ace, remembering a former coach's advice about avoiding cars when you can make it on foot, sets out for home at a gallop, with Bonnie in his arms. At home, he indulges in the ritual of combing his hair in an attempt to get the look of Alan Ladd, the popular film star. Worried about Evey's impending arrival, he turns on the television, opens a beer, and finds the newspaper article, which states that a current basketball player has come within eighteen points of the county scoring record set by Olinger High's Fred Anderson in the 1949-1950 season. Ace is angered at being referred to as Fred, however, and the article only increases the tightness in his stomach, which is similar to the pregame jitters of high school days.

When Evey arrives, Ace feigns nonchalance, but she has already heard about the loss of the job from his mother. Ace sees that Evey is in a sarcastic mood ("thinking she was Lauren Bacall," he observes to himself—again, the unreal world of films, television, and popular music provides his frame of reference), and an argument is in-evitable. She states that she is fed up with his stunts. She is ready to let him run right out of her life. He ought to be making his plans for the future immediately.

Ace attempts to divert Evey's anger by turning on the charm and turning up the volume of the radio, which is playing romantic music. The mood of the moment seduces Evey into her husband's arms. As they dance, Ace seems to return to greatness. He imagines his high school friends forming a circle around them; in this fantasy world, he is once more the center of attention.

Themes and Meanings

The major conflict in "Ace in the Hole" is between the juvenile mind of Ace and the business mentality of Evey. Like John Updike's Flick Webb in the poem "Ex-Basketball Player" and Harry "Rabbit" Angstrom in Updike's novels *Rabbit, Run* (1960), *Rabbit Redux* (1971), *Rabbit Is Rich* (1981), and *Rabbit at Rest* (1990), Ace suffers from the former-jock syndrome. He is unable to cope with life after his athletic career is over. The excitement of life during the high school basketball seasons makes everything else seem anticlimactic. There is nothing in the ordinary world of making a living that can compare to being a hero. All of his basketball skills, however, are irrelevant in his current situation. Thus Ace feels uncomfortable, perhaps incompetent, in the job market. In his effort to overcome his feelings of inferiority, he reverts to the past. In his dress, hair style, language, and mannerisms, Ace is still existing in the teenage environment of his days of glory. He is a victim of the emphasis that society puts on sports. Now that he is no longer a sports hero, there is no place for him. He fails to make the adjustment from the realm of a high school star to the business world. Besides Flick Webb and Rabbit Angstrom, Ace is similar, in his predicament, to Christian Darling in Irwin Shaw's short story "The Eighty-Yard Run," and to Tom Buchanan in F. Scott Fitzgerald's classic novel *The Great Gatsby* (1925).

Evey, on the other hand, is concerned with more practical matters—such as why her husband got fired and what he is going to do for employment. She proclaims that he is no longer the most important thing in her life. She has a life of her own, and, if he wants a part in it, he will have to change. There will be no Fred, Junior, in their lives because Ace has trouble adequately supporting one child. Evey's values are centered on money and social position. Because Ace has been a failure in the business world, he is a handicap in her plans for upward mobility. Although Ace lives in the past, she exists in her dreams of the future. There is no room in her world for a loser. At the end of the story, she momentarily yields to Ace's charisma, but she is too obsessed with business to linger for long.

The tension between Ace and Evey, then, is not likely to disappear. Ace's romanticism, involving a glorification of the past, is supported by his mother. She apparently has been overprotective of Ace during his childhood, and she refuses to help make him an adult. Her attack on Evey's Catholicism and her invitation to Ace to move into her house illustrate her disruptive influence on the marriage. Evey is not the right wife for her wonderful son. It is doubtful if any woman could live up to her expectations. Ace's mother consciously puts more pressure on her son's marital situation in an effort to win him back.

The baby daughter also creates added pressure. To the obsessed Evey, she represents the further necessity of economic security. The loss of the job is made more critical by Bonnie's presence. Evey has to work to keep the family solvent, and now her husband has increased the problem. She is saddled with a spiteful mother-in-law and an incompetent husband. Evey does not want to spend her time cooking, baby-sitting, or dancing. She wants to get ahead in what she perceives as the real world.

Ace, who is indeed "in the hole," pulls out one more ace from his deck of tricks to divert Evey's wrath temporarily. However, her version of his domestic responsibilities is still the trump card. Thus, the battle continues.

Style and Technique

Updike is particularly proficient in choosing words and gestures to emphasize the outstanding qualities of his characters. In depicting the immaturity of Ace Anderson, the author uses words that are associated with the teenage milieu of about 1950. Ace feels crowded by Evey and his mother. He feels threatened by the teenager in the next lane and calls him a miserable wop. When he tries to turn on the charm, Evey becomes "Baby." In his view, it is not his fault that he was fired. In the lingo of the jock, Ace calls attention to the terrific hands of Bonnie, claiming that she is a natural.

Ace resembles a teenager, too, in his gestures. He flicks on the radio and beats time to the popular song. He sucks on a cigarette and snaps the match out the window, scoring two points in the perennial basketball game in his mind. He runs from his mother's house to his own with Bonnie in his arms. Ace makes a ritual out of combing his hair. He whips it back and flips it out of his eyes. He seizes Evey and spins her into a dance routine in the concluding scene. He is continually in motion, as if his physical activity will conquer the strength of Evey, who prefers to see his energy channeled into the proper course of making money. Thus, the details of the story unobtrusively work together to create a coherent pattern of imagery.

Noel Schraufnagel

ACROSS THE BRIDGE

Author: Heinrich Böll (1917-1985)
Type of plot: Social realism
Time of plot: After World War II
Locale: Germany
First published: "Über die Brücke," 1950 (English translation, 1956)

> *Principal character:*
> GRABOWSKI, the narrator and protagonist, a German who has
> survived the war

The Story

As the narrator Grabowski rides across the railway bridge that was part of his regular three-day-a-week routine ten years before the war, he recalls his earlier life. At that time he worked as a messenger for the Reich Gun Dog and Retriever Association. He had little education, knew nothing about dogs, and had only to transport urgent correspondence, money, and a large manila folder of "Pending Cases" between the Königstadt head office and the Gründerheim branch office.

The trip required crossing the Rhine River at one of its widest points. Although he crossed on a wide four-track railway bridge, the crossing always frightened him. With nothing able to convince him that the bridge was safe, he fixated on the first house on solid ground on the far side, a two-story house just before the town of Kahlenkatten.

On his regular trips to Gründerheim on Mondays, Wednesdays, and Saturdays, he always saw the same woman scrubbing the floor by the windows on his left side. When it was not raining, a young girl would be sitting on the front steps holding a large clean doll, frowning at the train. On his return trips from Gründerheim, he saw the woman washing the windows in the rear of the house, always in a certain order.

Gradually Grabowski became obsessed wondering which windows the woman washed on Tuesdays, Thursdays, and Fridays, when he did not ride past her house. He drew up a cleaning timetable for the week, and from what he had observed on three mornings, tried to fill in the other three mornings and all the afternoons.

So preoccupied was he with the house-cleaning schedule that on one occasion he forgot to deliver the "Pending Cases" folder and was duly admonished. At first the district manager threatened to fire him, then suddenly became human and instead gave him a day off to sort out his troubles. On that day, a Thursday, Grabowski rode the usual train route four times in each direction, from 8:00 A.M. to 6:00 P.M., and worked out the woman's whole Thursday timetable, which included cleaning the front steps. On his last trip, he also saw a stooped man humbly digging in the garden, watched by the little girl.

The remainder of the story takes place after the war. Passenger cars have been replaced by boxcars, the four-track bridge has been reduced to a one-track temporary bridge that wobbles dangerously. Whereas previously only the narrator feared the crossing, now everyone is afraid, and car after car of passengers falls silent as they leave firm ground and head precariously out over the Rhine.

Only after his car has safely made the crossing does Grabowski suddenly realize that he is on his old familiar route. He wonders if the house is still standing. It is, and is still very clean. Gripped by an indefinable emotion as thoughts of the past rage within him, Grabowski sees a woman washing the steps of the house. It is not the mother now but the daughter, and it is in fact Thursday.

Themes and Meanings

"Across the Bridge" has attracted little critical notice and makes an unostentatious beginning to the twenty-five stories that Heinrich Böll published in 1950 as *Wanderer, kommst du nach Spa* (*Traveller, If You Come to Spa*, 1956). Indeed his narrator introduces the story with the remark that "maybe it isn't really a story at all." Böll offers no interpretive guidelines for the reader. He does not even say precisely what it is that Grabowski feels so intensely: "an indefinable emotion." If indeed "it isn't really a story at all," one is left with an account of a coincidence. Authors frequently have their narrators utter such disclaimers, however. The reader is expected to have more insight into their circumstances than the narrators do, and thus participates in the act of fiction by supplying the ending and its rationale.

If one regards "Across the Bridge" as primarily a contrast of things great and small, then one may see that by taking a second snapshot ten tears later, Böll cleverly inverts their relative positions. Much goes without saying. Reference to the Reich Gun Dog and Retriever Association, for example, suffices to conjure up all that was associated with the Third Reich—which Adolf Hitler claimed would last a thousand years. Böll can afford to understate the irony. Everyone knows the Germans lost the war.

Böll was as disinterested in National Socialism as Grabowski is in the contents of the "Pending Cases" folder that he carries. Böll was the only student in his class who chose not to join the Hitler Youth. From the start, he seemed to understand that the systems thought out by philosophers and politicians and struggled for by armies are transient, and any hope or expectation of a better future that one invests in such works is futile. To Böll the machineries of history and the dicta of those who would change it were ephemeral, treacherous, and capricious. By contrast, a humble house that is occupied continuously by successive generations of the same family has its own rules. The simple acts of sweeping the steps and digging the garden and the daily maintenance of a home and family embody the only values that truly last a thousand years.

Postwar German literature has been dubbed *Trümmerliteratur*, or "Rubble Literature," because it shows how, with almost everything in ruins, it took an extreme effort just to survive, to get food every day, and to keep from freezing in the winters. Against that backdrop, the intact Kahlenkatten house and family in "Across the Bridge" seems to be a miracle.

In 1952 Böll wrote an essay titled "In Defense of 'Rubble Literature,'" which argues that "it is our task to remind the world that a human being exists for something more than to be bureaucratized." "Across the Bridge" does just that. The narrator's obsessive interest is necessary to highlight the small and ordinary tasks and rituals that make up human lives and have more durability than the mightiest empire.

Style and Technique

Böll was able to write in the late 1940's only because his wife's income as an English teacher was enough to support their family. He was aware that he was working with a radically changed language. It was *Stunde null*, the "zero hour." He had to work without and around all the words whose meanings had been changed by Nazi propaganda. Hence his relatively simple, straightforward language and conversational tone. The voice that he uses is that of the common man, and his viewpoint is that of private, personal experience. He narrates in the first person without interpreting. He portrays without preaching. He is kindly. This style and attitude greatly impressed his fellow writers in the Group of 47, although he neither feared their criticism nor sought to win their favor. As a result, he won their prize in 1951, the first of many.

One distinctive feature of Böll's style that is much in evidence in "Across the Bridge" is his tendency to end paragraphs with ellipses. He avoids going into more detail than is necessary, leaving open multiple meanings that may or may not contribute to the advancement of his story. For example, after mentioning the large manila folder of "Pending Cases," Böll ends his second paragraph with the sentence: "Being only a messenger, of course, I never was told what was in the folder. . . ." This ellipsis serves both to characterize Grabowski as uninterested in the Third Reich's bureaucracy, and to let the reader engage briefly in historically based tangential speculations of a more sinister nature.

Although Grabowski's reaction to seeing the familiar house still standing and the girl cleaning its steps is one of positive relief, Böll stops short of making a virtue out of German cleanliness. "It was a clean and yet unwelcoming house." At the end of the story, in fact, the cleaner is given a decidedly negative description. Grabowski recognizes the girl by her "pinched, spidery, frowning face, and in the expression on her face something rather sour, something disagreeably sour like stale salad. . . ." It is ironic that someone who has more than most should seem so dissatisfied and that so mundane a scene should elicit so emotional a response. This is early Böll, who went on to become a superb satirist.

Finally, the title of this story is an important key to its interpretation. Despite Grabowski's fears, he not only safely crosses the Rhine repeatedly before the war but also gets across unscathed after the war, when the makeshift bridge seems no stronger than a thread. Although there are literally two bridges in this story, the bridge of the title is figuratively neither of these structures but rather the ten years that span Grabowski's past and present. Grabowski is one of the Germans fortunate enough to have made it across that bridge. He has reason to rejoice.

Jean M. Snook

ACROSS THE BRIDGE

Author: Mavis Gallant (1922-   )
Type of plot: Domestic realism
Time of plot: Around 1950
Locale: Paris
First published: 1991

Principal characters:
> SYLVIE CASTELLI, the narrator and protagonist, a young woman
> who has not yet left her parents' home
> MADAME CASTELLI, her mother
> MONSIEUR CASTELLI, her father
> ARNAUD PONS, her fiancé
> MONSIEUR PONS, her fiancé's father
> BERNARD BRUNELLE, a young man with whom Sylvie has been
> corresponding
> MONSIEUR BRUNELLE, the father of Bernard

The Story

Sylvie Castelli recalls the time when she and her mother walked together near the Place de la Concorde in Paris. As they cross a bridge, Sylvie shocks her mother by saying that she does not love her fiancé, Arnaud Pons, and that she would rather marry another man, Bernard Brunelle. Madame Castelli questions her daughter, and is misled by Sylvie's vague, diffident answers, which convince her that Bernard Brunelle has written Sylvie a letter proposing marriage. Believing that Sylvie can marry Bernard instead of Arnaud, Madame Castelli impulsively dumps her daughter's wedding invitations into the Seine River.

As Sylvie dreams about a perfect, enchanted life with Bernard, her parents cancel her scheduled wedding and break her engagement to Arnaud. Sylvie's fantasies suddenly collapse, however, when Bernard's father states emphatically in a letter that Bernard has not promised to marry Sylvie and that Bernard has no interest in Sylvie. When Madame Castelli demands that Sylvie show her the letter in which Bernard promises marriage, she realizes that the proposal existed only in Sylvie's vivid imagination. Furious with his daughter, Monsieur Castelli blames his wife for the family's humiliation. He and his wife both believe that they have allowed Sylvie too much freedom, and that had Sylvie been restricted as daughters were a generation earlier, the "fiasco" would never have occurred.

Uncertain what to do next, Sylvie considers putting aside the idea of marriage and going to work instead. There are few career opportunities for women at this time, however, and Sylvie does not know how properly to pursue permanent employment. She drifts through the days until her mother persuades her to have her hair cut and to buy some new clothes. With short hair for women once again fashionable, Madame Castelli thinks that a makeover will make it easier for Sylvie to find a husband.

Madame and Monsieur Castelli approach the Pons family, hoping that Sylvie's former fiancé might mend the broken engagement. Arnaud, who has been working in the city of Rennes, agrees to meet Sylvie for lunch in Paris, where he calmly tells her that he is no longer possessed by passionate feelings of love but still wishes to marry her.

Afterward Arnaud and Sylvie walk together back to the train that will return Arnaud to Rennes. Arnaud, who is conservative with money, wants Sylvie to work after they are married, as his own mother did. He also suggests that after they have children, he will tend the children during the summers, so that Sylvie, an amateur artist, will have time free to paint (an offer that is extraordinary for the time). Shocked at the idea of a man's taking care of children, Sylvie says nothing but thinks slightly the less of Arnaud.

After Arnaud's train leaves, Sylvie decides to walk home, going far out of her way in order to arrive at approximately the same time that Arnaud reaches Rennes. In her mind this binds her to Arnaud. For the first time she begins to think of herself as part of a couple and as an adult woman. In deciding not to tell her parents why she is so late returning home, she subtly but symbolically breaks with her parents.

Themes and Meanings

Of several "bridges" that are crossed by the story's characters, the most important is the bridge between childhood dependence on parents and the adult realm of independent action—a crossing that Sylvie makes at the end of the story. She moves toward adulthood by rebelling against her parents, first by refusing to marry Arnaud and then by choosing Bernard. After she makes clear her preference for Bernard, she avoids showing her mother the letter from Bernard that supposedly contains a promise of marriage. She does this because she does not want to "share" Bernard with her family. In contrast to Arnaud, the son of a family friend, Bernard is someone whom she has met on her own. By rejecting Arnaud and keeping Bernard to herself, Sylvie has a taste of adult independence.

For a female child, the crossing into adulthood also means joining the company of mothers and wives. Some months after her original engagement is broken, Sylvie realizes that mothers conspire to control events. Her mother reveals that she has been privately seeing Madame Pons, who admits that she still wants Arnaud to marry Sylvie. The implication is that the two mothers will subtly pressure their children to reconcile. This conspiracy between women to achieve goals mutually beneficial to their families is necessary because social conditions in postwar France limit their ability to act more openly and directly. Sylvie says that she is ignorant of world events because her father does "not like to see young women reading newspapers." Her family wants her to have a small collection of accomplishments that will increase her desirability as a potential bride—such as the ability to paint attractive watercolor copies of famous artworks. At the same time, her accomplishments should not be too impressive, lest they make her appear needy or plain. Older married women are subject to other restrictions. Madame Castelli, for example, must ask her husband for money because she cannot legally have her own bank account or sign checks without her husband's consent. This legally mandated dependence of women on their husbands makes Sylvie's choice of husband vitally important to her future happiness.

Style and Technique

"Across the Bridge" looks back on the events that lead to Sylvie's marriage. The story is constructed out of her memories, which are surprisingly uncolored by emotion, given the circumstances of her engagement. Sylvie describes what she has thought and done, but her feelings are expressed only in the actions that they motivate. For example, when she is berated by her mother for Bernard's nonexistent proposal, Sylvie remembers that "I put my napkin over my face and began to bawl"; her strong underlying emotions are not otherwise described. The absence of feelings accentuates Sylvie's passivity as a young woman. This passivity makes her not entirely sympathetic as a character; the reader waits for her to take charge, to do something. Ultimately, however, dissatisfaction with Sylvie's inaction distances her from the reader. Such distance is a primary characteristic of Mavis Gallant's fiction, and has been both praised and condemned by critics.

In addition, the veracity of Sylvie's story is suspect because it is reconstructed out of memory. Sylvie tries to assemble a smooth coherent story from her past, and some memories trouble her because she does not know either where to place them or if they are entirely true. She hints that she has pared away the memories that do not connect well with others. Truth in a person's life is not always neat and well contained, however, so Sylvie's story will necessarily be false in places. The combination of the inherent "falseness" of her story together with her highly subjective viewpoint make Sylvie an unreliable narrator.

The story is also a reinvention of the Sleeping Beauty fairy tale, in which the heroine is awakened from a deep slumber that resembles death by a prince who will take her away from the life that she knew as a child. After Sylvie is rejected by Bernard, she feels ashamed and falls into a kind of sleep, drifting through life seemingly without real desire or purpose. In one of the few places in which Gallant provides Sylvie with the memory of actual feelings, Sylvie says that she was waiting for her "true life" to reveal itself. She longs for it passionately but does not see it as something that she can create through her own thoughts or actions. Ultimately this "true life" is provided indirectly by Arnaud, who plays the role of the fairy-tale prince waking the sleeping maiden when he agrees to become re-engaged to Sylvie. It is important to note, however, that this "true life" is something that Sylvie holds inside her, and not a direct gift from Arnaud, even though his action precipitates the internal processes that allow Sylvie to find it. Ironically, this "true life" with Arnaud can only properly begin when both he and Sylvie put aside romantic dreams and fairy tales. Gallant suggests that they can do this at the end of the story, when Sylvie acknowledges the present, and implies that she has had a happy life with Arnaud.

Kelly Fuller

ACROSS THE BRIDGE

Author: Graham Greene (1904-1991)
Type of plot: Psychological
Time of plot: The 1950's
Locale: A Mexican village on the U.S. border
First published: 1949

> *Principal characters:*
>> JOSEPH CALLOWAY, an English millionaire wanted on charges of
>> investment fraud
>> THE NARRATOR, an unnamed foreigner who waits in a Mexican
>> town for a lift to the Yucatán
>> TWO ENGLISH DETECTIVES, who are trying to catch Calloway

The Story

Joseph Calloway, a rich Englishman indicted on investment fraud charges in his own country, has led authorities on a chase through several Latin American countries. He is now taking refuge in Mexico, hoping that its disordered government will make it easier for him to dodge officials. The narrator, an aimless drifter who is passing through a small border town where Calloway is hiding, sympathizes with the tedious boredom that Calloway feels, with nothing to do but sit in the dismal town's square all day.

Each day, Calloway strolls to the bridge that joins the Mexican town with a U.S. town and wistfully looks across the river. On one occasion, he expresses the idea that life begins on the other side; however, the narrator mocks Calloway's view that the other town has more life and excitement than the Mexican town. He knows that it is the same thing over again. The American town even has the same layout; it differs only in having paved streets and taller hotels and in being a little cleaner and much more expensive. On his way back from his walks to the bridge, Calloway routinely kicks the dog that has accompanied him from England as if he is venting some private frustration. Everyone in the town sees everything that Calloway does and knows his entire story, but he is unaware of this.

When two foreign detectives come to the town searching for Calloway, everyone but Calloway knows who they are. People anxiously gather at the town square, watching in amazement as the detectives—who carry only an outdated photograph of their suspect—chat amiably with Calloway over drinks. They all get along well and speak familiarly of their mutual homeland. After the detectives learn that Calloway is the man whom they are chasing, he and they go to Mexico City. The detectives seek an extradition order so that they can arrest Calloway, who wants government protection. Although Calloway is a criminal, the narrator suspects that Mexico has admitted him to the country because his millions have made him a celebrity in this part of the world.

Calloway returns to the northern village on a train; as he rides in a first-class car, the detectives ride in second class. The detectives have not obtained the extradition order that they want, so they try to lure Calloway out of Mexico. They kidnap his dog and take it to the American town, expecting Calloway to come looking for it. The narrator follows the detectives across the bridge to the American town, where he sees Calloway strolling around. It is not clear whether Calloway is looking for his dog or is merely fulfilling his desire to see what lies across the bridge. Unaware of Calloway's proximity, the two detectives chat with the narrator in a nearby store, where he learns that one of them is a dog-lover.

When the dog sees Calloway heading toward the bridge, he bounds after him. The detectives get into their car and chase the dog, which ends up in the middle of the road, dangerously close to the speeding car. The driver—the detective who loves dogs—swerves to avoid the animal and hits Calloway. The mortally injured man throws his arm toward the dog then dies of shock and a weak heart. The detectives believe that Calloway's gesture was a caress, but the narrator thinks it was meant to be a blow.

Themes and Meanings

Typical of Graham Greene's fiction, "Across the Bridge" examines human motives and desires under a surface political intrigue. Like many of his works, Greene infuses this story with a deep sense of religion and morality. In Greene's world, the worst kind of person one can be is the kind that Calloway is: neither truly good nor truly evil but merely petty. Throughout the story, a reader can have little sympathy for Calloway's life or even his death. Although he is a criminal, he does not strike one as evil. His crime is a white-collar crime—merely a manipulation on paper done by a mild-mannered man behind a desk. Calloway is far from being good and generous either. His feelings for his loyal dog can scarcely be called love, as his habit of daily kicking the animal reveals. His ambiguous gesture at the end of the story symbolizes the essence of his character. The detectives like to believe that his thrust of his arm is a loving gesture toward his pet, but the narrator sees it as a hard, spiteful blow. Very likely, the gesture is neither; it is Calloway's very lack of good or evil conviction that makes him so pathetic. His story is laughable when it should be tragic.

The story consistently depicts Calloway as a hapless old man who is easily taken advantage of by a Mexican boy, who cleans his shoes several times a day for money. The fact that everyone in the town but Calloway knows what is going on is another example of his pathetic quality. He appears at his worst, however, when he kicks his dog, "not in anger," the narrator points out, but as if he "were getting even for some trick it had played him a long while ago." Calloway's pettiness gives the story a comic quality. Several times the narrator comments on Calloway's oddly comic nature; he even goes so far as to say that Calloway's death would not make the story less comic.

Many Greene characters are motivated purely by evil, but their stories involve a fall and salvation. Although he often depicts them as evil incarnate, he also makes them sympathetic, preferring the fervor that they embody to the weak-willed and self-deceiving manner of a character such as Calloway. For Calloway, there is no salvation in his death, not even dignity.

Style and Technique

Greene's stories frequently demonstrate a liberal use of irony, providing both a comic turn and poignant message. The irony in "Across the Bridge" is expressed through the personal observations of the narrator, who knows more than the other characters, thus providing the reader with an informed point of view. Through the narrator, the reader can find irony by contrasting what other characters believe and what is actually true. The reader becomes part of the audience in the story who watches Calloway's story unfold. Comic scenes such as that in which the detectives fail to recognize their suspect are made funnier by the presence of the knowing, incredulous audience in the square, of which the reader is a part.

The narrator also expresses the irony in Calloway's dying gesture: What he may mean as a blow is seen by others as a kind, loving motion to his dog. Calloway, who has habitually kicked his dog, is now the loving master reaching out to hold his loyal pet to his very last breath, even though the dog is the key to Calloway's demise. Readers may believe that they know better, but in the final paragraph, the narrator changes his tone. After having looked skeptically on Calloway's "caress," he now concedes that this gesture could actually have been a loving one. Here, the narrator assumes a "humble" position, which for Greene symbolizes the limited knowledge that human beings have.

Although the narrator generally seems to know more than other characters, he is not omniscient. He is simply a third-person limited narrator, who is consistent with Greene's religious beliefs that human individuals cannot know everything. In the final paragraph, the narrator pulls away from assuming that he knows Calloway's true motives behind the ambiguous gesture. He lets the reader think that Calloway was going to hit the dog in that movement but then concludes that it could possibly have been a gesture of love.

This sudden shift in the narrator's view, along with his concluding comments about "a human being's capacity for self-deception," makes the reader aware of an underlying sense of irony that permeates the story. People are self-deceived because they believe that they know or control some part of their future, but this, according to Greene, is laughable in the eyes of God. In the difference between what humans, whether they be ignorant characters or knowing audiences, can know about human life and what only God can know is a comic irony. This larger kind of irony adds a profound religious implication to Greene's story while providing many humorous moments as well.

Susan Hwang

ACT OF FAITH

Author: Irwin Shaw (1913-1984)
Type of plot: Social realism
Time of plot: Summer of 1945, immediately after the surrender of Germany
Locale: France
First published: 1946

> *Principal characters:*
> NORMAN SEEGER, the protagonist, a twenty-one-year-old Jewish
>   sergeant in the U.S. Army
> OLSON and
> WELCH, his friends, both army privates
> SEEGER'S FATHER, an economics professor in Ohio
> CAPTAIN TANEY, Seeger's commanding officer

The Story

The war in Europe is recently over. Sergeant Norman Seeger and his friends, having survived the Normandy invasion at Omaha Beach and the capture of Strasbourg from the Germans, are struggling to collect enough money to enjoy their weekend passes to Paris. Olson and the taciturn Welch hold Seeger in considerable esteem. Seeger has won the Purple Heart at Saint Lo and, despite his youth, Olson affectionately refers to him as *"Mon vieux."* Likewise, both Olson and Welch call him "Sir"; they know that Seeger's noncommissioned status does not warrant the title but believe that his experience and valor do. A remark by Olson reveals that Seeger has saved the lives of his comrades. When a young second lieutenant who is obviously untested by battle passes the three friends, Olson stares him down and offers no salute. It is thus that the two "kids" in the threesome put their trust in Seeger to get a loan against their late pay from Captain Taney.

When Seeger can only put together two hundred francs, the three men are at a loss to locate adequate funds, until Welch remembers that Luger pistols taken from German soldiers are going at nearly premium prices; he can get sixty-five dollars for Seeger's Luger if Seeger will part with it. Both young men recognize that Seeger may not want to surrender the pistol, but they cannot appreciate the value of the Luger to Seeger, who took it from an SS major whom he killed at close quarters in Coblenz. Seeger has five hours in which to measure the value of the weapon against the importance of going to Paris.

As Seeger struggles to make his decision, he receives a letter from his father, who is anguishing over his other son Jacob's break with reality, brought on not so much by the boy's leg wounds taken at Metz as by Jacob's having recently "devoured . . . concentration camp reports." The father cannot dismiss Jacob's fear that a bazooka-armed mob is coming after Jews. He has been experiencing antagonism toward American Jews and indifference to those brutalized in Europe.

The letter unleashes Seeger's repressed memories of his own experiences with anti-Semitism—which he encountered even as soldiers were hitting the beaches at Normandy for the last great assault on Hitler's armies. Most strikingly, he recalls an old Jewish couple who were amazed that he was both a Jew and powerfully armed in the service of their liberation. These memories and the old couple's belief in him and his Garand rifle magnify the burden of selling his Luger. He resolves the dilemma in an ostensibly simple fashion, asking Olson and Welch what they think of Jews. Olson's response and Welch's concurrence end Seeger's turmoil, "Jews? . . . What're they?" This retort helps Seeger to put other memories in perspective, recollections of how his casual pals unhesitatingly put themselves in harm's way for him, risking their lives without question for a friend and comrade in arms. Finally, Seeger gives up the Luger with an ease that masks the agonizing he has gone through: "What could I use it for in America?"

Themes and Meanings

At the heart of this story is the struggle of American Jews, at midcentury, to keep faith with their nation and the ideals of the U.S. Constitution in the face of both German death camps and the U.S. national reaction to what is now called the Holocaust. Soon after World War II, it became apparent that the U.S. government had chosen not to confront the conditions of the German concentration camps or to inform the citizenry of Nazi genocide during the course of the war. Into the bargain, anti-Semitism was virulent in the United States both during and after the war. Irwin Shaw is at pains to reveal the spiritual turmoil and agony of American Jews in the wake of these social currents. He accomplishes this especially by showing his readers that Jews bore their share of suffering in the defeat of fascism and also reminds the reader that anyone who fought in Europe was, during the summer of 1945, a candidate for being shipped to the Pacific war zone for more combat. One must remember that Seeger is one of three sons called to service. His brother Leonard has been killed; he and his other brother, Jacob, have been wounded. Such manifest signs of sacrifice should discredit the anti-Semitism that the living sons and their father have so keenly experienced.

At another level, the story reveals how the young among a class of scapegoats in an ostensibly democratic nation, and especially under conditions of extreme trial, must struggle with the antithetical social messages of this society in order to establish bases of trust and confidence. In order to contain his exhaustion and to enhance his infrequent pleasures, Seeger has buried a long list of hateful messages: They concern the naval officer who would not eat with a Jew; the combat engineer who remarked about Jews' profiting from Europe's agony; the soldier in the PX who said their bayonets were going to be used on the "Yids" when the war ended. At the story's climax, it is memories such as these and their many parallels in his father's accounts that Seeger must overcome if he is to keep faith with the commitment that he has made for four harrowing years. Seeger does not turn to the fine ideals of the Bill of Rights for reassurance but to the clear message of Olson's, Welch's, and Taney's brotherhood with him in combat. His act of faith rests, finally, on their proven disregard for anything but his humanity. This is the faith proper to confronting the bigotry waiting in Ohio for Seeger. The story thus makes a case that even the rich symbolism of a Luger taken from the SS itself is not so powerful as this trust.

Style and Technique

As a conventional slice-of-life story recounted from the third-person point of view, this story has plotting that is adroit but simply linear. The straightforward technique is controlled by the presentation, in evolutionary stages, of the compressed and layered conflict within the protagonist. Shaw plots the story to highlight the subtle texture of this conflict and to embody his theme of faith precisely within its resolution. In so doing, Shaw hooks conflict and theme to several profoundly meaningful objects. Money is entirely positive; it represents nothing more than access to well-deserved pleasure and its enjoyment with genuine friends. It is important that the money stands for something as emotionally and spiritually valuable as the Luger. The Luger, on the other hand, stands equally for access to that fraternity and for Seeger's sense of ongoing security in the face of the death camps. His view of the war has left him with a commitment never to be victimized by any kind of fascist. His is not a pistol picked up idly at a roadside; it belonged to one of those responsible for the camps, a murderer of Jews who was vanquished by Seeger himself. It thus stands for Seeger's personal and ethnic duty. Through it readers see Seeger as an instrument not only of American national integrity but of Jewish justice. The reader should then see its emblematic affinity with Seeger's rifle, which the old Jewish couple so clearly perceived in terms of their liberation. The sale of the Luger is untainted by any interest in financial profit. Rather, it affirms a brotherhood between honorable citizens of a free society and a faith in the capacity of that bond, above even the legitimate use of force, to secure the rights of those endangered in a democracy.

Two complementary objects alluded to in his father's letter serve to increase Seeger's anxiety and the pressure on his confidence in Olson's and Welch's fidelity. The bazookas of Jacob's fantasy are the traumatic extensions of the Luger, the SS, and the death camps into the troubled postwar Jewish-American scene. Jacob's Bronze Star is equally significant; his ambivalent attitude toward it reflects the vacillation within him of hope and despair concerning the meaning of his and his brothers' service to America. The father's despondency and Jacob's tortured relation to these objects push Seeger to the furthest limits of potential disillusionment. It is especially this matter in Ohio that he must set beside Olson and Welch, "who were like his brothers," in the test of his belief in both his service and America's character. His friends have sufficiently more weight in his imagination than his fears of injustice, thus making his choice to sell the Luger "an act of faith."

David M. Heaton

ADAM AND EVE AND PINCH ME

Author: A. E. Coppard (1878-1957)
Type of plot: Fantasy
Time of plot: The early twentieth century
Locale: England
First published: 1921

Principal characters:
GILBERT CANNISTER, a young husband
MILDRED, his wife
JAFFA CODLING, Gilbert's alter ego in his fantasy dream
GABRIEL, the unborn child of Gilbert and Mildred

The Story

The narrative begins in mid-sentence in the reverie of Jaffa Codling, who walks in the English countryside and remarks on the beautiful light, which reminds him of a euphonic name. He enters his garden and sees three children playing, then goes into his house. Upstairs he hears his wife Mildred speaking affectionately to a man. When he looks into his room, he sees his wife caressing a man in a rocking chair. The artificial scene troubles Codling. Why is his wife kissing another man? Why does he himself feel so disembodied?

As the maid brings something to the couple in the room, Codling tries to communicate with her, but she stares through him. When Codling goes outside, the gardener walks through him. Gradually, he realizes that he is a spirit cut loose from his body. As a writer, he realizes he has often tried to plumb the depths of evil in his writing and has felt cut loose from his true self at these moments. Suddenly he feels happy and declares himself a new Adam in an old Eden.

At this moment his three children, Adam, Eve, and Gabriel, come into his view and pester the gardener with questions. Gabriel has a toy sword that the gardener thinks is dangerous as it can cut a lock of Eve's hair. Codling grows more confused. He throws a flowerpot at the gardener that flies right through him and breaks on the ground. As Codling watches his children play, it becomes clear that the youngest child, Gabriel, can see Codling and the spirit of a fish, which the other children cannot see. After the children run off, Codling is left alone with his dreams until Mildred comes into the garden to call him to dinner. His odd manner frightens her.

He goes into the house and picks up a book with his name, "Gilbert Cannister," in it. Suddenly Jaffa Codling and Gilbert Cannister are fused, soul and body. When Gilbert goes with Mildred to see his sleeping children, he is surprised to see only two, not three, and exclaims, "only two." Mildred then confesses that she is pregnant. Gilbert now realizes that he has met the spirit of his third child, Gabriel, in his own spirit form of Jaffa Codling and tells his wife of this unusual happenstance, declaring that the new baby will be named Gabriel.

Themes and Meanings

"Adam and Eve and Pinch Me" seems to suggest that an immense spirit world surrounds the literal world. Gilbert Cannister is a professional writer who is used to delving into the psyches of his characters. The story describes an out-of-body experience in which he is forced to plumb the depths of his own psyche. He notes his own Jekyll and Hyde nature.

One moment Cannister's alter ego, Jaffa Codling, is noting the beauty of nature and his children, the next he is jealous because he thinks his wife is kissing another man. He mistrusts her and feels enraged. Later he is annoyed at the maid and throws a flowerpot at the gardener. Still later he seems to communicate with the child Gabriel. This mixture of anger, beauty, joy, and jealousy deeply disturbs Codling. In truth the range of emotions in an individual is disturbing indeed, but one's conscious mind often denies the disturbing elements.

Jaffa Codling's world is also a highly symbolic one. The children's names, Adam, Eve, and Gabriel, take one back to the Garden of Eden, while the title of the story recalls the nursery rhyme "Adam and Eve and Pinch Me Tight." Throughout the story, Codling keeps pinching himself trying to understand what is real and what is not. Gabriel's sword is the one that barred Adam and Eve from reentering Eden after the Fall; it is indeed dangerous, just as the gardener warned the little boy Gabriel about his sword. Gabriel is also the biblical messenger who announced the impending birth of Christ to Mary, just as Mildred tells her husband of her own impending delivery at the end of this story. The singular beauty of the countryside and the colors created by the sun recall an Edenic past and the seemingly endless summer of childhood.

As Jaffa Codling journeys through the spirit world, he analyzes his own actions and intentions and finds them to be a "little spurious, counterfeit." When he merges into the body of Gilbert Cannister at the end of the story, the brief conversation between him and his wife seems quite prosaic compared to the extraordinary adventure that has preceded it. Mildred promises to give Gilbert a new baby, "if you are a very good man"—a remark that sounds almost like baby talk. Gilbert retains a glimpse of the spirit world that he has just visited, however, as he begins to tell her about the child Gabriel.

Style and Technique

The style of "Adam and Eve and Pinch Me" owes something to the stream-of-consciousness style made popular by James Joyce and Virginia Woolf during the period when A. E. Coppard wrote this story. Like the fictional characters of Woolf and Joyce, Jaffa Codling flits from image to image in his mind: from Edenic images of Adam and Eve and Gabriel to William Shakespeare's Isabella in *Measure for Measure*; from birds, to fish, to ships, to stars—stars that fall in your hand and burn you and do not leave a mark.

Coppard's story goes a step beyond stream-of-consciousness, however, because Codling the spirit becomes separate from Cannister the physical body. Cannister can speak as well as Codling, however, and Codling can critique Cannister's speech. Codling/Cannister thus has a dual personality.

"Adam and Eve and Pinch Me" also recalls William Wordsworth's "Lucy" poems in which he has "strange fits of passion" and fears that Lucy has come to harm. Codling seems to have irrational fears about his wife's faithfulness. Charles Lamb's early nineteenth century essay, "Dream Children," also comes to mind in connection with Coppard's story. In Lamb's reverie the children are a complete figment of his imagination and sadly vanish from his real world. Although Lamb's reverie is more sentimental than Coppard's, it may be thought of as a forerunner to "Adam and Eve and Pinch Me."

One of Coppard's great strengths as a writer is his ability to raise many questions in the mind of the reader, answer a few easy ones, and leave the reader to puzzle out the rest. For example, Coppard lets the reader know that Codling is Cannister's spirit and that Gabriel is his unborn child, but the reader never fully understands why Codling has become disembodied, why he is suspicious of his wife, or why he is ecstatically happy one moment and in despair the next. Much of the story revolves around unstated questions about the meaning of these contradictory states.

When Cannister's wife startles him back into a conscious state, he runs up to his room and finds that he can open doors that seemed to be locked when he was a spirit. He is trying to work these contradictions out when Mildred takes him to see the children and tells him of the expected third child. Cannister says that they will name the child Gabriel and tells his wife that he already knows about him. Then Coppard ends the story with the words "and he told her a pleasant little tale." Once again Coppard has planted ambiguity in the reader's mind. If Cannister tells Mildred the whole story, it will not be pleasant; if he glosses over areas less favorable to himself, it will not be the whole truth.

Perhaps the ultimate meaning of "Adam and Eve and Pinch Me" is contained in the manner in which Coppard chooses to write the story. The contradictory emotions felt by Gilbert Cannister when he is separated from his body in the spirit Jaffa Codling show the reader that life itself is contradictory and confused, mean-spirited and lighthearted, and beautiful and rich. Coppard embodies the meaning of his story in his method of writing it.

Isabel B. Stanley

THE ADMIRAL AND THE NUNS

Author: Frank Tuohy (1925-1999)
Type of plot: Social realism
Time of plot: 1952
Locale: Brazil
First published: 1960

Principal characters:

BARBARA WOROSZYLSKI, an English-born housewife living in
Brazil
STEFAN WOROSZYLSKI, her Polish husband
FERNANDO FERREIRA, their neighbor
DORALICE FERREIRA, his wife
THE NARRATOR, an English visitor to Brazil

The Story

An unnamed English visitor to a South American country that seems to be Brazil unintentionally becomes involved in the lives of Stefan Woroszylski, a Polish laboratory assistant at a remote industrial development project, and Barbara, his English wife. Barbara insists on inflicting on her fellow Englishman the "emotional confusion" built up over two years in a strange country. In contrast, Stefan is relatively comfortable in Brazil because several Poles are there.

The daughter of an admiral, educated in a convent, Barbara desperately misses the active social life associated with her upper-middle-class background. Even with a husband, three children, and a fourth on the way, she is lonely in a place so different from that to which she has been accustomed, not only in Kensington but also in such places as Malta, Gibraltar, and Alexandria. "Perhaps I'm just not the pioneering type," she explains to the narrator. Barbara does all she can to inform the narrator of her former status so that he will "perhaps, later, commiserate with her for her present circumstances."

The narrator can sympathize with Barbara up to a point, especially when he accompanies Stefan on a hunt for wild dogs: "You can judge your distance from civilization by the state of the dogs: Tonight we were very far away." This distance becomes even clearer when Stefan declines to finish off a dog he has wounded because of the expense of the extra bullet, explaining that the dog's "friends will kill him for us." The distance increases when Stefan interrupts a dinner conversation between Barbara and the narrator to tell his guest about the quality of the local prostitutes.

The Woroszylskis live only one hundred yards from Fernando and Doralice Ferreira, but Barbara is almost entirely isolated from them and everyone else in the settlement. The wives consider Barbara an incompetent housekeeper and mother and feel only contempt for her. Barbara looks forward to a ball at the local British Club in celebration of the coronation of Queen Elizabeth II. She imagines that she will find there those who will "accept her in the way she wanted to be accepted as a person."

Stefan takes the narrator on a tour of his world: a meal of cabbage and sausages, heavy drinking, and the Polish prostitutes at the Bar Metro. The narrator narrowly escapes spending the night with one of the whores. Barbara later thanks the narrator for looking after her husband: "You boys seem to have had a whale of a time together."

The Woroszylskis have difficulty getting into the ball because Stefan, in his shabby brown suit, is not dressed properly. Inside, because Stefan flirts with a seventeen-year-old blond, Barbara tries to make him jealous by dancing closely with the narrator, but they are forced to leave shortly when the girl becomes upset by Stefan's advances.

The narrator suspects that Barbara's patience with her philandering husband has finally come to an end. When Fernando brings her to him looking forlorn, the narrator expects her to say that she is leaving Stefan. Instead, she reveals that her husband has decided to return to Poland. Stefan's exile will then have ended; Barbara's will continue, probably for the rest of her life.

Themes and Meanings

Because Frank Tuohy taught in Finland, Poland, Brazil, Japan, and the United States, his stories and novels frequently contrasted cultures and examined how social, sexual, and cultural distinctions alienate people from one another. Tuohy's characters who attempt to embody two cultures at once are seen as absurd for doing so. Fernando Ferreira is "the traveling salesperson of a progressive North-Americanized civilization" yet is "full of Latin prejudices, without having any idea they made nonsense of his smart Americanism." The humorless, unimaginative Fernando judges the Europeans he encounters as types rather than individuals: "He accepted every remark one made as a representative national judgment." Seeing himself as a sophisticated man in a primitive land, Fernando devotes himself to "preserving the formalities" of civilization but is bewildered by the Woroszylskis because they, as Europeans, should be at least as civilized as he but seem much less so. Barbara, as usual, is oblivious to the possibility of any superiority on the part of the Ferreiras and acts like one who considers "it her right to intrude into the houses of her inferiors," thereby lowering their opinion of her even further.

Stefan is perhaps more at home in South America than Fernando because he refuses to acknowledge the distinctions observed by his wife, the Ferreiras, and even the Bar Metro prostitutes. He is "perpetually the peasant arriving in the great cities of the world and staring uninvolved at the palaces or skyscrapers." He cannot understand the people at the British Club because getting drunk and chasing women is the most natural behavior for him regardless of his surroundings. The narrator admires Stefan for being himself, for being immune to alienation, and sees him, ironically, as having "more standards" than those who expel him from the British Club.

Barbara's standards, on the other hand, intensify her isolation. It is clear from the beginning of "The Admiral and the Nuns" that her background has left her unprepared for life in Brazil and perhaps for marriage as well. However, Barbara has more complexity, if not depth, than the other characters. She seems stupid to the narrator but has a strength the others lack. She has committed herself to a marriage with a man completely unlike herself and will try to make the best of it not only because her Catholicism will not allow her to consider divorce but also because of her personal code of behavior. This code makes her outraged when other Englishmen dare to slight her husband in her presence, and she stands up for him even when he embarrasses her at the coronation ball.

Barbara lacks self-knowledge, persisting in considering herself the best possible thing that could ever have happened to Stefan, yet she refuses to ask for help from her family or friends because she would be letting them down: "I feel kind of responsible to them all. I'm sure they've all been praying for me such a lot." Her marriage makes her an exile whether she is in Brazil or Poland. However, she becomes almost admirable to the narrator for her willingness to endure everything that life throws at her. Her philosophy that "everything'll turn out right in the end" is too shallow to help her do much more than survive, but Tuohy knows, even if his narrator does not, that such self-deception is an inescapable part of life, a necessary weapon against the sterility and isolation of the human condition.

Style and Technique

"The Admiral and the Nuns" begins with Barbara's pearl necklace breaking for the second time since the narrator has known her. The pearls are the main symbol in the story, signifying Barbara's superficial, pretentious values. "They're artificial," she explains to the narrator. "But good artificial, if you see what I mean." They also suggest that Barbara's life is more than only her ill-suited relationship with Stefan and her endless talking about the convent nuns; she tells the narrator that the pearls have a sentimental value, and he guesses this sentiment is not connected to her husband. The story ends with this same second breaking of the pearls, ironically providing it with a structure missing from Barbara's life. The pearls underscore her inability to use her background to impose any order on her life.

Tuohy's other major stylistic device is the use of his sympathetic yet impatient, judgmental narrator. This character cannot decide what to make of Barbara. One minute he despises her arrogance; the next he feels sorry for the predicament into which she has gotten herself. As he is kept off balance by her, so is the reader. When she says she must keep Stefan from sin, the narrator wonders if she truly believes this or has "returned to her usual game of lying to herself." The narrator wants a simple explanation for everything, but his intelligence makes him realize the foolishness of this need.

Michael Adams

THE ADMIRER

Author: Isaac Bashevis Singer (1904-1991)
Type of plot: Domestic realism
Time of plot: 1975
Locale: New York City
First published: 1975

>*Principal characters:*
>"I", the narrator, a writer
>ELIZABETH ABIGAIL DE SOLLAR, a thirty-three-year-old woman
>who admires the narrator's work
>OLIVER LESLIE DE SOLLAR, her husband
>MRS. HARVEY LEMKIN, her mother
>HOWARD WILLIAM MOONLIGHT, Mrs. Lemkin's lawyer
>DR. JEFFREY LIFSHITZ, an assistant professor of literature at the
>University of California and an admirer of the narrator

The Story

Elizabeth Abigail de Sollar writes to the narrator to express her admiration for his books. Then she calls to arrange a meeting. In the course of the conversation, he mentions his fondness for Thomas Hardy; she soon sends him a beautifully bound set of Hardy's works. Finally, after a number of delays, she arrives at the narrator's West Side Manhattan apartment.

As she had in her letter, Elizabeth tells the narrator how much she likes his writing. She also gives him another present, a Ouija board, because he seems interested in the occult.

He asks about her life, and she willingly replies. She is the granddaughter of a Polish rabbi but has married a Christian. Her husband taught philosophy but has quit his professorship to write about astrology and numerology. Soon she is revealing more intimate details, including the information that she is a virgin, that she has never slept with her husband, and that she daydreams about "passionate affairs" with the narrator. She adds, however, that she has not come to seduce him.

The visit is repeatedly interrupted by telephone calls. Even before Elizabeth arrives at the narrator's apartment, her husband, Oliver Leslie de Sollar, calls, saying that their daughter (his child from a previous marriage, Elizabeth claims), is suffering an asthma attack and that Elizabeth must come home with the medicine that she carries in her purse. Later, Mr. de Sollar calls again to warn the narrator to beware of Elizabeth: "She lives in a world of illusions. . . . If . . . you became involved with her, your talent would be the first casualty." He denies that he is writing about astrology; he claims that his book concerns Isaac Newton's religious views.

The narrator hangs up and goes looking for Elizabeth, whom he finds in his bedroom. She has overheard her husband's statements and vows never to return to him. She and the narrator begin to act out her passionate daydreams when the phone rings yet again. This time her mother has called to repeat Mr. de Sollar's warning. Elizabeth grabs the phone, shouts insults at her mother, and then crashes to the floor in an epileptic fit.

The narrator desperately seeks help. In a nightmarish sequence of events, his phone goes dead. He then knocks at a neighbor's door, but no one answers. Turning to go back to his apartment, he notices that the door is closed, locking him out. The elevator will not come, so he runs down eleven flights of stairs to the superintendent's office, but when he reaches the lobby his path is blocked by furniture. He races back to the sixth floor to ask a friend to call the superintendent, but further complications ensue. The narrator finally returns to the lobby, secures a duplicate key, and gets into his apartment, where he finds Elizabeth lying on his couch. She looks at him "with the silent reproof of a wife whose husband has left her sick and alone and gone off somewhere for his own pleasure." She tells him that she wants to stay with the narrator and offers to type, clean, and cook for him.

Before he can reply, someone knocks at the door and again the phone rings. The call is from the lawyer of Elizabeth's mother; the narrator mistakes the visitor at the door for Elizabeth's husband and begs him to take her home. In fact, the man proves to be Dr. Jeffrey Lifshitz, a professor of literature and another admirer of the narrator's work. Elizabeth, realizing from what the narrator has told Lifshitz that she is not wanted, leaves, promising to call if she does not go mad. The narrator never hears from her again.

Themes and Meanings

On one level, the story is a comic portrayal of the harried life of a popular writer. The constant ringing of the phone, the appearance of one admirer at the beginning of the story and a second at the end, the narrator's frantic efforts to secure help for Elizabeth, who recovers without assistance and seems to reproach him for going off on a lark, all these incidents are the stuff of farce.

However, the story has its menacing aspect. Elizabeth may be viewed as the stereotypical crazed admirer and the narrator the conventional beleaguered writer who wants to be polite—and left alone. On a deeper level, though, Elizabeth suggests the Lilith of Jewish legend. In the Cabala, Lilith was the first wife of Adam and the archseductress. She has also been identified with the Queen of Sheba, who, like Elizabeth, journeyed to see a man she admired and put questions to him. Like the Queen of Sheba and Lilith, Elizabeth tests the narrator's knowledge. She asks him to explain the theological tract that her grandfather wrote, and, more subtly, she challenges him to decipher her true character. Is she telling the truth about herself and her husband? Is her husband's version the correct one? What about her mother's account?

Isaac Bashevis Singer's use of the Lilith legend stresses a recurring idea in his fiction: Man is never free from the struggle between the divine and the demonic, not even in a West Side Manhattan apartment. Elizabeth represents temptation, particularly of the flesh but not limited to that. She has apparently cost her husband his teaching job and has caused her mother to leave New York for Arizona. Combatting her are other forces, apparently providential. Elizabeth's mother calls just as the narrator is about to go to bed with his visitor; the second admirer comes as Elizabeth is trying to persuade the narrator to let her stay with him. His apartment thus becomes a battleground between the forces of light and dark fighting for his very soul.

The narrator escapes. Or does he? Tomorrow he has an appointment with another admirer, whom he has mistaken for Elizabeth's husband. Lifshitz is not in fact Mr. de Sollar, but might he be Asmodeus, king of the demons and the legendary husband of Lilith?

Style and Technique

As he so often does, Singer has woven a complex message into a seemingly simple tale. "The Admirer" finally—and finely—questions the narrator's ability to judge and perceive. Perhaps Providence does intervene to save him from the destruction that befell Oliver Leslie de Sollar. Certainly, the narrator would not have been able to save himself because he repeatedly demonstrates his lack of judgment. He mistakes Dr. Jeffrey Lifshitz for Mr. de Sollar. He misdiagnoses Elizabeth's fit. He gets no answer when he knocks on his typesetter's door because he has sought him on the wrong floor.

However, is the narrator saved? Might he be wrong to reject Elizabeth, who offers services he needs? His apartment is a mess, and his larder is decidedly limited. Because Singer tells the story through the filter of a first-person narrator who is obviously flawed, the reader cannot be certain that sending Elizabeth away is the right decision.

Like the narrator, the reader must decide about Elizabeth. He knows no more than "I"; for the reader, as for the narrator, Elizabeth comes and then vanishes, leaving behind questions about herself. Ultimately, she also leaves doubts about the realms of appearance and reality.

Joseph Rosenblum

THE ADULTEROUS WOMAN

Author: Albert Camus (1913-1960)
Type of plot: Fable
Time of plot: The early 1950's
Locale: Algeria
First published: "La Femme adultere," 1957 (English translation, 1958)

> *Principal characters:*
> JANINE, a childless married woman in her forties
> MARCEL, her husband of twenty years, a textile merchant

The Story

Taking its ironic title from the parable that is related in John 8:3-11, "The Adulterous Woman" describes a day of sensual and spiritual crisis in the life of a middle-aged, faithful wife who, until the time of the story, has had little reason or occasion to question the basic facts of her existence. Narrated in the third person, although from the limited viewpoint of the title character, known only as Janine, the story tells of Janine's inner and outer adventures during the course of a business trip on which, however reluctantly, she has agreed to accompany Marcel, her husband.

Although French by origin and culture, both Janine and Marcel are *pieds-noirs* (black feet), presumably born and reared in Algeria during the period of French domination that still continues. Neither Janine nor her husband has ever managed to master the language of Algeria's Arab majority; throughout their marriage, Janine and Marcel have lived all but confined to their apartment in one of Algeria's northern, Europeanized cities, intent on the precarious textile trade that Marcel has inherited from his family. The trip described in the story is in fact their first venture into the Algerian interior, prompted by Marcel's long-planned determination to eliminate the "middleman" in his transactions with rural Arab merchants.

During the course of a long, difficult bus ride, Janine finds herself recalling the years of her marriage to Marcel and, for the first time, questioning her attachment to him. Marcel is shorter than she is, with irritating mannerisms; what is more, he has long since abandoned his legal studies in favor of the business in which Janine often assists him. Under the frank gaze of a jackal-faced French soldier seated across from her on the bus, Janine begins simultaneously to doubt and to reaffirm her sexual desirability: Tall and far from slender, she is, she reasons, probably still attractive.

At one point, the soldier distractedly offers Janine a hard candy from a box in his pocket, proceeding thereafter to lose interest in the woman as he stares at the road before him. Janine's preoccupation with the soldier, never fully acknowledged, gives way to her visual and tactile impressions of the trip, and of their eventual stop at a somewhat drab and inhospitable hotel. Janine, feeling somewhat spurned by the soldier, becomes increasingly aware of her weight and clumsiness, her thoughts returning as before to the athletic fitness and well-being of her adolescent years, before she joined her future to that of the law student Marcel whom she may have loved.

Despite the ironic "promise" of the story's title, Janine's adultery is and remains purely internal and symbolic, quite possibly informed and infused by her own recollections, however unconscious, of the biblical parable deliberately recalled in the author's choice of title. Like the biblical adulteress who is about to be stoned, Janine feels a strong sense of guilt, if only for perceiving vague intimations of a freedom of which she has never even dreamed. As her thoughts run on, for once unchecked by habit, she is increasingly aware of her femininity, incongruous in a male-dominated world. The language of the story, reflecting Janine's thoughts, grows increasingly sensual, culminating in a scene of almost ritual abandonment. Janine, having encouraged Marcel to visit with her the ramparts of a fortress recommended for its sweeping view of the desert, returns alone to the fort after Marcel has fallen asleep in their hotel room. Surprisingly light of step, running faster than she dreamed possible, Janine seeks desperately to reexperience the sense of release, that had briefly overtaken her there hours earlier, at the side of her reluctant, uncomprehending husband.

Returned to the fort, Janine experiences an even greater sense of freedom than before, a simultaneous revelation of fitness and release: "After so many years of mad, aimless fleeing from fear, she had come to a stop at last. At the same time, she seemed to recover her roots and the sap rose again in her body, which had ceased trembling." Increasingly filled with "the water of night," Janine begins to moan in ecstasy. "The next moment, the whole sky stretched over her, fallen on her back on the cold earth."

Back in the hotel room with her sleeping husband, Janine watches as Marcel rises from the bed in a nearly somnambulistic state. By the time he returns, having slaked his thirst from a bottle of mineral water, Janine is weeping uncontrollably. "It's nothing, dear," she attempts to reassure him, "It's nothing." The story thus ends on an intentionally ambiguous note, raising more questions than it answers. Will Janine return to her "normal" state, assailed by guilt, or profit from her newly discovered freedom?

Themes and Meanings

First in the series of thematically linked short stories gathered in *L'Exil et le royaume* (1957; *Exile and the Kingdom*, 1958), "The Adulterous Woman" adumbrates and announces the prevailing themes of the collection. Janine, "exiled'" like Marcel among the ethnic French born and reared in Algeria, perceives on both of her visits to the fort a greater "kingdom" of nature and humanity than she has hitherto even suspected. The innumerable Arabs, predominantly male, and the rockbound, evidently hostile land that they inhabit provoke in the sheltered Janine a sudden awareness of human possibility, of unnoticed opportunity, occasioning a "moment of truth."

Despite his repeated rejections of the "existentialist" label, followed by repudiations on the part of the existentialists themselves, Albert Camus's mature work developed from, and significantly contributed to, the postwar intellectual climate most commonly associated with Jean-Paul Sartre and his followers. Faithful in spirit to Camus's own early essay *Le Mythe de Sisyphe* (1942; *The Myth of Sisyphus, and*

Other Essays, 1955), "The Adulterous Woman," like most of the tales in *Exile and the Kingdom*, delineates the contrast between freedom and habit, between "authentic" response and "conditioned" human behavior. Janine's "moment of truth," however unique and memorable, demonstrates both the "authenticity" and the unpredictability of human behavior "in situation," a theme frequently encountered in the works of both Camus and Sartre. Presumably, Janine's incipient discovery of her "authentic" self will uproot her from the "inauthenticity" formed by years of habit; the author, however, is careful to leave the situation open.

Like Camus's novel *La Chute* (1956; *The Fall*, 1957), originally planned as a short story to be included in *Exile and the Kingdom*, "The Adulterous Woman" derives no small part of its impact and resonance from the author's skillful infusion of biblical themes and references. Although a professed unbeliever, Camus often tended to reinterpret his observations in terms and structures drawn from Scripture; in the present story, the parable related in John's Gospel is inscribed within the narrative or, more specifically, within Janine's recorded observations: In symbolic replication of the scriptural stoning, the bus on which Janine and Marcel are riding is frequently pelted by wind-driven sand; on reaching the heart of the desert, Janine is surprised to find that it is composed largely of rock. The predominance of male characters, mostly faceless, who fail to notice Janine's imposing female presence recalls the tribunal of men who would stone the biblical adulteress. An even deeper inscription of the parable occurs when Janine perceives undecipherable writing in the sand, recalling Jesus's "earthly" rewriting of the Law as described in the Gospel verses. Should Janine be "condemned" like her biblical predecessor, Camus strongly suggests, the condemnation would be of her own doing, a voluntary if unconscious choice to resume the patterns of behavior that have promised her security, however false that security may be. At the end, having glimpsed the "kingdom," Janine is, ironically, still "free" to prolong her lifelong "exile" by forgetting what she has seen and felt.

Style and Technique

An acknowledged master of many styles and voices, Camus in "The Adulterous Woman" chose to use the neutral, "affectless" third person. Although limited to Janine's "uninformed," instinctive, often uncomprehending viewpoint, the narrative hints often at the presence of an omniscient, objective, yet generally sympathetic observer and recorder. The style is generally terse, matter-of-fact, yet as Janine travels deeper into the desert and farther from home, her thoughts are set down in increasingly sensual, even erotic language, culminating in the frank and lyrical description of her symbolic seduction when she returns to the fort. By implication, the subject of language itself also figures prominently in the story's development: Janine and Marcel are "exiled" from the Arab majority by their dependence on French, yet at the end of the story they experience an even wider "communication gap" within their common language, a gap widened still further by their perfunctory lovemaking.

David B. Parsell

THE ADVENTURE OF THE DANCING MEN

Author: Arthur Conan Doyle (1859-1930)
Type of plot: Mystery and detective
Time of plot: The late 1890's
Locale: London and Riding Thorpe Manor, Norfolk
First published: 1903

Principal characters:
SHERLOCK HOLMES, a private detective
DR. JOHN H. WATSON, his roommate and trusted friend
HILTON CUBITT, a wealthy landowner
ELSIE CUBITT, his wife
ABE SLANEY, a Chicago gangster
INSPECTOR MARTIN, a Norfolk constable

The Story

Like almost all the Sherlock Holmes stories authored by Arthur Conan Doyle, this one is presented as a memoir written by Watson, the first-person narrator. The story begins in Holmes and Watson's Baker Street apartment in London. Holmes, who appears to be deeply engrossed in his chemicals and test-tubes, surprises Watson by apparently reading his mind: "So, Watson . . . you do not propose to invest in South African securities?" Watson, astonished by Holmes's remark, demands an explanation, and Holmes complies, relating an intricate chain of reasoning that begins with the presence of chalk on Watson's left hand the previous night and concludes with his investment decision.

Holmes then hands Watson a sheet of paper bearing some stick figures and asks him what he makes of it. Watson believes it to be a child's drawing, but Holmes tells him that a client, Mr. Hilton Cubitt, is calling on them soon to seek an explanation of the stick figures drawn on the paper, figures that seem to resemble dancing men. When Cubitt arrives, he explains that he has been married for about a year to a young American woman. He knew little about his wife, Elsie, when they met, and she requested that he not ask her about her past, a past she says she would like to forget. He has honored her request, but recently she seemed quite shaken after receiving a letter from the United States. Shortly after she read and burned that letter, the dancing men hieroglyphics were found written in chalk on the window sill. Cubitt washed them off but noticed his wife's dismay when he told her about them. Then the paper that Holmes had shown Watson was found on the sundial in the garden. When Cubitt found it and showed it to Elsie, she promptly fainted. He does not wish to violate his promise to his wife and ask whether these dancing men are related to her unknown past, so he has come to Holmes for help in understanding this apparent mystery involving the woman he loves so dearly.

Holmes asks Cubitt some questions about the neighborhood and sends him home, asking him to watch for more dancing men drawings and urging Cubitt to copy down faithfully any that he finds. Holmes studies the drawing silently and makes no remarks about the case to Watson. About two weeks later, Cubitt returns with more hieroglyphics; some have been written in chalk on a door, others have been scrawled on a paper left on the sundial. One night, Cubitt reports, he saw a figure moving through the darkness in the yard; he took his pistol and, despite his wife's protests, went after the man. He did not find anyone, but the next morning more dancing men, apparently drawn by this mysterious visitor, were found chalked on the door. Cubitt believes that his wife possibly knows who this man is; he remains true to his promise, however, and refuses to interrogate her about the matter.

Cubitt returns to his home—Riding Thorpe Manor—on the train, and Holmes puzzles over the drawings some more. When Cubitt mails him another set of drawings found on the sundial, Holmes examines them and decides that he has the key to the mystery and needs to visit Norfolk immediately. When he and Watson arrive at Riding Thorpe Manor, they find Inspector Martin of the local police. Martin reports that Cubitt has been shot dead; Mrs. Cubitt has also been shot but remains alive in critical condition. It is assumed that Mrs. Cubitt murdered her husband and then attempted to take her own life. Holmes is stunned by this news and immediately examines the scene of the crime and questions the staff about the shooting. After close scrutiny of the room where the murder took place, Holmes discovers that three shots were fired, rather than only two as the police assume. Because only two bullets were fired from the revolver found with the bodies, Holmes concludes that another person with a gun was present at the time of the murder. The third person perhaps fired into the house through an open window, he reasons, a thesis confirmed by a spent cartridge found in the garden. Testimony from the staff that they heard a loud explosion, followed by a second explosion not nearly so loud, establishes that there were two shots fired almost simultaneously, followed shortly by a single third shot.

Holmes questions the stable boy about the inns and farms in the area and then sits down and writes a brief note, which he sends off to a nearby farm, addressed to a Mr. Abe Slaney. Holmes remarks that they will have about an hour before anything happens; he uses the time to explain the secret of the dancing men. The individual dancing figures are symbols substituted for letters of the alphabet. Because the most frequently used letter in the English alphabet is "E," Holmes assumed that the dancing man hieroglyph that appeared most often stood for the letter "E." By substituting other letters for symbols, using the frequency with which these letters normally appear in the language as a guideline, Holmes was able to break the code and decipher the messages. Finding the name Abe Slaney in one of the messages, and, knowing that the original letter that had disturbed Mrs. Cubitt had come from the United States, Holmes then cabled New York to ask a police friend there whether Abe Slaney was known to him. When the response indicating that Slaney was "the most dangerous crook in Chicago" came on the same night that Holmes received the last dancing man message from Cubitt, a message saying "Elsie prepare to meet thy God," Holmes realized that there was no time left to waste. Unfortunately, he explains, he and Watson arrived too late to prevent a murder.

Holmes's explanation is interrupted by the appearance of Slaney, who is immediately apprehended. He was summoned to the house by Holmes's message, written in dancing man hieroglyphics; Slaney had assumed that Elsie Cubitt had sent the message. The dancing man code was developed in Chicago by Elsie's father, the leader of the criminal gang to which Slaney belonged. Elsie was at one time engaged to marry Slaney but decided that she wanted no part of his criminal life, so she fled the country and attempted to start over in England, marrying Cubitt, who agreed to raise no questions about her past. When Slaney finally tracked her down and began to leave her messages in the code she had learned as a child, she panicked. She wrote him and asked him to leave, then asked him to meet her so she could attempt to bribe him into disappearing.

It was during this late-night meeting that Hilton Cubitt surprised his wife and Slaney arguing. Slaney and Cubitt exchanged shots, but Slaney ran without knowing whether Cubitt had been seriously wounded. Elsie Cubitt, unknown to Slaney, shot herself with her husband's revolver when she saw that her secret past had indirectly brought the life of her trusting husband to an end.

After explaining how the pieces of the puzzle fit together, Holmes hurries Watson off for the train back to London. Slaney is given a life sentence, and Mrs. Cubitt survives her self-inflicted wound to live out her life as a despondent widow.

Themes and Meanings

This story resembles many other stories in the Holmes series in that it revolves around a secret past, an apparently forgotten indiscretion. Time and again Holmes is called on to piece together a series of seemingly unconnected clues. The key to these puzzles is frequently, as it is here, a past action—a love affair, a theft, a personal injury—that one of the participants hopes will remain undiscovered. Past secrets always have a way of coming back to haunt people, Doyle believed. In this story, for example, Mrs. Cubitt will not be able to escape her past, no matter how badly she wishes to do so. If she had told Cubitt about her involvement with Slaney in Chicago, her husband would probably have loved her just the same. Because she attempts instead to keep the past concealed, she loses her husband and is condemned to live out the rest of her life without the one man who loved her so dearly that he would never break the promise he had made.

Style and Technique

It is generally agreed that one of the most important factors in the success of Doyle's Sherlock Holmes stories is the use of Watson as narrator. Doyle wrote a few stories with Holmes himself narrating, but they are not successful. Watson is a pleasant sort, but he is not terribly perceptive when it comes to understanding the puzzles he is called on to investigate. His guesses about the significance of clues are frequently wrong, as they are in this story when he first assumes the dancing men are a child's drawing. Watson's stolid and somewhat plodding personality provides a reassuring contrast to the brilliance of Holmes. Readers can identify with Watson's misperceptions because they themselves cannot follow Holmes's lightning-quick deductions. Watson's literal-mindedness provides an anchor that both secures Holmes to the world of plausibility and accentuates the marvelous powers of the famous detective's mind.

Watson's narration also maintains the suspense of the mystery that is unfolding. In this story, for example, Holmes works out the secret of the code, but the answers are kept from Watson (and the reader). The ominous message contained in the last set of hieroglyphics and the fact that Holmes has been in touch with New York and knows of a gangster named Slaney are not revealed until Doyle allows Holmes to explain the case to Watson. The structure that Doyle developed for the Holmes stories—an opening in Baker Street, the appearance of a client with a mysterious problem, a visit to the scene of the crime, misperceptions of the clues by Watson, the sudden revelation of the mystery followed by a detailed explanation by Holmes—was a formula that was repeated fairly consistently throughout the sixty adventures that make up the Holmes and Watson series. Using an omniscient narrator (who would have to tell the reader all the facts) or using Holmes as narrator (and thereby revealing how the detective is working his way through the puzzle) would not keep the reader guessing the way that Watson's narration does. If people read mysteries so that they can attempt to solve the puzzles before the characters in the stories do, then Doyle discovered the nearly perfect technique for prolonging the suspense and mystery by using Watson as first-person narrator; the proof is that the Holmes stories are the most famous, and most widely read, detective stories in the world.

Don Richard Cox

ADVENTURE OF THE GERMAN STUDENT

Author: Washington Irving (1783-1859)
Type of plot: Gothic
Time of plot: The late eighteenth century, during the French Revolution
Locale: Paris, France
First published: 1824

Principal characters:
GOTTFRIED WOLFGANG, the German student studying in Paris
THE MYSTERIOUS WOMAN, found seated on the guillotine steps
THE NARRATOR, the "old gentleman with the haunted head"

The Story

This story, one of a number of tales and sketches collected in *Tales of a Traveller* (1824), is narrated by an old man to a group of listeners. The story concerns a young student from the German university town of Gottingen. The student, Gottfried Wolfgang, is described as a man of good family but also as one given to intense speculation on the dark, mystical side of existence. Indeed, he is shown to have dedicated himself to these studies to such an extent that both his physical health and his imagination have become "diseased." As the narrator tells his audience, "He took up a notion, I do not know from what cause, that there was an evil influence hanging over him; an evil genius or spirit seeking to ensnare him and ensure his perdition."

To combat Wolfgang's melancholy and morbid obsessions, his friends and family send him off to France to continue his studies at the Sorbonne. They hope that, removed from the gloomy German environment, he will be more happily influenced by the new surroundings of the school and by the "splendors and gayeties of Paris." Unfortunately, Wolfgang arrives in Paris at the beginning of the Reign of Terror, and the scenes of butchery and cruelty that follow cause him to withdraw even more into his own private, dark world of the imagination. Again, in the words of the narrator, "Sometimes he spent hours together in the great libraries of Paris, those catacombs of departed authors, rummaging among their hoards of dusty and obsolete works in quest of food for his unhealthy appetite. He was, in a manner, a literary ghoul . . ."

In addition to his constant musings on the metaphysical and demonic, the student is also sexually obsessed. Although he is too shy actually to approach a woman, he gives himself over to romantic and erotic dreams when safely ensconced in his room. One female face in particular becomes the focus of his desires; he dreams about her night after night until he nears the point of madness. Finally it happens that on one stormy night Wolfgang, making his way from the library to his room, finds himself at the Place de Greve, the site of the daily executions performed on the guillotine. As he reluctantly crosses the square, he sees a dark figure collapsed on the steps leading up to the horrible instrument of death. Motivated by an uncommon feeling of sympathy, he approaches the figure to offer help or condolence, but when he speaks he sees, to his amazement, that the person is the haunting and enticing young woman whose face has filled his dreams. He asks her if she has a home, a place to stay on such a stormy night. "Yes—in the grave!" she answers, and Wolfgang, touched by her despair, impulsively offers his own room as temporary shelter. The beautiful woman accepts.

Once Wolfgang and his guest reach his boardinghouse, he is better able to appraise her appearance, which is both alluring and disturbing. She has long, raven-black hair, eyes "large and brilliant," and a striking figure. Most remarkable, however, is the "broad black band . . . clasped by diamonds" that she wears around her neck. Although somewhat perplexed, Wolfgang is immediately captivated by the strange woman. As they talk, he gives over all of his doubts and fears; soon he expresses his love and passion for her, and she in return avows her desire for him. "I pledge myself to you forever," he tells her. "Forever?" she asks seriously. "Forever!" he answers, whereupon she gives herself to him as his bride for the remainder of the night.

The next morning Wolfgang goes out before his bride awakes, but when he returns he finds her sprawled across the bed, her head hanging over one side, her face "pallid and ghastly." Horrified, he calls for help and waits in shock for the authorities. When a police officer arrives, he, too, is stunned at what he sees, for he recognizes the corpse as that of a recent victim of the guillotine. As the police officer unclasps the black band around her neck, the strange woman's head drops onto the floor, and Wolfgang shrieks in despair, remembering his old nightmare of damnation. Driven now into total madness, he is finally placed in an asylum, where he remains until his death.

Is the story true? "I had it from the best authority," the narrator replies. "The student told it me himself. I saw him in a mad-house in Paris."

Themes and Meanings

The stories in *Tales of a Traveller* strongly reflect the influence that the European gothic horror story, with its emphasis on psychological as well as physical terror, played on Washington Irving. Gottfried Wolfgang is an "enthusiast," one given to extremes rather than carefully reasoned actions. He has devoted himself to unhealthy studies, and they have made him into a kind of monster—a "literary ghoul," as Irving bluntly puts it, feeding on dead and putrid thoughts just as an actual ghoul would feed on dead bodies. Thus, the student is shown from the beginning to be of unsound mind, bordering precariously on the edge of madness.

Irving also makes clear, however, the student's sexual obsession, which is equally unhealthy. His lack of restraint as he thinks about women, and especially about the one ravishing female of his dreams, shows yet again the diseased state of his imagination. Indeed, these two fascinations—mystical speculation and sexual fantasies—are linked in the student's mind: His ghoulish tendencies are easily transformed into necrophilic desires.

Finally, when Wolfgang gives himself to the mysterious woman, he does so by denying time-honored social and religious beliefs and ceremonies. "What need is there of sordid forms to bind high souls together?" he asks before consummating his mar-

riage night with his "bride." Because the woman is most likely dead, although possibly inhabited by an evil spirit, this sexual consummation is an act of incredible horror:
Wolfgang becomes a necrophiliac and must pay for his rashness with his sanity.

Thus, in addition to being a thrilling horror story, "Adventure of the German Student" is a warning against enthusiasm, loss of balance, lack of reason. For Irving, who
grew up in the Age of Reason, Wolfgang represents the dangers of extreme liberality,
whether in philosophy, sex, or religion, just as the French Revolution illustrates the
madness of a society that rejects a rational manner of government. The story shows
Irving's uneasiness with many aspects of the Romantic movement.

Style and Technique

The most striking aspect of the story is its use of narrator. The chief speaker is the
"old gentleman with the haunted head," who tells the story to a group of other men.
Among them is the "inquisitive gentleman" who questions the truth of the story after
the narrator has finished. The narrator then replies that he heard it from the most reliable source, Wolfgang himself. Thus, Irving gives the reader several possible explanations for the events in the story and also imparts a fascinating ambiguity to the tale.

The reader may, for example, simply accept the student's story as a true example of
demonic possession: The woman was indeed a reanimated corpse sent specifically to
ensnare Wolfgang's soul. Given the student's already established precarious mental
state, however, the reader might address even more disturbing possibilities. Was the
woman ever truly alive in Wolfgang's presence? Because he has necrophilic tendencies, could he have appropriated a corpse and imagined it alive? The fact that the
portress at his hotel sees Wolfgang and the woman arrive might bring this reading into
question. Is it then possible that Wolfgang himself murders the woman after he brings
her to his apartment? Perhaps, but the police officer identifies the woman as one executed previously on the guillotine, so once again this rational answer seems unlikely.

The reader, however, must remember that the source of all this information appears
to have been Wolfgang himself, a madman incarcerated in an insane asylum. The narrator says that the student is the best authority, but how reliable can Wolfgang be?
Moreover, what does the reader make of the narrator himself: the "gentleman with the
haunted head"? What relationship is there between this man and Wolfgang? Why was
he in the asylum in the first place? Why is he "haunted"? Should not the reader, like
the "inquisitive gentleman," wonder at the events he relates?

"Adventure of the German Student," then, is a deceptively complex story, suggesting a great deal more than Irving chooses to make clear. It is the forerunner of the psychological horror story that Edgar Allan Poe would perfect in such works as "Ligeia"
and "The Fall of the House of Usher," stories in which the mental state of the narrator is often as intriguing as the events he relates. Although Irving uses traditional folklore in this story, he employs it to reveal his awareness of terrors that hide inside every
man.

Edwin T. Arnold

THE ADVENTURE OF THE SPECKLED BAND

Author: Arthur Conan Doyle (1859-1930)
Type of plot: Mystery and detective
Time of plot: 1883
Locale: London and Surrey, England
First published: 1892

Principal characters:
SHERLOCK HOLMES, the world-famous English detective
DR. WATSON, his companion and confidant, the narrator of the story
HELEN STONER, a young English lady who fears for her life
SIR GRIMESBY ROYLOTT, Helen's stepfather and the master of Stoke Moran

The Story
Sherlock Holmes and Dr. Watson rise unusually early one morning to meet Helen Stoner, a young woman who fears that her life is being threatened by her stepfather, Sir Grimesby Roylott, a doctor who practiced in India and who was married to Helen's mother there. Helen's sister has died almost two years earlier, shortly before she was to be married. Helen had heard her sister's dying words, "The speckled band!" but had been unable to understand their meaning. Now Helen, too, is engaged, and she has begun to hear strange noises and to observe strange activities around Stoke Moran, the estate where she and her stepfather live.

Sir Grimesby Roylott does keep strange company at the estate. He befriends a band of Gypsies on the property and keeps as pets a cheetah and a baboon. For some time, he has been making modifications to the house: Before Helen's sister's death, he had modifications made inside the house, and now he is having the outside wall repaired, forcing Helen to move into the room where her sister died.

Holmes listens carefully to Helen's story and agrees to take the case. He plans a visit to the manor later in the day. Before he can leave, however, he is visited by Roylott, who threatens him should he interfere. Undaunted, Holmes proceeds, first to the courthouse, where he examines Helen's mother's will, and then to the countryside.

At Stoke Moran, Holmes inspects the premises carefully inside and out. Among the strange features that he discovers are a bed anchored to the floor, a bell cord that does not work, and a ventilator hole between Helen's room and that of Roylott.

Holmes and Watson arrange to spend the night in Helen's room. In darkness they wait; suddenly, a slight metallic noise and a dim light through the ventilator prompt Holmes to action. Quickly lighting a candle, he discovers on the bell cord the "speckled band"—a poisonous snake. He strikes the snake with a stick, driving it back through the ventilator; agitated, it attacks Roylott, who had been waiting for it to return after killing Helen. Holmes reveals to Watson that Roylott plotted to remove both daughters before they married because he would have lost most of the fortune he controlled when the daughters took with them the money left them by their mother.

Themes and Meanings

To understand the theme of "The Adventure of the Speckled Band" and to appreciate the levels on which the story operates, one must view it as representative of its genre, the detective story. Like all formula fiction, it is intended by its author to conform to the traditional requirements of that genre.

Formula fiction provides its readers a certain kind of satisfaction: Those familiar with the formula know what to expect, in a general sense, from any story that follows the pattern. In the case of detective fiction, readers may not know how a particular case will be resolved, but they are assured that certain common elements will be present in every such story, and that certain expectations will be raised and satisfied. Most readers seek out detective stories to satisfy their inquisitive nature: People like to have their intellectual faculties challenged. They like to attempt to solve the mystery before the hero does. This they do through careful reading and clever analysis of clues presented by the author, often through a narrator who is aware of the facts but not always able to make the proper deduction. Hence, the "meaning" of most detective stories is usually discoverable on the surface: The denouement gives the reader a sense of completeness, and rereadings simply provide better opportunities to discover carefully disguised clues that make the solution of a particular case more plausible. Readers are not usually challenged to think about larger issues, as they might be by stories dealing with more complex social or philosophical issues.

At the end of the tale, Holmes himself supplies the moral, observing that "Violence does, in truth, recoil upon the violent, and the schemer falls into the pit which he digs for another." The events of the story support this claim, as Roylott dies by the agent he had planned to use against his stepdaughter. Although such an explicit conclusion might be out of place in other forms of literature, it is expected in detective fiction, especially in early examples of the genre.

This is not to say that the story itself is simplistic, or that Doyle is interested only in showing that "good will out." "The Adventure of the Speckled Band" explores a universal problem that transcends its genre: the tendency of individuals to jump to conclusions based on insufficient or misleading evidence. Even the great Sherlock Holmes is temporarily led to a wrong conclusion by evidence that suggests a solution that, in reality, is far from the truth. Not only can physical evidence be misunderstood—the sinister combination of the Gypsies, the cheetah, and the baboon in this story certainly provides a wonderful opportunity for such misguided reasoning—but also words themselves are subject to misinterpretation, with potentially deadly results. Only by examining every piece of the puzzle and carefully evaluating each item in relationship to all other clues and circumstances is Holmes able to solve the mystery and, in this case at least, save an innocent life. "The Adventure of the Speckled Band" provides its readers with a vivid lesson in the importance of sound reasoning and careful, unprejudiced observation—something that is not simply the purview of detectives.

Style and Technique

Doyle's works provide a touchstone for the reader seeking a guide to the formula for good detective fiction. Many classic elements of style and technique are used with great success in the Holmes stories.

Characteristic of this story and of other Holmes adventures is the use of the first-person narrator who is not the detective. Watson, less observant than Holmes, presents the clues for the reader's benefit; part of the thrill of reading is in solving the crime, using information provided by Watson without benefit of the doctor's analysis. The first-person narrator also allows Doyle to mask information from the reader because Watson is limited in knowing what Holmes discovers when he is away, or of knowing what Holmes is thinking.

This tale also contains another familiar device of the detective story: the presence of "red herrings," false clues drawn across the trail to distract the unwary reader from evidence that is germane to solving the crime. The baboon, cheetah, and band of Gypsies are all false clues. In this story, though, the false clues serve a dual purpose: They also throw Holmes off the trail momentarily, adding to the suspense and, ultimately, to the realism of the adventure.

Extensive dialogue is the primary method for presenting background information and for revealing the detective's method of operation, providing readers with details essential to solving the crime and explaining how evidence should be interpreted. This dialogue is balanced with extended, minute descriptions of locale and character. The thrill of reading such stories is in making proper deductions from this plethora of information—and misinformation. As in all first-rate detective stories, the evidence provided in "The Adventure of the Speckled Band" allows the careful reader to arrive at the right answer. No tricks are introduced at the end of the tale. One need only exercise one's skills in inductive reasoning to become equal in skill to the world's most successful detective.

Laurence W. Mazzeno

THE AEROPLANES AT BRESCIA

Author: Guy Davenport (1927-   )
Type of plot: Surrealist
Time of plot: 1909
Locale: Riva, Austria, and Brescia, Italy
First published: 1970

> *Principal characters:*
> FRANZ KAFKA, the protagonist, a young lawyer and aspiring
>   writer, on vacation from Prague
> MAX BROD, his friend, also on vacation
> OTTO BROD, the younger brother of Max, also on vacation
> BLERIOT, a French aviator at Brescia
> G. H. CURTISS, an American aviator, the winner of the Brescia
>   airshow

The Story

Standing on a seawall in Riva, Franz Kafka, the story's protagonist, and Otto Brod, his friend, conclude their morning walk. They are on vacation from Prague and decide to finish their discussion over a beer. En route, their conversation turns from moving pictures to the modern, cubelike architecture of Riva. This style creates, in contrast to Prague's older architecture, a sense not only of freedom but also of emptiness. As the two arrive at the cafe, they learn from Max Brod, Otto's brother, that there will be an airshow at Brescia. The attraction of the new flying machines, and the possibility of seeing internationally recognized aviators, convinces the three vacationers to travel to Brescia.

On the first stage of their journey, the trio board an ancient steamboat that ferries them across the lake to Salo. More important, the miniature odyssey is a mental one: Kafka, recalling the previous evening's conversation about the Wright brothers, falls into a daydream that mixes people, places, times, and themes. He wonders about what Orville and Wilbur's plane looked like, imagines what they could see while flying above an American community, and thinks about their pragmatic study of previous pioneers of flight—Leonardo da Vinci, Benjamin Franklin, and Samuel Pierpont Langley. He considers also the influence of the brothers on each other, and he hints at a rivalry between the Wright brothers and another early American flyer, G. H. Curtiss.

More pessimistically, he thinks of the loneliness and monotony that could be inspired in modern classrooms. Unlike the Brods, who are "modern men" (Otto is comfortable with the "hollow thought of Ernst Mach," and Max dreams of a new Zionist state in Tel Aviv), Kafka is burdened by this modern sense of loneliness. Although he is becoming a successful lawyer, and although he can mentally create stories, he is deeply frustrated by his inability to put his ideas onto paper.

At Salo, the journey shifts from boat to train, and the three soon arrive in Brescia. There a comic interlude gently satirizes the bustle of this modern city. Newspapers are not read privately here but are rather declaimed from the sidewalks; the militia has been called in to keep order in the restaurants; that night, several police officers frantically chase two individuals down a street outside the trio's hotel. The three travelers also experience a similar distortion of reality: Their driver takes a convoluted path to a building where the airshow's organizing committee assigns them to a dirty hotel; later, through a hole in the floor of their room, they observe a pizza being cut with such an enormous knife that it causes Otto to indulge in unexplained hysterical laughter.

Still, this surreal world has a darker side, as Kafka begins to realize. Spatially, the streets of Brescia seem to come together at one focal point. Temporally, the "Italian continuity of things" is one in which "accident and order were equally impossible." This is juxtaposed to Berlin and Vienna, where there is a facile dichotomy between the new and the old. However, now Kafka is confused: He believes that any narrative produced in an Italian setting would be devoid of meaning—"gratuitous figures in an empty piazze" or "an empty room in an empty building in an empty novel." Thus, Kafka's nightmare that evening, instead of providing insight, only further confuses him. In his dream he is alone (when he had expected to be in the company of statues of poets and statesmen), and Kafka hears Johann Wolfgang von Goethe reciting a poem in a language so alien that it is incomprehensible.

In the morning, however, the humorous tone returns. Resuming their train journey to the aerodrome, the three pass a comic melange of travelers: goggled automobile drivers desperately trying to maintain their composure in speeding cars, passengers in carriages swaying along the road, and a strange congregation of bicyclists. Others like these individuals have already created a carnival atmosphere at Brescia itself. All Europe, apparently, has joined in the festivities. There are Gypsies and royalty, the obese Countess Carlotta Primoli Bonaparte; the musician Giacomo Puccini is there, as is the philosopher Ludwig Wittgenstein. The planes seem incongruously insignificant; the great Bleriot's craft is "alarmingly small, scarcely more than a mosquito magnified to the size of a bicycle."

Counterpoised with this comic commotion is the composure of the aviators. Bleriot, the Frenchman who successfully overflew the English Channel after eighty unsuccessful attempts, has an "athlete's sureness." Before the competition, the American Curtiss displays a "professional nonchalance" by remaining detached, with his feet propped on a gasoline tin, reading a newspaper. Even when mechanical problems frustrate Bleriot, the first flier, he simply removes himself from the aircraft until the plane is ready to be flown. Curtiss, in contrast, starts his engine on the first attempt and taxis smoothly across the field, becoming airborne almost effortlessly.

However, if Otto is entranced with the ground operations, clearly it is Kafka who learns the most from the airshow. To be sure, Curtiss performs cleanly, almost magically, and looks, as he flies overhead, "peculiarly familiar and wildly strange" simultaneously. Indeed, his five circuits in less than fifty minutes virtually assures his victory in the Grand Prix de Brescia. His performance is important, yet it is two other fliers—Bleriot and another Frenchman, Rougier—who teach Kafka something more immediately relevant. In flying his ungainly machine, Bleriot appears to be dividing his attention equally among three activities simultaneously; to Kafka, he seems like a scholar working heroically at his desk. Rougier, who also has difficulty controlling the many levers and gears of his flying machine, manages successfully and seems, ultimately, "like a man for whom writing with both hands at once is natural." Still, Kafka's understanding of what he has learned from these three aviators is imperfect at this stage; in the last line of the story, he tells Max that he does not know why he is quietly crying. The ending is thus problematic: It remains unclear, in this open-ended narrative structure, whether Kafka will return from the airshow, and from his vacation, with the ability to work as a writer in the modern world. If he can, then Kafka's tears become tears of joy.

Themes and Meanings

In his important essay "Ernst Machs Max Ernst," Guy Davenport points out that when he collected the stories for *Tatlin!* (1974), in which "The Aeroplanes at Brescia" appears, he consciously arranged these narratives to circumscribe the history of flight, from its early days to Commander Neil Armstrong's first step onto the moon. His purpose, he notes, is to demonstrate that the "logos hides in technology in our time." This view makes the airplane, the technological symbol of the twentieth century, representative of the essence of this society. It is at once both an exciting attraction and a fear-inducing new technology.

That the twentieth century's predicament is troublesome for Kafka may be seen in the dichotomy Davenport establishes between Prague and Riva. In the former, older city, there is a "glittering richness," yet one may discover only the "half-truths of the cut-glass sunlight"; in the latter, there is "truth in the light," but as Kafka himself notices in Brescia, there is a disturbing emptiness and loneliness in this modern existence. Indeed, Kafka is the only character who shows, in his quiet tears at the story's end, any emotion. In addition, his contact with others—including his good friends, the Brods—seems curiously sterile. Although many of the incidents in Brescia have a comic tone, Kafka is unable to communicate his innermost concerns—his daydreams, his nightmares, and his meditations about the aviators—to his fellow travelers.

As Davenport mentions in his essay, "The Aeroplanes at Brescia" evolved from a previous study of the writer Franz Kafka, who was, in 1909, actually suffering from a serious writer's block. Davenport thus transmutes a real historical event—Kafka's attendance at the airshow—into an imaginative re-creation of his protagonist's inspiration from the aviators. Davenport's Kafka begins to learn from those he watches: from Bleriot that perseverance is needed; from Rougier that a beginning writer must concern himself with many actions simultaneously; from Curtiss that a polished writer can gracefully provide fresh insight about familiar subjects. He learns from those he sees only imaginatively as well: from the Wright brothers of the need for study and pragmatic practice; even from Leonardo da Vinci's and Icarus and Daedalus's early errors. By examining these aspects of flight, he discovers that technology, like the writer's imagination, must be actively employed if one is to survive in the modern world.

Style and Technique

As might be expected from a writer who announces that "a page could be dense in various ways," the style of "The Aeroplanes at Brescia" is one that challenges the reader. On the one hand, Davenport uses similes and metaphors often, and in this way he helps the reader visualize unfamiliar objects. Such, for example, occurs when he describes Bleriot flying "around them like an enormous bee." Conversely, Davenport's numerous passing allusions to figures as diverse as the Goncourt brothers, Alfred Lowry, and the Roman poet Cinna require the reader to pause to consider their implications. It is important to note that these allusions encapsulate individuals from a wide variety of historical and cultural contexts, and thus Davenport brings many disparate epochs together. In essence, he is conflating time and space as the architecture of Brescia seems to do.

The reader, then, is invited to perform an imaginative act that links him with the writer. The surreal images of life in Brescia, combined with Kafka's dreams and thoughts, begin to make sense when the careful reader correlates these ideas and facts in new ways. The main theme—how an imaginative individual is able to survive in a culture based on technology—only gradually surfaces, from Kafka's daydreams and nightmares, as the central concern of the story. Davenport's answer is optimistic but conditional: The legacy of the past and the technology of the present must be combined in new, imaginative ways.

Charles J. Gaspar

AFRICA KILLS HER SUN

Author: Ken Saro-Wiwa (1941-1995)
Type of plot: Satire, epistolary
Time of plot: The late 1980's
Locale: A prison in Nigeria
First published: 1989

> *Principal characters:*
> BANA, one of the bosses of a gang of armed robbers
> SAZAN and
> JIMBA, his co-bosses and cellmates
> ZOLE, childhood girlfriend of Bana
> THE PRISON GUARD, bribed to convey Bana's letter to Zole
> THE HIGH COURT JUDGE, surprised at the plea of guilty by the
>   three robbers
> A GERMAN PROSTITUTE, a role model for Bana

The Story

Written in the form of a condemned man's last letter to his former girlfriend, "Africa Kills Her Sun" constitutes a dark satire on the effects of all-encompassing corruption and pervasive graft in Nigerian society and Africa in general. In ironic form, it denounces the economic immorality that took hold in Nigeria under a continuous military dictatorship that began in 1983 and did not end until 1999. Democracy came too late to save the author. Saro-Wiwa was imprisoned first in 1993 and again in 1994 for his political activism on behalf of his native Ogoni people and was hanged on November 10, 1995, by the military regime.

In the story, Bana reveals himself to be somewhat of an existentialist. From the outset, he tells his girlfriend Zole that she and the others who remain after his death have the worse fate because they have to suffer the injustices of an uncaring world. Bana and his two companions, Sazan and Jimba, who are both sound asleep as he is writing on his last night on earth, will soon have nothing left to worry about. Bana reminds Zole of their unconsummated love, which ended ten years ago but still inspires him.

Bana and the others feel that they have outwitted their corrupt society. Caught and brought to trial, the three robbers agreed to plead guilty to all charges immediately and to demand capital punishment. They did this, Bana writes Zole, to deny the high court judge the power to choose their penalty. They prevented the judge from exercising his corrupt power by being more lenient to one or two of the three equally guilty robbers. For once, Bana insists, the judge had to pass an honest judgment in accordance with the law.

Next, Bana writes of why he became a robber. As a merchant marine, he met a prostitute in Germany. She told him that for her, women's professions—whether secretary, nurse, or prostitute—were all the same. Impressed by what he felt was the clarity of her convictions, Bana quit his job to work for the Ministry of Defense. There, he learned that every official was bent on robbing the country blind through corruption, so he decided to become an armed robber, which he viewed as a more honest alternative to being part of a corrupt society. At least, he writes, he stole openly.

Bana tells Zole that corruption is endemic in contemporary Africa, where corrupt regimes degrade society and bring misery to their people. He writes that he went to jail only because the corrupt superintendent of police botched their last robbery. He reveals that they always worked in collaboration with the police. However, during their last job, a police officer escorting a money transport shot at the robbers, who returned fire. Although the police wanted to punish some of Bana's minions, the three bosses decided to face the penalty instead of playing this corrupt game. Bana reveals that he considers himself a kind of Nigerian Robin Hood, who shares his loot with the poor of his gang.

As Bana envisions his upcoming execution in the sports stadium, his letter becomes a bitter reckoning with corruption, which robs the continent's people. He asks Zole to have a statue sculpted of him because his body will be dumped in an unmarked grave. As Sazan and Jimbo wake from their sleep, Bana implores Zole to have an epitaph inscribed at the base of this sculpture. As the bribed prison guard awakens, Bana finishes his letter, telling Zole his epitaph is to read "Africa Kills Her Sun," an allusion to the historical lines, "Africa kills her sons," spoken by an African leader over the grave of a favorite officer. Bana affirms his love for Zole and says good-bye as he is about to be shot.

Themes and Meanings

"Africa Kills Her Sun" is a serious reckoning with the corruption and lawlessness that the author saw as being among the major forces responsible for robbing African people of their chances for a happy, decent, and productive life. The story is full of allusions to real-life cases of corruption and the economic mismanagement and political brutality of failed historical leaders such as Idi Amin of Uganda or Jean-Bedel Bokassa, who made himself emperor of the Central African Republic and was deposed after allegedly eating the flesh of murdered schoolchildren.

Against a near-universal pan-African pattern of corruption, Saro-Wiwa's protagonist sets the example of a ruthlessly honest man. Bana chooses to be true to the nature and laws of his society. Instead of working for wages on which he cannot live without taking bribes or participating in the system of stealing under the guise of performing civic services in a state ministry, Bana becomes a boss of a gang of armed robbers. The story strongly argues that his taking of workers' salaries by ambushing money transports, after coordinating his actions with a willing and paid-off police force, is identical to the devious actions of state officials who steal vast amounts of public money that should have benefited society and provided for economic development.

For Bana, personal honesty and high ethics require that he stand by his actions and be prepared to pay the price for his behavior. He even implies that he could have bribed the prison guard to let them escape but declined this dishonest act.

However, behind Bana's somewhat existentialist act of accepting straightforwardly and without excuses the idea that the world of human society is random, harsh, and cruel and that only death brings liberation, there is the equally strong underlying theme of extreme moral outrage at this sorry state of affairs. Bana's letter also blames the Africans who have the power to change things for failing to do so. These include the leaders who betray their people; those who participate in corruption, from the highest to the lowest levels; and the apathetic public, which drinks beer and watches imported television instead of challenging society and demanding change and action.

An undercurrent of prescient despair as well as black humor charges Bana's apparently willing and nonchalant acceptance of his sentence, for Africa itself has allowed the killing of its metaphorical "sun," representing a better tomorrow for the continent. By not resisting corruption and injustice at every level of occurrence, from the top to the bottom, the author implies, Africans become complicit in this crime of murder.

Style and Technique

The choice of a short story is especially appropriate for the material, as a short story's few pages represent approximately what condemned prisoners could write on their last night. Having Bana write to his childhood girlfriend lends credibility to his confession to his cellmates that he wants to explain the meaning and significance of their pleading guilty to a sympathetic human being. Because Bana and Zole are not really close anymore, the primary bond that ties them is something like the universal human sympathy the author may hope for from his readers. Therefore, the letter is as much directed to the general human population as to a fictional character.

This stylistic idea is reinforced by Zole's name. The phonetic closeness of "Zole" to "soul" immediately strikes Saro-Wiwa's fellow English readers. It may also represent an allusion to the writer's Nigerian friend, fellow author Wole Soyinka, who chose the alternative of exile over possible death at the hands of the military dictatorship, leaving Nigeria in 1994 and not returning until after democracy was restored in 1999.

Bana's moral stand to face capital punishment for his actions, even though the application of the law is clearly unjust, is built on a model with long Western literary tradition. In Plato's famous account of the Greek philosopher Socrates, the philosopher's friend Crito is prepared to offer a bribe so that Socrates will be released from jail and spared execution, but the philosopher refuses this option because of his absolute belief that citizens have to obey the legal system of their country, even when its sentences are unjust. In addition, Albert Camus's existentialist hero Meursault, in *L'Étranger* (1942; *The Stranger*, 1946), faces his death sentence rather than shedding a few hypocritical tears for his dead mother. In the hands of Saro-Wiwa, Bana becomes a kind of African Socrates and Meursault by his own valiant refusal to give in to the temptation of corruption in his native Nigeria.

R. C. Lutz

AFTER SATURDAY NITE COMES SUNDAY

Author: Sonia Sanchez (1934-   )
Type of plot: Social realism
Time of plot: April in the late 1960's
Locale: Indianapolis
First published: 1971

Principal characters:

SANDY, the protagonist, a single black mother with twin baby boys, who lives with Winston

WINSTON, the antihero, a thirty-eight-year-old unemployed black man, a former convict, and a heroin addict

ANTHONY SMITH, the antagonist, a middle-aged white drug dealer

The Story

As the story opens, Sandy has gone indignantly to the bank to correct what she believes to be a bank error showing her checking account to be three hundred dollars overdrawn. To her humiliation, the bank officer confronts her with five checks—all bearing the signature of Winston, the man with whom she lives. She reacts to the officer's condemning stare with a stupor of silence and immobility, so that someone must be called to drive her home. Ironically, Anthony Smith, Winston's drug connection, arrives and Sandy rides silently home while contemplating the first spring with Winston, wondering "if it wud be beautiful."

Amid Sandy's own despairing confusion and Winston's crying, he confesses that "I'm hooked again on stuff." Having been first addicted at seventeen, he explains that he realizes that he "shouldn't have done that" this time: He has used heroin with his friends from prison because he felt sorry for them and because he had wanted to help them overcome their self-hatred and their addiction. He claims, however, that he has not been addicted long and that he will withdraw from the habit the next day, on Saturday. Swearing that he loves Sandy and her children, Winston begs her forgiveness and promises to stop hitting her, to get a job, and to spend more time at home.

Sandy's first response is to ask about the welfare of her children, but she stutters so badly that she must resort to writing Winston a note; learning that her babies are asleep, Sandy writes that she is tired, has a headache, and wants only to sleep. As Winston leaves to get sleeping pills for her and for himself (to use in his withdrawal the next day), Sandy drifts off to sleep. When she awakes, it is already dark and Winston has returned but, instead of sleeping pills, he has brought her a morphine tablet, and she realizes that he is high again. While Winston explains alternative ways in which Sandy can use the tablet, she sees his needles and blood-soaked cotton.

Again Sandy attempts to speak, only to suffer once more her childhood malady of extreme stuttering. She writes another note, demanding that Winston throw away the tablet and promising to help him through the withdrawal. He reads her note meekly, and she hears the toilet flush before he returns with two cold beers. Believing that Winston has resigned himself to the difficult struggle of withdrawal, Sandy hears a cry upstairs and feeds the twins their bottles.

When she finishes, Winston is in the bathroom, but he will not permit her to enter. A half hour later, he comes out, high again. Sandy, out of sorrow and desperation, tries to make love with him. Winston, however, cannot perform because of the drug's effects; Sandy feels guilty and ashamed, "as if she had made him do something wrong." Still unable to enunciate clearly, she listens as Winston tells her that she is "unlucky," having lost her husband to "a rich/wite/woman" and now having a "junkie" as an inept lover. Before they slip into an uneasy sleep, Winston once again proclaims his love and begs Sandy for help.

When Winston awakes the next morning, he kisses Sandy in the kitchen, where she is feeding the boys, and she watches him go outside and throw away the envelope containing his drug apparatus. In order to be with Winston throughout most of the day, Sandy has arranged for a baby-sitter, so that they can go to the country. The car will not start, however, and Winston is too weak from the initial withdrawal to push it to a service station for help in starting it. Instead, they walk to a park, where Winston's attention and their horseplay suggest to Sandy that he will finally conquer his addiction. When he grows too weak from the progressing withdrawal to continue their play, she helps him walk home.

After Sandy has cooked supper, she checks upstairs on Winston, who is now bedridden, engulfed in his "Saturday/nite/pain." Proud of his struggle, she massages him and brings sherry to ease the pain; as he thanks her, she says "any ol time, man" and realizes that she has not stuttered for the first time in twenty-four hours. Having fed the babies, she returns to check on Winston, whose condition has deteriorated to nausea and chills. Sandy adds an extra blanket and, taking off her clothes, tries to warm him with her body. Fearful and crying, she is unsure how to comfort Winston, so she sings to him as if he were a child. Having quieted him, Sandy succumbs to her own exhaustion, falling asleep while calling his name as he gets up to regurgitate in the bathroom.

When one of the babies wakes her, it is very early Sunday morning. While she hands the baby his bottle of milk, Sandy realizes that the house is dark and silent. Frantically, she turns on the lights to find an empty bed and, downstairs, her open purse with an empty wallet. Knowing that Winston has failed, she walks out on the porch and, despite her nakedness, stares for a moment at the empty street. Vulnerable but strengthened by the ordeal, Sandy returns to the children.

Themes and Meanings

Although Sonia Sanchez has worked in several genres, poetry is her primary craft; "After Saturday Nite Comes Sunday" might then best be considered an autobiographical prose poem, for her childhood years were spent in a New York tenement, where drug addiction was an everyday reality. In her essay "Ruminations/Reflections," she asserts that "the poet is a creator of social values." The story, without recourse to blunt didacticism, addresses from "a Black woman's view of the world" the struggle to avert the breakdown of the black family in the social context of white oppression.

The story's opening clarifies that context when Sandy is confronted by "that under-sized/low expectation of niggahs/being able to save anything" at the bank. When she discovers that Winston is responsible for the missing money, she must confront not only his drug addiction but also the legacy of his frustrated dreams, "like some child-hood disease," which have culminated in heroin fantasies from an early age. Those fantasies, based on the fear of failure and a sense of hopelessness, have led to drug-related crime, conviction, and prison—metaphors for being born black, for racism, and for exclusion. Having served his sentence, Winston remains criminally irrespon-sible and unemployed: He has confirmed the white stereotype of prejudice, which ig-nores the fact that he has grown up in a society that discriminated against him both le-gally and socially.

Sandy's self-induced silence, her stuttering, and her dependence on the white drug dealer Smith (an Everyman figure for racists) reenact symbolically Winston's entire fragmented life in the course of two hours and, further, the two days that follow. From the humiliating stare at the bank to her vacant gaze on the empty streets of the white world that consumes her lover, the story is framed by a white society that encourages blacks to become addicts to its own values, among which is the implicit inferior social status of the black man. As Sanchez asserts in her essay: "The most fundamental truth to be told in any art form, as far as Blacks are concerned, is that America is killing us."

Sandy's solitary struggle to free Winston from his cycle of self-hatred and self-destructive drug addiction is not a struggle against him so much as it is a loving strug-gle of selflessness for him. Despite his lies, theft, and betrayal, she respects Winston's attempt to affirm blackness, through his empathy for his friends and for her, far more than she respects her former husband, who has left her for a rich white woman and, subsequently, feeds the addiction to white values. Sandy, however, knows that Winston may fail again, and her struggle for a loving black unity of the family centers not only on him but also on her twin boys, who will inherit Winston's legacy. When Sunday—a day of thanks and rest—comes, Sandy will have practiced the black aes-thetic, which Sanchez defines in part as "a clarion call to the values of change while it also speaks to the beauty of a nonexploitative age." In the midst of the mutual despair, Sandy nurtures the destiny of the black male—and family—offering to her boys a model of care, attention, commitment, self-reliance and, most important, unwavering love.

Style and Technique

Although Sanchez's third-person narrator reflects Sandy's point of view, Sanchez gives both of the central characters voices in their own right. Italicized passages per-mit Winston a tenuous dignity appropriate to this desire for psychological freedom and trace Sandy's conquest of her stuttering as she becomes confident in her commitment to him. These passages blend indistinguishably dialogue and interior mono- logue; the characters speak directly from within to each other and to the reader. Con- sequently, the reader knows that these characters are aware of their efforts to shape their own lives. Just as Sandy must overcome her stuttering in favor of clear self- expression to endure the emphatic images of emptiness that close the story, Sanchez must subvert standard English to find a language suitable to her characters.

Sanchez's language alternates between clashing images of a harsh reality, such as the spots of blood seeping through the envelope that contains Winston's needles, and of tender commitment, such as Sandy's naked vulnerability of selflessness while he is in the throes of withdrawal. Within this imagistic tension, Sanchez develops her im- ages of drug addiction into a complex, dominant metaphor of nearly absolute evil: the living death of an individual or a people when they become dependent on values that they have had no role in creating. To underscore the need for self-definition in order to gain self-determination, Sanchez frequently uses unusual spellings, slang, and com- pressed phrasing: The spellings "wuz," "wud," "cuz," and "sed" echo not only black speech but also her devotion to the improvised sound poem in which her cries and moans are impossible to capture on the printed page, thereby affirming the black oral tradition; her phrases such as "wite/dude" and "yo/woman" indicate not only the pre- vious sound technique but also a semantic compression in which "wite/dude" con- notes a clever, exploitative bigotry—the mask of friendship worn by Smith, at whose "crib" Winston and his friends inject heroin. This latter example of slang contributes both to the frequent intermeshing of drug users' slang and black slang for realism in the speech rhythms and to the irony that Sanchez achieves through repetition; Smith's "crib" is the living death that awaits Winston, while the boys' crib is the living beauty that Sandy is determined to create for them.

Even straightforward repetition works ironically and symbolically, for as Sandy turns on lights all over the house, only to find emptiness, she gains an inner illumina- tion and a strength that allows her to stand naked boldly—not submissively—before the world. She returns to her boys with a greater resolve than ever to secure their fu- ture, whether or not Winston returns to continue his struggle. Like Sanchez turning her experience into a distinctive language of the black aesthetic, Sandy transforms her disappointment with Winston into an ethic for those who will follow her.

Michael Loudon

AFTER THE FAIR

Author: Dylan Thomas (1914-1953)
Type of plot: Sketch
Time of plot: 1933
Locale: Wales
First published: 1934

> *Principal characters:*
> ANNIE, the protagonist, a homeless young mother
> THE FAT MAN, a circus freak who befriends her

The Story

After the crowd goes home from a local fair and the booths and rides are closed down, a young girl named Annie remains behind. Surrounded by the shapes of wooden horses and fairy boats, she begins to look for a place to sleep for the night. Peeping into tents and behind stalls shrouded in canvas, she continues searching for a suitable bed but fails to find a comfortable place. When she comes to the Astrologer's tent, she discovers a bundle of straw in the corner. When she touches the straw it begins to move. She then kneels by its side, puts out her hand, and feels a baby's hand touch her own.

Having nowhere to sleep now, she decides to walk toward the trailers where the workers from the fair make their homes. Most of the trailers are dark, so she chooses to knock at the door of one of the only two that still have their lights on. The fattest man she has ever seen in her life opens the door and invites her in. After they share some buttered toast, the large host explains to Annie that he is the Fat Man. As he puts it, "I've always been a fat man . . . and now I'm the Fat Man; there's nobody to touch me for fatness." When he asks her why she left her home in Cardiff, Annie simply replies, "Money." He, in turn, tells her about the fair, the places he has been, and the people he has met. Annie finally tells him about the baby in the Astrologer's tent. "That's the stars again," he replies. Annie merely says, "The baby'll die."

When the Fat Man suddenly leaves the trailer Annie assumes he is going after the police, and the narrator explains that she does not want to be caught by the police officer again. It is not clear why she is sought by the police, but her earlier remark that she left Cardiff because of money implies that she may have stolen some cash. One is also led to assume that she is now down on her luck, a vagrant, and that the abandoned baby is hers.

The Fat Man, however, returns to the trailer smiling and carrying the baby in his arms. "See what the stars have done," he announces. She takes the child, which has begun to cry, and holds it against her small breast. She tells the Fat Man that a police officer is after her, but when he asks her why the police want her, she does not answer but holds the child closer to her "wasted breast."

As the baby's cries grow louder, both Annie and the Fat Man become distressed. Annie decides that the only thing they can do to silence the child is to take it on the merry-go-round. The three of them move through the darkness of the deserted fair toward the place where the wooden horses stand waiting. With the baby clutching her neck, Annie climbs into the saddle of one of the horses and calls out for the Fat Man to start the engine. The machinery set into motion, the Fat Man gets up by her side, pulls the main lever, and climbs into the saddle of the smallest horse of all.

As the merry-go-round picks up speed, the baby stops crying and begins to clap its hands out of sheer excitement and pleasure. The noise of the ride brings out the men from the other trailers who see this amazing spectacle: the Fat Man and a thin girl dressed in black with a baby in her arms, racing round and round on the wooden horses to the blaring music of the organ.

Themes and Meanings

In both his poetry and his fiction, Dylan Thomas celebrated the animal joy and vitality that human beings embody when they are in harmony with the cosmic cycle of life and death. As a young boy, Thomas took great joy in going to the local fairs. The spectacle of the crowds, lights, music, and exotic people (such as the Fat Woman) presented life in a rich, compressed form that dazzled the boy from Swansea. In his essay "Holiday Memory" (1946), he recorded the excitement that he and his friends had shared during a visit to the fair on a bank holiday.

In "After the Fair,' Thomas focuses on the intense loneliness experienced by a young woman when the bright wonders of the fair are closed down. Annie's life is one of fear and alienation from the community. Hungry and homeless, she leaves her baby in the Astrologer's tent, presumably hoping that someone will find it and be able to care for it. Thomas, who later emphasized the symbolic importance of the constellations in his poem "Altarwise by Owl-Light" (1936), suggests the providential nature of the stars in this story. When the Fat Man fetches the baby and announces, "See what the stars have done," he is simply being considerate of Annie's feelings by jokingly attributing the baby to the stars rather than to its actual mother. Thomas, however, implies that the stars do, indeed, help to shape the destiny of this lonely woman and her abandoned child.

Annie, her baby, and the Fat Man bring the sleeping fair to life when they start up and ride the merry-go-round. The wooden horses come alive as they are ridden by this bizarre "family." The story ends with the celebration of life as the baby claps its hands and Annie and the Fat Man become one through the ever-increasing music, speed, and exhilaration of the ride. The circular motion of the merry-go-round suggests the great cycle of life itself. The ecstacy of Annie, the child, and the Fat Man reflects the pulsing energy of primitive life force that drives all creatures under the stars.

Style and Technique

"After the Fair" was the first short story that Thomas published. Presented from the third-person, omniscient point of view, the narrative seems straightforward. There is, however, an interesting ambiguity in the story. The narrator never states outright that it is Annie's baby lying in the straw in the Astrologer's tent, and never explains why Annie is being sought by the police. The reader can, therefore, interpret the Fat Man's remark, "See what the stars have done," as having symbolic significance. As a "star child" the baby brings Annie and the Fat Man together in a symbolic union of life-giving energy.

The story has the form of a sketch, a small slice of life. The reader is never informed of Annie's background and only a few details are given about the Fat Man's past. The focus is on the present, and in concluding the story with the night ride of the merry-go-round still in progress, Thomas suggests the endless nature of this exhilarating moment. Thomas, displaying a Romantic sensibility (with his interest in children, freaks, common people, and mutability of life), freezes in a timeless action a circus fat man and a lonely girl clutching her baby. In so doing, he moves from his straightforward style to a lyrical, celebratory, poetic style rich in metaphors and rhythmic cadences.

Richard Kelly

AFTER THE STORM

Author: Ernest Hemingway (1899-1961)
Type of plot: Realism
Time of plot: The late 1920's or early 1930's
Locale: The Florida Keys
First published: 1932

Principal character:
THE NARRATOR, an unnamed sponger

The Story

The story opens with two men fighting over very little, something that has to do with making punch. One man is getting the better of the other by choking him. This man, however, manages to get his knife out, and he slashes the arm muscles of his attacker, after which he leaves the bar where the fight has taken place. He gets into his skiff, which is full of water from a recent storm, bails it out, and sails toward the open sea.

First he sees a three-masted ship that has sunk during the storm. He can see the stumps of the ship's spars sticking out of the water, but the vessel itself rests in water too deep for him to have any hope of reaching it and claiming the salvage. Then he notices a huge congregation of birds in the distance. He sails toward them and eventually comes on the wreckage of the largest steamer he has ever seen. The ship is lying on its side in sand, some of it close enough to the surface of the water that he can stand on it and be only chin-deep in water. He can see rows of sealed portholes as he looks at the side of the ship down through the clear water.

He speculates on what riches the ship might have been carrying. After he tries unsuccessfully to break one of the porthole windows with a wrench tied to a pole, he strips and dives into the water carrying the wrench with him. He gets a grip on the edge of one of the portholes and tries to break the glass, but it will not yield. He can see through the window. On the other side is a dead woman, her hair floating languidly in the water.

He makes several dives to the porthole and succeeds only in cracking it. He cannot break it. His nose is bleeding badly from staying under the water so long and from diving so deep. He cuts the grapple from his anchor to use as a tool and goes back under with it, but he cannot hold on to the grapple. Next he lashes his wrench to a pole and tries to use it to get into the porthole, but the wrench slips from the lashing and sinks to the bottom. He is forced to abandon for the time his attempts to penetrate the ship. He speculates that the liner must have had five million dollars' worth of loot on it. He wonders why there are no sharks in the vicinity.

When he gets back to port, he learns that the fellow he cut with his knife is all right except for his wounded arm. He is placed under a five-hundred-dollar bond for his part in the fight, but some of his friends perjure themselves and testify that the wounded man had come after him with an ax and that he had acted in self-defense, so he is not held culpable. The weather is foul for all the next week, and by the time he is able to return to the site of the wreck, "the Greeks had blown her open and cleaned her out. They got the safe out with dynamite. . . . She carried gold and they got it all. They stripped her clean."

The narrator speculates on what must have happened on the night of the storm. The night was too wild for anyone to be out on deck. The ship, out of Havana, could not make port. The captain was trying to get through a channel and missed it by only a hundred yards, but what the ship hit was quicksand. Probably the captain ordered the ballast tanks opened, and when that happened, the ship went down. The boilers then likely exploded, killing many of the 450 passengers on board as well as all the crew. Those who did not die in the explosion soon drowned.

The reader is told that the hull, which is still there, is now inhabited by huge jewfish, some weighing three to four hundred pounds. The narrator complains that he was first at the wreck after the birds, but that the Greeks got all the booty. He reflects, "even the birds got more out of her than I did."

Themes and Meanings

"After the Storm" tells about a catastrophic event, the sinking of a large ocean liner during a storm. The loss of life is in excess of 450 passengers as well as the entire crew. Readers are dependent, however, on the narrator to tell them about the catastrophe, and he views his loss of the booty as more catastrophic than the loss of life incurred in the sinking.

The narrator is a sponger, and the double meaning of the word is quite intentional. He makes a living harvesting sponges, but he also is not above living off carrion, just as do the birds that first attract him to the wreck. This man is willing to engage in a potentially fatal fight that is, by his own admission, not about anything. If he has any emotions about the deaths of those who went down with the ship, they are not revealed in this carefully controlled and tightly written story.

The story is essentially about predators: the narrator, the birds, the jewfish, and the Greeks. The narrator is an embryonic version of Harry Morgan in Ernest Hemingway's later novel *To Have and Have Not* (1937). He is a man whose only hope of real wealth comes from the possibility of plundering something. His only obstacle to doing this in "After the Storm" is that he does not have the equipment to carry out the job, so that others beat him to the plunder. It is not unusual in the Hemingway canon to find characters whose success in an important venture is blocked by their lack of equipment or, in the case of Hemingway's writing about wars, lack of adequate weapons.

The solitary qualities of this story remind one of those found in *The Old Man and the Sea* (1952), in which Santiago hooks his dream fish but does not have the equipment to land it, so he drags it behind his ketch while it is eaten away by sharks. By the time Santiago reaches the dock, little is left of the majestic fish with which he had his greatest and most threatening combat.

In "After the Storm," the narrator is a loser, the captain of the sunken liner is a loser, and all those on board are losers. The birds win by getting the carrion that first attracts them to the wreck, the jewfish prosper afterward by living in the battered hull, and the Greeks succeed best of all because they have the equipment necessary to salvage the treasure.

Style and Technique

Hemingway's mastery of understatement as a controlling literary device is evident throughout "After the Storm." Akin to the understatement is the strong irony within the story. Events that have cost the lives of all the people on the sunken ship are minimized by Hemingway's choice of narrator. Because the narrator's focus is self-serving, materialistic, and essentially meretricious, the information given about the shipwreck is minimal, and its scope is limited by the vision of the low-life person who tells it. The secondary action of the story, that of the actual shipwreck, is the larger, more dramatic action of the two story lines Hemingway develops here, but by downplaying it, he asserts his stylistic control.

The story's narrator is a crude, brutalized person, someone who will fight over nothing and whose moral code is as debased as his speech, which throughout the story gives subtle insights into his personality. The birds flock around the ship to eat carrion because they must live; they are morally neutral. The narrator, however, does not have their moral neutrality and is, hence, more culpable than they.

Despite the ironic contrast between the main action and the secondary action, in fact, perhaps because of it, the reader develops a growing sense of horror at what happened. This sense of horror continues to develop in one's mind long after one has read the story. The impact is remarkably long-lasting because the reader keeps supplying details from an imagination that Hemingway has piqued and set in motion.

Hemingway's language in this story, as in most of his work, is simple and direct. His sentence structure is unornamented. The ironies of the story are convoluted and intertwined with one another. Hemingway controls them with precision, as he controls the two story lines with a deftness and economy that one finds in few other authors.

R. Baird Shuman

AGHWEE THE SKY MONSTER

Author: Kenzaburō Ōe (1935-   )
Type of plot: Ghost story, frame story
Time of plot: The mid-1950's to mid-1960's
Locale: Tokyo
First published: "Sora no kaibutsu Aguii," 1964 (English translation, 1977)

> *Principal characters:*
> D, a young composer who sees a vision of his dead baby in the sky
> HIS NURSE, who is contemptuous of D's vision
> HIS FORMER WIFE, who returns a key to the locker storing D's compositions
> HIS MISTRESS, who is abandoned by D after the birth and death of Aghwee
> AGHWEE, his son, named after the only sound he made in his brief life
> THE NARRATOR, who is hired to look after D on his aimless wanderings through Tokyo

The Story

"Aghwee the Sky Monster" is one of Kenzaburō Ōe's first stories about children born with mental defects, written after his own son was born in 1963 with a cranial defect that would cause mental disability. In the story, the father, D, succumbs to traditional Japanese pressures and prejudices against raising a mentally disabled child and lets his newborn son starve to death. This is in stark contrast to Ōe's own decision to love and raise his disabled son. D's baby returns as a ghost and ultimately drives D to suicide, creating a haunting tale about the grave consequences of a father being unable to face the responsibility of raising a seriously disabled child.

The story opens as the unnamed narrator reflects back to a time ten years earlier. Then entering college, he is interviewed by a rich banker. The overbearing man is looking for a companion to keep scandal away from his twenty-eight-year-old son, the composer D, who has become obsessed with the idea that he is living with a monster. Once a week, the narrator is to accompany D on his wanderings throughout Tokyo.

When meeting D, the narrator is told that there is a being in the sky that is invisible to all people but him. Occasionally, it comes down to D when he is in the open. D asks the narrator not to act startled in such a case. The latter agrees. Toward the end of their first day, D acts as if he has an invisible companion while they are part of a crowd watching the frenzied solitary dance of an old businessperson.

The narrator asks D's nurse about the composer's monster. With clear contempt, the nurse explains that it is a huge baby as big as a kangaroo, dressed in a white cotton nightgown and afraid of dogs and police officers. When the narrator meets D again, D knows about the conversation with the nurse. D says that he is not living in the present anymore but is traveling through time and does not want to leave as much as a footprint or the memory of a conversation with anybody else in Tokyo.

The narrator's visit to D's former wife reveals the nature and name of the monster. D calls him Aghwee, after the first and only sound made by their son, who was born with what looked like a brain hernia. While his wife was in a feverish coma after her cesarean, D and the physician decided to starve the baby to death by feeding it nothing but sugar water instead of milk. After the boy's death, an autopsy revealed that he had an operable, benign tumor rather than a permanent defect. D divorced his wife and began seeing Aghwee in the sky. The composer's former wife gives the narrator a key to give to D. Eventually, the narrator mails the key and learns that it opens the locker in which D keeps his original scores, which D burns in the narrator's presence.

The narrator is sent to D's mistress, with whom D slept on the day his baby was born. He is instructed to tell her that D, who stopped visiting her after the baby's death, will never see her again. The mistress fails to seduce the narrator, who returns to Tokyo.

While on a bicycle outing in winter, D and the narrator run into a pack of dogs. Afraid that D may attack the dogs to protect Aghwee, the narrator bursts out in tears and suddenly feels Aghwee's hands on his shoulder. Later, D tells him that the sky is full of beings representing cherished things the living have lost and that one can see them only by making a sacrifice.

On Christmas Eve, D jumps in front of a truck, apparently trying to save Aghwee from being run over. The narrator visits D in the hospital before his death and wonders whether D made up the story of Aghwee to cover his suicide. Ten years later, after the narrator loses his right eye in an attack by vicious children, he again senses Aghwee's presence, brought on by his own personal tragedy.

Themes and Meanings

The meaning behind the haunting of D comes from his decision to let his baby die rather than to face the burden of raising a mentally disabled human being. Having failed to provide for his son while he was alive, D feels he has to make amends to Aghwee the sky monster by obliterating all traces of his once successful personal and professional life. By confiding his vision to incomprehensive others who judge him to be mentally ill, D assumes a creative punishment for his own actions. Ōe creates additional punishment for D by providing him with the knowledge that his son could have been cured. The theme of moral responsibility in a challenging world runs deep in all of Ōe's fiction, and this short story is no exception.

D is shown as a weak man who continues to betray people around him. He neglects his wife for his mistress, decides to starve their baby without consulting her, and even turns on the narrator by committing suicide while in his company. This makes the narrator lose face with D's father, who silently pays the narrator for his last day's service at the hospital with one thousand yen, which the narrator slips the driver of the truck that fatally hit D. By failing to face up to his human responsibilities as husband, father, employer, and companion, D represents modern humanity, which lacks a clear moral bearing.

Ironically, D assumes some responsibility for his actions only when it is too late. Making amends with Aghwee becomes his overriding concern in life. He wants to show the sky monster that Tokyo is a sort of paradise, creating a positive experience for the ghost while denying himself any further meaningful life. No longer composing any music and withdrawn from both his former wife and his mistress, D shuns even occasional human interactions such as the purchase of a subway ticket, leaving this task to the narrator. D's vision of himself as a time traveler careful not to leave any traces serves as a thematic parallel to his regret over having denied the experience of life to his newborn son.

Style and Technique

Stylistically, Ōe deals with the theme of parental and human responsibility through the medium of an effective ghost story. By limiting the point of view to that of the narrator reflecting back on past events, Ōe draws the reader into a magical tale. The focus is on the gradual revelation of D's deeds and his unique response to his guilt. What D did becomes clear as the narrator meets the people central to the composer's life. The frame story serves to bring the story to a satisfying close: At the beginning of the story, the narrator promises to reveal what happened to his right eye, and at the end, it is revealed that he was rewarded with a magical second sight of Aghwee for being partially blinded.

The choice of Christmas Eve for D's suicide may strike readers as a bit melodramatic, but then again D is engaging in a kind of performance for the narrator, who stands in for an audience, so it is convincing that D ends his own life with a maximum of emotional effect and chooses a day that means nothing religious to him but represents a culturally imported occasion for shopping and gift giving in contemporary Japan. In a way, D offers his own life as a gift of penance to his murdered baby son.

In "Aghwee the Sky Monster," Ōe deliberately leaves open the question of whether Aghwee is a real ghost or just the product of D's guilty conscience and the narrator's collusion in that perception. The reader has only the narrator's report that D acts as if Aghwee is there and that he himself sensed Aghwee's presence twice in his life. Beyond this personal account, there is no independent, objective confirmation of these occurrences, and a reader may side with D's nurse, who rejects Aghwee as the product of a lunatic's imagination.

On a deeper level, the monster functions as a manifestation of D's guilt over having starved his apparently brain-damaged son. The monster represents a magnified return of his suppressed memories of his own actions, whether it is meant to be a real vision or a metaphor of the enormity of D's bad conscience.

R. C. Lutz

THE ALBATROSS

Author: Susan Hill (1942-   )
Type of plot: Social realism
Time of plot: 1968
Locale: A fishing village in northeast England
First published: 1969

> *Principal characters:*
> DUNCAN PIKE, the protagonist, a simple-minded workman
> HILDA PIKE, his mother
> TED FLINT, a fisherman

The Story

Duncan Pike is an eighteen-year-old man with limited intelligence and thus an outsider to himself and to the small fishing village in which he lives. His agonizing feeling of being an outcast is reinforced by his domineering mother, Hilda, who constantly reminds him, "We keep ourselves to ourselves in this town." His mother wants him to be alone; she clings to him for several reasons. For one, she is handicapped, like her son. Because she is confined to a wheelchair, she depends on Duncan to help her through each day. She also underestimates her son: She thinks him incapable of performing the simplest task without her instructions. This is also the attitude of the villagers toward Duncan; he can only feel further isolated because of this.

For Duncan, any contact with the villagers is extremely painful. "He dared not wonder what they really thought of him, or how they talked, as he went away. . . ." He has almost come to hate himself and doubt his abilities because he has listened too long to his mother and to the other residents of the village.

An incident at the opening of the story illustrates this well. Each Wednesday, Hilda sends her son to buy fish in the market for their supper. She writes down "not cod" as "she wrote everything down for him, every message, every demand, every list." Duncan resents this treatment; no matter where he goes, he thinks, he takes his mother with him. He has given up trying to defend or explain himself to her or anyone else. The villagers speak to him clearly, loudly, and slowly, thinking that he cannot understand them if they do not. He buys cod because that is all that is being sold, not bothering to ask for anything else or to go to another fish seller. Too mentally beaten down to explain the circumstances, Duncan endures the verbal abuse of his mother when he returns home.

Understandably, at eighteen, Duncan is beginning to want some independence, to break away from his mother and the village. His desire is particularly acute because of his isolation and his feelings of inferiority. He sits in rapture when his boss speaks of the outside world, which Duncan sees as "new, miraculous." He stands and looks out at the sea, longing for a new life. Slowly, reluctantly at first, Duncan begins to see that

"I could go anywhere." His mother seems to sense his desire to leave, for she repeatedly reminds him that he could not make it at sea or anywhere else. "You stay as you are," she chides him. Duncan's desire to leave his old life nevertheless remains strong. With each view of the sea he reminds himself that "he could go anywhere, by himself."

Ted Flint, a fisherman, is Duncan's idol. He has done everything and been everywhere that Duncan would like to go. Ted treats Duncan as an equal. He offers to take him out in his boat, but Hilda's relentless words, "You leave going in boats alone," stop Duncan.

He continues to be fascinated by Flint, and Flint befriends the boy because he feels sorry for him. He good-heartedly offers to buy Duncan a drink at the local pub. He does not fear Hilda Pike, but Duncan does, and so he does not accept the invitation. Still, Duncan is thrilled, for he has had the chance to go, to be with the men, to assert his independence. It reinforces his feeling that perhaps he could do something about his life.

The turning point of the story, and of Duncan's life, happens when Flint is drowned in a sea storm. The incident crystallizes in Duncan's realization that he, too, could die without ever having lived. He is so affected by Flint's death that he leaves his mother in her wheelchair alone at the funeral because she taunted him, saying that he understood nothing about death. It is Duncan's first act of defiance.

The act of ignoring his mother's abuse and leaving her helpless in church is followed by Duncan's going by himself to the pub to buy a drink. He repeatedly tells himself, as if to convince himself, that he can do what he wants. Ultimately, a sense of calm overcomes him. "He was no longer anxious, he felt a new person, strong, by himself."

"Duncan thought of nothing, felt nothing. He had decided what he should do and could not remember a reason." What Duncan decides to do is to free himself, and he does that by poisoning his mother and burning all the things in the house that he hates and that remind him of her. Ceremoniously, he removes her sewing materials, her furnishings, and burns them in the grate. Then he dresses his mother, places her in her wheelchair, and pushes her into the sea. Duncan then gets into a boat and goes to sea himself—something his mother would never allow him to do.

That Duncan is limited mentally is apparent in his solution to his problems. He can be free only by killing his mother. He makes no plans for his future beyond being at sea in a boat. He is later found huddled in a grainbarn. The reader must assume that he will be tried but found mentally incompetent.

Themes and Meanings

The title "The Albatross" immediately evokes Samuel Taylor Coleridge's poem *The Rime of the Ancient Mariner* (1798). In the poem, the mariner is cursed to wear an albatross, a seabird, around his neck because he has callously killed the bird. Only when he appreciates the beauty and power of nature and of life is the curse lifted: The albatross falls from his neck.

The two themes of burden and the power of nature are central to this short story. Susan Hill very carefully lets the reader decide who is an albatross to whom. Hilda Pike sees her son as a burden. She is ashamed of his limited mental ability. She believes that she has sacrificed her life to give him a home because he could not possibly make it in the world on his own. Similarly, Duncan sees his mother as the albatross. Her dependence on him and her constant harping on his inabilities to survive are his curse. Finally, he believes that in order to have any freedom he must kill her. The irony here is apparent in relation to the Coleridge poem: The mariner gains freedom through an appreciation of life, while Duncan thinks that he is gaining life through death; in fact, he has merely exchanged one kind of prison for another.

Style and Technique

Hill's straightforward, easy-to-read prose has the resonance of a folk ballad. In part, this effect is achieved by her use of traditional symbolism. The sea is the predominant symbol in the story. It represents both freedom and death. It gives life to the village, but it also takes life because of its power. Descriptions of the turmoil of the sea reflect the inner emotional turmoil of the characters involved. When Duncan sees the dead body of Ted Flint, he can only compare it to the deaths he has known, that of dead fish, "dead white cod."

Further symbolism of the sea and nature is achieved in the use of the characters' names. Hilda and Duncan Pike see each other and themselves as useless. A pike fish in England is a freshwater fish that is good for nothing, including food, and is bothersome and caught only by mistake. Ted Flint is as tough and strong as his name implies. He is the flint that starts the spark in Duncan, provoking him to want life.

The final words of the story show that life goes on just as nature endures. Hilda Pike is dead, Duncan Pike has been apprehended, but the land, the sea, the seasons, and the elements are eternal. "Later that day, the wind veered west, blowing in soft-bellied rain clouds. The thaw began."

Resa Willis

THE ALEPH

Author: Jorge Luis Borges (1899-1986)
Type of plot: Magical Realism
Time of plot: February, 1929 to March, 1943
Locale: Buenos Aires, Argentina
First published: "El Aleph," 1945 (English translation, 1962)

> *Principal characters:*
> BORGES, the narrator and protagonist, a writer
> BEATRIZ VITERBO, his beloved
> CARLOS ARGENTINO DANERI, her cousin and a writer of
>   questionable merit

The Story

"The Aleph" begins with the narrator, Borges, recalling that on the February morning of Beatriz Viterbo's death, a billboard advertisement in the Plaza Constitucion was being changed. The observation prompts him to vow not to allow himself to be changed by life, and thus he intends to consecrate himself to the memory of his beloved. Every year on Beatriz's birthday (April 30), Borges returns to the house of her father and her cousin, Carlos Argentino Daneri. Whereas in the past it had been necessary to devise pretexts for his visits, the new circumstances permit him to carry on his devotion to Beatriz while seeming to perform an act of courtesy and respect. With each successive visit, he arrives later and stays longer. Gradually he gains the confidence of Carlos Argentino.

Beatriz's cousin is in effect her antithesis: Beatriz possessed an ethereal quality that almost transcended reality, while Carlos Argentino is altogether too human, as is suggested by his entirely ordinary physical presence and his pointless existence. His remarks about modern humanity (that it is unnecessary for people to travel since the advent of the telephone, telegraph, radio, cinema, and so forth) cause Borges to make a connection between Carlos Argentino and literature: Both are equally inept, pompous, and vast. When Borges asks why Carlos Argentino does not write down his ideas, Carlos Argentino predictably responds that he has, in a poem entitled "The Earth." As Carlos Argentino reads and comments on the verses, the consummate mediocrity of the work becomes evident. The real task involved in the poem, decides Borges, has been, not its composition, but rather the invention of reasons to explain why it is so admirable. Carlos Argentino's purpose in his encyclopedic enterprise is to versify the face of the earth, which he does in a boring, unskillful, and chaotic way.

Several Sundays after Borges hears about the poem for the first time, Carlos Argentino unexpectedly requests a meeting between the two, which is to take place in the establishment of Zunino and Zungri. After censuring critics and the practice that he refers to as "prologuemania," Carlos Argentino comes to the point of the interview:

He would like Borges's assistance in securing a prologue for his poem from Alvaro Melian Lafinur, a literary figure of renown. Borges agrees to help but without any actual intention of doing so.

The following October, the protagonist receives the second call that he has ever received from Carlos Argentino, who this time is extremely upset because Zunino and Zungri are about to demolish his house in order to expand their business. Borges thinks that he understands the cousin's consternation until Carlos Argentino explains the real cause of his distress: He cannot finish the poem without the Aleph (one of the points in space which contains all points), which is located in the basement. An accidental discovery of his childhood, it now serves as the source of material for the poem.

Borges tells Carlos Argentino that he will be over immediately, and, on hanging up, it occurs to him that Carlos Argentino is insane, which would account for his seemingly inexplicable behavior. Once in the house, Borges engages in a conversation with a large portrait of Beatriz until he is interrupted by Carlos Argentino, who is obsessed with the idea of losing the Aleph. After a glass of wine and some instructions about how to view the phenomenon, Borges goes down to the basement and settles into the position that Carlos Argentino has designated. Just when he fears that he has been poisoned and buried by a madman, he sees the Aleph, a small, iridescent sphere of nearly intolerable brilliancy, which reveals the inconceivable universe. He gropes for some emblem or image that might enable him to communicate the experience of witnessing the ineffable, infinite, and vertiginous Aleph, but at the same time he fears contaminating his report with the falseness of literature. Also, he feels despair in the knowledge that the successive nature of language makes it an inadequate vehicle for conveying the simultaneity of spectacle that is the Aleph.

Overcome by feelings of veneration and pity, Borges is once again rudely interrupted by the voice of Carlos Argentino. At that moment, he plots his revenge: He refuses to talk about the Aleph with Carlos Argentino and recommends repose in the serenity of the country. However, despite his pretense, Borges has indeed been transformed by the experience: All faces seem familiar and nothing surprises him; all is return. Fortunately, however, memory yields to forgetfulness after a few nights of insomnia.

A postscript from the first of March, 1943, updates the report. Carlos Argentino's poem has won the Second National Prize for Literature, something that Borges ascribes to misunderstanding and envy. Finally, he poses some questions about the Aleph: Did Carlos Argentino choose that name for the sphere, or did he see it used elsewhere applied to the same sort of phenomenon? If, as Borges suspects, the latter is the case, does a genuine Aleph exist, and did he see it and forget it?

Themes and Meanings

"The Aleph" is a fictional rendering of a universal metaphor as outlined by Jorge Luis Borges in an essay published in 1952 entitled "La esphera de Pascal" ("Pascal's Sphere"). The essay traces the development of the image of God as an endless sphere from six centuries before the Christian era to Blaise Pascal. Borges first cites Xenophanes of Colophon, who proposed to the Greeks the concept of one God who might subsume all the gods of their mythology, a single, perfect divinity in the form of a sphere and conveying solidity. Analogous images are found in the classical verses of Parmenides of Elea, in the Egyptian *Hermetica*, in the twelfth century poem *Roman de la rose*, and in the Book of Kings. The medieval interpretation of this idea was the presence of God in all of his creatures without being limited by any one of them, a re-affirmation of Scripture. When the cosmic vision represented in Dante's *La divina commedia* (c. 1320; *The Divine Comedy*, 1802; the earth as the immobile center of the universe around which nine concentric circles revolve) ceded to Copernican space, the initial sense of liberation eventually turned into anguish: Humankind felt lost in time and space, alone in a universe that resembled a labyrinth and an abyss.

As Beatrice led Dante through the spheres to a vision of God, so does Beatriz Viterbo serve as the link between the character Borges and the Aleph: Her clairvoyance helps Borges to see. Images of light, agony, ecstasy, and eternity are common both to her and to the sphere, which is also prefigured by the collage of photographs that capture Beatriz's multiple attitudes in frozen time. Her death removes her from time or its passage (which is marked through change). The large portrait that Borges addresses shows her smiling out of time rather than out of date. She stands still, so to speak, while life goes on; she has entered eternity.

If Beatriz expresses the Aleph, Carlos Argentino misunderstands it. Her notable lack of interest in books and her desire to live life contrast with his obsession with literature, which, in his case, equals an avoidance of contact with life. His conclusions about twentieth century man show an enthusiasm for substituted forms of experience and an inability to distinguish them from reality. During all the years that he has spent in the basement observing the Aleph, he has been incapable of interpreting it because his deficient intellect dwells on its millions of individual details, which he then records. His attempts to turn revelation into reason are misdirected, a distortion of the original subject. The poem presumes to be a faithful reproduction of life but merely accumulates facts at the expense of essence.

Borges's description of the Aleph is an unrhymed enumeration in which events are seemingly unordered and unrelated—in other words, meant to simulate the experience itself. He despairs of communicating what he has witnessed because he is acutely aware of the limitations of language and the falseness of literature. The religious and literary precedents that he invokes do not betray the verbal ostentation of Carlos Argentino but rather are intended to refer to a shared past. At the same time that he relies on that past, however, he also recognizes the importance of forgetting: As the twilight blurs distinctions in the photographs and the colors of the portrait fade, so does time corrupt his memory of the Aleph—a release for which Borges is grateful. To him, this godlike knowledge is an intolerable burden to be forgotten.

Style and Technique

One of the most striking aspects of "The Aleph" is the quantity of allusions made to the world outside the text, be they literary, historical, religious, philosophical, or geographic. Most are explicit, such as the epigraphs that preface the story or the numerous proper names mentioned, but implicit reference is also made, for example, to *The Divine Comedy* by the presence of certain structural and thematic elements (Beatriz, the sphere, the descent, and the name Daneri). Literary precedents are summoned by Carlos Argentino as well as by Borges, although their respective reasons for doing so differ substantially: ostentation versus the quest for answers. In addition to texts, place names appear with some regularity, contributing to the would-be veracity of Borges's report (a veracity that is completely at odds with the report's fantastic central episode).

The range and quantity of factual information are complementary to the story's elaborate temporal framework, both being dimensions that would normally help to orient the reader with respect to the events recounted. Throughout, the narrator remains highly conscious of years, months, days, hours, minutes, times of day, and segments of time, thereby enhancing the illusion of accuracy. There is also a thematic function involved: The contrast between time and eternity, like that between geographic locations and infinity, manifests the arbitrariness and artificiality of those human inventions.

Carlos Argentino is the symbol of such absurd endeavors, the epitome of misguided activity, and through him the futility of humanity's efforts becomes amusing. Meaninglessness, insignificance, affectation, obsession, mediocrity, and complacent stupidity are identified as humankind's characteristic traits and as a way of coping with existence: Human beings focus on small, immediate concerns because the larger questions cannot be answered. The somber, melancholy tone set by the agony and death of Beatriz is pervasive and bespeaks other losses (of innocence and faith, for example). In juxtaposing two elements as incongruous as profound sadness and absurdity (a technique that recurs throughout the story), the author illuminates otherwise undiscernible qualities and relationships in an ironically humorous way.

Krista Ratkowski Carmona

THE ALIEN CORN

Author: W. Somerset Maugham (1874-1965)
Type of plot: Realism
Time of plot: The early 1920's
Locale: London and Sussex, England, and Munich, Germany
First published: 1931

> *Principal characters:*
> FERDY RABENSTEIN, a worldly and affluent London Jew
> GEORGE BLAND, his great-nephew
> SIR ADOLPHUS (FREDDY) BLAND, a country squire of Sussex and
> George's father
> MURIEL (MIRIAM) BLAND, Sir Adolphus's wife
> LADY HANNAH BLAND, the mother of Sir Adolphus and the sister
> of Ferdy Rabenstein
> LEA MAKART, a concert pianist and a friend of Ferdy Rabenstein

The Story

The narrator, a successful middle-aged novelist, tells the story from his point of view in episodes that span about three years. He reminisces about his long-standing acquaintance with Ferdy Rabenstein, a cultured and affluent Jewish bachelor of London who moves in the best social circles. From Ferdy, the narrator learns that the Blands, who have invited him to Tilby, their estate in Sussex, are Ferdy's relatives, Sir Adolphus Bland being his nephew. Unlike Ferdy, they have concealed their Jewish identity and have led the lives of English country gentry.

Eminently successful, Sir Adolphus, a conservative member of Parliament, served as minister of munitions during World War I. Muriel, his wife, has converted to Catholicism. Their two sons, who bear the quintessentially English names George and Henry, are enrolled in elite educational institutions. Henry attends Eton, and George, the elder son, has just been sent down from Oxford, where he wasted his time and his father's money. Family ties with Ferdy have been broken, in part because he would not change his name during World War I and also because the Blands want no association with unassimilated Jews.

Because George will inherit the estate, his father wants him to follow a suitable profession, such as the diplomatic service. George has other ideas. He asks permission to go to Munich to study languages and prepare for an Oxford examination, a request his family reluctantly grants.

A few days after his return from the Blands, the narrator sees Ferdy in London and is invited to dinner. At the dinner he finds George present, a surprising turn because George's parents have rejected Ferdy's invitation, sent through the narrator himself.

Ferdy has interceded with his sister, Lady Hannah Bland, George's grandmother, who arranged the meeting. However, the dinner is not a success because Ferdy embarrasses George, whom he has just met for the first time, by telling humorous Jewish stories.

When the narrator next sees Muriel, he learns that George has spent his time in Germany studying music in the hope of becoming a concert pianist. The parents turn their energies to discouraging him from a course that they regard as unsuitable and demeaning. When George returns to Tilby for his twenty-first birthday celebration, however, he is heaped with gifts. On this occasion he causes consternation when he informs his family that he intends to return to Munich, saying that he knows he has genius. Even Ferdy, who is now on speaking terms with Sir Adolphus, sides with the family against George's ambition. After George remains unmoved by pleas and threats, his grandmother, Lady Bland, suggests a compromise. He will be allowed two years' study in Munich and will return home at the end. If it is not apparent by then that he has genuine talent, he will give up music and assume the duties of an elder son on a landed estate.

Later, the narrator visits George in Munich at the request of his mother because the agreement with George stipulated that members of the immediate family would not visit him. He finds George living a bohemian lifestyle but conscientiously applying himself to his piano. He also learns that, unlike his parents, George is concerned with his Jewish identity and heritage and takes pride in his friendship with Jewish students, artists, and intellectuals. He no longer thinks of himself as English. The narrator hears George play the piano, and, although he is no critic of music, concludes that George's hands are not well coordinated. When he returns to England, he tells the family only that George is well.

At the end of two years George returns to Tilby, and the family gathers to judge his talent. With his concurrence, they have invited the concert pianist Lea Makart to hear him play and to make the judgment about his career. The narrator notices the same lack of coordination that he had noticed before. When George finishes playing, Lea Makart inquires, "What is it you want me to tell you?" He replies that he wants to know whether he can become a first-rate concert pianist. Her devastating response is, "Not in a thousand years." George accepts this profoundly disappointing news in good form. When she suggests that he ask for another opinion, he admits that her assessment agrees with that of his teacher in Munich. She points out to him that he does not have a pianist's hands and, before leaving for her scheduled concert, plays for the assembled family. In her performance, the narrator clearly discerns the difference between the professional artist and the amateur.

Sensing his son's deep pain and disappointment, Sir Adolphus offers to give him another year in Munich or to send him around the world with a friend from Oxford. Deeply moved, George embraces his father and says he will take a walk; instead, he goes to the gun room. Afterward, hearing a report, servants go to the room and find George shot through the heart.

Themes and Meanings

W. Somerset Maugham's title is taken from John Keats's "Ode to a Nightingale," which contains a poignant reference to the biblical character Ruth, who stood with heavy heart in Judah amid the alien corn. Although Maugham finds his chief talent in telling a story in a memorable way, he considers characters that are alienated from society the most interesting. In other narratives he writes of unassimilated but changed Englishmen in the colonies, particularly in Asia and the South Pacific. He likes to depict characters who are in a sense outsiders, who have a kink or unusual streak in their personalities.

In this story, the narrator identifies with the Blands, calling himself an alien because of his aesthetic detachment, yet he shows the reader, by probing beneath the surface of the characters, by catching them off guard, that they are not as assimilated as they think. As self-conscious outsiders, the Blands (the name they have chosen seems symbolic) are unusual because they strive so hard for assimilation. Their very striving to shut themselves off from their past creates tensions within the family involving three generations and leading to their son's tragic death.

More than alienation, however, the quest for an ideal contributes to the tragedy. Another common and significant theme in Maugham is art, especially its power to attract absolute commitment. Although the Blands think the performing arts too trivial for their son, Lea Makart, the gifted pianist, expresses the view embraced by George. Artistic genius is all that matters. Other people are only the artist's raw material in the creation of beauty. If one has genius, all sacrifices to further it pale into insignificance. Like other characters in Maugham's works, George is willing to pin all of his hope on artistic success. A character such as Charles Strickland in *The Moon and Sixpence* (1919) takes a desperate gamble and succeeds, establishing himself as a renowned painter. In *Of Human Bondage* (1915), however, Fanny Price, seeking to become a painter despite her lack of talent, experiences a fate similar to George's. When George discovers that he cannot attain his only ambition, he comes to the conclusion that life is not worthwhile, despite the wealth, status, and security that is assured to him by his doting family.

Style and Technique

The story is narrated in the lucid, fluent, and idiomatic English that one usually finds in Maugham, who is not known for figurative language or for poetic passages. However, one passage from the story, that describing the narrator's response to the playing of Lea Makart, has been noted as one of Maugham's most artful. It is filled with images, associations called up by the music, and flights of imagination, leading up to generalized impressions. Its rhythm is artfully complex. The plot reveals extensive use of foreshadowing and irony.

However, Maugham's narrative art is perhaps most evident in the narrator, a type often designated a Maugham persona because he bears a striking resemblance to the author. He is an established and successful author who moves with ease in upper-class society. He is tolerant, urbane, skeptical, and somewhat detached. The narrator interacts with the characters, advising them, even disagreeing with them but never becoming insistent or intense. Some of his comments are only for the reader, differing from those he addresses to the characters. He sizes up situations and characters in frank and critical revelations to the reader.

The narrator tells the story in episodes, beginning with a leisurely account of his acquaintance with Ferdy Rabenstein. A series of episodes exploiting dramatic conflicts then follows, with effective and sparkling dialogue. It is typical of Maugham that much of this dialogue occurs during dinners with Ferdy, with the Blands, and with George. Maugham's early success as a dramatist appears to have exerted a strong influence on his later fiction.

Stanley Archer

ALL SHALL LOVE ME AND DESPAIR

Author: Jean Thompson (1950-   )
Type of plot: Social realism
Time of plot: The late twentieth century
Locale: The Oregon coast
First published: 1995

> *Principal characters:*
> EDWARD, a twenty-year-old Chicagoan nicknamed Scout
> ANNIE, his girlfriend, also from Chicago
> PHIL, their neighbor in Oregon
> ACE, a drug dealer

The Story

A young couple leaves Chicago to begin life anew on the Oregon coast. The twenty-year-old man, whose real name is Edward but is called Scout, is hooked on drugs. He and his girlfriend, twenty-one-year-old Annie, head west. Scout, who in his twenty years has never seen the ocean, is ill during most of the trip, and Annie does all the driving.

On the trip, Scout exists on milk, milk shakes, and jelly doughnuts, but eating makes him nauseated. He frequently throws up, filling the car with the wretched, sour smell of vomit. At one point, Annie pulls into a service station and gets him to freshen up in the rest room. She considers leaving him there and continuing the trip herself, reasoning that someone would surely come along to help him. She thinks better of this, however, and they continue their journey.

Scout is experiencing withdrawal symptoms, which explains his illness. He certainly is hooked on drugs. Reading between the lines, one finds strong indications that Annie has persuaded him to leave Chicago to wean himself from the drugs on which he depends. When the story opens, the two have been in Oregon for two months, and Scout is shooting up. If his motive for moving was to rid himself of his addiction, his efforts have failed. Annie, afraid of drugs, does not join Scout in his illicit drug activities.

Annie does not consider herself pretty. She values Scout because he does not much care about people's faces. When the two of them lived in Chicago, they frequently walked to Belmont Harbor on cold winter days and watched the boats bobbing about in the marina on Lake Michigan, a body of water Scout considers a fraud. Why sail on a lake that cannot take one anywhere? It is far more sensible to sail on an ocean, he argues.

Annie does not share Scout's disdain for the lake, which she considers bottomless and shoreless. She will, however, not disagree openly with Scout, whom she considers the most intelligent person she knows. Rather, she makes small noises in her throat as her response when he rants on stupidly, rationalizing that even intelligent people sometimes say stupid things.

When Scout is high on drugs, he turns silent, giving the impression that he is contemplating profundities. At times like this, Annie sometimes is tempted to take drugs herself to keep from being lonely, but she never succumbs to this temptation. She thinks that Scout appreciates her abstinence, that he needs to have something to withhold from her. Yet she sometimes feels guilty about not sharing the drug experience with the man she loves.

Scout and Annie walk the Oregon beach. Scout goes out into the frigid Pacific, which frightens Annie, precisely as he intends. At this point, Annie has an epiphany: Despite their long journey, they are the same people they were but are merely in a new place. The hovel they inhabited in Chicago, with its smell of gas and sugar, has now been replaced by a converted garage closer to the highway than the beach. However, they are the same people; Scout has not kicked his habit.

Mysterious telephone calls come in constantly when Scout is not there, frightening Annie. Then Ace, a drug dealer, appears, and Scout tells Annie he owes Ace a large sum and tries to get her to help even accounts by going off with Ace.

Phil, their neighbor and only friend in Oregon, works filling vending machines with soft drinks and gets stoned every morning before going to work. Phil's brother owns the *Lazy Day*, an eighteen-foot boat that Phil takes Annie and Scout to see. He suggests they take it out, but the idea scares Scout. Annie demurs, saying it is not much of a boat.

In the end, Annie realizes that she is no longer in love with Scout. She packs her things and plans to leave but cannot. Shortly afterward, Phil comes to tell her that the *Lazy Day* is missing. Apparently Scout has taken it into the ocean and will never be seen again.

Themes and Meanings

Jean Thompson's stories are consistently ironic and often cynical. In "All Shall Love Me and Despair," the lead story in *Who Do You Love: Stories* (1999), she explores the theme of love and views young love cynically. In doing so, she chronicles the transformation of Annie from a doormat to an independent woman. As the story progresses, Annie realizes that Scout is a hopeless junkie and always will be.

Annie shows her uncertainty about building a future with him during their trip across the country to Oregon. When she pulls into the service station and gets Scout to clean up, the idea of abandoning him crosses her mind, but she drops the idea. Once in Oregon, Scout is wholly negative. Annie whispers to him that she loves him, then urges him to say that he likes Oregon. Instead, he complains about the rain.

Thompson shows the differences between the two young people's outlooks in a scene that involves flying kites on the beach. Scout, indifferent to Annie and her feelings, all at once twirls her around and says that he will buy a big kite, one so big that it can eat all the other kites. Annie wants to tell him that this is not what a kite is for, but she remains silent.

As the theme of fading love advances, a turning point occurs after ghost telephone calls come into Scout and Annie's cottage when Annie is alone. She is so frightened that she stops answering the telephone. Shortly thereafter, Ace appears, and the tension is palpable.

Scout tells Annie that Ace has a car and asks her if she wants to go for a ride. When he suggests that just she and Ace go, Annie realizes that Scout is trying to get her to provide sex for Ace. Humiliated, she retreats into the bathroom while Scout tries to convince her how important it is for her to go with Ace, to whom he obviously owes drug money. He thinks he can clear the ledger if Annie allows herself to be used as barter.

Annie now wants only to keep Scout away from her. She threatens him with scissors, and after he departs, she packs her things and leaves. It is past midnight. At that moment, however, the telephone rings, and Annie returns to the apartment to answer it. Then she lies down and awaits the dawn. When Scout returns, he has the keys to a stolen car, and they head out in it, but when the car breaks down, much as their relationship is breaking down, they sell its tires to buy bus tickets back to the coast.

Soon Phil takes them to see his brother's boat. They discuss going out in it, but neither wants to go. For the first time, Annie views Scout without love. She goes so far as to call him ignorant. Thompson here demonstrates how love necessarily involves respect, a condition that Annie had overlooked until now. Then she learns that Scout and the *Lazy Day* are missing. This news frees her to live her life.

Style and Technique

Thompson tells the story of Annie and Scout in the third person, using the author omniscient point of view, making herself the observer of all that happens. Her mode of telling the story is direct and sequential except for two brief flashbacks to Chicago after the couple has arrived in Oregon.

Thompson uses these flashbacks to provide background details about Scout—he is of Polish descent, his father drove a bakery truck, and the family was not affluent—and to set the stage for Scout's venture into the Pacific on the *Lazy Day* by including the scene at Belmont Harbor on Lake Michigan during which Scout expresses his disdain for any body of water short of an ocean.

As the story unfolds, one begins to glean the ways in which some men demean women. When her love for Scout blinds her, Annie is robbed of her self-respect. Scout calls Annie his cupcake but lacks any deep feeling for her. She is his woman, his bed partner, and always, in his eyes, his inferior. She plays up to his misconceptions, convincing herself that he is much smarter than he is. It is only when she calls him ignorant close to the end of the story that she frees herself from his clutches.

R. Baird Shuman

ALL SORTS OF IMPOSSIBLE THINGS

Author: John McGahern (1934-   )
Type of plot: Realism
Time of plot: The mid-twentieth century
Locale: Rural Ireland
First published: 1978

> *Principal characters:*
> JAMES SHARKEY, a schoolmaster
> CATHLEEN O'NEILL, his former love interest
> TOM LENNON, an agricultural instructor
> MRS. LENNON, Tom's wife
> CHARLIE, a barkeeper
> A PRIEST

The Story

"All Sorts of Impossible Things" is told in the first person, primarily through the point of view of the main character, lonely schoolmaster James Sharkey. The story begins with Sharkey and his friend Tom Lennon spending a Sunday afternoon hunting rabbits with two hounds; one, Coolcarra Queen, is a retired racing dog belonging to Lennon, and the other is a mongrel that Sharkey has borrowed from Charlie's bar. Though they are unaware of it, this will be their last Sunday spent hunting because of Lennon's failing health. After an afternoon without seeing any rabbits, the dogs finally raise one, which leads them on an exhausting chase before eventually eluding them.

An agricultural instructor, Tom Lennon is currently employed on a temporary contract and is preparing for exams to determine whether he will be offered a permanent job. His knowledge of his profession is not the problem; rather, he is concerned that his congenital heart defect will cause him to fail the required physical exam. As a husband and father, he needs the security for his family that a permanent position would provide.

After Lennon leaves for home with his dog, whose paws are wounded from running on the hard ground, Sharkey returns the mongrel to Charlie's bar and observes Charlie's elaborate way of hiding his drinking from his wife. He also indulges in a moment of resentment and jealousy over Lennon's apparently successful marriage, followed by an inward expression of concern over the possibility that his friend will lose his job. The narrator makes special reference to the fact that Sharkey has not removed his hat.

The sequence that follows is a flashback that reveals and explains Sharkey's notable idiosyncrasy: his refusal to remove his hat, even in church. Once, Sharkey was in love with Cathleen O'Neill. In their happiness, they were blissfully unaware of the passage of time. Then Sharkey began to lose his hair, which made him feel the urgency of securing their uncertain relationship while they were still young. His proposal to Cathleen took the form of an ultimatum, as he would prefer rejection to uncertainty. When she refused to be pressured, their relationship was over.

Since that time, Sharkey has refused to remove his hat in public. In conversation with the priest who came to find out why Sharkey did not remove his hat in church, Sharkey compared his hat to the priest's collar: both are sublimations of *timor mortis*, the fear of death. As a schoolmaster in the employ of the church, Sharkey was risking not only his standing in the community but also his career. The priest, to avoid conflict, stationed Sharkey at an offering table outside the sanctuary, where he could wear his hat without breaking the rules.

Back in the story's present, Tom Lennon's health takes a turn for the worse, and when James Sharkey goes to visit, the reader is introduced to Lennon's wife and baby. Sharkey feigns optimism even though he detects impending death in Lennon's sickroom. As the weeks pass, Lennon's health does not improve. Sharkey takes both dogs hunting again, and this time they catch and maul two rabbits; Sharkey finishes the rabbits off by striking them, giving one to Charlie when he returns the mongrel and taking the other to Lennon.

Lennon's health has deteriorated further, and Sharkey offers to take care of the hound Coolcarra Queen. Shortly thereafter, in spite of Lennon's sickness, Sharkey cuts Lennon's hair in preparation for the exam. Sharkey and Lennon's wife discuss the hopelessness of the situation, and as he watches Lennon's shorn hair falling to the towel draped around him, Sharkey feels the impulse to remove his hat, as if he is in the presence of something sacred. Lennon dies the next morning while attempting to crank-start his car.

After the funeral, Sharkey listens to men in the bar debating planting methods the deceased agricultural instructor had advocated and buys Charlie a drink. The story closes with Sharkey returning home to the dog, who welcomes him. He imagines throwing his trademark hat away and finding a girl with whom to go to the beach or training the dog to race again. Finally he dismisses both of these daydreams as impossibilities and turns back to his uneventful—and now lonelier—life.

Themes and Meanings

As in much twentieth century Irish literature, paralysis is a major theme in "All Sorts of Impossible Things." Cathleen O'Neill's silent rejection of James Sharkey's proposal was the defining moment of his life, and the hat he wears inside and out is a constant reminder of his permanent state of loneliness and isolation. His education is another factor that separates him to a degree from most others in the town and connects him all too briefly with Tom Lennon. Lennon's death underscores Sharkey's isolation and paralytic inability to change his situation (in contrast with Lennon's widow and her baby, who move away after Lennon's death). At the story's conclusion, it is clear that for Sharkey, there are no alternatives to the lonely life he leads. Shedding his hat, finding a new love, even training the dog to race again—all of these reasonable endeavors are classified as impossible options for the paralyzed protagonist.

Although Sharkey's attempt to find security in marriage is thwarted, two other marriages in the story suggest the range of possibilities that such an opportunity would have offered. The bartender Charlie's relationship with his wife is far from ideal; Charlie sneaks drinks of whiskey in secret to avoid her disapproval and perhaps to escape from the emptiness of the relationship. Tom Lennon's marriage, in contrast, seems ideal, at least to the lonely James Sharkey, who manifests bitterness and jealousy at the thought of the fulfillment (sexual and otherwise) that Lennon derives from the relationship.

From the story's opening scene, decay is a recurring theme. As Sharkey and Lennon follow the dogs during the first hunt, they pass a football field with only one goalpost standing. The river Shannon is described as sluggish, almost lifeless. Lennon's home is in a single tower, surrounded by bare trees, the remains of a larger building that has collapsed. The aura of death that Sharkey later detects in Lennon's bedroom is merely a focusing and an extension of the atmosphere that pervades the whole story.

Both paralysis and decay play roles in the theme that the story most explicitly identifies. *Timor mortis*, a Latin phrase meaning "fear of death," pervades the story even as it pervades Sharkey's life. The fear of death (suggested by his hair loss) drives Sharkey to force Cathleen O'Neill to decide between marrying him and breaking up with him. Similarly, the fear of death and the impulse to deny mortality cause Sharkey to wear his hat indoors and outdoors, even in church.

Style and Technique

The death of Tom Lennon is foreshadowed from the story's first sentence, when the narrator relays the information that it is the last time Lennon and Sharkey will go rabbit hunting. Though the story's point of view is generally located near James Sharkey, it reveals itself to be third-person omniscient when it provides information that the characters explicitly do not know. Throughout the story, the reader is given access to the inner thoughts of only one character, Sharkey. By providing analysis of his motivations that goes beyond Sharkey's own consciousness, however, the omniscient narrator leads the reader to a greater understanding of his motivations than could be revealed simply by relaying the protagonists' words and actions—certainly a greater understanding of Sharkey than Sharkey himself could attain.

Several objects, events, and conversations in the story serve to highlight the themes. The failed racing dog functions as a symbol for life itself when Lennon comments that the in-between kind, neither a dud nor a champion, is the worst kind to have. The hat that James Sharkey wears without fail, like the priest's collar, is a symbol of the sublimation of the fear of death. At times in the story, his hat comes to represent Sharkey himself, as at Lennon's graveside, when his hat is described as standing amongst the hatless men and women. Because Sharkey's life has been subsumed by his obsession with his own loneliness and inescapable mortality, the hat is a logical symbol, especially because the death of his only friend has reaffirmed both of these inevitabilities.

James S. Brown

ALL THE YEARS OF HER LIFE

Author: Morley Callaghan (1903-1990)
Type of plot: Domestic realism
Time of plot: 1935
Locale: Unspecified; probably New York City
First published: 1935

> *Principal characters:*
> ALFRED HIGGINS, the protagonist, a young man apparently
>   destined for serious trouble
> MRS. HIGGINS, his mother
> MR. SAM CARR, his employer

The Story

Late in the evening, a drugstore owner and his assistant are closing up for the day. Sam Carr, the small, gray-haired proprietor, stops Alfred Higgins, his adolescent helper, just as the young man is leaving for home. Alfred has worked there for six months, and this is the first time Mr. Carr has ever varied the evening routine of bidding his employee "good night" without even looking at him. Alfred is unnerved by his boss's softly menacing manner as he blocks his exit.

Mr. Carr asks Alfred to empty his pockets before he leaves. When Alfred feigns surprise and then indignation, Mr. Carr reveals that he knows the exact items that Alfred has stolen that evening: a compact, lipstick, and toothpaste. Moreover, he tells Alfred that he has suspected him of petty thievery for some time but wanted to be proved wrong because he liked him. Now, he believes, he has no alternative but to call in the police.

Mr. Carr pauses to let Alfred absorb the full impact of his sense of betrayal and disappointment. Alfred admits to himself that repeatedly he has been in serious trouble since leaving school and has been unable to hold on to a job. He feels afraid and ashamed. Mr. Carr seems to sense Alfred's emotional pain and decides to call Alfred's mother before summoning the authorities. Clearly, Alfred is at a decisive point in his life.

Anxious to appear indifferent and self-reliant, Alfred is nevertheless hoping desperately to be rescued from police and courts by his mother. He expects her to rush in, hysterical and pleading; while he hopes she will save him from the law, he anticipates his embarrassment at her abject behavior to Mr. Carr and her contempt for him. She soon arrives; although it is obvious that she has hurriedly dressed, her poise and calm dignity are a surprise to them both.

She confronts her son, who does not deny his guilt or attempt to mitigate it. She then speaks to Mr. Carr with such unaffected humility and understanding that he is somewhat awed by her. She asks for compassion, which she receives for her son. Mr.

Carr dismisses Alfred from his job but lets him go home. On their way home, Alfred's relief verges on hilarity, but he is restrained by his mother's obvious pain and anger. Her silence abashes him.

At home, Mrs. Higgins calls Alfred "a bad lot" and sends him to bed while she goes to the kitchen to make some tea. In his room, the fear and shame Alfred felt earlier in the evening begin to dissipate, and he longs to tell his mother how he admired her smooth handling of the situation. He quietly goes to the kitchen, and there, unde-tected, he observes his mother's face, the face behind the mask she had worn earlier in the evening. It is "a frightened, broken face utterly unlike the face of the woman who had been so assured a little while ago in the drugstore." Her hands tremble as she pours tea and draws the cup unsteadily toward her lips. At that moment, Alfred has a sudden, crucial insight. He comprehends the hard reality of his mother's life as well as the effect of his actions on her. He knows, too, that in an important sense his own youth is over. An evening that began with a shabby crime culminates in a moment of sympathetic identification that marks Alfred's passage to manhood and maturity.

Themes and Meanings

In this story, Morley Callaghan focuses on a rather commonplace and distressing experience during which a young man's character begins to take a definite moral form. The boy's petty thievery, false bravado, and emotional dependency are high-lighted early in the story. There is little to suggest the possibility of genuine moral growth except for the boy's capacity for honest self-evaluation when he is first con-fronted by his employer, and his ready admission of guilt to his mother.

Alfred does mature, however, and it is important to recognize that his moral devel-opment owes very little to the fear and shame that suffuse him on being caught and imagining his punishment or his mother's contempt for him. Fear and shame prompt him at first to indulge in some defensive role-playing, and these emotions quickly dis-sipate once the immediate threat of arrest is removed. In this interlude of relaxation from tension, however, Alfred is surprised by an insight that transforms him.

When he discovers his mother alone and vulnerable, he sees for the first time the hard path she has walked "all of the years of her life." This capacity for responding deeply and fully to the imagined life of another is, Callaghan implies, the beginning of maturity. Thus, for Callaghan, maturity depends essentially on a sense of solidarity with others as opposed to a feeling of anarchic individualism, which sees others as simply obstructions or conveniences. All Alfred's anger, shame, despair, and elation earlier in the evening subside eventually, allowing his innate capacity for sympathetic identification with another to reach expression. This capacity may seem as common-place as the crime that Alfred commits, but Callaghan convincingly suggests that it is at the root of the moral imagination.

Style and Technique

As in most of his stories, Callaghan's style here is objective, concise, and un-adorned. He strives to present the essential, illuminating experience directly to his reader. Much depends on the reader's sensitivity to implications and undercurrents, which is entirely consonant with a story about a young man's discovery of the poignant reality underlying his mother's apparently routine existence.

The story is written in the third person, with Alfred as the central consciousness, as befits a story about his moral growth. The clipped dialogue, unmetaphorical prose, and paucity of specific details regarding time, place, characters, atmosphere, and so on allow Callaghan to highlight those moments when the central character's consciousness expands under the impact of experience.

Structurally, "All the Years of Her Life" develops through a series of surprises moving toward a crucial revelation. Alfred is surprised by his employer, surprised by Mr. Carr's inexplicable reluctance to prosecute, surprised by his mother's deft handling of the situation, and finally, surprised by his discovery of the pain and suffering his mother endures. Though compact and spare, the story convincingly suggests the potential in humanity for significant moral development.

Michael J. Larsen

"ALL YOU ZOMBIES—"

Author: Robert A. Heinlein (1907-1988)
Type of plot: Science fiction
Time of plot: 1945-1993
Locale: Cleveland, Ohio; New York City; somewhere under the Rocky Mountains
First published: 1959

Principal character:
THE NARRATOR, an agent of the Temporal Bureau

The Story

"'All You Zombies—'" takes full advantage of the cause-and-effect paradox inherent in the concept of time travel. The tale assumes not only the existence of time travel but also its necessity. To forestall the atomic destruction of the earth, for example, agents of the Temporal Bureau must selectively manipulate what becomes the past, taking care not to leave too many anachronisms. Temporal agents do not change the past, for that is impossible; rather, it is their hidden presence in past events that ensures that history turns out as it really does. For example, the intervention of a temporal agent turned what could have been the nuclear disintegration of New York into what became known as the Fizzle War of 1963. The Mistake of 1972 (which apparently led to forced labor and a shortage of food in 1974), however, did take place. It is history, and no temporal agent can undo it.

More temporal agents are needed to prevent another Mistake. Thus, the narrator is sent from 1993 back to 1970 to recruit a likely candidate: himself. Central to the fun of the story is the revelation of how significant a part the agent played in the very existence of the raw recruit. The recruit actually comes into the world as a baby girl, Jane. She is stolen from the hospital in 1945 by a mysterious man, the temporal agent, who places her as a foundling on the steps of an orphanage in Cleveland. Though she is determined to keep her virginity until she is married, Jane realizes after lonely years in the orphanage that her rather severe, mannish appearance will do little to attract a potential husband. The alternative is to enlist in W.E.N.C.H.E.S., the Women's Emergency National Corps, Hospitality & Entertainment Section, to provide on-board relief of sexual tensions for pilots who must spend years in space. The Corps takes good care of its own, and many end up getting married to pilots.

Jane's dream, though, is shattered in 1963. She is seduced by a mysterious man and becomes pregnant. Her baby girl is delivered by cesarean section, and the surgeon points out to Jane that she has apparently grown up with both male and female organs. In fact, though Jane did become pregnant, "she" is really a man. Worse, a month later Jane's daughter is stolen from the hospital nursery. Jane is determined to find the man who seduced her and brought ruin to her life. Now maturing as a male, Jane changes his name and moves to New York, where, unable to secure a decent job, he becomes a

confession writer. Now, in 1970, at twenty-five, he spills out his life story to the bar-
keeper at "Pop's Place" in New York. The man behind the counter, the temporal agent,
offers this potential recruit a chance to come face-to-face with the seducer.

That requires a time jump for both of them back to 1963. Sent out by the agent, the
potential recruit finds not a mysterious man but Jane. She is irresistible. As the agent
later reflects: "It's a shock to have it proved to you that you can't resist seducing your-
self." After such a realization, the young man is ready to be recruited into the Temporal Bureau. The agent returns to 1993 with his recruit, who is sent off for processing.

The agent returns to his own quarters, determined to give up recruitment for some
other work at the Bureau. Thirty years of recruiting have soured him on the job. Besides, once one has recruited oneself, completing the circle, what is there left to accomplish? The young man will make a good agent, of course; he already knew that.

Self-doubt and loneliness wash over the agent. He glances down at his belly, finding the scar from the cesarean section, and something in him aches for Jane. Those
around the agent, and presumably the readers of the story as well, are to him little
more than zombies, animated corpses, less than human, with their origins unknown.
Now, in the darkness, the agent has a frightening thought, and he addresses the reader:
"You aren't really there at all. There isn't anybody but me—Jane—here alone in the
dark. I miss you dreadfully!"

All the main characters in the story—the agent, the recruit, the baby girl, the
woman, the seducer—are the same person. A few other supporting characters are
briefly mentioned in the story, such as the doctor at the hospital and an officer at the
Temporal Bureau, but the question of their identity is left open. The events in the story
form a closed loop, and it is in that loop that the agent is caught. Everyone else is excluded from that loop; the very existence of others, from the agent's perspective, is
questionable indeed.

Themes and Meanings

Robert A. Heinlein has dealt with the convolutions of time travel before, most notably in the novel *The Door into Summer* (1957) and in "By His Bootstraps," a story
published in 1941. "'All You Zombies—'" takes full advantage of those convolutions
but is much more than the work of a gifted writer who has taken on an imaginative
challenge. At the beginning of the story, the temporal agent refers to the odd ring he is
wearing. A gift from another operative, it pictures the World Snake consuming its
own tail, symbolizing the time-travel paradox. It is in a sense also symbolic of a favorite kind of Heinlein character, the self-made individual, one who by force of intellect
and will is able to create his own environment. In *Starship Troopers* (1959), for example, published the same year as "'All You Zombies—,'" Heinlein glorifies the individual combatant in his fight against the Bugs. The world of the starship trooper is all that
matters.

It is to the author's credit that he realizes the darker side of the self-made individual.
In the end, such a person is condemned to a solipsistic universe. A culture that exalts
individualism, self-achievement, and even eccentricity also produces alienation, dis-

enchantment, and loneliness. The ultimate end of the work ethic, the pressure for individual accomplishment, is the salvation of the world, over and over and over again, by the temporal agent. It is at once the highest calling and yet the most meaningless of tasks, for if all but the agent are mere zombies, for whom is the world to be saved? Fittingly, the word "zombie" refers not only to talking corpses, the soulless ones, but also to a snake, the python god of West African origin.

Style and Technique

The story is told in a brusque, no-nonsense manner, with each of its seven divisions headed by time and location. There is playfulness in Heinlein's depiction of the young recruit, who as a confession writer has taken to calling himself the "Unmarried Mother," reminiscent perhaps of the author's own early days as a pulp writer at four cents a word. "Unmarried Mother" refers not only to the point of view taken in the young man's published stories but also to his experience as Jane, pregnant (it turns out) with himself. Here the writer is truly the creator. Heinlein peppers his story with intriguing glimpses of a future society. In his version of 1970 (the story was published eleven years earlier), space travel is routine, with the need for female companionship spawning such organizations as W.E.N.C.H.E.S. and, in 1993, the elite Women's Hospitality Order Refortifying & Encouraging Spacemen. At Pop's Place in 1970, a song entitled "I'm My Own Grandpaw!" keeps blaring from the jukebox. The mysterious Temporal Bureau headquarters under the Rocky Mountains hints of increasingly complex loops. Are operatives from the farther future at work in 1993 to ensure the workings of temporal agents in 1970?

Against this background, the events leading to the Unmarried Mother's self-creation are played out. The agent recounts his activities with a serious, though wry, tone. His emotions at the end of the story suggest a lonely, world-weary cry, yet even here the cry is for the self, for Jane. "'All You Zombies—'" is a cautionary tale as well as one of the finest time-travel yarns in science fiction.

Dan Barnett

AN ALPINE IDYLL

Author: Ernest Hemingway (1899-1961)
Type of plot: Realism
Time of plot: The early 1920's
Locale: The Austrian Tyrol
First published: 1927

> *Principal characters:*
> NICK ADAMS, a young American man
> JOHN, his friend
> AUSTRIAN INNKEEPER
> SEXTON
> OLZ, an Austrian peasant

The Story

"An Alpine Idyll" belongs at the end of the Nick Adams cycle of stories. A now mature Nick has come down from a month's skiing in the mountains with a friend, John. They witness a peasant burying his wife and the reader experiences an epiphanic moment of recognition shared with Nick, though not with his friend.

The story opens in the early morning with two young men carrying their skis as they are climbing down from the mountains into the valley. They pass a churchyard just as a burial is ending. The narrator, who remains unnamed throughout the story but who is clearly Nick Adams, greets the priest but does not receive a greeting in return. The young men stop to watch the sexton shoveling earth into the new grave. When the sexton rests, a peasant standing at the grave takes over, spreading the soil as evenly as he would manure in a garden.

The grave filling looks unreal to the young men, and they cannot imagine being dead on such a beautiful May morning. They walk up the road to the town of Galtur; the narrator explains that they were skiing in Silvretta for a month but that with the coming of the warmer weather the skiing was spoiled. It was too late in the spring to be up in the Silvretta; they stayed too long, and the May morning in the valley seemed more natural than the spring in the high mountains.

They arrive at an inn, and, after greeting the owner, who gives them their mail, they go inside to drink beer while they read the accumulated post. During an exchange of conversation, John notes that it is no good doing a thing too long, such as skiing in the mountains in the spring. The open window draws Nick's attention to the white road and dusty trees and the green field and stream beyond. Inside, the sunlight filters through the empty glasses. John is asleep with his head on the table. Two men come into the inn: the sexton and the bearded peasant from the burial. Both order drinks, for which, after a brief argument, the peasant insists on paying, and he abruptly leaves to drink at a *gasthaus* up the road. The innkeeper, after a brief exchange in a local dialect with the sexton, asks when the young men want to eat. John is still asleep on the table, but he awakens when the menu is brought by the waitress. Nick asks the innkeeper to join them for a drink.

As the innkeeper is taking a seat, he calls peasants beasts. Nick confesses that he and John saw the funeral as they were coming into town; he is informed that it was for the peasant's wife. Again, the innkeeper calls the peasant a beast. "How do you mean?" asks Nick. The innkeeper calls over the sexton to meet Nick and John, and the sexton accepts a drink and agrees to tell the two gentlemen about the peasant; he must do so, however, in a dialect unintelligible to John. The peasant, the innkeeper begins, brought his wife in for burial that day. She died the previous November. No, it was in December, the sexton corrects him, but the peasant was not able to bring her to be buried until the snow was gone from the pass over the Paznaun, for although the peasant lives over the mountain, he belongs to their parish. The sexton explains that some difficulty arose when the priest saw the condition of the dead woman's face. The priest asked her husband if she had suffered much (because she was known to have had a heart condition, nobody was surprised by her death); no, she had not suffered, the priest was told. Then the priest asked how her face had got into such a condition.

The peasant responded that, after his wife died and he realized that he could not move her body across the pass until spring, he placed her body in the woodshed on top of the big logs. Later that winter, when it came time to use the big logs, he stood his wife's body against the wall. Her mouth was open and, when he came in to cut wood at night, he started hanging his lantern from her frozen mouth. He did this every time he went to the woodshed to work. On hearing this, the priest was furious and told the man that he had done wrong. The peasant, however, claimed that he loved his wife and apparently felt little remorse.

John interrupts the story to ask when they are going to eat. Nick tells him to order and asks the innkeeper whether the story is true. Certainly, he is told; the peasants are beasts. Again, John says that they should eat, and Nick agrees.

Themes and Meanings

Although several critics have noted the importance of this grotesque Tyrolean tale, "An Alpine Idyll" contains more than the mordant humor of the folk story. The central theme, which is introduced in the opening paragraphs, is the need to return to an active life after a period of rest and pleasure. Nick and John have already stayed too long in the mountains and are regretting that they did not leave earlier: It is not good to extend pleasure beyond a certain point. This theme is reinforced by the references to descending from the mountain into the valley, where the May sunshine seems more natural. The accumulated letters that the two young men read while drinking beer also recall the outside world awaiting them. It is a world of obligations and responsibilities.

Little attempt has been made to understand the macabre story-within-the-story as in any way integrated with such larger themes. However, there are many connections. The first and most obvious is to see the folktale also reflecting the theme of something overstayed or prolonged beyond what is natural. The peasant, like the young men, had to remain too long in the mountains with his dead wife before he could descend into the valley to discharge his duty and bury her, thereby putting a closure to her death. With the funeral completed, he is free to get on with life's obligations.

"An Alpine Idyll" was first published in book form in the collection *Men Without Women* (1927), and the peasant's story may also suggest the grotesqueness of men living without women, providing a clue to some of the unmentioned obligations to which Nick must return—namely, those of wife and family. The "unnaturalness" of the spring skiing also makes a connection here with the unnaturalness of the peasant's behavior in using his wife's dead body as a lantern stand. In both cases, the light of the past experience illuminates something strange in the mountains, a something put into perspective in the cleansing light of the valley below.

Style and Technique

It is commonplace to notice that Ernest Hemingway used nature as a reflector of his characters' moods and feelings. "An Alpine Idyll" is a story whose meaning hinges on an evocative description of a pastoral scene out a window that Nick observes while reading his mail. It is an especially telling scene because it so expertly illustrates Hemingway's pictorial style, a style he likened to the paintings of Paul Cezanne.

This passage opens with the sun streaming through the window and through the half-full beer bottles on the table. It ends with Nick's attention drawn back inside the window to the empty beer glasses on the table and to John asleep with his head resting on his arms. What Nick sees outside the window does indeed look like a painting described plane by plane: the white road and dusty trees, the green field and stream beyond, the mill with the untended log bobbing in the water, the five crows—one separate (like Nick) looking at the others in the green fields—the porch of the inn and the men sitting on it and finally, John asleep at the table. It is as though a motion picture camera were making an excursion out into nature and back in again; Nick ties together his own life and thoughts with the Cezanne-like outdoors, and the empty/full tension of the Jan Vermeer-like still life indoors.

The log rocking in the mill water recalls the peasant's wife, frozen and unattended in the woodshed. The wetness and greenness of the fields and stream contrast with the cold sterility of the mountains that Nick has left behind. All this is made clear through Nick's painterly synoptic vision. The scene is a moment of calm recognition that is broken by the arrival of the peasant and the sexton, who will tell their strange story of death—a story that, like the gravesite scene that greets the young men just down from the mountain, provides both protagonist and reader with a grim reminder of life's final obligation.

Charles L. P. Silet

THE ALTAR OF THE DEAD

Author: Henry James (1843-1916)
Type of plot: Psychological
Time of plot: The late Victorian period
Locale: London
First published: 1895

Principal characters:
GEORGE STRANSOM, the protagonist, who maintains a memorial altar to his dead friends
THE YOUNG LADY, a nameless female character who becomes a friend of Stransom and a fellow worshiper at the altar
MARY ANTRIM, Stransom's deceased fiancé
ACTON HAGUE, a former friend to Stransom and lover to the nameless female character

The Story

Fifty-five-year-old George Stransom is obsessed with observing the anniversary of his fiancee Mary Antrim's death, a fact that leads him to expand his commemorative pantheon to include all the other departed friends who live on in his memory. Imbued from an early age with what he terms "the religion of the Dead," he decides to provide a material sign of his remembrance in the form of a private altar in a church, which he endows on the condition that he be allowed to stipulate the number of candles to be lit there.

Stransom, after a time of worshiping privately at his altar, notices that a lady somewhat younger than he has been as frequent a worshiper at his altar as he. One day he notices her at a concert and inquires if she recognizes him, which she does. They strike up a friendship subsequently, although Stransom, in his reserve, takes considerable time even to learn her name. She lives with an elderly aunt, who acts as an obstacle to their further intimacy until her death, after which the young lady invites Stransom to her lodgings. On this occasion, in showing Stransom her room, it is brought out that the young lady was the lover of Acton Hague, and it is to his memory that she has been devoted in her observances at Stransom's altar. More powerfully than the deceased had in life, the ghost of Acton Hague rises up between Stransom and the lady and separates them for an extended period. This gulf is fixed between them because of Stransom's hatred of Hague (who injured him in a way that is never specified) and the lady's refusal to abandon the memory of her lover.

Separated for many months, the pious couple are reunited finally when Stransom journeys to his altar to complete the array of lighted candles that lacks but one more for perfect symmetry. Drawn by some mysterious instinct, the young lady discovers Stransom at the altar, now committed to adding a final candle to the group. The young lady believes at first that the addition is to be the memorial to Acton Hague that she had demanded of him, but she discovers her error on realizing that the final candle is to light the memory of Stransom's own death, which occurs as the story closes.

Themes and Meanings

The story is perhaps the most powerful presentation in Henry James's entire oeuvre of two of his most important themes: mourning and renunciation. Stransom's obsession with the memory of his departed friends is linked to his having abandoned any other form of living, to his characteristically Jamesian renunciation of an active life for one of contemplation and privacy. Even the bond that is forged, then broken, between Stransom and the nameless young lady depends crucially on their mutual recognition that the truly human act is the abandonment of life in favor of memorializing the dead. Her career as a writer and his vaguely specified affairs do not impinge in any significant way on the main action, which is focused on their mutual mourning and the conflict that arises out of their inability to share a single attitude toward one of their dead.

Like many of James's shorter tales, this one, too, is concerned with the life of the artist, although here the figure of the artist is represented in the pious Stransom, whose work of art is neither novel nor painting but the very altar that he endows and in a way even creates. The clear emphasis on the importance of symmetry and harmony among the lighted candles, on the price that Stransom must pay in order to achieve this perfection (his death is necessary to complete both the altar and the tale itself)—these in other contexts are characteristic features of James's conception of the artist's life and work. For James, the artist must renounce participation in the active affairs of the world and devote himself to the solitary and generally unappreciated labor of aesthetic understanding. The nameless young lady's profession as a writer serves to counterpoint the genuine devotion to art that she and Stransom share against the false labors of commercial scribbling. As in many other contexts throughout the James canon (most graphically in the short story "The Next Time"), public fame and commercial success are at absolute loggerheads with authentically aesthetic achievement. The price of such devotion, as the fate of Stransom illustrates, is ultimately life itself. One could say that Stransom's death is merely the logical and necessary outcome of a life that has effectively renounced the living from the moment that its focus became exclusively the mourning over the memory of departed friends.

Style and Technique

James was a notable theoretician of fictional technique, particularly of so-called narrative point of view. Taking his cue from the "free indirect style" inaugurated by Gustave Flaubert, James stipulated again and again that the adoption of a limited point of view in which the narrator was privy to the innermost thoughts of a single character but more or less deprived, except from the evidence of conversation and gestures, of any information about the thoughts and feelings of other characters was the key to realistic and aesthetically powerful narrative. "The Altar of the Dead" adopts exclusively the point of view of Stransom, whose speculations, emotions, and intuitions are all made entirely lucid for the reader, at the same time that he acts as what James often called the "reflector" of the deeds and the possible thoughts of the other principal character. Her remaining unnamed throughout the story is possibly mannered, but it does reinforce the point that for the reader she is never fully embodied but remains an object of attention only insofar as she is of interest to and helps to illuminate the character of Stransom.

The adoption of limited omniscience serves other purposes in the tale as well, and James characteristically practices his craft with consummate skill. The entire narrative turns, in one sense, on the meaning of the character of Acton Hague, who is both the bond and the barrier between Stransom and the young lady. Given Stransom's long-standing grievance against Hague, and his effectively having written Hague out of existence (for Stransom himself, that is), it is perfectly plausible that the reader will never learn any more about Hague than Stransom's vague feeling of having been wronged. A different view of Hague would have been possible were the reader to have access to the nameless young lady's thoughts, but this is precisely what the narrative technique, rigorously limiting point of view, denies the reader. The mystery of Hague, which is in a way the mystery of the entire tale, is protected by the device of narrative technique.

James's major fiction (the bulk of his novels and some two dozen of the tales, including "The Altar of the Dead") is dominated by the device of the secret. Diane Arbus's famous remark about a photograph's being "a secret about a secret; the more it tells you, the less you know," applies with equal rigor to the fictional world of James. In learning that Acton Hague was the lover of Stransom's younger friend, one is more, not less, in the dark about Hague than before. This is made clear in Stransom's puzzlement over what his lady friend might have loved in his enemy, as well as in Stransom's desire to know precisely the details of their relationship. All that the revelations in this story, including the final revelation of Stransom's own death as the fulfillment of the design of the altar, reveal is the extent of the reader's ignorance about the meanings of the lives of the characters. There would have been a variety of ways in which this sense of ultimate and irresolvable mystery could have been achieved, but surely the device of limited narrative point of view is one of the more effective means of maintaining the sense of ignorance and wonderment that animates James's fiction. James's stories manifestly reach a point of climax, customarily in the final paragraphs, but they signally lack any definitive factual or diegetic resolution. In this way, his narratives are less contemporary with those of Arthur Conan Doyle than with the antinovels of Alain Robbe-Grillet.

Michael Sprinker

ALYOSHA THE POT

Author: Leo Tolstoy (1828-1910)
Type of plot: Fable
Time of plot: The nineteenth century
Locale: Rural Russia
First published: "Alyosha Gorshok," 1911 (English translation, 1944)

Principal characters:
ALYOSHA, the protagonist, a simple, good-hearted, and
uncomplaining peasant lad
HIS FATHER, who is selfish and neglectful of his son
A TOWN MERCHANT, Aloysha's employer, who, as well as his
family, overworks the lad
USTINYA (OR USTINJA), the orphaned young cook for the
merchant's family, who is in love with Alyosha

The Story

In simple language, this compact narrative presents the correspondingly uncomplicated and short life of Alyosha, from his early years with his family in a village to his
death at age twenty-one from an accident while working in town. The plot can be divided into three phases, in each of which the protagonist is abused in some way. The
first phase shows Alyosha's life from early childhood through his eighteenth year, as
the spindly lad grows up with his peasant family in a village. Despite his build, he is
hardworking and is abusively overtaxed with farm chores by his mother and father,
leaving him little if any time for school, which Alyosha has found difficult from the
beginning.

Because of his cheerfulness (derived from good-heartedness, the narrator implies),
Alyosha uncomplainingly bears his labors, his parents' habitual, overly severe chas-
tisement, and the mockery from other youths about his homeliness and clumsiness.
The latter occasions his nickname, when after accidentally breaking a pot filled with
milk Alyosha is not only beaten by his mother but also tauntingly dubbed "the Pot" by
his peers, whose childhood cruelty complements that of the adults.

In the second phase of the plot, Alyosha is apprenticed by his father to a town merchant, replacing Alyosha's brother, who has been drafted into the army. Despite initial
doubts and insults about Alyosha's physical capacity for labor, the merchant, along
with the rest of the household, quickly falls into the pattern of Alyosha's parents, as-
signing the ever-cheerful and obedient youth an unending series of toils. Once again,
Alyosha is incessantly criticized and taken for granted, never thanked, and shown
kindness only by the young cook, who, though working Alyosha like the rest of the
household, makes an effort to see that he is properly fed and clothed.

In the third phase of the plot, Alyosha discovers for the first time a relationship not based on family or necessity but on love. Though his clumsy marriage proposal is accepted by the cook, Ustinya, who returns his feeling, the couple is thwarted by the callous self-interest of those around them.

The merchant and his wife object to the marriage, fearing a lessening of productivity in their servants. When their complaint is made to Alyosha's father, who has only been interested in collecting the entirety of his son's wages and has even reproved his son for the expense of a new pair of boots (the old ones, hand-me-downs from his brother, were literally worn out in Alyosha's ceaseless labors), the father forbids the marriage. Always obedient, Alyosha agrees, though both he and Ustinya are grieved, and for the first time in his life, Alyosha's smiling gives way to weeping when he answers affirmatively the question put to him by the merchant's wife about whether he will mind his father.

The narrative states that Alyosha's life returns to what it had been, but the reader knows that Alyosha suffers the added injury of losing his loved one in addition to his regular maltreatment by family and employers. Only a short time later, Alyosha falls from the rooftop of the merchant's store, where he has climbed to clear off snow, as ordered by the merchant's clerk. At the conclusion of the story, Alyosha's simple piety is demonstrated when on the third day of his incapacitation Alyosha thanks Ustinya for her kindness, vindicates the thwarting of their marriage (because his fatal injury would have ended it anyway), prays wordlessly with the priest who has been summoned, and then dies peacefully.

Themes and Meanings

The fundamental goodness, patience, meekness, and altruism of Alyosha highlight in satiric contrast the moral defects of the story's other characters. The impatience and ungentleness of Alyosha's mother are stressed by the opening picture of her thrashing of her son for dropping the pot, though later in the story Alyosha fleetingly recalls moments of maternal kindness or pity. Alyosha's father is depicted as self-interested and materialistic, concerned only with how much work and money he can get out of his son.

Similarly, the merchant and his wife care only about how much labor they can be spared as a result of Alyosha's toils, at the least possible expense. The rest of the household, with similar lack of compassion, take advantage of Alyosha, even (in the beginning) the sympathetically portrayed Ustinya, whose acceptance of Alyosha's proposal by striking him on the back with a towel (or a ladle, depending on the particular translation of the story) seems to symbolize her partial affiliation with the world of force and self-assertiveness for which Alyosha is a foil.

Alyosha's noteworthy special definition of love as not only being affectionate or tender but also serving or looking after another emphasizes altruism. Another inner value from the "heart" (a key word in the story) is the simple uneducated piety of the peasant class, a theme in several of Leo Tolstoy's works. Like the three hermits (the title characters of Tolstoy's story "The Three Old Men") who show their inner holiness by running on top of the sea after an educated bishop because they have forgotten the formal prayer that he has taught them, Alyosha merely folds his hands in prayer twice a day, and finally at his death, and lets his heart speak, having long forgotten the words his mother taught him.

Alyosha's meekness, or not talking back, is repeatedly emphasized in the story. The prevention of his marriage and his sadly premature death cut Alyosha off from the pleasures of earthly life, but the story implies that Alyosha will gain entry into Heaven (which he thinks of only as "the world beyond" or "there"). All of Alyosha's attributes enable him to accept death peacefully, an encounter that preoccupies Tolstoy in many of his stories.

Style and Technique

Symbolism is pervasive in the story, including many religious allusions. References to Shrovetide and Lent put Alyosha's death at Easter time, and Alyosha's death on the third day after his fall (as well as his final request for something to drink) also suggests an analogue to the gospel story of Christ. Ironically, while Jesus arose to life, the downtrodden Alyosha falls and dies; yet if a cruel material world has been persecuting Alyosha in life, death promises escape and possibly reward, which parallels Jesus's life and message. Even a mark of Alyosha's homeliness, his large or lop ears, which evoke the ridicule of the other village children, by implication of the simile "stuck out like wings" may ironically suggest not only the manner of his death but also his angelic qualities and future.

The most far-reaching symbolism in the story is that embodied in Alyosha's nickname, "the Pot." The pot corresponds to many of Alyosha's physical features: the prominence of his nose and ears, giving his head a pot or pitcherlike appearance; a certain clumsiness, resulting in the dropped milk pot at the beginning of the story and Alyosha's own fall and breakage at the end; and a poignant reference to his physical slightness, contrasting with the fullness or heaviness of a filled pot. Furthermore, the pot symbol conveys many attributes of Alyosha's personality or spirituality. It intimates his capacity to bear, both in physical labor (Alyosha's incessant hard work) and in suffering or endurance (his toleration of all the injustices continually heaped on him). It suggests that despite his appearance of empty-headedness, Alyosha, whose mouth gapes in a perpetual grin (comparable to the open mouth of a pot or jar), has the capacity to be filled by pleasure from simple things in life or by the tranquillity from an influx of the spiritual.

Finally, the pot symbol points to the cycle of emptiness and fullness in Alyosha's discovery of love, its removal, and his final transcendence to "the world beyond." Alyosha's true love is a cook, whose occupation revolves around pots; after the opening paragraph, she is the only character who explicitly mentions Alyosha's nickname, doing that, significantly, when she accepts his marriage proposal. At the end of the story, after the loss of Ustinya and any earthly pleasures, the dying Alyosha repeatedly asks for something to drink, reminiscent of Jesus's words in John 19:28-30 and suggestive of a different sort of fulfillment that is to become Alyosha's.

Contributing to the story's fablelike or fairy-tale quality are its telling in simple language and its purposeful deletion of much realistic specificity. All other characters besides Alyosha, his brother, and Ustinya are unnamed, being referred to merely as "Alyosha's father," "the merchant," "the merchant's wife," or "the clerk." Moreover, places are similarly unspecified (only "the village" or "the town"), nor are there any references that would pinpoint the time. Such devices also help to create the satiric dimension of the story, which does not have the conventionally happy ending of the prince and princess getting married and living happily ever after. Perhaps most important, this parabolic quality contributes to the universality of the story, which was a principal aim of Tolstoy's last works, including among them many children's or fairy tales, folktales, and legends.

Norman Prinsky

AMANDA

Author: Roberta Fernández
Type of plot: Domestic realism
Time of plot: The 1950's
Locale: South Texas
First published: 1990

Principal characters:
THE NARRATOR
HER MOTHER
AMANDA, the dressmaker

The Story

The narrator recalls moments as a five- or six-year-old girl when she would spend her days watching Amanda work at her sewing machine, transforming cloth into fantastic dresses, and spend her nights thinking about Amanda's creations until she fell asleep. Amanda was her connection to the world of creation, as well as a link to the larger social world that Amanda relayed to her through provocative gossip about the men and women she knew in South Texas.

The narrator is not completely comfortable, however, in Amanda's presence. Although she can speak freely with other people, with Amanda she is rendered almost speechless because she is sure that Amanda is indifferent to her.

The narrator has other apprehensions about Amanda. It is rumored around town that Amanda and her friends Librada and Soledad are associated with magic. Although no one considers Amanda a real enchantress, her special powers make the children, at least, believe that she has little figurines that are exact replicas of everyone who had ever crossed her.

When Librada visits the narrator's house, she leaves behind a slimy substance in which the narrator puts her arm. The narrator and her mother both think the substance is associated with Librada's status as a witch, so the mother takes the substance outside in newspapers and burns it.

The narrator believes that Amanda is part of a complex plot that she cannot figure out. Although out of fear she wears a scapular and blesses herself before she enters Amanda's house, she still is attracted to Amanda because she believes that Amanda is her only link to exciting possibilities that lie beyond the everyday world of others. In order to enter this world of hidden powers, the narrator requests an outfit from Amanda, one that a witch would give her favorite daughter, so horrible that it would enchant everyone. By the time that Amanda gets around to creating the outfit, the narrator has almost forgotten about it.

Eventually, Amanda makes an ankle-length black cape from cat fur, sparrow bones, chicken feathers, and cat paws. The narrator's mother is upset when she sees her daughter wearing the cape, and forbids her to wear it.

One night during a full moon, the narrator puts the cape on and has her moment of transcendence: She gazes at the moon and familiar surroundings that glow luminously, as the chirping of crickets and cicadas reiterates the permanence of everything around her. The mother catches her and again urges her never to wear the cape again.

Years after this singular experience of perfection in the universe, the narrator goes to the storeroom and discovers the cape. It is stiff from the dryness of the trunk, but she recognizes that it was made as an expression of love by Amanda.

When the cape is lost as the narrator travels west, no one can understand why she is so upset. It is clear, however, that she mourns the loss of the witch's daughter's cape because of the closeness she felt with Amanda. The narrator confesses that she cannot imagine that anyone would ever again take the time to create something as personal for her as Amanda had done.

Themes and Meanings

In telling the story of a Mexican American girl who grows up in South Texas and moves to California, Roberta Fernández is replaying her own life story. Whether the events of the story are autobiographical or simply imagined, its themes are universal.

The story focuses on the extremes of experience: plenitude and loss, presence and absence, youth and adulthood. The narrator is privileged to have her encounters with Amanda, to be surrounded by the strength and special powers of older women, including her mother, and to have her moment of epiphany beneath the full moon when she recognized the harmony and perfection of the universe. Because the story leaves childhood behind and ends with the narrator far from Texas on the foggy coast of California, it contains elements of sadness. The cloak has been lost, Texas has been abandoned, and the narrator has not seen Amanda in years, but the narrator's memory is keen, and her imagination, kindled by Amanda, is still strong. The past may be unretrievable in reality, but in memory and in storytelling it endures and has power.

Amanda is the narrator's first hero as an artist, the first creator to inspire the narrator to imagine a world separate from the prosaic world of logic and practicality. The story begins: "Transformation was definitely her specialty"—precisely what the artist must learn in order to be successful. Amanda teaches the narrator how to create, transform, believe in the world of the senses mixed with imagination. It is crucial for this artist, this narrator, that the teacher is a woman because Fernández's search as a writer has been for a feminist aesthetic. The larger work of which "Amanda" is a part, *Intaglio: A Novel in Six Stories* (1990), presents a narrator who, according to critic Nicolás Kanellos, is "trying to piece together her own adult identity by remembering the women who most influenced her." Amanda's genuine love for the narrator is expressed in the cape that she pieces together from cat fur and chicken feathers, and the narrator's love for Amanda is pieced together out of the memories she has stored away over the years.

Style and Technique

The epigraph from Fernández's story comes from the Chilean poet Pablo Neruda. She intentionally leaves the quotation in Spanish, not translating it, and in this way she announces her identity: She will braid together her two traditions, her experiences as a girl in the Mexican American society of South Texas, and her life as a woman in California, where no one can understand her sense of loss when her cape disappears.

Roughly translated, the epigraph says, "Where is the child that I was? Does it continue inside of me or has it gone? Why do we spend so much time growing just to sever connections?" These questions are answered dramatically within the story. Fernández's narrator focuses on the past in order to preserve it, in order to keep the child inside alive. The narrator will not accept a world in which the child that she was will disappear, not only because the past contained magical experiences but also because the past is part of her unique heritage as a Mexican American.

Fernández, who earned her Ph.D. in Romance languages from the University of California, Berkeley, does not turn her back on her past; through her writings she creates connections between herself as a writer and the women of South Texas who were her first models as artists and artisans. If Neruda wonders why one must spend so much time severing connections, Fernández posits a world in which people need to spend time forging connections between the past and the present, between the Latin American and the North American literary traditions, between the role models of childhood and adult heroes. Neruda may be an important poet for Fernández, but the type of character that Amanda is also serves as a significant source of inspiration, an example of how to live in this world that seems to encourage people to cut ties, move forward, and become adults who can function adroitly in a world based almost entirely on reason and consumerism. In "Amanda," alternative models are held up for scrutiny and for applause.

Kevin Boyle

AN AMATEUR'S GUIDE TO THE NIGHT

Author: Mary Robison (1949-   )
Type of plot: Domestic realism
Time of plot: The 1970's or 1980's
Locale: Phoenicia, Indiana
First published: 1983

> *Principal characters:*
> LINDY, the seventeen-year-old narrator
> HARRIET, her mother
> GRANDPA, her grandfather, a retired tailor

The Story

Lindy, a high-school senior about to graduate, has a job waitressing and busing tables at the local Steak Chateau restaurant. An average student and an amateur astronomer, she has a Frankus reflector telescope that she bought with her own money so she can watch the night sky. She enjoys examining Jupiter and the constellations but notes that on a clear night the stars are so bright that they are swimming in their own light.

Lindy often double-dates with her mother, a young-looking thirty-five-year-old. On these dates, they pass themselves off as sisters, and it is the mother who always gets the best-looking men. Lindy's parents are divorced, and her father has remarried and is living in Toledo. When Lindy wonders aloud what it would be like if her father came back, both her mother and grandfather respond that he had better not. As her grandfather observes dryly, it would cut down on her mother's dating.

The two women share a home with the mother's father, a retired, self-employed tailor. Although he claims that he sometimes forgot to tie off the threads, so that some of the clothes he made fell apart, his business was successful, and he now has enough money to take care of all three of them. Because they are all night owls, the grandfather keeps them informed of the late-night horror movies on television. The grandfather is seldom serious about anything, often resorting to juvenile responses such as "Poof you're an egg" when the girl asks him to make her an egg for breakfast, and "Not I, said the pig" when asked if he has seen something that is missing. He lies, too: He insists that Harriet, Lindy's mother, attended Lindy's graduation ceremony but sat back in one of the cooler seats, under the trees. The narrator knows that he lied to her and that her mother did not go because "She was scared of the 'going forward into the world' parts of the commencement speeches."

Lindy's mother is one of the fastest comptometer operators in the state but quits her job because she thinks people at work do not like her. Besides pretending to be her daughter's sister, the mother fantasizes other things; for example, she usually decides after two dates with a man that he must be married or running away from someone. She makes up a story about a ring of thieves stealing cars from the neighborhood; she talks about poison, taking "light pills," and having a brain tumor; and she determines that a stranger on a bus is a police detective on the bus for them. She also tries to have herself admitted to a nearby institution, but the hospital "didn't have space for her, or they didn't think she needed to get in right then." The narrator observes, "The problem I saw was that Mom really needed to keep occupied."

Themes and Meanings

The most important event buried among the seeming trivia of Mary Robison's story and the apparent triviality of its characters' lives is the young narrator's graduation from high school. The quest that begins for each person leaving the protection of school is daunting, even for those well prepared. As the title suggests, the narrator is an amateur (a novice) searching the darkness (night) of the future with much less light (knowledge, direction) to guide her than one her age should have. Not even for her daughter's sake can the childlike mother face this ceremony that represents going forward into the world, for she herself has gone nowhere and is going nowhere. The grandfather—usually a symbol of ancestral knowledge, giving wisdom to his progeny—is hardly more mature than the mother. He is symbolically defined by his loose threads. Neither adult can function as the narrator's guide. The father-figure is totally absent, both from the configuration of the family and from Lindy's special occasion—except for his note, which spells out all too clearly the narrator's plight, "Happy Graduation, Good Luck in Your Future."

Many people look to the stars as a guide to their lives and future. The narrator looks to the stars, the light, for when they are connected, they form patterns or models. Understanding exactly what one sees is difficult because on a clear night the "stars are too bright . . . swimming in their own illumination"; especially because she is an amateur, the narrator is overwhelmed by the light and cannot make sense of it. Rather than admit ignorance, most often she makes up answers. Who can she ask to help her understand what lies ahead, what is in her stars, her future?

Graduation is a moment of transformation: No longer a student, now what will she be? With a cap and gown and piece of paper, with one stroll across a stage, at the end of this magical ceremony, "Poof you are an—": transformed from child to adult. Within the story, the changes that parallel this idea of transformation are all grotesque: In the horror movies the family watches, the Creeper is half-man, half cat-beast; Zombies are the living dead; a man changes into a werewolf, and the werewolf becomes a person again. The young girl is trying to become an adult, but she admits that she could lie on the couch forever and go nowhere, like her mother and grandfather.

There is a chance, however: She lives in the town of Phoenicia, named for the mythological Egyptian bird that consumed itself by fire and rose, renewed, from its own ashes; the constellation of Phoenix in the Southern Hemisphere looks much like a stork, the symbolic bringer of new life. Like the narrator, all high-school graduates are amateurs in life and can either lie on their parents' couches, going nowhere, or choose to rise like a Phoenix from the ashes of their spent childhood into their own individual lives.

Style and Technique

Robison is most often considered a minimalist. The minimalist style produces deceptively simple and realistic fiction that, at its best, offers a concentrated and uncluttered narrative. Minimalism reflects the major characteristics of the short story, the genre in which it is most often employed. Both minimalism and the short story rely heavily on figures of speech and the baggage of connotation that comes with each, especially metonymy, in which one thing symbolizes another with which it is associated. Here, the title of this story is the key to the symbolic connection between the narrator's hobby and her need for direction and answers to puzzling questions about the future.

Some readers may find this story more cluttered than most minimalist fiction, but the clutter of the story represents the clutter that fills these characters' lives, and the trivia with which many people fill their lives so that they can believe they live full lives. The irony is that their lives are empty shells of existence filled with empty echoes of life. Here the mother and grandfather especially are going through the motions of life but at most are only existing.

In addition to the internal connection between the narrator's hobby and her role as a high-school graduate, the story reflects the universal situation of graduates poised on the brink of their futures. It also mirrors the duality of choice, the duality of cause, the duality of change, and the duality of consequences.

This final image of a universal truth reflected in a deceptively simple short narrative is the greatest achievement of the minimalist technique as well as that of the genre of the short story. For both offer what appears to be the simplest of stories. Both offer what appears to be the slightest view—a keyhole. Both offer the appearance of realism, and both use metonymy as the major figure of speech. A single event becomes the symbol for a particular human condition. Both minimalism and the short story create an inverse relationship between a singular event and the universal experience, or the trifling incident and the significant occasion.

Cynthia Whitney Hallett

THE AMBITIOUS GUEST

Author: Nathaniel Hawthorne (1804-1864)
Type of plot: Domestic realism
Time of plot: The early 1800's
Locale: Notch of the White Hills, Massachusetts
First published: 1835

Principal characters:
THE AMBITIOUS GUEST, a visitor to a remote cottage inhabited by
a gregarious family
MOTHER
FATHER
ELDEST DAUGHTER
AGED GRANDMOTHER
YOUNGER CHILDREN

The Story
"The Ambitious Guest" begins in a moment of great tranquillity, with a family co-zily gathered around their hearth. Father and mother, eldest daughter and aged grand-mother, are briefly described as assuming the guises of persons of their ages who are filled with great contentment. Although they are entirely comfortable, mention is made of the harsh winter weather and the dangerous position of the cottage, over which towers a mountain. The noise of stones tumbling down the mountain has often startled the family at midnight.

Throughout the story, a contrast is made between the cozy harmony within and the stormy conditions of nature outside. The wind rattles their door, and they are glad of the company of a young traveler, who proceeds to make himself at home in the wel-come atmosphere of the friendly family.

The Ambitious Guest is "frank-hearted" and quickly engages the family in a dis-cussion of his plans to make a reputation for himself. He finds in them a responsive mood that encourages his conversation about how a person must make his mark on life. As they are caught up in his enthusiasm, several family members express very personal feelings about their lives. The father would like a better property and a better title (Squire)—in short, a station in life that would command the respect of his com-munity. One of the younger children, excited by all this discussion of life's possibili-ties, calls out to his mother that he would like everyone, the guest included, to "go and take a drink out of the basin of the Flume!" His seemingly extravagant notion of visit-ing a brook that spills over into a "deep precipice" amuses the others, who cannot imagine leaving the presumed safety and comfort of the cottage.

One by one, however, the family members forsake their usual placid acceptance of things as they are and admit to various fancies, so that, as the mother says, "we're in a

strange way, to-night." The guest himself is portrayed as having "a high and ab-
stracted ambition." A solitary wanderer, his dreams of making his mark are just that—
dreams, reveries removed from the concreteness of domestic life as it is evoked at the
beginning of the story.

The talk turns to death, as the grandmother confesses to a strange preoccupation
with a superstition of her youth, that a corpse cannot rest in the grave if it suspects that
something about its appearance is awry. She asks her children to make a point of holding a looking glass over her face to get a glimpse of herself after she is laid out for the
grave. "Old and young, we dream of graves and monuments," murmurs the guest, who
has stimulated the whole family to think about how it wants to be remembered.

Reminders of the roaring wind and of the harsh, inhospitable elements outside finally culminate in the "awful sound" of a slide. The family rushes from the cottage
seeking a safer haven but, in fact, flees "right into the pathway of destruction." The
whole mountain falls on them. In the aftermath, their cottage remains intact and the
circumstances of their lives are apparent to all who observe the tokens the family has
left behind. Only the identity of the guest remains in doubt, his ambition having come
to nought.

Themes and Meanings

The title of the story focuses on the disturbing element: ambition. The guest's ambition is equated with his solitariness, his wandering, and his separation from the
community of feeling enjoyed by the family. Ambition, in itself, is abstract. It seems
to have nothing to do with the way this family lives; indeed, as the mother remarks,
she feels a sense of strangeness when the family begins to talk in the guest's terms
about what it wants as opposed to what it already has.

The eldest daughter is aware of the guest's disturbing ideas when she replies, "It is
better to sit here by this fire . . . and be comfortable and contented, though nobody
thinks about us." The guest, on the other hand, thinks of "Earthy Immortality," as the
narrator puts it. The guest rejects her acceptance of the status quo in favor of a sense of
destiny. He ignores, however, the signs of fate that Nathaniel Hawthorne infuses into
the sounds of nature: "There was a wail along the road, as if a funeral were passing."
What the family has forsaken, under the temporary influence of the guest, is its own
attunement to the world.

By not naming his characters, Hawthorne gives his story a universal dimension. It
is about the family, about ambition, and about how human beings both place themselves in and abstract themselves from the world at large. As the narrator remarks of
the family in this story, "Though they dwelt in such a solitude, these people held daily
converse with the world."

"The Ambitious Guest" is a fable, but it is also a folktale with its origins, the narrator implies, in fact—not in fancy or in abstractions. Of the family, for example, the
narrator comments: "All had left separate tokens, by which those who had known the
family were made to shed a tear for each. Who has not heard their name?" They have
become the subject of poets, the narrator notes, so that their fate becomes everyone's

fate, human fate—or, as the narrator puts it earlier in the story while commenting on the affinity of the family for the guest, "Is not the kindred of a common fate a closer tie than that of birth?"

Style and Technique

Hawthorne's style is ironic. The common fate he speaks of at the beginning of the story, for example, is not simply the meeting of minds between the guest and his hosts but also the death they will share, that everyone must ultimately share. Such a terse style allows the narrator to comment subtly on the characters without ever seeming intrusive or impeding the flow of the story. His technique is to understate the theme, giving over most of the narrative to description and dialogue. Nearly every paragraph is carefully balanced between the ease with which the characters behave and speak, on the one hand, and the disruptive, saddening sounds of nature that punctuate the human conviviality, on the other hand.

Always a master of sly, subtle repetition, Hawthorne is able to insert several references to discordant sound that serve as a counterpoint to the human harmony. Even that human harmony is usually shaded by qualifying phrases, such as the one that introduces the lively guest: "His face at first wore the melancholy expression, almost despondency, of one who travels a wild and bleak road, at nightfall and alone, but soon brightened up when he saw the kindly warmth of his reception." Thus, sentences as well as paragraphs are set off against one another, the first part establishing a mood that gives way to its opposite in the second part.

Hawthorne's style, in other words, aims to capture the rhythms of existence itself, rhythms that are contradictory and reversible and that elicit the intense concentration of the ironist. The implication is that all human beings are on the verge of confronting the end of their world. As the grandmother thinks of her death, the guest thinks of how "mariners feel when the ship is sinking." It is almost as if these words occasion the story's ending—so tightly has Hawthorne constructed the denouement. The house trembles and the earth shakes "as if this awful sound were the peal of the last trump." The biblical phrasing here emphasizes the parabolic nature of the author's style and themes. In his mind, the short story itself becomes the synecdoche of human fate.

Carl Rollyson

AMERICA! AMERICA!

Author: Delmore Schwartz (1913-1966)
Type of plot: Social realism
Time of plot: 1934
Locale: Brooklyn
First published: 1940

> *Principal characters:*
> BELMONT WEISS, a musician recently returned from Paris
> MRS. WEISS, his mother
> MR. BAUMANN, the insurance sales representative
> MRS. BAUMANN, his wife
> DICK BAUMANN, their oldest son
> SIDNEY BAUMANN, their youngest child
> MARTHA BAUMANN, their daughter

The Story

Belmont Weiss returns from Paris to a world changed by the effects of the Depression. Unable to fit into the changed situation among friends whose hopes have been "wholly modified," he takes it easy by enjoying long breakfasts, during which he listens to his mother's stories. The story of the Baumann family is told to him one morning as his mother irons.

Mr. Baumann, a cultivated immigrant, was known for his sociability, his appearance, and his ease of living. With little effort, he sold insurance policies, consoled the grieving at funerals, and accumulated a comfortable income from the premiums. His life was leisurely. The family often took four vacations a year, often entertained, and indeed became celebrated for their Sunday evening gatherings, where immigrants shed the loneliness of people who have been cut off from the old country ways and then thrust into the "immense alienation of metropolitan life."

As his mother irons, she tells Belmont that Mr. and Mrs. Baumann "shared so many interests that there was naturally a good deal of antagonism between them." Other people might regard her husband as a sage, but Mrs. Baumann sought out the rabbi, read Sigmund Freud and Henri Bergson, and relished all things and people Jewish. Their children, Belmont is told, reflected the attitudes of their parents. The oldest, Dick, moved from job to job but made little headway, except by marrying a successful beauty-parlor owner, Susan. When Mr. Baumann and Dick became involved in a real-estate partnership with Belmont's father, Mr. Weiss soon tired of their casual attitude toward business hours and responsibilities, terminating the partnership with a summary letter of dismissal. This ended the Weiss-Baumann friendship only briefly, however, because seemingly no one could stay angry with affable Mr. Baumann.

The youngest child, Sidney, followed an even more disastrous course of action, finding some jobs unbearable because of the class of people with whom he worked, others because of the summer heat. Sent to Chicago to find his feet, he failed there and returned to a series of temporary jobs, becoming embittered by his father's "limited success." After a quarrel over the seemingly trivial—a pair of shoes—the father and son fought, and the son "unsuccessfully" attempted suicide and was sent to a mental asylum.

Only their daughter, Martha, the plain intellectual, managed her life by increasing her separation from the family and by marriage to a doctor who, despite her bitterness, enjoyed the family atmosphere at the Baumanns. Although twenty years younger, Mrs. Weiss had offered advice through the years to Mrs. Baumann and continues to share her insights with Belmont (though she would have preferred talking with her older lawyer son).

The reader learns only in passing that Belmont's father left the family in the 1920's, but as this short story draws to an end, Belmont's reflections shape the plot. Sitting in the bedroom that he is sharing for a time with his brother, he examines the conflicting emotions generated by the morning's saga of the Baumann family and the whole panorama of immigrant expectations about America. The reader hears no more about the Baumanns but turns inward to the real purport of the story—what Belmont has learned about others and about himself.

Themes and Meanings

Although Delmore Schwartz added a disclaimer that "the characters in this story are not to be identified with actual persons," and that it is "a work of fiction in the fullest sense of the word," readers will see possible parallels between the musician-listener (Belmont) and any poet-creator, especially in the concluding reflections concerning Belmont's sense of differentness, society's lack of appreciation, and its failure to acknowledge the importance of art.

Even if readers honor the disclaimer, they will still notice the juxtapositions of the personal and the social. Schwartz sets his story during the first part of the twentieth century, ending with the Depression, and fills it with details about the aspirations of a typical immigrant family. Himself a third-generation American, Belmont Weiss learns not only about the changes that affected the Baumanns but also about those that have shaped his own life. As he hears more and more about the Baumanns, he acquires a growing understanding of his own life until finally he is overcome by a "profound uneasiness" and realizes that the contempt that he had directed toward the Baumann way of life is in reality self-contempt.

Belmont finds it difficult to put himself in the place of his forebears. Gradually, however, he begins to see a pattern in the experience of the immigrants and their children—a pattern that is evident not only in the failure of the younger Baumanns but also in his own life. Mr. Baumann was satisfied with an unreflective materialism, but his children, the next generation, judged and weighed him, finding much out of balance. What once had succeeded for Mr. Baumann (hence by implication, for that generation of immigrants) no longer served. His sons' mistakes mirror the changing attitudes of society.

Thus, when Mrs. Weiss comments that "a certain refinement" could "be a severe and even a fatal handicap," the social and personal levels of meaning are joined. As Belmont's reflections on his mother's storytelling (her attitude, her "irony and cruelty") increase in length, the reader moves toward an understanding of the estrangement that Belmont had expressed at the start of the story. He now sees his own life from the same ironic perspective from which he has viewed the Baumanns and realizes that he, too, may have been ruined by his "finest qualities." No longer the passive listener to the story of others, he realizes that he is those others and that "their America would always be present in him."

Style and Technique

Schwartz establishes a framework of storyteller and listener, with the third-person point of view focused on Belmont Weiss so that the reader, too, increases his understanding of the "meanings" of what Belmont hears. As Belmont increasingly fits himself into the story that his mother tells, Schwartz can insert time clues. The reader sees the span of generations in the account of the two women, Mrs. Baumann and a fellow "shipsister," who came by boat to the United States in 1888, were separated in 1911, and reunited in 1930. These structural clues are kept within the plausible context of remembrance and event.

Because of Schwartz's repetition of the word "irony," the reader notices Belmont's interaction with his mother's narrative and her ironic perspective. His mother's aural memory captures the nuances of the speech of the earlier immigrant generation, their becoming "American," and Schwartz has Belmont note that the mother imposes "her own variety of irony upon the irony which sang in Belmont's mind at every phase of her story." Brief at first, Belmont's ruminations increase page by page until they consume the final two pages. At first uncertain "whether the cruelty of the story was in his own mind or in his mother's tongue," he is finally convinced that the irony and contempt with which he has listened to the story applies to himself and to his own awareness of self-contempt.

The telling concluding analogy has Belmont acquiring the "curious omniscience" gained by looking at an old photograph. Much as Belmont has judged the failure and waste of the Baumanns, so might the viewer of an old photograph look condescendingly on the people pictured there, finding their clothes and their very posture ridiculous—until, moving beyond this superficial vision of past time, he might recognize "that the very act of looking has . . . in its time, the same character."

The passive viewer of the photograph of past times, as Belmont has been the passive listener to tales of past times, achieves his enlightenment: "And now it seemed to him that all those lives inhabited the air he breathed and would be present wherever he was." The framework, therefore, embraces both the social and the personal, inviting all readers to reflect and to achieve awareness of the forces that have shaped them.

Eileen Lothamer

AMERICAN HISTORY

Author: Judith Ortiz Cofer (1952-   )
Type of plot: Coming of age
Time of plot: 1963
Locale: Paterson, New Jersey
First published: 1993

> *Principal characters:*
> SKINNY BONES, the narrator and protagonist, a Puerto Rican teenager
> EUGENE, an Anglo teenager known as the Hick because of his Georgia accent
> SKINNY BONES'S MOTHER, a housewife
> EUGENE'S MOTHER, a nurse

The Story

Skinny Bones is a teenage Puerto Rican girl struggling to adapt to life in a multi-family apartment building in Paterson, New Jersey. She lives in a former Jewish neighborhood that is now inhabited mostly by Puerto Ricans and African Americans. As a loner, Skinny Bones is attracted to marginalized individuals like herself. She finds her soulmate in Eugene, a shy teenager who has recently come from south Georgia. Because of his marked southern accent he is soon dubbed "the Hick," and he becomes the school's newest object of ridicule, joining Skinny Bones as an outcast. Skinny Bones falls in love with Eugene, and they soon become inseparable, despite their cultural differences. Eugene, a bright student, tutors Skinny Bones in several subjects. Although Skinny Bones is a good student, she is not admitted to advanced courses because English is not her first language.

The story's climax occurs when Skinny Bones accepts Eugene's invitation to a tutorial session at his home, immediately across from her own apartment building. She accepts gladly because she has been wanting to meet Eugene's family. After having watched his kitchen from her own apartment, Skinny Bones is particularly interested in Eugene's mother, "a red-headed tall woman." Their study date, however, is almost interrupted by the assassination of President John F. Kennedy. Skinny Bones must convince her grieving mother to allow her to go to Eugene's house instead of going to church to pray for the slain president.

At Eugene's house, Skinny Bones encounters another unexpected problem. When Eugene's mother answers her knock at the door, she regards Skinny Bones as one of those "people" who live across the street and immediately dismisses her. The mother also forbids her from studying with Eugene because he is smart and does not need any help.

Frustrated in what appears to be her first adolescent love, Skinny Bones returns home and tries to "feel the right thing for our dead president." Eventually she cries, but realizes that the tears coming up from a deep source inside are strictly for her.

Themes and Meanings

Puerto Rican American literature has shown a strong attachment to northeastern cities in representing the cultural clash that Puerto Rican immigrants have experienced in the United States. The characters most typically depicted by Puerto Rican authors are adult males—who experience the plight of living in poverty, isolated from the expected American Dream. Judith Ortiz Cofer deals with issues related to the Puerto Rican migration experience, but her characters are usually teenage girls or women, who—like the male characters of other Puerto Rican writers—confront ethnic discrimination. Her female characters also tend to abandon the traditional barrio of Puerto Rican culture and involve themselves in cultures that are foreign to the traditional Puerto Rican Caribbean lifestyle.

"American History" stands out particularly because the theme of cultural isolation and xenophobic attitudes in a large American city is viewed through the fresh eyes of a teenage Puerto Rican girl. During Skinny Bones's early struggles to adapt to life in Paterson, the theme of cultural isolation is explored on various levels. The problems that she has in adapting are geographical (she is unused to the bitter cold of the Northeast), interpersonal (she is still learning about another culture's codes), and familial (she confronts her mother's inability to provide feminine advice in this foreign society). Through narrating her daily-life experiences she discovers that all these issues are related to one another and are intricate parts in the forging of her own personality as a young Puerto Rican woman growing up in the United States.

Skinny Bones's interest in documenting her daily life leads her to create a journal in which she introduces the reader to a number of locales and characters. Her primary focus is her world at "Public School Number 13," the impersonal educational facility where she first experiences racial conflicts with African American students. They give her her nickname—which she loathes—in order to avoid using her real Spanish name, which never appears in the story.

Skinny Bones shows an inclination toward feminine issues, such as the process of becoming a young woman. These issues merge with the story's thematic axis, which revolves around how people from different cultures react to one another and what aspects of their behavior may be viewed as xenophobic. Skinny Bones does not assume a judgmental role even though all the non-Puerto Rican characters represent alien cultures that affect her life. African American teenagers stand out because they represent the struggle by both groups to avoid cultural assimilation into the nondescript American melting pot.

Style and Technique

Ortiz Cofer's commitment to document the Puerto Rican experience of adolescent female characters is evident in "American History." In fact, her female characters, unlike the male characters created by other Puerto Rican writers, move away from the traditional cultural and linguistic separation of life in the barrio, to allow a more direct interaction between the environment and the self. "American History" singles out the development of the feminine psyche of a teenage Puerto Rican in a feminist text that incorporates the young woman's voice into the struggle for racial equality.

As the narrator and protagonist in a story with few characters, Skinny Bones not only represents a transitional Puerto Rican generation, she also determines the literary devices. She narrates in a style that is clearly personal, fashioned after the popular female teenage practice of keeping a journal for careful recording of all of her daily activities. The technique resembles the *Bildungsroman*, a literary chronicle written from the point of view of a young character. As a *Bildungsroman*, "American History" introduces Skinny Bones's personal view as an outcast character of society at large, including her vision of American culture from her perspective as a Puerto Rican teenager. That personal view gives to the text its freshness of expression and its unbiased stands on the subject matter presented.

The authentic testimonial narrative devices of a *Bildungsroman* text reveal Skinny Bones's role as a young reporter of life in the barrio. Although young people are evidently the author's expected audience, both adults and youngsters react positively to her story's direct and austere writing style. That personal style, reflective of a young teenager's daily journal entries, presents issues to be discussed at a personal level— such as Skinny Bones's meditations on her life—inviting that analysis by the reader. Therefore, the reader, without much warning, learns from concrete examples about such controversial issues as racist attitudes among ethnic groups.

The story also offers a political view of popular American history. Skinny Bones's dual roles are evident: As a teenager, she confides to her journal details of her attempt at a romantic relationship outside of her ethnic group; as a historian, she records President John F. Kennedy's assassination. Ortiz Cofer recognizes her political dimension. She has remarked that she does "not know of any intelligent, thinking person, sensitive to what is going on in the world, who is not political. If my stories have serious lives being lived, that is, lives that are not being recounted for the sake of mere entertainment, then I am a writer with political intent."

In style, technique, and content Ortiz Cofer creates a new kind of Puerto Rican short story. The core of the narration is supported by her use of English, instead of Spanish or Spanglish (a mixture of the two languages). That linguistic decision has proved pivotal in bringing together characters of diverse ethnic groups not part of the Puerto Rican barrio.

Rafael Ocasio

THE AMISH FARMER

Author: Vance Bourjaily (1922-   )
Type of plot: Psychological
Time of plot: The twentieth century
Locale: Indiana
First published: 1980

> *Principal characters:*
> VANCE, the narrator, a university writing teacher
> KATIE JAY, a student in his class
> NOEL BUTLER, his friend during his graduate student days
> DAWN BUTLER, Noel's wife
> DANIEL, the Butlers' Amish landlord

The Story

Vance teaches writing at an Indiana university. He has a student named Katie Jay from whom he tries to elicit a particular response by telling his class a story. He instructs them to pay particular attention to the crucial function of his story's narrative point of view. His story goes back to a time ten years earlier when one of his fellow graduate students, Noel Butler, called begging to see him because someone had just tried to kill him. As Vance awaited Noel's arrival, he remembered the circumstances under which he had met Butler and his beautiful wife, Dawn. Noel was a competent and popular graduate student who was desperately in love with his wife. Vance had met Dawn at a departmental party, where her sexuality caused him—and most of the other men—to act like a foolish schoolboy. Despite being smitten, Vance was aware of Dawn's sexual ploys and instability. There was something dangerous about her intimacies—such as her tight gripping of Vance's wrist in seeming desperation.

Earlier, Noel had had to struggle to persuade Dawn to leave Boston to join him in Indiana with her five-year-old son, Jimmer (the son of a famous but cruel choreographer). He arranged for his family to live on an Amish farm, twenty miles—and three centuries—away from his campus. Dawn agreed to live in this remote place because of their previous "interesting experiences" in Boston. As Noel told Vance, the struggle of living through their first harsh winter on the farm made living there worthwhile.

The Butlers' thirty-two-year-old Amish landlord, Daniel, was the youngest and favorite son of an Old Order Amish patriarch. Daniel cared well for his farm, his wife and seven children, and his community of fellow believers. Although the Amish themselves do not use modern technology, he provided the Butlers' cottage with electricity and a telephone.

It was Daniel, Noel told Vance, who tried to kill him. Noel admitted that he had failed to recognize how strongly Dawn and Daniel were attracted to each other until he figured out when they first consummated their relationship. During a treacherous

winter storm Noel had had to leave Dawn stranded while he struggled back to the farm
to check on Jimmer's well-being and to get help. The only person available to help
was Daniel, who violated Amish precepts by driving an old tractor through the storm
to rescue Dawn. Vance suspected that the forbidding storm conditions placed Dawn
and Daniel into a situation in which they became "the only man and woman in the
world," and that their desire for each other became too great to resist.

After drawing this conclusion, Noel accused Dawn of unfaithfulness, but she denied it and mocked him. The following spring, Noel came home early one day and
saw Daniel leaving his house. He again accused his wife of unfaithfulness and told her
that he was leaving. When Daniel saw them fighting, he attacked Noel with a wrench.

Noel now wanted Vance to go back to the farm with him to help him fetch his belongings. Dawn then called him, asking her husband to talk with Daniel, who was in
an agony of shame. Together, they met with the farmer, who asked Noel to forgive him
and pray for him. Nevertheless, Dawn, her son, and Daniel moved to northern Indiana,
where they still live. Noel finished his graduate studies and later left the state.

Vance asks his class to analyze his story to assess what would change if it were told
from another perspective. His students, however, do not believe that anyone but him
could tell it. Katie Jay's failure to enter the discussion disappoints Vance, who hoped
to hear what she would say about Dawn because of what she has revealed about her
own casual attitude toward sex. Vance then lectures that if his story were to be a tragedy, it should be by Daniel's father, who would see the incident as a precursor to the
breakdown of his Amish community. Afterward, Katie does not leave with the rest of
the class. When Vance approaches her, she grips his arm—as Dawn did ten years earlier—and tells him haltingly that she needs an Amish farmer herself.

Themes and Meanings

The theme of this story is seeing, which Vance articulates to his class: "What I am
going to try to illustrate is the remarkable power of point of view." The narrator (who
shares author Vance Bourjaily's first name) controls his class's perceptions of his
characters' situation. Nevertheless, he carefully assures them that they should realize—
if they listen attentively—that he is projecting his own point of view on the story when
he tells them what he did not observe. "Imagine Daniel knocking then" or "I think an
embrace develops out of this" or "Perhaps she touches him."

Unlike Vance's students, the story's readers not only read his story of the love triangle from his point of view, they also read his rendition of how he tells his story to his
class, as well as the story of his interaction with Katie Jay—all from his point of view.
Vance asks his class to analyze the point of view of his Amish farmer story; in order to
understand its theme the reader must analyze the point of view for its classroom context. The class itself fails to get much beyond what they are given; they either dismiss
the possibility of other points of view or trivialize them with stock categories, such as
melodrama, romance, or comedy. They are left with Vance's assertion that only if it
were told from the point of view of Daniel's patriarchal father would it become a tragedy because the infidelity of his son foretold the breakdown of his community.

One might ask what would happen to this story if a class member, perhaps Katie Jay, were to tell it. Further, one might ask whether the story gains its power—as one class member suggests—from its narrator revealing how it has affected him. In asking such questions, the reader should ask about the reliability of the story's narrator. Noel tried hard to understand his relationship with Dawn. Did Vance understand his with Katie Jay? Although he was able to mock himself when he told about his first meeting with Dawn, that ironic distance seems lacking in the classroom. The relationship between professor and student is at least as tenuous as the Butlers' marriage, yet there is no evidence for Vance's diversionary counterclaim of Daniel's father's belief that Amish society is decaying. At the same time, both the class and the readers should ask themselves if even a flawed narrator can reveal truths about life. Katie, for example, learns a crucial truth about the inadequacy of her own sexual attitudes. If her professor cannot tell his story from all points of view, or even from the most important one, it is nevertheless a significant telling for her.

Style and Technique

Bourjaily, a post-World War II American novelist, is associated with the "after the lost generation" writers who use techniques pioneered by post-World War I writers. He is known primarily for his first novel, *The End of My Life* (1947), which explores the effects of the world war on his generation and culture. Although he experiments with style in each of his novels, "The Amish Farmer" is representative of the core of his work in its naturalistic realism and emotional detachment. What one critic said about his novel *Confessions of a Spent Youth* (1960) applies equally to this story: It has a "conversational style that moves easily from quiet humor to unobtrusive lyricism." In a few sure descriptive strokes, Bourjaily brings his varied characters to life. For example, the men who meet Dawn perceive her as "a wave of heat" with "brute magnetism" and "the look of a woman standing her ground and at the same time enticing you to share it with her." However, something is "missing from the voice despite the smiles and the flicking tongue. . . ." Another significant feature of this story is its strong narrative thrust. It moves ahead, compelling its readers with it; even the asides to describe the Amish worldview move the plot forward. The frame of the classroom for the "story within the story" fits naturally.

This style is particularly appropriate for Bourjaily's theme about the reliability and power of perception. The narrator does not have an omniscient point of view; his flaws as a narrator are highlighted by his flawed students. He sets up an interesting case study that readers can apply to both stories while being forced to confront the limitations of one person's perspective. Bourjaily himself once said that "the process of writing fiction is not a matter of describing directly a reality that one sees. It's much more often a matter of re-creating a reality which one recalls perhaps imperfectly which one remembers as having been in some way moving, and one almost has to re-create it in order to discover why it is that it still moves one to think about it."

Barbara J. Hampton

AMONG THE DANGS

Author: George P. Elliott (1918-1980)
Type of plot: Parody
Time of plot: 1937 to after World War II
Locale: The United States and the eastern foothills of the Andes
First published: 1958

> *Principal characters:*
> THE NARRATOR, a graduate of Sansom University in search of a
>   vocation
> DR. SORISH, his sponsor at Sansom
> REDADU, his wife among the Dangs
> VELMA, his North American wife

The Story

The narrator, the story's central character and only developed personality, is an Everyman with needs to satisfy. His quest depicts the relative capacity of two different societies to fulfill his needs and to bring him to full humanity. On graduation from Sansom, he requires a job and will take what he can get, no matter how unpromising it seems. When the doing brings him to a greater truth than he had aimed at and through a path of apparent improbabilities, the result is nothing short of miracle or comedy in the Dantean sense, but it is tinged finally by his reversion to the values of the lesser civilization. This story realizes the full potential of I-narration by bringing the unwitting modern through his society's delusions and his own limitations toward the will to faith. His dramatized example witnesses that, of all the stories having more than passing value, the deepest and most satisfying—toward which others lead—is the Christian mystery. His return to something less, though certainly human, is a letdown.

To run the course of his discovery, the narrator makes three trips to the primitive Dangs, about whom little is known except their appetite for prophecy and hostility toward intruders. Surprisingly, he makes three returns, though one seems unlikely, his qualifications to do anthropological research among the primitives being merely that he is a "good mimic, a long-distance-runner, and black." These seem less than sufficient, considering the problems: He has no zeal for the quest but goes because he needs money and has no other prospects; he doubts that the "brick dust" black Dangs will spot a relative in his "granite dust" black skin and ersatz primitive getup.

Surprisingly, virtually everything goes his way. Entering primitiveness, he makes enough errant gestures to get a troop of searchers killed but without that conclusion. Apparently, the Dangs are broader-minded about accepting other humans than he and his educated tutors had assumed; when he unwittingly assumes the "prophetic squat" and commits additional natural gestures in which the Dangs see significance, he has assured himself of success. Throughout his first visit, comedy issues from the Dangs' seeming gullibility in accepting his ways. They even bend the rules for his satisfaction. For example, when the narrator accepts the advances of the girl Redadu and satisfies himself prodigiously, the Dangs accommodate the couple by condoning their irregular mating, going so far as to find a substitute for his "Methodist mother" to sit outside the marriage hut and listen for the "orgastic cries" of consummation. Because these primitives honor naturalness and accept others easily, the narrator does not grasp the firmness of purpose beneath their smoothing of his way to prophecy. After all, the advanced civilization that has sent him forth is not particularly compliant or flexible; it bent him from his desire to study history into a tool of social science. Finally prepared for the vatic role, he chants *James Infirmary,* and the Dangs accept that good story by incorporating its rhythms into their daily drumming.

One might expect the narrator's departure to end this relationship as a grade-B comedy, but he returns to the Dangs and is accepted, as are his explanations, by this people who put so high a premium on artful telling. Given these conditions, he works toward greater efforts, shifting from the blues to the Christian Passion and moving toward an understanding of what he has been doing. The wisdom and patience of the primitives has produced an artist who satisfies his audience as well as himself.

The returns to modernity, handled briefly, serve to illustrate the superficiality of values in a civilization where marriage, money, and vocational acceptance fail to stimulate the passion and satisfaction produced by the narrator's relationships among the Dangs. Consequently, it is a sad irony that hovers over the ending. Back home at Sansom, he has employed his experience to make an "honorable contribution to knowledge" and has gained a "tenure to a professorship—thereby pleasing" his "wife." There are no "orgastic cries" from the bedroom, nor do his two daughters match the aspiring-prophet son he has left among the Dangs. The narrator's defense for his final return to Sansom—his fear that he would "revert" until he became "one of them"—is a spiritual letdown. The Dangs had led him into his vocation, a process of their primitive society, not his social science, being the power that promoted the loss of self "utterly" in religious truth.

Themes and Meanings

"Among the Dangs" is an argument for the primacy of story among humanity's ways of knowing and for the primacy of the vatic teller among the world's knowers and tellers. The story suggests that the data of the modern social scientist is not wisdom, that advanced civilization does not satisfy, and that the persistent ritual of primitives who know what they want can lead man, through the habituation of doing, to spiritual understanding. The "Dangs make no separation between fact and fantasy, apparent reality and visionary reality, truth and beauty," suggesting a connection between them and a more romantic stage of civilization that modern man has fallen away from—much to the chagrin of such thinkers as Matthew Arnold, William Butler Yeats, and W. H. Auden as well as George P. Elliott. The Dangs' seemingly "mindless holding of the same position hour after hour" and the monotony of their melodies can blot out the noise, however unique, of modern delusions and can make the prophet aware, through subtle rhythms, of the mystic truth.

The Dangs, so improbably helpful to the intruder, are so cast to call attention to the limitations of advanced society's assumptions and values; their behavior also represents an educational philosophy—help the willing to find the way by patience and flexibility—from which any society could benefit. There is also in the story a chastening of blind belief in uninterrupted progress. Because the religious knowing pictured here depends on a creative interaction between the individual and the whole society, when the individual flags in his pursuit of the truth and steps down to lesser values, the society may have to wait for another generation to produce a new performer. To be "among the Dangs" is to be within the possibility of integrity; to leave is to impede the best hope.

Style and Technique

Elliott's style, which promotes irony, satire, and other deflators of pretentiousness, thus functioning as a pathway to moral judgment, has been called "cool." Elliott himself has described his medium as "formal seeming, of a certain polish," and has explained that his didacticism depends on "the complex relationships among storyteller, characters, and readers" and an "aesthetic distance," without which "there is not likely to be much moral clarity." In "Among the Dangs," the narrator's discoveries act as adjustments of the moral focus until aesthetic distance is achieved.

The comedy of the narrator's encountering primitive humanity employs sharp contrasts between frightening expectation and actuality. Equally important for aesthetic distance are muted contrasts introduced at varying removes: Consider, for example, that a life of floating corpses and the possibility of mutilation and even sacrificial death brings the narrator only to the scratch-wounds of sexual ecstasy and a stubborn rash, whereas a return to civilization involves him in World War II, in which his right hand is "severed above the wrist," a fact he relates almost incidentally among a list of supposed accomplishments.

Moral clarity increases when, through the narrator, truth momentarily shines forth from beneath the mix of styles. Modern man in need bares his motives: "After I'd got them to throw in a fellowship of some sort for the following year I agreed. It would pay for filling the forty cavities in my brothers' and sisters' teeth." The budding anthropologist describes a primitive event: "They could not possibly just assimilate me without marking the event with an act (that is, a ceremony) signifying my entrance." Then the growing prophet discovers real values: "If the conditions of my being elevated, I said to myself, are the sufferings of the people, Redadu's death, and the sacrifice of an old man, then I must make myself worthy of the great price."

Then the moral instrument achieves its full aesthetic distance by the deflating rhythm of the ending: "if I had stayed there among the Dangs much longer I would have reverted until I had become one of them, might not have minded when the time came to die under the sacrificial knife, would have taken in all ways the risk of prophecy—as my Dang son intends to do—until I had lost myself utterly."

William P. Keen

AMY FOSTER

Author: Joseph Conrad (Jósef Teodor Konrad Nałęcz Korzeniowski, 1857-1924)
Type of plot: Psychological
Time of plot: The 1890's
Locale: East coast of England
First published: 1903

> *Principal characters:*
> YANKO GOORALL, an Eastern European; the sole survivor of a
> shipwreck
> AMY FOSTER, the Englishwoman whom he marries
> KENNEDY, the country doctor who relates their story to the frame
> narrator
> SWAFFER, the farmer for whom Yanko works

The Story

An unnamed narrator recalls a time several years earlier, when he was staying with his friend Kennedy, a country doctor in the English coastal village of Colebrook, near Brenzett. One day as he accompanied the doctor on his afternoon rounds, they came upon a dull-looking woman named Amy Foster, who was hanging out her wash. Kennedy asked after her son's health. As he continued his rounds, he told the narrator about this woman's recent life.

Although Kennedy agreed that the woman looked passive and inert, he confided that this same woman once had enough imagination to fall in love. The oldest child of a large family, Amy was put into the service of the Smiths, the tenant family at New Barns Farm, where she worked for four years. Meanwhile, she occasionally made the three-mile walk to her family's cottage to help with their chores. As Kennedy explained, Amy seemed satisfied with this drab life until she unexpectedly fell in love.

After the narrator and Kennedy passed a sullen group of men trudging along the road, Kennedy resumed his story, this time telling about a man who used to walk the village paths with such a jaunty, upright bearing that Kennedy thought he might be a woodland creature. The man was an emigrant from central Europe who had been on his way to America when his ship went down near the coast. He could speak no English, but Kennedy guessed that he had boarded the ship in Hamburg, Germany.

Kennedy then described the railway journey that had carried the German to Hamburg. After riding a train for several days before changing trains in Berlin, he reached the mouth of a river, where he saw a ship for the first time. There he lost contact with the three men who had recruited him to immigrate to America with the promise of his earning three dollars a day there. Using a telegraph, the three men secured passage to America for the man, whose father paid for the passage by selling livestock and part of his farm.

Kennedy again digressed to mention that he had patched this story together from fragments gathered over two or three years. When the castaway first appeared in Brenzett, his wild language and appearance shocked the town. Taking him for a gypsy, the milk-cart driver lashed him with his whip and boys pelted him with stones. The man ran to New Barns Farm, where he frightened Mrs. Smith. Amy Foster, however, responded with kindness. Though Mr. Smith thought that the man's wild appearance and indecipherable speech proved that he was a lunatic, Amy implored the Smiths not to hurt him.

Several months later, reports of the shipwreck appeared in newspapers. The emigration agents were exposed as confidence men who had cheated people out of land and money. Townsfolk speculated that the German may have floated ashore on a wooden chicken coop. At New Barns, he showed his appreciation for Amy's kindness by tearfully kissing her hand.

The stranger went to work on the farm of the Smiths' neighbors, the Swaffers, who had Kennedy examine the man. Observing the man's verbal and emotional isolation, Kennedy wondered why he did not go mad. The castaway's nightly thoughts returned to Amy Foster, who had treated him kindly. Eventually, the stranger learned a few words of English. One day he rescued Swaffer's infant grandchild from a pond into which she had fallen.

Kennedy could not describe exactly how the stranger made a new life for himself. The villagers still found his customs odd; his favorite songs, his religious habits, and his clothes all marked him as an outsider. He was a mountaineer from the eastern Carpathians whose first name was Yanko. His last name, as best as the locals could tell from his speech, was Goorall. This name, Kennedy recalled, survived in the parish marriage register.

Yanko began his courtship of Amy with a present of a green satin ribbon, and he persisted in spite of the warnings and threats of the townspeople. After Yanko asked for Amy's hand, Mr. Swaffer gave them a cottage and an acre of land—the same land that Kennedy and the narrator passed during their rounds—in gratitude for saving his granddaughter from drowning.

After Amy bore Yanko's son, Yanko told Kennedy about problems that he was having with Amy. One day, for example, she took their boy from his arms when he was singing to him in his own language. She also stopped him from teaching the boy how to pray in his own language. Yanko still believed that Amy had a good heart, but Kennedy wondered if the differences between them would eventually ruin their marriage.

After breaking off this story, Kennedy said that the next time he saw Yanko, the man had serious lung trouble brought on by a harsh winter. When Kennedy treated Yanko, he was lying on a couch downstairs, suffering from fever and muttering in his native tongue. Kennedy asked Amy to move Yanko upstairs to get him away from the drafty door, but she refused. Kennedy saw fear in her eyes but had to leave to treat his other patients. That night Yanko's fever worsened. Perhaps thinking he was speaking in English, he demanded water, but Amy could not understand him. As his demands increased in intensity, she took her child to her family's farm three miles away.

The next day Kennedy found Yanko outside his cottage. He took him inside and called for Amy, but Yanko told him she had fled the night before. Yanko weakly wondered why and then said the word "Merciful!" just before dying of heart failure. Over the years that followed, Amy never mentioned her husband.

Themes and Meanings

The tragedy of Yanko Goorall probes the modernist theme of isolation and alienation. This idea also figures prominently in Joseph Conrad's major works, such as the novels *Lord Jim* (1900), *Heart of Darkness* (1902), and *The Secret Agent* (1907). Yanko is an unwilling loner whose free and easy nature undergoes repeated assaults until even the only person who has offered him love abandons him at the moment of his greatest need. His first ordeal was physical confinement in crowded trains, the boxlike berths aboard a ship, and the dungeonlike lodge at New Barns.

Kennedy senses, however, that Yanko's most painful ordeal is his verbal and psychological confinement. He notes that "an overwhelming loneliness seemed to fall from the leaden sky of that winter without sunshine. He could talk to no one, and had no hope of ever understanding anybody." The story repeatedly contrasts Yanko's nobility with the prejudice and insensibility of the townspeople, whose rejection intensifies his feelings of estrangement. Amy's father, for example, opposed Yanko's marriage partly because he heard him mutter to himself in his native language. Told by Kennedy that Yanko was dead, the father responded with indifference: "I don't know that it isn't for the best."

Like much of Conrad's writing, this story has autobiographical roots. As a Pole, Conrad knew isolation during his years at sea on British ships. He learned English in his twenties, but other problems contributed to his loneliness during his residence in England. In addition to his problems establishing himself as a writer, he had nagging financial worries and a growing emotional distance from his English wife. He personally had an experience similar to that of Yanko in 1896, when he suffered from a fever and rambled incoherently in Polish, frightening his young wife.

Style and Technique

The use of multiple narrators and repeated flashbacks are techniques that Conrad carried to even more complex levels in other works. In "Amy Foster," the technique permits Conrad to minimize the elements of his story that interest him the least (such as melodrama, the sea adventure, and the budding romance), while concentrating on Yanko's isolation, rejection, and personal despair. Conrad's artistic choices, as in many of his other works, break up the linear development of plot in favor of character analysis and psychology. Kennedy's disjointed narrative thus supports Conrad's conscious artistic design. The strategy allows Conrad to emphasize fragments of Yanko's life that lack proper chronological unity but reflect the larger thematic unity. This technique also enables Conrad to introduce brief comments from the other characters whom Kennedy quotes to round out the picture of Yanko.

Kennedy is an ideal narrator to relate Yanko's story. His training as a physician, his analytical mind, and his professional duties in towns outside of Brenzett distance him from other villagers. The unnamed narrator who begins the story introduces Kennedy by remarking that

> the penetrating power of his mind, acting like a corrosive fluid, had destroyed his ambition, I fancy. His intelligence is of a scientific order, of an investigating habit, and of that unappeasable curiosity which believes that there is a particle of a general truth in every mystery.

Such detachment provides Kennedy with a growing appreciation and understanding of Yanko's rejection and anguish, as well as a measure of shared guilt in its outcome.

Glenn Hopp

THE ANATOMY OF DESIRE

Author: John L'Heureux (1934-   )
Type of plot: Fantasy
Time of plot: An apocalyptic future
Locale: Unspecified
First published: 1981

Principal characters:
HANLEY, a victim of war
THE NURSE, also known as the saint, who loves Hanley
THE GENERAL, who orders Hanley's flaying

The Story

Hanley has been flayed by the enemy and is unable to find anyone to love him; not even his wife and children will spend time with him because he is raw, and he will never be any better. Only one nurse, known as the saint, stays with him and applies blood retardant to his flesh. Although he does not find the woman pretty, he does find her saintly. He asks her to love him, to possess him. She says that she will perhaps love him if sometime she finds out that she must.

The narrator recalls how Hanley's flaying occurred. He was sleeping in a trench when soldiers found him and brought him back to their camp to serve as an example of what happens to infiltrators. When Hanley was taken to the general's tent, he captivated the general, who caressed his skin, saying that he had a beautiful face. He apparently performed a sexual act with his prisoner. When Hanley was led out for his punishment, the general told the men who carry the knives to spare Hanley here and there because he could be his own son. Hanley's face and genitals were spared but the rest of his skin was flayed and hung on the barbed wire. Hanley was left to die, but after the enemy retreated, he was taken by his own unit to the hospital, where he met the nurse.

After some time passes, the nurse agrees to make love with Hanley. While they are in bed, he decides he does not miss his wife and children; in fact, he does not even miss his skin. The nurse, meanwhile, whispers to Hanley that she cannot live without him, after he wakes her to apply some blood retardant on his body.

Hanley soon recognizes that he wants more from the saintly nurse. He is in love and is loved, and wonders why that is not enough. The nurse replies that nothing is ever enough. After making love, Hanley recognizes that even sexual intimacy is not enough; it is only a metaphor for what he wants.

At the close of the war, the general is made mayor of the capital city by the occupying forces, and then he is elected senator and made a trustee of three nuclear arms conglomerates. Despite his achievements, he feels an absence. He longs for Hanley: "I wake in the night and see your face. . . . You could have been my son. . . . I can endure no more. I am possessed by you."

Hanley finally recognizes what it is that he wants from the saint: He asks for her skin. Feeling resigned, even satisfied, she consents. Hanley, for a brief moment, feels completely fulfilled. Just as the general gazed deeply into his eyes, traced the lines of his eyebrows, and pressed his palms lightly against his forehead before he ordered Hanley's skin to be removed, so too Hanley, wearing the saint's skin, now gazes deeply into her eyes, traces the lines of her eyebrows gently, and presses his palms lightly against her forehead.

Hanley's happiness soon shifts to sadness and tears because he recognizes that despite the love he feels from the saint, there can never be possession, only desire.

Themes and Meanings

In early Aztec society, a ceremony was performed each year to honor the goddess of grain. A young virgin selected from the group became the embodiment of the grain goddess; her reign was brief, however. After a short period of ritual fasting and prayer, the young girl was sacrificed to the goddess, her skin was flayed, her blood sprinkled on the crops, and then the priest who performed the ritual would wear her skin. John L'Heureux offers a similarly gruesome tale in "The Anatomy of Desire," but his story is perhaps even more unsettling than the Aztec ritual because it begins and ends not with purification and hope but with absurdity and despair.

Hanley is flayed because of some soldiers' absurd notion of duty. Soldiers loyal to the general come across the sleeping Hanley and make an example of him. He is accused of being an infiltrator, but it is clear that he is dragged across the arbitrary demarcation line by the soldiers; he has infiltrated nothing. He is simply a random victim of war, a war whose origin and purpose are never shared with the reader. His sacrifice is related to no larger myths of the society, no purpose.

The French psychoanalyst Jacques Lacan has said that "what is desired is always displaced, always deferred, and reappears endlessly in another guise." L'Heureux's male characters, especially Hanley, seem to reflect Lacan's belief. Happiness and contentment are absent in the story because, as the nurse says, nothing is ever enough. There is always desire, and no matter how arduously one fights for satisfaction, one's desire will always remain, will always be transferred to some other object. Even if one can somehow enter into another person, either metaphorically or by literally wearing the other's skin, one will still feel a need, a lack, or at least Hanley will.

There is an exception, however, to this schema. The nurse perhaps serves as another model. She is neither transfixed by desire as the general is, nor constantly frustrated by her inability to satisfy her longing as Hanley is. She is resigned, even satisfied, when she gives her skin to Hanley. The reader is not given any other glimpse into her mind before the story ends, but she seems to be able to reach some kind of contentment through sacrifice. Perhaps she, as a nurse among soldiers, as a woman among men, is able to achieve a rapprochement with desire; perhaps nothing is ever enough, as she says, but in her own saintly way she is able to find satisfaction, or at least resignation, despite the seemingly unquenchable nature of desire.

Style and Technique

Johanna Kaplan, a critic for *The New York Times*, has called L'Heureux's style "spare, witty and elegant." Those words certainly apply to "The Anatomy of Desire"; it is spare and witty and, despite the gruesomeness of certain scenes, the language remains elevated. Even the saint's flaying is described in an elegant fashion: "Hanley lifted the shroud of skin from her crimson body." This elegance and spareness create a tension within the story simply at the level of style. If fiction needs friction in order to achieve its effects, L'Heureux creates friction by yoking together the understated style with the sensational aspects of the story.

The technique that gives this story added complexity is L'Heureux's use of the double, or counterpart. He avoids relying on the simple dichotomies of good and evil by carefully plotting the story so that the difference between victim and victimizer becomes muted. The villainy of the general is clear: He is a pointlessly cruel power-monger who serves as a trustee for nuclear arms conglomerates. Because his actions are mirrored almost exactly in the actions of his victim, Hanley, the reader can see the general not as an individual with serious faults, but as a type, a representative of humanity. Certainly he is cruel, but he suffers as well. Just as Hanley caresses the face of the nurse whom he has flayed, so too the general caresses Hanley's skin before he orders his flaying. The general and Hanley both yearn for an end to desire, for a level of satisfaction that they never achieve. The general and the soldier, the two enemies, the innocent victim and nasty victimizer are one, it seems, under the skin.

This use of the double allows the character of the saint to stand out in full contrast. Unlike the general and Hanley, who are united by similarities, the saint is shown in relief despite her similarities to Hanley. When she is flayed, her face and genitals are spared, just as Hanley's were. She is caressed by Hanley and told she has a beautiful face, just as Hanley was. She has the blood retardant applied to her skin, just as she applied it to Hanley's. These similarities only suggest the differences between her and Hanley, between her and the general. They are horribly human, desperately human, whereas she is resignedly a saint.

Kevin Boyle

. . . AND THE EARTH DID NOT PART

Author: Tomás Rivera (1935-1984)
Type of plot: Vignette
Time of plot: The 1950's
Locale: Chiefly Texas
First published: ". . . y no se lo trago la tierra," 1971 (English translation, 1971)

> *Principal characters:*
> A CHICANO BOY, the protagonist
> HIS COMMUNITY, Chicano migrant workers

The Story

". . . and the earth did not part" is the title story in a book of linked stories, a sequence of vignettes in which an unnamed Chicano boy confronts his memories of the past year in an attempt to define himself and to understand more fully the lot of his people. In each of these brief pieces, averaging four or five pages in length, Tomás Rivera presents one facet of the life of a community of migrant workers. The workers and their children—who are indeed workers themselves—are exploited by seemingly uncaring or blatantly callous American bosses. Brutality, however, is not limited to Anglo-Chicano relations, and the author also shows Chicanos exploiting their own people. ". . . and the earth did not part," which appears midway in the sequence, recounts a crucial experience in the young protagonist's life, a decisive change in his outlook.

The story begins with a directness characteristic of the volume: "The first time he felt hate and anger was when he saw his mother cry for his uncle and for his aunt." The fate of the aunt and uncle is quickly sketched: Having contracted tuberculosis, they were sent to separate sanatoriums, their children "parceled out" among various relatives; the aunt died, and the uncle, allowed to go home, was spitting blood. The boy's mother was "crying all the time," and it was then, he recalls, that he began to be angry—"angry because he could not strike back at anyone."

These emotions clearly signal the onset of critical awareness, the full development of which is traced in the course of the story. When his father is temporarily felled by sunstroke, the boy becomes angrier—even his father is not exempt from pointless suffering—and he is angrier still when both his mother and his father repeatedly call on God, asking for his mercy. The boy confronts his mother, raging against her, against their fate, against God. Frightened by his words, she tells him that he must not blaspheme: "The ground might open up and devour you for talking like that." Her fatalistic faith, however—"Only death can bring us rest"—does not persuade him.

The climax of the story comes when the boy goes out to work in the fields with his brothers and sisters; their father is still too sick to work, and their mother must stay with him. The day is hot, and the youngest brother, nine years old, becomes sick, vomiting and then fainting. The boy must carry his sick brother home, and as he does his anger comes to a head. Finally, he finds an outlet, someone to "strike back at": He curses God. For a moment, he feels "the fear instilled in him by time and by his parents," but the earth does not open; indeed, he "felt himself walking on very solid ground; it was harder than he had ever felt it." His anger rises again and, emboldened, he again curses God; far from suffering retribution, he notices that his brother appears to be better.

That night, he feels a sense of peace, and he goes to work the next morning with a man's self-confidence. The story concludes with a symbolic expression of that confidence and of his mature awareness of life and death; he kicks at the ground and taunts it: "Not yet, you can't eat me yet. Someday. But I won't know."

Themes and Meanings

Many Chicano stories and novels present an adolescent character, usually a boy, in the throes of discovering his own identity in a world that is not of his making but that he must make sense of. This adolescent moves between two worlds, that of his parents and that of his own adulthood, and in the process often confronts the relative nature of good and evil, deception and reality, morality and immorality; in short, he must rethink and reevaluate what he sees and experiences. The position of the Chicano, caught in the tension of his dual (Mexican and American) heritage, is analogous to that of the adolescent in that the Chicano must evaluate the cultural trappings passed on to him and must decide which ones to keep and which to reject as he sets about defining himself anew.

This is precisely the issue faced by the nameless Chicano character who recalls, synthesizes, and eventually evaluates the experiences of a year in his and his community's life. Paramount in the young Chicano boy's recollections is the cyclical pattern of suffering and disillusionment suffered by the boy's community. At first, he is unable to understand why he and his community suffer, but his review of the year allows him to discover that suffering is not unique to Chicanos and that brutality and exploitation know no boundaries of race, place, or time.

Indeed, these vignettes are above all directed at Chicano readers, urging them to self-awareness. The periodic ills of the Chicano community are caused by the economics of migration and peasant labor, neither of which fosters the building of strong individuals or communities and both of which prevent the acquisition of a good education. Ignorance of the lands where the migrants work and of the world beyond their community exposes them to economic exploitation, while an almost stereotypical passivity, ingrained by the free admixture of superstition and a Catholicism that leaves all events in the hands of God, prevents the members of the community from acting to change their lot. With his curses, the protagonist redefines himself as a young man capable of decisive action; it is this liberating knowledge that gives him hope both for his own future and for the future of his community.

Style and Technique

   . . . and the earth did not part (1971), the volume in which this story appears, was one of several works published in the 1970's that brought to the tradition of Chicano fiction a new degree of artistic quality.

   Chicano fiction, that literature by and about Americans of Mexican descent, began to make great strides in the 1960's. With the founding in 1969 of Quinto Sol, a publishing house dedicated to Mexican American, or Chicano, literature, and the subsequent institution of the Quinto Sol Prize, Chicano fiction of high artistic quality received a needed boost. Rivera's *. . . and the earth did not part* was one of the first works to receive this prize.

   In terms of structure and narrative technique *. . . and the earth did not part* is highly unusual. As noted above, it is a cycle of linked stories: twelve vignettes, formed by a very brief opening "chapter" (about a half-page long) and a longer concluding chapter. The opening chapter presents the problem of the young boy's confusion and his need to resolve the problem through recalling the events of the past year. In the last chapter, he recapitulates the contents of the twelve vignettes and forms his conclusions. Each of the vignettes (and the concluding chapter as well) is preceded by a self-contained, brief italicized passage, only a few lines long, which plays against the piece that follows.

   The author employs a wide variety of narrative techniques, among them dialogue, interior monologue, contrapuntal setting of both, and a number of third-person narrators. His combination of some of these within any one vignette or chapter allows for a variety of points of view of a particular incident; this in turn allows the incident or the character to acquire new dimensions and to free itself from the control of the author.

   Multiplicity of point of view, however, introduces the possibility of ambiguity. In the opening chapter, the author consciously blurs the lines between reality and dream and reinforces this ambiguity with multiple points of view; one is never quite sure whether what is reported actually happened.

   Rivera, as a true Chicano writer, shows the influences of both American and Mexican writers: of Sherwood Anderson and William Faulkner in his use of monologues and the creation of a community with mythic proportions, and of Juan Rulfo, the Mexican novelist and short-story writer, in his use of simple peasant language in dialogue combined with an overwhelming variety of narrative techniques.

St. John Robinson

ANGEL LEVINE

Author: Bernard Malamud (1914-1986)
Type of plot: Fantasy
Time of plot: The twentieth century
Locale: New York City
First published: 1955

> *Principal characters:*
> MANISCHEVITZ, a tailor
> FANNY, his wife
> ALEXANDER LEVINE, a black angel

The Story

Manischevitz has lost everything. His son was killed in the war, and his daughter left home. After a lifetime of work, his tailor shop burned to the ground and could not be rebuilt; his own health is so broken that he can work only a few hours a day as a clothes presser; his wife, Fanny, ruined her own health by taking in washing and sewing, so she is now confined to her bed. Always a religious man, Manischevitz cannot understand how God can have allowed such unreasonable suffering to come to him. In desperation, Manischevitz first prays for an explanation from God, but he quickly changes his prayer to a simple appeal for relief.

Later, while reading the newspaper, Manischevitz has a premonition that someone has entered the apartment. Entering the living room of his small and shabby flat, he discovers a black man sitting at the table reading a newspaper. At first Manischevitz assumes that the visitor is an investigator from the welfare department. When this proves not to be the case, the tailor again asks the man's identity. This time the man answers with his name, Alexander Levine. Manischevitz is surprised to discover that the black man is a Jew, and even more surprised when Levine tells him, "I have recently been disincarnated into an angel. As such, I offer you my humble assistance, if to offer is within my province and power—in the best sense."

Manischevitz is unwilling to accept Levine's characterization of himself, suspecting that he may be the butt of some joke or prank, so he tests him with such questions as "Where are your wings?" and "How did you get here?" Levine answers rather lamely, and even though he is able to recite correctly in Hebrew the Jewish blessing for bread, Manischevitz is unconvinced of his visitor's authenticity. As the interview reaches a conclusion, Manischevitz accuses Levine of being a fake, and the angel, disappointment registering in his eyes, announces, "If you should desire me to be of assistance to you any time in the near future . . . I can be found . . . in Harlem." He then disappears.

For a few days after Levine's visit, both Manischevitz and Fanny seem better, but their condition soon reverts to its former state. The tailor laments his fate, questioning why God should have chosen him for so much unexplained and undeserved suffering. Eventually he comes to wonder if he was mistaken in dismissing Alexander Levine, who indeed might have been sent to help him. In his desperation, he decides to go up to Harlem in search of Levine.

At first he cannot find Levine in Harlem. When he goes into the familiar setting of a tailor shop and asks for Levine by name, the tailor claims never to have heard of him. However, when Manischevitz says, "He is an angel, maybe," the tailor immediately remembers Levine and indicates that he can be found in a local honky-tonk. Making his way there, Manischevitz peers through the window to see Levine dancing with Bella, the owner of the bar. As they dance by the window, Levine winks at Manischevitz, and the latter leaves for home, convinced of the failure of his mission.

When Fanny is at death's door, Manischevitz goes to a synagogue to speak to God, but he feels that God has absented himself. In his despair, Manischevitz suffers a crisis of faith and rails against God, "cursing himself for having, beyond belief, believed." Later that afternoon, napping in a chair, the tailor dreams that he sees Levine "preening small decaying opalescent wings" before a mirror. Convinced that this may be a sign that Levine is an angel, he makes his way again to Harlem in search of him. This time, before arriving at Bella's honky-tonk, he enters a storefront synagogue, where four black Jews sit studying the Holy Word. Again he asks for Levine— identified by one of the congregation as "the angel"—and is told to look at Bella's down the street.

Since the previous visit, when Levine was shabbily dressed, things appear to have changed. He now is attired in fancy new clothes and is drinking whiskey with Bella, whose lover he appears to have become. As Manischevitz enters the bar, Levine confronts him, demanding that he state his business. First the tailor acknowledges that he believes Levine is Jewish, to which the black replies only by asking if he has anything else to say. When Manischevitz hesitates, Levine says, "Speak now or fo'ever hold off." After an agonizing moment of indecision, Manischevitz says, "I think you are an angel from God."

Levine changes back into his former clothes and returns to the tailor's flat with him. When Manischevitz asks him to come in, the angel assures him that everything has been take care of and tells him to enter, while he "takes off." Instead, Manischevitz follows him to the roof, only to find the door padlocked. Peeping through a broken window, the tailor believes that he can see "a dark figure borne aloft on a pair of strong black wings." A feather drifts downward, but when Manischevitz catches it, it proves to be only a snowflake.

Returning to his flat, Manischevitz finds Fanny up and about, busily cleaning. "A wonderful thing, Fanny," Manischevitz says, "Believe me, there are Jews everywhere."

Themes and Meanings

Perhaps the most ubiquitous figure in Bernard Malamud's fiction is the person, usually Jewish, who suffers, like Job in the Old Testament, without any apparent reason. Manischevitz is not a bad man; no sin accounts for his fall. As he complains, he suffers far more than would seem to be just.

The tailor's mistake is in wanting to understand why he should suffer, and in expecting there to be some cause and effect in life. Just as he will want proof that Levine is an angel, he wants some sign that God exists. When he fails to achieve either of these assurances, Manischevitz undergoes a crisis of faith when he renounces his belief in God and surrenders to despair. It is then that his dream vision of Levine preening his wings gives him new hope and sends him in search of the angel. Still, his faith must be tested, so Levine forces him to acknowledge before the assembled crowd in the honky-tonk that the black is an angel. At this point, not only is Manischevitz's problem solved, Levine casts off the clothes of a pimp and becomes the angel he is meant to be. Faith is necessary both for God and for humankind.

Manischevitz's final realization that there are Jews everywhere reflects Malamud's theme that all men are Jews. Jews, in Malamud's fiction, are those who suffer without cause and who maintain their faith in humanity (or in God) despite the injustice of their plight. Manischevitz does not suffer because he is a Jew; he is a Jew because he suffers. He does not believe because he is a Jew; he is a Jew because he believes.

Style and Technique

Though it deals with purely imaginary events, Malamud tells his story in the straightforward manner of literary realism. The language and grammar are those appropriate to someone of Manischevitz's background because, though the story is told in the third person, Manischevitz is clearly the center of consciousness, and the dialect in the story is his. This is an appropriate method, as it enables the reader to reach his own determination as to whether he is reading of an episode imagined by this broken old man or whether the event occurred as reported. In the final analysis, it makes little difference, as Malamud's theme does not rely for its effectiveness on the "reality" of the situation so much as on the reader's understanding of the humanizing quality of faith.

William E. Grant

THE ANGEL OF THE BRIDGE

Author: John Cheever (1912-1982)
Type of plot: Psychological
Time of plot: The mid- to late twentieth century
Locale: New York City
First published: 1964

>*Principal characters:*
>THE NARRATOR, a businessperson and the protagonist
>HIS OLDER BROTHER, also a businessperson
>HIS MOTHER
>THE HITCHHIKER, a young woman and folksinger

The Story

The story begins with the narrator being embarrassed that his seventy-eight-year-old mother likes to ice-skate in Rockefeller Center in New York City. He shortly discovers, while he is waiting with her in the Newark airport to put her on a plane to visit some friends of hers in Ohio, that she is mortally afraid of flying. His next revelation is that his older brother, more successful in business than he and their mother's favorite, has recently developed an intense fear of high buildings, especially the elevators in them. Although the narrator's confrontation with his mother's phobia has given him an insight into her fragility, his brother's neurosis—perhaps because the narrator feels in competition with him—strikes him as absurd.

The narrator is afraid of neither heights nor planes. His business requires that he fly frequently to the West Coast and to Europe. He romanticizes flying: He enjoys comparing the simultaneous activities in different time zones, the way the sky appears at high altitudes, and the way night moves across a landscape seen from the air. Without warning, however, on the way back with his wife and children from a visit in New Jersey, the narrator undergoes a strong emotional and physical reaction to the George Washington Bridge as he drives across it. From then on he is afraid of large bridges, especially high ones.

He informs the family doctor, who in effect informs him that he is being cowardly. When a psychiatrist suggests that the anxiety behind his fear will need long-term analysis, the narrator backs off, unwilling to spend the time and money, or to entrust his problem to psychiatric procedures.

The narrator's phobia changes his view of himself and of the world. He begins to doubt the joy that he finds in living and to see the world as emotionless and chaotic. He senses that the high point of a bridge symbolizes for him his loathing of the complexity and banality of modern civilization. He tells no one of his phobia other than the doctor and the psychiatrist, and he takes extravagant means to avoid driving on bridges; he drives twenty miles out of his way on a trip to Albany, New York, and he leaves his rented car in San Francisco to take a cab across the Oakland Bay Bridge.

The narrator's fear comes to a head on a Sunday morning when he drives his daughter back to a convent school in New Jersey. He does not remember his phobia until he is actually on the George Washington Bridge. Managing to hide the symptoms, he makes it across. He decides to return on what he thinks is the easier Tappan Zee Bridge farther north. Everything he thinks of either to avoid the bridge or to console himself fails. His wife might send someone for him, but the shame he would feel would damage his marriage. He might stop at a friend's house for a drink, but he would have to explain why he needed one so early in the day. When he stops for gas, he finds the gas station attendant too withdrawn for conversation. He might wait for the bars to open in the afternoon, but he has spent all his money on gas.

Finally, he arrives at the bridge and begins to cross. It upsets him more than he has ever been upset on a bridge since his phobia began, and he is forced to pull over. A young woman gets into his car, thinking that he has stopped to pick her up. She is a hitchhiker and a traveling folksinger who plays in coffeehouses. Besides her cheap suitcase, she carries a harp with her. She turns out to be the "Angel of the Bridge," for she sings him a folksong as he drives, and this not only calms him completely but also leads him to see order and beauty in the bridge and the river. The singer leaves at the toll station, and the narrator from then on is able to cross bridges without fear, though he still avoids the George Washington Bridge.

Themes and Meanings

One of John Cheever's favorite subjects is the middle class, and the locale of many of his stories is New York City and the suburbs north of it. His stories often focus on the eccentricities and failures of these people, and on how they endure. The major motif of "The Angel of the Bridge" is fear, and it is pictured as both an eccentricity and a failure. The story presents eccentricity as odd behavior in the early scene in which an elderly woman is committed to doing something that the young normally do: ice-skating. It is soon clear that the narrator's mother's odd behavior includes her phobic reaction to flying. The narrator and his older brother are also eccentric in their respective phobias. The fears of all three have two things in common besides their eccentricity: all three are afraid of heights and—if their disinclination to talk about their phobias is any sign—they regard their fears as personal failures.

In the narrator's case, his fear of heights not only is triggered by bridges but also signals a change in his vision of the world from a romantic to a terrifying one. Before the change, he was safe in his habits and regarded aberrant behavior as partially distasteful, partially amusing. The world was beautiful because his life was orderly, if somewhat boring. After the change, the world seems chaotic to him, a failure resting on his own failure to take in stride such implicit dangers in it as high bridges. His comfortable expectations and habits are turned upside down as he goes to extravagant lengths to avoid bridges.

It takes an example of courage in an eccentric form to reverse the fear and horror in the narrator. The appearance of the young folksinger when the narrator is finally all but paralyzed by his fear is enough to cure him. She is eccentric because she pursues an abnormal—that is, an adventurous—career. She is courageous because she does this on her own, hitchhiking from place to place, enthusiastically taking what the world has to offer rather than imposing meanness or paranoia on it. Her daring is what makes her angelic to the narrator and what saves him from his phobia, restoring him to a sense of well-being and giving him a new appreciation of daring behavior such as his mother's. He has realized, in short, that the human world is lovely precisely because of the unpredictability in it, and that the function of fear and failure is to make one see this.

Style and Technique

Paradox is the chief stylistic device that Cheever uses in this story. The characters demonstrate it to a marked degree. The narrator's mother is old yet pursues a sport that is dangerous for someone her age. Moreover, she radiates youth and a kind of sexiness by putting herself on display in a skating costume that reminds the narrator of "a hat-check girl." The paradox continues in his mother's case in that she is not afraid of the real danger of falling in the ice-skating rink but is afraid of the remote danger of falling in an airplane. The narrator's brother is also paradoxical. Although he is "higher," so to speak, than the narrator in their mother's esteem, and higher than the narrator on the scale of worldly success, he is also so terrified of high buildings and of elevators falling that he interrupts his career and success by quitting his job when the firm for which he works moves to the upper level of a skyscraper.

The paradox in the narrator is twofold. His own success in life is fairly humdrum and earthbound, yet it involves much flying, which at first gives him, despite the mild discomfort he feels toward the end of flights, a sense of well-being. After his phobia develops, the second part of the paradox shows itself. Not only does the fear he shares with his mother and older brother fail to draw them all closer together, but also he is returned to his normal way of life by an abnormal event—the appearance of an "angel" (the young folksinger with her harp). She is paradoxical in the narrator's mind in that her beauty and power do not fit into his original vision of the world's order. Finally, the paradox embedded in the narrator is meant to suggest that modern civilized humanity itself is paradoxical, pursuing a restricted and orderly life but projecting a romantic vision on the world and, on the other hand, experiencing chaos and profound anxiety.

Mark McCloskey

ANGELS AT THE RITZ

Author: William Trevor (William Trevor Cox, 1928-   )
Type of plot: Psychological
Time of plot: The early 1970's
Locale: Suburbs of London, England
First published: 1975

Principal characters:
GAVIN DILLARD, a thirty-eight-year-old man
POLLY DILLARD, his thirty-six-year-old wife
MALCOLM RYDER, the host of a party
SUE RYDER, Malcolm's wife

The Story

"Angels at the Ritz" is set in the outer suburbs of London in the 1970's. Gavin and Polly Dillard are about to attend a spouse-swapping party. Although spouse swapping has been practiced in the suburb since the 1950's, the Dillards have never participated in it before now. They usually simply leave before the game begins at about one o'clock in the morning. This occasion, however, proves to be a little different.

The party the Dillards have been invited to is hosted by their oldest and closest friends, Malcolm and Sue Ryder. The Ryders have never participated in the spouse-swapping game, in which partners are chosen at random, and Polly wonders why they are starting now.

On the night of the party, the Dillards leave their two young children with a baby-sitter. As they set out, it is eight-thirty on a rainy November night, and they decide in advance not to stay long at the party. When they arrive, about sixty well-dressed people are in the spacious house, standing around in groups as tape-recorded music plays. The Dillards know most of the guests. Food is served and wine flows. Then dancing begins.

Polly dances with a man whose name she does not know, while Gavin drinks and chats with Jack and Sylvia Meacock and a woman in an orange trouser suit. Sue joins them and soon takes hold of Gavin's hand, which makes Gavin feel uneasy. He reminds himself that he is in love with his wife and could not bear to hurt her. The thought of another man making love to his wife or of himself being expected to make love to another woman fills him with distaste. Meanwhile, Malcolm is attempting to seduce Polly. Taking her into his den with the excuse that he is fetching brandy, he kisses her. They both pretend that the kiss was merely an expression of friendship, but Polly feels apprehensive.

As Sue dances with Gavin, she reminds him of a special occasion in the past, an evening that Gavin, Polly, Sue, and Malcolm spent together in 1961 at the expensive Ritz restaurant to celebrate Polly's birthday. In his den, Malcolm begins to caress

Polly's leg, tells her that he has always been sexually interested in her, and then starts talking about sex. He admits that he has not always been faithful to Sue, but Sue knows about his affairs. Now they are planning to approach that aspect of their marriage differently.

Sue puts on some music that reminds them of their evening at the Ritz, which prompts Malcolm and Polly, who have emerged from the den, also to recall that night. Polly also notices that Sue is trying to seduce her husband, and for the first time in her life, she dislikes her. At the same time, Malcolm asks her to dance again, and it is clear he has not given up on his attempt to seduce her. Polly realizes that the Ryders must have decided in advance that this would be their strategy. They wanted to bypass the game of chance in which the men threw down their car keys and the women were blindfolded as they made their choices. The plan was for Malcolm to drive Polly home and make love to her while Gavin remained at the party. When it came time to play the game, Gavin and Sue would not participate, so they would be available for each other.

Gavin resists Sue's plan, and they exchange harsh words. Gavin and Polly drive home, and Polly is pleased that her husband has rejected their friends' idea. Gavin feels he should return to apologize to Sue. Polly says it is not necessary, but then when he still seems troubled, she allows him to go back and apologize, which he does after he has taken the baby-sitter home. Polly knows very well what she is permitting her husband to do; however, as she goes to bed she is resigned to it and not unhappy. She has rejected the spouse swapping because it was distasteful to her, her husband has stayed loyal to her, and the unfaithfulness that she has permitted him seems a fair reward for his constancy.

Themes and Meanings

The underlying theme of the story is the loss of innocence, a "fall" from an earlier state of purity. It is a tale of paradise lost. The state of innocence is symbolized by the evening at the Ritz that the two couples spent together in 1961, fifteen years before the party at the Ryders' home. Their recollections of the occasion emphasize its innocence and spontaneity. All four of them were happy and carefree; Malcolm was at the peak of his rugby career, Gavin was on the brink of a breakthrough in television, and the two women felt themselves to be physically attractive, pleased to be spending such an extravagant evening in such a happy group of friends. For Polly, it was the nicest thing that ever happened to her. Everything then was genuine, untouched by jealousy or impure motives; love and affection were freely given between friends. The subject of swapping partners could never have come up.

They all instantly remember the evening at the Ritz when they hear the song "A Nightingale Sang in Berkeley Square," which tells of an enchantingly perfect evening spent by lovers in London's Mayfair district. The song includes the line, "There were angels dining at the Ritz." Those four young people were angels then, but time has transformed them into fallen angels. It is Sue who jokingly asks the question about whether they have fallen since that famous night at the Ritz. She does not mean the question to be taken seriously, but as Gavin and Polly drive home, Polly clearly realizes that they have indeed fallen. They have done so, not only in the obvious sense that Sue and Malcolm now want to indulge in spouse swapping, or that Malcolm, formerly a fit sportsperson, has allowed himself to become overweight, or that Sue has become treacherous. The fall runs even deeper than that. Polly knows that their lives in the outer suburbs are nothing to celebrate. They are all living a lie, pretending in their upper-middle-class superficiality and materialism not to see the falseness of it all, the emptiness of their values. Polly herself is not fooled; she knows the game they are all playing, and she regards the Ryders' party not as an occasion of innocent fun but as a sordid mess.

However, she excepts herself from this fall—that is, until the end of the story, when she realizes that she too has fallen, because she is resigned to the fact that her husband, although he initially restrained himself for her sake, was in the end only too willing to make love to her best friend.

Style and Technique

The story is told by a limited third-person narrator who has insight into the thoughts and feelings of Gavin and Polly. The other couple, Sue and Malcolm, are seen only through the eyes of Gavin and Polly, although their motivations are made unmistakably clear through their words and actions.

Although William Trevor's style is naturalistic, and the dialogue and setting ring absolutely true to their time and place, there is also a symbolic element that reinforces the main theme of the loss of innocence. This is in the contrast between the lives of the couples when they lived in the center of London and when they moved to the suburbs. The city center is associated with authenticity of life, the outer suburbs with false values. For example, ten years ago the two couples used to go regularly to Tonino's Trattoria on Greek Street in the city, and Gavin fondly recalls those lazy evenings of fine food and drink and amiable companionship. A branch of Tonino's has opened in the suburbs, and Gavin has convinced himself that it is very like the original. Polly, however, knows better. She knows that the Tonino's in the suburbs is just a joke, a sham compared with the original on Greek Street. Nothing in the suburbs can match what they left behind in the city, including the quality of their lives. They are like the fallen angel Lucifer, thrust out from the burning center of life in which everything is true to itself, to the outer suburbs (the equivalent of the outer circles of hell), in which everything is a lie, however prettily it is dressed up.

In many of Trevor's stories, the moment of greatest significance comes near the end. It is often an internal realization by the protagonist that reflects a profound shift in understanding of his or her own life and sometimes of life in general. Usually this is presented as a surprise or an unexpected twist. So it is in this story, when Polly, having convinced herself that she has not fallen like the others, realizes that in fact she has, although in a different and quite unexpected way.

Bryan Aubrey

ANOTHER PART OF THE SKY

Author: Nadine Gordimer (1923-   )
Type of plot: Social realism
Time of plot: The 1940's
Locale: Rural South Africa
First published: 1952

> *Principal characters:*
> COLLINS, the white principal of a reformatory for black African
>   youths
> HIS WIFE
> NGUBANE, one of his black assistants
> THE BOY, an inmate who has run away

The Story

The protagonist walks across a compound to his house, considering the appearance of the place for which he is largely responsible. He is Collins, the idealistic white principal of a reformatory for young African men. When he first arrived there, it was surrounded by high walls topped with jagged pieces of glass. Now the walls are gone and the grounds are marked with edged pathways and flower beds. He has had playing fields built and musical instruments brought in, and he has given the inmates more freedom.

The newspapers call Collins "the man who pulled down the prison walls and grew geraniums in their place"; however, he reflects that it was not really geraniums but roses that the boys have planted. Whenever people think that they understand something, there is always a small inaccuracy waiting to be revealed. The world is simply more complicated than most people realize. Collins understands—or thought he did—the complexity of his own position, the benefits and disadvantages of tearing down the prison walls.

Now one of Collins's boys has run away and is suspected of beating and robbing an old woman. During the two days since he has heard of the assault, Collins has tried to convince himself that this boy could not have committed the crime. He reminds himself that to the police all blacks look alike and that the police think that the offender is his boy because they know that he is missing. They do not know, however, the quiet discipline that Collins has imparted; they have not studied boys for nine years as he has.

Collins's worry will not go away. Every minute, he expects to hear the phone ring, the police calling to say that the boy has been arrested. As he worries silently, his wife worries in her own silence. Over the years she has supported his work, stayed in the background, and kept silent. Now, as Collins climbs into bed, he knows that his wife is awake and worrying; however, they do not speak to each other. Both fall asleep, worrying.

In the middle of the night a knock at the door awakens Collins, who immediately thinks that they have come to tell him about the boy; however, the man at the door is Ngubane, one of Collins's assistants. The man is in shock, frightened. Collins thinks that Ngubane is bringing news of the boy. Instead, Ngubane tells him that he and his brother Peter have just spent their day off in Johannesburg, where Peter has been killed in an accident. Collins comforts the grieving man, gives him a sleeping pill, and tells him to take the next day off to arrange for the funeral.

After Ngubane leaves, Collins and his wife go back to bed. In the darkness, just before dropping off to sleep, the wife admits, "I thought he'd come to tell us bad news about the boy." Lying alone and worrying again, Collins suddenly realizes that he was actually relieved when he heard the reason for Ngubane's coming. So focused has he been on his own boys, on his "system," that he has ignored the rest of his life—his very humanity. He did not comfort Ngubane out of compassion but only mechanically, without feeling any of the man's pain. Furthermore, he has not for years considered his wife as anything more than a part of his work. He may have been a good principal, but he has not been a good man. "If you search one face," he realizes, "you turn your back on another." The epiphany is so devastating that he shuts his eyes against burning tears.

Themes and Meanings

A dominant theme throughout Nadine Gordimer's fiction is the unusual complexity of life and politics in South Africa before it abolished apartheid. In her stories there are no easy solutions to the problems that history created in South Africa. Even though it is clear that the system of apartheid is wrong, there are often no clear moral choices for the whites living under the system.

Collins is in many ways a typical Gordimer protagonist. He tries, in his own way, to offer respect and human kindness to the African boys under his care. He tries to give them more freedom, to teach them discipline and hard work, and to help them become productive. Nevertheless, he cannot escape his own racism. He offers them the best that he knows, but does it in a patronizing way. Once, for example, he stumbles over the brick edging of a pathway and reflects that the boys laid the edging "with all their race's peasant pleasure in simple repetitive patterns." He smiles at their simpleness. Wanting to teach them good values, he turns to his own religion, Christianity, and makes his charges attend weekly church services. He cannot imagine that developing a spiritual life within their own systems of belief would strengthen them and is puzzled every time that a boy runs away. Why should anyone choose to live by a paraffin-tin fire instead of a warm reformatory?

Collins truly wants to help Africans. He mentions no friends, no colleagues, no pleasures or recreations of his own. He has given up his personal life to devote himself to the reformatory. Further, he has taken professional risks by converting the reformatory from a harsh prison to a nearly normal school. However, the only methods that he can imagine are those that will help the boys to become more like him.

Despite Collins's limitations, "Another Part of the Sky" is not about a misguided principal and a saintly boy. The boy, after all, has committed some kind of offense that is the reason for his being in the reformatory in the first place. Eventually the reader comes to realize, as Collins and his wife do, that the boy is in fact the person who has assaulted and robbed the old woman. Clearly, some form of control and some discipline is necessary. This is not a simple case of whites trying to transform innocent Africans.

The prison wall is an important symbol in this story. Gordimer repeatedly states that walls separate people from one another, making real communication impossible. The story demonstrates how walls exist not merely between black and white people but also between a reporter and the truth, between a governing board and a principal, and between a man and his loyal wife. Although Collins can tear down bricks and broken-glass barriers, he cannot establish real contact with another person.

The story leaves the reader with more questions than answers. Is oppression under a well-meaning and caring master any less oppressive? What is the best treatment for youthful offenders? Can a dominant culture teach without dominating? How can a man care about a community without caring about its individual members? How can people—individually and in groups—reach out to one another? Most important, can a man search one face without turning his back on another?

Style and Technique

Although there are other characters and actions in the story, the focus of "Another Part of the Sky" is internal. To help focus attention on Collins and his thoughts, Gordimer uses a limited third-person narrator who knows nothing that Collins does not know, presenting all the action only as Collins experiences or remembers it.

The reader may begin to question Collins's understanding of the world and his part in it, but the narrator does not push this questioning. No overt judgment is made of Collins—no words such as "patronizing" or "selfish" are allowed. Working within these constraints, Gordimer allows hints about Collins's flaws to emerge subtly from his own reflections, without his even noticing them.

Because the story unfolds late at night when Collins's wife pretends sleep, there is little need for talk in the story. What little speech there is—the governing board's consoling words to Collins, his own conversation with the grieving Ngubane—flows naturally into the paragraphs with neither indentations nor quotation marks. The only objects mentioned are those that Collins sees or touches. Gordimer chooses not to put the reader into the moment but instead to keep the reader inside Collins's mind, to give only his reflections on a moment.

When the sudden moment of insight comes, it surprises the reader as well as Collins. The realization has to do with Collins's humanity, not just his politics. By filtering every image and speech through the lens of Collins's own mind, the story demands that the reader see Collins as an individual, not merely a representative of his race.

Cynthia A. Bily

ANOTHER TIME

Author: Edna O'Brien (1930-   )
Type of plot: Psychological
Time of plot: The 1980's
Locale: An Irish seaside resort
First published: 1988

Principal characters:
NELLY NUGENT, the protagonist, a former television announcer
VINCENT, an older teacher whom Nelly recalls having loved
GERTIE, the sultry young woman who married Vincent
CAIMIN, a dim-witted hotel waiter

The Story

On the verge of a mental breakdown, Nelly Nugent decides to escape London by vacationing at a small seaside resort some twenty miles from the village where her family lived when she was a child. She fancies that this new place, full of mystery and romance, will lead to some kind of personal "redemption." The dismal reality of the dingy hotel and its provincial inhabitants sets the stage, however, for a series of bitter disappointments that drive her into an even deeper depression.

Nelly's hotel room is both tiny and shabby; instead of looking out on a sweeping ocean expanse, she can see only a sliver of the shoreline. Matters worsen when Nelly's before-dinner drink with her hosts proves awkward; her refusal to have a drink at the local pub with another guest sends the man into a rage, and her solitary candlelight dinner is disturbed by a large crowd of unruly children. After beginning her journey wanting to escape London, Nelly now counts the days until she can escape her vacation site.

When Nelly walks along the seashore the next morning, the peaceful scene revives her until she is recognized by a vacationer as a former television announcer. This encounter forces Nelly into another unpleasant reverie as she recalls that she gave up a promising career to marry a man with a "black heart." Predictably, the marriage ended in divorce and a bitter custody battle for the children, who are now grown and no longer integral parts of Nelly's life.

Having shrunk from all possibilities of human contact, Nelly encounters a young calf that engages her sympathies because it is being driven mad by flies that are swarming into the wounds left by the removal of its horns. She orders its owner to hold the animal while she digs the flies out. After they put the calf in a dark shed away from the flies, the calf's pathetic shrieks make it plain that it prefers the torment of the insects to the isolation of the unlit cell. After taking care of the calf, its lonely owner asks Nelly to marry him. She realizes that the young man is not serious, as he simply wants some company, but pretends that she is married and flees back to her hotel.

At her hotel, Nelly is greeted with the unwelcome news that she has had a visitor named Gertie. The mere mention of Gertie's name forces Nelly to recall a painful event that happened more than thirty years earlier. After getting a sophisticated black dress from an older friend, Nelly mustered the courage to visit a man named Vince, the new teacher at a nearby technical college who had set all the feminine hearts of the village aflutter. Unfortunately, her audacious visit turned into a disaster when Gertie appeared from the kitchen and sensuously claimed her man.

Now, Nelly cannot avoid meeting with the adult Gertie, who generously admits that Nelly has "kept her figure," while she has not. Gertie also confides that Vince, now dead, always bragged about knowing Nelly, especially after she became a television celebrity. For the first time in the story, Nelly reaches out to a fellow human being by inviting Gertie to stay for tea. Unfortunately, Gertie must leave, but she promises to return another time.

Themes and Meanings

Lantern Slides (1990), the story collection in which "Another Time" appears, features a series of lonely older women who have been either widowed or jilted. Most of them have experienced rewarding love affairs, but these affairs are in the past. The present is dreary and the future looks even bleaker. Most attempts at rekindling love end in bitter loneliness. For many of them, loneliness is imposed by family or society; Nelly Nugent's isolation is different—it is self-imposed. During her seaside visit, she spurns the overtures of two men—her neighbor at the hotel and the calf's owner. She even makes Caimin, the dim-witted waiter who likes her, feel like "a dog that knows it has done something wrong." When she walks on the almost deserted beach, she embraces solitude by reveling in "the isolation, the sense of being alone."

When Edna O'Brien enters Nelly's mind, it becomes clear why this former television celebrity is so determined to be alone: All of her relationships have caused intense suffering. Her marriage ended in divorce and a painful custody battle; the departure of her firstborn to boarding school caused a "rupture" resulting in "raw pain"; and her mother's death led to a bitter struggle with her "maggot brother." The past has such a powerful impact on Nelly that she is clearly on the verge of mental collapse. She dreams that one of her children had "stripped her of everything, even her teeth"; her visit to the travel office fills her with "doom"; an invitation to a sing-along causes her to shudder inwardly; and a compliment from poor Caimin makes her feel that she is about to "break down."

Instead of breaking down, Nelly experiences a kind of resurrection. Ironically, it is her former nemesis Gertie who is the catalyst that releases her from her "welter of rage." Gertie's generous admission that her husband Vince had cared about Nelly prompts Nelly to feel "as if doors or windows were swinging open all around her and that she was letting go of some awful affliction." All the pent-up rage that had poisoned her soul and relationships finally appears to be released.

As an epigraph to *Lantern Slides*, O'Brien uses a quote from Thomas Mann: "Each human life must work through all the joys and sorrows, gains and losses, which make up the history of the world." In "Another Time," Nelly Nugent, having been released from the sorrows and losses of her past, is poised to embrace a brighter future. Although it is clear that Nelly and Gertie will never meet again, Nelly now has a chance to give meaning back to her life.

Style and Technique

O'Brien's straightforward chronological structure with flashbacks into Nelly's past belies the subtlety of her story's multilayered motifs. The story's most prevalent motif, consisting of both physical and mental cages, reinforces Nelly's desperate mental state. The travel agent's posters depict cities surrounded by walls, the hotel closet hooks remind Nelly of "skewers," and a hotel window's slanted view of the ocean seems like a barred prison window. Reminiscences of her childhood are even more imprisoning, especially when Nelly recalls her brother's padlocking a hall door to keep her out and Gertie's standing in Vince's doorway to shut her off from her would-be lover. Those painful memories of her childhood cause Nelly to "put an iron grille" over her former life as she tries to keep "the weed and bindweed of the past" from pushing "up through the gates of her mind." Neither the present nor the past offers any consolation to Nelly.

Even more subtle are the various motifs that O'Brien uses to hook the present to the past, especially as the past relates to Vince—the love that Nelly never managed to forget. Nelly's selection of a seaside resort—with which she associates happy newlyweds—is the same place where Gertie and Vince were supposed to have honeymooned. The red clothing of the people on the beach stands out, as did Vince's dashing red sweater. The shifting green, blue, and violet of the sea mirror the colors of the "stained-glass fanlight" in Vince's front door.

The third motif, water, is at once the most complicated and most central to O'Brien's theme. Although the "liquid silver" stream that young Nelly crossed on her way to pick up the black dress represents a transition from girlhood into womanhood, the sea is both comforting and terrifying. Nelly selects a holiday getaway surrounded by ocean on three sides, but one that maintains a reassuring jetty to the mainland. The sea is by turns "gentle," "bright, like a mirror with the sun dancing on it," and "sulky." After Gertie's visit, Nelly feels "like a river that winds its way back into its first beloved enclave before finally putting out to sea." Although this last line of the story appears to suggest that Nelly has released all of her bitter feelings, her future is not entirely secure. Nelly's attraction to the sea suggests release; however, the sea is also a traditional symbol for death, or at least the unknown.

Sandra Hanby Harris

APOCALYPSE AT SOLENTINAME

Author: Julio Cortázar (1914-1984)
Type of plot: Autobiographical
Time of plot: The mid-1970's
Locale: Costa Rica, Nicaragua, and Paris
First published: "Apocalipsis de Solentiname," 1977 (English translation, 1980)

Principal characters:
THE NARRATOR, an unnamed but renowned writer and the
protagonist of his own narration
CLAUDINE, his companion

The Story

The narrator, a celebrated Latin American cultural figure—he shares with Julio Cortázar the honor of having written the short story "Las babas del diablo" ("Blow-Up")—recounts a journey that he has made to Central America. On arriving in Costa Rica, he is met by several friends who are important members of the Sandinista movement, some of whom escort him to the island of Solentiname, off the coast of Nicaragua. During his visit, one of the purposes of which is to demonstrate solidarity with the Sandinistas in their protracted armed struggle against the Somoza dictatorship, he notices some naïve paintings done by the humble inhabitants of Solentiname. Struck by their unashamed innocence and enthusiasm, he photographs the paintings as souvenirs. After several intermediate stops, he returns to his home in Paris, where his life resumes its normally hectic rhythm. One day, when he recalls having left the roll of film to be developed, he retrieves it and settles down for a comfortable and nostalgic viewing.

Approximately halfway through the roll of slides, however, just when the pleasantly ingenuous pictures should appear, the narrator is dismayed to witness projected scenes of unspeakable violence and cruelty: Soldiers murder peasant children in cold blood, cadavers are piled in tall mounds, women are tortured and raped. The arrival of his companion Claudine coincides with the end of the brutal spectacle. Too upset to speak, the narrator reloads the projector for her and retreats hastily to the bathroom, where (here his memory fails him) he may have vomited, cried, or simply sat in disbelief. After recomposing himself, he returns to Claudine's side and learns that she has seen nothing but the charming paintings that the narrator photographed when at Solentiname. Not wanting to appear foolish before Claudine (or the reader), the narrator says nothing to explain his uncanny experience. This apyretic conclusion is highly appropriate because for those who share his revolutionary social concerns there remains nothing to say, and for those who do not, the whole matter is inexplicable and, perhaps, meaningless.

Themes and Meanings

Cortázar's writing generally sorts itself into one of two categories: the fantastic-mythical, as characterized by many of his early stories in such collections as *Final del juego* (1956; *End of the Game, and Other Stories*, 1963) and *Todos los fuegos el fuego* (1966; *All Fires the Fire*, 1973), or the political-historical, best seen in his novel *Libro de Manuel* (1973; *A Manual for Manuel*, 1978). "Apocalypse at Solentiname," which first appeared in *Alguien que anda por ahi* (1977), constitutes an extraordinary synthesis of these two major tendencies within one brief tale. The ascending portion of the narrative is uniformly in the historical mode. Easily recognized and politically significant names (Sergio Ramirez, Ernesto Cardenal, and Roque Dalton) and places (San Jose, Solentiname, and Havana) inform the reader of the theater and the principal actors in this highly charged ideological drama. The narrator's deep affection for the Sandinista leaders and his admiration for the unpretentious artwork of the common folk of Solentiname create reader sympathy for the insurgents' cause (in 1976, when the story was composed, the Somoza regime still held absolute power in Nicaragua). Fantasy would appear to have no place in this palpable and contemporary conflict.

Only when the narrator attempts to relive his trip does an irrational element enter. No logical explanation for the intrusion of the scenes of officially sanctioned atrocities is possible because the first half of the roll of film offers the narrator no surprises, and Claudine sees nothing unusual in her viewing of the same roll. This overlaying of the marvelous on the mundane is quite characteristic of Cortázar's fiction (he contends, in consonance with the surrealists, that a more real superreality is always there, lurking below or behind our everyday, impoverished conception of existence). Some of his most frequently anthologized stories, such as "La noche boca arriba" ("The Night Face Up") and "Instrucciones para John Howell" ("Instructions for John Howell"), follow that very pattern. What is especially well achieved in "Apocalypse at Solentiname," however, is the creation of a highly tendentious but still verisimilar initial setting, the political impact of which is enhanced rather than undercut (or rendered irrelevant) by the climactic revelation (implicit in the term "apocalypse"). The literary mode of socialist realism is thus dealt as severe a blow by the Utopian visionary as is capitalist market theory.

The playful treatment that Cortázar affords so serious a theme as civil war finds an antecedent in his master piece *Rayuela* (1963; *Hopscotch*, 1966), in which the author uses a puerile game as a stunning metaphor for mankind's search for identity and meaning in life. A highly fragmented and polymorphous text (the reader has endless options as to the inclusion and ordering of the parts), *Hopscotch* irreverently calls into question some of the classical tradition's most cherished assumptions: what constitutes literature, the wisdom or possibility of exercising free will, the value of reason itself. Bridging such discrete domains as theory and practice, on the one hand, and the metaphysical and the physical (erotic play is not the least of Cortázar's concerns), on the other, *Hopscotch* has come to enjoy the status of a secular bible of the contemporary Latin American novel. It lacks, however, the explicit commitment to social justice of "Apocalypse at Solentiname," a story that captures in miniature the major issues in the author's mature, politicized worldview.

Style and Technique

Without a doubt, Cortázar has one of the most kindly authorial personas in modern literature. An analysis of that benignity, on whose convincing portrayal the story's success is greatly dependent, reveals three chief components: colloquial diction, intimacy with the reader, and self-deprecating humor. The illusion of a spoken rather than a written text is achieved by the first-person narration through the frequent use of diminutives (which are extremely common in spoken Spanish) and slang (especially with respect to nationalities: Nicas, Ticos, and Gringos for Nicaraguans, Costa Ricans, and Americans, respectively). The reader's confidence is gained principally through direct address ("You're probably saying I'm boiling over with false modesty, but let's face it, old man"), and by means of the "vos" (a very familiar form of the second-person singular pronoun that is archaic in mainstream Spanish but still current in Argentina, among other places). In addition to several humorous asides along the way and a confession of incredible naïvete where Polaroid cameras are concerned, the author makes himself the butt of his own joke at the conclusion. He confides to the reader his temptation to ask Claudine if she did not see a picture of Napoleon on horseback, in essence a confession of the absurdity of his situation vis-à-vis his companion.

A fourth ingredient in the author's winning repertoire, no less significant but certainly more diffuse, could be called deceptive simplicity. Although there are numerous instances of recognizable cultural allusions (the references to the author's story "Blow-Up," to Roque Dalton and Ernesto Cardenal, as well as to other lesser known writers, for example), Cortázar is sure to avoid appearing bookish or excessively cerebral, as might his compatriot Jorge Luis Borges, the immensely respected but much more politically conservative dean of postmodern Latin American literature. Despite the story's brevity and folksy tone, though, the simplicity is decidedly deceptive, for the layers of representation evoked in the final scene outstrip many a full-length novel. When the narrator (who is and is not Julio Cortázar: his wife at the time was named Carol) describes his hallucinatory vision, the reader receives a verbal (sequential) rendition of iconic (spatial) perceptions or conceptions. These images, in the normal course of events, should have been mere filmic reproductions of the amateur pictorial artwork produced in Solentiname, and those canvases, in turn, would be based on the imagined or lived experiences of their painters. The multiple intermediate levels of interpretation, both actual and hypothetical, between the reader and the event related in the text disclose the true complexity of the author's thinking. A master ironist and rhetorician, Cortázar means in "Apocalypse at Solentiname" much more to the "accomplice reader" (a term he coins in *Hopscotch*) than meets the untrained or passive reader's eye.

Jonathan Tittler

APPROXIMATIONS

Author: Mona Simpson (1957-   )
Type of plot: Coming of age
Time of plot: The 1960's and 1970's
Locale: Illinois, Nevada, and California
First published: 1984

> *Principal characters:*
> MELINDA, the narrator, a Midwestern teenager
> CAROL, her mother
> JOHN, her father, a waiter in California
> JERRY, her stepfather, a professional skater

The Story

Melinda imagines a scene in which her parents are holding each other closely as they dance to music. She has had this same fantasy since she was four years old, when she learned that the man in the black-and-white photograph was her father. She has no real memories of her father, only this fantasy. When Melinda once asked her mother where her father was, her mother replied vaguely, telling her that her father was gone but would be back sometime. Melinda remembers other people asking about her father, but she has never met him.

Melinda's mother, Carol, refuses to face reality, drifting along, waiting for Melinda's father to return. Melinda and Carol are now used to living alone. On Saturday nights they dress in identical outfits and go ice-skating together. Carol points to the empty seats, telling Melinda that when she is older she can bring boys there to watch her skate so that they will know that she is more than simply another pretty girl, that she can really do something. Carol's advice to her daughter emphasizes physical appearance and the importance of attracting men.

Melinda first hears from her father, John, in 1963, when he calls from Las Vegas to invite her and her mother to join him at Disneyland. When Melinda finally sees him, she finds that he is an ordinary balding man. He works as a waiter in a hotel restaurant and shares an apartment with three roommates. He introduces her to his friends, making Melinda feel that he is proud of her. As he touches her hair, she thinks that she loves him blindly. He gives her a cheap package of headbands, but she is so pleased with this token of her father's love that she does not even open the package.

When Carol asks John when they will go to Disneyland, he replies that he has lost the money "on the tables." This revelation provokes a fight, but they sleep together in the bedroom that night while Melinda sleeps on a couch in the living room.

The next morning Melinda and her father have breakfast at a coffee shop. At his invitation she tastes her father's soft-boiled egg and then tells him how good it is, hoping to share it with him. Instead of sharing the egg, however, her father orders another one for her. He promises that they will visit Disneyland on their next trip. As Melinda holds his hand tightly, she dreams of other trips so that she can spend time with her father. On the plane ride home Carol notices how much the package of headbands means to Melinda. She then reminds her daughter that while she works to pay for the rent, skating lessons, school, and books, all her father has given her is a seventy-nine-cent package of headbands.

The following year Carol marries Jerry, an ice-skating professional whom she has met during a Saturday night skating session at the rink. Melinda and her mother skate in a few ice shows but eventually drop out, while Jerry continues to go to the rink every day just like any other man going to a job. On one Saturday Carol insists that Melinda accompany Jerry to a Girl Scout father-daughter banquet, telling her that Jerry wants to adopt her. Refusing to attend the event, Melinda goes outside to play. When Melinda sees Jerry dressed up for the dinner in a turtleneck sweater and paisley ascot, she feels sorry for him but does not change her mind about attending. As she rides off on her bicycle, she tells herself that none of the other fathers would be wearing ascots.

When Melinda is ten years old, her natural father asks her to visit him in California by herself, but Carol talks him into sending two airplane tickets so that she and her daughter can make the trip together. She thinks that she can persuade John to buy her a television set that she wants. In California, Carol, Melinda, John, and John's rich new wife tour Disneyland, eating in restaurants and buying souvenirs. Melinda and her father have little to say to each other, and Carol makes no progress in getting John to buy her a television. On their last night in California, Carol coaches Melinda on how to dress and behave in order to get her father to buy the television. The next morning when John buys a candy bar, he asks Melinda if she wants anything. Melinda wants only to stand there eating candy with her father but knows that this moment will be only a memory next year when her father forgets to write or call her. Instead, she follows her mother's advice and tells John that she is saving up for a television set, realizing as she says this that she is cutting the ties with her father.

After they return home, Carol is still angry with Melinda for failing to get the television and takes out her frustration by telling Melinda that she is ordinary and belongs with the mill workers' children. To escape her mother's yelling, Melinda goes to the ice rink. When she sees Jerry, she runs toward him and throws herself into his arms. She now realizes that while her dream of being reunited with her natural father is gone, Jerry is there for her. The story ends with Jerry teaching Melinda how to do loops on the ice.

Themes and Meanings

As the story's title suggests, the characters' lives are full of approximations. Jerry settles for an "approximation" when he buys the used Cadillac that he can afford instead of the new Lincoln Continental that his wife wants. As a stepfather Jerry is himself an approximation; he is not the perfect father of Melinda's dreams but a shy steady man who is willing to take care of her. Some of the individual scenes are approximations. At the beginning of the story, for example, Melinda imagines her father holding Carol and closing his hand over her ear. At the end of the story Jerry embraces Melinda and holds his hand over her ear. Melinda's imagined scene of her parents dancing is replaced by a real scene in which Carol and Jerry skate together. As Melinda matures, she gives up her fantasy of a perfect family, and learns to appreciate the "approximations" that are the realities of life.

Melinda fantasizes about her father and so longs to know him that she takes each small gesture of his affection and holds on to it tightly, hoping for a relationship with him. Disneyland is important to her only because it provides an opportunity for her to be with her father. She wants to share an egg with her father in the restaurant, but he prefers not to share. When they walk together hand in hand, it is John who releases Melinda's hand. After a number of disappointments, Melinda realizes that she will never be a part of her father's life.

This is the story of a young girl coming of age in a fragmented family. With an absent father and a critical, self-absorbed mother, Melinda is shut off from a normal family life. In a number of scenes Carol shows a callous disregard for Melinda's feelings. When they go to California in order for Melinda to meet her father for the first time, Carol monopolizes his time, first by fighting with him, later by sleeping with him. When she closes the door, she leaves Melinda alone on the couch. At the skating rink, Carol is so absorbed with Jerry that she forgets to give Melinda the cue to begin skating, and Melinda falls on the ice. This is, however, also a story of survival, and Melinda survives in spite of her mother's selfishness and her father's indifference.

Style and Technique

Through flashbacks and reminiscences provided by a first-person narrator, Mona Simpson shows a character growing from childhood to adolescence. Instead of simply telling a story, she provides scenes as vivid as snapshots. Melinda has only a vague idea of what her father looks like, but when she comes face to face with him, she describes him in realistic detail, noting his bald spot and even the way that his chin sticks out from his face. At times Melinda appears to be taking a mental picture of her father so that she can remember him. She watches him working in the restaurant, balancing dishes on the inside of his arm or standing at the candy counter buying Lifesavers. John's casually dressed roommates form a picture as they lean on the iron banister of the porch to their apartment. These and other scenes are brief but vividly portrayed. Melinda describes how Jerry tries to impress her mother by doing a "t-stop . . . shaving a comet of ice into the air." Jerry and Carol laughing at the stage exit, or skating under the spotlight, Carol twirling in Jerry's arms—in these scenes Melinda is excluded. Taken together these snapshots tell the story of Melinda's life.

Judith Barton Williamson

THE APRIL WITCH

Author: Ray Bradbury (1920-   )
Type of plot: Fantasy
Time of plot: The 1920's or 1930's
Locale: Green Town, Illinois
First published: 1952

>   *Principal characters:*
>   CECY ELLIOTT, the protagonist, a remarkable seventeen-year-old
>   with magical powers
>   ANN LEARY, the nineteen-year-old girl whose body Cecy
>   possesses
>   TOM, a twenty-two-year-old man who is in love with Ann

The Story

In April, the spring of the year when gentle breezes blow and flowers begin to bloom, young girls everywhere dream of falling in love. Young seventeen-year-old Cecy Elliott, from whose point of view the story is told, also desperately desires to fall in love. Cecy, however, is unlike other girls. She possesses magical powers. She can travel through space and time, she can soar in doves, stop in trees, and she can become one with frogs, dogs, grass, moles, and every living thing. She sleeps by day and flies by night. She can leave her plain, bony body and spiritually possess any living thing. However, Cecy cannot marry a mortal. As Cecy's parents warn: "We'd lose our magical powers if we did."

Despite her parents' warnings to be careful, to be patient, telepathic Cecy satisfies her longings for love in a special way. Because Cecy cannot experience love for herself, she decides to experience love through a human. She promptly dispatches her mind and quickly possesses the body of nineteen-year-old Ann Leary, a girl quite unwilling to have Cecy possess her. When Ann drinks from a well, Cecy enters her body and, through Ann, comes to cherish human love.

Cecy must work hard to experience and to maintain this love, however, and herein lies the story's intrigue. Cecy forces Ann to accept a date with an admirer, Tom, a twenty-two-year-old whom Ann has never really liked. While inhabiting Ann's body before and during the date, Cecy faces a constant struggle in trying to develop and nurture the relationship between Tom and Ann. When Ann spills water at the well, Tom wipes her shoes with a kerchief. Unappreciative of his kind gesture, Ann kicks at Tom and then thanks him only because Cecy forces her to respond.

Cecy is ecstatic when Tom asks a reluctant Ann to the dance that evening. Cecy has never worn a long gown, and she has never danced. Cecy controls Ann's movements as Ann prepares for the dance. They heat water for a bath, iron a gown, and prepare for Tom to arrive with his horse and buggy. During the evening, Ann and Cecy dance with

Tom. Both have a wonderful time even though Tom wonders about Ann's new demeanor.

As they return home from the dance, Tom confesses that he still loves Ann, despite her fickle nature and despite his fear of being hurt. Inside Ann's "roundly fleshed" body, Cecy tries to force Ann to return Tom's love. Nothing happens. Tom reveals that he plans to accept a job a hundred miles away and asks Ann whether she will miss him. Both girls reply in the affirmative. When Tom asks Ann if he may kiss her good night, Cecy answers affirmatively "before anyone else could speak."

After the kiss, Ann sits motionless, unwilling to move and unwilling to embrace Tom despite Cecy's pleading. At this point, a lonely Cecy realizes that, despite her parents' warnings, she would indeed risk everything—all of her magical powers—for love. "I'd need only to be with him. Only him. Only him," she decides.

As Tom and Ann approach her home, Ann, directed by Cecy, makes Tom promise to visit a friend of hers a few miles away in Mellin Town, Illinois. Reluctantly, Tom finally agrees. On a piece of paper, Ann scratches the name of her friend: Cecy Elliott.

When midnight approaches, a tired Cecy, like Cinderella just returned from the ball, feels her magical powers waning. Before she leaves Ann's body, though, Cecy and Ann again kiss Tom good night. During this kiss, Cecy tells an unsuspecting Tom, "This is me kissing you."

As Tom sleeps, he clutches the paper Ann gave to him and never stirs when a blackbird pauses wondrously at his windowpane and gazes softly at him before flying away toward the east.

Themes and Meanings

In "The April Witch," Ray Bradbury readers will recognize familiar themes: initiation into maturity and metamorphosis. Bradbury's young people, whose emotions largely control their actions, frequently struggle for rather than against adulthood.

Nostalgic Cecy, who can metamorphose at will according to her desires and needs, has a large capacity for wonder. During her journeys through time and space, she looks at the world, wonders at the world, participates in the world, and cannot look away. She yearns desperately for her innermost desire: to be loved. This love, as she has been warned by her parents, surely will destroy her magical powers; nevertheless, as a typical teenager, she fails to heed their warnings and rushes to embrace life and experience a love she has never known. At the end of the story she wonders whether Tom will love her "with all his heart for all time" as she loves him. Symbolically, Bradbury suggests that he will. The bird that gazes softly at Tom flies toward the east, a symbol of new beginnings and of renewal.

Because of Cecy's special qualities, reality in this story is relative. To the readers, reality is determined by what Cecy needs and wants. First she flies into the air, then she lives in blossoms, perches in frogs, and lives in new April grasses. Finally, however, she embraces the reality of a teenager in love, a young lady who yearns for a special kind of love: one that will last forever.

Style and Technique

A lyrical writer, Bradbury uses strong sensory images, particularly nature imagery, which he combines with rich metaphors and similes, with a poet's attention to the sound of words, with nostalgic scenes, and with frequent juxtapositions. An impressionistic writer, Bradbury builds his scenes via a deluge of images that suggest rather than directly relate.

Bradbury begins his story with nature imagery: Cecy inhabits air, valleys, stars, rivers, winds, fields, and various animals. These images convey both the advent of spring and the magical powers of Cecy; they suggest spring and, by extension, the season of love. Cecy longs to embrace both love and life despite her parents' warnings. Cecy views the world through sensory imagery: She sits in Ann's eyes, and in the eyes of insects and animals. These images also form similes. Cecy is "invisible as new spring winds," she "soars in doves as soft as white ermine," and she perches in a frog "cool as mint."

Moreover, Bradbury juxtaposes Cecy with Ann Leary, a girl who shrinks from life and love. Ann's body is "roundly fleshed," whereas Cecy's body is plain and bony. A pretty girl, Ann stands in direct contrast to the less attractive Cecy, who, like most people in springtime, wants to dance, to kiss, and to fall in love.

Bette Adams Reagan

ARABESQUE—THE MOUSE

Author: A. E. Coppard (1878-1957)
Type of plot: Psychological
Time of plot: The early twentieth century
Locale: England
First published: 1921

Principal characters:
FILIP, a middle-aged man
HIS MOTHER
CASSIA, a young woman he met years earlier
THE MOUSE

The Story

Filip, a middle-aged man, sits in his room on the fourth floor of an old house in the commercial area of a city. He is reading a Russian novel, as is his late-evening habit. After becoming aware of a small mouse scurrying about the room, he baits a trap to catch it. There are many mice in the building; he knows he must try to eradicate them but feels pity for the bright-eyed rodent. He says, "Mean—so mean, to appeal to the hunger of any living thing just in order to destroy it." This sentence becomes a key to the flashbacks that follow.

Filip remembers having been a sensitive child who was upset at having to carry dead larks, tied by the feet, home for supper. When he got home, his face stained with tears, he discovered his mother expressing breast milk into their fire; she was weaning his baby sister. As his mother allowed him to help squeeze out her milk, he noticed her heart beating, then felt his own heart beat. His mother noted that the heart must beat for one to live. Filip kissed his mother and cried out, "Little mother! Little mother!"

The next day Filip's world changed forever when his mother was knocked down in the street by a horse, and a cart ran over her hands, crushing them. Her hands were amputated and she died shortly thereafter.

Haunted by the image of his handless mother, Filip grew into a questioning man who found justice and sin and property and virtue incompatible. His rebellious spirit was rebuffed by others and he became timid and misanthropic, easily offended by small slights and moved by imagined grievances.

As Filip's awareness of the mouse returns momentarily, his mind flashes back to another moment when he was a young man and met a beautiful young woman named Cassia at the village festival. During their only meeting, Filip and Cassia were exuberant and full of life. They danced and strolled together; then he carried her home. When he set her down on her porch, she put her hand on his heart and remarked on its beating. He cried "Little mother, little mother!"

Hearing a snap, Filip is brought back to the present by the realization that the mouse has sprung the trap. The mouse, however, is not caught; it stares at him mutely. Horrified to see that the trap has amputated both of the mouse's forefeet, Filip picks it up, and it promptly bites him. Uncertain what to do, he flings the mouse out the window. Filled with remorse, he runs outside and searches unsuccessfully for the mouse until he is chilled to the bone. He returns to his room, retrieves the mouse's feet from the trap, throws them into the fire, and rebaits the trap.

Themes and Meanings

The title of A. E. Coppard's story, "Arabesque—The Mouse," is a cue to both its meaning and its style. An arabesque is an ornamental object, such as a rug or mosaic, in which flowers, fruits, animals, and other figures are represented in fancifully combined patterns. Coppard's story is just such an arabesque. Filip's present encounter with the mouse is arranged by his imagination and memory into a pattern of warmth, violence, and loss—which explain his misanthropic personality and constricted life.

The line, "Mean—so mean, to appeal to the hunger of any living thing just in order to destroy it," explains the pattern, or arabesque, his life has formed. Filip was evidently a sensitive, needy child who drew warmth and solace from his mother as a nursing mother. Her warm breast and heart were especially reassuring to a fearful child. This reassurance was snatched from Filip by the unspeakable violence and poignance of his mother's maiming and death.

Filip's brief encounter with Cassia is similarly affirming to him. At that moment he is strong, virile, and seems assured. When Cassia remarks on his heartbeat, however, he is cued to the memory of his mother's discussion of his heartbeat the day before her death. He even repeats the phrase, "Little mother, little mother!" The reader does not learn what broke off his relationship with Cassia but does learn that they only met one time. Filip's psyche seems to have been warped by his mother's death, and he is unable to connect to others on a permanent basis.

In Filip's fourth-floor room is a color print by the Japanese painter Utamaro of a mother breast-feeding her child in front of a mirror. This picture tells the reader that Filip has chosen objects for his home that reinforce his memories of his mother and of Cassia.

The amputation of the mouse's feet by the mousetrap, recalling Filip's mother's amputated hands, creates a tragic irony almost too great for Filip to bear. He is cut off from others because of his nervous sensibility and critical rectitude about matters of property and justice. His only positive life experiences are connected to his mother and Cassia. The maiming of the mouse seems part of an inexorable pattern in his life.

Filip's relationships deteriorate from a major one with his mother, to a minor one with Cassia, to a minuscule one with the mouse. In like manner, Filip's world has shrunk to a tiny sphere with little human contact. When he goes out into the cold to find the injured mouse, he is trying to reconnect with life; however, his search fails and he returns to his old ways—calmly rebaiting the trap and returning to his Russian novels, which are emblematic of another, far away world.

Style and Technique

The style of "Arabesque—The Mouse" is that of an arabesque, a carefully woven Persian carpet or Byzantine mosaic. By using this technique, Coppard is suggesting that people's lives are patterns of their own weaving made from the circumstances and events that happen to them. The circumstances of Filip's life are not his to choose, but the pattern is his. All memory is selective, and his memory selects warmth followed by loss.

Coppard's style resembles the techniques of James Joyce and Virginia Woolf, who wrote during the period in which Coppard wrote "Arabesque—The Mouse." Joyce and Woolf employed a stream-of-consciousness style, however, which differs from Coppard's work. The arabesque technique uses all materials remembered to form the pattern of the whole; there are no loose threads or unconnected memories as is so often the case with stream-of-consciousness writings.

Coppard's technique leaves many unanswered questions in the mind of the reader. Were there no other nurturing influences in Filip's life? Why did his relationship with Cassia fail? Why does he read Russian novels? Characteristically, Coppard gives the reader some hints about Filip's life but leaves the reader to sort them out and form conclusions about Filip. In his studied stinginess with the reader, Coppard points toward other minimalist writers who succeeded him later in the twentieth century.

At the close of the story, Coppard refers to the mouse twice as "the little philosopher." Is Coppard suggesting that the mouse has something to teach Filip, or does Filip himself see the mouse as a little philosopher? The reader cannot be sure. Filip certainly rushes out to rescue the mouse, but what would he do with it if he found it? It has no forefeet, just as Filip's mother had no hands. Perhaps Coppard uses the many indeterminants in "Arabesque—The Mouse" to show just how precarious the task of building a secure self is. After chance kills Filip's mother, Filip becomes a wounded, maimed person just as she was; however, unlike her, he must live without the metaphorical hands to reach out to others. The incident with the mouse reminds Filip of his own incompleteness. Coppard's arabesque technique makes the tenuous life-maiming events in his story the pattern of Filip's psyche.

Isabel B. Stanley

ARABY

Author: James Joyce (1882-1941)
Type of plot: Symbolist
Time of plot: About 1894
Locale: Dublin, Ireland
First published: 1914

> *Principal characters:*
> A YOUNG BOY, about twelve years old
> A YOUNG GIRL, the sister of a playmate named Mangan

The Story

The little boy lives with his aunt and uncle on a dead-end street in Dublin, in a house formerly occupied by a now deceased priest. The boy is impressed and somewhat mystified by the moldy books—a historical romance, a pious tract, and a detective autobiography—and other reminders of the previous tenant.

The action of the story begins with the children's games, played in the lanes and backyards of the neighborhood during the winter twilight. These games end when the sister of one of the boys—named Mangan—calls her little brother in to his tea. The image of this girl standing in the lighted doorway so fixes itself in the boy's imagination that he begins to pursue her shyly in the street. Even in the bustle of the weekly grocery shopping, he carries with him a feeling about her that amounts to something like mystical rapture.

Then, one day, while the other little boys are playing, she asks him if he is going to a bazaar, named Araby. She is unable to go because of religious activities at her school, but he undertakes to go and bring her a gift instead. This brief conversation and the prospect of the trip to the bazaar causes the boy to lose concentration on his lessons and regard his playmates with disdain.

The Saturday of the bazaar is acutely agonizing for the boy. He has to wait all day long for his uncle to come home and give him the required pocket money. He withdraws from play and wanders through the upper empty rooms of the house, dreaming of the girl. His apprehension during suppertime is compounded by the chatter of a visiting woman. Finally, at nine o'clock, his uncle arrives home, somewhat drunk, for his dinner. He greets the boy's anxious reminder of his trip with some patronizing cliches.

When he sets out at last, the boy finds that he is alone on the special train arranged for the bazaar, and finally arrives there at 9:50 P.M. In his haste, he pays the adult fee at the turnstile, only to find that the bazaar is just about to close and the day's take is being counted. Hesitantly, he approaches one of the few stalls still open, one selling pottery. The young lady in charge of this stall pauses momentarily in her flirtatious banter with two young men to attend to the boy's diffident interest in her wares. He is so put off by all his disappointments and her tone of voice, however, that he at once decides not to buy anything. Instead, he simply stands there in the middle of the darkening bazaar, incensed at the betrayal of his hopes and the shattering of his illusions.

Themes and Meanings

This is a story of the loss of innocence and the frustration of first love. The young boy's exaggerated expectations about the emotional rewards of his devotion to the little girl are cruelly deflated. He interprets the disappointing circumstances of his journey as a sign of the hollowness of the ideals with which he undertook that quest. He thus connects the frivolous banter among the young people and his own earlier brief conversation with Mangan's sister and thinks that he has perceived the banal reality behind the romantic image. However, his perceptions in each case are unreliable: His immaturity causes him to overreact in each direction. The story, then, shows that the temptations to both the romantic inflation and to the cynical devaluation of experience are but two sides of the same false coin.

"Araby" is the third of the fifteen stories in *Dubliners* (1914). These stories examine the hazards of the various stages in life, and "Araby" marks the end of childhood and the beginning of adolescence. This protagonist begins his story as a boy amid his peers, full of childish energy and short-lived attention. The image of Mangan's sister gradually emerges from these confused impressions, however, gathering itself into a vision of desire, both erotic and religious. The growth of these feelings soon sets the boy apart from his fellows, and becomes even more consuming at the mention of the bazaar. He now connects his attitude toward the transcendent with the popular mystique of the Orient, each with an awakening sexual longing. No sooner are these connections made, however, than they are compromised: The girl cannot be possessed (because of her "retreat"), and in the compromise—the material gift—lie the seeds of the destruction of the dream. The rest of the story dramatizes the painful deflation of that dream: the human limitations of his uncle and aunt and the natural limitations of time and space all conspire to thwart the boy's search for fulfillment. He is therefore emotionally disposed to interpret the material elements of his adventure (the adult admission fee, the falling coins, the extinguishing lights, the casual talk of fibbing) as the signs of the end of the childish idealization of human values. From such a point of view, this is a story of initiation, marking the rites of passage from the Edenic domain of home to the uncertain terrain of adult life.

Similarly, the story can be viewed as a version of the medieval romance. The hero sets forth from surroundings of blissful innocence in pursuit of a distant ideal. In his solitary adventure through dark places, his spirits are buoyed up by the vision of remote beauty with which he hopes eventually to commune. He encounters and overcomes various obstacles and adversaries on his journey, finally gaining possession of the symbol of the truth that liberates him from ignorance and unites him with the beauty he desires. This literary mode is predominantly melancholic and nostalgic, focusing on the consciousness of the narrator or hero, emphasizing the chivalric virtues, and embracing a sense of Christian mystery. In its broad terms as well as in scores of details, "Araby" may be seen as designed in accordance with this story type, though rendering it in an ironic vein. The promise of spiritual bliss is made but not delivered: The hero's aspirations are cultivated and then denied. The cacophony of the modern city clashes and breaks the harmony of the mood of nostalgia for a faith in an ideal order of nature and grace. Thus, the story conjoins the personal and archetypal stories in a beautiful blend of realistic detail, tonal control, and symbolic design.

Style and Technique

Told from the first-person point of view, the story is a convincing representation of the voice of an observant, impressionable, naïve young boy. At the same time, through the deft use of language, symbol, and allusion, a world of feeling beyond the boy's experience is conveyed to the attentive reader.

First, the story is firmly rooted in time and place: The Joyce family lived on North Richmond Street in 1894, and the young James (then twelve years old) attended the actual Araby bazaar held between May 14 and 18 of that year. All the historical, geographical, and cultural references in the story are true to life.

Second, the language is carefully designed so as to convey a complex, yet highly controlled range of meanings. Consider, for example, the use of the words "blind," and "set . . . free" in the first sentence, the various uses of "stall" in the body of the story, and "driven" and "eyes" in the last sentence. These motifs support the chivalric and religious themes in the story and subtly link them to its emotional core.

Third, the story is rich with the symbolism of romance, Roman Catholicism, and the Orientalism popular at the end of the last century. The various allusions—to Sir Walter Scott, James Clarence Mangan, Caroline Norton's poem *The Arab's Farewell to His Steed*, the Freemasons, Mrs. Mercer—can enlarge the relevance and appeal of the boy's private adventure for the attentive reader.

Finally, the story reaches its climax with what Joyce calls an "epiphany": a term borrowed from theology and applied to a moment of unexpected revelation or psychological insight. Such moments are not conventionally dramatic, nor are they explained to the reader. Here the epiphany occurs in the boy's consciousness when he overhears the petty and incomplete conversation at the bazaar. He believes himself to have been self-deluded: He has placed too much faith in Mangan's sister and the values she represents. His early religious training and ignorance of human relations have caused him to adore a mere petticoat.

Coilin Owens

THE ARGENTINE ANT

Author: Italo Calvino (1923-1985)
Type of plot: Fable
Time of plot: The mid-twentieth century
Locale: A coastal village in Liguria, Italy
First published: "La formica argentina," 1952 (English translation, 1957)

Principal characters:
THE UNNAMED NARRATOR
HIS WIFE
THEIR INFANT SON
SIGNORA MAURO, their landlady
SIGNOR REGINAUDO, their neighbor
CAPTAIN BRAUNI, a nearby neighbor
SIGNOR BAUDINO, from the Argentine Ant Control Corporation

The Story

Acting on the advice of his uncle, a man moves his wife and infant son to a small rented cottage in a Ligurian coastal village in Italy. At first, all seems idyllic, but on their first night, as they prepare for bed, they discover that their kitchen is swarming with ants. "Argentine ants," the narrator informs his wife, and he remembers being told that this is the country of the Argentine ant. After the narrator calms his wife, they retire to bed; they are awakened by the cries of their baby and find his bed is filled with ants.

The next day, the narrator considers the situation, noting that the yard, which he had planned to convert to a garden, is alive with ants. He visits Signor Reginaudo, their nearest neighbor, for advice, and finds that the old man and his wife have used, and found practically useless, every ant spray, poison, and powder available. Still, the Reginaudos are not discouraged and actually laugh at themselves, the ants, and the ridiculous situation. They arm the narrator with a variety of concoctions, carefully chosen to be harmless to the baby, and return him to his family.

The narrator then rushes off to see Captain Brauni, another neighbor with his own way of fighting the ants. Captain Brauni has transformed his house and yard into a maze of ant traps. Some ants are destroyed when they fall off a narrow wire into a can of gasoline; he kills an average of forty ants a minute, Captain Brauni says with almost comic precision. Many other devices are scattered about. Captain Brauni orders his wife to bring out a sack; it is filled with dead ants. His insanely rational plan is to kill enough worker ants so that the queens will begin to starve and leave their nests; only then can the problem be solved. He promises to construct a device for the narrator.

As the days progress, the narrator and his wife discover that neither poisons nor contraptions are effective. One afternoon a strange man comes through their property, leaving small saucers of molasses scattered about. It is Signor Baudino, known as the ant man, from the Argentine Ant Control Corporation. Supposedly he is spreading poison, but most residents agree with Signor Reginaudo that the corporation is actually feeding the ants to keep business thriving.

The narrator and his wife call on Signora Mauro, their landlady, to ask why she failed to mention the ants before they rented the house. Signora Mauro insists that a truly clean house should have no problem with ants; hers certainly does not. As they sit in her large, dark house, they notice that she is subtly moving and twitching; the narrator realizes that ants are crawling under her clothes and that her house is even more thoroughly infested than their own.

When they return to their house, they find an ant has crawled into the baby's ear. It is flushed out with warm oil, but the situation is intolerable for the wife. She rushes down the street with a crowd of women behind her and the narrator tagging along; they arrive at the office of the Argentine Ant Control Corporation and confront the ant man, who first makes general denials and then runs off. There is nothing to be done. That evening, the couple and their baby walk down to the coast, to the sea and a fresh wind but no ants. They sit and watch the ocean.

Themes and Meanings

Writing about "The Argentine Ant," American author Gore Vidal said that the story "gives us the human condition today. Or the dilemma of modern man. Or the disrupted environment. Or nature's revenge. Or an allegory of grace. Whatever." A great part of the strength and appeal of Italo Calvino's story is that it can plausibly support each of these interpretations, as well as others. At the same time, the details of setting, characters, and action are so realistically rendered that the story is securely anchored in reality; the reader has the visceral understanding that these events actually happened, or could have happened, in just the way Calvino recounts them, whatever elusive meaning they may possess.

Although the story can be interpreted on several levels, it is clear that it is an allegory of the difficulty for human beings to achieve freedom and choice. As Vidal implies, the world may be defined through a number of approaches: theological, philosophical, artistic, social, economic, or political. For each approach human beings are inherently limited. The Argentine ants can be seen as symbols of those limitations.

For example, some critics have seen the story as a political parable, with the ants representative of the modern conformist trend, a trend that reached its nadir during Calvino's younger years with the triumph of the Fascists in Italy and the Nazis in Germany. Their mindless obedience can easily be traced in the relentless, thoughtless, and unstoppable onslaught of the ants. Calvino fought with the Italian Resistance during World War II against the Fascists and their Nazi allies, and later joined the Italian Communist Party, only to leave it in protest of the brutal suppression of the 1956 Hungarian uprising. He was familiar with the evils of totalitarianism, and the ants in his story may be seen as a symbolic expression of such a political system.

However, like the insects that are so important to the story, "The Argentine Ant" refuses to be pinned down. The story could also be interpreted as a satire on modern faith in technology, with the Reginaudos and Captain Brauni compulsively chained to their unworkable powders and sprays and intricate traps, which have no real impact on the problem. On the other hand, "The Argentine Ant" could be about the existential role an individual must play in the contemporary world, with the unnamed narrator caught between an indifferent nature (the ants) and an inauthentic society (his neighbors). There are numerous other interpretations, more or less plausible.

The essential theme of this ambiguous yet realistic story is ambiguity itself. Just as art can have many meanings, Calvino implies, so can life, and vice versa. As Vidal would annotate, "Whatever." The ultimate meaning of "The Argentine Ant" is that "The Argentine Ant" has many different meanings, all plausible, all important.

Style and Technique

"The Argentine Ant" is written in a style of scrupulous realism. Its descriptions are given in precise, simple language that is utterly clear and, in its surface meaning, unambiguous. The reader has no doubts about what is happening; what it means is another matter, and that level of ambiguity is actually reinforced by the clarity of Calvino's presentation. For example, Captain Brauni's activities in building his increasingly intricate ant-trapping devices are easily followed, and even their most complicated workings are clearly presented. It is what Brauni's activities signify that is puzzling: Are they actions for their own sakes, or do they represent something universal in human nature or human society? In a similar fashion, Signor Baudino, the local representative of the Argentine Ant Control Corporation, is described in a short, precise vignette, making him an easily imaginable individual. That description, however, emphasizes his antlike appearance. Does this mean that Baudino, and perhaps the other characters in the story, has somehow become like the ants? Can this identification be extended to include modern human beings in general? The very simplicity of the prose that suggests such a connection denies an easy answer.

Calvino's deceptively forthright style presents its most subtle considerations in its treatment of the ants, which makes it difficult to understand if they are symbolic and, if so, what they represent. For example, throughout the story they are often compared to sand. Considering the seemingly inevitable onslaught of the tiny creatures, the narrator admits that he was "face to face with an enemy like fog or sand, against which force was useless." Later, when the narrator visits Captain Brauni, the captain has his wife bring out bags filled with ants slaughtered by the captain's devices. As Brauni lifts handfuls of ants from the bag and lets them fall back, they appear "a soft red-black sand of dead ants." At the end of the story, the narrator, his wife, and their child are at the seaside, at last free of the ants, and he gazes on the ocean and thinks "of the infinite grains of soft sand down there at the bottom of the sea where the currents leave white shells washed clean by the waves."

Is the sea a refuge from the ants, or has it, too, become part of their domain? The clear, simple style suggests a response but refuses to answer. From such clarity and subtlety does Calvino fashion "The Argentine Ant."

Michael Witkoski

ARK OF BONES

Author: Henry Dumas (1934-1968)
Type of plot: Fable
Time of plot: Probably the mid-twentieth century
Locale: The Rural American South, probably Arkansas
First published: 1971

> *Principal characters:*
> FISH-HOUND, the narrator, a young black male
> HEADEYE, his friend, another young black male with the powers
> of a seer

The Story

Because the actual language of "Ark of Bones" is its primary virtue, the story is difficult to describe. It is a first-person account of Fish-hound, a young black male, who goes fishing one day and is followed by his friend Headeye, who claims to have supernatural powers because he possesses a mojo bone, a totemistic object of African superstition. The story attempts to create the rhythm and idiom of southern black dialect and to emulate the syntax and digressions of an uneducated black youth. Although the ages of Fish-hound and Headeye are not revealed, their language and actions suggest that they are in their early teens.

The plot of the story at first seems aimless, with Fish-hound describing how Headeye follows him to the Mississippi River and how Fish-hound tries to dodge him so as not to reveal the best fishing spots. Events take a turn toward the metaphoric, however, when Headeye catches up with Fish-hound and tells him that the mojo bone is a key to the black experience, the only one in the world. Headeye recounts the story of Ezekiel in the valley of dry bones, in which it is foretold that the bones shall be bound up and shall rise again. Headeye himself prophesies that Noah's Ark will come again and seems to be watching for it to appear on the river, while Fish-hound tries to ignore him and continues fishing. The story moves into fable when Fish-hound indeed sees a gigantic boat floating on the water, moving and standing still at the same time.

Fish-hound assumes that they are both dead and that the boat is the glory boat to take them to Heaven—until he sees a rowboat drawing up to them (rowed by two black men), which takes them to the Ark. After climbing aboard on steps that seem to be numbered for various years, they meet an old, long-haired black man dressed in skins, who talks to Headeye while Fish-hound hangs back frightened. When Fish-hound and Headeye go down into the Ark, they find bones stacked to the top of the ship; crews of black men handle the bones as if they were babies, while the old man reads from a long parchment. The men on the ship speak in a foreign tongue, which sounds as if it might be an African dialect and which Fish-hound cannot understand. As Fish-hound watches the men haul bones from the river and lay them out, he recalls a sermon about Ezekiel in the valley of dry bones, a theme frequently repeated throughout the story.

The old man tells Headeye that he is in the house of generations, that every African who lives in America has a part of his soul on the Ark and that God has called Headeye to be anointed. The old man makes Headeye promise to consecrate his bones and to set his brother free. He then engages in a ritual ceremony with the mojo bone before the two leave the Ark. Several days later, Headeye comes to tell Fish-hound that he is leaving, that he will someday be back, and that Fish-hound is his witness. The story ends with people asking Fish-hound where Headeye has gone, but he answers only by telling them about Ezekiel in the valley of dry bones, which makes people think he is crazy.

Themes and Meanings

Although "Ark of Bones" is based on a common short-story convention of a central character who undergoes a mysterious and unexplained experience, and although it makes use of a fablelike form common to the short story since its beginning in biblical parables, Henry Dumas adapts these conventions to a uniquely black idiom and theme. The story depends on that unique blend of African black magic and Christian religion that creates the spiritualism that often characterizes black religion in the United States. The black magic of the mojo bone is connected to the idea of the dry bones in the Old Testament, and Headeye is both an Old Testament prophet and an African witch doctor. Dumas combines these two folk traditions of the supernatural to create a parable of the black experience in the United States. The notion of the dry bones being like little babies combines the idea of the death of the black man in white America with the promise that he will rise again and take his rightful place; thus, the bones are scrupulously cared for, as if they were incubating for a rebirth. Although the story does not make clear how Headeye is qualified to fulfill such a role, he is the chosen prophet for black resurrection, a seer who hears the moans and cries of his people and sets off in the end to fulfill his sacred promise to "set my brother free."

Fish-hound is the one who remains behind to tell the story of the sacred encounter and of Headeye's holy mission. Headeye is special because, as his name suggests, his eyes are large enough to see what no one else can or wants to see—the soul and spirit of the black man in the United States. The notion of the Ark still traveling the water is a metaphor for the idea of there being no place for the black man to land, no home for him until his bones can be bound up together and he can rise whole again. Fish-hound has several intimations of the meaning of Headeye's encounter and mission, but he keeps them to himself, for he is a sacred witness, the one allowed to see the encounter, although he is unable to understand or explain it fully. He never tells anyone about the Ark, only the story of Ezekiel in the valley of dry bones. Indeed, "Ark of Bones" strangely combines black versions of both the Ezekiel story and the Noah story to serve as a subtle and submerged metaphor of the black experience in America. Thus, although "Ark of Bones" is not an explicit outcry against injustices against the black man, it is a sly and sacred parable of those injustices.

Style and Technique

Style is crucial in this story. Fish-hound tells the tale in a manner and dialect that is typically black. Dumas creates the feel of oral speech, even as he gives Fish-hound's spoken tale a biblical rhythm. Thus, the story combines the oral with the written, the informal with the formal, the everyday with the ritualistic. "Ark of Bones" also blends the naturalistic with the fabulistic and the everyday with the supernatural. The linking of these two realms of the profane and the sacred is typical of short-story technique, and Dumas makes use of the combination to address the black experience.

The story is somewhat difficult to read, not because the dialect is hard to understand but because of the elliptical nature of Fish-hound's speech and the abbreviated and cryptic nature of the dialogue between Fish-hound and Headeye. It is also difficult to determine the nature of Headeye's experience because so much of the story depends on a religious view of reality in which signs are manifested in everyday life, in which ordinary objects have totemistic value, and in which Old Testament religion is taken literally and thus is very much a part of external reality.

To respond to the story appropriately, one must be willing to enter completely into the seemingly aimless but actually quite formal and stylized language of the young narrator. As in many similar first-person narrator stories (for example, those by Sherwood Anderson), one must accept the values of the narrator, at least temporarily, as a way into the worldview of the story. Fish-hound is a young man trying to understand, trying to make sense of his experience and to communicate that experience to others. That Headeye's confrontation with his own special destiny goes beyond commonsense understanding adds poignancy to Fish-hound's apparently stumbling and wandering story line. Consequently, more than simply a commonsense understanding is required to accept this highly stylized spiritual/social parable.

"Ark of Bones" is the title story of Dumas's only short-story collection, published after his death at age thirty-four. It is typical of other stories in the collection in its focus on the oral nature of the African American culture in the United States, particularly the Gospel tradition and the tradition of black blues. Thus, although the language of the young narrator may appear uneducated and aimless, there is a sense of ritualized music, almost a chant, in the sound of his tale. What the story ultimately attempts to do is create a sense of the very source of folktale and legend as Fish-hound watches the birth of a heroic figure for the twentieth century black, as Headeye is consecrated to go out and "set my people free."

Charles E. May

THE ART OF LIVING

Author: John Gardner (1933-1982)
Type of plot: Social realism
Time of plot: The early 1970's
Locale: Upstate New York
First published: 1981

> *Principal characters:*
> ARNOLD DELLER, the protagonist, a cook in an Italian restaurant
> FINNEGAN, the narrator, a member of a motorcycle gang
> ANGELINA DELLAPICALLO, a high school senior and cocktail
> waitress in the restaurant
> FRANK DELLAPICALLO, the owner of the restaurant
> JOE DELLAPICALLO, a bartender in the restaurant, Frank's son and
> Angelina's father

The Story

An Italian restaurant in a town in northern New York State has acquired a certain lo-cal fame because of its cook, Arnold Deller. A veteran of World War II, in which he was an army cook in Europe, Deller is fascinated by the art of cooking, and though the special dishes he prepares each week for the restaurant are not elaborate, they are un-usual and meticulously researched. Deller has worked in the restaurant for twenty years. He is an avid reader, something of a philosopher, and a political idealist. He has three young daughters, and his son Rinehart has been killed in the Vietnam War.

Finnegan, the narrator, belongs to a teenage motorcycle gang called the Scaven-gers. Beneath their braggadocio, they are a harmless bunch; their custom is to visit the Italian restaurant in the afternoon to have a beer and listen to Deller hold forth in his eccentric but literate manner while he takes a break from work.

One afternoon, he harangues the boys with his notion of "the art of living." Also present are Joe Dellapicallo, the owner's son, a bartender, and Joe's daughter Ange-lina, a cocktail waitress in the restaurant. Although Joe seems indifferent to, and Angelina coldly irritated by, Deller's lecture, Finnegan is nonplussed by its intensity. Deller's argument is that the art of living is the ability to absorb rather than fight for-eigners and foreign ways of thinking. His assumption is that man has always been both a social and a warlike creature. The need to have and protect children is at the root of this dual aspect of man's nature, according to Deller. The social contract has arrived at the point, however, where a man has to accommodate those he once re-garded as his enemies if children are to be successfully nurtured in the modern world.

The emotional force behind Deller's point is the fact that his son has been killed in a war that is primarily racial, and therefore anachronistic. That is, the social instinct is now more important than the warlike instinct, for if children are to be given a chance to survive, the former must be enlarged deliberately (through "art," a willfully intentional process) and the latter must be forsworn.

That evening, Angelina approaches Finnegan in his father's garage, where he is working on his motorcycle. Finnegan has been attracted to Angelina for some time, but he has kept the attraction a secret—or so he believes. At dinner earlier, his sister Shannon teased him about it and his mother suggested that he invite Angelina to dinner. So far, Finnegan has expressed his interest only by driving his motorcycle by Angelina's house at night or near the places where she might be attending a party. He is, in his own eyes, concerned for her safety, as though he were a surrogate for her father. They have not been together—even to talk—before she arrives at the garage.

Angelina tells Finnegan about an ancient Chinese dish called "Imperial Dog." It requires a completely black dog, and she asks him to find one that night so that Deller may prepare the dish. Vaguely scandalized but not wanting to alienate Angelina, Finnegan, along with the other Scavengers, breaks into a pet shop, steals a black dog, and brings it to the restaurant after hours. Deller is waiting for them, and as he continues his harangue from the afternoon, he butchers the dog and cooks the exotic dish. Besides the Scavengers, his audience consists of Frank Dellapicallo, his son Joe and granddaughter Angelina, Deller's three daughters, and his kitchen helper Ellis. Frank insists that, according to the long contract Deller has with him, the dish must be eaten. He himself eats nothing but spaghetti, and after he sees that everyone present except his son has sat down to eat the dish, he leaves, as does Joe himself.

The story ends with Finnegan commenting on how good the Imperial Dog tastes, and with various toasts and the approval—as Finnegan reports—of the shadows beyond the candlelight, which are the ghosts of Deller's son and of numerous Asians.

Themes and Meanings

This story's theme concerns the meaning of art: Art is essential to life itself, John Gardner believes, for it connects human beings to one another. Not only is it social in this respect but it also requires that artists practice their art with this concern in mind, controlling their instinct to be defensive and allowing their instinct to benefit humankind to predominate. There are various kinds of art in the story that serve as examples of "the art of living." The main one is Arnold Deller's cooking; it is meaningless unless there is someone for whom to cook. The Scavengers work, like Finnegan, to make their secondhand motorcycles function well, and they do this to cement the social bond among them: This, too, is art. Angelina is not only a work of art in that she is beautiful and attracts others to her but also an artist insofar as she actively promotes social ideals (especially, as the reader learns, when she goes to college) and functions as mediator between clashing social units (Deller, her father, and the Scavengers).

Art is based on the love for children—that is, on concern for the future of humankind. Those who are without feeling and who mechanically accept the status quo, and those who thoughtlessly hate strangers and unfamiliar customs, are against art in its true social sense. These are the antagonists in the story, and they are represented by Joe Dellapicallo, Angelina's father. He pretends not to listen to Deller when the latter is talking about art in the bar; he seems not to care, but it soon becomes clear that he is passionately against the idea of cooking a dog, and later, when the dish is ready to eat, he refuses to take part and walks out of the restaurant. Ironically, as Finnegan notes, Joe is civilized (to the extent supporting the idea of art as the suppression of the primitive destructiveness built into the human psyche) in refusing to eat "man's best friend," but he is also the servant of unexamined assumptions, suggested by his robotlike movements as he withdraws from the banquet. His father, Frank, represents a middle position: He accepts art and its social function by allowing Deller to prepare special or unusual dishes as part of the restaurant's menu, but he refuses to eat these dishes himself. He is the kind of conservative (a condition underlined by the fact that he is old, sick, and withdrawn) who supports art but does not act on its implications—who does not, in short, partake of art.

Style and Technique

"The Art of Living" uses two aspects of plot, foreshadowing and climax, to embody its meaning. The potential merging of perspectives in the story is foreshadowed by what some of the major characters are and how they behave. Arnold Deller is a cook, which means that his art is to do something for others; he also makes his appeal to those who are much younger than he—Angelina and Finnegan. Angelina is a social idealist, which means that she is open to Deller's appeal. Though she belongs to a tightly knit Italian family, she acts on the basis of Deller's values by putting in motion the theft of the dog for his recipe. Finnegan himself is half-Irish and half-Italian, a mixture to begin with, and because his mind and his attraction for Angelina enlarge his perspective beyond the confines of his gang he procures the dog for Angelina and Deller.

The climax of the story is the ultimate realization of all these tentative mergings, the moment in which the barriers between the characters (with the exception of Angelina's father) break down. They all participate in the same difficult dinner: The young gang members cooperate with the older and more established Deller; Deller's daughters come out of their seclusion to be with the others; Finnegan and Angelina cement a friendship; the shadows of the dead merge with the high spirits of the living at the ceremonial dinner.

Mark McCloskey

THE ARTIFICIAL FAMILY

Author: Anne Tyler (1941-   )
Type of plot: Domestic realism
Time of plot: The 1980's
Locale: Baltimore, Maryland
First published: 1975

Principal characters:
TOBY SCOTT, a graduate student
MARY GLOVER, an art gallery worker
SAMANTHA GLOVER, Mary's daughter

The Story

When Toby Scott meets Mary Glover at a party, he is immediately impressed by her long hair and old-fashioned gingham dress. Afraid that he might not see her again, he asks her to dinner immediately. Mary tells the eager bachelor that she has a daughter, but Toby does not know if this means that she is married or is simply unwilling to date.

Samantha Glover, Mary's daughter, is a somber five-year-old who dresses like her mother, in floor-length dresses. The impression that Mary and Samantha make together is that of stoic pioneers riding a wagon train across the prairie.

Samantha accompanies her mother when Toby asks her out. On a trip to the Baltimore zoo, Samantha sits between Toby and Mary as they look at animals. Mary never volunteers any information about her first marriage or Samantha's father. When Toby inquires, Mary refuses to answer any questions, revealing only that she ran away after two years of marriage. Her previous life remains mysterious.

Toby's feelings for Mary and Samantha deepen. When Mary mentions that she has child-care problems, Toby volunteers to watch Samantha himself. Mary works in an art gallery with fixed hours, while Toby can easily adjust his own schedule. Despite Toby's offer to watch Samantha, Mary keeps paying her teenage baby-sitter. Toby fears losing Mary because his graduate student life lacks warm human relations.

After knowing each other only five months, Toby and Mary are married. Toby's parents object to his brief courtship and the fact that Toby is acquiring a ready-made daughter. Although Toby questions his ability to love his own biological children—were he ever to have them—he finds that he can easily warm to loving Samantha.

Toby envies the resolve with which Mary carried Samantha from her presumably troubled first marriage. She took no clothing, jewelry, or personal belongings of any kind. As if fleeing from a burning building, Mary simply snatched away the only thing that really mattered: Samantha. Toby wonders about the strength of the relationships that he is forming with Mary and Samantha. For some reason, Mary is reluctant to enter compassionately into their marital union. Overly concerned with Toby's privacy, she never even enters his office—the spare bedroom. She even places a no-entry sign above his door, even though he has said that he was always alone at his lab and does not want to be alone at home. Although Toby attempts to bond emotionally with Mary and her daughter, Mary scrupulously avoids close personal contact.

Toby becomes a model father, playing games with Samantha, reading her stories, and giving her piggyback rides each night before bedtime. Samantha returns Toby's affection more readily than Mary does. Every evening she walks to his lab, calling him to dinner. Her attention, smiles, and warmth flatter Toby, who wonders if he would feel differently about her if she were his own daughter.

At Christmas, Toby's parents visit the newlyweds. The four days of their visit seem to drag out forever because of their tactless remarks about Toby's "artificial" family. Not knowing that the topic is forbidden, the Scotts ask many questions about Samantha's father. They also comment on the way that Mary has taken over Toby's life. Toby, Mary, and Samantha form an alliance against the Scotts, seeking refuge together in Toby's study to play dominoes. They even sneak off to the movies together.

Gradually, Toby's once private study becomes a gathering place for the new family. Toby reads, Mary sews and places her pottery around the room, and Samantha plays on the floor. Finally, the ice thaws and the marriage seems to form strong emotional, spiritual, and physical bonds. Under the influence of Toby's playfulness, Samantha grows unruly with her mother, talking back and roughhousing, in contrast to her former sullenness. Mary complains that Toby's attention is spoiling Samantha. Toby dotes on Samantha, giving her everything she wants. Toby's feelings for her strengthen. On one occasion, Toby becomes angry when Samantha steps into the street without looking; he pulls her back, feeling a deep sense of shock and nervous helplessness.

Toby becomes so confident about his fathering that he asks Mary for another baby. Toby loves Samantha so much that he wants more children to love, but Mary insists that women have less love to give than men because of the demands of housekeeping. Toby and Mary also disagree over Samantha's Easter basket. Toby gives Samantha a big prepackaged basket with chocolate, jellybeans, and candy rabbits, but Mary insists that she and Samantha observe Easter differently, and she resents having to be the parent who says no to treats. Although Samantha enjoys receiving the candy, Toby senses that he has lost the battle. Once again Mary grows distant and emotionless.

After Samantha finishes the first grade in school, Mary leaves Toby for good. The only message that she leaves for him simply says, "I've gone." Devastated, Toby puts his head in his hands and thinks about how he can find his family. After eating a sandwich that Mary has made for him, he runs to Samantha's school, dodging cars. He feels the same kind of grief felt by a parent whose child has died. After Samantha's teacher tells him that she has not been at school, Toby walks home in a daze. He lies down on the sofa without turning on lights. He knows that he will find Mary's and Samantha's clothes in their closets. Once again, the only things that they have taken away are their gingham dresses and themselves.

Themes and Meanings

The first question that this story poses is exactly what is meant by "artificial" in its title? Toby's desire for a family has an artificial easiness about it. Perhaps he savors the idea of a family more than the reality of complex people with mysterious pasts. Mary's commitment to Toby seems even more clearly artificial and dishonest. She and Samantha appear artificial or unreal; they appear out of nowhere and disappear equally mysteriously. However, Mary is overly concerned with the artificial quality of the Easter basket that Toby buys in a store instead of making it himself.

In exploring definitions of love and the struggle for power within a family, "The Artificial Family" addresses the sanctity of marital love—a love that demands willing, imperfect, vulnerable partners engaged in forming a more perfect union. Toby, the character most concerned with his ability to love, seems to exemplify unconditional love and acceptance. His courageous act of saving Samantha from being hit by a car and his grief after her later departure indicate that he has fully entered into the relationship. Toby desires to have more children and unconditionally accepts Samantha despite his own parents' misgivings.

Mary prizes her independence and her ability to abandon a bad marriage without hesitation. Her hardened "survivor" mentality prevents her from displaying vulnerability or showing her true personality. Toby notices that her face seems artificial, like a mask, after they fight over the Easter basket. Mary resists Toby's offer to help with child care and resents depending on him.

Toby's concern with his ability to love, his high regard for family, and his desire for children—all qualities that are generally regarded as feminine—stand opposite to Mary's masculine independence, unresponsiveness, and refusal to invest in the relationship. Mary seems to lose authority over her daughter because of Toby's abundant attention and lax discipline; her leaving may be read as an attempt to reassert her control. Mary and Toby attempt to love each other, but too many "artificial" impediments bring their marriage to an end.

Style and Technique

Anne Tyler tells this story in a straightforward, realistic, and unsentimental style. "The Artificial Family" avoids both an overtly didactic message or a conclusive, tightly wrapped ending. Instead, readers must guess why Mary leaves Toby. The story leaves many unanswered questions: What is the meaning of Toby's desire for children? Was this experience artificial or real for Toby and Mary? How will Toby cope with his loss? What will Mary and Samantha's new life be like?

American novelist John Updike once described Tyler as a southern writer because, like Flannery O'Connor or Carson McCullers, she evokes a solid sense of family, place, and region. Tyler's characters seem isolated from the large currents of change in American culture and evoke nostalgia for an earlier, simpler time. Tyler is preoccupied with character psychology but not corrupted with the modern idiom of clinical psychotherapy. The motives and desires of Toby and Mary are deftly implied and lightly sketched, leaving much room for creative interpretation.

Jonathan L. Thorndike

THE ARTIFICIAL NIGGER

Author: Flannery O'Connor (1925-1964)
Type of plot: Psychological
Time of plot: Probably the 1940's or 1950's
Locale: Atlanta, Georgia
First published: 1955

> *Principal characters:*
> MR. HEAD, a sixty-year-old man living in rural Georgia
> NELSON, his ten-year-old grandson

The Story

Flannery O'Connor's own favorite among her stories, "The Artificial Nigger" is really two stories in one: the saga of Nelson's initiation into the world of experience and the tale of Mr. Head's fall from righteousness to emptiness. The two journeys parallel each other, just as the railroad tracks, which play an important part in this story, parallel each other; unlike the tracks, however, which never intersect, Mr. Head's and Nelson's journeys coalesce in their shared visions of the mysterious statue that provides the title of the story.

In the opening scene, Mr. Head and Nelson, who live together in rural Georgia, are preparing for a trip to Atlanta, each motivated to make this monumental expedition for different reasons. Mr. Head, proud of his independence and omniscience (he does not even need an alarm clock to awaken him), sees the trip as a "moral mission" during which he will guide his grandson through the complexities of the city, helping him see everything so that Nelson will never again want to visit the city and will, instead, be content to live forever with his grandfather. Nelson, for his part, wants to see the city where he believes he was born; for him, the trip is a journey into his past.

Traveling to Atlanta by train, the pair experience their first shared event—an event that, ironically, separates them. Mr. Head has been warning Nelson about seeing "niggers," telling him that the city is full of these people, who were run out of the county two years before Nelson was born. Nelson, confident that he will be able to identify a black person when he sees one, observes but does not recognize the first black man he sees on the train. Mr. Head asks him, "What was that?" and Nelson responds, "A man." Pushed to be more specific, Nelson says that the man is "fat" and that he is "old," but never does he identify him as black. As Nelson tries to rationalize when told by his grandfather what he was supposed to have seen, "You never said they were tan. How do you expect me to know anything when you don't tell me right?" Mr. Head, the guide, righteously enjoys his knowledge at the expense of his grandson's ignorance.

The next episode continues to distinguish the guide from the follower. The two weigh themselves on a scale in front of a store, and though the machine is inaccurate in its numbers, Mr. Head is sure it is accurate in its words because the ticket says that he is "upright and brave" and that all of his friends admire him. Nelson's fortune, by contrast, is ominous: "You have a great destiny ahead of you but beware of dark women."

As the two pursue their journey, Nelson becomes increasingly enamored of the wonders of the city, horrifying his grandfather by his positive reaction to the place Mr. Head believes is evil. To shock his grandson, Mr. Head takes Nelson to a sewer entrance and forces him to look into the depths of the underground system. Explaining to him the terrors of that underbelly, Mr. Head unknowingly teaches Nelson that there is indeed a dark underside to the wonders of existence. The lesson, however, requires more experience before Nelson truly understands its implications.

One of these experiences occurs when Nelson and his grandfather, lost in the city, meet a black woman whose presence confuses Nelson because of her maternal yet sensuous presence. Wanting to be comforted and seduced by her, a feeling he has never had before, Nelson nearly collapses from the sensation, remembering the fortunes on the scale that told him to beware of dark women but told his grandfather that he was upright and brave. Nelson decides to trust his mentor once again.

His mentor, however, betrays that trust. In a subsequent episode, Nelson collides with a woman, knocking her down and incurring her wrath. She accuses Nelson of breaking her ankle and tells Mr. Head that he will have to pay the doctor's bill. When Mr. Head responds that Nelson is not his boy, that he "never seen him before," the biblical echoes of Peter's and Judas's betrayals resound. Nelson is devastated.

Guide and follower are now separated by a monumental chasm. The relationship between the two is literally and figuratively severed, with Mr. Head walking ahead of his grandson, the young boy trailing behind. As the two individuals proceed in this fashion, they see a statue whose image and significance provide the climax of the journey and the story. A plaster figure of a black boy about Nelson's size, the statue has "a wild look of misery," and its misery, viewed by two human beings who are themselves miserable, becomes the vehicle by which Nelson and Mr. Head transcend their particular situation. Grandfather and grandson sense that they are "faced with some great mystery, some monument to another's victory that brought them together in their common defeat. They could both feel it dissolving their difference like an action of mercy."

The two return to their life in rural Georgia, Nelson having been initiated into the world of good and evil, Mr. Head having been initiated into the world of humanity. Each recognizes his need of the other; both realize that they do not understand the mystery of a world that contains sewers and illuminating visions.

Themes and Meanings

Two worlds are juxtaposed in "The Artificial Nigger": the world of the machine, with its alleged accuracy and predictability, and the world of mystery, with its ambiguity and spontaneity. In the first world, the railroad train arrives on time and, like the best of technological inventions, transports its passengers efficiently and safely to their destinations. The scale, another mechanical device, provides weight and fortune, both for a mere penny. The train, however, delivers Mr. Head and Nelson to a place that they had not expected to visit—their inner selves—and the scale gives numbers that are not accurate and fortunes that are ambiguous.

In the other world, the world of mystery, there is no pretense of accuracy or clarity. A black man on a train is not really black; he is tan. A black woman leaning in a doorway is not simply seductress or mother; she is both. A statue, appearing miraculously on the lawn of someone's yard, is not merely terrifying or purifying; it is an ambiguous combination of both emotions.

Like William Faulkner, another southern writer, O'Connor celebrates those qualities that distinguish human beings from machines, those qualities that are most closely connected to mystery and ambiguity. When Mr. Head and Nelson return from their trip to the city, they are interdependent because they have been touched by the mysterious, shared vision that connects them.

Style and Technique

O'Connor adapts various traditional literary devices to her story of Mr. Head and Nelson. The most obvious strategy is the idea of a journey, which provides both the structure and the content of the tale. Just as Don Quixote and Huckleberry Finn travel to make external and internal discoveries, so grandfather and grandson in "The Artificial Nigger" voyage to foreign territory and see not only new sights but also new selves.

In the classical version of the journey, a guide plays an important role in helping the traveler find his way and his goal. Ironically adapting the figure of the guide, O'Connor describes the grandfather as "Vergil summoned in the middle of the night to go to Dante, or better, Raphael, awakened by a blast of God's light to fly to the side of Tobias." Mr. Head does indeed lead Nelson, but he guides him to wonders that neither mentor nor follower anticipates.

Still another traditional image is that of moonlight, which both distorts and illuminates. At the beginning of the story, when Mr. Head awakens to discover "half of the moon five feet away in his shaving mirror," he finds in its "dignifying fight" confirmation of his delusive self-image, his self-righteous notion that he is "one of the great guides of men." At the end of the story, when the travelers return from their trip, the moonlight is once again shining, but this time the light is clarifying, not misleading. Nelson and Mr. Head have returned, a reminder of T. S. Eliot's words in *Four Quartets* (1943): "Home is where one starts from/ . . . And the end of all our exploring/ Will be to arrive where we started/ And know the place for the first time." Nelson says this in his own words: "I'm glad I've went once, but I'll never go back again!"

Marjorie Smelstor

THE ARTIST OF THE BEAUTIFUL

Author: Nathaniel Hawthorne (1804-1864)
Type of plot: Allegory
Time of plot: About 1840
Locale: New England
First published: 1844

> *Principal characters:*
> OWEN WARLAND, the protagonist, a watchmaker, dreamer, and
> the artist of the beautiful
> PETER HOVENDEN, his former employer, now a retired
> watchmaker
> ANNIE HOVENDEN, Peter's daughter, whom Owen loves
> ROBERT DANFORTH, a blacksmith, Owen's childhood friend and
> rival for Annie's hand

The Story

Even as a child, Owen Warland enjoyed carving intricate figures of birds and flowers and showed mechanical ability. Hence, he is apprenticed to Peter Hovenden, a master watchmaker, with whom, his relatives hope, he will be able to make practical use of his delicate talents.

Peter, however, is not impressed with Owen's character. He recognizes his apprentice's considerable talents but senses that Owen does not care to apply them in a conventional way. When failing eyesight forces Peter to surrender his shop to Owen, the young man confirms his master's fears. Owen's business declines because his customers do not appreciate the way he trifles with their beloved timepieces, which he tends to embellish fancifully.

Far from regretting this lack of customers, Owen rejoices in the free time he now has to pursue his goal of creating an object so like its natural original that it will be indistinguishable from it. The first attempt fails after Robert Danforth comes to deliver a small forge ordered from the blacksmith. Danforth's brute strength so disturbs Owen that he carelessly demolishes the artifact.

For some months Owen returns to watchmaking, abandoning any artistic pretense. Slowly, however, he recovers his interest in his project and is about to begin again when Peter visits him. His former master's skepticism toward anything lacking utilitarian value so upsets Owen that he relinquishes his dream.

In the summer he once more takes up his task but again he is frustrated, this time by Annie Hovenden, who has come to his shop to have her thimble repaired. Owen loves her and wonders whether she might be a worthy partner for him. She provides the answer by touching Owen's delicate device, thus ruining it. Enraged and disappointed, Owen sends her away and resigns himself to a winter of dissipation.

With the return of spring, Owen resumes work on the intricate device. One evening Peter comes to tell him of Annie's engagement to Robert Danforth. Though Owen does not betray his disappointment to Peter, he himself destroys the mechanism in a fit of despair. For a while he ridicules his former dream of rivaling nature, but at last he decides to produce his imitation as a wedding gift for Annie.

By the time he delivers the present, Annie and Robert already have a child. As Annie, Robert, Peter, and the child look on, Owen opens an elegantly carved ebony box; out flutters a butterfly, more beautiful than any to be found in the woods or meadows. Although all admire Owen's handiwork, none recognizes its true genius. As it hovers about the room, the infant grabs it and crushes it in his fist. Owen is not troubled, though, for in creating the butterfly he had achieved his dream.

Themes and Meanings

As in many of his works, Nathaniel Hawthorne here explores the artist's life, which Hawthorne defines in true Romantic fashion. Owen takes nature as his model, devoting his summers to the careful observation of butterflies. His examination is not scientific; he does not dissect or analyze. Rather, he draws inspiration from the butterflies and seeks to comprehend their essential qualities.

This quest for understanding has no monetary or utilitarian value. Again showing himself a product of the Romantic era, Hawthorne stresses Owen's desire for self-satisfaction. Owen rejects the practical: He has no interest in using his talents to regulate machinery, and the sight of a steam engine, that most useful of devices, makes him physically ill. His concern is with the spirit, chiefly his own. Hence, he feels no regret when the physical manifestation of his art is destroyed; all that matters is fulfilling his dream.

However, if Owen enjoys the success of the Romantic artist, he also suffers from the artist's failure. To become an artist of the beautiful he must sever his ties with his fellow men. He cannot be bothered with customers, with would-be friends like Robert Danforth, even with love. He creates the artificial butterfly, but he loses Annie. Because Owen does not isolate himself for any evil purpose, Hawthorne does not condemn him as he does Ethan Brand (in the story of that title) and Chillingworth (*The Scarlet Letter*, 1850), who have also cut themselves off from humanity. Still, Owen pays a price for his victory, and Hawthorne leaves open the question of whether it is too high.

Style and Technique

To make his point about art and the artist, Hawthorne uses allegory. Each of the characters in the story represents an attitude or principle. Owen embodies the artistic quest. Robert Danforth, strong and earthy, is brute force. Peter Hovenden, who devotes his considerable skill to regulating the temporal world rather than changing it, stands for materialistic skepticism; Annie is the force of love. Each of these last three challenges and threatens Owen, and each is responsible for the destruction of the mechanism in the course of the story. Owen's self-doubt also threatens his success, as indicated by his destroying the artifact after he learns of Annie's engagement when, presumably, he questions the value of his enterprise if it costs him so dearly.

Owen's device takes the form of a butterfly emerging from a black box, an allegory of the soul escaping, transcending, the body. Owen has worked to release his spirit from its prison, and he finally succeeds. Because the butterfly is only the physical manifestation of the concept, its fate, once the dream has been made real, cannot affect Owen, who remains free—and alone.

Nature, too, assumes an allegorical aspect. In the winter, symbol of the soul's dark and unproductive period, Owen abandons his project. When spring returns, Owen's creative spirit is renewed, indicated by the reappearance of butterflies in the fields. Owen's struggles, his periods of doubt and achievement, are those of any artist who would create beauty. "The Artist of the Beautiful" demonstrates Hawthorne's faith in the artistic principle and also his clear-sighted understanding of the struggles that the artist must endure.

Joseph Rosenblum

AS BIRDS BRING FORTH THE SUN

Author: Alistair MacLeod (1936-   )
Type of plot: Magical Realism, fantasy
Time of plot: The nineteenth and the twentieth centuries
Locale: An unspecified place by the sea and Toronto, Canada
First published: 1985

> *Principal characters:*
> THE GRAY HOUND
> THE GRAY HOUND'S MASTER
> HIS TEENAGE SON, who helps his father on the fishing boat
> HIS YOUNGER SON, who also helps on the boat
> HIS GREAT-GREAT-GREAT-GRANDSON, the narrator
> HIS ELEVENTH SON, the narrator's great-great-grandfather

The Story

"As Birds Bring Forth the Sun" begins as the story of a man whose family name, which is never revealed, indicates a Scottish Highland heritage. He lives by the ocean and has a large family whom he supports by fishing and farming. The man has a huge gray dog, that is devoted to him. He adopted her when she was just a small puppy that someone had left on his doorstep. Later, he saved her life again by nursing her back to health after she was run over by a cart. Though he has never given the dog a name but simply calls her *cù mòr glas*, or "the big gray dog" in Gaelic, he is very much attached to her. When she comes into heat, he searches out a male large enough for her and helps them breed. However, shortly before her pups are to be born, the big gray dog disappears. The whole family worries about her, her master most of all, but she never returns.

More than a year later, while the man and two of his sons are out in their boat fishing, a sudden storm blows up, forcing them to take refuge on a nearby island. Suddenly they see the missing dog, standing on a hilltop. Her master is so overjoyed that he jumps out of the boat and wades toward shore; spying him, she rushes headlong down the hill, jumps up on him, and in her enthusiasm knocks him down. Suddenly six more gray dogs rush down to join in what they assume is an attack on this strange man. Before their mother can drive them off, they have killed her former master. The next day, when the sea is calmer, the sons take their dead father home. Later searches of the island reveal no trace of the dogs, though periodically a sighting is reported.

At this point the narrator reveals that the man who died was his own great-great-great-grandfather. This tragic incident had grave consequences. Because of it, the narrator's great-great-grandfather, born a few months after the dogs' attack, never had a chance to know his father. Moreover, neither of the two boys who witnessed their father's death ever recovered from the shock. The younger of them had terrible nightmares about the gray dog, which he associated with death; after a particularly vivid dream, he killed himself. The older son lived to be forty, but only by drowning his memories in drink. His end came one night in a Glasgow pub, when something he said about the big gray dog resulted in his getting into a fight with a large, gray-haired man. According to the story, when the two took their quarrel outside, six more gray-haired men appeared. The seven of them beat the son to death, then vanished.

The narrator admits that all of this happened in the distant past. However, he insists, each of the succeeding generations of his family has had visitations by the gray dog, and always they were followed by someone's death. What has reminded him of these stories is that he and his five brothers, all gray-haired, are at their father's bedside in a Toronto hospital. They all worry that their father may have a dream or a vision of the gray dog and give up his attempt to survive. However, what they fear most is that the gray dog will appear to them, for in their hearts they know that the tales are true.

Themes and Meanings

Like many of Alistair MacLeod's other stories, "As Birds Bring Forth the Sun" deals with the appearance of the supernatural in ordinary life. The title is taken from a sentence near the end of the story when, after asserting that he and his brothers are afraid, the narrator admits that there are some people who call faith in the supernatural mere foolishness. They would lump it with the beliefs some still hold that Earth is actually flat or that it is the flight of birds that causes the sun to rise. The brothers are not simple people. They also might be expected to equate the supernatural with superstition; however, they cannot. As the narrator points out, even his most skeptical sibling arrives at the hospital uneasy, and once there, he is no less afraid than his brothers that the gray dog will appear.

MacLeod does not offer the supernatural as an alternative to the real world. The dog's master is an ordinary person, the father of eleven children. He is a man who knows about birth as well as death and about domestic happiness as well as sudden violence. He gets dirty. He plants crops, breeds animals, casts out nets, and keeps his eye on the sky. The narrator, too, is rooted in reality, as can be seen in the matter-of-fact way he describes his great-great-great-grandfather's terrible death. The narrator also offers a plausible explanation as to why the dog was unable to return home with her pups. The farm is a real place, so is the Glasgow pub, and so is the hospital room where the story ends. However, and this is the point of the final paragraphs, although the gray dog began as an ordinary dog living in the real world, in some mysterious way she has transcended that world to become not only a part of the ancestral memory but also a presence just outside the door.

Style and Technique

During the three decades before the appearance of his prizewinning novel *No Great Mischief* (1999), MacLeod had published only sixteen stories. However, in them he had displayed such a high level of craftsmanship that he was consistently described as one of Canada's finest fiction writers.

MacLeod's stylistic dexterity is evident in "As Birds Bring Forth the Sun." He begins writing as if his story were a folktale. There is an unnamed hero living in an unspecified location. In keeping with the oral tradition, all but one of the sentences in the first paragraph are short and simple; three of them begin with "and," the connective so often used by storytellers. However, MacLeod soon changes to a more complex and more formal style, with the modifications and afterthoughts that one would expect from a well-educated narrator, switching to simpler sentence patterns only in the action scenes, such as the dog-breeding episode, the savaging of the master, and the murder of the older son. The author moves easily from the realistic depiction of farm life to lyrical descriptions of nature to philosophical musings such as those in the final sentences of the story. Always the style suits the subject, and always the transitions are seamless.

MacLeod is just as deft in his handling of point of view. "As Birds Bring Forth the Sun" is especially interesting in that as the story progresses, the narrative voice keeps changing. At first, the voice is that of a storyteller so distanced from events that he knows very little about his central character. It is as though the narrator is simply reciting a story that has already passed through many hands. Even when the voice changes to that of an educated man, the stance is still one of detachment. Not until the story is two-thirds told does the narrator admit that it involves his own family, and from that time on, there is no attempt to distance himself either from the tradition or from the reader. In fact, the reader becomes a confidant, someone to whom the narrator confides his uncertainties and his apprehensions.

One reason that MacLeod is so admired is that he leaves his readers certain about what has happened in a story but uncertain about its full significance. In "As Birds Bring Forth the Sun," there is little doubt that the big gray dog exists; what is not so evident is what the presence of such beings implies not just for a single family but also for the whole human race.

Rosemary M. Canfield Reisman

ASSORTED FIRE EVENTS

Author: David Means (1961-   )
Type of plot: Antistory, metafiction
Time of plot: The 1990's
Locale: Hudson River Valley, New York
First published: 2000

> *Principal characters:*
> A WRITER, the narrator
> HIS AUNT, who immolates herself
> SHANK, a boy who likes to burn living creatures
> FENTON, a boy who accidentally starts a fire and is terribly
>   burned

The Story

There is no single unified plot in "Assorted Fire Events." Instead, as its title suggests, the story is a series of events about fire, related to one another only insofar as they are of interest to the narrator writing about them.

In the first paragraph, the narrator recalls one winter when he was thirteen and living in Michigan when a man set fire to several cottages. In the spring when the snow melted, the narrator loved the sight of the black charred remains of one of the cottages and adds it to his "line-up of memorable images."

For the second fire event, the narrator describes sitting in his study writing and listening to his children playing outside when a fire breaks out at a nearby house because of the spontaneous combustion of varnish-soaked rags. In a footnote, the writer provides a biographical basis for this event, saying that in the previous spring when a house near him was reduced to rubble, he heard the children hollering for joy.

The third fire event focuses briefly on a boy named Shank who pours gasoline on a dog and sets it on fire. The fourth event, which the narrator says in another footnote is a horrible tragic fact, describes how his aunt pours gasoline on her head and body and sets herself on fire, dying a few hours later, her flesh consumed. The aunt has left a note written in the first person from the point of view of the gas can.

In the final and most detailed fire event, the narrator tells of Fenton, a boy who builds a makeshift cardboard rocket ship, douses it with gasoline, and lights it in a narrow space between the garages of his parents and their neighbors. When the flames roar up his legs, he drops and rolls, but there is little room between the two garages, and he keeps rolling back toward the fire. Although he screams, a neighbor is mowing his lawn and cannot hear him. Both garages and part of the two houses also catch fire.

The last section of the story describes Fenton crawling on all fours, his skin smoking, his sneakers having melted into his feet, a "ghastly sight that no one gets to see." When the firefighters arrive, he is still smoldering like a heap of campfire residue. The narrator then describes the aftermath of the disaster, Fenton lying in a flotation tank with his arms outstretched, like Christ. This fire event is "a holy event," says the narrator, for Fenton walked into the hot fire of hell and came out with a face hard to recognize as human. When people pass him on the street, they do not want to look at him, for his face is like that of a clown in a circus; a goofy smile has been painted over the face of the saddest clown-school dropout they have ever seen.

Themes and Meanings

"Assorted Fire Events," the title story of David Means's second book of short stories, which won the 2001 Los Angeles Times Book Award for fiction, is a poetic meditation on the universal fascination with fire, describing and pondering the significance of several events in an attempt to explore what drives people to "play with fire" or "follow the fire truck" to a burning building.

The first event does not focus on the person who started the fire but on the boy's fascination with the effect of fire on a house. What he likes is the way the fire makes its way from the inside out until there is no more inside, only outside. He also likes the way the pine trees around the cottage are reduced to brittle towers. The skeletal remains after fire has ravaged a house and its surroundings create a poetic image of something being stripped to the bone.

The narrator introduces the second fire event by saying that the sound of fire, like popcorn in hot oil just before the kernels explode, makes him laugh. He tries to find a metaphor for the sound, noting it was like a "huge hunk of brittle cellophane crumpled by the hand of God." However, he says he will never use that metaphor, but rather the metaphor of a giant weed whacker. The ironic juxtaposition of this sound against the sound of his children whooping and hollering with joy is what interests him in this event. When he finds out that the fire started from spontaneous combustion from varnish-soaked brushes, he creates an additional metaphor of sound in which the brushes sitting in the hot sun begin to sizzle and talk to one another, until "drunk with the elixir" of the varnish, they are ready to "burst forth in the song of fire."

The next two events focus on the burning of living flesh, first by a boy named Shank, who burns a dog, and then by his aunt, who sets herself on fire. The previous metaphor of the singing fire is extended to a metaphor of dance. The dog's body writhes in a heat wave, and no one is sure if the movement is the dog's or an illusion produced by heat distortion; it is like the monks "doing their sit-down self-immolating dances during Nam." The narrator muses that the plot of fire is both wildly fanatic and calm at the same time, taking its own sweet time and then becoming logarithmic, until it "sings sweetly the fantastic house-burning lament."

The final and most extended fire event combines the horror and beauty of fire. When a young boy named Fenton tries to launch his homemade rocket ship with gasoline, the fire quickly gets out of control and engulfs him. The ironic juxtaposition of horrible destruction and comic effect is then suggested by a description of Fenton on fire, looking like an actor in a fire suit, a stunt person like a Charlie Chaplin tramp. This image of opposites is echoed at the end when the boy is so scarred that people try not to look at him for fear of laughing out loud. The narrator says that he looks like a clown whose goofy smile is painted over the face of the saddest-looking, most pathetic clown-school dropout.

Ultimately, the narrator sees Fenton as resembling Christ, who has walked into the fires of hell to suffer for all humankind. Thus, the fire is a holy event, for the boy has experienced that extreme mystery that he cannot explain and that the writer can only create assorted fire events to try to capture.

Style and Technique

Style is everything in "Assorted Fire Events," for the story is an example of a writer's attempt to use language to explore the basic paradoxical mystery of fire as a powerful force that can burn away the extraneous and reduce an object to its pure essentials. Means's method for achieving this exploration is to reject linear narrative altogether and describe various fire events in such a way that even as they are horrifying, they are somehow eerily beautiful. If one is concerned with images rather than physical actuality, what is horrible becomes abstractly beautiful. If one focuses only on the sound of the fire, it is "lively and spunky" like popcorn. Consequently, although there is nothing particularly funny about fire, if one divorces its sound from its destructive power, fire is comic. Also, if one perceives the immolation of a dog or indeed a human being as being like a dance, then that too, divorced from its physical horror, can be beautiful.

In this way, the narrator moves from one fire event to another, describing them as purely aesthetic objects. The aunt's first-person note written from the point of view of the gas can serves as a grotesque parallel to the aunt's body and mind. The narrator thinks of the meaninglessness of the can's life; as the can is used for mundane tasks, all the while the vapors inside it are pushing against the roof of its mouth, "singing, making little arias to the instability of their bonds."

The final event of the burning of the young boy, as terrifying as it may be in actuality, is transformed into an emblem of paradox, like that of the mythic transformation of Christ from mere body into spirit. Although it seems cruel to laugh at the scarred face of the boy, what one is really laughing at is the mystery of the sadness that underlies the painted smile. Thus, the basic technique of the story is to use the essential methods of poetry, which, like fire itself, transforms the merely physical into the aesthetically meaningful and beautiful.

Charles E. May

AN ASTROLOGER'S DAY

Author: R. K. Narayan (1906-2001)
Type of plot: Social realism
Time of plot: Probably the 1920's and 1930's
Locale: Southern India
First published: 1947

Principal characters:
THE ASTROLOGER
HIS WIFE
GURU NAYAK, a client of the astrologer

The Story

The story begins with a description of the place and environment in which the astrologer meets his clients and does his work. He begins his work every day at midday in a public place under a large tree that is close to a public park in his town. The place chosen for his work is generally full of people who pass by or gather there, such as customers attracted by vendors of nuts, sweetmeats, and other snacks. It is a place poorly lighted in the evening, and because the astrologer has no light of his own, he must depend on what light comes from the flickering lamps kept by neighboring vendors; a dully lighted, murky place is best for his purpose. He is not an astrologer by profession but was led into it by circumstances that forced him to leave his village, where, if he had stayed, he would have settled down to a life of tilling the land.

He has a practical knowledge of the common problems of most people: "marriage, money, and the tangles of human ties." His sharp eyes, used to scanning for customers, make people believe he has an unusual ability to tell people's fortunes.

"An Astrologer's Day" opens as its title character arrives at his workplace, at midday, and as usual spreads his charts and other fortune-telling props before him, though no one comes seeking his aid for many hours. Later, with nightfall approaching, he begins preparing to go home when, all of a sudden, he beholds a man standing in front of him. In the exchange of talk that ensues, the astrologer carefully tries to spread the net of his craft around the client, and the client, Guru Nayak, responds with a challenge: Would the astrologer tell him whether he, Guru Nayak, will be successful in a search he is carrying out, returning double the fee he has paid if the prediction cannot be made? The astrologer alternately accepts, declines, and feigns indifference, all the more to whet Nayak's appetite and make him press his offer. The astrologer then catches a glimpse of Nayak's face (previously shrouded in darkness) in the light of the match Nayak has struck under his cheroot, and, though at first chilled by the sight, decides to play out Nayak's game: The astrologer tells him that he was once left for dead by another man, who had attacked him with a knife; Nayak, astonished, bares his chest to show the scar and wants to know if his assailant is alive. The astrologer, addressing him by name (to his further surprise), adds that his assailant is now dead and that he, Guru Nayak, should go back to his village and live out his life peacefully. To placate the still angry Nayak, who demands to know if the assailant met the kind of death he deserved, the astrologer replies that he was crushed under a lorry (truck). Nayak pays him the fee and hurriedly departs. The astrologer returns home late to his anxious wife and gives her the money he earned that day, adding that it all came from one client. The wife is happy but notices a slightly changed expression on her husband's face; she asks him if there is something wrong. "Nothing," he says but after dinner tells her that he is relieved that the man he thought he killed in a drunken brawl many years earlier is, in fact, alive. He says that it is late and goes to sleep on a pyol (mat).

Themes and Meanings

The story turns on a most important human weakness: the desire to know the future. This weakness is greater among the sick, the suffering, and the poverty-stricken. In a poor country such as India, astrologers, palmists, and numerologists, as well as others who claim to know the future (for example, fortune-tellers assisted by birds in drawing cards), assume a great significance in society. Fortune-tellers offer hope to those leading tragic lives, giving them reason to continue their existence, and offer solace where it otherwise does not exist. They also find a means of survival in taking advantage of the misfortunes of millions, by listening to their tales of woe (particularly significant in a culture where psychiatrists are not common and would not command confidence even if they were). Astrology, in particular, has played a crucial role in the lives of many, and has long been an integral part of Indian life (so much so that, tradition has it, the horoscopes not only of Buddha—who lived five hundred years before the birth of Christ—but even of epic heroes dating back at least a thousand years before Christ have been maintained). In "An Astrologer's Day," Narayan not only touches on a tradition that has existed since antiquity but also comments on its debased modern version. Emphasizing a social reality, Narayan exploits, with a comic eye, a common foible of Indians and writes a happy-ending story with a double twist and double surprise. The astrologer in the story is not a Brahman (a traditional astrologer) but one of the more common kind found on the roadside who has been forced to run away from an appointed role to a new destiny, and who adroitly uses the opportunity to thwart permanently a calamity that was hanging over his head. Even as others have their ups and downs, the astrologer has his ups and downs in life, and as the narrator says, "He knew no more of what was going to happen to others than he knew what was going to happen to himself next minute." In the story, significantly enough, the astrologer's would-be assailant unwittingly comes to the man whom he is seeking in revenge and misses the opportunity to kill him. Astrology deflects him from his violent purpose, giving him the illusion of tasting revenge, and also helps the astrologer to resolve an old, burning conflict; so, both are happy.

Style and Technique

"An Astrologer's Day" is the title story of a collection by Narayan published in 1947 (in Great Britain but not in the United States); it is also the first story in *Malgudi Days* (1982), a retrospective volume that includes stories from several decades. It is typical of Narayan's work not only in its themes but also in its style and structure.

The distinctive appeal of Narayan's stories derives in part from tension between their strong emphasis on plot and their extreme brevity. "An Astrologer's Day," like most of Narayan's stories, is very short, less than five pages long. Most modern short stories of its length are sketches, tending toward the plotless; in contrast, Narayan's stories almost always have a clear dramatic action in which (in Narayan's words) "the central character faces some kind of crisis and either resolves it or lives with it."

"An Astrologer's Day" features a plot twist worthy of O. Henry, but the brevity and conciseness of the tale and its low-key ending save it from the air of contrivance to which O. Henry was prone. Also notable is the irony that can be appreciated only in reading—particularly the exchange in which the astrologer assures Guru Nayak that his enemy met the fate he desired.

K. S. Narayana Rao

ASTRONOMER'S WIFE

Author: Kay Boyle (1902-1992)
Time of plot: A summer around 1930
Type of plot: Domestic realism
Locale: A European mountain villa
First published: 1936

> *Principal characters:*
> KATHERINE AMES, the protagonist
> MR. AMES, her husband, an astronomer
> THE PLUMBER

The Story

Early in the morning, Katherine Ames steps quietly out of bed, trying not to disturb her husband—who either is still asleep or pretends to be. Mrs. Ames—as she is called throughout the story—comes "into her own possession" by beginning the day with brief exercises. She will stay busy with household duties, deeply ingrained habits that absent her from her husband's constant, unknowable silence.

Silence is her astronomer husband's dominant characteristic. The couple's relationship is built on the understanding that he is a man of the mind, who spends his days studying, meditating, contemplating the heavens through his rooftop telescope, or wandering through the mountains. His constant silence informs his wife that she is part of his life only in the sense that man is "the new arching wave, and woman the undertow that suck[s] him back." Mrs. Ames feels chided and shamed by her husband's silence, which constantly reminds her that he is preoccupied with mysterious ideas that she can never comprehend. As a result, she has forgotten her youth; no light shines from her gray eyes.

The serving girl announces the arrival of the plumber, who has come to repair an overflowing toilet. Mrs. Ames discusses the problem with him in a grave, dignified manner. She delicately avoids using the name of the offending appliance, referring to it not as "the wash basin," but as "the other." After studying the situation, the plumber suggests that the pipes are stopped up, rebukingly adding that the problem would not have occurred if there were a valve. During this discussion, Mrs. Ames speaks in nervous, hushed tones, reminding the plumber that her sleeping husband should not be disturbed. She is unsettled by the "relentless eye" of the plumber, who has been looking at her directly. His face softens a bit as he tells her he will check the pipes from the drain opening in the garden.

Suddenly, from behind the closed bedroom door where he has listened to the plumbing conversation, the astronomer's voice rings out (the only time in the story that he speaks): "Katherine! . . . There's a problem worthy of your mettle!" Her only apparent reaction to his scorn is the heightened color of her face, which the plumber notices as they step into the sunlit garden, which is full of a profusion of flowering plants.

For the first few moments in the garden, Mrs. Ames is in despair, still hearing her husband's taunt. She tells herself that a man's mind is concerned with great problems, dreams, and illusions, rather than with tangible things, while for woman, life is like the ocean where she must cling to floating debris for survival. When she looks down she sees the plumber gazing up at her from the trapdoor to the drains. His hair is "as light as gold." He suggests in a bitter voice that perhaps her husband, a man of knowledge, would like to come down into the drains. Confused, Mrs. Ames responds that her husband never goes downward, only up—on rooftops or mountaintops. She notices the plumber's lean, rugged build, his firm, clean, and tanned flesh. She can understand his strong hands holding the trapdoor rings.

Like a star, the plumber's light-gold hair glows from down in the drain. Understanding what this man is saying to her about the stopped-up elbow drain, Mrs. Ames is surprised to be able to comprehend anything that a man says. She sits motionless on the ground trying to make sense of this discovery that some men go "up" and others "down." She concludes that her husband is "the mind," this other man "the meat," of all humankind.

When the plumber emerges from the drain, Mrs. Ames questions him softly, looking up at him as he answers, smiling, that the elbow joint can easily be fixed, as can "everything a-miss." She begins to feel youth and delight as he talks of problems solved, his eyes full of "insolence, or gentleness, or love." Mrs. Ames stands up and calls the servant, telling her to report to Mr. Ames that she has gone "down." Then she enters the earth with the plumber, knowing that what he has said is true.

Themes and Meanings

Kay Boyle is especially well known for her intense psychological portrayals of people who long for meaning and love in a disordered world. In that vein, "Astronomer's Wife" is concerned with the relationships between men and women and the effects of emotional manipulation and control. The important men in Mrs. Ames's life have apparently all been cold and domineering. She assumes that all men are like her husband, who makes her feel that men are strong, intelligent, and important, while women are weak, incompetent, and irritating. When Mr. Ames makes his only utterance, he reaffirms his idea that his wife is spiritually incapable of understanding anything more complicated than a stopped-up drain. This insult has a double effect: It undermines Mrs. Ames's already-shaky self-confidence, thus reinforcing her dependence on him, and it announces her general inadequacy to the plumber and the servant.

For obvious reasons, Mrs. Ames prefers her husband's usual ominous silence to his actually speaking to her. His silence keeps distance between them and reminds her constantly of his superiority. Her mental and emotional state, as a result, is characterized by confusion, frustration, loneliness, and ineffectualness. The plumber, a man of sensitivity, holds out a metaphoric hand to rescue her. At first, he is brusque in discussing the plumbing problem; however, after hearing Mr. Ames's humiliating remark to his wife, he feels compassion for Mrs. Ames and anger toward her husband. Initially, when the plumber looks directly at Mrs. Ames, it disturbs her. Gradually, however, she grows more aware of him as a man and realizes that he is entirely different from her husband. When she consciously decides to go down into the drains with the plumber, she frees herself from the bondage that her husband has imposed on her. Love, hope, and meaning have come back into her life.

Style and Technique

Boyle's short stories are characterized by fluency of language, whose fresh, striking images and metaphors give her characters' lives a sense of immediacy. This story unfolds through a gradual revelation in relation to these metaphors rather than through crises of action. For example, the occupations of the astronomer and the plumber are metaphorically significant. An astronomer is concerned with a study of heavenly bodies, and as such, has his eyes fixed upward. Boyle's astronomer seems completely disconnected, mentally and spiritually, from earthly matters. Furthermore, he keeps himself physically remote from even his wife, seldom speaking to her. Throughout the entire story, he remains behind his bedroom door. Mrs. Ames realizes—and tells the plumber—that her husband only goes "up," never "down."

The plumber's vocation suggests several things about his role. A plumber's attention is fixed, literally, on the earth—buried pipes and drains and such. This story's plumber, who remains nameless, seems completely at ease with his strong, capable body and with his mission in the cavernous drain. He goes "down" readily into the earth and speaks to Mrs. Ames from within the drain. Amazed, Mrs. Ames sits "down" on the grass, and during a meditative few moments, begins to see the plumber, always "down," as a symbol of the physical body of man, in contrast to her husband, always "up," representing man's mind. Through simple word choice—"up" and "down"—Boyle represents opposing planes of living. As she and the plumber enter the earth together, he has begun, metaphorically, to plumb the depths of her despair and will remedy it as easily as he repairs drains, with simple human love and communication.

Judith Callarman

AT THE BAY

Author: Katherine Mansfield (Katherine Mansfield Beauchamp, 1888-1923)
Type of plot: Domestic realism
Time of plot: The early twentieth century
Locale: New Zealand
First published: 1922

> *Principal characters:*
> LINDA BURNELL, a woman who embodies a female mystique
> STANLEY BURNELL, her husband
> ISABEL, their oldest daughter
> KEZIA, their middle daughter, much like her mother in temperament
> LOTTIE, their youngest daughter
> MRS. FAIRCHILD, Linda's beloved mother, the stabilizing female force in the household
> BERYL FAIRCHILD, Linda's unmarried younger sister
> ALICE, the servant girl

The Story

Although written four years later, "At the Bay" was conceived as a continuation of "Prelude." Like the earlier story, "At the Bay" is organized around time in all of its various aspects, the design of the story functioning symbolically as part of the overall meaning that derives from the integration of themes. The story begins at the moment the sun rises over Crescent Bay and concludes on the evening of the same day.

The meticulous record of that day in terms of time and the household routines of the Burnell family provides a summary of the action of the story, the careful delineation of sequential time causing plot to become symbolic action. Stanley, the first to arise, goes to the beach to swim in the bay, but he finds his brother-in-law, Jonathan Trout, there before him. After his swim, Stanley returns to the cottage and dresses while breakfast is being prepared by Beryl and Mrs. Fairchild. Stanley allows twenty-five minutes to have breakfast with them and the children. Linda remains in bed. After much frenzied activity, Stanley leaves for work, and the children are sent out to play. The women relax with another cup of tea. At exactly eleven o'clock, they all go to the beach—except Linda, who sits in the garden while the new baby sleeps. The children play at the beach with their cousins, Rags and Pip, and Beryl, despite her mother's disapproval, leaves the family group to swim with Mrs. Harry Kember.

After lunch, Mrs. Fairchild and the children take an afternoon rest. Beryl washes her hair and then goes out to play bridge with Mrs. Kember. Alice, the servant girl, has the afternoon off and goes into town to visit with Mrs. Stubbs. After tea, the children go out to play in the garden, while Mrs. Fairchild gives the baby his bath. Linda walks in the garden until sunset, when Jonathan comes to take the boys home, and Stanley returns from the city. After dinner the day has ended for everyone except Beryl, who, late at night, after everyone is asleep, walks with Mr. Kember in the garden.

Although in both "Prelude" and "At the Bay" it is difficult to name a protagonist (all the female characters seem to merge into a collective identity, with each single character suggesting an aspect of the female psyche), if it is necessary to name a protagonist, it is arguable that in "At the Bay" Beryl emerges as the principal figure. For Beryl, the day is one of disquieting discovery and frustrated attempts to find a life and a lover of her own.

Early, at breakfast, Stanley is aware that something is wrong with Beryl. She is unmindful of him and cross with Kezia. Her mood changes when she stops the coach and has the chance to talk and laugh with one of the passengers. She is happy to have Stanley leave, to be free from his demands and authority. At the beach, Beryl disregards her mother's wishes and moves beyond the family circle to join Mrs. Harry Kember. Fascinated by what she sees as masculine qualities in Mrs. Kember, Beryl becomes shy and reckless. Defiant of the other women on the beach, she undresses boldly and goes into the water with Mrs. Kember. For Beryl, Mrs. Kember's face in her black bathing cap as it emerges from the water is an image of Satan, constantly shifting form in a manner that is for Beryl both horrible and fascinating.

Later that night in her bedroom, Beryl recalls the day and in her imagination puts Mrs. Kember's compliments on the lips of a lover. In the midst of Beryl's fantasy, a real man appears, Harry Kember. When he calls to her, Beryl goes out to him, but she is not prepared for his aggressiveness, and she runs inside. Kember is a horrible caricature of a fantasy lover; the episode seems like a dark and disturbing dream.

Themes and Meanings

From the moment "At the Bay" opens, readers are introduced to the geographical area where the story takes place and to the emotional climate that will prevail. From the merging images of earth and sea arise the major symbol of the story. Throughout the narrative, the activities of the characters will be seen against the background of the rise and fall of the tides of the ocean, and, as in "Prelude," are in time with the movement of the sun and moon through the heavens. Life moves along a path between birth and death and is no more than the rising and setting of the sun. As the images of sea and earth merge, so life and death are unified; the manifestations of sex, male and female, merge also, so that distinctions disappear.

The opening paragraph of the story, in which sea and earth are merged, is a metaphorical statement of the mutability of time and life. In the microcosm, the members of the Burnell family react to the symbolic situation and setting with varying degrees of awareness and acceptance. In "Prelude," the house and garden are surrounded by the dark bush, and the story moves back and forth between them. In "At the Bay," the action moves in and out of the house to the sea and seashore. The characters continue the same concerns, seeking answers to the same questions.

Style and Technique
  One of the characteristic devices used by Katherine Mansfield in her fiction is the disruption of normal time sense. Often within a sequence of events defined in terms of clock time, Mansfield provides knowledge of another time, one not bound by ordinary rules of motion and space but rather existing apart from perception or the record of time passing. Thus, immediately at the beginning of "At the Bay," when Jonathan calls out to Stanley, the reader experiences a dislocation from normal sequential time. Jonathan's voice is totally unexpected as it booms over the water and thus destroys the normal time sequence, which has been carefully built up. Time doubles back; other doors are opened; another character has emerged and made his way to the water to join Stanley. The time in which this has happened is unexperienced by a reader because the author has not provided necessary sense data to fill in the interval.
  Another, and more striking, example of the disruption of the normal time sense, when time is stripped of its ordinal and metrical qualities, occurs in the scene with Linda in the garden under the manuka tree. In the garden there is an abrupt shift of geographical place that ignores the ordinary relationships of distance, time, and motion. Without transition in the narrative, Linda is seen as a child leaning against her father's knee. The reader's imagination accomplishes the sudden movement into past time because Linda's does, but simultaneously the reader is led to experience events that never took place, that existed only in Linda's imagination. As a result of this manipulation of time, the reader experiences a release from normal sequential time perception. The ordinal and metrical limitations are destroyed, and when they cease to exist, so do the boundaries that separate the real from the unreal and life from death.
  Mansfield's role in the development of the short story was profound. Concentrating on a single moment in time, eliminating a strongly plotted action fine, and using imagery and metaphor to expand the moment and give it significance beyond itself, Mansfield helped move the short story away from the formulaic, shaping it as an art form whose aesthetic value was sufficient to place it beside the other and older literary genres.

Mary Rohrberger

AT THE BOTTOM OF THE RIVER

Author: Jamaica Kincaid (Elaine Potter Richardson, 1949-   )
Type of plot: Pastoral
Time of plot: The mid-twentieth century
Locale: St. Johns, Antigua, West Indies
First published: 1982

> *Principal characters:*
> THE UNNAMED PROTAGONIST, at times the first-person narrator, a
> young adult woman
> THE UNNAMED MAN, and
> THE UNNAMED WOMAN, her parents at middle age, seen from a
> child's perspective

The Story

In the first of the six sections that constitute this story, the third-person narrator defines a "terrain" that is at once external and internal. From the mountains of its origin to the flat plain of its mouth, the river poses a philosophical riddle of its own cycle of creation and destruction, which awaits the human sensibility "that shall then give all this a meaning." The unnamed narrator then shifts abruptly to describe "a man who lives in a world bereft of its very nature." As an individual, the man is incapable of reconciling his own alienated existence with his participation in the larger cycles of natural and human history. He "cannot conceive" of a contentment that comes from "the completeness of the above and the below and his own spirit resting in between." Further, he is unaware even of his own alienation or of a contradiction within him; consequently, he "sits in nothing, in nothing, in nothing."

Although the second section continues the third-person narration, the mood and tone of the narrative voice become more familiar, even autobiographical, than they were in the first section. The scene shifts to a detailed but detached domesticity: a man, his wife, and his child. As the father, a skilled carpenter and a subsistence farmer, contemplates what he has accomplished, he meditates on the joy and futility that seem to possess him: "First lifted up, then weighed down—always he is so." He delights in the beauty of ordinary events—the color of a sunset, the flight of birds, and the dance of insects—but he mourns the passing of the natural world. Despite a loving family and his domestic stability—he has built his own house, read books, planted fruit trees, educated his child, and provided food—the father seems to stand uncertainly "on the threshold" of spiritual identity, for he "imagines that in one hand he holds emptiness and yearning and in the other desire fulfilled." Analogous to the first section, which offered a universalized figure, this section offers a particular man who succumbs to the futility of an amorphous but vast silence, to "Nothing."

As the third section begins, the tone becomes even bleaker: The narrator recites a litany on the inevitability, the ultimacy of death. The mood deepens from futility to despair as the narration changes in mid-paragraph to the first-person interior monologue of the man, who decides that "life is the intrusion," and, subsequently, so, too, is his sense of beauty and truth in his own accomplishments and in his love for his family, an intrusion into the absolute context of death. Sorrow, grief, and regret as well as joy, innocence, and knowledge are "bound to death." The speaker here, however, claims to regret, not this awareness of the pervasive presence of death, but the powerlessness of "my will, to which everything I have ever known bends." The fragility of human will and achievement constitutes despair, not the fact of death itself.

Midway through this third section, a folk parable intervenes in the manner of a riddle. An exotic caterpillar is stung by a honeybee; its pain becomes pleasure as it balances "remembering and forgetting" in its life "inside and outside" the mound in which it lives, until it vanishes, leaving only a faint glow in the darkness around it. The speaker, still in the first-person voice, says that she has "divined this" and wishes to share her knowledge with "a monument to it, something of dust"; yet this interior monologue is not that of the man, her father, but that of the daughter, who feels that she has been mocked by her father's explanation: "Death is natural." She rejects death as a natural occurrence: "Inevitable to life is death and not inevitable to death is life." In her own echoic parable, she describes—amid a tentative, majestic imagery—a worm (symbolic of death) overcome by a bird (symbolic of the soul's flight), but a boy enters the scene and shoots the bird with his bow and arrow. Bluntly, she concludes that the boy's own "ends are numberless." For the child's sensibility of the speaker, all life yields to death, but she rejects the inevitability as a natural process.

The brief fourth section clarifies the point of view of the first-person speaker, who now reveals the reflection in process: "I see myself as I was as a child." Here, focusing on the innocence of love in the memory of her mother rather than on the alienation of her father, the recollection is one of unquestioned contentment; yet the mature narrator notes that even as she sang harmoniously with other girls at a celebration, she and the others did so with "minds blank of interpretation." They were oblivious to an image of the grave within the song.

In the complex epiphany of the fifth section, the narrator stands on the river's bank looking below into the mouth of her own experience. At the bottom of the river, she sees a detailed vision of her childhood house, her personal memory, situated "near the lime-tree grove," her cultural memory. (Limes were a principal crop of the colonial economy.) In the motionless world that she views below, she realizes that she experiences "something new: it was the way everything lit up." This illuminated, expansive sense of the past brings her a sense of unity with her mother, the natural world, and her own destiny. As she watches the woman below looking to the horizon, she, too, sees what the woman sees: the simultaneous shining of the sun and the moon beneath the water. In the transparent light of the epiphany, "the sun was The Sun, a creation of Benevolence and Purpose," and "the moon, too, was The Moon, and it was the creation of Beauty and Purpose." Having symbolically reconciled her father's alienation (the sun) and her mother's innocence (the moon), her vision of harmony expands to embrace the whole of the natural world, and she is "blessed with unquestionable truth" in a "world not yet divided, not yet examined, not yet numbered, and not yet dead." Simply viewing this world, however, is not enough; she yearns to enter it in order to discover her purpose. Although still in the first person, the narrative perspective once again shifts—to a vantage point from the bottom of the river: "I stood above the land and the sea and looked back up at myself as I stood on the bank of the mouth of the river." Disassociated now from the egocentric self, the narrator sees herself merging with her cultural history and the natural world. Although she burns in transforming flames, she experiences herself as an enlightened, pure will over which she has "complete dominion," and she enters the sea, merging fearlessly with it to touch "the deepest bottom." In the freedom of "a mind conscious of nothing," she embodies the paradox of the creation of being out of nothingness. She becomes an unnamed medium of light, beyond contradiction and time, much like the glow of the caterpillar.

In the brief closing section, the narrator questions the new light of which she is made, a light that might lead her "to believe in a being whose impartiality I cannot now or ever fully understand and accept." From the "pit" of her paradoxically liberating repressed memories, primordial as well as personal and cultural, she steps into a room and, in the light of a lamp, sees a few simple things: books, clothes, a table and a chair, and a flute and a pen. At this moment, she knows that she is bound to the history of "all that is human endeavor" and to all that will perish without a trace. Uncertain but assured, she asserts the will to purpose that she has experienced as her spiritual identity: "I claim these things then—mine—and now feel myself grow solid and complete, my name filling up my mouth."

Themes and Meanings

What remains unanswered at the end of Jamaica Kincaid's imagistic yet abstract story is the question of the name that creates her identity anew. When the narrator's final persona emerges from her transforming vision at the bottom of the river, she accepts her own inevitability of death in the knowledge that she can create herself beyond it: She accepts the mature artist's role of creating works in the midst of a modern world marked by alienating futility. To achieve the confidence of the creative will, the narrator had to endure passage through a number of identities, which led from her own childhood innocence through the pain of both her father's and her own experience of pain and death to the uncertainty with which she must live. Seized by the reluctance to acknowledge the limits of creation, to face death, the narrator must immerse herself in the unconscious psychological and spiritual turmoil that she imagines in her father and experiences within herself.

The reader is privileged, then, to witness the birth of an artist and to experience—through an empathetic identification with the narrator—the struggle of the creative will to come into being. Obliquely autobiographical, the narrator describes an island world where natural beauty threatens to overwhelm the creative energies of humanity. Constrained by an implied experience of isolating poverty, the narrator knows too well the agony of her father's alienation and the futility that has imprisoned him. Consequently, once she can move beyond the naïve rejection of death, created by the sheltering love for and from her parents, the narrator is free to enter the sea, symbolic of both the unconscious and death itself. Her epiphany is the dissolution of the ego and the death of the body, a vulnerability that, conversely, opens new possibilities of power; experiencing primordial, cultural, and personal unity, she is capable of seeing herself anew, organizing an informed innocence—through her creations—of light, the spiritual awareness of truth, which she now reflects to achieve beauty and purpose. Nothingness, however, has been prerequisite to that light; interpretation and meaning originate in darkness, consistently calling the self into question. To create being is to name it, and to name is to engage continuously in the creative will necessary to both aesthetic and spiritual being: They are one and the same. The artist overcomes death by creating even as the creations disappear into death, into nothingness. The artist achieves the will to purpose by giving up the will to immortality, thereby—paradoxically—gaining immortality for the creative process itself.

Style and Technique

Kincaid's style embodies the very process of creation that the story describes, for she re-creates elements from traditional and modern genres. On one hand, she draws on the pastoral mode of the idyll, framing scenes of a rural, tranquil beauty that are emblematic of a simple happiness; yet, in contradiction, she further extends her pastoral images into biblical echoes of incantatory repetitions to emphasize the complexity of those magical moments of earthly content. Moreover, she evokes the historical development of the idyllic mood, perhaps reminiscent of Robert Browning's *Dramatic Idyls* (1879-1880), to juxtapose psychological crisis and the innocent rapture of the Caribbean folktale. On the other hand, the haunting images and fractured narrative voices recall the surrealism of the early twentieth century, which sought to heal, through disruption of ordinary perception, the fragmented consciousness of modernity. With narrative perspective that ranges from a detached observer through the alienated unconscious of the father to the naïve, the disembodied, and the mature selves of the narrator herself, these rapidly transforming personas demonstrate the very growth—through creation and dissolution—of the artist.

Kincaid's creative process, then, consists of reconstructing the various elements of passing traditions and "monuments," works of art, in a "terrain" that contradicts them, within the creative will and without, on the page (the story at hand), so that what constitutes making something new is also the unmaking of it, which, in turn, is the preservation of the traces of the past. The author achieves exactly what the young girl wishes to do in remembering the caterpillar and inventing the story of the boy who kills the bird: She compounds a compressed, concise language that is at once intensely concrete and profoundly abstract into a self-definition of the artist and, in so doing, illuminates the contentment in the process of fiction itself. However, to underscore the death of the author, she appears as the mature artist only when the fiction is complete.

Michael Loudon

AT THE JIM BRIDGER

Author: Ron Carlson (1947-   )
Type of plot: Domestic realism, frame story
Time of plot: The 1990's
Locale: The Cascade wilderness and a resort lodge
First published: 2000

> *Principal characters:*
> DONNER, a man on a fishing trip
> HIS MISTRESS, who accompanies him on the trip
> RUSTY PATRICK, a man Donner once saved from freezing

The Story

In "At the Jim Bridger," Donner has just come out of the mountains after a week fishing with a woman identified only as "not his wife." They are looking forward to eating a huge steak and a baked potato at the Jim Bridger Lodge's end-of-season New Year's Eve party. As the couple pulls into the parking lot of the lodge, Donner sees a familiar truck with a dog he recognizes in the back. He tells the woman that it is the dog from the story he has told her about saving a man from freezing; when they enter the lodge, he sees Rusty, the man from the story. Although he is not sure why, Donner feels differently about the woman from the way he did before they went on the fishing trip; he feels "ruined and hollow."

In September of the previous year, on his annual fishing trip, Donner was trapped by a snowstorm in the Cascades and made a bad decision. It is now his favorite story. Seven months earlier, he told it to the woman who was not his wife, "and it was the story that kindled all of the rest." The bad decision Donner made was to break camp in the afternoon during a steady snowfall instead of staying where he was and waiting for the storm to stop. That particular year, he felt a special pressure, for his fourteen-year-old son had run away. Donner soon knew that he had made a mistake because the snow was so heavy he could not see the trail. He stopped and built a large fire and took off all his clothes and hung them to dry. At this point, a dog burst into the ring of light made by the fire and a man followed it, saying, "Well, here's Adam. Is Eve in the tent?"

The man, Rusty Patrick, a thirty-three-year-old truck driver, told Donner about falling in love with a woman dispatcher, Darlene, where he worked. However, Rusty's boss became interested in Darlene and talked against Rusty until he split them up. Rusty said that with a broken heart, he bought a gun and came up to the mountains.

During the night, Rusty began to develop hypothermia. Donner cut off Rusty's damp underwear, slipped into his sleeping bag with him, and tried to revive him by massaging him and covering him with his own body heat. As Donner talked to Rusty, he began to talk to his son, telling him to come on home. He put Rusty's hands in the warmth between their legs and found himself sexually aroused. In the morning, the snow stopped, it began to warm up, and the two men walked out of the wilderness.

At the Jim Bridger Lodge, after Donner and the woman finish their meal, Rusty sees them and hugs Donner. The woman tells Rusty she has heard the wonderful story, but Donner has not told her about the sexual arousal he felt when he and Rusty spent the night naked in the sleeping bag. Rusty asks about Donner's son and is happy to find out that the boy returned. While Rusty and the woman dance during the New Year's Eve party, Donner goes outside with Rusty's dog and watches a huge bull moose standing on the other side of a pond.

Themes and Meanings

Although he has published two novels, Ron Carlson is one of those rare writers who has remained true to the literary form he seems to love best and at which he excels— the much-maligned short story. "At the Jim Bridger" is the title story of his fourth collection, published in 2002.

Echoing many short-story writers before him, Carlson considers each story he writes an investigation and a surprise. For example, he has said that when the woman tells Rusty she has heard the wonderful story about the rescue, it surprised the writer himself, for he did not realize that he was writing a story about stories. In many ways, the nature of story is one of the predominant themes of "At the Jim Bridger." The story Donner tells the woman who is not his wife about being caught in a snowstorm and saving Rusty by keeping him warm is what began their affair. Similarly, the story that Rusty tells Donner about losing his girl to his boss is a story that bonds them in the sleeping bag in the snow.

The woman's love for Donner results in part from the story he tells her. However, when he sees Rusty's pickup in the parking lot, he senses something false in his relationship with the woman, something not as genuine as the night in the sleeping bag with Rusty. That the erotic experience with Rusty seems more real than his sexual experience with the woman does not suggest that Donner has homosexual longings. His lying down flesh to flesh with Rusty is a life-or-death experience, and the erotic nature of the encounter is not narrowly sexual but somehow broadly mythical.

Donner told the woman the story to seduce her, but he now feels that this use of the story has cheapened it. At the end of the story, as Rusty and the woman dance in the New Year and Donner goes outside and watches the magnificent moose across the lake, he thinks that to use the story as he had, "to show it to her, burn it like a match, had led to this new darkness and the longer night."

It would be easy to oversimplify Donner's encounter with Rusty either by reducing it to the perhaps meaningless term of latent homosexuality or by putting it in the category of masculine bonding typical of locker-room banter and towel slapping. However, Carlson risks this, and by his no-nonsense style and the very seriousness with which he describes the encounter, he succeeds in suggesting that an erotic experience can occur between two men without being narrowly sexual and can instead lead to a profound realization of what it means to hold someone else as if it meant life or death.

"At the Jim Bridger" suggests that genuine stories about such bonding encounters, regardless of the gender of those engaged in them, are all people have to protect them from the cold that surrounds them.

Style and Technique

Carlson says that the title story of *At the Jim Bridger* is his tribute to Jack London's "To Build a Fire" (1902). However, its tight-lipped style, its focus on doing things with care, and its emphasis on telling a story well make it a more likely descendant of Ernest Hemingway's "Big Two-Hearted River" (1925). Donner is a Hemingway character who does everything with care, with a kind of exactness that borders on ritual. He tells the story of his encounter with Rusty with the same kind of precision that he uses in the wilderness to build a fire. When he told the story well, "something in him knitted up taut and he felt centered and ready." This sense of exactitude, of getting it just right, is part of the Hemingway style that dominates the story. Moreover, there is the same sense of the significance of being "alone in real places," often suggested by Hemingway. The tight-lipped style in which the story is told reflects the masculine bonding theme that holds it together.

The Hemingway style can most clearly be seen in Carlson's description of the physical encounter between Rusty and Donner in the sleeping bag. After Donner takes Rusty's hands and puts them in his own groin to give them warmth, "he felt himself stirred, a reflex he gave in to." Donner identifies Rusty with his son and wants to rescue him with his own body, for as he talks to Rusty he also talks to his son. As Rusty falls asleep in Donner's arms, "Donner knew that Rusty had taken him into his hands and they were together that way in the mountain tent."

The story that Rusty tells Donner makes him sick, for he imagines the boyish Rusty being betrayed by his boss, an older man he saw as a father figure. The seemingly irrelevant story of Donner's son running away is actually a reflection of Donner's seeing Rusty as a son who has been betrayed by a father and who now can be rescued by another father. These parallels, like the parallel of the two fishing trips, create a balanced structure of significance for the story.

Charles E. May

AUNT CARRIE

Author: Rita Dove (1952-   )
Type of plot: Social realism
Time of plot: The mid-twentieth century
Locale: An unnamed city and Fort Myers, Florida
First published: 1985

> *Principal characters:*
> THE UNNAMED NARRATOR
> AUNT CARRIE, her father's sister
> ERNEST PRICE, her father
> BELLE PRICE, her mother
> SAM ROGERS, Aunt Carrie's dead husband
> EDNA ROGERS, Sam's first wife
> GRANDMA EVANS, Belle Price's mother

The Story

"Aunt Carrie" is told in two parts, first from the perspective of the narrator as a child and later as the childhood experience is re-evaluated by the narrator as an adult.

The setting for the first portion of the story is a train station. The nine-year-old narrator is excited by her first visit to a train station. She is awed by the dark and noisy trains and by her imaginings of Pittsburgh, the point of departure for her father, whom she, her mother, and her Aunt Carrie have come to meet. Ernest Price has been away attending a convention and is about to return. Before her father's train arrives, the girl is confused by the odd behavior of her mother, who is acting tense and speaking in a weird tone of voice; somewhat inexplicably, she has brought Aunt Carrie along to the station.

The young narrator has difficulty believing that her aunt is just a few years older than her mother although she realizes that Aunt Carrie is not considered physically attractive, and that she seems old and worn. She senses that the older woman wears lipstick to make herself pretty but that her effort is ineffective. Part of her impressions are formed by offhand negative comments about Aunt Carrie that her mother has made, so her own views of her aunt are not sympathetic.

When her father arrives, the girl runs into his arms. While he holds her, something happens among the adults that she does not understand. Aunt Carrie seems upset; pulling distractedly on a hankie, she is covered by her coat and retreats behind the large pregnant physique of Mrs. Price, where the girl can barely see her. Belle Price confronts her husband, but her words are meaningless to the child. She refers to Aunt Carrie as his "lovely sister" and informs Mr. Price that she once read a letter that Aunt Carrie wrote to him years ago. All three adults are immobilized by this announcement, and the child fears that her parents are about to have an argument. Her father looks like he is about to cry, and Aunt Carrie is actually crying. She decides that it was not nice of her mother to call Aunt Carrie lovely when she is not, and that this must be the source of the tension.

The story then shifts from the vignette at the train station to a moment years later, when the narrator is grown up and living in the same city as Aunt Carrie. She has just asked Aunt Carrie to tea. Their dialogue sheds light on the cryptic scene on the station platform and answers some other questions about her parents that have stayed in the narrator's mind.

Soon after the incident at the station the narrator and her parents moved to Florida, and the narrator has always wondered why. She asks Aunt Carrie if she knows. After some encouragement, Aunt Carrie tells her niece her family history: how her father deserted their family when she was thirteen and how she raised her younger brother Ernest while her mother and the older siblings went out to work. Homely and untalented, she had little status within the family. At seventeen she was married off to an older man and kept house for him until he died. Left a widow without means at nineteen, she moved back into her mother's home. One day while hanging laundry there, she was forcefully attracted to a young man coming down the street.

As she recalls this attraction and the sensuality and sexual consummation that accompanied it, the story is revealed to be a tale of incest, for it is her brother Ernest with whom she became involved. After confessing this secret, she tells her niece that she ended the affair because she realized it was crazy. Ernest went on to meet and marry the narrator's mother and to establish a successful career and family. Carrie then became the caretaker of the neighborhood, baby-sitting her brother's and other children, and generally being available for people in need. After Carrie and Ernest left the brief incestuous period of their lives behind them, it came to seem as if it had actually happened to other people. When Ernest was away in Pittsburgh, his wife discovered a letter that Carrie had written to him after their first sexual encounter, reassuring him about his worth and encouraging him to hold his head up with pride. All this immediately preceded the encounter at the train station, the move to Florida, and Carrie's ostracism from the family.

The narrator then asks Carrie how she knew the details about her mother's finding her letter. Carrie explains that after the narrator's maternal grandmother, Grandma Evans, was widowed, she called Carrie one day, befriended her, and told her the story. The story of Aunt Carrie ends with the niece and the aunt bonded together and the narrator pledging to see Carrie again in the future.

Themes and Meanings

Rita Dove's story is about the senses and human passions, most especially love, mercy, compassion, anger, and unforgivingness. It is also a story of awakening and memory, of the revision of a childhood incident into a mature adult context, and the breaching of alienation as various characters reach out to one another in different ways. It is a tale of identity, most importantly Aunt Carrie's identity, the perception of which changes markedly from beginning to end.

As in much of her poetical work, Dove takes her themes and meanings from the context of family history. One major theme of "Aunt Carrie" is the passage of knowledge, memory, and respect from one generation to another through oral tradition or the telling of a tale.

Style and Technique

When asked why she uses the details of the everyday and familiar in her writing (in "Aunt Carrie," a cup of tea, the roses on a hankie, the smell of pomade, a bedsheet blowing in the wind, or the touch of a dry palm), Dove has explained that the more specifics you know about someone, the harder it is for you to kill that person. Poetry, she says, springs right out of life and makes you feel more connected. So it is with "Aunt Carrie."

There are two references, one in each part of the story, to the narrator's love of drawing. This is used as a literal and metaphoric device: The picture the girl draws of her father in the first part of the story serves to show that the Ernest that the child knows is a different person from the one with whom Carrie is so familiar. The narrator draws out Aunt Carrie in the second part of the story, gently pleading with her to tell her the truth behind her parents' actions. Indeed, the story is crafted like a drawing— the first part functions as a sketch or framework that is later filled in with detail. The first section is sketched from the "outside," through the astute observations of the child. The true meaning of what she has observed is then revealed through the carefully wrought confessions of Aunt Carrie. As she tells her tale the narrator and the reader learn the specifics of Aunt Carrie's life, its pathos, and its yearnings and losses. In the process Aunt Carrie is transformed. When she first appears, she is an unattractive, cowering figure about whom not much is known and who exists on the fringes of the scene, obscured by the dominant and controlling position of the narrator's mother. In the second part of the story, rather than reacting to others, she is the actor or central figure, and we come to see things from her point of view. Through the details of her life she is sympathetically transfigured into a fully human and humane person whose experience has been tragic. Through the telling of her life some of the exile and ostracism she has experienced at the hands of the narrator's unforgiving mother is healed. Her niece, in effect, takes her back into the family and reverses the invisibility to which she has been subjected by reaching out to her after she has heard her story and telling her she wants to see her again. Identity is revealed and coupled with identification. Similarly, Grandma Evans, widowed and alone, knows of the taboo that has been broken but can identify with Aunt Carrie's loneliness, and befriends her, leaving the past behind them.

Barbara J. Bair

AUNT GRANNY LITH

Author: Chris Offutt (1958-   )
Type of plot: Regional
Time of plot: The 1960's and 1980's
Locale: The Appalachian Mountains of eastern Kentucky
First published: 1990

> *Principal characters:*
> BETH, an Appalachian mountain woman
> CASEY, her husband
> NOMEY, her mother
> LIL, a neighbor woman
> AUNT GRANNY LITH, a wizened witchlike woman who lives in
>   the woods

The Story

This modern folktale of the Appalachian Mountains of eastern Kentucky begins in the present time with Beth retrieving her drunken husband from the clutches of a local woman of dubious reputation. Casey has made his yearly batch of moonshine and has gone on a two-week bender, ending up at the house of Lil, their nearest neighbor. After a knockdown, hair-pulling fight between the two women, Beth begins the trip home with Casey but has an accident that sends the pickup truck into the creek.

When Beth walks the two miles home to get the mule and some chains to pull the truck out, the story shifts to the past, when Casey's first wife died the day after they were married from a broken branch that pierced her face and when his second wife was found dead of a broken neck at the bottom of a cliff. A year after his second wife's death, Casey met Beth, but her mother, Nomey, warned her he was hexed and gave her a charm to wear. After the wedding, Beth saw an old woman with ragged clothes and long hair scurry into the woods near her house. She followed the old woman, who crawled into a hollow log.

When she described the old woman to Casey, he told her a story of something that happened twenty years before when he and a friend were playing in the woods. When he saw his friend hiding in a log with his hand sticking out, he put a ring he had made from a buckeye with his initials on it on his friend's finger as a joke and said, "I take you as my wife . . . 'til death do us part." However, it was not his friend in the log but rather a dried-up little old woman. Beth's mother told her that the old woman was the last granny woman, or midwife, in the area, who stopped delivering babies when a hospital was built in the nearby town and who went to live in a cave with a log over the face of it.

After Beth became pregnant, she went to the cave and spoke to an unseen Granny Lith, telling her that Casey belonged to her, not to Granny. When she found what was left of the buckeye ring Casey put on Granny's finger, she knew that Granny still held Casey to his promise. Her mother told her the only way to break the promise was for him to go and spend the night with the old woman. After much urging from Beth, Casey stayed the night with Granny Lith and then lay in bed for two weeks with a fever. He told Beth that after he spent the night with Granny Lith, the old woman begged him to kill her.

The story then shifts back to the present with Beth pulling the truck out of the creek and rescuing Casey. That evening, with both of them safe in bed, she remembers the night Casey spent with Granny Lith and thinks they did the right thing; their four daughters are proof of it. The story ends with Casey and Beth making love.

Themes and Meanings

Although "Aunt Granny Lith" is a modern story about Appalachian folkways, its plot and theme derive from the ancient legend of "the demon lover." The tale has many variations, but the basic story involves a man or woman who makes a love promise to another. However, either because of an error, as in Chris Offutt's story, or because the loved one dies in battle, the one who makes the promise tries to break it. A typical plot line is that after several years of grieving, the loved one decides to marry someone else. Then on the day of the wedding, the ghost or corpse of the lover to whom the promise was made returns to claim the one who made the promise. In the anonymous poem "The Demon Lover," the lover comes to claim the woman who promised herself to him, even though she now is married and has two children. Soon after she sails with him she spies his cloven foot, and he breaks the ship in half, causing them to sink into the sea.

Another ancient story from which "Aunt Granny Lith" derives is the rabbinical legend of Lilith, who was Adam's first wife before Eve. When Lilith would not submit to Adam's wishes, she cursed him and went back to her home in the Red Sea, where she mated with demons and had demon children. From there she flies through the night to prey on children or to lie down with sleeping men. She has sometimes been said to be the wife or grandmother of Satan. In Offutt's story, Aunt Granny Lith is first associated with children through her role as a midwife and then with the boy Casey, who makes his mistaken promise to take her as his wife "'til death do us part."

The story's modern theme focuses on the strength of women to protect weak men from being lured away from their family responsibilities by temptation. First Beth rescues Casey from Lil, another form of Lilith, and then she rescues him from alcohol and from the accident in the creek. In the past, with the help of her mother, Beth saved Casey from the archetypal temptress woman Aunt Granny Lith, or Lilith. This is a story of archetypes, in which the man is weak and easily taken in by women, whereas women are of two types—the hard-to-resist temptress, who represents sexuality, and the strong and dependable wife, who represents the mother/protector. The superiority of women over men is indicated by Beth's mother, Nomey, when she says things are always harder for women than for men and that is why they are smarter than men.

Style and Technique

"Aunt Granny Lith" makes use of superstitions and folkways of the Appalachian Mountains to give this modern story of a woman trying to keep her man the archetypal authority of an oral folktale. To make the combination plausible, Offutt situates his story in a remote mountain area of eastern Kentucky where belief in the old ways is still quite strong. Nomey, Beth's mother, has knowledge of charms and tokens from her own mother and passes this knowledge on to Beth.

Although for the most part, the story seems to take place in the real world, albeit a world only lightly touched by modern civilization, there is still something supernatural about Aunt Granny Lith herself. Her old ways as a midwife have been superseded by the new hospital that has gone up in the region, and it may be plausible that she now lives in a cave. However, it is unlikely that she is able to maintain a hold on Casey without the story assuming some supernatural element, suggesting that Aunt Granny Lith has magical powers.

The story maintains a sense of plausibility while at the same time allowing something of the magical. Therefore, while not strictly a folktale, it is not strictly a modern realistic story either, but rather a careful balancing of both. The blending of the two elements is achieved by the dual time frame of the story. In the past, Casey has mistakenly pledged himself to another woman, the folklore figure of Aunt Granny Lith. In the present, Casey, now under the influence of alcohol, goes to the mythic descendant of Lith, named Lil. Just as Beth uses sympathetic magic in the old story, boiling the buckeye ring to bathe Casey clean after his one night with Lith, in the present story she throws the hair she has pulled from the head of Lil into the stream to free Casey from being drawn back to Lil.

The story ends with Beth providing the ultimate female "cure" for Casey's drinking and being tempted by other women—her own sexuality. The pervasive irony throughout the story is that whereas Casey thinks he is the strong one because he is a man, it is Beth who triumphs because of her feminine strength. The final indication of this irony occurs when Beth groans from a hip injury received during her fight with Lil and Casey says she always did hurt too easy. The final image of Beth is the knowing smile on her face as she embraces him.

Charles E. May

AUNT MOON'S YOUNG MAN

Author: Linda Hogan (1947-   )
Type of plot: Coming of age
Time of plot: The early 1950's
Locale: Rural Oklahoma
First published: 1988

> *Principal characters:*
> THE NARRATOR, a young Chickasaw woman
> AUNT MOON, an older Chickasaw woman who lives alone
> ISAAC, a young stranger who becomes involved with Aunt Moon

The Story

On an autumn day in rural Oklahoma a town prepares for its annual fair. The event attracts people from neighboring towns who have goods to sell, thereby breaking the monotony of life in Pickens. Among the new attractions in town is a magnetic young man whom the narrator immediately identifies as a full-blooded Indian. Remarking that most of the people in Pickens are of mixed blood, the narrator explains that she feels somehow inferior to a pure-blood. After the narrator and her mother eye the drifter, the narrator thinks about Aunt Moon, an older woman whom she admires.

Aunt Moon lives alone with her dog, Mister, in a house that her father built on a hill. There is something mysterious about Aunt Moon, who seems to have a special kind of vision, an ancestral wisdom. Aunt Moon dries medicinal herbs, upholding a tribal tradition that most townspeople have discarded. The narrator is attracted to Aunt Moon because the old woman seems more alive than the rest of the people in Pickens.

When the narrator and her cousins visit the fair, they see barnyard oddities such as chickens that lay green eggs. The narrator wants Aunt Moon to look at the strange chickens, but Aunt Moon seems distracted. The narrator realizes that Aunt Moon has spotted the young drifter and is drawn to him. That night the narrator's mother and father dress for a waltz contest. At the dance, the narrator notices that the local women seem especially animated because of the presence of the young man. When Aunt Moon arrives, she dances with the young man, causing the other women to raise their eyebrows and whisper. Soon, the town of Pickens is scandalized by the affair carried on between Aunt Moon and the young stranger. The women shun Aunt Moon in public but go to her in secret to buy her ancient remedies. The narrator's father forbids her from visiting Aunt Moon's house so long as the stranger, Isaac, is there.

At this point, the narrator digresses by telling the reader how she came to call Bess Evening by the name of Aunt Moon. Bess Evening seems to fit her nickname because sometimes she is full of strength and light and at other times seems pale and weak. The narrator's mother tells her the story of the freak accident that took the life of Aunt Moon's daughter. The narrator understands that her friend must cope with the tragedy each day of her life. Aunt Moon experiences another loss when her dog Mister, frightened by an electrical storm, runs through town twitching and crashing into things. Thinking that Mister has rabies, men shoot him. This new loss devastates Aunt Moon, but Isaac comforts her. By the next fall, Aunt Moon is pregnant and Isaac has disappeared. With Isaac gone, the local women are not jealous; they offer Aunt Moon their sympathy and cluck their tongues over what a snake Isaac has turned out to be. The narrator is looking through Aunt Moon's window, however, when Isaac returns. Aunt Moon and Isaac hold each other like true lovers. The narrator learns that Isaac has escaped from jail, where he was sent for selling illegal herbal remedies.

The story ends as the narrator sets out for Denver, where she will live with her cousins. She hopes to find work and go to school. Carrying a bag filled with Aunt Moon's herbs and an eagle feather wrapped in a scarf, she leaves Pickens not knowing whether she will ever be back.

Themes and Meanings

"Aunt Moon's Young Man" explores the theme of spiritual well-being. The role of storytelling, the importance of ancestry, the nature of relationships among women, and the difficulty of coming of age are all issues in the story that contribute to the narrator's development of inner strength.

Two kinds of storytelling exist side by side. Mean-spirited gossips spread the details of Aunt Moon's questionable parentage. This malicious narration seems to wound the communal spirit. By contrast, the narrator's mother tells stories about Aunt Moon's life that help the younger woman understand and respect her elder. The narrator's fascination with Aunt Moon is linked to her curiosity about the mostly forgotten ways of her tribe. Aunt Moon inherits from her parents the knowledge of the medicinal value of dried herbs. The narrator seems to understand that, in a quest for identity, one's heritage is an important area of investigation. Healing is not Aunt Moon's only power. She is a strong woman both physically and intellectually: The narrator respects her for her ability to deliver Holstein calves, as well as for her analysis of American culture. The narrator delights in this model of feminine strength. Aunt Moon sets an example that the young woman cannot find in any other person, even her mother.

The narrator's mother is a strong woman in the sense of being a stern authority figure. She seems to read her daughter's mind and rein in her fantasies. In contrast to Aunt Moon, who opens up new worlds, the mother represents restriction. Although the narrator may not revere her mother, she at least does not hold her in contempt, as she does the other women of Pickens. The narrator learns to despise the women in town because they are not loyal to one another and do nothing to foster an authentic sense of community. When the gossips turn on Aunt Moon, the narrator lashes out at them.

Estranged from her neighbors, uneasy around her mother, and unsure of her place in Aunt Moon's life now that the older woman has a lover, the narrator feels a sense of isolation in Pickens. She craves new experiences and opportunities—the kind that she hopes to find in Denver. This is the coming-of-age that the narrator is poised to undergo. She lets one of the local boys kiss her, but the experience seems hollow and pales in comparison to the image of passion she sees between Isaac and Aunt Moon. Her own passage is to be spiritual, not sexual. With her last words the narrator describes the "small, beautiful woman" in her own eyes. This is the emblem of feminine pride and strength that the narrator learned to see by watching Aunt Moon. By telling her own story, the narrator provides a role model for other women in search of self. She passes on the gift that Aunt Moon has given her.

Style and Technique

Linda Hogan is a poet as well as a fiction writer. It is with a poet's sense of imagery that she details the images in "Aunt Moon's Young Man." Description does double duty in this story, creating a tableau that is both earnestly real and deeply symbolic.

From the narrator's first descriptions of Pickens, the reader comes to understand that the Chickasaw are a people with inescapable and uneasy relationships to the land and the forces of nature. The livestock carted to the fair slump in the oppressive Oklahoma heat. Biting flies bring back not-too-distant memories of unpleasant days past. White chicken feathers remind the town of the cotton crop that has all but failed them. The air is still in the wake of a recent tornado, and thunderclouds on the horizon threaten to turn the dusty roads to mud. The environment is stagnant but expresses the potential for turmoil. The people of Pickens evidence a similarly paradoxical set of attitudes and emotions. They show the strain of monotony, yet seem poised to experience the chaos that the full-blooded drifter will create. Nature serves as an index for human behavior.

This fusion of physical and psychological elements becomes an important motif as the story progresses. One example of this is the description of the women avoiding Aunt Moon on the street. Hogan sends the gossips scurrying "like swallows swooping into their small clay nests." The swooping motion conveys the women's fear of the unique and sometimes powerful Aunt Moon. The small clay nests represent the narrowness of the women's minds and lives. The narrator employs just this sort of metaphor when she gives Bess Evening a name that corresponds to the many emotional phases that the older woman goes through. Linda Hogan's skillful use of poetic imagery lends a remarkable depth and texture to "Aunt Moon's Young Man."

Nick David Smart

AUNT ROSANA'S ROCKER

Author: Nicholasa Mohr (1935-   )
Type of plot: Domestic realism
Time of plot: The 1970's
Locale: New York City's Spanish Harlem
First published: 1985

>*Principal characters:*
>CASTO, a Puerto Rican immigrant
>ZORAIDA, his wife

The Story

Casto and Zoraida, two Puerto Rican immigrants living in New York, have been married for nine years and have four children. For two months, Zoraida has acted as if possessed by a demon lover during her sleep. As she moans and mimics sexual behavior in bed, Casto paces the floor in the next room trying not to hear her passionate sounds and vainly trying not to imagine her lascivious gestures. Casto married Zoraida because she was frail, sickly, and somewhat plain, not loud and coarse like other girls. He now believes that his wife's nightly behavior is lewd and vulgar, not the kind of behavior in which a decent husband and wife should engage. He believes that his wife enjoys her dream sex, and calls her a happy victim, an animal, and a hypocrite.

After telling his parents about how he is being cuckolded by a spirit possessing Zoraida, Casto is urged to take his wife to a spiritualist who can exorcise the demon lover that visits her nightly. Although the spiritualist's incantation works, Zoraida still does not become the kind of wife Casto wishes to have. Although she is a wonderful housekeeper and a devoted mother, serving dinner on time every night and attending to the children without any problem, whenever Casto approaches her for sex, she sits in a rocking chair and stares into space like a zombie. Casto calls another meeting of the family to help him decide what to do next. His mother, Dona Elvira, thinks that her healthy son is too good for the sickly Zoraida, and Dona Clara, Zoraida's mother, thinks that Casto is a brute of a man who does not deserve anyone as delicate as Zoraida.

Purencia, Casto's sister, thinks that it serves her mother right that because she never thought anyone was good enough for Casto, he now has a sickly wife. She is puzzled about Casto's problems with Zoraida and wonders if Zoraida, whom she calls goody two-shoes, is one of those quiet ones who hide the action. She is curious whether Zoraida is doing something about which nobody knows. Don Isidro, Zoraida's father, can only lament that his daughter still looks like a sickly child. Having been born prematurely, Zoraida was called a miracle baby by the doctors; thus, her parents gave her the middle name of Milagros. Confused by the marital difficulties between Casto and

Zoraida, Don Isidro thinks that his daughter is lucky to have found a man that would have her at all.

The rocking chair in which Zoraida sits when Casto wants sex originally belonged to her great-aunt Rosana, who was very beautiful and had many suitors. Part of her family history, the chair reminds Zoraida of Puerto Rico and is the one place where she now feels she can be herself and be free. Her parents decide that to solve Casto's marital problem they will take the chair back home with them. After they leave, Zoraida falls asleep thinking, as if she were her great-aunt Rosana, that she will not be able to sit in the chair any more and meet her suitors. When Casto comes to bed, he feels that a great burden has been lifted from him. He touches Zoraida but, finding her asleep, he turns over, thinking that he can always try again tomorrow.

Themes and Meanings

Stereotypical male expectations of female sexuality is the central subject of Nicholasa Mohr's story of Zoraida and her obsession with her dream lover and her great-aunt's rocking chair. The theme is first suggested by the fact that Casto believes that the kind of sex that Zoraida is having with her demon lover is not the kind of sex in which a decent husband and wife should engage. Although the story does not make explicit what Casto means by normal, healthy sex, it seems clear that it does not include a woman's wanton enjoyment of the sex act. Casto finds Zoraida's total delight in her hallucinatory sex acts disgusting. A hypochondriac who is obsessed with his health and who takes handfuls of vitamins and spoonfuls of tonic every day, Casto justifies his need for sex as necessary to keep him from becoming ill. He feels that he is the master of his home, but he will not touch Zoraida as long as she seems under the control of something unhealthy. Zoraida's enjoyment of sex makes Casto call her a whore and an animal, vulgar and common. When he married her, her shy behavior and ill appearance, like that of a "sick sparrow flirting with death," made him think of her as a lady.

Throughout the story, Casto insists on his rights as a man to have sex when and how he wants. Zoraida's conscious views about sexuality are not made clear in the story, but the fact that she can take pleasure in sex only while she is asleep, and therefore has no conscious control over her behavior, further suggests the stereotype that women are not supposed to enjoy sex but only to be concerned with what pleasure they give to their husbands. Although this is a common Western stereotype, Mohr suggests that it is particularly prominent in Hispanic cultures.

When Zoraida is denied her dream fantasy sex by the spiritualist, she retreats to the rocking chair every time her husband wants sex, becoming invisible or zombielike to him. Her mother tells her that women have to humor men, that they are like babies and that sex helps them relax. She recommends that Zoraida pretend that she like sex, for that makes men get it over with very quickly. Only at the end of the story does the reader fully realize that Zoraida has been possessed by the spirit of her great-aunt Rosana, a beautiful woman who had many lovers and who, therefore, embodies the kind of female freedom denied to Zoraida. When Casto comes to bed after the rocking chair has been taken away, he feels that he is once more in control of things. Retreating into her one remaining role, Zoraida tries not to think of the rocker or of Casto; she reassures herself that her children are safe in bed in the next room.

Style and Technique

The focus of "Aunt Rosana's Rocker" is primarily on Casto, but it is clear that the narrator's sympathy is with Zoraida, who is the victim of stereotypes that control her life. The story communicates these stereotypes primarily by focusing on Casto's sense of being treated as less than the man of the house, first by Zoraida's sexual pleasure with a dream lover and second by her retreating into the rocking chair and becoming invisible to him when he wants to have sex. Casto's macho expectations are presented by the narrator as if they are perfectly reasonable, and Zoraida has no right to her own pleasure or her own identity.

Although the story is told in a realistic style, the fact that a spiritualist is called in to exorcise the demon that seemingly has possessed Zoraida and, more important, the fact that the reader learns at the end of the story that Zoraida has somehow been taken over by the spirit of her dead great-aunt Rosana, suggest some of the elements of Magical Realism that characterizes the fiction of such Latin American writers as Isabel Allende. As Zoraida lies in bed at the conclusion of the story, she thinks that without the rocker she will not be able to sit there and meet all of her suitors. She recalls that the last time she sat in the chair she was dancing to a very slow ballad, but without the rocker she cannot remember it, nor can she sit in the rocker again and pick up her memory where she had left off the time before. Mohr purposely leaves the end of the story inconclusive. Although Casto feels confident that he can now have Zoraida sexually any time that he wants, Zoraida's final posture of lying in bed with her back turned toward him indicates that even without the rocking chair, she will continue to be invisible to Casto.

Mohr is one of the few Hispanic women in the United States to overcome the often-closed world of New York publishing to present realistic images of the situation of Hispanic women and children growing up in New York City. "Aunt Rosana's Rocker" is a fine example of Mohr's depiction of the Puerto Rican woman's struggle to overcome stereotypes of race and gender.

Charles E. May

AUTUMN IN THE OAK WOODS

Author: Yuri Pavlovich Kazakov (1927-1983)
Type of plot: Psychological
Time of plot: The 1950's
Locale: Northern Russia
First published: "Osen v dubovykh lesakh," 1961 (English translation, 1963)

Principal characters:
THE UNNAMED NARRATOR
HIS GIRLFRIEND

The Story

A young man living in a hut above the Oka River in northern Russia goes down to a makeshift dock, at which he is expecting a woman to arrive. He is apprehensive because he is not sure she will come. After he has waited anxiously for a few moments, the river boat finally docks, and she steps gingerly ashore. They are shy with each other at first as they climb the hill back to the hut, but the initial discomfort goes away as he shows her the beauties of the area even in the darkness, relying mostly on the sounds and smells. Using his lantern, he points out to her the white feathers of the chicken eaten by a fox and the mountain ash berries he uses to make his own vodka. Her reserved reactions reveal that she comes from a different region—that of the White Sea and the frozen tundra.

Back in the hut, the cozy stillness and the crackling fire enable them to deepen the friendship they fleetingly established when they first met in her native town on the North Sea. They are still awkward, however, as shown when she asks him to turn around while she is undressing and not to keep the light on all night. They listen to a jazz melody in English that comes over the radio from an unknown source. He interprets the various instruments as acting out an unknown drama, in a way resembling the quiet drama of their meeting in the oak forest. They talk and reminisce, finally falling asleep at dawn, while the first real snow of the autumn sprinkles the windows.

The day breaks sunny and cheerful, and they go out to explore the surrounding area. He proudly shows her the heifers grazing on the gray winter grain shoots, the hardly faded dandelions, frozen mushrooms, and various kinds of trees. Despite this bravado, it becomes apparent that he is anxious to impress her so she will not be disappointed and leave him. She allays his insecurity by agreeing that it is good there. When a tug appears on the Oka River and goes away—a potential harbinger of her departure—they look at it from above, "quietly, silently, as in a white dream." They are together at long last, and the rustic beauty around them mirrors their happiness.

Themes and Meanings

Yuri Pavlovich Kazakov was a leading short-story writer in the so-called thaw period in Russian literature from the 1950's through the 1970's when, after decades of

strict Communist Party control, writers felt free to write as they pleased and not follow party dictates. One group of writers concentrated on village life, presenting the
struggle of the peasants to preserve their moral fiber and to survive the intrusion of the
urbanites trying to remake their way of life. Another group depicted life in the big cities under the onslaught of political, moral, and technological progress. Kazakov positioned himself in the middle. Although most of his stories deal with urban characters
in their city environment, many of them want to escape from urban life and hope to
find solace in nature and the countryside. "Autumn in the Oak Woods" is a perfect example of such a balancing act.

It is not clear from the story why the young man, the protagonist and narrator, has
chosen to live away from big cities. There are indications that he once lived in a large
city or at least had an opportunity to do so, and his female companion comes from a
large city. However, they have come to the pristine environment of the countryside
and prefer it to the hustle and bustle of city life. Whether this is a rebellion against the
constraints of an urbanized society is not made clear, but judging from the pleasures
the two characters derive from their sojourn in the country and by their final decision
to stay there, it can be surmised that they are turning their backs on urbanization.

Their determination goes further than that. The characters not only prefer the country life but also approach the newfound, enjoyable ambience from an almost philosophical position. Their every step, word, and thought makes it clear that they are after
something much deeper than making a simple change. That something is a search for
a union with nature. They want to be a part of nature, not merely accidental visitors
and consumers. The young man enjoys his stay in the hut with every sight and sound
he perceives and every happening he witnesses. To him, everything is wonderful.
How glorious it is that his friend has arrived, that there is snow to greet her, that they
have a little music, and that everything is so promising. He draws hope and strength
from the beauty of nature, convinced that when he shows his friend the Oka River, the
fields, the hills, the forest, and the ravines, she will conclude that this is the place for
both of them to live and be happy.

Such an attitude does not stem from the mere enjoyment of the beauty in nature,
however. When he shows his friend the feathers of the chicken devoured by a fox, he is
not angry or vengeful and does not think first of killing the fox, as his friend, seemingly logically, suggests. He tacitly admits that a constant struggle for survival is a
part of nature, just as the white snow, the blue sky, and the steamy river are. His hut has
almost no furniture, only the necessities, just as nature is often frugal and functional.
All he needs is a tea kettle, a modest amount of food, a little radio music to keep him in
touch with the world, and the warmth of his beloved next to him. Even when he has
doubt about whether his friend will stay with him, he trusts nature to convince her, and
it turns out that he is right. His actions and gestures appear to be natural, as, for example, when he refuses to kiss his friend on her arrival in the light of the boat searchlight.

The characters sought the best place under the sun for themselves, and they found it
in nature, in the countryside away from big cities.

Style and Technique

Kazakov accomplishes his task and advances his main theme through an accomplished style and technique that have rendered him one of the best short-story writers in Russian literature. He begins his story with, "I took the pail to get water from the spring. I was happy that night because she was coming on the night boat." He then proceeds, step by step, through the important events of the plot: descending to the river dock, meeting his friend, bringing her back to the hut, and showing her around, while all the time worrying whether he could convince her to stay with him. When it finally is clear that she will stay, the reader feels the satisfaction of a completed story. At the same time, instead of telling everything to the last detail, he allows readers to draw some conclusions on their own.

Sometimes it seems that not much is happening. In this sense, Kazakov often has been compared with the greatest Russian storyteller, Anton Chekhov, who has also been criticized for the fact that not much happens in his stories and plays. The author believes, however, that telling everything explicitly is not necessary. In the same way, it is unnecessary that the story have a clear-cut ending—a hint is enough. Thus, Kazakov does not say that she is staying, he only shows a tug come and leave again without her.

Kazakov is especially adept at creating characters. Slowly and unobtrusively, in an almost impressionistic manner, he completes the portraits. The narrator emerges as a taciturn but strong man, somewhat sentimental and romantic, showing weaknesses but with enough hope to carry him through perhaps the greatest challenge of his life. His friend also is shown as a strong person, "of the sea," as he characterizes her, with a husky voice and a mind of her own. The blending of the characters with their environment is perhaps the strongest artistic point of the story. The two characters emerge at the end as a part of nature, which may have been Kazakov's main goal in writing this story.

Vasa D. Mihailovich

AXOLOTL

Author: Julio Cortázar (1914-1984)
Type of plot: Fantasy
Time of plot: Spring during the 1950's
Locale: Paris, France
First published: 1956 (English translation, 1963)

Principal characters:
THE NARRATOR
AXOLOTL, an aquatic salamander into which the narrator
metamorphoses

The Story

An unnamed man living in Paris becomes fascinated by an axolotl, a creature that he observes in the aquarium of the Jardin des Plantes. (A salamander noted for its permanent retention of larval features, such as external gills, the axolotl, or axolote, is found in lakes near Mexico City, where it is considered edible.) Despite its association with the everyday, the creature gradually assumes a mysterious quality as the narrator's fascination with the animal intensifies. He visits the exhibit every day and feels a growing affinity between himself and the creature. His description of the axolotl is realistic (the axolotl is like a lizard, about six inches long, with a delicate fish tail and paws), but he adds some eerie details. The creatures have humanlike nails and eyes with unfathomable depth.

After the narrator describes the axolotl in the fourth paragraph of the story, the first hint appears that the affinity between him and the axolotl goes beyond that of a naturalist's love for the object of his study. Suddenly the narrator starts speaking in the first-person plural, as if he himself were an axolotl: "We don't like moving around too much, and the aquarium is so cramped; we hardly move and then we bang our tail or our head into another one of us; then we get problems, fights, tiredness. Time is less oppressive if we stay still." The narrator is projecting himself into the mind of the creature that he is observing; it is the first indication that he is slowly being sucked into the axolotl's universe.

As the narrative continues, it moves—more and more disconcertingly—between the objective eye of the human observer and the internal universe of the axolotl. The narrator goes on to describe his fascination with the creature's eyes, in which he glimpses a "sweet, terrible light" and "an unfathomable depth which made me dizzy." As he becomes intrigued by the idea that the axolotls are, deep down, human, he imagines that their eyes are telling him: "Save us, save us." He visits them religiously every day, behavior so odd as to cause the guard to take notice. The narrator cannot keep his mind off the animals; he starts dreaming about them, feeling that they are devouring him with their eyes.

Then the unthinkable happens. One day, as the narrator is pressing his face against the glass, looking into the eyes of an axolotl, he suddenly turns into one and sees his own, human face pressed against the glass instead of that of an axolotl. At this point the narrative takes a new tack by focusing on the narrator trapped within the body of an axolotl.

The last paragraph of the story is ambiguous; it raises the possibility that the narrator and the axolotl are the same person, leaving the reader wondering who is who. The man visits the aquarium less frequently now because "the bridges between him and me are broken." The narrator is consoled by the thought that perhaps the man will "write about us, that he will write all this about the axolotls down believing that he is imagining a story."

Themes and Meanings

This story centers on Argentine writer Julio Cortázar's favorite theme: the monstrous, the bestial as mysteriously attached to human destiny. The main meaning of this particular story, "Axolotl," is that it raises the question of the mysterious relationship between the human subject and the animal kingdom. After all, we cannot look into the heads of other creatures; for all we know, they may be thinking about philosophy and are simply unable to express their thoughts. "Axolotl" also explores the question of the empathy between creator and reader; in a sense readers are being sucked into the text. If the story is successful, according to Cortázar's criterion, readers will feel sucked into its plot and arrive at a meeting of minds similar to that between the narrator and the axolotl.

Also present as a theme in this story is the notion of unease with the human body. In an essay on the short story and its environment published in 1969, Cortázar explains how writing serves as an exorcism for him, a way of "casting out invading creatures," and this seems to fit "Axolotl" in the sense that it appears to exorcise a feeling of nausea created by a sense of entrapment within the clumsy heaviness of the human body. "Axolotl" is gripping precisely because it speaks to its readers about a more elemental feeling, that of the soul being trapped within a body, or spirit being trapped within matter. This is an archetypal idea to which many religions have appealed.

The main reason Cortázar uses the axolotl as a focus for his story is that it is one of the few species in nature that dies before completing its metamorphosis; it reproduces during its larval stage, and thus is a curious example within the natural world of an incomplete life-form. (When the Austrian scientist Alexander von Humboldt brought the first specimen from Mexico to Paris in the nineteenth century, the discovery that it could reproduce in its larval stage caused a sensation in the scientific world.) The axolotl's incomplete metamorphosis also makes it appropriate for Cortázar's story: Stunted in its growth, it mirrors the human mind trapped within a body and forced to a basic, "animal" level of existence.

Style and Technique

In an essay on aspects of the short story published in Cuba in 1962, Cortázar defined the short story as "a mysterious brother to poetry" in which fantasy is shown to rule supreme, as opposed to the false empirical realism created by the Western notion of logic and causality. This definition applies to "Axolotl" because the story shows how a fantastic reality bursts into the realm of the everyday. In this short story, as in many others, Cortázar first gains the reader's confidence, putting readers at their ease by creating a normal setting and conventional characters in familiar situations. Soon, however, readers find themselves trapped by a strange, nightmarish turn of events that threatens and ultimately destroys the logical, routine reality described up to this point. Cortázar has also likened the short story to a photograph. Unlike novels and films, which provide abundant details and complete, well-rounded plots, the short story—like a photograph—limits its scope to a single frame, a fragment of reality that forces the reader to supply the missing pieces. One of Cortázar's finest stories, "Axolotl" is elegantly written. It uses suspense well and explores the mysterious boundaries between the human and the animal kingdoms.

Stephen M. Hart

BABETTE'S FEAST

Author: Isak Dinesen (Baroness Karen Blixen-Finecke, 1885-1962)
Type of plot: Domestic realism
Time of plot: 1883
Locale: Berlevaag, Norway
First published: 1950

Principal characters:
    MARTINE and
    PHILIPPA, the adult daughters of the founder of an austere
        religious sect
    BABETTE, their French servant and cook
    LORENS LOEWENHIELM, an army officer who once fell in love
        with Martine
    ACHILLE PAPIN, a famous opera singer who once fell in love with
        Philippa

The Story

This story focuses on a lavish dinner that a French servant woman named Babette prepares for a group of pious ascetics in an isolated Norwegian village on Sunday, December 15, 1883. The events leading up to this feast take many years to develop.

Martine and Philippa's father founded a religious sect respected throughout Norway that strictly denied the value of all earthly things, insisting that charity toward the poor and preparing for heaven were the only meaningful activities on earth. In their small and isolated village, Martine and Philippa adhere to their father's teachings along with a small group of his followers. The two beautiful sisters pass from their childhood into adulthood facing only two earthly temptations: At eighteen Martine is wooed by young Lieutenant Lorens Loewenhielm; a year later, Philippa spurns the advances of the famous opera singer Achille Papin, who meets her while vacationing near their village. Having rejected earthly love in order to maintain their focus on spiritual matters, Martine and Philippa continue to lead the small group of ascetics after their father dies.

Fifteen years after rejecting their suitors, Martine and Philippa are joined by a French woman named Babette, who appears at their doorstep exhausted, wild-eyed, and impoverished after escaping political turmoil in Paris. A letter from Achille Papin states simply that Babette "can cook." For twelve years Babette serves Martine and Philippa without pay, preparing for them and their flock the austerely simple meals that their religion demands.

One day, Babette receives a letter from Paris informing her that she has won ten thousand francs in a lottery. Her news coincides with Martine and Philippa's plan to celebrate the one-hundredth birthday of their father on December 15. Babette makes her first request in twelve years—to prepare a real French dinner for the celebration at her own expense. Although Martine, Philippa, and their followers fear sinful luxury and extravagance in such a meal, they reluctantly accept her offer, secretly vowing among themselves to take little notice of the food and drink.

When the feast day arrives, Lorens Loewenhielm, now an aging general, becomes the twelfth guest. In the village to visit his aunt, an original member of the religious sect, he attends the dinner with her to honor Martine and Philippa's father. As a member of the French aristocracy, Loewenhielm is the only guest at the table who appreciates the magnificence of Babette's meal. By its end, he realizes that Babette was once a renowned Parisian chef.

After the feast and the departure of the guests, Martine and Philippa expect Babette to announce her return to Paris, where she can live as a rich woman with her ten thousand francs; however, Babette declares that she will stay with them in Norway. In any case, she has spent all of her winnings on the feast. She explains that as a chef she is an artist and that she is happy to remain as their servant because she has been a great artist one last time.

Themes and Meanings

Well into Babette's sumptuous meal, General Loewenhielm makes a speech that captures the story's main theme. In this celebratory feast, he says, "righteousness and bliss shall kiss one another." By this he seems to mean that spirituality can be achieved in this world as well as in the next and that spirituality may be closely related to human pleasure without lapsing into sinfulness.

In dedicating their lives to spirituality, Martine, Philippa, and the other members of the sect have denied themselves the wonders and delights of this world. For example, both Martine and her sister have forsaken excellent chances for earthly romance. Martine's spurned lover, Loewenhielm, is more than a victim of her rigorous self-denial. According to a legend in his family, another Loewenhielm married "a female mountain spirit of Norway," thereby gaining "second sight." When Loewenhielm met Martine during his youth, she appeared to him to be the embodiment of the family legend and suddenly "there rose before his eyes a sudden, mighty vision of a higher and purer life." Frightened by this possibility, Loewenhielm felt uncharacteristically inadequate in Martine's presence, so he returned to France, where he chose worldly pleasures and advancement over "second sight." He then rose as a military and court figure until his chance return to Norway for the feast in 1883.

Anticipating seeing Martine again, the now aging Loewenhielm is plagued by doubts. Did he make the right choice? He goes to Babette's feast in a combative mood, resolved to dominate where he once felt intimidated, determined to prove that he made the right choice—that "the low rooms, the haddock and the glass of water on the table" that typified Martine's ascetic world "would very soon have become sheer misery." Instead, Loewenhielm finds a wondrous meal produced almost magically in this remote Norwegian village. When he rises to leave, he seizes Martine's hand and tells her "I have been with you every day of my life" and will "be with you every day that is left to me." Babette's feast has taught him that the miraculous can come to one through earthly experiences, that his spiritual kinship with Martine was never lost, diminished though it might have been by their physical separation.

Loewenhielm serves as a foil for the ascetics: They want to achieve spirituality so badly that they deny the world in order to attain it; he wanted spirituality so badly that he ran away from it because it frightened him and instead embraced worldly pleasures. The achievement of spirituality is a compromise between these two positions, symbolized in the willingness of Babette to remain in this Norwegian wilderness, supported by her memory of the one evening when she created a meal fit for the gods.

Style and Technique

Isak Dinesen presents weighty themes with a delightfully subtle sense of humor that surfaces most noticeably during the feast and its aftermath. Appropriate to the main theme, everything works by opposites. The ascetics come to the feast prepared to endure and resist the temptations of the world but end up getting tipsy and discovering the brotherhood and true spirituality they had been losing. General Loewenhielm comes to the feast determined to prove his superiority to the rustics but is humbled by the Parisian magnificence of Babette's meal. Although Babette creates the meal only for her own satisfaction (not knowing that Loewenhielm will be a guest), she transforms the lives of many in a single evening.

The comedy during the meal arises from Loewenhielm's wonderment at the fare and the nonchalant responses of the ascetics. Although they do not understand what so excites him, they manage to appear sophisticated in their nonchalance. For example, as Loewenhielm expresses incredulity at being served Blinis Demidoff (a kind of blintz), he looks around at his fellow diners, only to see them all eating their own Blinis Demidoff, "without any sign of either surprise or approval, as if they had been doing so every day for thirty years." Once the ascetics become slightly drunk, they readily accept more drink. They know that what they are drinking is not wine because it sparkles. "It must be some kind of lemonade," they guess. The "lemonade" agrees with "their exalted state of mind and seem[s] to lift them off the ground, into a higher and purer sphere."

Before Babette's meal, the aging ascetics grow so quarrelsome and petty that Martine and Philippa worry about their group's spirituality. During the feast, however, the wine so loosens their tongues and the food so warms their hearts that by its end they are forgiving old quarrels and building new intimacies. Soon the house is "filled with a heavenly light," as if they have "been given one hour of the millennium." After the dinner the disciples stagger out of the house and stumble together in the snow, giggling and playing like small children in a "kind of celestial second childhood." In a monument to comic understatement, Martine enters the kitchen after the guests depart and says, "It was quite a nice dinner, Babette."

Terry Nienhuis

BABYLON REVISITED

Author: F. Scott Fitzgerald (1896-1940)
Type of plot: Social realism
Time of plot: 1931
Locale: Paris
First published: 1931

>*Principal characters:*
>CHARLIE WALES, a thirty-five-year-old businessperson, formerly
>   from the United States, now from Prague, Czechoslovakia
>HONORIA WALES, his nine-year-old daughter
>MARION PETERS, his sister-in-law
>LINCOLN PETERS, Marion's husband
>DUNCAN SCHAEFFER and
>LORRAINE QUARRLES, friends of Charlie from his former days in
>   Paris

The Story

Charlie Wales has returned to Paris after a three-year absence in the hope of taking his nine-year-old daughter, Honoria, back to live with him in Prague. He remembers with regret that his former life in Paris was a life of dissipation and wildly extravagant spending. Paris then was awash with Americans who had achieved almost instant wealth on the stock market. The Paris to which Charlie returns, however, is a changed Paris, now almost empty of Americans because most of those who had lived so extravagantly had lost everything in the stock market crash of 1929. Charlie himself has come back a changed man. He has replaced his wild, drunken sprees with the stable life of a successful businessperson who consciously takes only a single drink each day to help keep the idea of alcohol in proportion in his mind. He hopes that the change will convince Marion Peters, his sister-in-law, to relinquish to him the legal guardianship of Honoria, which Marion assumed at the death of Charlie's wife, Helen.

Marion has persisted in unfairly holding Charlie responsible for the death of his wife. Charlie and Helen had argued while dining out one night in February, and he had gone home without her, locking the door behind him, not knowing that she would arrive there an hour later, wandering about in slippers in a sudden snowstorm and too drunk to find a taxi. As a result, Helen had barely escaped pneumonia, and Marion has never forgiven Charlie, taking the scene as typical of their turbulent life together. Charlie must now break through Marion's reservations to the maternal part of her nature, which Charlie knows must acknowledge that Honoria's proper place is with her father. Charlie fears that if he does not get his daughter soon, he will lose all of her childhood and she will learn from her aunt to hate him. He is relieved and gratified when, on an outing with him, Honoria expresses a desire to come and live with him.

Charlie knows that he can win his battle with Marion if he shows her that he is now in control of his life. She is skeptical about his even entering a bar, after his earlier extravagances, but he convinces her that his drinking is under control. During Charlie's lush years, Marion and Lincoln had ample reason to envy his wealth, but now it is clear that his is not a precarious income based on the fluctuations of the market but rather the stable income of a hardworking businessperson and that he can indeed provide a good life for Honoria. Charlie makes it clear that he is in control of his emotions when he listens to Marion attack him one more time for his role in Helen's death, and he calmly responds, "Helen died of heart trouble."

Charlie has the battle won when suddenly there intrude two ghosts from his past in the form of two friends whom he cannot control. Early in his visit to Paris, Charlie leaves his address at his brother-in-law's with a bartender in case some of his former friends want to get in touch with him. Later, when he actually encounters two of these old friends, Duncan Schaeffer and Lorraine Quarrles, he realizes how far he has progressed beyond where they still are and how uncomfortable he is in their presence. He shocks them with his sobriety and amuses them with his fatherly concern for Honoria, but they are drawn to him because he possesses a strength that they know they do not have. Charlie avoids giving them his address, but they get it from the bartender, and just as Charlie is making arrangements for Honoria's move to Prague, into the Peterses' home they burst as drunken reminders of Charlie's dissipated past. Charlie, as angry as his relatives about the intrusion, rushes them out, but it is too late. The damage has been done. Marion is so upset that she retires to bed, and any further arrangements have to be postponed. The next day, Lincoln informs Charlie that they must put off any decision about Honoria for six months. Charlie sits in a bar, disillusioned and alone, but still in control of himself as he says no to a second drink and tells himself that he will come back for Honoria some day, that they cannot keep her from him forever.

Themes and Meanings

In this story that recalls F. Scott Fitzgerald's own alcoholic existence in Paris in the 1920's, Charlie Wales learns how truly relative wealth is. In losing, for at least a while longer, the future that he hopes to share with Honoria, he is paying for his past.

Charlie recalls his earlier dissipated life and suddenly realizes the meaning of the word "dissipation": to make nothing out of something. As Charlie sits alone in a bar at the end of the story, he seems left with nothing. He is not without wealth. He now makes through hard work as much money as he made through luck during the boom days of the stock market. The way of life that came with sudden fortune, however, destroyed his chance to enjoy things of more lasting value. He remembers the money frivolously thrown away on wild evenings of entertainment and knows that it was not given for nothing: "It had been given, even the most wildly squandered sum, as an offering to destiny that he might not remember the things most worth remembering, the things that now he would always remember—his child taken from his control, his wife escaped to a grave in Vermont." Just when he hopes to get Honoria back and establish a future with her, his past intrudes, and he is unfairly kept from doing so. The ill-timed appearance of Duncan and Lorraine convinces him of the impossibility of ever outliving his past.

Charlie is alone and frustrated at the end, but he is not defeated. He has learned to "trust in character again as the eternally valuable element" and he has faith in his own reformed character. He knows that he has much to offer Honoria: a home, love, and values. He is disillusioned, but in his new strength, he will not slip back into the destructive habits of his past. For the time being all that he can offer Honoria are things, and he knows how little value there is in the things that money can buy.

Style and Technique

Contrast plays a major part in Fitzgerald's technique as he presents both Charlie and Paris as they were before the crash of 1929 and as they are at the time of the story. The language of the stock market adds a note of irony as Charlie applies it to the rise and fall of his fortune—both his monetary fortune and his fate in general.

On his return, the reformed Charlie sees Paris through new eyes. With the majority of the wealthy Americans gone, Paris is indeed a changed city, but even what remains unchanged looks different to Charlie when seen with the clarity of sobriety rather than through a drunken haze. He sees his former outlandish behavior from a more serious point of view and shies away from contact with his friends, who seem never to have changed. He can even see his old self as he must have appeared to the Peters, who did not share in the wealth that seemed to come to him so easily. Helen's death is presented from two different perspectives—Charlie's and Marion's. Her obvious jealousy and his remorse shift the balance in favor of support for Charlie and belief in his version of the story.

Charlie sees the error of his former ways and the ephemeral nature of his life prior to 1929. He recalls the snowstorm that almost caused Helen's death and the fantasy world that surrounded the incident: "The snow of twenty-nine wasn't real snow. If you didn't want it to be snow, you just paid some money." Money was not a problem during two dazzling, extravagant years in Paris: "He remembered thousand-franc notes given to an orchestra for playing a single number, hundred-franc notes tossed to a doorman for calling a cab." Having too much money, ironically, was the source of Charlie's greatest losses. As he sits in a bar realizing that he has once again lost Honoria, at least for a time, the bartender offers his regrets for a different loss: "I heard you lost a lot in the crash." Charlie responds, "I did" and adds, "but I lost everything I wanted in the boom."

Donna B. Haisty

THE BABYSITTER

Author: Robert Coover (1932-   )
Type of plot: Antistory
Time of plot: The 1960's
Locale: Suburban United States
First published: 1969

> *Principal characters:*
> HARRY TUCKER, a middle-aged man
> DOLLY TUCKER, his overweight wife
> JIMMY TUCKER and
> BITSY, their young children
> THE BABY-SITTER, an unnamed schoolgirl
> JACK, the sitter's boyfriend
> MARK, Jack's friend

The Story

In just over a hundred paragraphs presenting several different points of view, the story recounts the confusing events of a single evening, between 7:40 and 10:30 P.M. The multiple viewpoints frequently collide and even merge as the story revises itself, offering concurrent and competing plots. In other words, several plots occupy the same time and space and involve the same characters, whose fantasies influence reality. The story seems to ask the question, what would the world be like if everyone's competing fantasies were to come true?

As Harry and Dolly Tucker dress for a cocktail party, the baby-sitter arrives at their house. Harry imagines that the girl is arching her back, jutting out her pert breasts, and twitching her thighs just for him. After the Tuckers leave, their young children, Jimmy and Bitsy, attack the baby-sitter playfully, jumping on her and tickling her. Jimmy fantasizes that his baby-sitter will overpower him and spank him.

Meanwhile, the baby-sitter's boyfriend, Jack, and his friend Mark are playing pinball in a nearby arcade, discussing the idea of visiting her. Although the boys have carefully studied the pinball machine, they still cannot easily beat it. Jack would like either to collaborate with Mark in the seduction or rape of his girlfriend or protect her from Mark's advances—or possibly both.

The story soon becomes an exercise in multiple choices. Does Mr. Tucker return home to discover the baby-sitter watching television alone, or has she been having sex with Jack and Mark, or is she giving Jimmy a bath? Does the baby-sitter spend a quiet evening alone, or is she harassed all night by anonymous phone calls and Peeping Toms? Is she raped and murdered by Jack, or by Jack and Mark, or perhaps by Mr. Tucker? Does the baby choke on a diaper pin or drown in the bathtub? Does everyone die at the end of the story, or does everyone quietly go to bed?

The answer to all these questions is yes. As one critic has pointed out, there are at least five hundred possible plot lines in this story.

Themes and Meanings

In American culture and literature, baby-sitters have long been the objects of lust and fantasy, especially for middle-aged men. One need only turn to John Irving's novel *The World According to Garp* (1978) and John Cheever's story "The Country Husband" (1954) to find examples of baby-sitters who have become the targets of lustful married men. Robert Coover's "The Babysitter" explores this fascination. The title character serves as the object of desire for three generations of males: pre-adolescent Jimmy, teenage Jack, and middle-aged Harry Tucker.

In a role reminiscent of the pot-belly stove in Stephen Crane's 1898 short story "The Blue Hotel," the Tuckers' living room television set functions as an extension of the characters. It commands their attention, participates in their activities, and even vies with them for narrative control. The characters regard the television not only as a source of entertainment but also as a reward for obedience, an employment perk (in the baby-sitter's case), an alibi or excuse, and a companion-protector. So conspicuous is the television's presence and role that "The Babysitter" can be interpreted as an indictment of television for its harmful effects on viewers. In the course of his intentionally confusing narrative, Coover examines television's coupling of sex and violence, its tendency to desensitize people, its tacit encouragement of voyeurism, and its function as a surrogate baby-sitter.

Not only do the television programs bombard the characters with images of violence (for example, the fighting cowboys in a western), they also combine sex and violence. In one program, a detective stares "down at the body of a half-naked girl" who has been strangled and presumably raped. Coover's characters also link sex with violence. In one plot line, the baby-sitter experiences an orgasm as she watches a television gunfight. Other characters fantasize about rape or being raped. At times, the television actually participates in the violence and promiscuity of the characters. When Mr. Tucker returns home unexpectedly, he finds the baby-sitter's "panties hanging like a broken balloon from the rabbit-ear antennae on the TV." As Jack and Mark rape the baby-sitter, "the television lights flicker and flash over her glossy flesh," as if the television were touching her. During one violent scuffle, in which two figures—perhaps Mark and Jack—try to rape a girl—probably the baby-sitter—the television set crashes to the floor, ironically becoming a victim of the violence.

Desensitized by years of television viewing, the characters feel little compassion for other people's suffering and tend to dehumanize their objects of desire, as Jack and Mark do when they treat the baby-sitter as a pinball machine. Possessing short attention spans, they expect "commercials" at intervals and change channels frequently. They engage in voyeurism, spying on the baby-sitter through the bathroom window or the keyhole in the door. They may not prefer to watch, as Chance does in Jerzy Kosinski's novel *Being There* (1971), but they watch anyway, conditioned by their television experience. Television has an especially tragic effect on children, who are more impressionable than adults and spend more time in front of the television. Since its proliferation in the 1950's, television has indeed earned the epithet "The Great American Baby-sitter." It is television's role as a surrogate baby-sitter, which indoctrinates Americans from a young age, that Coover attacks in this story, just as the story is a statement on human sexuality, the art of fiction making, and American culture generally.

Style and Technique

Structurally, "The Babysitter" follows the chronology of a television schedule. It is divided into five sections, each of which corresponds to a program on television. The first section, which covers the time period from 7:40 to 8:00 P.M., is dominated by images and sounds of a musical on television. This section complements Mr. Tucker's "musical" fantasy of the baby-sitter. In the second section, which corresponds to Jimmy's "spanking" fantasy, a western organizes and informs the events between 8:00 and 8:30. The third section, unified by a spy show, encompasses the period from 8:30 to 9:00 and corresponds to Jack's "spying" fantasy. Between 9:00 and 10:00, the baby-sitter changes channels constantly, switching back and forth among three programs: a love story, a ball game, and a murder mystery. It is not easy to associate any of these programs with a specific character, but the murder mystery, which receives the most attention in the various plots, seems to parallel the actions of Mark and Jack, while the love story seems to parallel the triangle of Harry, Dolly, and the baby-sitter. Covering the period from 10:00 to 10:30, the last section repeatedly mentions the news, the only "real" or nonfiction program on the television. Whereas the fictional programs feed the fantasies and influence the actions of the characters, the news program assesses the damage of the Great American Baby-sitter.

The shifting points of view in the story simulate the changing of channels and television's fragmentation of reality. At the beginning of the story it is relatively easy to identify and distinguish the various points of view. The first paragraph, for example, is probably told from the point of view of the baby-sitter; the second from that of Mr. Tucker; and the third from that of Jack. Jimmy's point of view is not represented until the fifth paragraph and Mrs. Tucker's not until the eleventh. It is uncertain whether any of the paragraphs represent Mark's, Bitsy's, or the Host's point of view.

Early in the story, Coover uses tag phrases to help the reader link the individual paragraphs to characters. For example, the recurring phrase "light brown hair" identifies Mr. Tucker, while "enough's enough" or "that's enough" identifies Jack. As the story progresses, however, the points of view begin to conflate, frustrating attempts to distinguish among them. By the end of the story, chaos has replaced clarity and coherence. The shifting points of view and the steadily increasing confusion make "The Babysitter" a particularly effective satire on television and justify its classification as an antistory.

Edward A. Malone

BAD CHARACTERS

Author: Jean Stafford (1915-1979)
Type of plot: Psychological
Time of plot: The early twentieth century
Locale: Adams, Colorado
First published: 1954

> *Principal characters:*
> EMILY VANDERPOOL, the narrator and protagonist
> LOTTIE JUMP, an eleven-year-old vagabond
> JACK, Emily's brother
> STELLA and
> TESS, Emily's sisters
> THE VANDERPOOLS, Emily's parents

The Story

The bad characters in this fictional autobiography are two young girls: Emily Vanderpool, the protagonist and narrator, and Lottie Jump, an eleven-year-old vagabond from the lower-class section of town. A brash, impudent, yet privileged girl, Emily has not yet learned to maintain friendships. Because she believes that she needs frequent solitude, she insults her friends until she loses their friendship. Always Emily repents of these impetuous actions, but always too late; she indeed alienates all of her friends. Even her brother and sisters are targets of Emily's vituperation.

Emily has one friend—her cat, Muff. Muff dislikes all humans except Emily, mirrors Emily's need for self-inflicted privacy, and, by extension, mirrors Emily herself. Because Muff and Emily are mirror images, Stella, her sister, frequently refers to Emily as "Kitty" whereas Jack, her brother, calls Emily "Polecat."

As the Christmas holidays approach, Emily, without a friend, sits home alone with Muff. When she investigates a sound coming from the kitchen, she quickly discovers a young girl stealing a piece of cake. Tall, sickly looking, ragged, and dirty, this girl, Lottie Jump, is the antithesis of Emily. Lottie frequently lies, steals, has ragged teeth, and comes from a lower-class family. Lottie's mother is a short-order cook in a dirty café; her father has tuberculosis; her brother has received no education. By contrast, Emily has a good home, wears nice clothes, attends a good school, attends church regularly, and has educated, healthy parents. However, during the course of one afternoon's conversation, the spirited Lottie, who explains that she appeared in Emily's kitchen not to steal but to visit Emily, manages to convince the vulnerable Emily to become her friend. Incredible as the story may appear, Emily acquiesces.

That afternoon, the girls search through Emily's mother's bureau drawers. Emily, however, fails to notice Lottie stealing Mrs. Vanderpool's perfume flask. Emily's many advantages make Emily feel guilty, which is why, perhaps, she succumbs so easily to Lottie's proposition. To remain friends, Lottie threatens, Emily must not only join in a shoplifting spree at the local dime store but also bring along money for the trolley fare. Reluctantly, Emily agrees to the plan.

Before she leaves the Vanderpool home, Lottie steals the cake she initially sought earlier that day. That evening, Emily allows her parents to believe that a vagrant stole the cake and, because of her guilty conscience, has a tantrum when her mother worries about the loss of the perfume flask.

In the following few days, ordinary events cause Emily to feel even more conscience-stricken with regard to her approaching day of shoplifting. Her dad's visiting friend, a respectable judge, discusses vandalism and punishment of criminals. Emily steals her Sunday-school offering to pay for both trolley fares, and on the fatal day, she begs off from baby-sitting for her younger sister. Most of all, she worries about the Sunday-school offering she has taken to pay for the trolley ride, money intended for widows. Ironically, she does not want to steal anything and certainly does not need anything. Repelled by Lottie's suggestion, she does not even wish to see Lottie again. However, she feels mesmerized and fascinated by this clever girl's persuasive personality, by her thieving, by her unfortunate background, and by her colloquial Oklahoma dialect.

On Saturday, Emily meets Lottie and is astounded to discover Lottie wearing a huge hat. Emily does not realize that Lottie's hat is a repository for the day's stolen articles. In the trolley car, Lottie, adept at stealing, carefully explains Emily's role. In exchange for half of the stolen articles, Emily is to divert the clerk's attention while Lottie steals the articles and hides them under her huge hat.

By late afternoon, and after several articles have been successfully stolen, Emily suddenly and characteristically needs to be alone. This time, however, she insults Lottie at the same moment Lottie attempts to hide a string of pearls. Whirling around to notice the target of Emily's insults, the clerk catches Lottie in the act of stealing the pearls.

Although she has been caught stealing, Lottie cleverly pretends to be deaf and dumb and points an accusing finger at her young accomplice: Emily Vanderpool. Because the authorities believe that a more powerful and advantaged Emily has victimized an obviously handicapped Lottie, they reward Lottie with a bag of candy and send her home.

Because this is Emily's first offense, she is remanded to her father's custody. Subsequently, she faces her father's friend, Judge Bay, who lectures to her on the subject of thievery. Then she faces her wounded mother's recriminations and those of her brother and sisters.

Emily, however, has learned important lessons from this experience. She no longer thoughtlessly insults her friends when she wishes to be alone. Instead, like adults, she feigns a headache or a dentist appointment. She has also learned to maintain more than one friendship.

Meanwhile, her mirror image, Muff, has also grown up. Rather than miss Emily's infrequent companionship, Muff has been busy herself—having kittens.

Themes and Meanings

Jean Stafford depicts two young girls who are approaching puberty. One girl, who has every advantage a girl could desire, is trapped by her antithesis, a girl who has had no advantages in life. By contrasting the girls' backgrounds, values, manners of speech, and personalities, Stafford can examine Lottie's corrupt, emotionally bereft nature. When she is caught stealing, Lottie, who has initiated the dishonesty, pleads a physical handicap and allows Emily to bear the responsibility alone. Lottie has clearly taken advantage of Emily and has felt her expertise superior to that of Emily's. By revealing her obvious disadvantages and thereby appealing to Emily's propensity for guilt, Lottie, left unpunished for her crimes, does not mature or learn from the experience. For Emily, this has been an important learning experience: She faces a crisis in her young life, resolves that crisis, and, as a result, gains both experience and maturity.

Style and Technique

Stafford employs both dramatic irony and symbolism to give the story resonance. Through the device of dramatic irony, the reader learns immediately important information that Emily learns only at the end of the story. More pervasive is the use of symbolism. Muff and Emily, for example, are symbolically compared: Both are unkind to humans; Emily is referred to as Kitty and Polecat; Lottie dislikes cats. Moreover, Jack insists that Emily likes fish. As Muff matures, she becomes less dependent on Emily and, finally, has kittens. At the same time, Emily matures and spends her time maintaining friendships.

Other uses of symbolism are Lottie's stealing devil's food cake, which foreshadows her tempting Emily and further suggests Lottie's devilish nature. At Emily's house, Lottie admires herself in the mirror as if she has never really seen herself. Symbolically, she has not. The evening before the shoplifting spree, Emily does cross-stitch embroidery, a symbolic foreshadowing of the next day's deceit. Also, the story takes place during the Christmas holidays, a time for renewal. Together, these and other symbols create a pattern that reinforces the story's themes.

Bette Adams Reagan

THE BALLAD OF THE SAD CAFÉ

Author: Carson McCullers (1917-1967)
Type of plot: Realism
Time of plot: The 1930's
Locale: Central Georgia
First published: 1943

Principal characters:
MISS AMELIA EVANS, the owner of the Sad Café
COUSIN LYMON WILLIS, her hunchbacked, beloved cousin
MARVIN MACY, her former husband

The Story

The action of the story covers the period from the time Cousin Lymon arrives in town until his departure with Marvin Macy almost seven years later. The narrative, however, includes incidents and explanations of circumstances from Amelia's early childhood until several years after Lymon and Marvin have gone. The story begins with a description of the dreary, isolated town, the hostile climate, and the central building there—a shabby, boarded-up former café. From the upstairs window the dim, grief-stricken face of Miss Amelia can occasionally be seen gazing out. The story of the café and the story of Miss Amelia are one. She was born there in the upstairs living quarters, was reared as a solitary child by her widowed father, and was heiress to both the property and the business when her father died. She is a woman of many talents: a sharp business negotiator, a renowned liquor distiller, a compassionate and knowledgeable doctor, and a strong and independent person.

Amelia's independence and solitary habits of existence are well known, and when Lymon, the little sickly hunchback, arrives and claims to be her cousin, the townspeople are astonished and baffled that she takes him in. He quickly becomes the center of her life and encourages her to convert the store into a combination store-café, where not only the traditional supplies and moonshine are dispensed but also meals are served and a general festive gathering of the townsfolk takes place on Saturday nights. Lymon is the center of the café activities. He enjoys the company of the townsfolk, and Amelia becomes more sociable and friendly, even to the extent of wearing dresses instead of the rough, masculine work clothes she had always worn before.

Her love for Cousin Lymon is obvious, though incredible, to the townspeople, especially as they recall her one previous experience with love, when she was courted and wed by Marvin Macy. Marvin was a wild young man who had been abandoned by his parents when he was a small child. He was handsome, reckless, and a notorious seducer of romantic, trusting young women. When Marvin Macy met Amelia, however, his life changed. He fell in love with her, reformed his character and behavior, and patiently waited two years before declaring his love and asking her to marry him.

Amelia did marry him but with the belief that the marriage was a business arrangement, and she aggressively resisted his efforts to consummate the marriage physically. In his efforts to win her over, he gave her all that he owned: his money, property, and gifts that he bought for her. After ten days of this uneasy relationship, with Marvin the lover trying earnestly to win over his beloved, she threw him out but kept all that he had given her. He left town, and rumors subsequently went around that he was in the penitentiary for robbery. Amelia's life continued as before until the arrival of Lymon.

After six years of happiness and contentment between Amelia and Lymon, during which time the café flourishes and the townsfolk enjoy the social activity each Saturday night, Marvin Macy abruptly returns. Lymon is entranced; he adores this arrogant, swaggering, handsome outlaw. Marvin, for his part, ignores and even abuses the little hunchback.

During the winter, Lymon, undaunted by Marvin's scorn, invites him to come and live in the café. Amelia makes no protest, not daring to insist that Marvin leave, for fear that Lymon might go with him. Instead, she begins to practice boxing. She is an inch taller than Marvin Macy and solidly built; the townspeople speculate that she will precipitate a fight when she feels confident that she can whip Marvin.

Finally that day arrives, and the townspeople gather to witness the fight. Amelia and Marvin exchange hundreds of blows over the course of a half hour or so; they are so nearly equally matched that no apparent advantage can be seen. Then the fighters shift to wrestling, grappling in intense effort and concentration. Finally, Amelia proves to be the stronger and pins Marvin to the floor. Just as she has her hands around his throat and is on the verge of victory, however, Lymon, who has been standing on the counter in order to see better, leaps onto Amelia's back and grabs her around the throat. This intervention turns the course of the fight, and Amelia is decisively beaten—left lying on the floor of her café. Marvin and the spectators leave, and Lymon hides underneath the back steps outdoors.

Later that same night, Marvin and Lymon return and with Amelia closeted in her small office, they ransack the café, destroying what they do not care to take. As a final expression of their hatred, they prepare Amelia's favorite dish—grits and sausage—mixed with poison.

Amelia becomes more and more isolated. She raises her prices, and people can no longer afford to eat at the café or shop at her store. She loses her interest in healing and in helping small children. For three years, she simply sits on the front steps, waiting, but Lymon never returns. Finally, she has the building boarded up, and she retreats to the upper story, whence she occasionally looks out over the town.

The town itself loses its spark of life as the life goes out of the café. It becomes a dispirited and isolated place, and the only pleasure the people find is in walking out to the highway, where a chain gang of twelve men is working at patching the road. The men in the gang begin singing, and as they sing, their song fills the listeners and the earth and sky with the music of human voices telling of the joys and sorrows of life. It is the music of men chained together.

Themes and Meanings

The love theme is unquestionably the most important of several themes interwoven in this richly symbolic story. The author not only demonstrates through her characters her distinctive view of love relationships but also, at one point in the novel, digresses into a brief essay on the nature of love and how it affects people who love and are loved. She distinguishes the lover, who is free to love and to demonstrate this love and is thus in control of the relationship, from the beloved, who is in danger of being possessed by the lover. The lover is the happier one in the relationship always, and the beloved fears and even hates the lover.

There is no place for reciprocal relationships in this concept of love. Marvin Macy loves Amelia and she rejects him. Amelia loves Lymon and he uses and finally attacks her. Lymon loves Marvin, but Marvin despises and abuses Lymon. Love is a pleasure for the lover as long as the beloved will tolerate the lover. For the beloved, the relationship is no pleasure at all, and the only reason to tolerate it is for some perceived material gain.

A very insistent theme is that of isolation. The town is isolated, Amelia is isolated in many ways from the other people of the town, Marvin Macy was isolated in prison, the members of the chain gang are isolated from other people in society, Lymon is isolated by his handicap and ill health. All attempt to overcome the isolation by love, social intercourse with other people, and singing in harmony, as the case may be. However, the story ends with Amelia in ever more profound isolation, with the townspeople seeking to relieve their loneliness by leaving the town to go listen to the chain gang singing. Love, the author suggests, can overcome this sense of isolation, and being together, even in a chain gang, is preferable to the intolerable loneliness of isolation. Amelia's isolation is destroying the life of the town as it has destroyed the social center of the town.

Another important theme is that of the grotesque. Each of the major characters is manifestly grotesque in certain ways. The little hunchback who is less than four feet tall is certainly grotesque. To add to his oddity, he dresses in grotesque clothing not at all appropriate to the time, place, or climate. Amelia is grotesque also. She is not built like an ordinary woman, being too tall, too strong, too brawny, and she dresses and acts like a man. Amelia's talents for commerce, healing, moonshining, fighting, and self-sufficiency all set her apart from the ordinary. Marvin Macy is also grotesque, in his outlaw behavior, his defiance of social mores, and his cruelty to people who care about him. Indeed, the town and the climate itself seem grotesque in that they depart manifestly from the usual. The author seems to suggest that isolation stems from differences and that love does provide a bond to enable people to share and be together, but as the love is not reciprocated, the chain is weak and will be broken, incurring even more profound isolation, and even more grotesque behavior.

Style and Technique

The author is acutely concerned with presenting an atmosphere within which rather bizarre characters can interact and seem plausible. She undertakes detailed descriptive passages to bring into focus the aspects of the town, the café, and the people that enable the reader to comprehend and believe the action of the story. Although the story is told from a third-person point of view, there is not an omniscient narrator but rather one who observes acutely and from time to time digresses to comment on the action, or even on the philosophy of the events of the story.

The strength of the story's characterizations depends to a large extent on the author's skillful control of descriptive passages. The movement of the story's action is well paced, and the flashbacks to earlier episodes in the major characters' lives are never intrusive but seem necessary and well integrated into the overall story line.

Betty G. Gawthrop

THE BALLOON

Author: Donald Barthelme (1931-1989)
Type of plot: Metafiction
Time of plot: 1966
Locale: New York City
First published: 1966

Principal character:
THE UNNAMED NARRATOR

The Story

A seemingly purposeless balloon suddenly appears in New York City. The balloon, which was inflated by the narrator one night while people were sleeping, covers almost the entire southern half of Manhattan—from Fourteenth Street in Greenwich Village to the southern edge of Central Park, near the Plaza Hotel on Fifth Avenue, covering twenty-five blocks on either side of Fifth Avenue. The narrator first refers to the appearance of the balloon as a situation but then qualifies this idea because, by the narrator's definition, situations imply sets of circumstances that lead to some resolution. This balloon, however, is merely a "concrete particular" passively hanging there.

The balloon provokes a series of reactions from various people in the city, including a flood of original ideas and milestones in the history of inflation. Impressions about the balloon run the gamut of responses from the banal to the creative. The balloon's meaning is disturbingly elusive, and this lack of purpose, of cause, of a fixed reason for the balloon, creates in the authorities a lack of trust, frustration, even hostility. Experts conduct secret tests to determine ways of removing or destroying the balloon, but because the narrator has cleverly hidden his pumps, they decide that nothing can be done.

In contrast to the suspicions of the authorities, the general public responds warmly to the balloon. Children enjoy bouncing on it, and others begin to locate themselves in relation to it. Opinions vary, but even people who are ambivalent toward the balloon experience an "admixture of pleasurable cognition." The balloon affords them a unique opportunity for contemplation, even though the balloon's meaning can never be known absolutely.

Each person's response to the balloon becomes a reflection of his or her general outlook on life. One man thinks the balloon is inferior to the sky, but the narrator concludes that the balloon is actually an improvement on the dark, ugly January weather. Another person considers the balloon to be an unanticipated reward, as if just being in its presence was a gratifying and positive experience. No matter the response, the balloon provides the citizens a reprieve from the ordinary grind of their lives; its shifting forms and malleability are pleasing, especially to those whose lives are rigidly patterned.

Having reviewed the public's and the public officials' reactions, the narrator reveals the reason for having inflated the balloon. The narrator has been romantically involved with a person who has been visiting Norway, and the balloon was the narrator's way of disclosing the unease felt at the partner's absence. When the narrator's partner returns, the narrator decides that the balloon is no longer needed. The balloon is dismantled, awaiting another time that they again feel angry with each other.

Themes and Meanings

"The Balloon" is a good example of metafiction, a postmodern literary movement in which a writer explores the process of writing by writing stories about how stories are written. Critic Patricia Waugh, in her book *Metafiction* (1984), states that the purpose of metafiction is "simultaneously to create a fiction and to make a statement about the creation of that fiction." For a practitioner of metafiction, conventional story forms are exhausted, so new techniques are created in self-conscious narratives— narratives that reveal themselves as narratives per se—exploiting the old conventions to create fresh ways of telling stories.

In a metafictional sense, this is a story about writing stories, and it also explores the relationship between the author and his work, and the public's response to it. The balloon itself is an allegorical representation of the story that contains it, so that the reader is forced to confront and respond to the story in the same way that the citizens of New York City must confront and respond to the balloon. The balloon can represent any artistic creation—a song, a painting, a sculpture—and allusions to the balloon as having a "deliberate lack of finish" and its being a rough draft reinforce the idea that the balloon is an art object designed to provoke public and private reactions.

The balloon, like Donald Barthelme's story, provides the community—and the reader—an opportunity to express several alternative, often contradictory, perspectives regarding its significance. The naïve point of view is represented by the children who accept the balloon at face value, without expecting it to mean anything more than the pleasure it offers them as a plaything, something to be enjoyed simply for what it is. The implication is that art may be enjoyed in its immediacy, without the need to establish any significance other than the fact of the object itself. Other views expressed in the story represent more mature or professional expectations and center on the need for substantial meaning. Although the narrator claims the need for meaning is out of fashion because we have learned not to insist on meanings, many citizens demand that the balloon have some practical utilitarian value. One response, for example, suggests that the balloon be used as an advertising vehicle. Barthelme remains neutral as to which view is correct, implying that all views are correct and that the importance of art is relative to the expectations of the viewer.

The idea of content-neutral art, which provokes a series of equally valid if contradictory perspectives, corresponds to the precepts of much of modern art. Barthelme, an art critic himself, is suggesting that his balloon, like modern art—with its emphasis on abstract images and nonspecific content—allows imaginative engagement precedence, in terms of meaning, over the need for rational explanations. Modern art, like

Barthelme's balloon, resists analysis, and private reactions are as meaningful as any critical consensus as to its significance. Ironically, "The Balloon" illustrates the common reactions of the public and professional literary critics to Barthelme's stories when they first began to be published in *The New Yorker* magazine.

The only attempt to expose the narrator's purpose for the balloon (and by extension, that of the story), or to ground the reason for the balloon in any personal aspect of the narrator's private life, occurs in the enigmatic last paragraph. The narrator claims that the balloon was inflated simply as an emotional diversion to alleviate stress during the absence of the narrator's partner. In the end, the narrator implies that the purpose of art is ultimately always personal, but private motives have nothing to do with the public's reaction to it.

Style and Technique

In writing "The Balloon," Barthelme intended that readers not familiar with metafiction would duplicate the confusion of the citizens when they first encounter the balloon. Conventional fiction usually relies on a sequence of episodes, sustained by cause and effect, that lead through a series of complications, culminating in a climactic event and resolution of the action. Barthelme deliberately dispenses with these devices to subvert a reader's expectations. In his minimalist approach, he uses a truncated narrative that presents only the essentials of the story with very little comment on the action by the author. By foregrounding the form of the story, he develops a metaphor, a critique of how to read, challenging common assumptions about what constitutes a story.

His style is playful; his plots turn more on chance than design. Details accumulate arbitrarily, composed of what Barthelme has called "drek," the leftover tidbits that litter contemporary life. In an interview with critic Joe David Bellamy, Barthelme states that in using drek he creates a collage that combines unlike things to make a new reality. This collage effect in "The Balloon" is constructed from surface details, advertising slogans, political jargon, and common elliptical phrases, all enhanced with irony. The implausible—the appearance of a huge mysterious balloon in the heart of New York City—is depicted with a calm, detached, matter-of-fact tone that belies the fantastic nature of the event. This ironic treatment of an unrealistic event in a realistic manner underscores Barthelme's attempt to reinvigorate worn-out fictional forms and hackneyed language. By exposing the profound ordinariness of life, Barthelme offers imaginative transcendence through his faith in the creative process of art.

Jeff Johnson

THE BALLROOM OF ROMANCE

Author: William Trevor (William Trevor Cox, 1928-   )
Type of plot: Psychological
Time of plot: The early 1970's
Locale: Rural Ireland
First published: 1972

> *Principal characters:*
> BRIDIE, a thirty-six-year-old single woman
> JUSTIN DWYER, the owner of a dance hall
> DANO RYAN, a drummer with the dance band
> MADGE DOWDING, a thirty-nine-year-old woman
> BOWSER EGAN and
> EYES HORGAN, middle-aged bachelors at the dance

The Story

Bridie, an unmarried woman in her mid-thirties, lives in rural Ireland and spends much of her time caring for her crippled father. Bridie still hopes to marry, and on Saturday nights, she rides her bicycle the seven miles to a wayside dance hall. She has been going to the dances for years.

On this occasion, when she arrives at the dance, she greets Dano Ryan, the drummer in the band, and exchanges pleasantries in the cloakroom with her acquaintances among the girls. These include Madge Dowding, who is three years older than Bridie and is also unmarried. Madge tends to make a fool of herself chasing after the bachelors at the dance. Bridie dances with various men, sparing a thought for her father, who is probably falling asleep by the fire listening to the radio. She knows most of the men at the dance, and at various times over the previous decade, she has been kissed by some of them; however, this has never led to any possibility of marriage.

At ten o'clock, as usual, three middle-aged bachelors arrive at the dance, having cycled over from the public house. Bridie dances with one of them, Bowser Egan, who compliments her on her appearance. Another bachelor, Eyes Horgan, who is named for his bloodshot eyes, dances with Madge.

As she dances, Bridie's thoughts turn to Dano Ryan. She thinks that he might make an acceptable husband. Once she had pretended to have a puncture in her bicycle tire as she was about to go home from the dance, and he had pumped up the tire for her. It is well known in the dance hall that Bridie is interested in Dano, who works as a laborer for the County Council and lodges with a widow named Mrs. Griffin. He is said to be kind to Mrs. Griffin's disabled son.

Bowser pays great attention to Bridie, buying her a lemonade and complimenting her. After he goes to the bathroom to drink from the whiskey bottle he carries around with him (no alcohol is allowed at the dance), Bridie watches Dano. She imagines him sitting in her father's farmhouse kitchen, and the three of them eating a meal together that she had prepared. She imagines what her life would be like under such circumstances.

As a group gathers, the talk is about a new cement factory that is being built in a nearby town, but Bridie tries to talk to Dano on a more personal level. She tells him she will get him medicine for his eyes, which have been bothering him. However, he politely refuses, saying that Mrs. Griffin has arranged for him to have an eye test. Bridie immediately assumes that Mrs. Griffin is planning to marry Dano. She thinks back to two decades ago, when she was dancing with a young man named Patrick Grady. She had assumed they would one day marry, but he had married someone else. She feels about to cry. She dances some more, and Bowser Egan whispers that he would marry her tomorrow, but his mother would not allow another woman in the house. Bridie is not interested. Her attention is still on Dano.

As the evening draws to an end, Bridie decides that she will never dance there again. She thinks she is a figure of fun to the others. As everyone leaves, Bowser Egan rides his bicycle alongside hers. As they alight to walk up a hill, he drinks from his bottle of whiskey. Bridie knows that he will always be drinking and lazing around, wasting his time, although he says that when his mother dies, he will sell his house and pigs and buy something better for them both. Bridie knows that he will waste whatever money he inherits and will want to get married because he will want a woman to cook for him. She also knows full well that eventually she will marry Bowser Egan because she will be lonely after her father dies.

Themes and Meanings

The theme of the story is loneliness and the extent that people will go to relieve it. Bridie is a woman who was disappointed in love early in life and has since made sacrifices so that she can stay at the farmhouse to care for her crippled father. However, she is lonely and isolated. Had her father not lost a leg, she would have preferred to get a job in the town, where there is more of a social life. In the evenings, alone with her father, she often thinks of the activities that would still be going on in the town, but the town is eleven miles away and too far to cycle just for an evening.

Bridie has been going to the same wayside dance hall for twenty years, but she never manages to make the romantic connection for which she longs. She is friendly and seems to be on good terms with everyone at the dance, but the intimacy she desires escapes her. In spite of her loneliness and her poor prospects, however, she cannot keep her hopes from springing up again, even if they are unrealistic. She tries in a gentle way to turn her somewhat distant relationship with Dano Ryan, whom she has known for twenty years, into something closer. Although she is not in love with him, she regards him as a decent man, but Dano Ryan is not interested in her.

Bridie's loneliness stands in stark contrast to the bright lights and bustle and the banter and the camaraderie that pervade the dance hall. However, even that is deceptive, because the dance attracts many lonely people from the remote hill farms and villages. These are people who do not often see other people, and many of the men are settled permanently into bachelorhood. They cannot connect with women in any meaningful way but prefer to enjoy themselves superficially. This is only a cloak to hide the loneliness that has been a part of their lives for so long they perhaps no longer even notice it. Nothing much will ever change in these lives until necessity forces it. Madge Dowding will go on coming to the dance even though she is a figure of fun; Dano Ryan will go on playing the drums in the band; the bachelors will continue to drink and to live with their widowed mothers.

The irony of Bridie's situation is that the only man who seems to be genuinely interested in her is someone in whom she has no interest. This is Bowser Egan, and the fact that Bridie knows that life will eventually maneuver her into a situation in which marriage to him will be inevitable only serves to heighten her loneliness and turn her into an almost tragic figure. Both she and Bowser Egan will want to alleviate the loneliness that can only increase over the years. Faced with the acuteness of isolation, people will make their compromises, forget their original hopes and what they really desire, and try to endure as best they can what life has brought them.

Style and Technique

The story is told from a limited third-person point of view. Although the narrator reveals considerable information about the other characters at the dance, the story is mostly experienced through the consciousness of Bridie. The narrative itself is fairly straightforward. A brief exposition is followed by the scene at the Saturday night dance, where all the crucial thoughts and events take place. Occasional flashbacks in Bridie's mind give the reader insight into her past disappointments.

The rural Irish setting, the atmosphere in the dance hall, and the characters who gather there are all created with a deadly accurate realism: the colloquial, cheery dialogue; the vulgar gaudiness of the dance hall; the puritanical outlook of its owners, Justin Dwyer and his wife; the seedy unattractiveness of the men; and the forced gaiety of the women.

Trevor's stories often crystallize around a single moment of realization or decision, in which the protagonist gains insight into his or her situation and makes some kind of bargain with life. Usually this is a completely internal process, and no one knows about it but the protagonist. Nevertheless, the moment is crucial and vitally affects the protagonist's attitude toward his or her life. So it is with this story. As she leaves the dance, Bridie realizes that she will never go there again. She has for a moment seen herself as she thinks others might see her, and she wants none of it. Looking at Madge Dowding, another single woman only slightly older than she, she realizes that like Madge, she is a woman approaching middle age who is making a fool of herself by chasing after unavailable bachelors. The second, more serious revelation, is her knowledge that eventually she will marry Bowser Egan, a man for whom she appears to have no feelings of affection. At least she has acquired some self-knowledge, and she awaits her fate with resignation.

Bryan Aubrey

THE BAMBINO

Author: May Sinclair (1863-1946)
Type of plot: Psychological
Time of plot: About 1920
Locale: London and a country house in Buckinghamshire, England
First published: 1920

Principal characters:
ROLAND SIMPSON, an artist and the narrator of the story
THE BAMBINO, a five-year-old boy, the title character
ADELA ARCHDALE, the Bambino's mother
JACK ARCHDALE, Adela's husband and the Bambino's father
FRANCES ARCHDALE, Jack's sister, an artist and the painter of a
portrait of her sister-in-law and nephew

The Story

Told in the first person by artist Roland Simpson to an unidentified listener, "The Bambino" is less a plotted story than a sketch revealing a dramatic situation and a set of characters. The anonymous listener prompts the story by asking Simpson if he painted a portrait hanging on his studio wall. Simpson replies that it is a study of Adela Archdale and her infant son painted by Frances Archdale, sister of Adela's husband and at one time Simpson's fiance. Jack Archdale collects modern pictures, and Simpson explains to the listener the circumstances that explain why he has not purchased this one.

According to Simpson, the key to the situation can be seen in the composition of Frances's portrait of Adela and her son. The child is naked, standing between his mother's knees, but the visual focus of the picture is Adela's hands. "They're in the centre of the picture, large and white and important, as if Frances had known." For Simpson, the portrait captures the deadly combination of Adela's chief traits. The first is her beauty; he describes her as a "slender Flemish Madonna" and implies that Jack Archdale married her because she appealed to his collector's taste. The second is her clumsiness, both verbal and physical. Adela's hands are always in motion and always dropping things; she does not seem to understand the extent of the damage she does when she drops an antique Chinese bowl, left to Simpson in the will of a friend, and replaces it with a modern blue and white bowl from a department store.

The conflict Simpson observes between Jack and Adela is objectified in a dispute in London about who should hold the baby, thirteen months old at the time. Jack is angered when Adela says that the boy is "more mine than yours" and confides to Simpson that he cannot wait until the baby, whom they both call the Bambino, grows up. "I can't wait twenty years to know what he's going to do, the sort of things he'll say, what his mind'll be like." On the other hand, Jack continues, Adela would like to keep the boy a baby for the rest of his life. Although this tension between Jack and Adela, on the surface, represents the rather normal friction between the mother and father of any child, Simpson sees the conversation with Jack Archdale as ironic in the light of the Bambino's fate.

Four years later, Simpson meets Jack in his sister Frances's studio and accepts an invitation to drive down to the house in Buckinghamshire that Jack had purchased as a family home. Simpson, who has been out of touch with all the Archdales, notices a great change in Jack. He is short-tempered, withdrawn, and clearly under some sort of strain. The reason becomes clear when Simpson, on their arrival, asks to see the Bambino, who is now five years old. He was not prepared, he remarks to the listener, to see Adela return "with a baby in her arms—a baby too young to display excitement, too young to talk." It is the Bambino, however, and not a second child. Simpson perceives immediately, "She had got her way. The Bambino would be a baby all its life. Its mind had stopped dead at fifteen months." Adela, however, seems not to acknowledge this fact, attributing the child's physical and mental slowness to the size of his brain, but Jack Archdale is fully aware of the significance of his son's condition.

Frances Archdale explains to Simpson that when the Bambino was fifteen months old, Adela dropped him down a staircase. "She was coming down [the stairs] with the Bambino on one arm and the tail of her gown on the other. He caught sight of Archdale in the hall, and was struggling to get to him." Jack clings to every shred of medical evidence that suggests that the effects of that accident will not be permanent, and he struggles with his negative feelings for his wife. Simpson tells his visitor of the terror on Jack's face when, during that visit to Buckinghamshire, he saw Adela enter a room with a burning lamp in her hands. Frances explained then to Simpson that Jack lives in fear of the consequences of his wife's every action. He does not want her to have any more children, Frances added: "He simply couldn't stand seeing her hold them." Painful as the effects of the Bambino's condition are on Jack, Simpson tells his listener, he agrees with Frances that the greater potential for tragedy lies in Adela's situation. Oblivious to the consequences of her actions, as she has been throughout her life, Adela faces the most painful realization when the Bambino is too old for her to rationalize away his mental retardation. She will have to face the terror and hatred she engenders in the husband who cannot bear to look at her hands.

Themes and Meanings

In its broadest sense, the theme of "The Bambino" is the artist-observer's capacity to see the truth more clearly than do the participants in a particular situation. This generalization is supported by May Sinclair's use of Simpson as the narrator of this and a number of the other stories collected in *Tales Told by Simpson* (1930). Simpson and Frances Archdale, both of them painters, arrive at the insights concerning Jack and Adela with which the story ends; indeed, the entire story hangs on Simpson's assumption that the pose that Adela and the Bambino take in Frances's portrait provides a key to understanding the Archdales' situation.

The emphasis on the psychology of Jack Archdale is characteristic of Sinclair's novels and stories. She has a nearly scientific interest in the interplay of biological heredity and environment in the development of human personality. This is seen in Jack Archdale, the man who married a woman who was an art object and whose son becomes in time "like a porcelain idol, doing nothing but wag his head." One of the ironies at work in "The Bambino" is the fact that Jack gets exactly the wife and son his aesthetic taste craves, and then learns how life-denying aestheticism is. Sinclair's treatment of psychology is less complex in "The Bambino" than in *The Three Sisters* (1914), *Mary Olivier: A Life* (1919), and *Life and Death of Hariett Frean* (1922), novels written at approximately the same time she was working on the Simpson stories. All three novels discuss the relationship of child and adult; like the protagonists of the novels, the Bambino is shaped by factors of heredity and environment beyond his control.

Style and Technique

In "The Bambino," Sinclair does not use the stream-of-consciousness narrative technique that she employed in novels such as *Mary Olivier: A Life*. The style of the story develops from her use of Simpson as first-person narrator and of the painting as the visual focus of Simpson's conversation with the unidentified listener. In technique, the story most resembles the dramatic monologues of Robert Browning; Simpson, like the speaker in "My Last Duchess," uses the art object as a point of departure.

As a narrator, however, Simpson is more self-aware than the speaker in Browning's dramatic monologue. His sensitivity to the irony in the situation, and to the nuances of character found in the simplest words and actions, betrays his affinity with the narrator of Ford Madox Ford's *The Good Soldier* (1915). Essential to each is achievement of insight into others and into self. Simpson tells the story of "The Bambino" because he is reliable and honest, and is able to show the dishonesty with which others live.

Robert C. Petersen

BARBADOS

Author: Paule Marshall (1929-   )
Type of plot: Psychological
Time of plot: 1958
Locale: Barbados
First published: 1961

Principal characters:
MR. WATFORD, the seventy-year-old owner of a coconut
plantation
MR. GOODMAN, a local shopkeeper
THE GIRL, an eighteen-year-old who is sent by Goodman to keep
house for Watford

The Story

The title suggests a story that treats life in the Caribbean island of Barbados, perhaps on the microcosmic scale that suits the scope of the short story. However, the main character, Mr. Watford, deliberately lives far outside the mainstream of Barbadian society. He lives alone in an ostentatious plantation house with stone walls, large windows, and a columned portico, which is set far back from the gate that separates it from the crude wooden houses of the village. He tries to live like a white man. His house is an emblem of such a life, with size and pretense, with its furniture from Grand Rapids, Michigan, and its enormous parlor, where in the evenings he reads the newspapers from Boston. He is pleased when the boy who comes to order coconuts for Mr. Goodman shows him deferential gestures usually reserved for whites. Although he worked in a Boston hospital until he retired at sixty-five and although he has kept his American accent, furniture, and newspapers, he had been as detached from American life as he is from life in Barbados, the homeland to which he returned to buy his plantation and live five years before the story begins.

Alone, he works his five hundred trees all day, from dawn to dusk. At seventy, his vigor is fading, though he works ever harder to deny it, driving his body to perform as it did when he was much younger. His lean body is filled with tension, as if he could clench into himself all of his strength and prevent himself from breaking down in exhaustion and despair.

His solitude, his independence, his routine, and his forced energy all isolate him from the village. His disdain for his own people lies in his inability to hate the white family who forced him into servility when he worked for them as a yard boy. His hatred was redirected toward his own race, even toward his mother, who had given birth to nine stillborn children and whose only child to survive was himself. His terrible fear of death, his racial disgust, and his self-loathing drive him to work like a young man, a slave to his weakness and fear.

The antithesis to Watford is Goodman: corpulent, full of lusty vitality and magnanimity, with a rum shop and a coconut booth at the racetrack, a wife, two mistresses, and fourteen children. Goodman dispensing coconuts to the loud, sweating vulgar crowd at the track is the very image of sociability—an image that disgusts Watford. When Goodman comes to buy Watford's coconuts for resale, Watford criticizes as an idler the young man whom Goodman had sent to order the coconuts. Goodman replies that people such as Watford and himself, who have money, must provide work for those who need it. Watford balks at Goodman's assertion that they are responsible for helping others and becomes nauseous with rage when Goodman says that he will send a girl the next day for Watford to hire as a servant.

To have a servant in the house would violate the isolation that Watford has built around himself, would deny his complete self-reliance. To reveal the slightest need for the aid of another human might well lead to his confronting his true self as a mortal, black, aging man.

The servant appears the next day, a young woman barefoot in the driveway, standing as she must have stood, in the sun, from her arrival until his return at noon from the grove. Her stillness and self-possession contrast with Watford's frenetic activity. He tries to send her away, but she replies that she will be beaten if she does not work at least one day. After she fixes his lunch, he decides to send her back at the end of the day with a dollar in payment. She prepares his tea and a late supper, but when he looks for her to send her away, he finds her in an unused room under the stoop, asleep on a cot. He feels like an intruder in his own house. He decides to send her away the next morning.

When he descends at his customary 5:00 A.M., he smells breakfast and finds her sweeping the corridor. He thrusts the dollar at her and orders her out, but she tells him that it is raining. Her faint trust dies at that moment. Though she remains to cook and keep house, she becomes silent and more a part of the house than a human presence because Watford refuses to converse with her.

He preserves his isolation even in her company, yet something about her, the tilt of her head, which reminds him of his mother, works on his affections. After many weeks of her working every day, she goes on a bus excursion on the August bank holiday. Her absence is suddenly more of a disruption than her presence ever was. He feels betrayed by her eagerness to take the day off. He dresses carefully for her return, cleans his nails, and brushes his hair. The feelings mounting in him are those that he has repressed all his life, those of both father and lover, wanting to punish and to protect her.

After watching for some time for her return, he sees her in the moonlight with the boy whom Mr. Goodman had sent, the two of them laughing and frolicking and dancing. The tension with which Watford has held himself together as he has grown old goes limp, and he is unable to speak or act. Unnerved and unmanned, Watford sinks into his bed, aroused and tormented by the thought of the two outside. Sensing them inside the house, he dashes toward her room, preparing his anger for his discovery, but she is alone instead, her clothes twisted about her, and womanly in a way he has not seen before in her. His anger fails him, and he supports himself against the wall. In his weakest moment, he recognizes that she is his last chance to live, but he cannot find the strength to win her, to approach her as a man. He must first defeat her, so he reproaches her and flings her onto the cot. That is the last exercise of his strength. She stands and slaps his hand aside, halting him with her first assertion of selfhood, calling him a "nasty, pissy old man." Her greatest condemnation of him is uttered in language that sums up his predicament exactly, the result of his own confused racial identity: "You ain't people, Mr. Watford, you ain't people."

The charge crushes him. The audacity of her rebellion strikes him hard, but even harder is the epiphany of the "waste and pretense which had spanned his years." His heart gives out, and he dies with a great moan that fills the house and yard with his anguish.

Themes and Meanings

Paule Marshall identifies two sources for the character of Watford. In her 1983 essay "From the Poets in the Kitchen," she recalls a West Indian custodian at the public library in Brooklyn who would give her orders as if he were the librarian himself. The other model, as she wrote in the preface to "Barbados," was her landlord for a year in Barbados, an old man who scarcely spoke to her and who lived in a plantation house such as a black man "playing white" would have.

These two sources suggest that Marshall is examining in her main character the weakness that underlies a particular kind of angry, arrogant, male authority. Watford is portrayed as a strong, energetic man who is accustomed to having things exactly his way. His essential isolation undermines his power, until finally the girl brushes him aside and he collapses. His hatred of his people, his mother, and even himself prevents him from participating in his community, both in the United States and in Barbados. He holds himself above everyone through his cold, facile cynicism. He will not converse with the girl or even ask her name because he cannot allow anyone living so close to him her own personhood. Significantly, her first self-assertion destroys him. The kind of black manhood that is based on racial loathing corrupts every aspect of Watford's personality. His authority is hollow, his strength a mask for weakness.

Style and Technique

Marshall embodies her theme in her characters' physical surroundings and in their physiques. Watford's estate and house are a barrier between himself and the people he despises, but even that distance is not enough. He hardens even his body against the world, but the tension with which he holds himself eventually squeezes the life out of him.

His leanness is the opposite of Goodman's expansive robustness, the physical equivalent of Goodman's outgoing nature and his embracing of the life available to him in Barbados. What Goodman has dissipated through luxurious, sensuous living, Watford has hoarded, but it has dried up in his arid spirit. The house that he has built remains unfinished, the walls unpainted, the furniture unarranged. The magnificent but excessive exterior hides his loss of purpose. He has no one for whom to finish the house. His work in the coconut grove is obsessive, joyless, and dull, his movements mechanical.

Into that life comes the young woman, and as sternly as he tries to drive her off, her humble trust, ease of being, and grace embody a self-acceptance that undermines the basis of Watford's self-contempt. She is the ultimate danger as well as his only possible salvation. Only by letting her destroy his pretenses can he hope to stop wasting his life. To the end, he cannot unclench his body or his grasp on those protections he has built around himself. His strength has been exhausted in the effort, and when at last the girl's dismissive blow flings him aside, his very heart is squeezed dry.

Robert Bensen

BARN BURNING

Author: William Faulkner (1897-1962)
Type of plot: Psychological
Time of plot: After the American Civil War
Locale: Mississippi
First published: 1939

Principal characters:
COLONEL SARTORIS "SARTY" SNOPES, the protagonist, a ten-year-old boy
ABNER SNOPES, his father
LENNIE SNOPES, his mother
MAJOR DE SPAIN, a wealthy southern landowner, Abner's most recent employer
MRS. LULA DE SPAIN, Major de Spain's wife

The Story

As the story opens, ten-year-old Colonel Sartoris Snopes (he is named for Colonel John Sartoris, one of the central figures in William Faulkner's fiction) sits in a make-shift courtroom in a dry goods store and listens as his father is accused of burning a neighbor's barn. Young Sarty is called to the stand, but because the plaintiff is ultimately unwilling to force him to testify against his own father, the case is closed, and the father, Abner Snopes, is advised to leave that part of the country. As the family—Sarty, his parents, two sisters, an older brother, and an aunt—camp out that night on their way to their next home, Snopes, for whom barn burning seems to have become a habitual means of preserving his integrity in the face of men who have more power and wealth than he does, is absolutely cold and unemotional as he strikes Sarty and accuses him of having been prepared to betray his father back in the courtroom. He warns his son, "You got to learn to stick to your own blood or you ain't going to have any blood to stick to you."

Moving from one run-down tenant farmer shack to another has become a way of life for Sarty: He and his family have moved at least a dozen times within his memory. When Sarty and his father first approach the home of Major de Spain, on whose land they have most recently come to labor, Sarty finally feels that here are people to whom his father can pose no threat, that their mansion exists under a spell of peace and dignity, "rendering even the barns and stable and cribs which belong to it impervious to the puny flames he might contrive." Snopes, in his pride and envy, however, immediately forces a confrontation between the landed de Spain and himself, the landless tenant. As Snopes and Sarty walk up the drive, Snopes refuses to alter his stiff stride even enough to avoid some fresh horse droppings and then refuses to wipe his feet before he walks across the pale French rug that graces Mrs. de Spain's entrance hall. The shaken Mrs. de Spain asks the Snopeses to leave her house, and later in the day her husband brings the rug to their home, ordering that it be cleaned. In spite of his wife's pleas that she be allowed to clean it properly, Snopes sets his lazy and inept daughters to work cleaning the rug with harsh lye and, to be sure that it is ruined, scars it himself with a piece of stone.

Major de Spain seeks reparation for the damaged rug in the form of twenty bushels of corn from Snopes's next crop. He is amazed when Snopes, instead of accepting the fine, has him brought before a justice of the peace on the charge that the fine is too high. The justice finds against Snopes but lowers the fine to ten bushels. Any fine at all, however, is too much of an affront to Snopes's dignity. He goes home that night and, once more against his wife's protestations, gathers the kerosene and oil that he will use in burning de Spain's barn.

Sarty is faced with a decision that will shape the rest of his life. His father already knows what the decision will be. Snopes orders his wife to hold the boy so that he cannot warn de Spain. As soon as Snopes leaves, that is exactly what Sarty does. He wrenches himself free from his mother's grasp, warning her that he will strike her if necessary to free himself, and runs to alert the Major. As Sarty runs back toward the barn, de Spain, on his horse, passes Sarty on the road. Sarty hears first one shot and then two more. When he starts to run again, this time it is away from the fire, its glare visible as he looks back over his shoulder.

At midnight, Sarty is sitting on the crest of a hill, his back toward his home of four days and his face toward the dark woods. He tries to convince himself that his father was brave, that he even served nobly in the recent war. Later he will know that his father was in the war only for the booty it had to offer. For now, though, Sarty dozes briefly and then, near dawn, as the morning birds start to call, he walks off into the woods, not looking back.

Themes and Meanings

Young Sarty Snopes describes his own inner conflict as "the being pulled two ways like between two teams of horses." On one side is "the old fierce pull of blood"—family loyalty. On the other are truth and justice. The pull of family ties is strong, but Sarty is old enough to have started to realize that what his father does is wrong.

In the first courtroom scene, Sarty finds himself thinking of the plaintiff as his father's enemy and consciously has to correct himself: "Ourn! mine and hisn both! He's my father!" Leaving the courtroom, he attacks a boy half again his size who calls Snopes a barn burner. Throughout the story, a pattern is established. Sarty keeps trying to defend, through his speech and actions, the father to whom he knows he owes his life and his loyalty. His thoughts, however, and what Faulkner projects will be his future thoughts once he has reached manhood, reveal the ultimately stronger pull of truth and justice. When, after the first trial, his father strikes him and tries to convince him that the men who bring him to trial are only after revenge because they know that ultimately Snopes is in the right, Sarty says nothing, but Faulkner knows that twenty years later, Sarty will tell himself, "If I had said they wanted only truth, justice, he would have hit me again." The de Spain mansion immediately appears to Sarty as a symbol of hope that perhaps here is a power too great—a power with which his father cannot even hope to contend. What he cannot yet comprehend, in his childish innocence, is that the greater the wealth, the greater the gulf between the landowner and the landless Snopes, and thus the greater his father's jealous rage—a rage that Snopes keeps tightly in check until it bursts out in the flames of the fires he sets.

The battle goes on as Sarty continues outwardly to defend his father while inwardly his doubts grow stronger and stronger. When de Spain imposes the fine, Sarty protests to his father that de Spain should have told them how to clean the rug, that the fine is too high, that they will hide the corn from de Spain. When the fine is lowered, he still protests that the major will not get a single bushel. His outbursts in his father's behalf almost cause more trouble for Snopes when Sarty loudly protests, "He ain't done it! He ain't burnt." when the issue at hand this time is the damaged rug, not a burned barn.

Sarty still seems to be supporting his father when he runs to get the oil to burn de Spain's barn. During the short trip, however, he decides that he can neither simply run away nor stand by idly as his father burns the barn. He returns with the oil to defy his father openly for the first time, and he takes his stand firmly on the side of truth and justice when he runs to warn the major. By the end, he has turned his back both literally and symbolically on his home and on what remains of his family. His turning away from his family, however, is presented as a sign of hope as he walks off into the woods as dawn breaks and morning birds' calls replace those of the birds of night.

Style and Technique

The story is not narrated by the ten-year-old Sarty, but Faulkner calls attention to the boy's thoughts and thus to the inner conflict they represent by italicizing them. Subtle word choices also help trace Sarty's move toward maturity and responsibility. Hearing the shots that announce his father's death, Sarty first cries, "Pap! Pap!" but seconds later shifts to the more mature sounding "Father! Father!"

Images of cold and heat, of stiffness and metal, help characterize Abner Snopes. Snopes walks stiffly because of a wound suffered when he was caught stealing a horse during the war. However, stiffness describes his character as well as his walk. His voice is cold, "harsh like tin and without heat like tin." His wiry figure appears "cut ruthlessly from tin." This man who burns barns seems to save his fire for his crimes; all else he does without heat or emotion—whether it is talking, whipping a horse, or striking his son. Even the campfires he builds are niggardly. For him, fire is a means of preserving his integrity and "hence to be regarded with respect and used with discretion."

A little of Snopes's stiffness seems to have carried over to his son at the end of the story. When Sarty awakens after the night of the fire, he is described as being a little stiff. For Sarty, however, the stiffness will not last: "Walking would cure that too as it would the cold, and soon there would be the sun."

Donna B. Haisty

BARTLEBY THE SCRIVENER
A Story of Wall Street

Author: Herman Melville (1819-1891)
Type of plot: Psychological
Time of plot: The 1840's
Locale: New York
First published: 1853

Principal characters:
THE NARRATOR, a successful Wall Street lawyer
BARTLEBY,
TURKEY, and
NIPPERS, his scriveners
GINGER NUT, his office boy

The Story

"Bartleby the Scrivener" is narrated by a prosperous Wall Street lawyer who, in "the cool tranquillity of a snug retreat," does "a snug business among rich men's bonds, and mortgages, and title-deeds." Among his clients, the nameless narrator is proud to report, was John Jacob Astor, the richest man in the United States at the time of his death.

The narrator's employees, as the story begins, are Turkey and Nippers, who are scriveners, or copyists, and Ginger Nut, a young office boy. The Dickensian copyists present problems for their employer, for each displays a different personality during each half of the working day. Turkey, who is short and fat, works quickly and steadily before noon but becomes clumsy and ill-tempered after his midday meal. At the opposite extreme is the dyspeptic Nippers, nervous and irritable in the mornings but mild and productive in the afternoons. Because they are regular in their inconsistent behavior, the narrator reports that he "never had to do with their eccentricities at one time," and the work of the office proceeds, with Ginger Nut keeping the scriveners under some control by supplying them with cakes and apples.

The unusual order of the office is disrupted when the lawyer, because of extra work created by his being appointed a Master in Chancery, hires an additional copyist. At first, Bartleby works constantly, but one day he suddenly declines to compare a copied document and its original, offering no explanation, saying simply, "I would prefer not to." Gradually, he prefers not to perform any of his tasks. His employer also discovers that Bartleby has no home other than the office and is sleeping there nights and weekends, eating little more than ginger nuts (small, spicy cakes).

The lawyer pleads with Bartleby to work or leave, but the obstinate scrivener continues to pursue his preference not to do anything. Growing increasingly distraught over these circumstances, the lawyer finally moves his chambers to another building. When Bartleby is expelled from the office by the new tenant, he remains in the building. The lawyer makes final pleas, even offering to take Bartleby home with him. Still, the scrivener prefers not to make any change, and the narrator flees the city in his frustration. On his return, he learns that Bartleby has been taken to the Tombs, the forbiddingly named city prison, as a vagrant.

The lawyer bribes a Tombs employee to take care of Bartleby, but the prisoner refuses to eat, preferring to stand beside and stare at the prison wall. The narrator tries to convince him that his surroundings are not that depressing; the prisoner replies, "I know where I am." Eventually, he dies.

After Bartleby's death, the lawyer learns that he had previously been a clerk in the Dead Letter Office in Washington and thinks that such a melancholy duty explains the poor man's peculiar behavior. He ends his story by proclaiming its pathetic universality: "Ah, Bartleby! Ah, humanity!"

Themes and Meanings

The wealth of thematic possibilities in "Bartleby the Scrivener" has made it perhaps the most analyzed of all American short stories. Much of this analysis centers on the title character, who is seen as a forerunner of alienated modern man, as the victim of an indifferent society, as a nonconformist—perhaps even a heroic one—who becomes isolated simply for daring to assert his preferences. Another interpretation, built around Bartleby's role as a writer of sorts, claims that Herman Melville's story is a parable of the isolation of the artist in a materialistic society that not only is indifferent to its writers but also is bent on their destruction.

Such views, while having varying degrees of validity, ignore the fact that "Bartleby the Scrivener" is dominated by the sensibility of its narrator and his search for the truth, a search that is ironic because he is incapable of any objective understanding of Bartleby and his seemingly perverse preferences. Not Bartleby's actions or passivity but the narrator's responses to his copyist are what is important.

Early in the story, the lawyer describes himself as "an eminently safe man," one "who, from his youth upwards, has been filled with a profound conviction that the easiest way of life is the best." He makes allowances for Turkey and Nippers because that is the easiest way to deal with them, but he is unable to understand why he cannot similarly control Bartleby.

When his initial efforts with Bartleby fail, he attempts to turn the predicament to his advantage. The sentimental narrator tries to change the scrivener from an intractable problem to an opportunity for compassion. However, this compassion, as is appropriate for a man of Wall Street who exults in John Jacob Astor's name, "for it hath a rounded and orbicular sound to it, and rings like unto bullion," is selfish: "Here I can cheaply purchase a delicious self-approval. To befriend Bartleby; to humor him in his strange willfulness, will cost me little or nothing, while I lay up in my soul what will eventually prove a sweet morsel for my conscience." For him, the moral and the financial seem inseparable.

When compassion proves insufficient, the narrator resorts to philosophical explanations. Reading Jonathan Edwards's *The Freedom of the Will* (1754) and Joseph

Priestley's *The Doctrine of Philosophical Necessity Illustrated* (1777) convinces him that Bartleby has been "billeted upon me for some mysterious purpose of an all-wise Providence, which it was not for a mere mortal like me to fathom." This evasion of responsibility is not the answer, however, because people are talking about him. Because the good opinions of others are essential to his business and his self-esteem, the lawyer is finally forced to act.

Melville is satirizing the materialistic society of his time but in a much larger sense than merely its indifference to writers. Melville is attacking its smug morality, its pomposity, its sentimental, patronizing attitude toward its individual citizens, its simplistic view of the complex and the ambiguous, its persistent ignorance of its responsibilities. Not Bartleby but the self-deceiving narrator is the absurd, pathetic protagonist.

Style and Technique

Wall imagery dominates this "story of Wall Street." The narrator describes the location of his chambers in detail. At one end is seen the white wall of a large skylight shaft: "This view might have been considered . . . deficient in what landscape painters call 'life.'" At the other end is an ugly brick wall, blackened by age, ten feet from the window. Bartleby's desk is inside the lawyer's office, so that he can be within easy call, but is in a corner by a small window, which "commanded at present no view at all" because another wall is three feet from the panes. Bartleby stares at this wall when he prefers not to work. He is separated from his fellow copyists by a ground-glass door and is isolated from his employer, "a satisfactory arrangement," by a high, green folding screen, suggesting the lawyer's monetary obsession. Thus, there are walls within walls within walls within Wall Street.

The impossibility of the absence of walls is emphasized when Bartleby is removed to the Tombs, where he ignores the limited space in the exercise yard, choosing to stand beside the exterior wall, which both keeps him and protects him from society. He dies there curled into the fetal position (suggesting a possible tomb-womb pun), as if he could return to a state of innocence only in death.

These walls represent more than mere isolation; they are barriers to communication, to understanding, especially in a story told by a man who understands much less than he thinks he does. As in Melville's greatest achievement, *Moby Dick* (1851), the walls imply that humankind is incapable of true perception, that understanding the purpose of existence is impossible.

The other major stylistic device employed by Melville is his unreliable narrator, who sees only what is on the surface. It is ironic that in his quest for the easy explanation he decides that Bartleby refuses to work because something is wrong with his eyes. Melville helps establish the tradition of having a tale told by someone who is accurate about facts but who is very subjective in interpreting the motivations not only of others but also of himself. This self-justifying narrator creates the story's irony, its humor, its greatness.

Michael Adams

THE BASEBALL GLOVE

Author: Víctor Martínez (1954-   )
Type of plot: Social realism
Time of plot: The 1970's
Locale: Central California
First published: 1993

Principal characters:
THE NARRATOR, a Chicano teenager
BERNARDO (NARDO), his brother

The Story

The narrator, remembering when he and his brother Bernardo, or Nardo as the family calls him, were both teenagers, recalls the various jobs that Nardo held one summer: busboy, dishwasher, parking attendant, and short-order cook. Nardo managed to get himself fired from all of them, either for not showing up or showing up too often for a boss that hated him. Nardo's favorite job was working as a busboy for a catering service at the Bonneville Lakes country club, touching elbows with the rich and enjoying free drinks and other perks. He lost this job when, on a dare, he took off his busboy's jacket and asked a girl to dance. Unfortunately, his boss saw him.

There is not much left that summer for Nardo and his brother except the fields, and Nardo does not relish the idea of sweating over clods of dirt in temperatures more than 100 degrees, during one of the hottest summers in the history of California's San Joaquin Valley. Everyone in the family works, however—Nardo's sister Magda sweats in a laundry and Nardo's brother sells fruit door to door—so the pressure is on Nardo to get a job. Naturally lazy by temperament, Nardo is scolded, shamed, and threatened by his parents, especially by his father, but nothing seems to work. After a while everybody gives up on Nardo, who stays home lifting weights, exercising, and primping in front of a mirror.

The narrator, who is not at all like his brother, wants to work. Uncle Louie, with whom he sold fruit door to door, hurt his leg tripping over tree roots in the front yard, and the boy now feels empty without something useful to do. Besides, he needs money for school clothes and supplies. Most of all, he wants a baseball glove that he saw in the window of Duran's Department Store. His fantasies are filled with baseball, and he sees himself making spectacular Willy Mays-like catches with such a glove. When he tries to convince Nardo to go into the field with him to pick chili peppers, Nardo—to everyone's amazement—agrees. Nardo is going to prove to them all that he is not lazy.

At the chili field the next day, the two brothers find that most of the rows have already been taken because most of the fieldworkers got up while it was still dark, but the foreman agrees to give them a scrawny row that nobody else wants—a row coated with pesticide and thick with exhaust fumes from traffic on the nearby road. Their job is to fill a can with chili peppers and carry it to a nearby weighing area, where they will receive immediate payment. The weighing area, however, is sheer hell. Older women and young girls, some with handkerchiefs tied around their faces, sift through the peppers, and the scent of freshly broken peppers makes it almost impossible to breathe. At the weighing area is a company-owned vending truck from which workers can purchase snacks and soft drinks. Nardo is angered that he must pay eighty-five cents for a cheap soft drink that has gone flat.

The brothers endure this work, amazed at the Mexican working next to them. With a can in each hand, the man efficiently moves up and down the rows, pouring the cans into sacks he has stationed every twenty feet or so. Suddenly a van approaches, and workers begin to scatter. The brothers quickly realize it is the immigration authorities, come to pick up illegal aliens. Soon the Mexicans are all rounded up and herded onto a bus. The twenty or so workers who are left search the rows for filled sacks, confiscating them for themselves. Nardo claims the sacks belonging to the Mexican who was working the rows next to them; they contain more than the brothers could have picked in two days. Now, Nardo tells his brother, he can buy that baseball mitt.

Looking down at the sacks, the narrator feels weary and wonders how long it would have taken him to pick this many peppers. Then he envisions the baseball glove, clean and smelling of leather, and sees himself standing in the cool, green grass of center field, like the Bonneville Lakes golf course Nardo has told him about. He imagines he is already on the school baseball team with people looking at him with respect and admiration—not the people who pick peppers or those who were rounded up in the vans, but people he has yet to know.

Themes and Meanings

"The Baseball Glove" is not just a story about two brothers; it is also a story about two aspects of the Chicano experience. One involves first- and second-generation Mexican Americans; the other involves illegal immigrants from Mexico who come to the United States to work. The narrator and his brother, Nardo, are at the lower end of the American economic ladder, but at least they can get jobs as busboys, dishwashers, parking lot attendants, and short-order cooks. They dream of moving up someday among the rich at such places as Bonneville Lakes, and the narrator even dreams of success in that most American of all sports, baseball. The baseball glove embodies that dream; purchasing it represents for the narrator the beginning of his dreams of American success, which he intends to achieve by the usual American qualities of hard work, thrift, and rugged individualism.

Nardo, on the other hand, has been reared in the United States long enough to take it for granted. He casually loses job after job, loafs about the house, and sponges off his industrious family. Only as a last resort does Nardo undertake the most menial of jobs, picking chili peppers in the unbearably hot fields of the San Joaquin Valley—a job in which many Mexican Americans and illegal aliens are employed. The brothers discover in just a few hours what is a lifelong reality for many workers: The job is back-breaking, the wages are low, the conditions are terrible, and the company owns everything, even the burrito truck that sells snacks and soft drinks at exorbitant prices.

In contrast to the two brothers are the Mexican workers in the same field. They are not only capable workers, they are exemplary ones—fast, efficient, and uncomplaining. Although they earn less than minimum wage in the United States, they earn much more than they would make in Mexico and are among the few people in the United States willing to do such exacting labor. The chili growers, in fact, could not survive without them. When they are rounded up by the immigration authorities, the legal workers, rationalizing that the others do not live in the United States, confiscate the Mexicans' filled chili sacks for themselves, exploiting them just as badly as their employers do.

Although the narrator finds himself sympathizing with the illegals, hoping that they will get away, he, too, succumbs to the false dreams of American success. He ends up not thinking about the people carried away by the authorities but of the people he has yet to know, those who will admire him as he stands in center field, the center of attention. The implicit reality of the story, however, is that he and Nardo have few valuable skills, and that in an exploitative culture they may never get much beyond the chili fields, let alone onto cool, green baseball fields. The glove behind the window of Duran's Department Store may remain, like the American Dream of success for such boys, forever partitioned off, just beyond their reach.

Style and Technique

Víctor Martínez tells his story by suggesting much but declaring little. Although Nardo seems a lazy slacker at first, a little thought suggests that he is the victim of a society that offers him only dead-end jobs while enticing him with visions of unattainable society girls, golf courses, and opulent parties. Although Nardo has dropped out of the American Dream, his brother still fosters notions of conventional success: Someday he will be much admired, the focus of everyone's attention, a gifted baseball player. Although such things are possible in the United States, they are unlikely for Mexican American boys such as the narrator, who must rise above discrimination and his working-class background to attain anything at all. At the end of the story, he still retains his dreams, but the experience with the illegal workers has clearly unsettled him, perhaps even changed him.

Martínez tells his story with economical prose containing occasional figurative language, such as, "my weariness stretched as wide as the horizon," and poetic descriptions. The narrator gives the reader an account from inside the Chicano experience, forcing one to see his people as he does—with sympathy, humor, and affection—and that his dreams are the same as those of any teenage American boy. In the case of Nardo and his brother, however, Martínez makes it abundantly clear that those dreams will be exceptionally hard to achieve.

Kenneth Seib

THE BASEMENT ROOM

Author: Graham Greene (1904-1991)
Type of plot: Psychological
Time of plot: The 1930's
Locale: London
First published: 1935

> *Principal characters:*
> PHILIP LANE, seven years old, who loves Baines
> BAINES, the butler
> MRS. BAINES, the housekeeper
> EMMY, the girl Baines introduces to Philip as his niece

The Story

Left by his parents in the care of their butler and housekeeper, seven-year-old Philip Lane excitedly anticipates exploring the large Belgravia house while learning something about the adult world. Philip loves Baines, the butler, whose adventurous tales about Africa entrance him, but he dislikes and fears Mrs. Baines, whose very presence terrifies him in the same way that the demons that people his nightmares do.

Once his parents leave the house on their holiday, Philip seeks out Baines in the basement room, entered through a green baize door that separates the family rooms from the servants' quarters. In the basement room, Philip's fear and dislike of Mrs. Baines are reaffirmed as he watches Baines efface himself in her presence. Philip begins to appreciate the conflicting claims of adulthood in a world he yearns for yet fears to enter. He begins to understand fear and coercion and to intuit the meaning of evil. He suspects that undiluted joy, his feeling for Baines, can be threatened by the very presence of those such as Mrs. Baines.

Philip asks Baines to take him for a walk, but Mrs. Baines interferes. The boy escapes alone into the world beyond the Belgravia mansion rather than witness their disharmony. Too timid to venture far, he begins to retrace his steps. In a tea shop he sees Baines, not the cowering individual he recently left but a concerned and affable lover pressing jars of discarded cosmetics, rescued and then rejected by Mrs. Baines from the upstairs rooms in the process of housecleaning, on a young and unattractive girl. Philip thinks that it would be amusing to intrude on Baines and his "niece" in Mrs. Baines's voice. He invades their moment of happiness, returning them to reality with a fearful thud. Baines introduces Philip to Emmy, offers him a cake with pink icing, and asks him to keep Emmy a secret from Mrs. Baines.

Later, in the nursery, Mrs. Baines manages to trick Philip into revealing the secret he shares with Baines. She bribes him with a Meccano set. The pressures of adult responsibility invade his innocent sphere of love and trust, and he wonders about his place within the adult world. "Baines oughtn't to have trusted him; grown up people should keep their own secrets," he thinks. He betrays Baines by failing to tell him about Mrs. Baines's invasion of his dreams.

Mrs. Baines devises a simple plan to trap her husband and Emmy. She pretends to leave London to care for an ailing mother, then sends a telegram saying that she is delayed and will return the following day. Although she is gone, her presence pervades the house. Baines and Emmy and Philip spend a delightful day exploring London; that night, however, after Philip has been put to bed, Mrs. Baines comes once more into his room and confirms the reality of his nightmares. She again promises him a Meccano set if he will tell her where Baines and Emmy are. Terrified, Philip screams, then watches Baines grapple with Mrs. Baines on the landing. Philip sees her go over the banister "in a flurry of black clothes" and fall into the hall below.

Once again, Philip escapes into the world beyond the Belgravia house. He is found by the police, who learn of the "accident'" reported by Baines. They return him to the house.

In attempting to shield Emmy, Baines has moved the body from the hall into the basement room. When confronted by Mrs. Baines's death, Philip refuses Baines's mute plea to keep yet another secret. He has learned that to love is to accept the burden of trust in and responsibility for another, for which life has not yet prepared him. Philip extricates himself from Baines, from love and life. He dies sixty years later, still asking about the girl, Emmy, who had unwittingly unleashed fear into his innocent world and forced him to choose a life of lonely noninvolvement.

Themes and Meanings

"The Basement Room" is the dramatization of a traumatizing event that inhibits the individual from achieving human contact in the future. The situation presented deals with the souring of innocence and the consequent fear of life that it occasions. The theme is best expressed in the narrator's statement: "Life fell on him [Philip] with savagery and you couldn't blame him if he never faced it again in sixty years." Philip Lane is portrayed as an imaginative and sensitive boy who has not yet learned to distinguish good from evil and right from wrong. The story's central meaning has to do with his sudden awareness that life is a series of compromises, and that adulthood forces one into commitments and allegiances that one does not always understand. Philip learns that good and evil are not as clear-cut as his feelings for Baines, whom he loves, and Mrs. Baines, whom he fears. When he unwittingly betrays Baines, he does not understand that choice has been thrust on him too soon; rather than commit himself in trust and love to another human being in the future, he chooses to remain isolated from human life. The story focuses on the theme of betrayal, agonizingly complicated to the boy Philip, provocative to the reader.

Style and Technique

The action is presented by an omniscient narrator as he presents the events that inhibit the boy from fulfilling himself in the sixty years he lives following the traumatizing experience that constitutes the story's main action. The narrative shifts from

an acute and psychologically perceptive account of the boy's refusal to accept
Baines's appeal to keep yet another secret, to a view of the dying man who has managed, at best, a life of dilettantism. The contracting and expanding focus allows the
reader to appreciate the traumatizing incident and to realize its results on the character
of the man that the boy becomes.

The story can also be read as an exercise in meaningful symbolism. The house in
Jungian terms can loosely be seen as the integrated personality. The green baize door
through which the boy passes to the basement room serves as a Freudian device to distinguish between the conscious and the subconscious, while the sweet cake and the
Meccano set with which he never plays function as comments on the nature of existence. The experience of betrayal denies Philip both the sweetness of life and the ability to create. The city beyond the house can be interpreted as the region outside the
self, where good and evil exist in mutual tolerance of each other. Outside the house,
Philip agrees to keep Baines's secret. Mrs. Baines, however, invades his psyche and
catalyzes in the boy a fear of life. Insofar as Philip becomes Mrs. Baines's accomplice
by failing to tell Baines that he has inadvertently betrayed their secret, he is in complicity with evil; later, he suffers the death of the heart when he refuses the responsibilities and consequences of an adulthood that he is unprepared to accept. Dream and
nightmare, furthermore, afford a coherent imagery that emphasizes the power of evil.
As such, the story serves as an epitome of favorite themes and preoccupations that
characterize Graham Greene's fictional universe.

Perhaps the story's greatest accomplishment is the immediacy with which the
traumatizing episodes are presented. The reader is convinced of the tale's psychological validity as he appreciates and acknowledges the nature of a betrayal that destroys
innocence and dooms the individual to a life of waste and loss.

A. A. DeVitis

BATTLE ROYAL

Author: Ralph Ellison (1914-1994)
Type of plot: Social realism
Time of plot: 1947 and the late 1920's
Locale: Unnamed rural area in the American South
First published: 1947

> *Principal characters:*
> THE NARRATOR, an African American man
> HIS GRANDFATHER
> THE SCHOOL SUPERINTENDENT
> TATLOCK, a young man whom the narrator fights

The Story

The story consists of a frame in which the mature narrator remembers the advice that his dying grandfather gave to his son (the narrator's father) and his remembrance of a cruel betrayal that confirms the grandfather's advice.

The grandfather tells his son to "keep up the good fight," to continue the black people's war by guerrilla tactics, to be a traitor and spy in the enemy's country as he himself has been. He tells his son: "Live with your head in the lion's mouth. I want you to overcome 'em with yeses, undermine 'em with grins, agree 'em to death and destruction." The narrator and his alarmed family puzzle over the old man's last words, especially because the narrator has been praised by the town's powerful white men for his meekness and cooperativeness. He is secretly concerned that without meaning to he is already somehow carrying out his grandfather's advice.

The battle royal episode begins when white leaders ask the narrator to deliver a high school graduation speech on the virtues of humility to a gathering of leading white citizens, a "triumph" for the black community. The event, held in the ballroom of a leading hotel, turns out to be a "smoker," a male-only affair involving whiskey, cigars, and smutty entertainment. The latter begins with the battle royal of the title, a free-for-all boxing match in which blindfolded combatants punch at one another wildly. Because the boxers are all high school classmates of the narrator, he is recruited to take part.

Before the boxing match begins, a drunk woman does a nude dance before the equally drunk men, who try to grab her. After she escapes, the narrator and nine other African American high school boys are blindfolded and pushed into a ring, where they pound at one another to the blood-thirsty screams of the audience. By pushing his blindfold partly free, the sweaty and bloody narrator escapes some blows. He sees the other boys leaving the ring and realizes that he is being left alone with the biggest fighter, Tatlock. Because the custom is for the last two boxers to fight to the finish, the narrator tries to bribe Tatlock to take a dive, but he fails and is knocked out. Afterward, he and the other boys are invited to collect gold coins scattered on a rug for their payment, but the rug is electrified so they must endure shocks as they entertain the white men. The coins turn out to be brass advertising tokens.

Finally, the other boys are paid off and sent home, and the narrator is told to give his speech—which is a florid and conventional appeal to African Americans to be friendly toward whites and to accept the status quo. After gagging on blood from a cut in his mouth caused by a punch, the narrator inadvertently utters the phrase "social equality" instead of "social responsibility." The room goes quiet until he corrects himself. His return to meekness and humility is rewarded with thunderous applause, a calfskin briefcase, and a scholarship to the state college for Negroes. His family and neighbors are delighted, but he himself dreams about his grandfather, who shows him a message deposited in his briefcase: "Keep This Nigger-Boy Running." He awakens remembering the sound of the old man's ironic laughter.

Themes and Meanings

"Battle Royal" was first published as a short story in *Horizon* in 1947 under the title "Invisible Man." It later became the first chapter of Ralph Ellison's only novel, *Invisible Man* (1952), whose title comes from a phrase at the beginning of the story: "But first I had to discover that I am an invisible man!" "Battle Royal" provides a fascinating window into the creative forces that produced *Invisible Man*, which is recognized as one of the great American novels of our time, as well as a masterwork of the burgeoning black literature movement of the second half of the twentieth century. Grandfather episodes provide the thematic motor that drives much of the novel, which is a study of a naïve young man who is wounded by racism but unsure how to respond. He wants to be a good member of his family and community but fails to understand the poisonous effect that southern race relations have on even such simple acts as delivering a harmless graduation speech. The story makes clear just what the narrator will face in his maturity.

The battle royal episode itself introduces many of the themes with which the narrator deals later in his life in the novel. These include social Darwinism, which metaphorically encourages individuals to fight to the finish in order to receive rewards; the ways in which the black community's strongest and wiliest members take advantage of their fellows, refusing to cooperate against the common white enemy just as Tatlock refuses to fake defeat; the corrupting influence of prizes and praise on the narrator himself; and the need for the white establishment to maintain symbolic as well as literal power over the black community. If *Invisible Man* defines many African American responses to racism and politics, "Battle Royal" provides a capsule version of the thematic crux of the larger work, how to respond to the cruelty of racism while retaining one's decency and humanity.

Ellison involves the reader so deeply in the experiences of his narrator that one shares both his pain and his confusion and uncertainty. The innocence and decency of the narrator, who is simply trying to do the right thing, are so effectively conveyed that readers of all races and cultures can understand the special problems that he faces.

Style and Technique

One of this story's greatest achievements is successfully rendering the narrator's dreamlike and emotional memories, although these are often abstract in their lack of full detail—in contrast to the sharp, cinematic depiction of the "reality" of the battle royal experience, yet with each style reinforcing the idea of the other. The narrator's recollections tend to be simple declarative sentences using the first-person pronoun: "I was naïve. I was looking for myself." Through this highly personal medium the reader learns of the narrator's guilt and confusion about his grandfather's advice and his innocent lack of understanding of the mean-spirited intentions of the white establishment.

By contrast, the battle royal descriptions contain minute specificity, with details creating a word picture of place and setting: "It was a large room with a high ceiling. Chairs were arranged in neat rows around three sides of a portable boxing ring. The fourth side was clear, revealing a gleaming space of polished floor." Such straightforward description alternates with metaphors and similes that suggest the bizarre and exotic nature of what is happening: The blindfolded boys grope about "like blind, cautious crabs," their fists "testing the air like the knobbed feelers of hypersensitive snails." The nude dancer has yellow hair of "a circus kewpie doll," her breasts are "round as the domes of East Indian temples." The scenes in the boxing ring are especially effective, with visually descriptive phrases cutting quickly from image to image to convey the chaos of the blindfolded match: "The room spun round me, a swirl of lights, smoke, sweating bodies surrounded by tense white faces." The overly rhetorical style of the graduation speech slyly makes fun of the overwrought prose of that genre: "We of the younger generation extol the wisdom of that great leader and educator who first spoke these flaming words of wisdom."

Throughout, Ellison matches style and content, his medium conveying his message. Ellison's interest in and knowledge of jazz improvisation (he was a professional-level musician) is evident in the rhythms of his prose, which soars with a free exuberance yet still retains a tough-minded discipline. Even long after they were written, his verbal improvisations retain a freshness and newness assuring that this short story and the novel that grew out of it will remain essential reading.

Andrew Macdonald

THE BATTLER

Author: Ernest Hemingway (1899-1961)
Type of plot: Vignette
Time of plot: The 1910's
Locale: Michigan
First published: 1925

Principal characters:
NICK ADAMS, a young roustabout
AD (ADOLPH) FRANCIS, a punched-out former boxer
BUGS, an African American former trainer who looks after Ad
A RAILROAD BRAKEMAN

The Story

Nick Adams has been riding the rails in Michigan. Essentially innocent and by his own admission not tough, he falls for the ploy of a railroad brakeman on the freight train on which he has hitched a ride. The brakeman spies Nick and tells him to come close because he has something for him. The something that the brakeman has for Nick is a hefty punch that catapults him off the moving train to the earth below. Nursing a black eye, Nick washes up in a nearby tamarack swamp, then makes his way along the roadbed toward Mancelona, some three or four miles distant. As he walks along the tracks he sees a small fire in the distance and heads toward it.

Nick approaches the fire cautiously, hidden by the night and by the beechwood forest in which he lurks. Seeing a man beside the fire, he approaches stealthily. When he gets closer, he greets the man, who looks up and asks him where he got his shiner. Nick then unfolds his story. The hobo has a badly mutilated face and has lost one ear. Nick stares at him so hard that he asks Nick whether he likes his face. Introducing himself as Ad—and later as Adolph Francis, a former lightweight champion of whom Nick has heard—he invites Nick to eat with him. He also announces that he is crazy and that he has a heart that beats only forty times a minute—which he insists on having Nick verify by taking his pulse as he counts to sixty.

Just as this ritual ends, a third man, Bugs, stumbles down the railroad embankment. Ad's erstwhile friend, Bugs, is black. Ad insists that Bugs is crazy too, and Bugs does not deny it. After verifying that Nick neither is nor ever was crazy and that he comes from Chicago, Bugs begins cooking ham and eggs in a skillet. Ad asks to use Nick's knife to cut the bread, but Bugs intervenes, warning Nick not to give his knife to Ad. Instead, Nick cuts six pieces of bread for the three of them.

After they eat, Ad becomes pensive and goes off into a world of his own. Bugs addresses him but elicits no response. Suddenly, Ad turns on Nick, demanding to know who the hell Nick thinks he is to come and eat his food and then get snotty when asked to lend his knife. Ad challenges Nick to a fight, which Nick tries to avert. Ad is determined, however, and is on the brink of punching Nick when Bugs approaches him from behind and knocks him out with a blackjack wrapped in cloth.

Bugs then explains that he looks after the punch-drunk former boxer, whose career ended when he and his female manager—to whom he bore a striking resemblance—got married, causing all sorts of speculation about incest. Ever since, Ad has lived the hobo life with Bugs nearby to save him from disaster. His former wife sends him money for his subsistence.

Bugs advises Nick that he can revive Ad whenever he wishes but that it would be best if he were not around when Ad regains consciousness. Giving Nick a sandwich to take with him, Bugs bids him farewell and revives Ad, giving him a cup of hot coffee to help him wake up.

Themes and Meanings

Superficially, little happens in "The Battler," which was initially titled "A Great Little Fighting Machine." Although the story is little more than a vignette, it is touching in its simplicity and is remarkably psychologically sensitive and penetrating. Three unremarkable people come together by accident. Out of this brief chance encounter emerges a touching story of loyalty and camaraderie similar to John Steinbeck's *Of Mice and Men* (1937), in which George takes care of the retarded Lenny. Ad is not retarded; rather he is addled by the injuries he sustained in his fighting career. The character is based on two prizefighters whom Ernest Hemingway knew—Ad Wolgast and Bat Nelson. Bugs is based on Wolgast's black trainer.

"The Battler" is one of the many Nick Adams stories for which Hemingway gained early recognition. In these stories, Nick is consistently a catalyst rather than a central figure. He enters a situation, causes something to happen, observes it, then departs relatively unchanged. The story unfolding in "The Battler" belongs to Ad and Bugs. The basic conflict is that of a man, Ad, against the world. Life has not dealt him the best hand, yet his salvation comes from the loyal devotion of his friend, a sensitive, courteous, genuinely caring person. Bugs is unfailingly patient, yet he knows the limits that he must impose on Ad to save him from himself.

"The Battler" demonstrates how two men, each bearing his own burdens, can form a symbiotic relationship that enables both to survive. Bugs is called "nigger" and has undoubtedly suffered the humiliation of racial discrimination. Hemingway shows subtly that Bugs understands his place in a society that discriminates against him solely on the basis of his pigmentation. Hemingway always has Bugs refer to the other two characters in the story as "Mr. Francis" and "Mr. Adams," not as "Ad" and "Nick." Although Ad is the former prizefighter, Bugs is the story's strong character. Without him it is doubtful that Ad could continue his hobo existence. It is also possible that if Bugs were not burdened by the responsibility that he has accepted for Ad, he might have a better life for himself. Nevertheless, Bugs is committed to Ad for the long haul. He is uncomplaining, although he is realistic in dealing with Ad.

Nick Adams merely passes through a situation. He stumbles into it without planning to do so, is briefly engaged in it, then, having observed its dynamics, he departs at

Masterplots II

the appropriate time. The story is thematically tight. Hemingway wastes no words in its telling. He shows more than he tells, revealing character convincingly yet almost incidentally. The result is a story that has remarkable thematic and structural coherence. In this story, as in the other Nick Adams stories, the central character is one of society's rejects. Society has used and discarded Ad Francis. This is the fate, seemingly, of those who battle against society. Ad's descent began presumably because he passed his manager off as his sister. His eventual marriage to her evoked a public outcry that destroyed the marriage and essentially ended Ad's career. Outraged at the injustice of what happened to him, Ad then became uncontrollably violent, picking fights and eventually ending up in jail. On his release, Bugs rescued him and has devoted himself to controlling him to spare him further difficulties, yet coddling him like a dependent child.

Style and Technique

Known for his clipped, direct style, uncomplicated sentence structure, and simple vocabulary, Hemingway demonstrates in "The Battler" the effectiveness and appropriateness of depicting characters on the social fringe, essentially antiheroes, as unostentatiously as he can. Few of his sentences exceed ten or twelve words. Simple sentences predominate and, when Hemingway uses a compound sentence, it is usually held together by a simple "and."

During his post-World War I residence in Paris, Hemingway learned a great deal about style from Gertrude Stein, with whom he had a close friendship in the early 1920's. Stein, a careful observer of how ordinary people actually use language, experimented with dialogue and, especially in her experimental novel *Three Lives* (1909), captured the authentic means by which common, working-class people communicate. In so doing, she presented endless repetitions, often to the point of exasperating her readers. Hemingway's "The Battler" uses similar techniques. For example, Bugs tells Nick that Ad's wife "Looked enough like him to be twins," then, within half a page, repeats this information in almost the same words. Some authors would intrude on the actual language and would refine the dialogue to eliminate the repetition. Hemingway, however, prefers to allow his characters to speak the way real people speak, even if they repeat themselves.

In shaping his dialogue, Hemingway often avoids forms of the verb "to say." Rather, he uses such verbs as "advised," "warned," "finished," "asked," "smiled," or "came out." He draws attention to his most significant dialogue by using this device, reserving phrases such as "he said" for the more ordinary dialogue.

Hemingway developed a style unique among American writers, one easily distinguishable by its economy and directness. This style, an amalgamation of much that he learned from Gertrude Stein and of his experience as a journalist, has had a significant impact on more recent novelists, many of whom have striven to imitate Hemingway's controlled rhetorical simplicity.

R. Baird Shuman

THE BEACH UMBRELLA

Author: Cyrus Colter (1910-2002)
Type of plot: Domestic realism
Time of plot: Summer, around 1963
Locale: Chicago
First published: 1963

Principal characters:
ELIJAH, a forty-one-year-old warehouse worker
MYRTLE, his wife
RANDALL, his twelve-year-old son, who works at odd jobs to earn
spending money
MRS. GREEN, a young mother at the beach with her sons

The Story

On a hot Saturday in late summer, Elijah lolls in the sun on a Lake Michigan beach, like many others out to have a good time. Unlike them, however, he is alone and does not have a beach umbrella. Enchanted by the crowd of frolickers, he comes to the beach almost every Saturday, but his family has stayed home, where his wife is growing upset about his lack of ambition for his family. When she scolds him about getting a "real job," such as a high-paying job in a steel mill, he thinks of her as being "money-crazy."

Watching the smoke rising from a mill across the lake, Elijah ponders his job at the warehouse. After working hard there for nine years, he holds a position of responsibility. He wears a white shirt and a tie. The pay might be better, but he likes almost everything else about his job. Also, his pay would be enough, he thinks, if Myrtle did not want so much. A blue-collar job in the mill would be undignified and would leave him exhausted every night.

Feeling lonely and rejected by the groups of bathers, Elijah observes that beach umbrellas attract people to them—men and women who have come to the beach to have fun with others like themselves. Suddenly he feels that he must buy a flashy colorful umbrella.

By Monday evening Elijah has found an umbrella that would fulfill his dream, but he has less than half of the money that it costs. After dinner, his son Randy goes back to work at a store, and Myrtle again berates Elijah for not earning more money. The children, she tells him, will soon need clothes for school. Through the evening Elijah stares at the television, feeling oppressed by his alienation from his family. When Randy comes home, he avoids conversation by going to bed. Later, while Myrtle works in the kitchen, Elijah awakens his son and borrows fifteen dollars, telling Randy that he should not say anything to his mother about the loan.

On the next Saturday the sky is cloudy, but an anxiously hopeful Elijah carefully selects a spot on the beach where he raises his new red and white umbrella. When the sun at last comes out, people crowd onto the beach, and Elijah persuades two boys and their shy young mother to have a drink of lemonade in the shade that his umbrella provides. When the people under the umbrella next to Elijah's mistake this woman for his wife, she seems content when Elijah fails to correct their misimpression. Elijah is elated. As the conversation proceeds, however, his nervous laughter grows awkward until his new friends perceive that Mrs. Green is not his wife but probably is his girlfriend. There is some embarrassment over this confusion, but again the young mother does not correct the false impression. More bathers settle nearby, and soon Elijah is manic with delight at the boisterous party that he feels he has assembled. Life seems wonderfully different than it was just one week earlier. Elijah frolics in the water, flirting with the young single women and holding the young mother up as he teaches her how to float on her back.

As the sun lowers, Elijah's anxiety returns, and he tries to enlist friends for next Saturday's party. When the beach empties, loneliness sweeps over him; for the first time since morning he remembers his own family at home. He feels that he has done an awful thing for just one day of fun, and now he must face the problem of how to repay the money that he has borrowed. After sitting by himself for a long time, he decides that he must sell his umbrella, even if he retrieves only the fifteen dollars that he owes to his son. As he approaches prospective buyers, however, he soon learns that their needs do not match his, or that his offer to sell cheap makes people suspect that he is a thief who is trying to sell something that he stole. Humiliated, and chased off the beach by a self-righteous lifeguard, Elijah sits in his car, shaken, scared, and disillusioned. In this confused state, he feels that he truly has stolen both the umbrella and the joy of the day. Now everyone has gone home, there are no umbrellas in sight, and by next Saturday he will be too tired to enjoy the beach after pouring hot ore all week at the mill.

Themes and Meanings

This story presents a personal crisis of a kind that is common in the lives of working and middle-class men and women: the dilemma of choosing between satisfying their own personal needs and meeting the needs of their dependents. The immediate circumstances of their lives prevent them from having both. For example, for Elijah to meet the needs of the family to which he is committed by marriage and parenthood, he must sacrifice a personally satisfying worklife and the object that he sees as the means of fulfilling his dream of emotional satisfaction. If he chooses to serve himself, he will betray and neglect his family.

One approach to resolving dilemmas of this kind is to identify one's personal values and rank them, then choose what is the most valuable, even at the cost of losing what is less valuable. Clarification often involves a realistic look at one's life, in order to see if a valued aspect might actually be an illusion. Cyrus Colter's story dramatizes that process in the life of an ordinary person. In Elijah's case, everything that is at stake is strongly charged with emotion and seems to be very valuable; therefore the process of clarification, ranking, decision making, and right action is difficult and painful. Colter does not promise that his character's life will henceforth be entirely happy. The story leaves it to the reader to decide whether Elijah makes the wise choice.

Style and Technique

The style in which this story is told, featuring ordinary language and sentence structure, highlighted by vivid imagery, combines with its point of view and symbolism to allow the reader to see Elijah's life as he sees it. At the same time, it maintains distance as a thoughtful outside observer of what is actually going on. Although the narrative point of view is third-person omniscient, it focuses on Elijah's viewpoint, presenting almost everything as it is seen and understood by him. Even details that are especially important from the reader's outside point of view, such as the clownish shape of Elijah's legs and the near-hysteria of his laughter, with its chilling effect on the other bathers' perception of him, also are vaguely perceived by Elijah himself and contribute to his eventual realization that his dream of romance is an illusion.

Elijah's consciousness, like the story's setting, is divided between the beach and his home, but the powerful unifying force is his consciousness of family. He tries to deny the claims of his family at home, only to pursue his fantasy of romance, ironically, through a misunderstanding and falsification involving a quasi-family at the beach. The father of the boys at the beach is absent, just as Elijah himself is absent from his children.

The device that focuses the conflicting forces in Elijah's dilemma is the symbol that is presented in the story's title. The beach umbrella functions like another and more common symbol, a flag. Normally it carries only practical meaning and power, for persons sharing the culture of a time and place. It offers a kind of protection but may, at the same time, be merely a decoration. In a crisis, however, the visual thing may take on associations that charge it with emotional dimensions of meaning, so that it no longer merely stands for a thought about life, it now participates so fully in meaningful action that it becomes the thought itself. For other bathers, the umbrella remains a practical thing; however, they see Elijah differently when he owns one—as he knew they would. For both Elijah and the reader, however, the umbrella carries Elijah's full thought of escape into the colorful vitality of feeling free and desired. Like all effective symbols, its fullness as a thought includes the inescapable dark side of what gives it meaning. If Elijah continues to be thoughtful, thinking symbolically by means of the thing that, in his crisis, has drawn him to it, inevitably the umbrella will bring him to realize the necessity of surrender and the possibility of defeat. Perhaps he will also find an unexpected kind of victory.

Tom Koontz

BEARS IN MOURNING

Author: Adam Mars-Jones (1954-   )
Type of plot: Psychological, character study
Time of plot: The early 1980's
Locale: London and the suburb of Bromley, England
First published: 1992

> *Principal characters:*
>> VICTOR, a burly, bearded man in his forties
>> NARRATOR, the spokesperson for a group of men who share the
>> same physical type

The Story

This tale is narrated in the first person by a man trying to make sense of the life and death of his friend and erstwhile lover Victor. During the course of his musings, the narrator introduces the reader to the concept of the "bear," a physical type first delineated by the gay community and characterized by being slightly overweight and sporting a beard and perhaps body hair.

The narrator asserts that Victor was an ideal specimen of his type, a "bear absolute." At the time of their first meeting and their one and only sexual encounter, Victor was in his early forties. He had "heavy eyebrows and a startlingly dark beard," and his walk betrayed the recent acquisition of a "washtub stomach."

It becomes readily evident, however, that despite his attractiveness to other men who value these physical characteristics, Victor had not made a success of his life. He had moved back to his childhood home after the death of his mother to be near his father, with whom he had difficulty communicating. No level of understanding was ever reached between son and father before the latter's death not long after Victor's return.

At the time of his fateful decision to take his own life, Victor had just lost his job because of his recurring unreliability and was about to lose his license because of driving while drunk. He had lived with a succession of roommates, all of whom had left after a short while because living with Victor was "hard going by then." Without leaving a note to explain his intentions, he drove out into the countryside, selected a quiet spot of some significance to his dead parents, connected a hose to his exhaust pipe, and filled his car with the deadly fumes.

At the news of his death, his fellow "bears" are both "ashamed" and "angry." Immersed in the acquired immunodeficiency syndrome (AIDS) crisis, drawn together by their collective grief and outrage over the devastating repercussions of this human viral disease that undermines the immune system, the group cannot understand why Victor, healthy in body, should put an end to his life. His personal despair, his life of "squalor and misery," does not register on their consciousness, so inured are they to the one disease that has cast an omnipresent shadow on the gay community.

On the invitation of Victor's current roommate, the narrator travels to the cottage in Bromley to help clear out the dead man's effects. This act serves as the catalyst for his attempt to figure out the puzzle of Victor's unhappy life and his early death.

The narrator does not attend Victor's memorial service. Only in retrospect does he admit that he himself now begins to understand Victor's lack of "loyalty to life," the fact that "his despair was a gyroscope." At the time of Victor's death, however, such reflection was not the order of the day. Along with other "bears," the narrator does go to Victor's house for a post-funeral gathering at which most of the mourners get drunk and burn "bin-bags of Victor's papers and possessions" in a fit of resentment.

Themes and Meanings

Adam Mars-Jones has established a reputation as a chronicler of the AIDS crisis, an explorer in fiction of the consequences that the advent of the disease has had on the lives of gay people. With American novelist Edmund White, he cowrote the short story collection *The Darker Proof: Stories from a Crisis* (1987) as well as his own book, *Monopolies of Loss* (1992), which includes the story "Bears in Mourning."

One implication of the crisis at the time of this tale, in the early years not long after the human immunodeficiency virus (HIV) had been identified as the retrovirus that causes AIDS, involves how much this health threat obsessed and energized the gay community. Following a period of confused panic, gay people marshaled their forces in a collective effort to care for the sick, dispose of the dead, and memorialize loved ones. It was the author's own experience caring for AIDS patients that served as a catalyst for his writing about this subject.

By the end of the story, the narrator admits that perhaps at "any other time" the group might have grieved over Victor's unhappy end, but unfortunately he chose to take his life during a period when not only his fellow "bears" but also all gay men were overwhelmed with the collective tragedy of AIDS. "Didn't Victor know there was a war on?" the narrator asks. In this time of active contention between man and disease, the group saw Victor as a "traitor" who felt no "patriotism for the mortal country." Ironically enough, despite the meaning that his very name denotes, the condition of being a winner in a war or contest, Victor not only fails to play his part in the collective struggle but also loses his individual battle to his own personal adversary—despair.

Another implication of the disease was a reevaluation of body type. Before AIDS, the ideal male body was trim and toned, but the disease "that makes people shrivel away into a straight line up and down" put a premium in the gay community on carrying a few extra pounds. To be overweight offered the outward appearance of health, and the irony of Victor lying "plump in his coffin" was more than "any dwindling Bear" could comfortably countenance.

Another major theme of this tale is the disparity between the outer and inner life. A bear's identity, after all, is based on no longer "struggling all his life against his body" but adjusting to having hair and flesh to spare and settling comfortably into his life.

On the surface, Victor himself would appear to have promulgated this vision because he worked for a company that packages specialty magazines and had offered himself as a photographic model to augment the number of "bearded images in the media." These early magazine photos of Victor as a "slippered individual" stroking a dog and listening to "quadraphonic speakers" or a "genial chef" stirring a "golden sauce" do nothing to prepare the narrator for the middle-aged Victor that he had come to know, a man with a strong sense of personal failure and with "no loyalty to life."

Style and Technique

The author's skilled use of first-person narration not only provides the semblance of an eyewitness account but also supplies the story with an important character who participates in the action of the plot. On separate levels, the narrator is both a representative voice for the "bear" community and an individual with his own personal insight into Victor's fate. There are times, characterized by the plural pronoun "we," when the narrator defines and defends the bear way of life; there are other moments, identified by the singular "I," when the narrator grapples with his personal memories of Victor, such as their one-night stand and his voluntary effort to sort through Victor's things after his death.

Both voices, however, are marked at times by an almost comic detachment. There is, for example, the narrator's reference to the wake as a kind of "picnic," an allusion to the popular children's song "The Teddy Bear's Picnic" by John Bratton and James Kennedy. This particular "funeral feast" is anything but idyllic, however, since it ends in a bonfire, an attempted obliteration of Victor's memory.

The story abounds in such allusions to pop culture. The narrator, for instance, speaks of bear couples that consist of an older man and a younger man, "Daddy Bear and Baby Bear," a configuration that results, he says, perhaps from a wishful "filtering out" of the "female elements" of the fairy tale "Goldilocks." "What they are left with," the narrator asserts, "is a fuzzy fable of furry sleepers, of rumpled beds and porridge."

Shortly before he makes up his mind to end it all, Victor is also said to be obsessed with the popular song "The Living Years" recorded by Mike and the Mechanics in 1985. Presumably Victor hears and absorbs only the song's more negative message about a son's failing to communicate on a meaningful level with his father while he is still alive, and he ignores more hopeful aspects of the lyrics about holding on and waiting for the next day to bring a new perspective. To Victor, the next day never seemed to bring a change, only more of the same, more reminders of what he saw as his failed life.

S. Thomas Mack

THE BEAST IN THE JUNGLE

Author: Henry James (1843-1916)
Type of plot: Psychological
Time of plot: The late nineteenth century
Locale: England
First published: 1903

Principal characters:
JOHN MARCHER, an English gentleman of leisure
MAY BARTRAM, his friend and confidante

The Story

At a party in one of the stately homes of England, John Marcher meets May Bartram, and they realize that they had met years before in Italy. She recalls a strange confession he made on that occasion—that he had always felt the deepest thing within him was a sense of being reserved for a unique fate, "something rare and strange, possibly prodigious and terrible," that eventually would happen to him and perhaps overwhelm him. Whatever the fate is, it is not anything he is to do or accomplish; his role is to wait, and he asks if she will wait and watch with him. Like most people in Henry James's fiction, they do not have to work for a living; Marcher seems to be well-off, and Miss Bartram, though less well-to-do, can get by in a genteel fashion on a modest income. Whatever Marcher's fate is to be, it has not happened yet, and in response to her query, he says that it has not been to fall in love.

Thus they begin a long, intimate but uncommitted relationship, from which she gets nothing but the dubious pleasure of his company. He can give her nothing more because he must reserve himself wholly for the revelation of his destiny. At first, Marcher is as much hopeful as apprehensive; he believes that when it comes, his special fate will cause him to have "felt and vibrated . . . more than any one else." As the years go by and nothing happens, however, his feeling changes to dread, and he abandons the dream and waits for "the hidden beast to spring." He now sees this moment as the deadly leap of something sinister that "lay in wait for him, amid the twists and turns of the months and the years, like a crouching beast in the jungle." He does not know whether he will slay it or it will slay him; the crucial thing is the ultimate and inevitable spring. He has some qualms of conscience about having Miss Bartram accompany him on a "tiger-hunt," even if it is a psychological one, but he continues to exploit her, unable to give her anything in return.

As that moment continues to recede, they drift into the beginning of old age. (As the story opens, he is thirty-five and she is thirty.) Gradually, he becomes aware that she knows something about his fate that he does not. Her concern is to help him "to pass for a man like another," but he fails to understand her. While they continue to grope as if in a dark valley, he begins to feel that he has been cheated. However, May assures him that his fate is indeed special, that it is on the verge of happening, and that it is the worst thing possible. Still, she cannot tell him; he must find it out for himself. He will not consciously suffer, but his destiny is more monstrous than anything they could imagine. However, she assures him that the door is still open, that he can still escape. She is too ill to tell him how, however, and when he still fails to understand, she says that the beast has now sprung, the moment has passed. Perhaps he could have saved her, but he is too obsessed with himself to understand how, and she dies. So tenuous was their intimacy that Marcher is excluded from her funeral.

For a year, he travels around the world. On his return, he pays a visit to her tomb. At a nearby grave, he sees a man suffering from acute bereavement. From the other man's intense grief, he gets the revelation of his own fate. His life has been a void, untouched by passion; he is "the man to whom nothing on earth was to have happened." Too late, he realizes that May Bartram had loved him, that his escape would have been to love her, that had he done so, he might have saved her, that the moment when he failed to understand this was the moment when the beast sprang. Suddenly overwhelmed by despair, he flings himself on her tomb.

Themes and Meanings

James seems to have been going through an emotional crisis when he wrote "The Beast in the Jungle," for *The Ambassadors* (1903), the novel that he completed just before it and to which, in a way, the short story is a pendant, is also concerned with the waste of life. Its protagonist, Lambert Strether, has known love, but for a generation he has been a widower whose only role in life has been to edit a little magazine in a bleak New England town. When he goes to Paris at the age of fifty-five, he too has an emotional crisis that causes him to cry out, "Live all you can; it's a mistake not to. It doesn't so much matter what you do in particular, so long as you have your life. If you haven't had that what have you had?" Strether feels that for him, it is too late; he has, so to speak, missed the train. In fact, however, he still has a chance, whereas for Marcher, it is indeed too late. May Bartram is dead, the chance of love irrevocably beyond recall. His special fate is not to have had his life. The irony is that he has not even missed it until the final revelation. James valued his characters by their degree of awareness, and Marcher is supremely unaware until too late. His obsession with the special fate that he calls the beast in the jungle has so absorbed him that he has not realized that in waiting for it, he has lost everything else. At the end, he does not even have the beast to wait for any longer; it has already sprung, and he is left utterly bereft. A monstrous egotism has wasted not only his own life but also that of the woman who loved him and to whose love he was unable to respond.

Though classified as a realist, James wrote a number of ghost stories, the most famous of which is *The Turn of the Screw* (1898). In these tales the realism comes from the psychological subtlety, which makes it sometimes questionable as to whether the ghosts have any external reality or are only in the mind of one or more of the characters. "The Beast in the Jungle" has no ghosts, but it is generally included among the ghostly tales. The beast is purely in John Marcher's mind; he has, so to speak, conjured it up, but it destroys him just as surely as if this were an African or Asian adventure, not a story devoid of action and set on the fringes of British society. Marcher is surely haunted by his obsession, and May Bartram is the victim he has sacrificed to it. Though James enjoyed the adventure fiction of his friends Robert Louis Stevenson and Joseph Conrad, he himself preferred narratives in which very little happens externally, writing that "a man might have . . . an amount of experience out of all proportion to his adventures." Thus "The Beast in the Jungle" and *The Ambassadors* are full of the imagery of adventure fiction, though the only adventure in the narratives is in the mind. James said of himself that he stood "on the rim of the circle" of life and that "the only form of riot or revel ever known to . . . [him was] that of the visiting mind."

Despite an active artistic and social life, James ultimately found this life of the visiting mind to be inadequate. Critics said that James had the mind of an eavesdropper, and Max Beerbohm once drew a cartoon of James eavesdropping. The main deficiency in the life of the visiting mind, however, is the lack of love and of the sort of commitment to someone else that James could never give. Another novelist, Constance Fenimore Woolson (1840-1894), the grandniece of James Fenimore Cooper, was apparently in love with James, who could not wholly respond, and she committed suicide.

Style and Technique

"The Beast in the Jungle" is a product of what critics call James's third and final phase. Some consider this his richest phase; others find it flawed by excessive narrative and indirection, implausibly mannered dialogue, a fussy and cobwebby style, and a pretentious ponderousness. James Thurber, who admired James, parodied this style and technique in "The Beast in the Dingle."

"The Beast in the Jungle" does have some shortcomings. James's late works are an acquired taste, and though the denouement and message of the story are extremely powerful, they are delayed so long and the situation leading up to them is so farfetched that a reader unaccustomed to James may be frustrated. James was unable to place it in a magazine, and it had to wait a year to be published in a collection of his stories. Despite its length, the characters are never fully developed as three-dimensional individuals. Their lives and relationship are so anemic as to seem almost disembodied. May Bartram, as she is declining and trying to make Marcher aware of her love and his danger, does become poignant, but until the end, Marcher seems almost an abstraction, more the embodiment of an idea than a flesh and blood human being. He is wintry March; Miss Bartram is May. On the other hand, the story gradually generates considerable suspense as the reader waits to discover what the beast is and when it will spring, especially when Miss Bartram becomes aware of it and tries to warn Marcher, who continues to lack all comprehension. Even the labyrinthine style and the dialogue that seems more verbalized intuition than realistic conversation gradually take hold of the reader and appropriately create a sort of twilight world. Frustrating though its slow progress is, the story finally delivers a devastating conclusion.

Robert E. Morsberger

BECAUSE WE ARE SO POOR

Author: Juan Rulfo (1918-1986)
Type of plot: Social realism
Time of plot: The early twentieth century
Locale: Jalisco, Mexico
First published: "Es que somos muy pobres," 1953 (English translation, 1962)

> *Principal characters:*
> THE NARRATOR
> TACHA, his sister
> THEIR FATHER
> LA SERPENTINA, Tacha's cow

The Story

Swollen from torrential rain, the river near the narrator's village has been rising for three days. Everything is going from bad to worse. The rain has ruined the harvest, and the narrator's aunt has died. Moreover, La Serpentina, the cow belonging to his twelve-year-old sister, has been swept away by the river and drowned.

The noise of the river awakens the narrator. It is so loud that he thinks the roof of his house is collapsing. As he gets up, the noise grows louder and closer. The river has a rotted odor, and there is no sign that the rain will let up. When the narrator looks toward the village, he finds that the river has jumped its banks and is slowly rising along the main street. The water rushes into the house of a neighbor woman named Tambora. On the far banks of the river, a large tree in the dead aunt's yard—the only tamarind tree in the village—has been uprooted and swept away, dramatically proving that this flood is the largest in many years.

In the afternoon the narrator and his sister Tacha climb a ravine above the river, which they watch in fascination for hours. The river's roaring is so loud that it drowns out the voices of people near it.

From other people discussing the river's damage, they learn of La Serpentina's demise. A man has seen her washed away, although just why the cow drowned cannot be determined. Perhaps she tried to cross the river; more probably the water reached her while she slept, and the frightened animal cramped up in the water. She must have bellowed for help, but help had not come. She had a calf, but the narrator cannot tell if it survived. Tacha's father intended the cow to play a key role in his daughter's life; it was to be her dowry. While she was growing up, she could rely on the cow to attract a good husband who would always love her. Without a cow, finding a good man will be difficult.

Tacha's father is upset because the cow was intended to save her from the fate of her two older sisters. The sisters were reared to be God-fearing, obedient, and respectful, but they went astray. Their mother, who cries and prays for them, has racked her memory in vain trying to understand what misled them. Their father thinks they went bad because they were wild by nature and were poor. While adolescents, they started meeting men at the river at all hours of the night—and day. The men taught them bad things. The narrator saw his sisters rolling naked on the ground, each with a man on top of her. When their father could no longer tolerate his daughters' behavior, he ran them off, and they went to a nearby town to be prostitutes.

Now it appears that the same fate awaits Tacha, unless the calf is found. Any day now her pubescent breasts will attract a man. She stands on the ravine in her pink dress beside the narrator and cries. The water streaming from her eyes is dirty, as if the river has gotten inside her. The noise from her mouth sounds like the river. The rising river splashes its stinking water on her face. As she cries, her little breasts ceaselessly bounce up and down, as if they are suddenly beginning to swell, and she has started on the road to ruin. Whether the calf, now her only hope, will be found is unknown.

Themes and Meanings

"Because We Are So Poor" was first published in 1953 as part of Juan Rulfo's collection *El llano en llamas*. On one interpretation, the central focus of the story is the river and the damage it does to the impoverished lives of the narrator's Mexican village. It has ruined the harvest, carried off a large village tree, and rushed into a woman's house and threatened to drown her chickens, which must be of great importance to her.

The plain on which these people scratch out a living is arid. Through the Mexican Revolution's land distribution plan, the characters have received title to land on this plain, but it requires a pickax to plant even a seed. Ironically in this desert world, when rain does come, it comes as an unwelcome destructive force, engorging the river to flood levels.

In Rulfo's world, nature is never benign. It presents an overwhelming force against which puny human powers struggle and lose. The inevitability of this defeat constitutes the fatalism that threads its way through Rulfo's fiction, particularly in this story, in which nature's power literally engulfs humanity. For example, Rulfo describes Tambora's flooded house as "already part of the river." More ominously, the river has figuratively entered Tacha, whose crying resembles its roar. Her tears are the waters of the river already drowning the hope of her young life, as it drowned the cow that was to save her.

From another perspective, the story's focus is the fate of Tacha. Although her future remains uncertain, all signs point to her entering prostitution. The small chance of the calf's survival provides the slimmest hope that she will escape the degraded life of her sisters. Human nature conspires with external natural forces to place the girl a single step from the path trod so ruinously by her sisters.

The narrator remarks how Tacha is "shooting up like a rod," her breasts beginning to fill out. They are high and pointed, the kind that bounce around "promising to be like her sisters'." Such breasts will catch the attention of everyone, including bad men. Her father has seen Tacha's future in the pasts of his other daughters, and with the cow gone and her sexuality bursting, can find no barriers to her following in her sisters' path—"she'll end up going bad; mark my words, she'll end up going bad."

The theme of helpless humanity before the forces of nature within them as well as outside them pervades the story. For Rulfo, something seems dark, even rotten about physical as well as human nature. The river stinks, and tears are dirty water like the river. Human nature fares no better; lust lurks nearby, ready to destroy the family.

Perhaps nature is less threatening to the rich, who can build their lives on higher ground. Their homes do not become swamps; their daughters need not sell their bodies. If a crop fails, there are reserves. The fatalism of those who inhabit the Jalisco plain, on the other hand, is predicated on their poverty. Thus, Tacha's father believes there are two reasons for his elder daughters' fall. One is their wild nature, which the parents did everything to counter. The other is that "we were poor in my house." Poverty makes inevitable the triumph of hostile nature.

Rulfo intimates all this without moralizing or sentimentality. However, it is difficult to imagine one's not feeling sympathy for his characters. Such sympathy does not always arise in his stories, in which murder, vengeance, and the like abound. Here, however, decent people who are "very" poor strive for the good but are assaulted by uncontrollable forces that undo their painfully contrived attempts to improve their lives. The darkling plain gives no light and shows no compensation for those whose lives Rulfo paints so starkly.

Style and Technique

"Because We Are So Poor" (which has also been published as "We're Very Poor") takes the form of an interior monologue of the nameless brother of Tacha, whose fate dominates the story. The reader discovers at the end that the action takes place at virtually a single moment, as the narrator stands with his sister above the rising river, contemplating her situation and the river below. As in other Rulfo stories, time is frozen. The narrator speaks directly to the reader about the circumstances before him now. The title itself is the present tense, and the story artfully weaves past and present together.

The prose in all Rulfo's short stories is taut and spare, as if to mirror the grim reality he describes. In "Because We Are So Poor," he relates his story in little more than fifteen hundred words but manages to evoke the world of his characters and portray vividly their poverty and forlorn lives.

Augmenting the realism of life on the plain unrelieved by either joys or some final, comic victory of its people, is a sense that the narrator's thought process is woven into the narrative. He thinks out loud as he alters his account of the cow's drowning from one line to the next; he speaks of climbing the ravine with his sister in the past tense, but eventually one discovers that this past is actually the present.

Rulfo uses a fine sense of dramatic pacing. He shocks the reader and builds to a climax, although time is telescoped into a single moment. He introduces the loss of the cow at the beginning, but the impending fate of Tacha is evident only at the end, indeed, in the last line.

Charles F. Bahmueller

THE BECKONING FAIR ONE

Author: Oliver Onions (George Oliver, 1873-1961)
Type of plot: Horror
Time of plot: The early twentieth century
Locale: London
First published: 1911

>*Principal characters:*
>PAUL OLERON, a forty-four-year-old novelist
>ELSIE BENGOUGH, a journalist

The Story

In "The Beckoning Fair One," Paul Oleron, a novelist who has not catered to popular taste, becomes fascinated with the spirit that he detects occupying his apartment. He believes that the beckoning fair one is the spirit of a woman, and he tries to court her; the spirit appears, instead, to take possession of him and to drain him of his energy and his will. Under the influence of that spirit, he apparently murders the woman who loves him and nearly starves himself to death.

The process of Oleron's decline begins when he is attracted to an old, decaying building as an inexpensive way to solve his problem of living and working in different places. To unite living and working, he takes a single larger apartment in the otherwise abandoned building. He makes this move when he is fifteen chapters into what he believes is his greatest novel, *Romilly*. On completing the move, he discovers that he is unable to continue working on that novel.

The heroine is based on his journalist friend Elsie Bengough. As he attempts to continue writing, he finds himself dissatisfied with the heroine. He wants to begin again with a new heroine quite different from Elsie. Just as Elsie fits less well into his novel and his imagination after he moves, so too does she feel unwelcome in his new dwelling. She cannot be comfortable there. During two visits, she is injured in unaccountable ways, nails appearing where he is sure he had already removed them, and a step that had seemed perfectly sound to him suddenly breaking.

Oleron's attitude toward Elsie has always been ambivalent. Though he likes Elsie, she strikes him as too worldly for his austere taste. Similarly, his attitude toward his career has grown ambivalent. He confesses to her that he has become weary of his writing. He has not achieved the comfort and success that would make the effort seem worthwhile, and the effort itself has become an intolerable burden. Writing no longer provides him enough of the glow and thrill that it offered when he was younger.

Gradually, Oleron comes to believe that the opposition between the old and the new *Romilly* arises from an opposition between Elsie and a being occupying his rooms, a being whom he calls "the beckoning fair one." Her name comes from the title of a song that he hears in the sound of water dripping from a faucet and that is identified by a neighbor when he spontaneously hums it. This opposition also exists within himself, in his ambivalence toward Elsie and also in his desire both to live comfortably in the ordinary world and to enter into transcendent regions of artistic inspiration. The latter desire pushes him toward an exploration of the mysteries that he detects in his new rooms; the new tensions in his life seem to have their true spring in this division in his character. As he follows this impulse, he cuts himself off from Elsie, from his writing, and finally from the world.

Before he discovers an active spirit in his rooms, he believes that in his own love for them, he might create such a spirit. Not until after he learns of Elsie's desire to marry him does he discover that such a spirit already occupies his home. By the time that he learns of Elsie's love, he is already under the influence of that spirit; he finds that he does not want Elsie now. For days after this discovery, he is torn between a part of himself that would welcome her love and that fears for her safety, and another part that draws him toward the life that he feels in his rooms' hostility to Elsie. Then, one night when he finds himself as near as he has been to loving Elsie, he hears the sound of a woman brushing her hair, though no one is with him. Though he panics at first, he quickly accepts the possibility of a female spirit in his rooms, and he turns from Elsie to this beckoning fair one. At this juncture, a neighbor, a religious fanatic, accuses him of immoral activities with Elsie. Mistaken as this notion is, it proves an accurate estimate of Oleron's actual activity, which the narrator characterizes as treason against the ordinary terms and limits of human society.

Oleron begins to court the fair one, to dream of sexual union with her. Accepting her jealousy of Elsie and joining in excluding her, he concentrates on finding ways to coax the fair one into appearing. As he grows more desperate, he finally burns his manuscript, getting rid of his last connection with Elsie even as she stands outside his locked door, begging him to escape.

Eventually, he isolates himself in the womblike enclosure that his home becomes, receiving no visitors, no mail, and no food. He gives himself over to the invisible spirit. He finds the process of imagining her to be exhilarating, much as he found writing exhilarating in his younger days. This transcendent experience leads him into a slavery to the spirit that saps him; for days, he simply reclines, dreaming of the beckoner.

During this period of semiconsciousness, he seems to murder Elsie when she tries to rescue him. He has two experiences of this event. The first takes place when he is barely conscious; he then feels himself the instrument of the fair one when he strikes Elsie. In the second, he experiences a moment of apparent lucidity in which he is his old sane self. Then he seems to hear her murdered in another room. Oliver Onions never makes clear which of these is closer to the truth. Oleron quickly slips back into his insanity, in which state he is discovered by the police when they come searching for the missing Elsie.

The story ends with Oleron being carried to the hospital, accused of Elsie's murder, while his neighbors, stirred up by religious fanatics who seem to have dimly understood what he has been doing, call for his execution.

Themes and Meanings

"The Beckoning Fair One" is simultaneously the story of a man who becomes the victim of a vampiric spirit and the story of an artist who seeks to live wholly in the realm of imagination. Though there is sufficient ambiguity to lead a reader to suspect that the spirit may be merely a product of Oleron's imagination, Onions does not allow the reader to rest in such an opinion. Onions wants his ghost, ultimately, to be real. The main purpose of the ambiguity about the reality of the beckoning one is to emphasize the degree to which she is exactly the ghost most likely to entice an artist of Oleron's character. Indeed, he is the second of her known victims, an artist named Madley having previously died of starvation while living there. Because the fair one is the right ghost for an artist, the story communicates one main theme, the psychological dangers that threaten an artist who tries to conform his life to his work, to live in the ideal that he imagines.

Onions carefully details how Oleron's desire for the joy of the ideal blinds him to the absoluteness of the terror that he is pursuing: "To the man who pays heed to that voice within him which warns him that twilight and danger are settling over his soul, terror is likely to appear an absolute thing, against which his heart must be safeguarded in a twink unless there is to take place an alteration in the whole range and scale of his nature. . . . He is even content that . . . joy also, should for working purposes be placed in the category of the absolute things; and the last treason he will commit will be that breaking down of terms and limits that strikes, not at one man, but at the welfare of the souls of all." Onions represents Oleron's decline as a falling deeper into this treason until he loses his self and murders his human beloved.

Style and Technique

One of the most important features of Onion's technique is his handling of the ghost. Henry James's ghosts in *The Turn of the Screw* (1898) are seen only by the governess; that their very existence is therefore in doubt increases the psychological pressure on the reader to resolve the mystery. William Shakespeare's ghost in *Hamlet, Prince of Denmark* (pr. c. 1600-1601) is seen by several people, but it speaks only to Hamlet; that Hamlet doubts what the ghost tells him reveals the depths of Hamlet's character. The beckoner is more like Shakespeare's ghost than James's. Oleron's destruction reveals the fatal weaknesses of his character, but the ghost herself remains shrouded in mystery. What does she offer? Is she really an evil spirit, as Oleron finally, helplessly perceives her, or is she an absolute, amoral power, capable of raising him to transcendence had he a single will but instead giving him the strength to destroy himself by means of the normal human contradictions of his soul? In other words, does she appear evil because she is evil or because she empowers the evil in his nature?

Though the story may seem moralistic because Onions comments directly on Oleron's failures, it proves, nevertheless, a highly effective tale of terror, in part because of the ambiguities concerning the ghost's reality and its nature.

Terry Heller

THE BEET QUEEN

Author: Louise Erdrich (1954-   )
Type of plot: Parable
Time of plot: 1932, the Depression years
Locale: Argus, North Dakota, a fictitious town on the Minnesota-North Dakota border, and the northern plains
First published: 1985

> *Principal characters:*
> MARY LAVELLE, the narrator
> KARL LAVELLE, her brother
> ADELAIDE AND THEODOR LAVELLE, their parents
> SITA, a cousin
> FRITZIE AND PETE KOZKA, their aunt and uncle
> THE GREAT OMAR, "aeronaut extraordinaire"

The Story

In the opening episode of "The Beet Queen" (a six-paragraph prologue that displays the author's flair for the dramatic), Mary, a girl of eleven, and her fourteen-year-old brother Karl leap from a boxcar in the sugar beet valley of fictional Argus, North Dakota, and head for the home of their Aunt Fritzie, who, with her husband Pete, runs a reasonably successful butcher shop. As they walk through the streets, a fierce dog frightens them. Mary runs toward the butcher shop and Karl runs back to the boxcar in a scene reminiscent of the flight of Mendel and Isaac from Ginzburg in Bernard Malamud's short story "Idiots First." However, in "The Beet Queen," it is not Death pursuing the youngsters; it is Life.

Following this prologue, recounted by a third-person narrator, the rest of the story is told in the first-person voice of the little girl, Mary. She recounts the events that led to this fateful train ride, as well as her experience following it, beginning her story with the grain-loading accident that killed her father and the sad relocation of his pregnant widow and two small children to the Cities. There, they are reduced to penury and the new baby brother is born. "We should let it die," she recalls her mother telling her, "I won't have any milk. I'm too thin." Some weeks later, Mary recounts, with an eviction notice in hand they stumble on a country fair called "The Orphan's Picnic," where all three children are abandoned by their mother, who, in a moment of weakness and excitement and carried away by her ardor, flies into the sky with the dashing aeroacrobat "The Great Omar" and never returns.

Mary is left holding the baby, her older brother sitting beside her "gazing into the dark sky." A "sad man" whose wife has a "new baby of her own . . . and enough milk for two" simply sits beside Mary on the sidewalk and, waiting her out, finally takes the wailing baby from her arms and disappears into the crowd. The two children walk down the empty streets to their old rooming house, and the next morning they set out for Aunt Fritzie's, clutching their mother's small "keepsake box." During the train ride, the young female narrator sees her mother "flying close to the pulsing stars" and being thrown out of the plane by the selfish Omar when his fuel gets low. (Though readers never know whether the mother is really dead or whether, after abandoning her children, she is declared dead by the daughter, this fantasy scene contrasts with the next realistic scene of Mary walking toward the butcher shop.)

Mary is taken into the warm arms of Uncle Pete and Aunt Fritzie but is resented by her cousin Sita. She sets about making herself "essential" because she believes that she has nothing else to offer. Finally, in an effort to pay her own way, she opens the "treasure box" and is stunned to find only stickpins, buttons, and a worthless pawn ticket. Aunt Fritzie and Uncle Pete are silently sympathetic, but Sita gloats. In a conclusion worthy of all who discourse in parables, Louise Erdrich does not allow her protagonist's bad luck to overwhelm the virtues of experience and tolerance. Tenderly and unforgettably, the child narrator muses, "What is dark is light and bad news brings slow gain," acknowledging that her mother's legacy is both cruel and paltry and that the gain of which she speaks is intangible. Though disillusioned, she is not defeated.

Themes and Meanings

The function of a parable is to teach readers how, from the natural occurrences of life, one may discover moral and ethical attitudes essential to humankind. Erdrich's work is expressive of this tradition stemming from the oral traditions of American fiction, in which the journey becomes a metaphor for life, characters are archetypal, conflicts are gradually and slowly drawn and sustained, and endings are satisfactorily resolved. Themes that rise from the tradition of the parable are often predictable, but that does not make the story less interesting or the writer less skilled. On the contrary, these kinds of stories often loosen the spirit in ways that more complex stories do not. Erdrich is a member of the Turtle Mountain Chippewa Tribe of Indians, a cultural group whose storytelling traditions clarify the journey convention as deliberately as any other. "After that train journey I was not a child," says Mary Lavelle, her movement toward adulthood complete before she reaches her teens. "The Beet Queen" is clearly a story about a girl who has had no childhood, robbed of it by the circumstances of her grim environment.

A second theme, one of the significant recurring themes in twentieth century narrative fiction, is that of the loss of traditional values. Certainly, this story's events and ironic tone seize on this idea. It becomes apparent to the careful reader, however, that in the closing lines there is a hunger expressed by the youthful narrator for a fervent and passionate affirmation of life in spite of its cruelty and disappointments. She reassures her listener (the reader), "I could see a pattern to all of what happened, a pattern that suggested completion in years to come. The baby was lifted up while my mother was dashed to earth. Karl rode west and I ran east. It is opposites that finally meet." Even though the first of these events is assumed to be literal and the second hallucinatory, the reader has been carefully prepared to accept the voice of the narrator and to have confidence in her assessment of things, her oddly compassionate response to a cruel and undeserved fate. Wise beyond her years, Mary recognizes that life will not be easy for her, that time heals all wounds, and that conflicting forces are often suspended and united in ways that are not easily understood. Her attempts to fathom the mysteries of life, though not fully articulated and clarified, result in a transcendence.

Style and Technique

This is one in a series of Erdrich stories set in the fictitious town of Argus, North Dakota, a place that has been compared to William Faulkner's Yoknapatawpha County. The story's protagonist, Mary Lavelle, is not the Beet Queen of the title; indeed, the Beet Queen does not appear in this story at all and there is only scant reference to sugar beets. This absent persona, however, suggests a contrasting of values in the making of the character of Mary Lavelle, the daughter of failed farmers of the beet valley, forced out by foreclosure, now orphaned, clearly an outsider, returning to the rural region of her birth in a determined effort to find a place for herself.

Similes much like those found in Flannery O'Connor's short stories abound in this piece, but they are expressive of a much kinder, more compassionate outlook: "The train pulled like a string of black beads over the horizon"; "our faces stared back at us like ghosts"; "It was the baby, born heavy as lead, dropping straight through the clouds and my mother's body"; "over us the clouds spread into a thin sheet that covered the sky like muslin." Mary voices these comparisons during the train ride to Argus and as the details of life accumulate, these intricately woven similes, gentle and implicit, emphasize a transformation coming on and her metamorphosis from child to adult is given credibility.

The subtle tone of compassionate irony, rather than broad and brittle satire, is achieved by the author's careful interplay between the literal and the abstract. "After that we moved to a rooming house in the Cities, where my mother thought that, with her figure and good looks, she would find work in a fashionable store. She didn't know when we moved that she was pregnant. In a surprisingly short time we were desperate," Mary says matter-of-factly. Of being abandoned she says, "My mind hardened, faceted and gleaming like a magic stone, and I saw my mother clearly. . . . All night she fell through the awful cold. Her coat flapped open and her pale green dress wrapped tightly around her legs. Her red hair flowed straight upward like a flame. She was a candle that gave no warmth. My heart froze. I had no love for her. That is why, by morning, I allowed her to hit the earth."

Readers of such narrative fiction, who have come to expect a kind of unreliability of narrative voice in such writers as Flannery O'Connor, Carson McCullers, and Joyce Carol Oates, will notice a return to the traditional truthfulness of the storyteller in this Erdrich story. Indeed, the truth and purity in this narrative voice is one of the most charming devices in the story and, almost singlehandedly, it prevents the drawing of the demonic and grotesque characters so familiar in other contemporary works.

Elizabeth Cook-Lynn

THE BEGGAR MAID

Author: Alice Munro (1931-   )
Type of plot: Domestic realism
Time of plot: The early 1950's
Locale: Ontario, Canada
First published: 1977

Principal characters:
ROSE, a university freshman
FLO, her stepmother
DR. HENSHAWE, her landlady
PATRICK BLATCHFORD, a graduate student who is heir to a
    department store fortune

The Story

After growing up in the little town of Hanratty, Ontario, Rose wins a scholarship to a prestigious Canadian university. During her first semester there, she finds a comfortable place to live, a part-time job, and a male admirer. She meets Patrick at the campus library when she is working a weekend shift, reshelving books, and he is one of the few people studying there. When she asks him if he has seen a man who has just grabbed her in the almost deserted building, he rushes to her defense. Rose can tell at once that he is both high-minded and high-strung—a nervous man who wants to become a history professor. She also soon sees that he is infatuated with her. She does not know, however, that he is the heir to a family business. She dates Patrick partly to spite her landlady, a spinster former English professor who encourages her "scholars" to stay away from "boys." To Rose's surprise, the landlady likes Patrick and tells her that he is one of the most eligible bachelors on campus.

During the Christmas holidays, Patrick takes Rose to visit his family's luxurious home in British Columbia. Rose feels completely out of place among Patrick's parents and sisters, but so does Patrick. After returning to the university, they become engaged, and Rose takes Patrick to meet her family in Hanratty, where Patrick is taken aback by the working-class culture and the country accents. Rose increasingly wonders what Patrick sees in her or wants from her. Nevertheless, she finds herself saying all the right things to people who ask to see her engagement ring and ask about her wedding plans. As year-end exams approach, she breaks off her relationship with Patrick but relents when she meets him to return his ring.

They marry and have children but continue their pattern of separation and reconciliation, with subtle variations, for a decade. Eventually, they divorce. Another decade later, when Rose is a successful television interviewer and Patrick is a successful professor, they see each other in an airport. Rose smiles, realizing that she could throw herself at Patrick again but knowing better. He makes an ugly face. What remains of their relationship is this story, which she tells to many friends and lovers in the new age of honesty.

Themes and Meanings

The story's title is a cultural allusion of the sort that Patrick likes to drop on people, looking shocked if they do not understand it. He tells Rose that "The Beggar Maid" is the title of a famous work of art, a painting of a poor but beautiful young woman who wins the love of a king and marries him. Rose assumes that that is how he sees himself—as a gentleman rescuing a waif. It is not, however, how she sees herself. She feels no need to be rescued and often must reassure Patrick that he is not a weakling.

Rose only remembers one book from Patrick's shelves, but his fascination with that book says a good deal about his attitude toward her and her own difficulty with his attitude. The book is Robert Graves's *The White Goddess: A Grammar of Poetic Myth* (1948). It represents a genuine tribute to the goddess and the muse but also a dilemma for women interested in the arts, as it sees their job as being to inspire poets, rather than to be poets themselves. When Patrick insists on calling plump and dark Rose his "White Goddess," she calls him her "White God" and throws snow in his face to make her point. The snow jolts him into doing something manly for once, but when they climb out of the snowbank he returns at once to coddling apologies.

The dramatic question of this story is not whether Rose will win Patrick's love (she does so at once) or even whether she will win his family over (which she can do only when grandchildren are in the offing). The question is whether she will keep him. Even before Rose throws snow at Patrick, and especially after he apologizes for retaliating, she senses something wrong with their relationship. Their physical relationship is good, once she can stop pretending and start enjoying herself. Patrick's intentions are entirely noble, but he sees himself and Rose as being from "two different worlds." He says so, and she cannot forget. He thinks his own world is better, but Rose regards her own as equally valid and much more comfortable. Rose is uncomfortable in Hanratty only when she brings Patrick there and feels obliged to try to speak as he does.

Style and Technique

"The Beggar Maid" is the fifth in a series of ten stories about Flo and Rose. It appears in a collection with their names as a subtitle, and is the title story in the American edition (1979) and the British edition (1980). The original Canadian edition (1978) takes its equally suggestive title from the last story, "Who Do You Think You Are?" Alice Munro uses this technique of interconnected stories in other volumes, moving more than one reviewer to wonder whether she is writing novels rather than story collections. Each of her stories stands perfectly well on its own, but all belong to the larger fictional world of Hanratty, Ontario—much as William Faulkner's stories are about the people in a fictional Mississippi county. "The Beggar Maid" first appeared on its own in *The New Yorker*, but it has definite connections to the stories that come before and after it in Munro's collection. In "White Swans," Rose makes her first trip to Toronto after winning an essay competition, with Flo's warnings about white slavers ringing in her ears and the new surroundings being defined in contrast to the old. In "Mischief," Rose falls in love with a married man while she is still married to Patrick.

The whole cycle of stories, as one might call it, extends from Hanratty into the world at large and back again in Rose's memories. The first story gets its title from Flo's curiously poetic threats to Rose: "Royal Beatings." The last gets its title from Flo's nagging question: "Who Do You Think You Are?" Rose narrates all these stories, but she has learned the art of storytelling from Flo and, in telling stories to her friends and lovers, she comes to realize how much her life has been shaped by her small town origins. Munro is a provincial writer in the best sense. She finds God in the details of everyday life. The details are North American, to be sure, and Canadian even more so, but they come from the place where Munro grew up. Hanratty is a "ratty" little town of Munro's own creation, but it bears much in common with Wingham, Ontario, where she was born and raised. Her fictional university town is not named, but it is just as clearly modeled on London, Ontario, where she attended Western University for three terms before marrying a Vancouver man in 1951. Rose's story is not straight autobiography. Unlike Rose, Munro was not orphaned, and her marriage lasted a decade longer than Rose's. The parallels between Rose's life and her own, however, are unmistakable.

Fascination with details often pushes writers into longer works of fiction. Such fascination makes Margaret Atwood, a Canadian writer of Munro's generation, want to know what kind of appliances her characters have in their kitchens, and the answers make her best known fiction run to some length. Munro has found a way to give details associated with special moments in a life, and to remind the reader of those details in other stories. When Rose thinks about taking Patrick to Hanratty, readers know what she is up against if they have already read about her vivacious stepmother and the local butcher; Rose need only think of their names. When Flo returns Patrick's passion for history with a grotesque local story, the reader recognizes the stepmother who carries on in earlier stories. The reader also hears Flo as never before, through the mildly scandalized ears of her future son-in-law and the nervously horrified ears of her stepdaughter.

Munro writes in the language of the people. Some characters may be world travelers, such as Dr. Henshawe; others have not strayed far from Hanratty. Readers learn about Rose's development through the development of her language, and occasionally they hear the voice of experience, reflecting on her own story after many years. "The Beggar Maid" is very much a story of Rose.

Thomas Willard

BEGGAR MY NEIGHBOR

Author: Dan Jacobson (1929-   )
Type of plot: Social realism
Time of plot: The 1960's
Locale: A white suburb of Johannesburg, South Africa
First published: 1962

> *Principal characters:*
> MICHAEL, a white South African boy, about twelve years old
> FRANS and
> ANNIE, black South African orphans of Michael's age, brother
>   and sister
> DORA, the black cook in Michael's home

The Story

Michael, a white South African boy, is accosted by two black, raggedly dressed, almost emaciated children on his way home from school. Like so many impoverished black children, they are hungry and ask Michael for a piece of bread. At first he rejects them, but touched by their abject posture, he offers to give them bread and jam if they follow him home.

Dora, the black cook at Michael's home, grudgingly prepares the food, and Michael, experiencing the first flush of a power he has not hitherto known, gives them the bread and patronizingly demands a thank-you from the cowed "piccanins." The children begin to appear regularly, and the sense of his own generosity gradually helps to inflate Michael's ego and recently acquired power. He wishes, for example, that the children would be even more obsequious toward him. Michael, an only child, is lonely, and, compelled to rely on his own resources, he is much given to fantasizing. Michael's ambivalent feelings toward the black children—a sort of love-hate nexus—appear largely in his fantasies and the climactic dream sequence.

Yielding to a whim one day, Michael shows the children a particularly beautiful pen and pencil set, and the piccanins plead for it. Shocked by their desire for something other than food, Michael indignantly refuses and they leave, much to the delight of Dora.

Meanwhile, Michael's sense of his own importance and power increases, and his fantasies change rather noticeably: He begins to treat the children as if they were slaves, and in the real world he enacts these fantasies by deliberately keeping them waiting for bread and inflicting other acts of petty cruelty on them. Inevitably, Michael's scorn, which has been only partially submerged, surfaces and gives way to anger, and he summarily orders them never to return. The piccanins, however, are persistent, and time and again they return to haunt Michael, as if embodying his own imperfectly understood guilt.

Shortly after dismissing them, Michael is struck down by a fever, and in his delirium he sees himself brutally attacking the boy and sexually assaulting his frail sister. The delirium deceives Michael into thinking that he is awake, the fever broken, and he is leading the abused and rejected children into his room. Here Michael yields to the impulse of love, which has also surfaced in delirium, and he kisses and caresses the piccanins. They, however, have vanished into the dark world beyond the white, comfortable suburbs, and all of Michael's efforts to find them are futile.

Themes and Meanings

Michael's final rejection of the black children is at once a symbolic and a literal act. By ordering them never to return, he is trying to reject their dreaded Africanness, which gradually becomes a persistent irritant to him. Michael, therefore, may be regarded as the embodiment of the white South African's conscious or unconscious wish to rid himself of the gnawing demands of black intransigence.

To this extent the story may be read as an allegory, but it is also a sensitive and incisive treatment of the moral ambivalence dividing an essentially decent youngster. Michael's instinctive empathy for the black children is established early in the story. The children's touching dependence on each other is particularly appealing to Michael, whose need for a sibling as well as parental affection and attention is implicit in his behavior. Even though the children are "identical in appearance to a hundred, a thousand, other piccanins," they become increasingly individualized to Michael as his contacts with them increase. The apartheid system will not permit him to relate to the children on a personal, affectionate level, but his own sensitive humanity can safely do so in dream and fantasy. Even so, Michael does make tentative attempts to reach out to the piccanins in the harsh world of reality. For example, his questions, which are ostensibly innocent and paternalistic, conceal Michael's desire to know them as persons. Therein lies the source of the tragedy. Michael's revelation—it reminds one of a Joycean epiphany—comes, significantly, in dream: His hatred of the piccanins is mutual, and it is the inevitable product of the mores of his particular society. There is more: Michael understands that the piccanins require love as much as bread. This understanding comes too late; he has lost the moment. The human urge to give love, which does not recognize racial differences in its pristine stages, has been frustrated in both black and white.

Style and Technique

This is superbly controlled story. In a story full of political and moral resonances, the writer is undoubtedly tempted to indulge in authorial editorializing. In "Beggar My Neighbor," however, there are no authorial intrusions, and indeed the narrative voice is altogether effaced. All the moral conflicts and ambivalences in race relations are implicit in Dan Jacobson's carefully modulated references to the white boy's perception of his own intrinsic superiority and the piccanins' instinctive obsequiousness and silence. These are deployed in strategic, and therefore effective, places in the narrative. The first time Michael gives the children bread and jam is a good example. In this scene, the white superior-black subordinate relationship is conveyed in Michael's condescending, even supercilious posture and words. The tenor of his future relationship with the children is therefore established early in the story.

Jacobson also carefully controls his use of images. Images of light, shade, and darkness are embedded in the story's idiom. Fantasy and reality, love and hate, acceptance and rejection—all these antitheses tend to coalesce, then fade and separate, at various times in the story. In the same way, various intensities of light, shadow, and darkness are called up for the reader, and they are meant to complement and enhance the tenuous link between the moral antitheses and ambivalences. The juxtaposition of these antitheses is the hub around which the story turns. On the one hand, the social and political realities of race relations in South Africa forbid intimate contact with the piccanins; in his fantasies, however, Michael can give his deeply buried desires and fears and whims their widest scope. (It is worth noting that in most of his fantasies the black children are dependent on the white boy's courage and paternalistic assistance.)

Jacobson uses other methods to reinforce theme. Dora's hatred of the piccanins is a case in point. The author does not drive this hatred very hard; instead, he uses it rather subtly. In her role as cook in Michael's home, Dora is in a comfortable and decidedly preferred position, but her complacency and spurious security are jolted by the piccanins' inexorable persistence, which not only reminds Dora of her own dubious link with the white suburb but also, perhaps more pertinently, generates guilt feelings in her. Dora's conflicts are therefore suggested rather than stated with blunt directness.

The symbolic resonances of Michael's beautiful pen and pencil set are also worth noting. When Michael displays the set, it is a half-innocent, half-subconscious act of exhibitionism and flaunting from the middle-class white boy. When the deprived children linger over its shimmering beauty and then plead for it, however, Michael is shocked by the revelation that black children have aesthetic as well as physical needs. This undermines the assumptions about blacks that his society has nurtured in him, and so he perversely rejects them with noticeable severity. However, this severity is counterpointed when Michael suddenly relents and offers them more bread and jam as a substitute. It is a telling moment, for it tends to crystallize all of the boy's troublesome conflicts and ambivalences.

Harold Barratt

THE BEGGARWOMAN OF LOCARNO

Author: Heinrich von Kleist (1777-1811)
Type of plot: Ghost story
Time of plot: The fifteenth or sixteenth century
Locale: A castle on the edge of the Italian Alps, near Locarno
First published: "Das Bettelweib von Locamol," 1810 (English translation, 1934)

Principal characters:
THE BEGGARWOMAN, an old sick woman
THE MARQUIS, the lord of the castle
THE MARQUISE, his wife
THE NOBLEMAN, a Florentine knight

The Story

The apparent impetus for telling this strange history is the sight of a castle ruin as it might be noticed by a traveler descending into northern Italy from the St. Gotthard Pass. As if in reply to such a traveler's question of how the castle has fallen into disuse and ruin, the narrator tells the story of the beggarwoman of Locarno, in which an old woman comes begging at the castle gate, is taken in at the Marquise's orders, and is given a place to sleep for the night in one of the castle's unused rooms. When the Marquis returns from the day's hunting, however, he peevishly orders the beggarwoman from her place in one corner of the unused room to a spot behind the stove at the opposite side. In her effort to get up, her crutch slips on the polished floor, and she falls, injuring her spine. Laboriously and painfully, she finally stands and hobbles to the corner as bidden, but on reaching the spot, she collapses and dies of her injury.

The incident is evidently forgotten for some years, during which the Marquis's fortunes decline to the point that he begins to think of selling his domain, and the chance arrival of a Florentine nobleman seems to offer such an opportunity. Without further thought, the master and mistress of the house give their prospective buyer lodging in the same unused chamber for the amount of time that he may require to consider the purchase. However, in the middle of the night, the man comes downstairs, pale with fright, to report that his room is haunted by a spirit. He describes the ghostly presence as some invisible thing that arose from a corner of the chamber with a sound as if from a bed of straw, walked with slow, feeble steps across the room, and collapsed with moans and gasps behind the stove. The Marquis tries to reassure his guest and offers to spend the rest of the night with him in the uncanny room as proof that no harm could come to him there, but the knight declines the offer, asks to sleep until morning sitting in a chair, and with the new day continues his journey without delay.

From this time on, the rumor circulates that a ghost inhabits the castle, and several more prospective buyers are frightened off by the tale of what the first one experienced there. The Marquis therefore resolves to discredit the rumor by spending a night in the room himself. To his horror, he experiences, at the stroke of midnight, exactly what the Florentine knight had described. The following morning, he furtively tells his wife that a ghost does indeed inhabit the chamber. She is alarmed by the news but proposes that they confirm it beyond any doubt before acknowledging that the room is haunted. That same night, she, her husband, and a trusted servant all stay in the room, and all three hear the same inexplicable, ghostly sounds.

Now only their fervent wish to find an unwitting buyer and to be rid of the castle enables them to suppress their fear and insist that the uncanny events must have some harmless explanation. A third night, therefore, the husband and wife go to the room, this time with candles, sword, and pistol, and accompanied by the dog, which they decide at the last moment to keep with them. Again, at the midnight hour, the noises are heard. The sound of a crutch tapping on the floor arouses the dog, which backs, growling and barking, toward the corner, as if the animal could see what is invisible to human eyes. At this, the Marquise runs in terror from the room and orders horses hitched to leave at once for the town. Before she can pass through the gate, however, flames spring from the building. In his crazed fear, the Marquis has taken one of the candles and set fire to the place, "weary of his life." It is too late to save him from a gruesome death in the blaze, and, as the imaginary traveler is told at the conclusion, the whitened bones of the Marquis can still be seen lying in the same corner of the chamber from which he had commanded the beggarwoman of Locarno to get to her feet.

Themes and Meanings

It would be simple enough to draw from this story the lesson that a criminal act will eventually be punished, and that the punishment will fit the crime. In this case, the act amounts to murder, even if that was not the Marquis's intent, because his tormenting of the defenseless beggarwoman was gratuitous and mean-spirited. Heinrich von Kleist does not prevent his reader from inferring that the Marquis's economic circumstances worsened as a consequence of his heedless brutality, but he does not imply anything more than a coincidental connection, either. The Florentine nobleman, after all, seems quite prepared to buy the property, notwithstanding the ravages of "war and bad harvests" until his own terrifying experience in the guest room changes his mind and the minds of others who might also have come to the aid of the struggling owners.

The two ideas that are much more prominent here—and more characteristic of Kleist—are guilt and the guilty one's consciousness of it. The "several years" intervening between the beggarwoman's death and the decline in the Marquis's fortunes are also years in which he forgets the unfortunate incident, or at least obliterates it from his conscious memory. At no time in the story is any word spoken or sign given by the Marquis to acknowledge what he has done, either at the time of the old woman's death or in discussions of the frightening sounds in the fateful room. On hearing the nobleman's report, he is thus "frightened without knowing why himself" and treats the matter with forced unconcern. On the final night, he and the Marquise take the watchdog with them "without knowing exactly why, perhaps from an instinctive desire to have the company of some third living creature." "Perhaps" is a crucial word here, as it allows the possibility of reasons for taking the dog other than simply to have its company. The deeper "instinctive desire," especially on the Marquis's part, is to confront his tormenting spirit at last in some more tangible form. Thus, when the dog sees what the humans cannot, the Marquise flees in terror, yet her husband's fear compels him to stand and complete his struggle with the ghost he has summoned to his consciousness.

What the Marquis fears most is the guilt within him, and to know one's greatest fear as he now knows his is to be driven mad. He sets the suicidal fire "maddened with terror" and "weary of his life." The novelist Thomas Mann called the first of these two phrases thoroughly Kleistian and urged readers of "The Beggarwoman of Locarno" to ponder carefully Kleist's choice of words here. As for the Marquis's weariness of his life, there is only one thing clearly known about his life to which it can refer: his responsibility for the beggarwoman's death. The life Kleist has recounted here is the exhausting, doomed struggle to deny the knowledge of guilt.

Style and Technique

Because of length, and Kleist's reputation as an early nineteenth century master of the anecdote form, one might at first think of "The Beggarwoman of Locarno" as an example of this genre. Its narrator recounts a remarkable occurrence, building to the story's critical point with the objective economy that typifies the anecdote. However, despite its brevity, this work is almost always named among Kleist's novellas, stories that, on average, run to more than ten times the length of this short piece. Its dramatic character is what places "The Beggarwoman of Locarno" most decisively in the category of the novella.

That the story is told with objective economy does not imply stylistic simplicity. Kleist's prose is highly individual, some would even say perversely eccentric, whether to the modern ear or to that of his own time, and his translators seem able to succeed only by simplifying his syntax and punctuation to some degree. However, there is a strictly observed dramatic purpose in Kleist's idiosyncratic use of language. Whereas an epic narrator employs a grammatical style that is markedly sequential, emphasizing the discrete interest of the individual links of the narrative, Kleist's sentences depend heavily and crucially on interlocking grammatical subordination: hypotaxis rather than parataxis. The effect of his language in "The Beggarwoman of Locarno" is thus more nearly simultaneous than sequential; this is the essence of drama, in which the test of every element is in its purposeful relationship to the climatic moment.

"The Beggarwoman of Locarno" differs from the ghost stories of Kleist's contemporaries, such as Johann Ludwig Tieck and E. T. A. Hoffmann, in that it does not seek to generate the kind of ghostly atmosphere that is so effective in Tieck's and Hoffmann's tales of the supernatural. To do so would have risked creating moments or scenes with a substance of their own, which might divert or delay the reader's interest and thus slow the critically breathless pace of the story's events.

Michael Ritterson

THE BEGINNING OF AN IDEA

Author: John McGahern (1934-   )
Type of plot: Realism
Time of plot: The 1960's
Locale: Paris, France and rural Spain
First published: 1978

>*Principal characters:*
>EVA LINDBERG, a theater director
>ARVO MERI, a journalist with whom she is having an affair
>MANOLO, a Spanish police officer

The Story

"The Beginning of an Idea" is a story about a French woman's abortive attempt to fulfill her ambition to write an imaginary life of the Russian author Anton Chekhov. It begins with a passage from Eva Lindberg's notes, repeated throughout the story, about how the word "oysters" was chalked on the side of the wagon that brought Chekhov's body to Moscow for burial. His body was carried in the oyster wagon to preserve it from the heat.

Also among Eva's notes is an almost full translation of a very short story by Chekhov entitled "Oysters." The Chekhov story is about a starving father and son on the streets of Moscow; the father is trying to decide whether to beg for food. The boy, who Eva imagines to be Chekhov, sees a sign in a restaurant window with the word "Oysters" and asks the father what it means. When the father says an oyster is an animal that lives in the sea that people eat, the boy begs some people going into the restaurant for oysters; when they give him some, he mistakenly eats the shells while the men laugh. Eva wants to write an imaginary life of Chekhov, beginning with the day outside the restaurant and ending when the body reaches Moscow in the oyster wagon.

After this prologue, the story's action begins with the wife of Arvo Meri, with whom Eva has been having an affair, phoning Eva and calling her a whore after finding out about their affair. Later Arvo arrives with flowers to apologize for his wife's behavior. Eva wants them to have a life together and reminds him that once before when she got pregnant, he told her it was not the right time, so she had an abortion. Now when he tells her he cannot leave his wife, she says she does not want to see him again.

Eva, a theater director, decides to make a change she has long wanted: to leave the theater and try to write. She contacts some rich friends who have a vacation house in Spain and asks if she can use it. After having dinner with a poet she knows, who warns her about living in Spain alone with hordes of randy Spaniards, she takes the train to Barcelona and a bus to the house. On the bus she meets a Swedish homosexual who asks if he can stay in a room at the house, but she says she wants to be alone.

After arriving at the house, she tries to write, but although she has a beginning and an end to her story of Chekhov, she can write nothing. The only person she sees is a local police officer named Manolo who brings her a telegram from her old theater asking her to translate a Russian play, a task that she gladly undertakes.

When Manolo asks her to order contraceptives for him because his wife already has had two children in two years and they cannot afford any more, she agrees, even though it is a crime in Spain to have contraceptives. Manolo and his chief then come to her house drunk and threaten her with jail if she refuses to have sex with them. She does so and afterward cries with rage at being so stupid, packing up her things and taking a train to Barcelona. She thinks she tastes oysters and has the sudden desire to look out the train window to see if the word "oysters" is chalked on a wagon, but there is no wagon there.

Themes and Meanings

Trying to create a life is the central theme of "The Beginning of an Idea." Having reached a point at which she feels she must make a radical change, Eva Lindberg imagines beginning her own new life by creating an imaginary life of Anton Chekhov. She has the "beginning of an idea" in the fictional Chekhov story about a poor boy who mistakenly eats oyster shells and the end of an idea in the historical fact that Chekhov's body was carried to Moscow in an oyster cart. It is the symbolic symmetry of Chekhov's life that fascinates Eva; she even imagines that after the coffin is taken away for burial, some of the oysters in the cart are delivered to the same restaurant where the child Chekhov had eaten shells.

Actual lives do not have the same symbolic symmetry as imagined lives. Eva has asked her lover for a life and he offers her yellow roses instead. She realizes that what she yearns for is her own life, not his. She has not built a life with her lover, but she thinks she will now build something out of the opening sentences of her imagined book about Chekhov. She has a romantic idea that she can go away, be alone, and somehow be able not only to imagine a life of Chekhov but also to create that life and simultaneously create her own life by giving it meaning.

However, it is one thing to "try to write" and another to actually write; one either does it or one does not. Although Eva has the symmetrical beginning and end of her Chekhov story, she has no middle, no real sense of the human life lived between two conveniently symmetrical references to oysters. According to many critics Chekhov's genius was that he lopped off the beginning and end of his stories and left them with a meaningful middle. Eva is never able to achieve that. Thus, she finds it much easier to translate the work of Chekhov than to create an original work about the great writer.

The central disillusionment she experiences about her naïve assumption that her own life can become as ordered, symmetrical, and meaningful as what she imagines about Chekhov's life occurs when the young Spanish police officer she has befriended and trusted betrays and rapes her. What she calls the one real sin—stupidity—is her mistaken expectation that the order and significance of fiction can be duplicated in the unjust and unpredictable reality of life.

Style and Technique

The structure of "The Beginning of an Idea" is based on a parallel between a fictionalized life and an actual life. John McGahern initiates this parallel first by including as a story-within-a-story practically a complete translation of the Chekhov story "Oysters," which Eva plans as an opening to her imaginative or fictionalized life of Chekhov. However, the only two sentences she has written are her beginning sentences: "The word Oysters was chalked on the wagon that carried Chekhov's body to Moscow for burial. The coffin was carried in the oyster wagon because of the fierce heat of early July." Repeated five times throughout the story, almost like an obsessive mantra, the two sentences are indeed the "beginning of an idea" that gives the story its title.

Throughout the story, McGahern alternates accounts of Eva's actual life—her breakup with her lover, her trip to Spain, her encounter with the two police officers—with references to her idealized or "imaginary" life of Chekhov. Just as she never succeeds in translating her ideas into actuality by writing the life of Chekhov, she never really succeeds in creating her own life. Instead, she takes the path of least resistance, translating instead of creating, giving in to the rapists instead of resisting them.

The story ends with Eva's final romantic effort to equate the meaninglessness of her own experience with what she considers to be the significance of the life of Chekhov. By looking out the train window to see if there is a wagon with the word "oysters" chalked on the side, she hopes to identify with Chekhov. However, she never succeeds in creating an imaginary Chekhov, nor does she succeed in giving meaningful order to her own life. The final parallel between her own life and her projected life of Chekhov is that she too returns home, having suffered a kind of death and an ironic reduction.

As is typical of McGahern's short fiction specifically and of the modern Joycean tradition generally, "The Beginning of an Idea" is both realistic and lyrical at once, pushing mere description of the material to unobtrusive symbolic significance. Like McGahern's other stories, this one has a clear social context; however, he is not interested in confronting his characters with the abstractions of social limitations but rather exploring the universal challenge of responsibility, commitment, and guilt.

Charles E. May

THE BEHAVIOR OF THE HAWKWEEDS

Author: Andrea Barrett (1955-   )
Type of plot: Historical, realism
Time of plot: The 1930's to 1970's
Locale: Niskayuna and Schenectady, New York
First published: 1994

> *Principal characters:*
> ANTONIA, the narrator
> RICHARD, her science professor husband
> ANTON "TATI" VACULIK, her Czech grandfather
> OTTO LEINIGER, her grandfather's German boss
> SEBASTIAN DUNITZ, a teaching and research assistant from
>   Germany
> GREGOR MENDEL, nineteenth century pioneer in the science of
>   genetics

The Story

Andrea Barrett's interest in the history of science is reflected in "The Behavior of the Hawkweeds," a complex exploration of how the past is paralleled in the present. The story take place in several different time frames. The primary story focuses on the marriage of Antonia and Richard, who met in the late 1940's when he was finishing his doctoral thesis. As a way to get him to love her, Antonia tells him a story about her grandfather's personal relationship with Gregor Mendel, who she knows is Richard's hero; she tells him how Mendel was disillusioned in his research by a disastrous suggestion made to him by the well-known botanist Carl Nägeli.

When Richard becomes a professor, he tells the story to his students to impress them, identifying with Mendel as being unappreciated and misunderstood. Antonia believes Richard muddles the story and that he is more like Nägeli than Mendel. In the 1970's, when Richard invites Sebastian Dunitz, a bright young student scientist from Germany to come live with them, Antonia, bored with the tedium of her everyday life, is attracted to him. When he misunderstands her attraction as being sexual and rebuffs her, she calls him a German pig, the same name her grandfather called his boss when she was a child.

The second story is about Antonia's experience when she was five and working with her grandfather Anton (who she calls Tati) in a nursery in Niskayuna, New York. One day her grandfather came into the nursery and caught his boss, Otto Leiniger, a self-important and condescending German, trying to look down Antonia's dress. He called Leiniger a German pig, then struck him. Leiniger fell, hit his head on a heating pipe, and later died. Antonia's grandfather dies before he can be tried. Antonia does not tell this story to Richard until the 1970's, when she tells it in his presence to Dunitz.

The third story is the one that the grandfather tells Antonia about Mendel. After doing years of research on the hybridization of the edible pea, the Augustinian monk Gregor Mendel presented his findings to scientific societies but was ignored. When he sent his ideas to the famous botanist Nägeli, the expert on hawkweeds advised Mendel to concentrate on them rather than peas. Mendel spent years working on hawkweeds, but because the plant does not hybridize in rational ways, Mendel began to believe that his work was useless and gave it up.

Themes and Meanings

Barrett once told an interviewer that after doing graduate work, first in zoology in the late 1970's and then in history in the early 1980's, she began to see a way to weave science and history together with her love of fiction. The resulting elegant tapestry was her collection *Ship Fever, and Other Stories*, a surprise winner of the National Book Award in 1996. Although her stories focus on characters caught up in pursuits in the natural sciences, her real emphasis is on the vulnerable human element behind the scientific impulse. Many of the stories are historical fictions in the classic sense: They involve real people from the past, often very famous scientists such as Gregor Mendel and Carl Linnaeus, and they present the past as it impinges on and informs the present. All of Barrett's stories use scientific fact and historical events to throw light on basic human impulses and conflicts. "The Behavior of the Hawkweeds" is typical, for it focuses on the human story of Mendel's disappointment and loneliness and how such personal aspects bend and shape science.

A more pervasive theme throughout the story is the theme of heredity introduced by Mendel's research in genetics. More generally, the theme of heredity suggests the effects of the past on the present, first hinted at by the fact that the narrator Antonia is named after her grandfather Anton and thus replicates him in some way. It is further emphasized by the fact that her Czech grandfather hates his German boss not only because of his attentions to Antonia but also because of an old animosity between the two countries. Antonia echoes this effect of the past on the present when she asks whether she is supposed to hate Germans also. It is also reflected in the fact that Antonia's husband Richard is born with an extra finger and that he worries that their children will inherit the defect.

Style and Technique

The pervasive technique of the story is Barrett's presenting three separate but parallel stories to embody the theme of the persistence of the past on the present. First, there is the story of Mendel and Nägeli, then there is the story of Tati and Leiniger, and finally the story of Antonia and Sebastian. In all three, a misunderstanding results in a conflict or split as a result of one person treating the other with condescension. Antonia becomes confused about these relationships, jumbling together the various figures, reorganizing them as pairs of men who hated each other and pairs of friends passing papers.

This motif of misunderstanding is suggested by the metaphor of "The Behavior of the Hawkweeds." When Mendel tries to take Nägeli's advice and concentrate on hawkweeds instead of the edible peas he has been working on, his experiments fail, and he wastes years of work. The problem is that the hawkweed does not hybridize in rational ways, for it grows from seeds formed by parthenogenesis and therefore each new plant is an exact copy of the mother plant. The inexplicable behavior of the hawkweed, which cannot be classified or organized in a scientific or rational way, is reflected in the behavior of human beings who similarly often act in irrational and unpredictable ways. The best one can do, given the irrational nature of human beings, is to tell their story as accurately as possible, even though such stories may not always be as neat, organized, and predictable as science. This is why Antonia is upset that Richard retells the story she told him poorly, making Nägeli too black a villain and identifying himself too closely with Mendel.

A common technique of the "The Behavior of the Hawkweeds" is Barrett's exploration of the nature of story as a way of understanding human behavior. First, Antonia tells Richard the story that her grandfather has told her as a way to get him to love her, for he sees the story, torn from its personal and historical context, as a story about the beginnings of his discipline of genetics. When she tells the story to Sebastian because she cannot bear to hear Richard tell it badly again, she supplies for the first time the personal information about why her grandfather told her the story and thus is emotionally unfaithful to Richard by telling Sebastian something she had never told him.

When Antonia asks Sebastian to tell her about himself rather than to talk about science, she is simply affirming the importance of the personal over the objective, but Sebastian misunderstands it as a sexual overture and tells her, "you misunderstood." It is at this point that Antonia echoes the phrase that she heard her grandfather call his boss, muttering to Sebastian that he is a German pig.

Barrett is a consummate stylist who chooses words carefully. Mendel's paper on the hybridization of edible peas is held up by Richard, his present-day admirer, as a "model of clarity" representing everything that science should be. Similarly, Barrett's story is a model of clarity, representing everything that narrative art should be. She knows that science, history and storytelling all construct narratives to reveal connections, relationships, and the interdependence of all things.

Charles E. May

LA BELLE ZORAÏDE

Author: Kate Chopin (1851-1904)
Type of plot: Social realism, regional, frame story
Time of plot: Before the American Civil War
Locale: Bayou St. John, Louisiana
First published: 1893

Principal characters:
MANNA-LOULOU, a slave woman
MADAME DELISE, her white mistress
ZORAÏDE, the beautiful, tragic slave of Madame Delarivière
MÉZOR, the slave Zoraïde loves
MADAME DELARIVIÈRE, godmother and mistress of Zoraïde

The Story

On a warm and humid summer evening on the Bayou St. John in Louisiana, Manna-Loulou, a slave of Madame Delise, recalls the refrain of a Creole love song. The song reminds Manna-Loulou of the story of Zoraïde, and she decides that instead of making up a bedtime story for her mistress this evening, she will instead tell her this true tragic tale. Manna-Loulou then recounts the story of beautiful Zoraïde to her mistress in Creole patois.

Manna-Loulou's story beings with a description of the lovely Zoraïde, who is a Creole beauty with light skin and a slim graceful figure. She is the slave and goddaughter of Madame Delarivière. It is Madame Delarivière's desire that Zoraïde marry a mulatto, Monsieur Ambroise, who belongs to Dr. Langlè. Dr. Langlè is a friend and admirer of Madame Delarivière. However, Zoraïde despises the ugly Monsieur Ambroise, whom she describes as cruel and false. She cleverly contrives to avoid this match so often suggested by her mistress by claiming she is not yet ready to marry anyone. Madame Delarivière accepts this excuse because she does not really want to part with her dear Zoraïde, despite her insistence that this marriage take place.

Zoraïde eventually does fall in love but not with Monsieur Ambroise. Instead she loses her heart to Mézor. The first time she sees Mézor, he is dancing the Bamboula, a sensual Creole dance. The captivating dark-skinned Mézor is a field hand who also belongs to Dr. Langlè. When Madame Delarivière learns Zoraïde is in love with and intends to marry Mézor, she becomes distraught. She thinks Mézor is an unworthy match for her beloved goddaughter, so she demands that Zoraïde never speak to Mézor again. Zoraïde and Mézor, however, continue to see each other, and soon Zoraïde becomes pregnant. When she confesses this to Madame Delarivière, the white woman becomes very angry and persuades Dr. Langlè to sell Mézor to a plantation far away.

Devastated to be separated from her beloved Mézor, Zoraïde is comforted some-what by knowing that she will soon have a baby to love and cherish. However, after Zoraïde gives birth, Madame Delarivière arranges for the baby to be sent away. When Zoraïde asks for her baby, she is told the child is dead.

Zoraïde never recovers from this cruel blow, and after a few years of continual an-guish, she lapses into madness. She begins to clutch and carry with her a bundle of rags, the size and shape of a baby, convinced that this is her child. None of Madame Delarivière's attempts to persuade Zoraïde to part with this rag bundle is successful. Finally, desperate to restore her favored goddaughter to sanity, Madame Delarivière sends for Zoraïde's child, who is by now a toddler. Fearing a trick, Zoraïde rejects the child and lives the rest of her long life devoted to the rag bundle and forever tormented by her loss.

When Manna-Loulou finishes her story, Madame Delise makes only one comment. She says, rather sleepily, that she feels most sorry for Zoraïde's child.

Themes and Meanings

Kate Chopin's "La Belle Zoraïde" deals perceptively and sensitively with racism. Zoraïde's mistress believes she is acting in the younger woman's best interest when she forbids her to marry Mézor. Madame Delarivière has raised Zoraïde so that she possesses the elegant and refined manners so necessary to fit into cultivated society. It is her wish that her goddaughter marry someone who can appreciate these qualities. In her opinion, Mézor, who works barefooted in a sugarcane field, would not bring honor to her beautiful Zoraïde, or, consequently, to herself. What Chopin subtly reveals through Madame Delarivière's displeasure with Zoraïde's passion for Mézor is that the white woman, despite her claims to want only the best for the beautiful girl, is ac-tually insensitive and cruel. She does not have Zoraïde's welfare in mind when she in-sists that Dr. Langlè sell Mézor; she is motivated by her own selfish desire and need to control her goddaughter's future.

Chopin further dramatizes Madame Delarivière's callousness when the white woman schemes to deprive Zoraïde of her child. Madame Delarivière, bitterly resent-ful of her slave's melancholy and sorrowful disposition, believes that if Zoraïde thinks her child is dead, she will return to her former, light-hearted, charming self. By believ-ing this, Madame Delarivière severely underestimates Zoraïde's natural maternal in-stincts, reinforcing Chopin's main point. The white woman, who thinks of herself as a kind, charitable, and benevolent mistress, is really incapable of seeing Zoraïde as any-thing more than a possession. It never occurs to her how deeply the loss of the child will affect Zoraïde because Madame Delarivière has never thought of Zoraïde as any-thing more than her plaything. When Madame Delarivière's scheme does not produce its desired effect, Chopin seems to be further suggesting how such misguided and conceited attitudes as those of Madame Delarivière are condescending, dismissive, and dangerous to those who share Zoraïde's position.

Chopin concludes her condemnation of the society represented by Madame Delarivière with Madame Delise's inability at the end of Manna-Loulou's tale to sympathize with Zoraïde. She can think only of the child and how unlucky she believes it was to have ever been born. Her shallow response to Zoraïde's story again reinforces Chopin's indictment of the white women's insensitivity to their female slaves.

Style and Technique

With its emphasis on setting and character development, "La Belle Zoraïde" is an excellent example of American regionalism. Chopin effectively employs a lush Louisiana setting to develop and reinforce the story's theme.

As would be expected of the women of this time and place, Manna-Loulou and Madame Delise converse in Creole French, and Chopin describes their conversation as delightful and charming. Throughout the story, she intersperses phrases written in this dialect to demonstrate as well as accentuate the beauty of the language. This enchanting dimension of the story, though, is overshadowed by the other elements of the story's setting emphasized by Chopin. It is, for example, the oppressive atmosphere of this sultry summer night on the bayou that reminds Manna-Loulou of the story of the illicit passions of the ill-fated lovers, Zoraïde and Mézor. As Manna-Loulou begins her tale, the deep dark bayou rolls by outside Madame Delise's bedroom window, and the dark sky and still air foreshadow the story's unhappy ending.

Chopin's characters in "La Belle Zoraïde" exhibt those traits often associated with the story's locale. The white women in the story, Madame Delise and Madame Delarivière, are both depicted as beautiful and delicately cultivated. Their elegant manners and genteel background are also highlighted. Both are also attended by docile, eager-to-please female slaves. However, while these women are important to the story, it is their relationships with their slaves that is most relevant to the story's meaning. Although Madame Delise and Madame Delarivière appear to empathize with the black women who serve them, they do not truly nor fully feel compassion for them. For their part, the slaves are portrayed rather enigmatically. Although much of their outward appearance and many of their actions reflect a desire and willingness to conform to their mistresses' wishes, their docility masks their emotional complexity. Thus Chopin's portrayal of these characters undermines and challenges the stereotypes so prevalent in the American fiction written at this time. In Zoraïde and Manna-Loulou, the readers are allowed to see the humanity of characters who are so often overlooked or ignored by other writers. That the story "La Belle Zoraïde" is actually told from a slave woman's perspective further encourages readers to sympathize with both Manna-Loulou and Zoraïde and the roles they are forced to play in their society.

Traci S. Thompson

THE BENCH

Author: Richard Rive (1931-1989)
Type of plot: Social realism
Time of plot: The mid-twentieth century
Locale: Cape Town, South Africa
First published: 1963

Principal character:
KARLIE, a young man

The Story

After Karlie has lived all of his life in a remote rural part of South Africa, this is his first visit to Cape Town, a bustling metropolis in which all sorts of people rub shoulders. More obviously than in his more segregated home town, Cape Town shows the tensions that result from the rigid system of separation of races known as apartheid. Karlie sees people of all colors—some black, some white, and others mixed.

As the story opens, Karlie is standing in a large crowd that is listening to a black speaker who is proclaiming the rights of black majority, the working class to whom he refers as the proletariat. Karlie is impressed by what the speaker is saying because it seems to be the first time that he has even considered the possibility that blacks do, in fact, have any rights at all. He notices that two white detectives are taking notes on everything that is being said at the meeting.

As Karlie listens, he recalls the advice he received from elders in his own community. Ou Klaas, for example, taught him that God created blacks and whites separately, and therefore they should continue to live separately.

On the platform with the speaker is a white woman in a blue dress and Nxeli, whom Karlie recognizes as a famous trade-union organizer. As he watches, the white woman gets up and begins speaking. She encourages the black crowd to refuse to play by the rules imposed by the whites: Blacks, she says, should sit wherever they please, and go wherever they want.

As he leaves the meeting, Karlie is both confused by the new ideas and exhilarated. He doubts whether anything of this sort could ever be put into action in his own little town, but he is beginning to think it might be a possibility. At the train station that will send him home he notices, in a new way, a bench labeled "Europeans only." Inspired by all that he has heard and the sense of individual responsibility that the speakers have aroused in him, he decides to sit on the forbidden bench.

At first, no one seems to notice him. Time passes, and he thinks that his protest may go unheeded. After a while he eases into his new situation, and sits simply because he is tired. At that moment a young white man shouts at him to get up off the bench. Karlie neither speaks nor moves. As the white man continues shouting, a crowd gathers. Different people express different reactions. Some are outraged that Karlie will not sit on the benches reserved for blacks. Others declare that he should be allowed to sit wherever he wishes.

A police officer arrives and tells Karlie to move. Again, Karlie remains silent and stays where he is. As the officer begins shouting, the white woman who gave the speech Karlie heard approaches and defends Karlie's rights. Nevertheless, the officer begins beating Karlie; he puts handcuffs on him and drags him away. At first Karlie struggles and tries to hold on to the bench; when he sees that this is hopeless, he stands up and goes with the officer, smiling and asserting the arrogance that he now feels.

Themes and Meanings

This is the story of a young man's coming to consciousness of his rights and responsibilities. Richard Rive is focusing on a defining moment in Karlie's life, and the reader knows that the protagonist's life will never again be what it was before this fateful day. Whether he is treated badly in jail or not, he can never go back to his little village as the naïve fellow he was that morning. He has become a man.

The disturbing words that Karlie hears on his first visit to the city are described by Rive as if the young man had wandered into a church and had overheard a foreign revelation that was completely unexpected and totally liberating from his passing understanding of himself and of his possibilities. The notion that he might have all the rights of a white man seems, at first, far too good to be true, as if the political message was the good news that the word "gospel" actually means. Rive describes the young man as a young convert who is filled with the enthusiasm that follows from entrance into any new belief system. His somewhat precipitous action that soon follows the speech seems perfectly natural if viewed in this religious context: Karlie wishes to put into practice the invigorating message that has changed his interior life.

It is as though Karlie has been given a new set of eyes, and he views the world around him in much different terms. Those who had once seemed bigger than life— his elders in the village and, especially, the whites in the far-off city—now seem his equals. In some important sense, they also seem to be his inferiors because Karlie now recognizes that those who had advised him to cower timidly in the face of the unfair laws are, in fact, less-than-noble examples. They are frightened, small men who have grown accustomed to a limited domain for their lives. Unlike them, Karlie has taken the next step and asked the all-important question that leads to change in any society: Why are things this way? Karlie may be technically defeated in his act of civil disobedience, but he now finds himself identifying with a different group of role models: He now sees himself as one of those who proudly hold their heads high and smile as they are dragged off to jail.

Rive, whose father was an African American and whose mother was a mixed-race South African, is alert to the influence that the racial struggle in the United States has had in African politics. He dedicates the story to Langston Hughes, the African American short-story writer and poet. In this story, Karlie, although not from a cosmopolitan part of the country, nevertheless is aware of the Black Power movement and of the challenge that it presented to white authority everywhere. In some ways, Rive's story is an African version of the factual Rosa Parks story, in which a southern black woman in the United States refused to give up her seat in a bus to a white man as the discriminatory laws demanded.

Style and Technique

Part of the success of this story is its utter simplicity. The language is completely straightforward and the techniques are in no way complex. It is as though Rive looks directly into his character's uncomplicated system of logic and constructs his story as a perfect mirror of Karlie's mental processes. If the narrative were more subtle, or the vocabulary less accessible, the story would not have its powerful impact. Readers are shown Karlie's step-by-step movement from innocence to commitment, and nowhere along the path are they made conscious of the roadway itself. Rive thereby convinces them that Karlie, who might represent so many other young men like himself, can, in fact, take this uncharacteristic action and go against the timid advice of his elders.

Rive uses the bench as a symbol for arbitrary territorial borders that are used to maintain an unjust social structure. That an act as meaningless in itself as sitting on a bench could prompt such virulence in many of the whites points out that they see much more meaning in the bench than it deserves. For them, it is a symbol of their control of the rules of the game: They are the ones who have the power to define, quite arbitrarily, what this simple bench is. If a native African feels free to violate this definition, who knows how many others they might also choose to redefine, and some with far greater consequences. Rive's character, for all his simplicity, recognizes the power of symbols.

Rive constructs the story as an implied conversation between the speakers on the platform and the village elders who had counseled Karlie to know his place and to play along with the white overseers. As Karlie is won over to the words of rebellion, he begins to see Ou Klaas and the other accommodators in a less favorable light. He recognizes that they have been treated all their lives like pack animals, and he answers their implicit advice with a firm "No."

John C. Hawley

BENITO CERENO

Author: Herman Melville (1819-1891)
Type of plot: Adventure
Time of plot: 1799
Locale: The harbor of St. Maria, off the southern tip of Chile
First published: 1855

Principal characters:
> AMASA DELANO, a New England sea captain
> BENITO CERENO, the Spanish captain of the *San Dominick*
> BABO, the leader of the slave mutiny, apparently Cereno's devoted
> servant
> ATUFAL, Babo's lieutenant

The Story

Captain Amasa Delano anchors his ship, the *Bachelor's Delight*, in the harbor of St. Maria to take on water and food. The next day a Spanish ship, the *San Dominick*, also drifts into the harbor. Seeing the ragged state of the sails and the generally poor condition of the ship, Delano loads several baskets of fresh fish onto his whaleboat to present to the other vessel.

As soon as he steps on board, he is surrounded by blacks and whites lamenting their calamitous voyage marked by plague, hunger, thirst, and contrary winds. Moved by their story, Delano sends the whaleboat back for additional supplies while he remains to visit with the ship's captain, Benito Cereno. Because Delano knows the harbor and Cereno clearly does not, the American plans to act as pilot to lead the *San Dominick* safely to shore. He also intends to refit and refurbish the Spanish merchantman so that it can sail to its destination of Lima, Peru.

Throughout the daylong visit, Delano is repeatedly appalled by Cereno's behavior. The Spaniard never expresses gratitude for offers of help. He fails to maintain discipline, allowing crew members to fight, even to stab one another. However, be has ordered the docile Atufal to appear before him in chains every two hours until he begs forgiveness for some unnamed fault.

Delano is also troubled by Cereno's repeated private conferences with his constant black companion, Babo. The Spaniard and the black seem to be conspiring, and Delano derives no comfort from the tenor of Cereno's questions: How many men has the American on board? Is his ship well armed? Will all the men stay on board at night? Spanish sailors skulk about; a balustrade collapses, nearly plunging Delano into the ocean. Cereno's account of his voyage seems incredible—how could the *San Dominick* have taken months to travel the short distance the *Bachelor's Delight* traversed in only a few days?

Delano, however, dismisses his suspicions as unworthy, and his visit does seem likely to end uneventfully. After navigating the *San Dominick* into the harbor, he boards his whaleboat to return to his ship. At that moment, though, Cereno confirms Delano's fears. The Spaniard and his servant leap after him, followed by three Spanish sailors. Delano believes that they plan to murder him. The Americans overpower their assailants, only to discover that Cereno and the other whites have leapt into the water to escape the blacks, and that Babo has followed Cereno not to support an attack but to kill Cereno even at the cost of his own life.

At last Delano learns the true situation. On its way from Valparaiso to Callao, the *San Dominick* was seized by its cargo of slaves, who had been allowed to go about the decks unfettered. Led by Babo and Atufal, the blacks had killed all but a few Spaniards and ordered the rest to take the ship to Senegal. For their former owner, Don Alexandro Aranda, they reserved a particularly grisly fate. After murdering him, they removed all the flesh from his bones—probably by cannibalism—and substituted the skeleton for the ship's original figurehead.

Like Delano, the Spanish had come to St. Maria for water but were surprised to meet another ship. Babo then instructed Cereno as to what to say and do, threatening him with instant death if he refused. Babo intended to seize the American ship, but instead the Americans recapture the *San Dominick* and help it reach Lima.

There, Cereno offers a full, official explanation and then retires to a monastery, a broken man. Three months later, he is dead, and he is buried in the church where the remains of Don Alexandro Aranda were deposited.

Themes and Meanings

"Benito Cereno," like so many of Melville's other works, rejects the benevolent world view of the optimistic Transcendentalists, represented in the story by Captain Delano. Significantly, Delano comes from Massachusetts, the birthplace of Transcendentalism. Delano is charitable, well-meaning, compassionate, and trusts to the "ever-watchful Providence above." He is also a fool. Melville says as much at the beginning of the story when he describes the captain as rejecting the notion of "malign evil in man." The author then wonders whether "in view of what humanity is capable, such a trait implies . . . more than ordinary quickness and accuracy of intellectual perception."

The answer is no, as Delano repeatedly proves in the sequel. On board the *San Dominick* he sees repeated evidence that Cereno is not in control of the ship, yet he fails to draw the logical conclusion that if the Spaniard is not, the blacks must be. He notices that blacks abuse whites with impunity, that Babo uses the Spanish flag as a shaving towel, that at lunch Babo does not stand behind his supposed master but instead takes his station behind Delano, whence he can watch Cereno's every gesture. At one point a sailor tosses Delano an intricately wrought knot and urges him to "undo it, cut it, quick." Again Delano fails to understand the meaning of the scene; he does not equate the knot with the mystery aboard the ship.

Nor does Delano learn anything from his experience. Even at the end of the story, he believes that he is saved not by the actions of Cereno but by his own innocence and by Providence. He urges Cereno to forget what has passed and cannot understand why the Spaniard cannot share his happiness. "What has cast such a shadow upon you?" he asks naïvely. Cereno replies, "The negro." Though Cereno refuses to look at Babo after the rescue, he cannot ignore what Babo symbolizes. He has seen the heart of darkness that lurks in humanity, and that knowledge destroys him.

Style and Technique

Melville repeatedly uses irony to undercut the easy assumptions of Captain Delano. Observing Babo's constant attendance on Cereno, whom the black will not leave even for a moment, Delano comments, "Don Benito, I envy you such a friend; slave I cannot call him." Such envy is clearly out of place, but there is ironic truth in Delano's refusing to call Babo a slave, for Babo in fact is the master. Delano likens the ship to a monastery and the blacks to monks, analogies hardly appropriate to the situation. The American regards the black women as the pattern of docility, "pure tenderness and love"; later the reader learns that during the mutiny they were more vicious and bloodthirsty than the men.

Melville also employs irony to indicate that blackness is not a function of skin color. Babo demonstrates that blacks and whites are identical within when he mockingly shows the skeleton of Don Alexandro Aranda. To each of the Spaniards he puts the same question: Does not the whiteness of the bones prove that they belonged to a white man? The answer is no. Beneath the surface all people are alike, which means that all people are capable of the horrors committed aboard the *San Dominick*.

Ironic repetitions emphasize this idea. Babo's motto, "Follow your leader," is a warning to the Spaniards that if they refuse to comply with his orders they will share the fate of Don Alexandro. When the Americans recapture the *San Dominick*, the chief mate urges the sailors on with the cry, "Follow your leader!" When the blacks mutiny, they kill eighteen whites; in the recapture, "nearly a score of negroes were killed." Delano prevents Babo from stabbing the prostrate Cereno; later he stops the Spaniard Bartholomew Barlo (how close that name is to Babo's) from stabbing one of the chained blacks.

Even in death, irony rules. Don Joaquin hides a jewel to present at the shrine of Our Lady of Mercy in Lima as a gift of thanks for his safe passage. The jewel goes to the church, but only after Don Joaquin dies aboard ship. Babo warns Cereno that failure to obey will cause the captain to follow his leader, Don Alexandro, to death. When the *San Dominick* lands, Aranda's skeleton has been buried in St. Bartholomew's Church. Shortly thereafter, Cereno, too, is buried there and so does, indeed, follow his leader.

Kindness and Providence offer no protection against the blackness in humankind. Aranda was a kind master who allowed his slaves the freedom of the ship. His benevolence was his undoing, as it almost destroys Delano, who unwittingly guides Babo and his mutineers into a berth next to his own vulnerable ship. Though Delano emerges from his experience neither sadder nor wiser, the reader cannot be so untouched, for Melville has shown him the grimness of humanity's soul.

Joseph Rosenblum

THE BEST OF EVERYTHING

Author: Richard Yates (1926-1992)
Type of plot: Fiction of manners
Time of plot: The early 1950's
Locale: Manhattan, New York City
First published: 1954

> *Principal characters:*
> GRACE, the bride-to-be
> RALPH, the groom-to-be
> MARTHA, Grace's roommate

The Story

The Friday before Grace's weekend wedding, her coworkers give her gifts and treat her to lunch. Ralph gets a bonus from his employer, but when he calls Grace to arrange a date for that evening, he harbors a secret disappointment. His male friends have ignored the occasion. He has to stop by his friend Eddie's house to pick up a suitcase he is borrowing, and then he will travel into Manhattan to see his fiancé that evening.

With the wedding so near, Grace finds she still doubts her choice of a husband. Her sophisticated roommate Martha has been quick to point out Ralph's deficiencies. He comes from a working-class family (as does Grace) and has a menial job. His friends work menial jobs, too. His interests are limited to sports teams, and his command of English is substandard. He pronounces toilet as "terlet." Despite Martha's disapproval, Grace agrees to marry Ralph but silently fears that Martha is right. Grace attempts to elevate Ralph's status by calling him "darling" and giving him her best imitation of Martha's cultured smile.

When Grace returns home after work, she finds that Martha has cleaned the apartment, prepared dinner, and arranged to leave town immediately. Martha apologizes for her past, harsh judgment of Ralph and explains that she is leaving the apartment so Grace can be alone with Ralph that evening. She says her absence is a wedding gift. She gives Grace a knowing smile, implying that Grace has postponed sex with Ralph long enough. This night she should take Ralph into her bed. Grace grasps Martha's intent and makes it her own. After her roommate departs, she puts on a sheer, white nylon negligee she has been saving for the wedding night. She settles in with a glass of sherry to await Ralph's arrival, feeling like the female lead in a romantic film.

Ralph has doubts of his own. He fears that marriage will force him to give up the companionship of other males, which gives him great pleasure. When he is surprised at Eddie's house with a stag party, he regrets having made the date with Grace. His friends provide beer, heavy food, and a gift of a much-coveted new suitcase—along with a kinship and camaraderie Ralph knows he will never feel with Grace. Nevertheless, he leaves the party and goes to her, arriving late. Failing to notice Grace's negligee and seductive demeanor, Ralph never considers breaking the pattern of abstinence established during their courtship. Besides, he is having more fun with his friends than he has ever had with Grace. He makes his excuses and leaves hastily to return to his stag party. Before departing, he asks, "Mind if I use ya terlet?"

Themes and Meanings

This might be a story of domestic realism were it not for the predominance of social manners as determiners of character and behavior. Grace and Ralph are not free to love each other in the present, nor will they cement a solid relationship after marriage. Both are too bound up in the expectations they believe their peers have for them. They act not as they choose to—or even to please each other—but in blind accordance with the role prescribed for them by time, place, and circumstance. They have no sense of what is good or right, only what is conventional.

Many of Richard Yates's stories and novels unfold in three parts: fear, hope, and disappointment. This story is no exception. Early in the tale, Yates reveals that both bride and groom fear marriage, their choice of mate, and their amorphous future direction. However, when Grace dons her negligee, she hopes for a connection if not with Ralph, at least with the romantic dream she has assimilated from films and paperback novels. Her dreams, however, are to go unfulfilled. Ralph is too caught up in his desire for acceptance by other men to grasp the message Grace tries to send him. Grace resigns herself to this disappointment and—by implication—a future of still more disappointments.

This is a typical Yates story. His characters act without awareness of their motivations. Yates neither explains nor moralizes. He simply reports on actions lacking either substance or purpose. He has been called a pessimist, and this story shows why. Grace and Ralph have the potential to love each other, but that potential will never be realized. They define themselves and others by externals: a brand of suitcase, the cut of a suit, the pronunciation of a word. They will never achieve a meaningful relationship, because each is programmed by social convention to behave in ways that will prove frustrating to the other. They will remain as isolated from one another after their marriage as they are before.

In much of Yates's work, the characters are not characters, but actors playing a socially determined role. That role is often derived from popular films or novels, and Grace is a perfect example. She dresses, moves, and even adopts the gestures of an actress in a romantic film, assuming that Ralph will grasp her intent. Ralph, however, takes his models more from the playing field than from the motion picture house, and he is unmoved. The result is a return to Yates's favorite themes: unrelenting loneliness and despair.

Nevertheless, Grace and Ralph are sympathetic characters. The reader likes them, which cannot be said for many of Yates's characters. They are neither false nor duplicitous, only lost. Their social milieu controls them. Grace sticks with Ralph not because he is her soul mate, but because she fears she cannot do any better. If she is to live out any part of her romantic dream, Ralph will have to suffice. Both are victims of expecting—not too much—but too little.

Style and Technique

Yates prided himself on capturing his characters in revealing secrets about themselves they would have preferred to keep. He achieves that goal in this story through his selection of vivid details. For example, Carol receives predictable, impersonal gifts from her coworkers and boss on the eve of her wedding: a gardenia corsage, a silver candy dish, and a gift certificate from Bloomingdale's. At lunch, the women eat chicken and drink unfamiliar cocktails. Their work job is mundane. Grace labors as a typist—faceless among the ranks of those just like her who giggle and tease the afternoon away, seeking any relief possible from the boredom of their employment.

Yates divulges both character and social class through dialects and dialogue. Ralph, for example, reveals his blue-collar background and unsophisticated nature when he describes receiving his bonus: "The boss siz, 'Here, Ralph,' and he hands me this envelope. He don't even crack a smile or nothin', and I'm wonderin', what's the deal here? I'm getting fired here or what? He siz, 'G'ahead, Ralph, open it.' So I open it, and then I look at the boss and he's grinning a mile wide."

Yates also uses vivid details to disclose the norms of social class that constrain the characters. For example, Martha tells Grace that the right kind of man uses words like "amusing" and wears "small-shouldered flannel suits like a uniform." Grace's father works in a paper mill and drinks beer. Her mother repeatedly uses worn-out phrases such as "bright and early." Upper-class Martha, on the other hand, looks "very svelte in a crisp new dress."

Mannerisms and gestures also reveal character and conflict, much as stage directions do in a play. At the story's end, for example, Grace "blazes" to her feet and utters a cry of protest, but it sounds more like a whine than an appeal, so she capitulates quickly to Ralph's desire to return to his friends. As he leaves, she folds her arms across her chest and puts on a tired smile, agreeing without objection to meet Ralph on time the following day to carry out their wedding plans. The scene is so intimate and so pitiful, the reader is left feeling an intruder into a vast tragedy of the heart of far greater significance than the characters, setting, or dialogue import.

Faith Hickman Brynie

THE BET

Author: Anton Chekhov (1860-1904)
Type of plot: Fable
Time of plot: November 14, 1870-November 14, 1885
Locale: An unspecified Russian city
First published: "Pari," 1888 (English translation, 1915)

> *Principal characters:*
> THE BANKER, the host at the party, an elderly man
> THE YOUNG LAWYER, later the prisoner

The Story

"The Bet" is the story of a bet that stakes a banker's two million rubles against fifteen years of a young lawyer's life. As the story opens, the banker is recalling the occasion of the bet fifteen years before. Guests at a party that he was hosting that day fell into a discussion of capital punishment; the banker argued that capital punishment is more humane than life imprisonment, while the young lawyer disagreed, insisting that he would choose life in prison rather than death. As the argument became more heated, the banker angrily wagered two million rubles that the lawyer could not endure imprisonment, a challenge that the lawyer accepted, setting the term of his voluntary captivity at fifteen years, at the end of which he would receive the two million rubles.

The lawyer was imprisoned in the banker's garden house in complete solitude, permitted no visitors, no letters, no newspapers. He could write letters, however, and he was permitted books, music, wine, and tobacco. The banker observed the progress of the young lawyer's adaptation to his imprisonment. During the first year, he read fight books and played the piano. In the second year, he ceased being interested in music but turned to great literature. In the fifth year, he loafed, drank wine, and played the piano. Then for four years he studied languages, history, and philosophy before moving to the New Testament and to theology. Finally, his reading became eclectic.

At the beginning of the story, the day on which the banker is recalling the events of these fifteen years, he is within a day of the final accounting, when, no longer rich but oppressed by debt, he will be ruined by paying the two million rubles. Desperate, the banker resolves to unlock the garden house door and to kill his captive, throwing the blame on the watchman. When he enters the room, he sees an emaciated man, old before his time, asleep at his table. Before him is a paper, on which he has stated that he despises everything in human life, even the books from which he has learned about it, and that, therefore, he intends to leave his room five minutes before the fifteen-year period elapses, thus forfeiting the bet.

After reading the paper, the banker despises himself. The next morning, he learns that the lawyer has indeed left the garden house. So that no one will suspect him of a crime, the banker puts the paper in his safe.

Themes and Meanings

"The Bet" was written during a period when Anton Chekhov was greatly influenced by Leo Tolstoy, whose simple, didactic tales were popular during the 1880's. The theme of "The Bet" is clearly the vanity of human wishes. Before his imprisonment, the young lawyer believes that life on any terms is better than death. He thinks that he can find the inner resources to live in solitude for fifteen years, and that the promise of a fortune will sustain him during the period of complete leisure in comfortable surroundings. Like the eighteenth century travelers in search of truth—Dr. Samuel Johnson's Rasselas (from *Rasselas, Prince of Abyssinia,* 1759), for example—Chekhov's captive moves from one enthusiasm to another, discarding one by one those sources of human happiness that he is permitted under the terms of his agreement.

It is interesting that the lawyer alternates between self-indulgence and disciplined study, moving from light books and music to classical literature, then back to escape through music and wine, then to intense study, first of the human world and then of the divine. At the end, Chekhov's banker observes, he has no direction but strikes out erratically, obviously searching for something, anything, to give meaning to his life.

Unlike most truth-seekers in literature, the lawyer is deprived of human contact, love, family ties, friendship, and companionship. During the first year, Chekhov writes, the captive is lonely; evidently, solitude is less depressing during the later years. It might be said, however, that his exploration of all human possibilities is incomplete without an experience of personal relationships. Chekhov is aware of that omission and deals with it in the letter written by the lawyer at the end of his fifteen years alone. Through books, he says, he has experienced all human pleasures, from human love and the enjoyment of natural beauty to the exercise of tyrannical power, and though his emotional involvements have been vicarious, he believes that he can reject them on the basis of what he has learned.

The grounds of the lawyer's contempt for life, as expressed in the final letter, are several. First, everything is empty. Various interests last for various lengths of time, but none can justify a life. Second, all that man considers beautiful is ugly, and all that he considers true is false; in other words, man can like this world only if he sees it as it is not, and the captive has lost the capacity for illusion. Finally, nothing endures; death destroys everything and everyone. All is vanity, then, empty, illusory, and doomed.

It is significant that after he sees the shrunken, miserable captive whom he had intended to kill, after he reads the letter denouncing human existence, the banker feels contempt not for the world but for himself. Does he feel guilt because he has destroyed a life? Does he feel shame because he was ready to commit murder rather than lose his money? Does he feel that the captive has higher ideals than he? Chekhov leaves the banker's reaction unexplained. The banker, however, is not ready to renounce life; he locks the note in his safe as insurance against possible accusations.

One of the problems with this story is that the author seems uncertain as to his theme. Surely Chekhov does not agree with the captive that nothing is worthwhile, although he does realize that no enthusiasm in life seems to be permanent. The fact that Chekhov concludes "The Bet" with the banker's self-protective gesture suggests that the world is not ready to agree with the lawyer. Furthermore, the unnatural appearance of the captive leads readers to believe either that life has worn him down much faster than usual or that his life has been much harsher than the lives of most people. Is he truly wise? Or have fifteen years of solitary confinement warped his judgment? Again, Chekhov leaves the question open.

That Chekhov was uncertain about what he intended to prove in the story, other than the fact that human reactions are unpredictable, is indicated by the third section of the story, which he omitted in his collected works. In it, at a party a year after the prisoner's escape, the banker is expressing his admiration for the lawyer, the one man of principle whom he has ever encountered. Suddenly the lawyer appears, announces his love of life, declares books a poor substitute, and asks for a considerable sum of money, threatening suicide if he does not receive it. The banker agrees and then is overcome by the desire himself to renounce life, but realizing that his life is no longer happy enough to make the gesture meaningful, he rejects the impulse and declares the lawyer the winner of the bet.

Style and Technique

Because "The Bet" is cast in fable form, the characterization is not as individualized as in Chekhov's other stories, but rather, the banker and the lawyer serve as voices of two different viewpoints. Except for the letter written at the end of the fifteen-year period, Chekhov does not reveal the thoughts of the captive. On the other hand, the story begins with the banker's memories and observations, proceeds to his worries about money and his resolution to kill the prisoner rather than pay the bet, and concludes with the banker's self-contempt and with his self-protective gesture. The sequel discarded by Chekhov continues the focus on the banker's point of view. Thus it might be suggested that Chekhov is more interested in the psychological and ironic possibilities of his account than in a didactic point.

Usually Chekhov's imagery, too, reflects his psychological interest. Certainly in "The Bet" it is appropriate that the story begins on a dark rainy night and that the banker's temptation to murder occurs on a dark, cold, rainy night, that he passes a bare bed and a cold stove on the way to the sealed room, and that the prisoner's room is dark, with a dimming candle. All these images of death are consistent with the banker's resolution, as well as with the lawyer's death-in-life. Because they are seen through the banker's eyes, however, they are particularly important as reflecting his own psychological condition, a despair that is itself a death-in-life, and that may finally be Chekhov's particular interest in "The Bet." For although Chekhov followed Tolstoy in constructing his story in the form of a fable, both the story as he finally published it and the longer, earlier version emphasize psychological realism more than certain truths about human existence.

Rosemary M. Canfield Reisman

BEYOND THE GLASS MOUNTAIN

Author: Wallace Stegner (1909-1993)
Type of plot: Psychological
Time of plot: May during the late 1940's
Locale: Iowa City, Iowa
First published: 1947

Principal characters:

MARK AKER, the protagonist, a medical researcher on the Yale
University faculty

MEL COTTAM, his closest college friend, who runs his father's
former business in Iowa City

TAMSEN COTTAM, Mel's wife and a member of the same college
crowd

CANBY, Mel and Tamsen's twelve-year-old son

The Story

Superficially, the situation in "Beyond the Glass Mountain" is an American commonplace. It concerns a very brief reunion of Mark Aker, a Yale University medical professor and researcher, with his former college friend Mel Cottam, a small businessperson in Iowa City, Iowa, after a seventeen-year separation. The reunion begins for Mark with a nostalgic return to Iowa City and his recollections of the college town and the college world that gave him "the best days of his life." He returns, also, in response to what he perceives is a call for help from Mel. He hopes to repay a profound personal debt to the man who made those days possible. The reunion is cut short, however, when Mark cannot penetrate the wall that time and experience have put between them; he is unable to bring himself to pry into Mel's private world and unable to find the words that would set it all right with them again.

Mark's uneasiness about the long-delayed meeting is overcome, initially, by the power of Iowa City to trigger rich and complex memories of the good days of his youth, "the whole coltish . . . time handed back to him briefly, intact, precious." "The passionate familiarity of everything"—landmarks, names, sights, smells, and sounds—includes Mel's voice answering his phone call. Mark realizes that the poignancy of these "things" lies in the fact that they are all part of a storied past. The stories he recalls are made of modest material—sports, dating, eating, pranks—but they always involve Mel and suggest their closeness. Mark is reminded of how they had "made games of everything"; also, Mel's house had been home for both of them. The power of these memories invests Mark with the hope that the old Mel is not lost and their old relationship still lives.

However, Mark also fears the reunion. He fears the possibility that he will find Mel drunk rather than sober, that the drinking is a sign that his friend has been deeply hurt or betrayed. His evidence for believing that Mel is an alcoholic is slim—the reader hears initially only about two drunken phone calls. When Mark calls Mel to announce his unexpected arrival in town this particular Sunday morning in May, he is relieved to hear Mel's sober voice answer, but when Mark himself falls naturally into the bantering, clownish "talk" that characterized their college days ("Hello, you poop out. . . . This is Canby"), Mel responds by falling into his old role of happy-go-lucky, jocular sot, a role he sustains, to Mark's increasing distress, beyond the "point where it should have stopped."

Mark's initial fear is reinforced when he arrives at Mel's house to find Mel and his wife, Tamsen, having Sunday-morning cocktails. The source of Mark's concern for Mel becomes even clearer in the scene that follows: Tamsen, highball in hand but also "smooth and sober and impeccable," stands in striking contrast to spraddle-legged Mel; she gives every indication that she is "in command in this familiar house." In college, Mark knew Tamsen as shrewd but dishonest ("she could lie her way out of hell"), as well as a woman of easy virtue. He has learned that Mel found out about her infidelities and considered a divorce but that somehow the marriage was patched up.

In a brief moment the two men have together, Mark considers urging Mel to leave Tamsen, for the sake of their child as well as himself. He thinks of asking Mel to come away with him and kick his drinking habit. The plea, however, is never uttered: Despite his former closeness to Mel and his desire to be close again, Mark believes that "you simply did not say things like that. Even thinking about them made them sound self-righteous and prying." There is some invisible, transparent, but formidable barrier that separates them—a glass mountain. Even though Mel is as close as an animal seen by the hunter through the sights of his rifle, in fact Mark and Mel are as far apart as the two worlds separating the hunter from the animal he hunts—the animal seemingly indifferent to the hunter's presence.

To these unspoken reflections, Mel turns "his ear sideward like a deaf man." Mark, in turn, is shaken, refuses a second drink proposed by Tamsen, and begs the necessity of catching a 12:30 train. As the two friends part ways on the street corner, however, Mark tries once more to get his friend to "listen straight." The response is even more disturbing: He finally sees in his friend's eyes the "pained, intent, sad" expression for which he has been looking as evidence of the real Mel, but he also catches a "flicker of derision" on Mel's lips, indicating that he still does not fully understand the man behind the mask. The story ends with the reader still not sure that Mark has seen fully or judged fairly the situation or the relationship. Mel's derisive gesture marks his rejection of Mark as well as Mark's friendly overture.

Themes and Meanings

Initially the reader may see "Beyond the Glass Mountain" as Mel's story because his "problems"—drinking and marriage—preoccupy Mark. Mel's expression of contempt for Mark at the end of the story is consistent with his stoic resolve to hold on to his marriage, however compromising, and reject advances into his private life, even from a well-intentioned "friend"; it even implies a criticism of Mark's success. They both know that Mark has "gone up and out in the world," while Mel "has been ma-rooned behind." Mel signals his attitude toward Mark's success when he plucks at his sleeve and asks, "Where did you get that jacket?" Mark feels guilty in responding "Montreal," and shame when he finds himself justifying a trip there to attend a genetics conference.

The story is more centrally Mark's, for it presents a man of considerable worldly success facing a personal and private failure. Mark wonders how a man can act honorably when the past leaves him with debts and obligations. He fails to find an answer. Instead, he learns that his perceptions of reality are deceiving, that "friends" wear masks that hide their true feelings, and that communication between adult men is problematic.

Mark becomes angry when Mel draws attention to his worldly success: "Mel [who had everything then] had taught the whole unlicked lot of them something, how to win and how to lose, how to live with people and like them and forgive them. He had never owned a dime's worth of anything that he wasn't glad to share." Mark cannot repay his debt unless their youthful roles are reversed—with Mel the benefactor of Mark's largess. That reversal is effectively blocked by Mel's pride, the stigma of Mark's new status, and Mark's judgmental temperament.

Mark comes to the situation with strong moral biases. He can imagine pronouncing them, but he knows that it is inappropriate for a friend to voice them. His sensitivity is underlined by his unrehearsed response to the good life remembered and Mel's generous role in making it good. Faced with the present situation, however, he can only look uneasy. In his way, he is as reticent as Mel, withholding from his friend (if not the reader) his strongest sentiments about their relationship as well as his most strident judgments about Tamsen and dishonesty and bad marriages.

Both his moral probity and his success stand against him under the circumstances. Although part of Mark is convinced that he and Mel remain the people they once were, that "what we were is still here, if we peel off the defenses and the gag lines," the glaze that covers Mel's eyes is all but impenetrable. When it cracks for that moment at the end of the story, it does not give Mark the reassurance that he seeks.

Style and Technique

Meaning in "Beyond the Glass Mountain" develops out of the complex relation-ships between the characters and between the past and the present. Mark sees his college years with Mel as a Damon and Pythias affair—the allusion to the classical legend of the loyalty of two friends appropriately underlining the idealizing tendencies of Mark's memory. As this ideal collapses under the stress of the present moment, it is the legend of the mountain man Jim Bridger hunting elk in Yellowstone that comes to Mark's mind. The connotations of the wilderness and hunting—with their hint of alienation and even violence—suggest human relationships far from the ideal in the Greek legend.

Stegner uses quite different techniques to enrich the contrast between past and present. During Mark's initial nostalgic awakening, the reader watches him literally "soak himself in the sensations he remembered," the impressionistic images flowing from a man with the heightened sensibilities of a poet rather than a biologist. Later, at the Cottam home, Mark exposes an identity in his interior monologues quite at odds with the "civil" visitor who converses wittily with both Tamsen and Mel.

Indeed, talk is a major contributor to the dramatic tension that gradually emerges between Mark and Mel. The college talk into which the two drift—the caustic, sometimes ribald name-calling—is a code language that identified a camaraderie among young college strangers but keeps middle-aged adults at bay and estranged. Mark initiates it when he introduces himself as "Canby" ("In their college crowd everybody had called everybody else Canby"). Mel responds by dropping into the "clowning voice" of his college years, a voice that feigned drunken confusion and misunderstanding at every turn. When Mark tries to straighten out the conversation—"This is Aker. Remember me?"—Mel holds to his voice: "You mean Belly Aker, the basketball player . . . ?"

At the Cottam home, Mel's tomfoolery continues. Mark is unable to decide whether Mel has become a "drunken parody" of his former self or is using "double talk and affectionate profanity" as a defense to hide his feelings. When Mel and Tamsen's son innocently intrudes, Mel calls him "Canby" and treats him in the same roughhousing, jocular manner, suggesting that the son is being initiated into a kind of masculine, tribal discourse; as if donning the tribal mask, the son grins. Mark cannot escape the talk either, as well as the role it implies, despite his uneasiness. His farewell to Mel begins in the same spirit: "I wish you the best, you bum," he begins. When he tries to say more than this, however, he is met by Mel's pained expression and the "flicker of derision" that warns him to go no further. By invoking this series of contrasts—between ideal and real, past and present, thought and talk, the mask and the true self—Stegner reveals the difficulty of truly understanding another, of breaking through the "glass mountain."

Merrill Lewis

BEYOND THE PALE

Author: William Trevor (William Trevor Cox, 1928-   )
Type of plot: Domestic realism
Time of plot: 1979
Locale: County Antrim, Northern Ireland
First published: 1981

> *Principal characters:*
> DOROTHY MILSON (MILLY), the narrator and protagonist
> MAJOR R. B. STRAFE, her lover
> CYNTHIA STRAFE, the major's wife
> DEKKO DEACON, an old friend
> MR. and MRS. MALSEED, proprietors of Glencorn Lodge
> KITTY, the waitress
> UNNAMED YOUNG MAN

The Story

This tale of four English bridge players who habitually go on a summer holiday excursion to the same lodge in County Antrim, on the coast of Northern Ireland, examines what happens when something disrupts the "casual comedy" to reveal hidden unpleasant undercurrents in their lives. The story's narrator, Milly, insists on the perfection of the ritualized patterns of the foursome. For many years they have spent the first two weeks of June at Glencorn Lodge, hosted by Mr. and Mrs. Malseed. She notes approvingly that this year things are just the same as always at the lodge, and that all is well. Milly sees little outside the narrow field of her vision. The behavior of the foursome is equally unchanging. They go on drives and walks to the same locations; there is a day when Strafe and Dekko go fishing; they play bridge after dinner; and, most importantly, they maintain a tacit agreement never to talk about each other. Their reserve allows Milly and Major Strafe to carry on their love affair in the evenings after the major's wife Cynthia retires; the Strafes have separate bedrooms and the lovers assume that Cynthia does not notice them.

On the first night, an unwelcome stranger disrupts this comfortable routine. He is an unhappy young man whom the four friends and the Malseeds feel is out of place. When Milly and the men go walking the next day, Cynthia talks with the young man, who then commits suicide, leaving her terribly upset. The others immediately assume that the young man has made a pass at Cynthia, whom Milly mentally criticizes for her lack of assertiveness in "allowing" an improper advance. Indeed, the young man has approached Cynthia but not sexually. Rather, he has revealed to her that he has just murdered an old girlfriend to stop her from making bombs for the Irish Republican Army (IRA). He returned to Glencorn to kill himself because he and his girlfriend had frolicked there as children. As Cynthia recounts the man's story, the two later parted, with the girl growing up to make IRA bombs and the young man eventually killing her to stop the violence. He has committed suicide (by walking into the sea) to expiate his guilt. (The man's suicide resembles a famous Irish death—that of the legendary hero Cuchulain, who drowned himself after discovering he had killed his own son in combat.)

Cynthia strings together a narrative that links Irish history, the intimate history of the two young unfortunates, and British (and by extension, their own) culpability. Embarrassed and disturbed, the other three vacationers try to deny the validity of her tale, putting it down to shock, or to bad form on her part. Meanwhile, the Malseeds, parodies of hotel propriety, anxiously try to hustle Cynthia away from the scene. Before she is shunted away, Cynthia plays her trump card. Summoning Kitty, the dining room waitress, she announces that she knows all about the affair between Strafe and Milly, that Dekko and Strafe have never passed beyond the adolescent level of development, and that from the safety of their domesticity in Surrey or their idylls at Glencorn, they blindly ignore the horrors of murder and armed occupation in Ulster. She then departs, but the damage is done, and the illusory perfection of Glencorn Lodge is destroyed. Even then, however, Milly cannot bring herself to admit the justice of what Cynthia has said. Instead, she wishes that it had been Cynthia who had died in the sea. She dismisses Cynthia's narrative as "awful rigamarole" and sees the two children as having "grown up into murdering riff-raff."

Themes and Meanings

"Beyond the Pale" incorporates many of William Trevor's favorite themes: the loss of innocence (both real and false), the barriers and false fronts that people erect to hide from unpleasant truths, the intersection of the political and historical with the personal, the misery visited on people devoid of love, and the ways in which violence destroys both victim and perpetrator.

Although the children of Cynthia's Irish narrative grow up in a fallen world, it is more particularly the fall from a false and illusory Eden that fills the story's center. The Malseeds have created a garden setting in which the four English people can indulge their fantasy that life is perfect, that violence and unpleasantness exist elsewhere and that they all get along splendidly. The Malseeds themselves, however, are a transplanted English couple who affect a phony Irish manner; their very "tastefulness"—the studied effort to preserve the Georgian style of the building, the perfection of the garden, the resident pet Dalmations, the rooms not numbered but named after flowers—suggests rather questionable taste. However, even in the biblical Garden there was a serpent, and the Malseeds' garden, built as it is on falsehoods, cannot return them to a prelapsarian (before the fall) state. Even the Malseeds' name (*mal* is from the Latin for "bad") reveals that evil has entered this world already.

The world of Glencorn Lodge, like the implied social contract among the four friends, who never criticize each other or speak of anything more serious than old school hijinks, is a barrier, a "pale" erected around what they regard as their civilized existence—just as the English erected a pale around Dublin in 1395. Only Cynthia, with her interest in Irish history, understands that what lies beyond the pale is real life, that what is inside—no matter how desirable—is a tissue of deceit. The notion of actions that lie outside boundaries runs throughout the story, from the discussion of "unsuitable" guests being excluded from the lodge, the violence of the two former lovers, Cynthia's tirade, and, most notably, the violence of a decade of civil strife and military oppression in Northern Ireland and the spread of violence to London.

However, as Trevor shows repeatedly in his fiction, especially in the fiction set in Ireland, the personal cannot exist independent of the historical. Individuals who try to live by a private code of decency and compassion find themselves drawn into the quagmire of violence and revenge. Their own stories are taken over by stories much older and much bigger than themselves. So too in this story. Cynthia cannot fathom, nor can we, what caused the young girl of her story to become the bomb-making woman who drove her childhood sweetheart to kill her, nor what moved him to commit that desperate act. "Evil," as Cynthia says, "breeds evil in mysterious ways." The origins of the violence in Northern Ireland, as Trevor reminds us, go back hundreds of years. The "Pale" dates back nearly six centuries; the Battle of Boyne, which secured British rule over the island, took place in 1690; and the Act of Union binding Ireland to England was passed in 1800. However, the young couple dies scarcely even aware that they are fighting battles not of their own choosing.

The heartlessness of the actions of characters in the story is a by-product of an inability to love. Milly is driven by selfishness rather than passion, as is Strafe, while Dekko has never been able to commit himself to anyone on a mature level. The trajectories of the lives of the two young people demonstrate the ruin that comes about once love falls from their lives. More generally, Trevor implies, the horror and evil that Cynthia delineates stem from a more generalized inability to love one's neighbor.

Style and Technique

Trevor is a modern master of the realistic story whose narrative style is so smooth and understated that it rarely calls attention to itself. However, here, as in his other stories, that understatement is tied to an unreliable first-person narrator, and readers do not notice until late in the story just how much she has been hiding. The other notable feature is Cynthia's framed narrative, which veers away from quiet realism toward the mythic and the incantatory as she invokes Irish history and legend to indict herself and her friends for their lack of sympathy and understanding. Her nightmarish poetic style brings out the hostility in the more earthbound Milly, who attempts to see the embedded narrative as the ravings of a madwoman, and as a usurpation of her rightful place as the one who controls the story. However, Milly is fighting a losing battle: Her realism has masked a fantasy, just as Cynthia's fantastic narrative has unveiled a clearer version of reality. An act of imagination is required to arrive at truth, just as an awareness of violence is required to attain any hope of peace.

Thomas C. Foster

BEZHIN MEADOW

Author: Ivan Turgenev (1818-1883)
Type of plot: Sketch
Time of plot: The mid-nineteenth century
Locale: Province of Tula, Russia
First published: "Bezhin lug," 1852 (English translation, 1855)

Principal characters:
THE NARRATOR, a hunter
FEDYA,
PAVLUSHA,
ILYUSHA,
KOSTYA and
VANYA, peasant boys

The Story

As with all of Ivan Turgenev's stories in *Zapiski okhotnika* (1852; *Russian Life in the Interior*, 1855; better known as *A Sportsman's Sketches*, 1932), the plot of this one is simple and straightforward. After a day of grouse shooting, the hunter who narrates the story starts homeward but becomes lost as night approaches. Growing increasingly uneasy as he wanders beside a wood, then along the boundary of a field, around a knoll, and into a hollow, he stops short at the very edge of an abyss. At the bottom of the precipice he can barely perceive a broad river and a vast plain; he now knows where he is and descends to Bezhin Meadow, where five boys are clustered around two fires while keeping watch over a drove of grazing horses.

The narrator describes the boys, who range in age from fourteen to seven. The one who stands out from the others is twelve-year-old Pavlusha, who appears to be the leader, as the narrator, lying quietly apart from the boys, observes while listening to their conversation. They talk about goblins and water fairies and an apparition on a drowned man's grave. Suddenly, the dogs are roused, rush off, and are immediately followed by Pavlusha, who returns shortly, saying casually that he thought a wolf might have been the source of the dogs's excitement. The conversation around the fire resumes, again concerning tales about the dead, the supernatural, wood-demons, and water sprites. The boys share the few potatoes they have been cooking in a small pot, and Pavlusha goes off for some water. When he returns, they settle down to sleep in the deep silence that precedes dawn.

The hunter awakes just before sunrise, nods goodbye to Pavlusha, the only one of the boys who wakes up, and sets off for home as the sun rises and everything returns to life—the river, the hills, the creatures of the meadow. He hears a bell, then the drove of horses passes him, chased by the boys.

In the last paragraph, the hunter adds regretfully that Pavlusha died some months later in a fall from a horse.

Themes and Meanings

To understand the underlying ideas and significance of this sketch, one should consider the context in which this story appears. The book is a collection of landscape descriptions and character portraits based on chance encounters with peasants of all sorts and conditions. A few members of the gentry also appear occasionally but always in relation to the peasants, as in "The Bailiff," in which the narrator recounts an unpleasant and disquieting visit with an acquaintance who embodies the worst qualities of a cruel, self-indulgent landlord. It is perhaps in that story that Turgenev's opposition to serfdom is most strongly indicated. He never expresses this opposition directly, but the theme is perfectly clear, especially if one views the sketches as parts of a whole. Taken separately, the message in each sketch is presented so subtly that it almost disappears in the wealth of detailed portraiture and description, but even in the seemingly simple and straightforward account of a night spent observing five poor, ignorant, superstitious children, the author's ideas about his subjects are strongly implied. There is, however, a universality about the hunter's experience and the boys he describes that raises the sketch far above a merely sociological discussion.

The author's love of his native land is much more explicit, as be describes the countryside, the weather, and the various settings in which the hunter finds himself, such as a cottage, an inn, an estate, a hut, or a meadow next to a river.

Both themes—an indictment of serfdom and a love of the land—are present in "Bezhin Meadow," though in this particular sketch the latter seems predominant. However, in the tales the boys tell one another, the former is evident, too. For example, twelve-year-old Ilyusha describes the appearance of a goblin in the paper factory where he and nine other boys of his age work; quite matter-of-factly, he tells how the overseer makes the boys spend the night on the floor in the rolling room of the factory so that they will be on hand in good time the next day for an extra amount of work. Ilyusha is more interested in his account of the goblin's appearance than he is in the working conditions of the peasant, but the reader cannot ignore the significance of Ilyusha's barely mentioned details about his life. There is no complaining, no self-pity. If the reader, along with the silent hunter, observes the boys closely, the universal qualities of boyhood become evident in all their variety, humor, courage, intelligence, gullibility, and enjoyment of life, however difficult their circumstances. Their pleasure in one another's company and in the warm, starry night, with the two feisty dogs and the horses close by, is one that any reader can share.

Style and Technique

In this sketch, Turgenev uses a combination of lyrical description (particularly in the opening paragraph, in which a day in July is related in poetic detail) and a nearly total detachment, with such minimal, brief indications of the hunter's feelings that they go almost unnoticed. In the author's treatment of the boys, there is no sentimentality, no romantic idealization. They are real boys, and their conversation is natural: direct, candid, and unadorned. One can see the boys and hear them talk, just as one can feel the beauty of the night and hear its sounds—the snorting of the horses, the crackling of the fire, the eerie cry of a heron, and the splash of a fish in the river. However, one can sense, more from what Turgenev does not say than from what he does, the author's curiosity, compassion, and respect for his subjects.

The language Turgenev uses is genuine, never artificial, never overdone. The boys' stories of ghosts and goblins are given in their own words, with almost no commentary by the hunter. Their tales are mixed with references to the night and its sounds; the result is both realistic and poetic. There is a perfection in the choice of details and the dialogue that makes it possible for the reader to identify with both the hunter and the boys, and the night spent on "Bezhin Meadow" becomes a part of the reader's own memory.

Natalie Harper

BIG BAD LOVE

Author: Larry Brown (1951-   )
Type of plot: Domestic realism
Time of plot: The late twentieth century
Locale: A small town in Mississippi
First published: 1990

>   *Principal characters:*
>   LEROY, the narrator and protagonist, a lonely man
>   MILDRED, his wife

The Story

After the narrator (whose name is not revealed until the end of the story) states that his dog is dead, the rest of his narrative unfolds in its shadow, as its inert body lies in the front yard waiting to be buried. Other animals also play roles in the story. A cat belonging to the narrator's wife, Mildred, catches and slowly kills a young rabbit, while training its kittens to hunt. The narrator considers killing the cats because of their cruelty to the rabbit. He recalls a time when he raised rabbits for food but gave it up because having to kill them became too painful.

Mildred is sexually frustrated "because of her over-large organ." The narrator drives around in his truck and finds an old friend who gives him a beer. Then he goes home to shower and shave. Knowing that Mildred will return shortly, he drives off again to continue his drinking. In a crosstown bar, he drinks and plays pool with several women whom he would like to pick up. After failing in this endeavor, he drives home, following a circuitous route to avoid the police and to get home as late as possible so that he will not have to perform for his sexually insatiable wife.

Unashamed of himself, the narrator does not think of himself as inadequate; his wife simply needs more than he as an average man can provide. At the bar he recalls how he met Mildred: He was in Destin, Florida, recovering from his separation from his first wife. When he saw Mildred, he was sexually attracted immediately, so he divorced his first wife and married her. On their wedding night, he discovered that something was badly amiss. The next morning Mildred explained that she truly was virtuous and that it was not overuse that had made her organ so large. The narrator realized his predicament: Once again in an impossible relationship, as he knew that he would never be able to fulfill Mildred's desires. Throughout his narrative, he thinks about how sad he is, trying to make the impossible happen.

When he finally arrives home, he finds the house is dark and empty. Mildred has left a note saying that she has met another man and is going away with him: "He has the equipment to take care of my problem and we have already 'roadtested' it."

Leroy does not bury the dog. His sorrow and despair grow deeper as he realizes again that he could never satisfy his wife. He resolves to bury his dog in the morning and start looking for a new wife after that.

Themes and Meanings

Larry Brown's central theme in this story is that all creatures—humans, cats, rabbits, and dogs included—want to give and experience love. Giving and experiencing love is such a difficult thing, however, that no one and nothing can do it completely satisfactorily.

The dog dies in the first line of the story. It is therefore unable to provide any sympathy or help with the human characters' attempts at love and affection. The mother cat loves her kittens but shows her love by fetching a baby rabbit, which she teaches her kittens to stalk and kill. At first, the kittens do nearly nothing and the rabbit runs away. This happens several times before the kittens finally begin to attack it fiercely. In an act of compassion, a movement of brave existentialism, the narrator kills the rabbit.

The cats belong to Mildred, and the narrator once raised rabbits. Just as the cats slowly beat down the rabbit, Mildred is beating down Leroy. Just as the rabbit can do nothing about his situation but try to escape, only to be caught repeatedly and faced with an ever-worse situation, Leroy cannot escape his own predicament.

The underlying question that this story poses is not how to love, but whether love is possible at all in a world that is so cruelly unjust that people act without meaning or ability to gain spiritual or even physical gratification. Bad things happen to good people because bad things happen to everyone and everything. It is often not the fault of the individual who is only a very small force in an unpredictable and often unkind natural world.

Leroy married Mildred because of her sex appeal but soon learned that he could never reciprocate the sexual pleasure that he had hoped to gain for himself. Although Mildred does not blame him for being inadequate, she still wants him to improve and give her more. Leroy is the rabbit that runs away only to be caught and hurt slightly more each time.

This fatalistic, even hopefully fatalistic, type of existentialism appears frequently in the writings of Brown. When Mildred is found to be with another man, Leroy is not jealous. He is only saddened that he could not give her the sexual pleasure that is apparently the only means available for achieving a state of love or having a meaningful relationship. He wishes that he could give his own life meaning and that he could help others to do the same, but obviously, he cannot.

Style and Technique

Brown presents his protagonist here as a hopeful fatalist. Leroy's inability to change his condition in life is marked and poignant in that the character often declares hopeful wishes. He considers events that would help him to find a happier existence and these thoughts are very funny—in the same way that jokes are funny because they hurt. The protagonist is symbolized by traits of the rabbits that he mentions. He is running from his bad love relationship, just as the rabbit is running from the cats that will eventually kill it. In the bar, Leroy plays pool with three women but leaves when bigger and more burly men enter the bar. Then he drives his truck on backroads to avoid run-ins with the police, running and hiding again from those who would do him harm. Leroy is not cowardly, though, any more than a rabbit running from cats is cowardly. It is his position in life to be weak and timid. Leroy is living as well as he can, accepting his fate and drinking to relieve the pain inherent to the human condition.

Brown's ear for authentic dialogue is an asset to this story. His use of language is in the tradition of the deep South, genuine and honest, though no intensely obscure dialect or vernacular appears. Instead, the story is short and the style is quick and handy, easily readable and understood, and the turns of phrase and situations presented are mostly clear and funny. This is not written in an exceedingly wordy or old-world literary style; it is written as ordinary people speak and perhaps as they think.

Beaird Glover

THE BIG BEAR OF ARKANSAS

Author: T. B. Thorpe (1815-1878)
Type of plot: Tall tale, regional, frame story
Time of plot: The 1830's
Locale: Mississippi River steamboat *Invincible* and Arkansas woods
First published: 1841

> *Principal characters:*
> GENTLEMAN NARRATOR, who asks a hunter to describe his
>   greatest bear hunt
> JIM DOGGETT, the most skillful bear hunter in Arkansas

The Story

   The narrator, an educated gentleman knowledgeable about the people and manners of the frontier, describes a short journey by Mississippi River steamboat on which, he asserts, the entire gamut of humanity can be observed. Although he intends to avoid socializing with his fellow passengers, he and they become enthralled by the loud, bragging bear hunter who enters the cabin.

   Jim Doggett immediately introduces himself as the Big Bar of Arkansaw, ridicules New Orleans "green-horn hunters," and declares the superiority of life in Arkansas. His first tale involves a forty-pound wild turkey, and when a cynical Hoosier challenges his account of the turkey's size, Doggett explains that the exceptionally rich soil and air in Arkansas make all wild animals fat, so he habitually chases bears before shooting them because he wants their flesh and fat well mixed. After a foreigner questions his account of chasing a bear until his bullet released a ten-foot geyser of steam, Doggett insists his land is so rich that neglected beets and potatoes were mistaken for cedar stumps and Indian mounds and a stray grain of corn shot up so fast that the stalk killed a good-sized sow. He even brags about the ferocity of Arkansas mosquitoes.

   The narrator intervenes, asking Doggett to describe a memorable bear hunt. After Doggett mentions several large bears that he has killed, he promises to tell how "the greatest bar was killed that ever lived." First he establishes the tremendous size of the bear; then he demonstrates its superior cunning. In the first pursuit, Doggett realized this bear could outrun his horse and his phenomenal hound, Bowie-knife. For two years Doggett unsuccessfully pursued the bear, which brazenly killed his hogs but always eluded the hounds. Repeated accidents and bad luck caused the hunter to believe the bear might actually be a devil, hunting him.

   Determined to end this standoff, Doggett began a final great chase, but the bear seemed to taunt him by moving at a leisurely pace. Apparently trapped, the bear twice jumped over the encircling dogs and hunters, eventually plunging into a nearby lake, where Bowie-knife fought him and apparently killed him. Retrieving the bear's body from the lake, however, Doggett discovered that the dead bear was female. Once again the bear had embarrassed him because the hunter had to endure his neighbors' taunts.

Doggett vowed Monday morning he would again hunt the bear, not returning until he was successful. Sunday morning, however, when he went into the woods to relieve himself, the bear appeared, walking toward him. Doggett shot; the bear "gave a yell" and walked away. Attempting to follow, Doggett tripped over his own underwear, but he soon found the dead bear nearby. It took six men to load the bear on a mule, and the bear's skin, which Doggett used as a bedspread, was several feet larger than his bed on each side.

Doggett concludes his tale by suggesting this was an "unhuntable" bear, which merely "died when his time come." The narrator comments upon the "superstitious awe" common among "children of the wood" when they encounter extraordinary situations, but the spell is broken when Doggett invites everyone to "liquor" with him. During the night the narrator leaves the steamboat.

Themes and Meanings

"The Big Bear of Arkansas" strongly resembles other Old Southwest humor tales published in *Spirit of the Times* and similar gentlemen's magazines of the 1840's. Ostensibly its theme is a democratic glorification of the frontiersman's individualism, as he triumphs over genteel society. Entering a cabin filled with travelers more sophisticated than he, Doggett immediately captures everyone's attention; even the aloof narrator becomes interested in his accounts of his hunting prowess. Doggett's attractive appearance and good humor overcome the passengers' initial anger at his contemptuous remarks about "green-horn" city dwellers who cannot raise a crop of turnips or hit a barn door with a rifle shot. At first Doggett appears to be a loud, somewhat crude braggart, and several passengers express doubts about his tales, but he knows his listeners' expectations, and in each case he has an answer that both silences the questioner and reinforces his image as frontiersman and hunter.

From the beginning, the narrator seems disdainful of his fellow passengers; he hides behind his newspaper to avoid conversing with them. Doggett's arrival creates a type of social interaction, however, making the narrator also part of the storyteller's audience. Nevertheless, the narrator remains contemptuous of fellow passengers such as the cynical Hoosier, the "live Sucker" from Illinois, and the "timid little man"; only the "gentlemanly foreigner," presumably an Englishman, seems to gain his respect. Unlike those passengers who challenge Doggett, the narrator amuses himself by encouraging the hunter to spin an even more fantastic yarn. The narrator's condescension toward Doggett, implicit in the way he requests a story, becomes clear when he refers to Doggett as simple and speaks of frontiersmen as "children of the wood" who react with "superstitious awe." On the other hand, Doggett's comments, when he praises the narrator's willingness to learn and compares him with a litter of promising pups, raises the possibility that he may be subtly mocking the narrator.

Although the narrator somewhat sentimentally calls Doggett a child of the wood, the hunter's attitude emphasizes conquest and exploitation. For example, he seems to treat the timber and rich soil as resources to be consumed for his convenience. As his stories reveal, Doggett considers himself master of his land at "the Forks of Cypress," but he prefers hunting to farming. Like many frontiersmen, he raises hogs because he can allow them to forage in the woods and they require little or no care. Likewise, his story of the neglected beets and potatoes suggests that cultivating the land is not especially important in his lifestyle. Although the narrator may consider him a creature of nature much like the bears and wild turkeys Doggett hunts, Doggett clearly does not see any such kinship; he seems to derive satisfaction from the number and size of bears he can chase and kill, and even though the "creation bar" proves a worthy adversary, he is still merely a part of the nature Doggett wants to defeat.

Style and Technique
    The frame-story structure of "The Big Bear of Arkansas" is typical of the Old Southwest humor tradition. An educated gentleman narrator who speaks standard English introduces an amusing rustic, in this case a hunter, who recounts fantastic adventures in frontier vernacular. Doggett seems somewhat less crude than the stereotypical frontiersman, however, and his language also differs somewhat from that customarily attributed to such hunters. To create the impression of frontier dialect, Thorpe occasionally uses conventional misspellings such as "bar," "perlite," "sile," and "diggens," but most of Doggett's story is told in standard English. When he reinforces the accuracy of his statements by saying "may I be chewed to death by young alligators" or describes himself as "cross as a bar with two cubs and a sore tail," though, Doggett is using language appropriate to an Arkansas bear hunter.
    Generally Southwest humor was written for an audience of educated Eastern men who kept their humor magazines in their offices, far away from their wives and daughters. The earthy language and crude physical humor in most of these stories were considered unsuitable reading for women. Although Thorpe uses these characteristics rather sparingly, even Doggett's oblique reference to relieving himself, for example, would have been considered shocking and offensive, and his loud boasting would have been even more unacceptable than his putting his feet up on the stove.
    Frontier humor traditionally involves a central character engaged in an epic struggle with a foe associated with natural forces. Like Doggett, this hero boasts of his courage, skill, and cunning in defeating his larger-than-life adversary. Doggett's adventures also reflect Thorpe's formal education and frontier experiences, specifically the influence of both traditional epic heroes and Native American tales. Doggett outruns and outsmarts all bears until he encounters the "creation bar," which appears to be a character out of frontier folklore. After repeatedly defeating and embarrassing the hunter, though, this bear appears simply to give up, allowing himself to be killed. Doggett suggests that the bear may have realized the inevitability of his death at the hands of this superior hunter, but he also raises the possibility that the bear may have been fated to die at that particular time. Either way, Doggett seems awestruck and possibly even humbled by his final victory.

Charmaine Allmon Mosby

BIG BERTHA STORIES

Author: Bobbie Ann Mason (1940-   )
Type of plot: Domestic realism, war
Time of plot: The 1980's
Locale: A small town in Kentucky
First published: 1985

> *Principal characters:*
> DONALD, a Vietnam War veteran and strip-mine worker
> JEANNETTE, his wife and part-time waitress
> RODNEY, their preschool son
> PHAN, a young woman who was apparently Donald's lover in
>   Vietnam
> DR. ROBINSON, Jeanette's psychologist
> MISS BAILEY, a social worker who checks on Rodney and
>   Jeannette
> JEANNETTE'S PARENTS, the owners of a luncheonette

The Story

Set several years after Donald's return from Vietnam, "Big Bertha Stories" drama-tizes his inability to escape from his war experiences. The third-person narrative states directly the confused thoughts and feelings of Jeannette, but it reveals Donald's deeply troubled mind only indirectly. Thus, Bobbie Ann Mason shows Donald's iso-lation—his intense but unsuccessful attempts to communicate the horrors of com-bat—as well as the pain his problem inflicts on others.

Immediately after his tour in Vietnam, Donald seemed to adjust easily to civilian life. He had a good job at a lumberyard, enjoyed driving his classic Chevy convertible, and married Jeannette after a brief courtship. They lived happily for several years after the birth of Rodney. About two years before the time of this story, however, Donald deliberately collapsed a stack of lumber to get himself fired, sold his beloved automo-bile, and began to behave unpredictably. Now Donald works sporadically operating a steam shovel in the strip mines in Muhlenberg County, and he sees Jeannette and Rodney only during brief, unannounced visits home.

On these visits home, Donald tells Rodney bizarre stories featuring Big Bertha, a tall-tale heroine (based on a huge strip-mining machine) who is tall enough to see as far as Tennessee and whose powerful belches cause tornadoes. These fantastic stories both entrance and terrify Rodney, and they sometimes provoke nightmares. Just as the Big Bertha stories display Donald's earnest but ineffective attempts to communicate with his son, Donald's conversations with Jeannette repeatedly show his futile efforts to share with her his experiences in Vietnam. Using detailed descriptions, hand-drawn diagrams, and even a food-processor blade to simulate a Huey Cobra helicopter, he tries desperately to explain what happened but always concludes by proclaiming that she will never understand. In one long monologue, Donald describes Phan, a young Vietnamese woman who was apparently his lover before her village was destroyed. Powerless to tell Jeannette what the war was like and what he is feeling even now, Donald is also sexually impotent.

Separated from Donald both emotionally and physically, Jeannette seeks help from several sources. She consults a psychologist, but his inane questions anger more than comfort or clarify. When Jeannette visits her parents' luncheonette, her mother offers food along with shallow advice (that Jeannette should pray more and Donald should seek the Lord). Later, Miss Bailey, a visiting social worker, inquires about Rodney's bad dreams and examines his unusual drawings of Big Bertha's breasts but cannot even call him by his name.

After Donald's attempted explanations become more and more tearful and his nights more sleepless, he decides to enter the veterans hospital for treatment. This trip away from home he likens to a sea cruise with Big Bertha—a long, restful voyage that will presumably heal him. Meanwhile, Jeanette returns to work as a waitress and tries to make life normal for Rodney with trips to the mall and small gifts. One such gift is a miniature trampoline on which both of them play. The story concludes with a horrible dream provoked by the trampoline. After bouncing on it one day, Jeannette dreams that she is jumping up and down on a pile of dead bodies.

Themes and Meanings

Mason wrote this story while she was working on her best-known novel, *In Country* (1985), and these two fictional accounts of soldiers returning from war display obvious similarities in characters and themes. Like the classic story of Ulysses, these works portray warriors attempting to find their way home after battle, but Mason's modern characters are not honored as heroes, and the perils they must overcome are more psychological than physical.

As the title of this work indicates, Mason provides stories within her main story. Donald's accounts of Big Bertha's exploits are his efforts to make sense of his own chaotic experiences. Because Donald feels powerless, he creates a power of mythic proportions—a female equivalent of Paul Bunyan. In various embodiments, Big Bertha trains snakes to race, goes surfing, and leads a rock-and-roll band. Instead of creating order, however, Donald's stories are confusing and inconclusive. They usually begin with carefree delights but soon shift inexplicably to scenes of horror. For example, Big Bertha and other surfers are frolicking with dolphins on a California beach, but a neutron bomb suddenly destroys everyone except Bertha. In another story, the location of a joyous Big Bertha concert turns out to be a toxic-waste dump, and its contamination spreads throughout the country.

Such narratives reveal much about the workings of Donald's mind. He is searching for a super-heroic savior, but he finds nothing more than an implausible creation of his own desperate imagination. In their frenetic shifts from idyllic bliss to catastrophe, the stories about Big Bertha are veiled accounts of Donald's actual experience in Vietnam. With Phan during interludes between battle, he found that place almost edenic. However, the war completely destroyed both the country and Donald's innocence, leaving him to wander amid horrible memories. Just as he cannot bring his war experience to closure, he can never conclude his Big Bertha stories. These individual tales simply jerk to an abrupt and enigmatic halt, without any sense of orderly completion. Not knowing the fate of Phan, Donald cannot figure out the end of his own story. He feels compelled to keep talking to Jeannette about Vietnam, but any real conclusion eludes him.

Style and Technique

Along with the stories about Big Bertha, Mason uses details of work and setting to describe Donald's alienation and the resulting problems for his family. Although Donald initially seems able to cope with the aftermath of war, he works near his home at a job related to construction, moving and stacking lumber in neat piles. Soon, however, a destructive act costs him this job, and he also destroys a car by ramming it into a Civil War statue near the courthouse. Such an "accident" may, in fact, be a wordless but highly deliberate protest against the general horrors of war and the specific practice of publicly honoring the veterans of an earlier war while largely ignoring those of the Vietnam conflict.

Soon Donald's job itself becomes destructive. Operating a huge mining machine, he strips away vegetation and topsoil and leaves behind barren land. Donald himself compares this strip-mining operation to the destruction of Vietnam, and he notes that in moving the Kentucky earth, he keeps hunting for tunnels like those in which the Viet Cong hid. Thus, in this destructive job that takes him away from home, Donald seems to be reliving his experiences far away in Vietnam. On his brief visits home (described as periods of rest and recreation), he tries desperately to be a normal husband and father. Again and again, however, he returns to Muhlenberg County and reenacts the grim drama that has no concluding act. Occasionally Donald praises work of the mining companies to reclaim and reforest land, but such reclamation of his own psyche is still pending.

If Donald's efforts to return home from war recall those of Ulysses, Jeannette displays some of the fidelity of Penelope. She listens patiently to Donald's confused accounts of battle and pursues her job as literal homemaker. Capable and self-reliant (like most of Mason's female characters), she tries to recreate home by cooking meals that they can all share as a family, even when her main ingredients are bought with food stamps. After Donald leaves for the hospital, Jeannette's efforts are redirected. As her own home breaks further apart, she works as a server at the ironically named Fred's Family Restaurant. As she waits on families, she also waits for Donald to return so her own reunited family can eat there.

Albert E. Wilhelm

BIG BLONDE

Author: Dorothy Parker (1893-1967)
Type of plot: Satire
Time of plot: The 1920's, during the Prohibition era
Locale: New York City
First published: 1929

Principal characters:
MRS. (HAZEL) MORSE, the "Big Blonde," the central character
HERBIE MORSE, her first husband
MRS. MARTIN, her friend
THE BOYS, the men at Jimmy's bar

The Story

In the traditional sense, the story has no plot with a tight climax and resolution. It is primarily a history, an extended portrait of "Big Blonde." Hazel Morse, a big, fun-loving, peroxide blond, is a caricature. Amiable, empty-headed, given to tears at the slightest provocation, she is not so much a realistic character as she is a collection of traits and attitudes that the author holds up for satiric scrutiny.

She and her first husband, Herbie, begin married life isolated from any connections, utterly content with each other. Soon, Herbie—like Hazel, a collection of mannerisms, viewed by Dorothy Parker as a specimen—wearies of Hazel's moods, her "misty melancholy." When he can take no more, he slams the door, rushes out, and gets drunk. Once tender lovers, Hazel and Herbie (their names suggest Parker's attitude toward them) become enemies. Whenever Herbie stays out late, Hazel worries; in time, however, her worry turns to anger, and she is ready for an argument when he returns. Soon, loud, violent quarrels are a regular feature of their marriage.

Hazel begins to drink, and soon all of her days run together. Sure that she is losing Herbie, she begins to frequent Jimmy's bar, the haunt of "The Boys." Mrs. Morse, as she is known at Jimmy's, makes fast friends with a forty-year-old blond, Mrs. Martin; the two women drink together and enjoy the attentions of The Boys. One of them, Ed, from Utica and married for twenty years, plays poker with Mrs. Morse. His kisses lead the way to romance, and she becomes his "doll."

One day, Herbie packs to leave for a job in Detroit; he offers his wife, foggy with drink, the furniture and some stock. After he leaves, Mrs. Morse (so Parker refers to her for the remainder of the story) plays her favorite recording, "Ain't We Got Fun."

Ed gives her presents and suggests that she move. She agrees because her relations with Mrs. Martin and Joe, Mrs. Martin's boyfriend, are strained. Ed gives her a flat and a black maid, Nettie. Alcohol continues to keep Mrs. Morse fat; her moods keep her gloomy and melancholy.

At Jimmy's, Mrs. Morse finds the women monotonously the same: big, heavy, ruddy, healthy. Most are married, some divorced, some have a child. However, they are cordial and friendly. The Boys enjoy the women, above all Mrs. Morse. She needs money, so she passively responds to Ed, who continues to buy things for her. Finally, however, he is bored by her fits of gloom. He needs fun; the other women at Jimmy's are not so moody.

After three years with Mrs. Morse, Ed moves to Florida. He cries on leaving Mrs. Morse and gives her a check; she does not miss him at all, and each year when he returns to New York and rushes to see her, she remains passive.

A friend of Ed, Charley, has always liked Mrs. Morse, and now with Ed gone, he fills her life. She finds him "not so bad," but after a year, she lets Sidney, "a clever little Jew," take his place. Sidney likes her softness and size; with him, she feels lively and happy. Soon, however, he leaves her to marry a rich woman. Billy and Fred are next, but soon Mrs. Morse cannot recall how they came and went.

News comes that Herbie has a new woman, but Mrs. Morse is not moved at all. Several years have passed since she saw him; now, all the days blur together. One night, tired and blue, she sees horses stumbling and slipping, and she begins to think of death. With a drowsy cheer, she thinks "It's nice to be dead," and later she reads stories about suicides. In her drinking bouts, she has sudden intuitions of the nuisance of existing. She dreams all day of no more tight shoes, no more forced laughs, no more trying to be a "good sport." Whenever the idea of suicide becomes tangible and immediate, however, she flinches.

A new man, short and fat, comes on the scene; when he whispers "You're the best sport in the world," Mrs. Morse tries very hard to feel something. One night at Jimmy's with Art, she chats with a woman about insomnia and learns of a remedy: five grains of veronal. It can be purchased in New Jersey without a prescription. The next day, Mrs. Morse takes the train to Newark and easily buys twenty tablets of veronal. That night at home, she sends Nettie for Scotch; then, vaguely blurred, she goes to Jimmy's, where she meets Art, who has told her that he will be away for a week. Thus, the glow of the Scotch turns to gloom; this merely irritates Art, who leaves, impatient, with "Try to cheer up by Thursday when I'll be back." She returns to her room and swallows slowly the twenty tablets of veronal. Waiting for death to come, she says, "I'm nearly dead'" and chuckles at the words.

The next morning, Nettie the maid sees Mrs. Morse sprawled on the bed, making strange sounds. Nettie runs out and gets the elevator boy to run with her for a doctor. When the doctor sees the vials, he pumps out the drug, but Mrs. Morse remains unconscious for two days. When she wakes, she swears at Nettie, then apologizes. A pageant of sensations passes in her memory—Jimmy's bar, horses stumbling, men saying, "Be a good sport." Nettie gives Mrs. Morse a postcard from Art, urging her to cheer up for Thursday. Then Nettie and Mrs. Morse share a drink, with Nettie saying, "Cheer up now," and Mrs. Morse replying, "Yeah, Sure." Thus the portrait of "Big Blonde" ends.

Themes and Meanings

One of the central themes in "Big Blonde" is the futility of alcohol to fill an empty mind and heart. When Mrs. Morse cannot cope with disappointments, she has no remedy but drink and finds that ultimately it is no panacea. She also illustrates the old cliche about "laughing on the outside." While clinging desperately to her reputation as "a good sport" and struggling to laugh the easy laugh that attracts men, Mrs. Morse succumbs often to copious crying and soon loses her appeal. Closely related to her alcoholism and her oscillations between fun and melancholy is the theme of marriage. To endure, marriage requires a modicum of love and mature understanding. Mrs. Morse lacks these assets; her marriages are superficial or short-lived. This lack of love serves to intensify the emptiness of her relations with people and her failure to find true satisfaction in life.

Style and Technique

Dorothy Parker's style is direct, lively, and fast-paced. The third-person narration holds the characters at a distance: Mrs. Morse is an admonitory example, and while readers of the story may pity her, they are not invited to identify with her.

Dialogue is natural, quick, and immediate, though used sparingly. Much of the story is given to exposition, in the historical past, again enforcing a certain detachment. Parker offers few if any closeups of love scenes or hate scenes, or highly dramatic moments. Although the circumstances of the protagonist change, she does not undergo significant development; that is not the author's intention. Rather, Parker anatomizes a character type.

Ann Edward

BIG BOY LEAVES HOME

Author: Richard Wright (1908-1960)
Type of plot: Social realism
Time of plot: The early twentieth century
Locale: The American South
First published: 1936

> *Principal characters:*
> BIG BOY, an adolescent who becomes a man
> BOBO, his friend, who is tarred, feathered, and burned by a white
>   mob
> LESTER and
> BUCK, two black boys who are shot
> BERTHA HARVEY, a white woman who happens on the four boys
>   when they are naked
> JIM HARVEY, her husband
> LIZA MORRISON, Big Boy's mother
> SAUL MORRISON, his father
> LUCY MORRISON, his sister
> WILL SANDERS, a truck driver

The Story

    The story is divided into five distinct sections. The first opens on a hot day, as four adolescent African American boys laugh and play in the woods, singing and joking about sexually related matters and tussling and rolling around in the grass like young pups. In the second section, they arrive at a swimming hole, where they are determined to swim despite its no-trespassing sign, which clearly tells them that "Ol man Harvey don erllow no niggers t swim in this hole." After playfully frolicking in the water, the boys dry themselves in the sun—black and naked. Their innocence is accentuated by the black winged butterfly hovering near the water, the droning of a bee, and the twittering of sparrows. As the sun dries their skins and warms their blood, they laugh nervously about the risk they are taking, when a white woman suddenly appears.

    This woman's sudden intrusion destroys the boys' innocent frolic, forcing them to scramble about, hiding their nakedness and trying to get at their clothes behind where the woman is standing. The woman screams, calling for her husband. As Big Boy dashes for the clothes, he is as frightened as the woman is and stops three feet from her. Just then, her husband, Jim, arrives; he is wearing an army officer's uniform and is carrying a rifle. He immediately shoots Lester and Buck; the boys appear to be headed for his wife, but they are actually running toward Bobo, who is holding their clothes. When Jim points his rifle at Bobo, Big Boy lunges and grabs its barrel. As Big Boy fights with Jim, he accidently shoots him. When the man falls, Big Boy and Bobo turn to look at the woman, who screams and falls at the foot of the tree. Big Boy drags the crying Bobo through the woods.

In the third section, the boys head for home, leaving childhood behind them forever. Knowing that they will be lynched, Bobo can think of nothing else. Big Boy clings to the thought that he must get home to his parents. As he stammers out his story, his father, Saul, castigates him for not going to school and makes sure that the boys did not touch the white woman. Other black men arrive as Big Boy's mother presses his head to her bosom and comforts him. Elder Peters confirms everyone's fears by urging that they get Big Boy away immediately because there will be a lynching. Everyone understands that Big Boy is defenseless. When Brother Sanders says that his son Will is driving a truck to Chicago the next morning, Big Boy proposes to hide overnight in a brickyard kiln. His mother sends him away with hot cornpone, and he asks her to tell Bobo to join him where he is hiding.

In the fourth section, Big Boy runs toward the sunset clutching his hot cornpone. He goes over the crest of a hill and selects the largest of the kilns that he and his friends had dug the week before. Before he climbs into the kiln, he kills a big snake and stomps its head into the dirt. While imagining more snakes inside, he enters the enclosure and waits for Bobo, thinking over the events that have occurred. He regrets each and wishes that he had brought his father's gun—a thought that leads him to fantasize about killing several white men before he is lynched. He imagines newspaper headlines such as "Nigger Kills Dozen of Mob Befoo Lynched!" He smiles as he imagines stomping a white man as he has the snake. He knows, however, that any opportunity to display real courage and rebellion is only a fantasy.

When Big Boy hears a mob of white men and women looking for him, he overhears someone saying that they have already burned down his parents' home. He watches in helpless horror as barking dogs chase Bobo, whom the mob tars, feathers, and burns, after taking his finger and his ear as souvenirs. Someone in the mob says, "Ef they git erway notta woman in this town would be safe." Afterward the mob disperses, leaving Big Boy alone in his hole. As the mob passes his hole, a dog smells him and barks into the hole. Fearing that the dog will reveal his presence, Big Boy kills it and falls asleep holding its body in his arms.

The fifth section opens at daybreak, with Big Boy on his knees in a puddle of rainwater, staring at the dog's stiff body. He feels that he is waking from a dream, when he hears a truck approach. The driver, Will Sanders, opens a trapdoor behind his seat and pushes Big Boy into the truck, letting the trapdoor fall. As Big Boy rides off, he hears the lumber mill's six o'clock whistle. Later Will stops and gets him a drink of water in his hat. The story ends as the truck speeds Big Boy northward, jolting him, as he turns on his side to sleep. Initiated into violence, he is now a man.

Themes and Meanings

"Big Boy Leaves Home" is the first story in Richard Wright's 1938 volume *Uncle Tom's Children*. In his autobiography he says that this story poses a question: "What quality of will must a Negro possess to live and die in a country that denied his human-ity?" His story's sympathetic, omniscient narrator focuses on the imagined threat of black manhood to white people, the irrational violence with which white people con-front their fears, and the trap into which a black man matures. From the beginning of the story, the boys know that they will be lynched if they are discovered on the white man's property: Buck says that the no-trespassing sign means that there "ain no dogs n niggers erllowed." The dog parallel continues as Big Boy pulls off his clothes and calls out, "Las one ins a ol dead dog!" The white man kills Big Boy's friends just as Big Boy later kills the barking dog.

The boys' joking about the impotence of old man Harvey, the landowner, indicates that they also instinctively know that their threat to the white man is related to white perceptions of black virility. The white woman who inadvertently happens on them does not stop to think that she is standing between them and their clothes; she is so much a product of her own social conditioning that she cannot control her own igno-rant and unfounded fear. Even though her husband, Jim Harvey, stands behind the au-thority of his army officer uniform and holds a rifle in his hand, he is so helpless when Big Boy and Bobo confront him that he loses every pretense of rationality and reverts to fear and violence.

The only characters who take the time to think things through are Big Boy, his lov-ing, prayerful family, and their supportive brethren. However, they all know that his situation is hopeless and that his only alternatives are flight, emasculation, or death.

Style and Technique

When Wright lived in Chicago, he observed the callous brutality of a huge white mob that cut the heart out of a lynched man and dismembered his body. The fact that his story falls into five distinct sections that correspond to the five-part structure of a classical tragedy is a significant part of the tragedy of the circumstances.

The narrator skillfully associates images from nature with the boys' innocence, the lonesome train whistle that reoccurs with the unknown north, the battered snake with the fantasies of retaliation, the "bluesy" songs and spirituals with the slavery that still exists, and the truck with the freedom train of the underground. Wright's consummate artistry is reminiscent of the fourteen poems that he published in the two years just be-fore he wrote this initiation story; its success encouraged him to continue to write fic-tion.

Constance M. Fulmer

THE BIG-BREASTED PILGRIM

Author: Ann Beattie (1947-   )
Type of plot: Domestic realism
Time of plot: The 1990's
Locale: Florida Keys
First published: 2000

> *Principal characters:*
> RICHARD HOWARD MANSON, the narrator, a chef's assistant
> LOWELL, his boss, an internationally famous chef
> KATHRYN, Lowell's sister, who lives with him
> NANCY CUMMINS, an acquaintance of Kathryn, who jilts Richard
> LES, Nancy's cowboy boyfriend
> GEORGE STEPHANOPOULOS, assistant to President Bill Clinton
> BILL CLINTON, president of the United States
> HILLARY CLINTON, the First Lady

The Story

"The Big-Breasted Pilgrim," told in first person through the eyes of its protagonist Richard Howard Manson, focuses on a few, catastrophic days in his life. Richard is an assistant to Lowell, an internationally famous chef. Friends for more than twenty years, they live in a secluded house near Florida's Key West. At the moment, they have a visitor, Kathryn, Lowell's sister. Although Lowell has a girlfriend named Daphne, neither he nor his sister appears to be involved in long-term relationships or to have serious attachments. Nancy Cummins, an acquaintance of Kathryn, drops in to visit on her way to Miami. During the visit, Richard takes a phone call for Lowell from George Stephanopoulos, assistant to President Bill Clinton, requesting a dinner invitation so that the president and his wife can sample Lowell's renowned cooking. However, despite all the initial excitement in the house, the event is cancelled because it conflicts with an event in the schedule of Hillary Clinton, the president's wife.

As the story develops, its focus shifts to Richard and Nancy, who appears to develop an interest in Richard. She invites him to a high-society party at which people pass sarcastic judgments on various celebrities such as the singer Madonna, the designer Gianni Versace, and members of the presidential family. When Nancy announces that the president intends to eat a dinner prepared by Lowell, guests make jokes about the president's eating habits, particularly his preference for hamburgers over fine cuisine. During the course of the evening, Nancy tells Richard that she has come to Florida to attend a bris—the Jewish ritual of circumcision—because a psychic told her that she would find her true love. She suggests that Richard may be that man.

When Richard arrives home late that evening, Lowell and Kathryn tease him about his outing and the fact that he is becoming romantically involved with Nancy. Within moments of Richard's arrival, George Stephanopoulos calls to cancel the dinner engagement. Richard uses the opportunity to strike up a conversation with the caller. They discover that they have something in common; having lived in many places, they both share a feeling of disorientation. They end the conversation on a note of a developing friendship.

Later that evening, Richard decides to go to a bar before going to meet Nancy and her friends. He finds the biker crowd coarse and offensive and makes a hasty departure for his rendezvous with Nancy.

Nancy's friends eye Richard suspiciously, as if they see him as a threat to Nancy's happiness. Nancy recommends that they go to a party at a condo. Nancy's friend, Jerri, questions Richard about his association with Lowell. Richard tells her that years earlier when he was a chauffeur driving for a car service, Lowell was one of his customers. Because they got along well, Lowell invited Richard to come to work for him. Before going to the condo, they stop off at Jerri's so that she can check the alarm system and pick up a bottle of champagne. Richard notices that the place is filled with celebrity cardboard cutouts, everyone from Marilyn Monroe to Bill Clinton to Pilgrims, a joking form with a big-breasted woman and a man with his fly open.

While the group is playing with the cutouts and taking pictures, Jerri makes some sarcastic remarks about Nancy and the fact that she likes rich and famous men or people who hang around them. Another friend remarks that Les, the cowboy Nancy hung around with, was hardly rich or famous and had followed her all the way from Montana to New York. Nancy and her friends get into a heated discussion about this relationship. Through the quarrel, Richard learns that Nancy is still in love with Les. Nancy makes clear that the only reason she is not with Les is that she let him go. Nancy challenges Richard to protest the indignity of the revelation, but he does not. She walks out on him. Richard drives home to discover that Lowell is dead. He fell from a tree and broke his neck while trying to rescue a cat that Nancy had left with him.

Themes and Meanings

"The Big-Breasted Pilgrim" is a story told through the eyes of its main character, Richard Howard Manson. The allusions to the eighteenth century literary biographer James Boswell and to the novel by Kazuo Ishiguro, *The Remains of the Day* (1989), suggest a connection among Richard, Boswell, and the protagonist of *The Remains of the Day*, a butler named Stevens. Boswell's claim to fame is that he spent a good part of his adult life recording the words of the great eighteenth century English writer Samuel Johnson and wrote what became a classic literary biography, *The Life of Samuel Johnson, LL.D.* (1791). Boswell devoted his life to immortalizing his hero. Akin to Boswell, Stevens lives to serve his employers. In *The Remains of the Day*, Stevens recognizes that he has lost his opportunity to live. Life has passed him by in his devotion to serve others.

Both literary allusions have profound implications for "The Big-Breasted Pilgrim." Richard's relationship with Lowell is similar to the relationship of Boswell to Johnson and Stevens to his employers. Like them, Richard derives meaning and purpose in direct proportion to his service. In exchange for this sense of meaning and purpose, he allows life to pass him by. When Lowell dies at the end, Richard recognizes that he has lost the gamble in living his life through service to another. His reward is emotional destitution. If "The Big-Breasted Pilgrim" has a message, it might well be that people should live for themselves.

As with all first-person narratives, everything that Richard says is a reflection of his personality, limitations, needs, hopes, and aspirations. He states that his life had been a failure until he met Lowell. Since then, sometime in the late 1970's, Richard has lived with a sense of duty and obligation. He is grateful to Lowell for the quality of life he has experienced living with him. He has profited from Lowell's success, though at the sacrifice of his own unrealized aspirations.

Style and Technique

The technique of the story is first-person narrative; everything that Richard says is "unreliable," in that it reflects his personality, his limitations, needs, hopes, and aspirations. He sees what he cannot help seeing. Such a technique makes the narrator vulnerable and challenges the reader. The narrator is vulnerable because he can be blindsided by the limitations of his thinking and perception. Things happen to him that he cannot predict or protect himself against. The challenge for the reader is to evaluate and interpret events independently of what the narrator is saying in order to gain a better understanding of the action. For example, when Richard reports that Kathryn refers to him as Boswell or suggests he acquaint himself with *The Remains of the Day*, the reader realizes that Kathryn is making a comment on Richard and his life. Richard is aware of the meaning of the comment, but brushes it off, attributing it to her dislike of him. Only later, in the outcome of the book, does he realize that his life has turned out much like that of Stevens when he is left with nothing when Lowell dies. The reader is not so naïve.

The structure of the story leads to this revelation, or epiphany, a common device in short fiction. In the beginning, Richard denies that he lives to serve. Instead, he sees his current life as an escape from the past and an escape from a relationship with a woman that might end in disaster for him. Of course, that is precisely the course of the story. Nancy tempts him; he falls for her seductive ways and then finds out that she loves another man. In *The Remains of the Day*, Stevens, too, finds out that he has missed the chance to marry the one woman about whom he cared.

Besides allusion, Ann Beattie uses irony. One of the story's major ironies is Nancy's expressed purpose in coming to Florida: to attend a bris. She tells her friends that a psychic told her that by doing so, she would meet her "true love." However, she recognizes that she already has a true love, her former boyfriend Les and that she needs to go back to him. Here the Jewish ritual of circumcision is used ironically. In "Big-Breasted Pilgrim," bris can be understood to refer to circling around (the return to Les) and as a cutting off—the abandonment of Richard.

Richard Damashek

BIG FISH, LITTLE FISH

Author: Italo Calvino (1923-1985)
Type of plot: Fable
Time of plot: The 1940's
Locale: Italian Riviera
First published: "Pesci grossi, pesci piccoli," 1950 (English translation, 1984)

>   *Principal characters:*
>   ZEFFERINO, a boy who is a skillful fisherman
>   HIS FATHER, a man with a passion for limpets
>   SIGNORINA DE MAGISTRIS, a woman saddened by love

The Story

The boy Zefferino is completely at home in the ocean, moving effortlessly through it and relishing the beautiful denizens that he hunts and destroys. Speargun in hand, he trails a bream underwater and discovers an enclosed pond. Here he finds not only beautiful fish but also Signorina de Magistris, a fat woman wearing a bathing suit, who sits weeping on a rock. Zefferino's reactions are a mixture of sympathy and confusion: The sight of a woman crying saddens him, but he is unable to understand how the beautiful location, crammed with such a variety of beautiful fish, can fail to please her. Although she tells Zefferino that she weeps because she is unlucky in love, she knows Zefferino is too young to understand.

Zefferino first attempts to soothe his melancholy companion by inviting the woman to sample the pleasure of swimming underwater with his mask; when she proves incapable of enjoying this because of her tears, Zefferino switches tactics, hoping that the beautiful fish he catches will amuse her. He first catches a large silver and black bass and places it in a small, natural basin; but Signorina de Magistris is not pleased. Unhappy herself, she sees only the numerous tiny holes in its silver body made by sea lice.

With each new fish Zefferino hauls out of the sea, Signorina de Magistris detects the same indications of suffering and misery. What the inexperienced boy accepts as an inlet of unimaginable wonders, the heartbroken woman perceives as a "marine lazaretto, an arena of desperate duels."

After having caught or killed a gilthead, a bogue, and several other fish, Zefferino captures a big octopus. Reluctant to abandon his treasure in the small basin they find for it, Zefferino nevertheless swims off in the hope of catching the whole octopus family, while Signorina de Magistris stays and quietly observes the living octopus. While she absentmindedly caresses its coils, the octopus winds around her arm, seizing her, and she begins to scream.

Having ranged too far from Signorina de Magistris to come to her aid, Zefferino can only turn and observe that the octopus seems to be stretching out another tentacle to strangle her. Zefferino's father, who has wandered over in search of his son, easily dispatches the octopus with his knife as Signorina de Magistris faints. Zefferino's father has already cut the octopus into pieces when the woman awakens. Although Zefferino studies her features to determine whether she will begin to cry again, she appears able to suppress the overflow of her grief as Zefferino's father carefully explains to her the secret of a good octopus fry.

Themes and Meanings

"Big Fish, Little Fish" is a fable about illusion and reality, conveyed in contrasting perceptions. Zefferino perceives the world as an exciting novelty. "This was a place rich in fish, like an enclosed pond; and wherever Zefferino looked he saw a flicker of sharp fins, the glint of scales; his joy and wonder were so great, he forgot to shoot even once." A child, his perceptions are spirited and naïve.

By contrast, Signorina de Magistris's perceptions are darkened by her grief. When Zefferino first asks her if she appreciates how full of fish the pond is, she responds that she cannot see anything because she cannot stop crying. When Zefferino yearns to have her share his contentment with the size and beauty of the fish around them, Signorina de Magistris can only notice the evidence of suffering on their bodies. Afflicted with an agonized sense of herself as victim, she sympathetically regards the alcove as a refuge for animals sentenced to agony, while Zefferino, secure in his innocence, knows only the excitement of the hunt and the dazzle of the moment.

Innocence and experience offer conflicting points of view, but neither adequately comprehends reality: Both are solipsistic and illusory, based on expectations, falsified by projections of the self. Should the flicker of sharp fins arouse a throb of fear in Zefferino that perhaps a shark is near? It does not. Signorina de Magistris's perceptions are more knowing, informed by experience, but she indulges herself in a romantic fantasy about the sensitivity of fish, and thus strays into danger. Relieved because the octopus appears to be unblemished, she entertains thoughts of health and life, and thus carelessly becomes its intended prey. Ironically, her sense of herself as a victim seems to facilitate her becoming a victim. In the water, the fat woman resembles the big fish and Zefferino the little fish, but their points of view contradict their physical size. Zefferino views the world through the eyes of a hunter—a big fish—while Signorina de Magistris looks through the eyes of a victim—a little fish.

While Zefferino and Signorina de Magistris are one pair of opposites, together they present an additional contrast to Zefferino's father. The father, who is unnamed, never wore a proper bathing suit, and never strayed from the rocky shore; he appears as a human cipher, empty except for his passion for limpets. Having little identity, neither big fish nor little fish, neither hunter nor victim, Zefferino's father is comparable to a limpet, dryly tenacious in his hold on his life: a survivor. Accordingly, he is incapable of fantasizing that the octopus is a melodramatic villain or a delightful spectacle. He perceives the octopus simply and objectively, and his behavior, in contrast to Signorina de Magistris's paralyzing hysteria and Zefferino's wildness, is precise and efficient.

The perceptions of Zefferino's father, realistic though they might be, seem somewhat alien and comical. Presenting Signorina de Magistris with the octopus to eat, a highly pragmatic act, appears strangely inappropriate because of its cold irrelevance to her temperament and her emotions. Italo Calvino makes the humorous point that the concerns of Zefferino's father seem insensitive and unrelated to human experience, and therefore somewhat unintelligible. In composing a fable about perception, Calvino concludes with an enigmatic moral: Because human beings perceive relativistically, within relational frameworks comparable to oppositions, such as big fish-little fish, they mistake reality for their own interpretations; however, reality beyond the compass of their interpretations, our own human, undetachable identities, would be foreign, meaningless, and empty.

Style and Technique

"Big Fish, Little Fish" unfolds in a series of visual images, almost like a film montage. The reader learns about characters primarily by seeing the world through their eyes or by looking at them, often through one another's eyes. Zefferino's father is introduced in "rolled-up shorts and an undershirt, a white duck cap on his head." Signorina de Magistris is first described as "a white hand swaying" in the water, then, as a fat woman in a bathing suit. Zefferino, himself, is all eyes: "From every cranny of the rocks, or among the tremulous beards swaying in the current, a big fish might suddenly appear; from behind the glass of the mask Zefferino cast his eyes around, eagerly, intently." It is, of course, a chance to gaze through his mask that Zefferino hopes will ease the ache in Signorina de Magistris's heart. Later he wonders, if the sight of a bass or umbra will not make her stop crying, what will? The pronounced importance of seeing for Zefferino reflects its centrality to the story.

Contrasting visual images provide for characterization. Looking at the captured bass, Zefferino is thrilled by its iridescence, but Signorina de Magistris grieves instead to see evidence of parasites. Zefferino joyfully proclaims his bream to be a champion fish, and the narrator remarks that it was impossible for the boy to imagine seeing a bigger, more beautiful fish; but Signorina de Magistris sadly observes "the throat that had just swallowed the little greenish fish, only to be ripped by the teeth of the spear."

Even Zefferino's father's only perception of Signorina de Magistris as "the woman," contrasts tellingly with Zefferino's fixed perception of her as "the fat woman." By having the boy consistently describe Signorina de Magistris as "the fat woman," Calvino playfully reminds us that this is a story about subjectivity and points of view. Among the many possible interpretations of Calvino's title, "Big Fish, Little Fish," one may refer to Signorina de Magistris alone, as she is first perceived by Zefferino and later by his father.

Michael Scott Joseph

BIG ME

Author: Dan Chaon (1964-   )
Type of plot: Psychological
Time of plot: The 1980's
Locale: Beck, a small town in Nebraska
First published: 2000

> *Principal characters:*
> ANDY O'DAY, a thirty-two-year-old man recalling events that
>   occurred when he was twelve years old
> HIS FATHER, who dies of liver disease
> HIS MOTHER, who moves to Mexico
> MARK O'DAY, his brother
> HIS WIFE
> LOUIS MICKLESON, his childhood neighbor and perhaps his adult
>   double

The Story

"Big Me" is a first-person narrative, in which thirty-two-year-old Andy O'Day describes an odd series of events that happened when he was twelve years old, the year before his parents' marriage broke up. Andy explains that he has always been a dreamy child, living in a fantasy world.

In real life, the twelve-year-old Andy's parents run a bar in the small town of Beck, Nebraska, which has a population of fewer than two hundred people. To Andy, though, Beck is an imaginary town of two million, and he is the detective, protecting his city from crime. In his fantasy life, he performs feats such as saving the town from an evil werewolf, Mr. Karaffa, who in actuality is a high school teacher who dies of a heart attack.

One day, Andy notices a new neighbor is mowing the lawn. As he watches the man, he feels the man looks familiar. He comes to believe that the man, Louis Mickelson, is an older version of himself who has somehow traveled back in time. He does not know why Mickelson has done this and begins spying on him in hopes of discovering his secrets. Andy worries about the future and keeps a journal in which he writes to his future self, whom he addresses as "Big Me." He hopes his future self is happy, but if Mickelson is his future self, Andy worries that he has come back to warn of a disastrous future.

Andy goes as far as breaking into Mickelson's house and searching it. One day, as Andy is exploring a box of letters, Mickelson returns to the house. Andy knows he is invisible when he is the detective, and he creeps past Mickelson, who is staring at the television. However, as the adult Andy explains, that was the day Andy had his first blackout, a period of lost time.

Soon, Andy has collected evidence in a notebook, but it falls into the hands of Mickelson. As in any mystery story, the detective must confront his nemesis, who has been reading the notebook. Mickelson acknowledges that he has actually returned from the future and offers to whisper to Andy the secret of his future. However, Andy runs away and never sees Mickelson again, though he thinks of him regularly, whenever he lies to his family.

Interspersed with stories about his twelve-year-old self, the narrator describes his adult life. Andy is the only member of his family to have a successful, happy adult life. As he explains, he is happily married to a woman, whose name he never mentions, and they have beautiful daughters. Things have not gone well for the rest of his family. Andy is estranged from his mother, and his sister Kathy received a serious head injury in a car accident and now lives in a group home. Andy still sees his brother Mark, but Mark is bitter and obsessed with their terrible childhood. Mark insists Andy must remember events such as the time their father threatened them with a gun and the children had to hide in the junkyard behind their house. Andy has to admit that he recalls little of that time, except being the detective.

Andy's father is dead, but Andy had grown close to his dying father. They would meet and discuss Andy's time in law school and his girlfriend Katrina. However, as Andy explains, Katrina was just make-believe, a person Andy created so that his father did not worry about him. Andy acknowledges to his wife that he still has blackouts, and he admits that he still drifts off into moments of fantasy, but he is happy that his wife is there, speaking to him in a whisper.

Themes and Meanings

"Big Me" explores the contrast between the permanence of time and the imperfections of memory. The story raises questions of whether people can create their own identities or if they are trapped in their lives and their relationships to the people around them.

Young Andy worries about the future, that the world might be on the edge of disaster and that human life might come to an end. He has recently read *Het Achterhuis* (1947; *The Diary of a Young Girl*, 1952), a two-year record Anne Frank kept while hiding from the Nazis, and he begins keeping his journal so his words, at least, might live on, beyond him. As the adult who tells this story, Andy is haunted by the fates of the rest of his family, how he has lost touch with his mother, and how he has yet to visit his father's grave.

The only keepsake Andy retains is a plaque that once hung on Mickelson's wall. "I wear the chains I forged in life," it reads, which are Jacob Marley's words from *A Christmas Carol* (1843), by British Victorian author Charles Dickens. Jacob Marley is Ebenezer Scrooge's old partner, now deceased, who visits Scrooge to persuade him to change his ways just before Scrooge is visited by the three ghosts of Christmas. Andy, like Scrooge, is visited by what appears to be a ghost from the future, who warns him that his current actions may lead to a terrible future. Similarly, the adult Andy is haunted by the ghosts of the past and the permanence of what cannot be changed.

As an adult, Andy argues with his brother Mark about the events of their childhood. Mark recalls the children running for their life as their father chased them with a gun. Mark says their father tried to commit suicide, but Andy does not recall either event. Mark claims their parent had drunken fights every night, but Andy recalls these evenings as resembling scenes from a television comedy, in which people bicker as the audience laughs. The adult Andy sees that people are made up of many alternative versions and many different selves, some long forgotten and others that are haunting memories. Sometimes, these different versions are fantasies, dreams entered to avoid present troubles.

Style and Technique

With a first-person narrator, the reader must assess the validity of the narrator's perceptions and explanations. Sometimes a narrator may be too immature or too naïve to understand the unfolding events, and other times the narrator is intentionally trying to mislead the reader. The narrator of "Big Me" acknowledges that he is a liar and has misled his dying father with a story about a fantasy girlfriend. He has misled friends with claims that his mother is an actress and that his father is an archeologist in South America. Andy has admitted he still leads a fantasy life, and he recognizes that he still has moments when he blacks out and has no idea what he has done for the last forty-five minutes.

Part of interpreting "Big Me" is sorting through the claims of different characters. The adult Andy describes his brother Mark as paranoid; Andy says Mark exaggerates, but it is hard to trust Andy's version of events. The adult Andy describes his childhood days as spent spying on Mickelson as the detective, but one childhood scene that does ring true is that in which Andy is eavesdropping on his parents. He cannot quite hear what they are saying, but he worries that they are talking about him. In the end, "Big Me" is about the distances a person can go to avoid the truth. Although young Andy describes searching for clues about Mickelson, in the untold but underlying story, he is searching for clues to what his future holds.

His stories of spying on Mickelson have troubling aspects as well. He claims to have crept past Mickelson as the man sat in his chair, watching television, achieving this because he is invisible when he is the detective. The tale of his struggle with Mickelson culminates, as every thriller does, with a final confrontation. In this case, Mickelson states he has come back from the future to share a secret with Andy. However, as they face each other down, Andy feels as if he is standing in an empty field.

Mickelson never tells Andy his secret, but Andy acknowledges that he did not want to hear it. On one level, when Mickelson tells Andy that he has returned from the future, he may be joking with a young boy or he may just be part of a dreamy boy's fantasy life, but there is a sense that Mickelson is a warning to Andy. Mickelson's life is empty and lonely, thoroughly unhappy. The memory of Mickelson persists in Andy's mind as he grows up, so perhaps Mickelson has warned Andy away from a horrible future.

Brian L. Olson

BIG TWO-HEARTED RIVER

Author: Ernest Hemingway (1899-1961)
Type of plot: Adventure
Time of plot: 1919 or 1920
Locale: The woods of Michigan's upper peninsula
First published: 1925

> *Principal character:*
> NICK ADAMS, a young American who has recently returned from
> action in World War I

The Story

"Big Two-Hearted River" is one of the best stories by one of the greatest short-story writers of the twentieth century. "The story was about coming back from the war," as Ernest Hemingway later explained in *A Moveable Feast* (1964), "but there was no mention of the war in it." Unless the reader knows *In Our Time* (1924, 1925), Hemingway's first collection of short stories, "Big Two-Hearted River" will not make complete sense. The first five stories in that collection describe the young Nick Adams growing up in and around the northern Michigan woods, while the middle stories (and most of the interchapters that preface every story in the collection) concern Americans in Europe during and immediately following World War I. "Big Two-Hearted River" concludes the book and brings Nick Adams back from the wounds and trauma of war to the regenerative natural setting of woods and water, where, as a boy, he first learned about the world. "Big Two-Hearted River" is a boy's adventure of camping and fishing, but it is finally a story of a man's healing.

The story is broken into two parts (in *In Our Time*, they appear as separate stories in the table of contents and are divided by a brief interchapter), but there is very little plot in either. Part 1 opens as "The train went on up the track out of sight, around one of the hills of burnt timber." This is Nick's last contact (except in his thoughts) with other humans. Nick has been dropped off in what remains of Seney, a once thriving lumber town that has been deserted and burned over and now resembles (although Nick does not say so) the war zone that he has so recently left. "Even the surface had been burned off the ground."

At a bridge across the river, Nick looks down on "the trout keeping themselves steady in the current with wavering fins." Like the trout, Nick will try to hold himself together in the next days as he recovers from the war in the restorative environment of these north woods. Nick "felt happy. He felt he had left everything behind, the need for thinking, the need to write, other needs. It was all back of him." Hiking toward the woods, Nick finds that the grasshoppers "had all turned black from living in the burned-over land"; even the insects have learned to adapt here.

Little else happens in part 1. Nick walks away from the charred land into the woods, naps, and—like Rip Van Winkle—awakens to a new adventure. He finds a good camp-site by the river, pitches his tent, and crawls into it "happy."

> He had not been unhappy all day. This was different though. Now things were done. There had been this to do. Now it was done. It had been a hard trip. He was very tired. That was done. He had made his camp. He was settled. Nothing could touch him. It was a good place to camp. He was there, in the good place. He was in his home where he had made it. Now he was hungry.

Nick cooks dinner over his fire and, while he makes coffee, he thinks of Hopkins, a friend who deserted Nick and others when he became rich. "His mind was starting to work. He knew he could choke it because he was tired enough." Nick crawls into his tent and goes to sleep.

In part 2, Nick cooks and eats his breakfast, packs himself a lunch, and heads into the river. He hooks and then loses a huge trout ("He had never seen so big a trout"), but his "feeling of disappointment" slowly leaves him, and he catches two other trout. Nick sits on a log to eat his lunch and observes that the river narrows and flows into a swamp farther downstream.

> Nick did not want to go in there now. He felt a reaction against deep wading with the water deepening up under his armpits, to hook big trout in places impossible to land them. In the swamp the banks were bare, the big cedars came together overhead, the sun did not come through, except in patches; in the fast deep water, in the half light, the fish-ing would be tragic. In the swamp fishing was a tragic adventure. Nick did not want it. He did not want to go down the stream any further today.

Nick guts and cleans his fish and walks back to his camp. "There were plenty of days coming when he could fish the swamp," Nick thinks in the last line of the story.

Themes and Meanings

"Big Two-Hearted River" is perhaps the best example of Hemingway's theory of omission, which he discusses in *Death in the Afternoon* (1932):

> If a writer of prose knows enough about what he is writing about he may omit things that he knows and the reader, if the writer is writing truly enough, will have a feeling of those things as strongly as though the writer had stated them. The dignity of movement of an ice-berg is due to only one-eighth of it being above the water.

It is best if readers encounter "Big Two-Hearted River" first at the end of *In Our Time*, after reading the related stories of Nick Adams growing up, going to war, and being wounded. However, even if they read the story isolated in some anthology, readers should sense from the curiously tense surface that "Big Two-Hearted River," despite its content, is no boy's adventure story.

The meaning of the story lies in Nick's ability to build a good camp and to fish well and thereby tap the restorative powers that nature holds. Just as in the fishing scenes in *The Sun Also Rises* (1926), in which Jake Barnes and his friend Bill are able to escape the meaningless whirlwind of Paris life in the pure and tranquil fishing in the mountains of Spain, so Nick in "Big Two-Hearted River" can return to his Michigan woods to recover from the violence and trauma of war and to gain some control over his life. Although Nick shows no scars, his psychic wounds are deep. Nick in fact resembles the trout that he guts toward the end of the story: "When he held them back up in the water they looked like live fish." Nick has been gutted by the brutality and senselessness of war, but now, like Frederic Henry in *A Farewell to Arms* (1929), he is able to escape, at least momentarily, to a sanctuary from war and the world.

Nick is restored in two ways. First, the setting itself provides some kind of natural, almost mystical, healing power. Like Henry Thoreau at Walden Pond, Nick is able in the woods to return to the elemental activities of eating, sleeping, and fishing. Fishing provides the second restoration. In Hemingway's world, fishing is one of the ritualistic activities (like boxing and bullfighting) by which man establishes and maintains his control over an arbitrarily violent world. In such activities, there is a clear set of skills (a code) and by fishing well (and not, for example, "in places impossible to land" the fish), a man can be successful and achieve his limited goals. Fishing provides one means of erecting a scaffolding of skills over the essential meaninglessness of life. However, the story, in its brief twenty-four hours, recounts merely the first step. As Nick says in the last fine, "There were plenty of days coming when he could fish the swamp." The swamp thus represents human society, and, when Nick is whole again, he will be able to return to society for the painful task of human interaction. In the Hemingway cartography, society can be as violent and arbitrary (as "tragic") as the world of war. "Big Two-Hearted River" is about a man returning from the war, getting his psychological strength back through contact with nature and the ritual of fishing, and preparing to return to the world.

Style and Technique

"Big Two-Hearted River" is one of the most accomplished of Hemingway's early stories, ranked in the top half-dozen of this master storyteller's major achievements. The story is carried almost single-handedly through Hemingway's style. There is only one character in "Big Two-Hearted River" and very little plot or action. However, much occurs. Hemingway has written a story that is much like the Big Two-Hearted River itself—so spare and clean that the reader looks down into its clear water for meaning.

The power of the story comes in large part from its descriptions, which give the action with an economy of word and picture. There is no dialogue, and only a few times does Nick Adams allow himself to think. For most of the story, readers are observing Nick moving simply in this natural setting:

Nick went over to the pack and found, with his fingers, a long nail in a paper sack of nails, in the bottom of the pack. He drove it into the pine tree, holding it close and hitting it gently with the flat of the ax. He hung the pack up on the nail. All his supplies were in the pack. They were off the ground and sheltered now.

This lean, economical prose actually intensifies the psychological situation of the story. The prose is dramatic and objective, but right below the surface (or, in the other seven-eighths of Hemingway's "iceberg") is a man barely under control, who must cut off his own thoughts. The tightly controlled surface of the story, in other words, reflects the struggle that is going on within Nick Adams, and this surface tension is what gives the story its actual power. The simple declarative sentences, the repetition of sentence elements, and the lack of subordination—all these add up to the story's elemental weight and force. Beneath the story's simple actions, as Hemingway knew and as he expected his readers to know, is a story of recovery from war. As the tip of the iceberg stands for what lurks just beneath the surface, so the places and things on the surface of the story (the camp, the trout, the swamp) are symbolic and stand for the things, just below the surface, that Hemingway is not telling his readers.

To read "Big Two-Hearted River" right is to glory in the physical descriptions of making the camp and fishing, and to realize what a major psychic struggle is going on just beneath the surface of Hemingway's rhythmic, almost lyrical prose.

David Peck

BIJOU

Author: Stuart Dybek (1942-   )
Type of plot: Antistory
Time of plot: The 1980's
Locale: A film festival at an unspecified location
First published: 1985

Principal character:
AN UNNAMED NARRATOR, apparently a film critic

The Story

The narrator announces the screening of a foreign art film at a festival. The film challenges the audience in several ways; it is shot in black and white, with unpredictable light values, so that it often appears as a negative. Shades of gray are rarely used, and the narrator speculates that in the tropical country where the film was made, everything is vibrantly colored so that "even vanilla ice cream is robin's-egg blue." Black, white, and especially gray are colors that the narrator apparently associates with the West, industrialized Europe and the United States.

The film's "only acknowledged influence" is an obscure poem by Victor Guzman, "the late surrealist dentist of Chilpancingo" in Mexico. Guzman's poem "Laughing Gas" has given the director his inspiration for its one source of color, that of tongues. Eventually, the narrator says, the screen becomes "nearly technicolor with tongues."

Although the narrator describes the violent film—which tells of a failed guerrilla revolt against an oppressive military regime aided by the Central Intelligence Agency (CIA)—in some detail, it apparently has no plot. The most lurid moment of violence concerns the tearing out of the prisoners' tongues when they refuse to talk. The tongues, which bleed in various colors, are kept in a coffee can on the brutal colonel's desk. A young private vomits as he buries the can the next morning, and then the sound diminishes until it is reduced to the noise of the projector. Then fragmented subtitles race past, followed by freeze-frames of photos of the poor and of tourists, then shots of churches and universities with occasionally legible subtitles flashing political messages, such as "Where there is no freedom words fill the mouth with blood." Following what seems to be blurred documentary footage of violent scenes, during which the metallic background noise increases to a screech, the film apparently ends with another subtitle: "Even the hanged have no tongues to protrude!"

As the lights then go on, the stunned audience reacts in various ways, many applauding as if they have seen live theater. The narrator then predicts the critical reaction to the film, which is generally favorable but clichéd: "Uncompromisingly powerful, it demands to be seen" (from *The Village Voice*). The audience leaves as a final image appears on the screen behind them, "of an indigo tongue working at a husk of popcorn stuck in a gold-capped molar." In effect, the audience is presented with an "inside" image of a member of the audience doing something banal, despite the horror he or she has just witnessed. The film's credits list the actors, writers, director, and others, expanding to include the soldiers, students, and peasants actually involved in the world of the oppressive regime, the audience, and even "the myriad names of the dead."

Themes and Meanings

On the simplest level one might say that the readers and the audience of "Bijou" both get an obvious message about repression and violence, about the brutalization of peasants and the audience's involvement in the cruelty because of the CIA's role in overthrowing the rebels. The thematic thrust of the film also concerns freedom of speech, so it might be argued that the film is an allegory on that theme. The narrator speculates that although the audience may gasp and stare in silence, they have been conditioned to accept, even to expect, such violence on screen. Of course the same might be said for the readers, who also accept the violence of this story.

While the film audience within the story reflects on the significance of the terrifying film they have been watching, readers reflect on both the content of the film and the narrator's description of the audience's reactions. In effect, the story is about being an audience. Readers are told that members of the audience think they are at the festival not to "censor but to discern." That is, they see their role as essentially passive, simply to respond to what they see, not to think about it or to take action. They seem most concerned with issues that appear abstract and "academic." Is the film's violence a "statement," or "merely further exploitation"? "Is this perhaps the Cinema of Cruelty?"

The fact that the audience is so stunned and confused at the end (are they angry at the "oppressors" or at the film?) and that one critic even claims that the "ultimate praise" for a film is that it causes us "to confuse celluloid images with flesh and blood" suggests how powerful art, whether a film or a story, can be. It implicitly warns people against complacency or neutrality (the comfortable objectivity of the audience and critic). The image of the indigo tongue working on a husk of popcorn mocks the audience, which at the end is reminded that they, too, are actually part of the human drama they have witnessed. The readers might add their own names to the credits as well.

Style and Technique

In *The Coast of Chicago* (1986), the collection in which "Bijou" appears, Stuart Dybek, a Chicago native, mixes realistic narratives about urban life, usually involving young male protagonists, with a few unconventional stories like "Bijou." Bijou is a rather old-fashioned name for a movie theater, and that is ironic, given the avant-garde nature of the film being described. Bijou is also French for "jewel," and the word can be applied to anything, including this story, that is exquisitely wrought or well made.

Dybek gives his unnamed narrator the distance, if not the "aloofness," of the critic and commentator in the first sentence of his story, having him use the French phrase, *dernier cri* (the latest fashion). There is something pretentious about the narrator throughout. Note, for example, his overly elaborate description of the "modern hospital" in the wretched country where the film was made: "In the modern hospital, set like a glass mural against the sea, ceiling fans oscillate like impaled wings of flamingos above the crisp rhythm of nurses." The second simile in particular is the product of someone who is being precious about language, as in the use of "siren" as a verb in the following sentence: "As ambulances siren, they flash through color changes with the rapidity of chameleons."

Although the narrator has keen powers of perception, he shows no emotion in his account of the horrors. "Scene follows scene documenting torture in the modern military state," he says flatly. Throughout his narrative he exhibits his knowledge of film history, from Charlie Chaplin and Orson Welles to Sam Peckinpah, and at the end of the story he can anticipate the phrasing in various kinds of critical reviews. That is, the narrator, who is arguably the main "character," if not the only one, in this story, is presented as not only disinterested or objective but also as uncommitted and uncompassionate.

Dybek's story exhibits most of the characteristics associated with postmodernist fiction: a prevailing sense of irony; rejection of a clear specific setting, conventional plot, or character development; employment of the present tense in preference to the traditional narrative past; avoidance of a moral or ethical stance; and the use of absurd premises.

Literary theoreticians have observed that any story is in effect a "re-presentation" of reality. The levels of re-presentation in "Bijou," however, are multiplied. Readers experience the story of the film at second hand, while the audience actually experiences it. However, the film itself, as viewed by the audience, is a re-presentation of reality, so the audience is getting it secondhand, which means the readers are getting it thirdhand, and of course readers are well aware that the entire story is itself a re-presentation by Dybek. Part of what "Bijou" is all about is the distance that exists in art between the audience and actuality.

Ron McFarland

THE BIRTHMARK

Author: Nathaniel Hawthorne (1804-1864)
Type of plot: Allegory
First published: 1843
Locale: New England
Time of plot: The late eighteenth century

Principal characters:
AYLMER, the protagonist, a scientist
GEORGIANA, his beautiful wife
AMINADAB, his beastlike lab assistant

The Story

The protagonist of this tale, Aylmer, is a scientist "proficient in every branch of natural philosophy." The plot is set in motion when he marries a beautiful young woman, Georgiana, who bears a curious birthmark on her cheek in the shape of a tiny crimson hand. Envious women sometimes say it spoils her beauty, but most men find it enchanting. Aylmer, however, becomes obsessed with the birthmark as the one flaw in an otherwise perfect beauty. When Aylmer involuntarily shudders at the appearance of the birthmark, which waxes and wanes with the flushing or paling of the lady's cheek, Georgiana also develops a horror of her supposed blemish. Aylmer has a prophetic dream in which he seeks surgically to remove the mark, but it recedes as he probes till it clutches at her heart. In despair, Georgiana encourages Aylmer to try to remove the mark, even if it endangers her life to do so.

He secludes her in a lovely boudoir and entertains her with enchanting illusions and captivating fragrances. He and his gross, shaggy-haired assistant, Aminadab, labor mightily in Aylmer's laboratory to produce an elixir that will irradicate the imperfection of his nearly perfect bride. The laboratory's fiery furnace, its soot-blackened walls, its gaseous odors, and its test tubes and crucibles contrast grimly against the ethereal boudoir where his wife waits.

Meanwhile, Georgiana finds and reads Aylmer's journal, which records his scientific experiments. Her admiration and understanding for her husband's aspirations and intellect increase, even as she recognizes that most of his experiments are magnificent failures. Though she no longer expects to outlive the experience, she gladly and lovingly accepts the draft from her husband's hand. The birthmark does indeed fade, leaving her a vision of perfect beauty, a spirit unblemished in the flesh, but Georgiana is dead. The birthmark is mortality itself.

Themes and Meanings

Allegories seldom produce well-rounded characters because their purpose is primarily philosophical and didactic. Aylmer is undoubtedly the Faustian man who is never satisfied with his own limitations. Ordinary nature is never good enough to ful-

fill his idealistic aspirations, and like both Christopher Marlowe's and Johann Wolfgang von Goethe's Faust, he is entranced with the Greek ideal of perfect beauty. In
terms of visible beauty, Georgiana cannot compete with Helen of Troy, the supernatural succubus provided by Mephistopheles for Faustus. On the other hand, she can appeal to Aylmer's attraction to spiritual beauty and thus perhaps save his soul, like Gertrude, instead of assuring his damnation as the spurious Helen did for Faustus in
Marlowe's version. Aylmer's ultimate fate is not resolved in the story. Presumably, he,
like Ethan Brand, another of Nathaniel Hawthorne's protagonists, has found the one
unforgivable sin in himself: intellectual pride.

Aylmer is never covetous of evil pleasures. He aspires upward, always, toward the
ideal. In this sense, he is less believable as a human specimen than the Renaissance
Faustus, who craved sensual experience as well as knowledge and power. Aylmer
seems to have been corrupted by the idealist's tendency toward abstraction and dis-
content with reality. In fact, he hardly seems sufficiently empirical in orientation to
make a good scientist. However, the reader is assured that "he handled physical details
as if there were nothing beyond them; yet spiritualized them all, and redeemed himself from materialism by his strong and eager aspirations towards the infinite." Science is obviously closer to alchemy and magic at this time than to modern chemistry
and physics. Alchemy always had a spiritual element.

Georgiana is a one-dimensional heroine, as good as she is beautiful. In fact, the
story seems to support the Platonic assumption that perfect beauty is equivalent to
perfect goodness. Georgiana does gain some intellectual insight in the course of the
story, loving her husband more but trusting his judgment less. She has more common
sense than he but also more selfless devotion. Modern readers may complain that the
perfect goodness she attains, even before she is purified of her physical flaw, is simply
the absurd exaggeration of conventional female virtue: absolute self-sacrifice and
submission to the will of the beloved. Hawthorne casts all blame for the tragic outcome on the misguided husband, who is not satisfied with the blessings of nature.

The conflict is not really between good and evil; it lies, rather, in a fundamental in-
compatibility between the physical and the spiritual aspects of human beings. Georgiana recognizes that Aylmer's journal was "the sad confession and continual exem-
plification of the shortcomings of the composite man, the spirit burdened with clay,
and working in matter, and of the despair that assails the higher nature at finding itself
so miserably thwarted by the earthly part."

Style and Technique

Hawthorne inherited from his Puritan ancestors a brooding preoccupation with the
idea of Original Sin. He created several haunting symbols to suggest that human flaw:
the minister's black veil, the poisonous breath of Rappaccinni's daughter, the scarlet
letter that Hester Prynne wore on her breast. The birthmark is one of these symbols.
Although the tiny hand is expressly associated only with the "fatal flaw" of mortality,
Aylmer's peculiarly Calvinistic frame of mind expands its symbolic value to "his
wife's liability to sin, sorrow, decay, and death."

Hawthorne's symbolic mode sometimes explains too much for modern tastes, yet there are ambiguities lurking even in this most allegorical of tales. The fact that Aylmer connects the physical flaw to moral sin seems to be the reason for this abhorrence of the birthmark and thus his justification for, in essence, murdering his wife. This presents a moral ambiguity akin to the situation in "Young Goodman Brown," where the author carefully suggests that Brown may indeed have met his neighbors and his wife at the devil's sabbat but that he may have dreamed the whole episode. If the evil vision was a dream issuing from the tortured sense of his own guilt, then Brown casts a terrible blight on his wife and neighbors with the poisonous vapors of his Calvinistic imagination. Even more obviously does Aylmer blight his wife as though her physical imperfection were equivalent to sin.

However, Aylmer is explicitly aligned with the spiritual side of humanity. The shadow side of humanity, or the entirely physical element that presumably serves the spirit, is represented by the grotesque Aminadab. Lest the reader miss the point, Hawthorne pushes the contrast between the servant and his master. "With his vast strength, his shaggy hair, his smoky aspect, and the indescribable earthiness that encrusted him, he seemed to represent man's physical nature, while Aylmer's slender figure, and pale, intellectual face, were no less apt a type of the spiritual element."

In spite of the didactic instruction in the symbolic significance of such figures, one must remember that the villain of the piece is not the beastly shadow figure but the spiritual, intellectual Aylmer. This is true even though Aminadab chuckles ominously at the death of Georgiana, as though at the victory of earth over spirit. He contributes to the menacing gothic atmosphere of the alchemist's laboratory but is a relatively innocent collaborator in an intellectual crime. Who needs Mephistopheles when men can destroy in the name of perfection?

The obvious allegorical quality of "The Birthmark" makes it a less satisfactory treatment of the mad scientist theme than the more complex and polished "Rappaccinni's Daughter." They are both intermediate forms, however, between the religious allegories of the past and the science fiction of the present.

The traditional Satan or Mephistopheles has waned as literary symbol of evil, to be replaced by the machine or mutant monster that the mad scientist creates in his ambition to take over from God the control of natural forces. In "Rappaccinni's Daughter," the mutant form that in turn destroys the innocent maiden is the poisonous vegetation created by her father. In "The Birthmark," however, the scientist is described in persistently spiritual terms and creates no intermediate form, except of course the fatal potion, but brings death directly to his beloved. Although the menacing Dr. Rappaccinni seems closer to the devil in conception, Aylmer seems closer to God. Perhaps Hawthorne suffered from a dark suspicion that, after all, God must be responsible for humankind's imperfection and suffering. The tales of Hawthorne speak eloquently of a profoundly ambivalent mythic imagination.

Katherine Snipes

BIRTHMATES

Author: Gish Jen (1956-   )
Type of plot: Psychological
Time of plot: The 1990's
Locale: An American city
First published: 1995

> *Principal characters:*
> ART WOO, a thirty-eight-year-old, divorced Chinese American
> BILLY SHORE, a rival businessperson who shares Art's birthday
> CINDY, an African American mother living in an urban welfare
>   hotel
> LISA WOO, Art's former wife

The Story

In "Birthmates," an omniscient narrator representing the central character's consciousness affirms his financial responsibility for what transpires. In an effort to save money during an industry slowdown, Art Woo has booked the least expensive room he could find for a business trip, only to find himself in a strange city on a snowy December night in front of the locked door of a welfare hotel. His decision to stay at this hotel and his observations of and responses to these accommodations illuminate his character and his life situation. He is revealed to be a man profoundly alone, grieving, failing personally and professionally, and riding swells of inner terror. During this business trip, Art suffers acutely from fear, from anxiety about his job performance, from grief at his wife's departure, and from growing awareness of the pain of the loss of their unborn child.

Fearing for his personal safety, Art huddles in his dingy hotel room, scarcely able to sleep, clutching the handset of the clunky old phone as a weapon against imagined intruders. Still clinging to the disconnected phone handset in self-defense as he leaves the lobby in the morning, Art is tormented by children who use the handset to knock him unconscious. Cindy, an African American mother living in the hotel who nurses his injury, stimulates his sexual fantasies and stirs his impulse to care for others.

At the trade show later in the day, Art's physical fears yield to anxiety about business rivals and his professional future. He dwells on the unhappy prospect of seeing Billy Shore, a hearty, backslapping, mainstream competitor with whom he shares a birthday, but finds that Billy, the man he calls his birthmate, has beaten him once again by escaping to a new job. Ironically, Art is also offered the prospect of a new job, but when he returns to his hotel room, he discovers his phone now has no handset and the headhunter will not be able to contact him. Sitting on the bed, he wishes he could call Lisa, his former wife, to announce his new hopes. His final thoughts are at once denials and affirmations of all the deaths he is suffering: the death of his career, the death of his marriage, the death of his only child before birth, and his own profound sense that he is drowning in a sea of grief and loss he is unable to express.

Themes and Meanings

This is a story of hauntings, prosaic and profound. Locked inside his dismal room, Art Woo is comically haunted by horror-film images of invasion and physical assault. Ironically, while he projects these imaginary external threats on this hotel populated by mothers and children, the workings of his mind reveal he is suffering very real inner assaults of memory, inner deaths of love and hope. Art is haunted by images of his wife who left him because he was unable to comprehend her grief or feel his own grief at the loss of their unborn child to brittle bone disease. At the end of the story, Art is also haunted, dimly, and most poignantly, by the shadowy image of that fetus, his lost opportunity for fatherhood.

In his professional life as an employee of a dying minicomputer business, Art is haunted by the racial humiliations inflicted on him by his violent and crude boss and by the taunts of chauvinistic colleagues who exclude and disparage him. Ever the outsider as a Chinese American, Art silently envies the apparent power and ease of those around him. Indeed, the narrator reveals that Art's professional life, like his personal life, has been deficient in affect and action. He does not rage at the boss who injures him. He does not quit. He pragmatically uses the injury to passively extort a promotion. Failing to feel and failing to act when his child died, insisting on pragmatic acceptance and continuance of the fertility treatments, Art passively alienates his own grieving wife.

On this trip, Art again fails to take action. Instead of leaving immediately, Art moves into the humiliation and isolation of the squalid hotel. There, locked inside his own consciousness, he symbolizes his own disconnection from the world by removing the handset from the phone and imagining it a viable defense against all harm. The images of haunting and death accumulate until it becomes apparent that it is Art who is dead to the world and to himself. The comic assault by rampaging children in the lobby of the welfare hotel and Art's loss of consciousness when thumped on the head by the flying phone handset result in Art momentarily feeling awakened both physically and emotionally. He suggests he feels reborn when he regains consciousness in Cindy's room, but even that violent shock does not move him to action. He merely leaves for the trade show with a headache and new sexual fantasies aroused by Cindy's nursing. He ends as he began, haunted, still in that hotel room, still locked inside himself

Style and Technique

Gish Jen's stories often blend tragic and comic elements. In this story, the omniscient narration allows the reader distance enough to see Art Woo as both profoundly tragic and touchingly funny. His mind is powerful and continually inflates the trivial into consequence. A brass sign about injuries suffered in the hotel evokes his speculation on the hotel's potential dangers and leads to his reflection on the tendency to invest signs with significance. He recalls that his wife read the end of their marriage in the experience of seeing a tree split by lightning. Funnier still, as he sets off for the trade show, Art's anticipation of breakfast leads him to protracted rumination on his resolve to never eat a croissant in public because its awkward shape makes its consumption not only messy but vaguely emasculating. To this principle and others like it, Art attributes his ability to survive in the workplace.

However clever, articulate, and observant Art seems, the narrative discloses his is a mind that resists connection to other people and denies impulses to explore profound issues of love, pain, and loss. Jen acknowledges using her own pain at the loss of a child before birth as the seed of Art's most extreme instance of emotional denial. Art exists in the story in a world without clear coordinates in time and space, in a kind of private universe of unacknowledged pain at once denied and endured. Art Woo's social identities as a Chinese American, a businessperson, a former husband, and a father without a child are lost in the final grim landscape of a soul in emotional isolation. The narrative inside his mind is symbolic of how trapped he is and how little connection he has ever made to others. He says little to other people in the story although he fantasizes saying important things to Lisa, Cindy, and Billy. He has disconnected himself for protection just as he disconnected that telephone handset in his room.

The title "Birthmates" arises from Art's identification with his business rival, Billy Shore, who was born on the same day as Art but is four years younger. Art feels like an ineffectual shadow of Billy, a hearty white man who seems to get along with everyone and float through his days and his work effortlessly with all the jokes and male behaviors and colloquial language of drinking and sports that Art lacks. However, the many hauntings of the story, the many forms of birth and death, resonate and expand the title's expression of Art's failing professional life to include Art's feelings of inadequacy in his personal life as well, his failure to understand his mate, Lisa, and his failure to share her grief at the loss of the birth they had worked toward for so long.

Virginia M. Crane

THE BISHOP

Author: Anton Chekhov (1860-1904)
Type of plot: Philosophical realism
Time of plot: The late 1890's
Locale: A nameless Russian provincial capital
First published: "Arkhierey," 1902 (English translation, 1915)

Principal characters:
BISHOP PYOTR, the suffering bishop of a diocese and the
    protagonist
MARYA TIMOFEEVNA, his mother
KATYA, his niece
FATHER SISOY, his aide

The Story

Against the solemn background of Holy Week, the most important week in the liturgical year, Anton Chekhov recounts the last days in the life of the protagonist, Bishop Pyotr, including his illness, the accompanying crisis and "awakening," and death.

Bishop Pyotr officiates at vespers as the story opens on the eve of Palm Sunday. To the bishop, who is unwell, the congregation is an indistinguishable blur with "all faces alike," "heaving like the sea." That the congregation seems shrouded in mist suggests his isolation from his flock. Even as his own mother approaches him, he is unsure of her identity. When the bishop begins to weep, and the congregation with him, his tears are no doubt brought about by these imaginings of his mother as well as of his impending death. Suddenly the weeping stops and the narrator notes, "everything was as before"—words that are echoed at the end of the story following the bishop's death. On his return to the monastery, the bishop identifies with objects in nature even if these evoke sterility and deadness. To the bishop, "everything seemed kindly, youthful, akin . . . and one longed to think that so it would be always." Despite this desire for continuity of existence, his identification with such forms of nature strengthens the motif of his estrangement from his personal identity.

Returning to the monastery, the bishop rejoices to learn that his mother was indeed in town. The news quickens memories of his "sweet precious childhood . . . which seemed brighter, fuller, and more festive than it had really been"—a childhood when "joy was quivering in the air," when he had had "naïve faith," had been called Pavlushka, and had been "infinitely happy." His pleasant reverie is rudely interrupted by the snoring of his aide, Father Sisoy, in the adjoining room—a sound that to him suggests "loneliness, forlornness, even vagrancy." Descriptions of ominous nature—the "moon peeping" into the bishop's window and a "cricket chirping"—intensify this mood; in Chekhov, such images are often associated with death.

Chapter 2, which begins on Palm Sunday, describes the everyday routine of Bishop Pyotr's office, interrupted by lunch with Marya Timofeevna, his mother, and Katya, his niece. In this setting, surprisingly, his mother treats him as a bishop rather than as her son. Surprised and disappointed by his mother's reserve, the son once again "cannot recognize her," she who was so tender and sympathetic when he was ill as a child. Cut off from warmth and simple human intercourse, the bishop feels estranged from reality and is increasingly aware of his illness. Even as he overhears the banal conversation between his mother and Father Sisoy, he recalls the course of his clerical career. The life that, eight years before, seemed to him to have "no end in sight" has now "retreated far away into the mist as though it were a dream."

Chapter 3 further details the bishop's daily routine. Illness has intensified his sensitivity toward the clergy's lack of spirituality and the ignorance, triviality, and pettiness of his suppliants. People's awe at his rank annoys him. No one speaks to him "genuinely, simply, as to a human being." Church is now the only place where he feels peace. During Tuesday's vespers, the past rises before him again, and he recalls having heard in his youth the readings about the Bridegroom who comes at night and the Heavenly Mansion. He is satisfied with his success, acknowledges having faith, and contemplates life hereafter. However, some things remain unclear to him; he senses that something most important is still missing and that he does not want to die.

Chapter 4 opens with a lyric description of nature. Mention of "awakening trees smiling a welcome" foreshadows the bishop's "awakening" and identification with nature before dying. A visit from his eight-year-old niece, Katya, leads to genuine spontaneous communication. His mistaken impression of hearing the opening and shutting of doors, identified by Katya as the noise in his stomach, provokes his laughter and offers a moment of relief, yet it also indicates the progress of illness. His mother also visits him, observes that he is ill, and adds that, when Easter comes, he shall rest—words prophetic of his death the day before Easter. Similarly, the announcement that the horses are ready, that it is time for the Passion of the Lord, foreshadows the bishop's own approaching suffering and agony. Once again he finds relief in church, where he discovers a sense of continuity and thus a meaning to life—he sees the congregation as unchanged since the days of his childhood and senses identity in the church. At home, however, the feeling of oppression returns. He is even prepared "to give his life" merely to escape the monastery and the surrounding banality. His loneliness reaches its greatest intensity as he yearns for someone with whom he could talk openly. On the next day, Good Friday, final relief and release come in the form of a hemorrhage. He imagines himself thinner, weaker, and more insignificant than anyone and concludes "How good!" signifying his acceptance of death and the discovery of true peace. Realizing that the bishop is dying, his mother begins to comfort him and addresses him as her son, Pavlushka. However, he no longer hears her. Rather, having identified himself with nature, he imagines that he is a simple, ordinary man, free as a bird.

Easter Sunday, the day after his death, is celebrated by everyone with no particular notice of his passing. In fact, he is "completely forgotten," and some people do not believe of his mother that her son was a bishop. Thus, the bishop's deathbed vision of being at last a free man appears to agree with a reality where no one even remembers him.

Themes and Meanings

"The Bishop," Chekhov's penultimate short story, is the tragedy of a member of the intelligentsia whose pursuit of a highly successful clerical career cuts him off from genuine human intercourse. Not until he faces death does the bishop realize that something important is missing from his life—namely, a love and respect for himself, not for his rank. His existential feeling of loneliness and isolation is evidenced by his thoughts: "If only there were one person to whom I could have talked, have opened my heart."

The bishop has two identities: a private one associated with Pavlushka, the name from his youth, and a public one associated with his present name, Bishop Pyotr. He has been unable, however, to defend this private identity against the forces of his career. His mother's nearness during the last week of his life (after a nine-year separation for which he must share the blame) has made him painfully aware of the lack of genuine love and closeness in his life. Even his mother addresses him with the formal "you" and "Your Holiness."

Now that he is dying, he wishes to return to the simple existence of his youth (clearly a Tolstoyan idea). His metamorphosis occurs both physically and spiritually. He imagines that he has become thinner, shorter, and more insignificant than anyone (the Latin root of Pavlushka means "little"). The bishop and his mother agree, whereupon his mother kisses him, calling him Pavlushka and "darling son." Then, during his final, more spiritual, thoughts, he imagines himself a simple, ordinary man, walking cheerfully through the fields under a sky bathed in sunshine, free as a bird to go anywhere he likes. His awakening before death enables him to die peacefully, thinking "How good!"

The author notes that the bishop died and was forgotten, yet this conclusion is not despairing, for the story suggests that a simple, genuine existence guided by love and respect is far more important than rank and fame. Throughout the text, an analogy is drawn between Bishop Pyotr and Christ. This likeness rightfully stops with the quiet death of the bishop. The point is, the bishop is not Christ and need not be remembered. He is only a link in a continuous chain created by Christ. Before he dies, the bishop perceives this continuity and is happy that he is part of it. His faith assures him of the Resurrection promised by the one whose own Resurrection is celebrated the day after the bishop dies. The pealing of church bells that the bishop so enjoyed on Easter morning is testimony to the perseverance of his spirit.

Style and Technique

Chekhov's impressionistic style, evident here, consists in juxtaposing complete scenes with a minimum of authorial comment. Multiple perspectives lend the story ambiguity, and a variety of rhythmic structures combined with a variety of artistic devices such as contrast, parallelism, carefully chosen metaphors and similes, dreamlike sequences, and recurring formulas make it an excellent example of the musicality of Chekhov's prose. Among the story's many symbolic elements are the ubiquitous sound of bells, the mysterious moon, the smell of pine, and the chirping cricket. The language is a masterly blending of levels of diction, including journalistic, Church Slavonic, and standard and substandard Russian (for example, the language of Father Sisoy and the mother).

Guiding the course of the story is the fatal typhoid that controls Bishop Pyotr's thoughts and actions. "The Bishop" ranks as one of Chekhov's best works portraying illness. Sharing numerous thematic and compositional features with Chekhov's mature plays, it divides into four parts: The first chapter describes the onset of the malady; chapters 2 and 3, its duration; and chapter 4, the crisis followed by death. Hints throughout suggest that the bishop will die. Besides the symptoms of his disease that are scattered here and there, each chapter contains references and allusions to death.

Leonard Polakiewicz

A BIT OF A SMASH IN MADRAS

Author: Julian Maclaren-Ross (1912-1964)
Type of plot: Social realism
Time of plot: Probably the 1940's
Locale: Madras, India
First published: 1965

Principal characters:
ADAMS, the narrator and central character, an Englishman working in Madras, India
STANTON, a friend with whom he shares quarters
SHANKRAN, an Indian lawyer
HOLT, the assistant commissioner
SIR ALEC, Adams's boss
DR. MENON, the company solicitor
KRISHNASWAMI, witness to the accident
TURPIN, a jockey and Krishnaswami's cohort

The Story

The flippant title of this story about an Englishman who seriously injures an Indian laborer in a drunken automobile accident is the first clue to its ironic social criticism. The very fact that the central character and narrator of the story calls such an accident merely "a bit of a smash" says more about the British arrogance and indifference to native Indians that led to the crumbling of the British Empire than do volumes of history or social commentary.

The story begins with the narrator's admission to his unidentified listener that he was so drunk when the accident occurred that he knew nothing about it until told about it by his roommate the next morning. His prejudicial attitude toward the Indians is made obvious when the police inspector arrives and the narrator identifies him as an Indian but a "nice chap" anyway. Adams's white acquaintances are equally indifferent to the feelings of native people. All are eager to "fix" things for him—his roommate, who buys off his bar bill so there will be no evidence that he was drunk; his drinking buddy, who pays for his bail; and his boss, who retains the company lawyer for him.

Native figures influenced by British rule fare no better in this story. Adams's first act is to retain an Indian lawyer whose main claim to fame is that he once defended an Englishman who crashed into a Muhammadan funeral, killing five; the lawyer was able to get for him a sentence of only three years. After Shankran the lawyer re-assures Adams not to worry, he goes off thinking that, except for his skin, Shankran is much whiter than many Englishmen in India. The one witness to the accident, Krishnaswami, is interested only in extorting money from Adams, but he masks this by insisting that he believes the caste system should be abolished and that all men are brothers, even the poor laborer who was injured. He tries to ingratiate himself with Adams by suggesting that he should play middleman and take money from Adams to give to the laborer's family.

The British influence on Indians is further criticized by Adams's description of the company lawyer, Menon, and Krishnaswami, who negotiate a deal about the amount of the proposed payoff, both talking in Oxford English and trying to outdo each other. Shankran, who corrupts the courts and witnesses, ironically accuses Menon of corruption when the company lawyer tells him to get as much out of Adams as possible. In fact, the entire story is a complex and distasteful web of corruption, prejudice, and indifference by Englishmen and English-educated Indians alike. The only time Adams himself shows any sign of regret for his injuring the Indian laborer is when he visits him in the hospital and sees the man's family weeping and wailing around his bedside. Adams's prejudice is so deep-seated, however, so much a part of the British attitude toward the Indians, that his telling his listener that he "bloody near wept himself" rings false.

By the time the actual trial comes up, after Shankran has postponed it by fixing Adams up with a false doctor's report that he has dysentery, Shankran has frightened off Krishnaswami, has bribed another witness, and has promised to pay off the Inspector, all the while cursing his Indian countrymen as being corrupt and thinking only of money. The final judgment of the trial judge is that Adams pay 350 rupees to the injured man as compensation and two hundred rupees to the court as a fine for not stopping after the accident. He also must pay the Inspector three hundred rupees as a bribe, as well as his lawyers' fees. Instead of being chastened by his experience, Adams goes on a drinking binge for a month, is finally fired by his boss (although he is given good references), and goes back to England. His last line shows how oblivious he is of the moral weakness of his character: "Don't know of any good jobs going, do you?"

Themes and Meanings

The social criticism leveled at the British influence in India, both in terms of white people's attitudes toward the Indian and in terms of British corruption of the educated Indians, is clear in this story. The Indian who is seriously injured by the drunken accident and who is reported close to death remains anonymous and in the background. There is no real concern for him as a human being; rather, he is merely a nuisance, the cause of the Englishman Adams's being in trouble. The only real issue at hand seems to be who is going to get paid off to get Adams off the hook.

The story paints a thoroughly distasteful picture of prejudice and indifference so deeply seated that those guilty of it are completely unaware. It is not that the central character, Adams, is a particularly bad man, although there is little to like about him, but rather that he at no time sees his responsibility; his only concern is to get things fixed. If he is the central figure of obliviousness to his own prejudice and thus the central ironic voice of the story, then his Indian counterpart is the lawyer Shankran who, even as he bribes and threatens others to win his cases, accuses his countrymen of being corrupt, ironically, for accepting the very bribes that he offers. The other corrupt figure who spouts talk of brotherhood and democracy, even as he tries to extort money from Adams under the guise of giving it to the injured man's family, is Krishnaswami, who carries a card identifying himself as the holder of an Oxford bachelor of arts. The company lawyer, Menon, also parades his Oxford degree and what Adams calls his BBC accent as a badge of superiority to his fellow countrymen.

Characteristic of the story is the word-of-mouth network among the Indians (what Krishnaswami calls "systems of communications" unknown to the Europeans) that makes it seem as though everyone is watching the unfolding of a corrupt series of events without surprise but only with a sense of inevitability. Everyone is an impostor here, from Krishnaswami, who pretends he is the son of a trade commissioner, to Shankran, who pretends he is "straight," to Adams himself, who poses as a "good bloke" who only had a bit of a smash that has made things somewhat messy but requires simply some "fixing" to make it all right. Money is the oil to smooth over whatever problems the "bit of a smash" has caused. The reader comes away from the story with a clearer understanding of the imperialist attitude that doomed British control in India.

Style and Technique

The single most significant aspect of the style and technique of "A Bit of a Smash in Madras" is the fact that it is told solely in the first-person voice by Adams in a sort of extended dramatic monologue. However, even though the story is presented as if it were told to someone orally, rather than written down, the listener is never really defined or directly referred to. This technique of allowing the central figure, a character who is oblivious to his moral culpability, to tell the story, is a typical device to serve the purpose of social satire and criticism. It is obvious that the issue of slavery is all the more horrifying in Mark Twain's *The Adventures of Huckleberry Finn* (1884) because it is so easily accepted by everyone in the novel, even Huck himself. Such a technique of allowing a morally oblivious character to tell his own story is often used as an effective means to allow the reader to make the moral judgment that the narrator himself cannot make.

The voice of Adams, revealing as it does his values and his attitude toward the Indians (even though he himself sees nothing extraordinary about it), is sufficient to condemn him in the eyes of the reader. His slang and idiom reveal him to be middle-class in the caste system that makes up British society, a fact he reveals further by his scorn for those Indians who have been to Oxford or who at least affect such Oxfordian airs. Adams respects only the lawyer Shankran but only for his ability to "fix things" and get people off the hook by his political pull and bribery.

The tone of the narrator convinces the reader that corruption and prejudice are so integral to British life in India that no one in the story questions it. It simply is the way things are. At the conclusion, when Adams asks his listener if he knows of any "good jobs going," there is no reply. To the reader, who has been a close listener to the voice of prejudice, arrogance, and indifference, the very offhandedness of the question is the final repulsive indication of Adams's moral obtuseness.

Charles E. May

BITTER HONEYMOON

Author: Alberto Moravia (1907-1990)
Type of plot: Psychological
Time of plot: An August during the early 1950's
Locale: Anacapri, Italy
First published: "Luna di miele, sole di fiele," 1952 (English translation, 1956)

> *Principal characters:*
> GIACOMO, the bridegroom
> SIMONA, his wife, a member of the Communist Party
> LIVIO, a work associate of Simona, also a communist

The Story

Giacomo found the first night of his honeymoon unsatisfactory. His wife had complained that she was tired and still suffering from the effects of the boat trip to Capri and had put him off. Now, on this second day of their marriage, she is as much a virgin as she was before. The thought of his failure to accomplish this prime marital responsibility preys on Giacomo's mind, as he and his wife, Simona, are walking along a path winding through a field on the heights of Anacapri. He looks around at this place that he has selected for his honeymoon with a jaundiced eye. Several months before, when he was here last, the air was clear and the fields were fresh with flowers; now the weather is sultry and oppressive, the fields have turned to dust.

He walks several paces behind her, reflecting on their relationship, a love match "based rather on the will to love than on genuine feeling." Giacomo, however, is convinced that his wife views him with physical repulsion and that she regrets being married. He would like to take possession of her with one, single, piercing glance, a technique that has served him well with other women, but he realizes his chances are not good. He tries to figure out what he had found in her that was so physically attractive. Her legs are long and skinny, and chaste, shiny, and cold; her breasts droop and seem like extraneous and burdensome weights.

When she complains that she is being made to walk ahead, Giacomo goes on ahead, brushing her breast with his elbow as he walks past her "to test his own desire." The path winds around the summit of Monte Solaro; it goes through stretches of vineyards before descending sharply toward the sea. His wife complains, "Have we far to go? It's so hot. . . . I wish we could go home." Giacomo promises that soon they will have a swim, and to pass the time, he gets her to recite some poetry. She chooses the third canto from Dante's *Inferno*. They pass a villa that once belonged to Axle Munthe, a very fashionable doctor practicing in Rome at the turn of the century. Giacomo tells his wife a story about one of Munthe's famous treatments. A woman came to him with all sorts of imaginary ailments. Munthe responded by telling her to look out the window; when her back was turned, he gave her a swift kick in the rear. Simona remarks that that is the way she should be treated because she is slightly crazy for having acted the way she did last night. She says that she was neither tired nor seasick but simply afraid, "afraid of the whole idea." She allows that she will have to grow accustomed to the idea, and remarks, "Tonight I'll be yours."

The promise is insufficient to cure Giacomo's doubts about her and about his own virility. He decides that her aloofness has something to do with her political beliefs. She is a communist, while he is "too much of an individualist." In fact, he has no interest in politics whatsoever, and the only thing that bothers him is "the fact that his wife did have such an interest." He taunts her by saying that if the communists ever came to power, she would inform against him. She tells him not to worry about something that does not exist. The fact that she did not categorically deny his charge confirms Giacomo's suspicions and makes him angry. He continues to blame her for how he feels.

They continue their walk, now going down the slope toward the water. Giacomo watches her run ahead of him and wonders what could be the importance of a political party when compared to the act of love. "And he was sure that in the moment he possessed Simona he would drive out of her every allegiance except that of love for him." Nevertheless, his jealousy of the party continues. They reach a small inlet, but their continued togetherness is prevented by the presence of one of Simona's young Communist Party associates, Livio, to whom Giacomo takes an instant dislike. Giacomo cannot tolerate the nonchalant way Livio and his wife talk with each other. It is not so much what they say, mostly small talk about various party workers and vacations, but the note of complicity with which it is said, the "tone of voice of two monks or two nuns meeting one another." He senses that Simona will escape him through her party connections, but he does not want to show his annoyance and explains his scowl to her as a result of the heat.

The two honeymooners soon go off toward the shelter of some rocks to change their clothes for a swim. The sight of Simona's naked body prompts him to suggest that they make love "right here and now," but she puts him off, again promising that tonight things will be different. They put on their swimming suits and go back to the basin to take a swim. Livio is still there, now sunning himself. Livio springs into action, suggesting that Simona race him over to a distant rock. They dive into the water and swim off. Giacomo does the same, but he is no match for their athleticism; as he struggles out of the water near a rock on which they are sitting, Livio suggests that they race back. Giacomo tries to restrain his anger as he follows.

When all three are together again, Simona serves lunch, which she shares with Livio. The conversation about party associations continues. Although Livio's observations are commonplace, Giacomo notices that his wife seems to like them. After they have eaten, Simona decides to take a sunbath, but she refuses to allow Livio to rest his head on her lap. Now Giacomo senses that she is beginning to pay some attention to him, however, and his spirits soar. Once more he believes that there is "a possibility of love between them." At his suggestion, she accompanies him on a stroll among the rocks. They go to a more private beach to sunbathe and she allows him to rest his head on her lap. He sleeps for about an hour. When he wakes up, the sky is dark and they have to hurry back to their villa before the rain starts. Livio is gone.

Before they arrive home, it starts to thunder. Simona confesses that lightning scares her to death. She runs on ahead, feeling safe only when she is inside and the door is shut. She immediately goes to the bedroom. He delays joining her, drinking a glass of white wine before he enters the bedroom. Now he goes to his wife, removes her dressing gown, and orders her into bed. He then takes off his own clothes and lies down next to her. He tries to arouse her with soft caresses, but these produce a strong desire to possess her, which he impulsively tries to do. His vigorous approach prompts a strong refusal on her part. He tries to prevail by force, but she fends him off. Finally, after a somewhat prolonged tussle, he loses his patience and gets up. He goes to the bathroom and cuts his finger with a razor blade. Returning to the bedroom, he smears blood from his wound on the sheets and announces to her that she is no longer a virgin. He shows her the bloodstained linen as evidence. She seems unsure, but when she sees his cut finger, she knows he is lying.

Giacomo goes into a rage. You will be a virgin forever, he shouts. He accuses her of always being hostile, of being closer to Livio than to him; he repeats that, if the party came to power, she would inform on him. These charges reduce her to tears; she sobs that she would rather die than inform on him. Still distraught, she gets up from the bed and goes over to the window. As she looks outside, the sky is suddenly illuminated with a flash of lightning, followed by the metallic-sounding crash of the thunderbolt. Simona returns to the bed, frightened, and throws herself into her husband's arms. While she is still weeping, he has sex with her. He feels his accomplishment is somehow comparable to the power of the sun. Later, though, he decides that nothing really was settled, but he is satisfied that she had said she would kill herself for him. That will do for the time being.

Themes and Meanings

Giacomo's relationship with his wife is shaped by his sense of what is proper. He believes that love, especially marital love, is above all an act of submission that begins with his wife letting him deflower her on their wedding night. The prescribed copulation has not been accomplished, and Giacomo is extremely bitter. The feelings of his wife matter little, whether she was tired, or seasick, or anxious, or terrified. Giacomo, brooding on the consequences of his failure, fears that his whole marriage was a mistake. To get even for this insult to his masculine pride, he begins to badger his wife, accusing her of not caring about him, taking her to task for her political beliefs, which he says could lead to his betrayal.

Giacomo's sexuality cannot be separated from his ingrained belief that sex is an instrument of male domination over women, a device for the achievement of total possession. A wife is there for constant reassurance that the husband is the only person who matters. Livio is therefore immediately seen as a threat. Livio is part of his wife's life to which Giacomo has not, and probably will not, be able to gain entrance. The shoptalk of Simona and Livio appears conspiratorial and sinister. Giacomo's resentment of Livio is increased because Livio is also a symbol of the very virility that

Giacomo apparently lacks. Giacomo sees Livio as "a bronze statue on a stone pedestal" and observes his "trunks pulled tightly over his voluminous pubis and all the muscles of his body standing out." These thoughts continue to plague him. Livio, he decides, is "the sort of a fellow that goes in for purposeful tanning, and then wanders about showing it off, wearing skimpy tights designed to exhibit his virility as well." Livio is a worse menace because he comes from the working class, while Giacomo is bourgeois. Giacomo, preoccupied with Livio, worries that his wife will renege on her promise to give herself to him.

When the moment of truth finally comes, Giacomo's wife does refuse to go through with it. This prompts Giacomo to stain the wedding sheets with his own blood. If he cannot have the reality, he will at least have the appearance of reality. His wife refuses to cooperate in his subterfuge. Thanks to the timely intervention of the night storm, she allows herself to be "penetrated." In the aftermath of his conquest, Giacomo glories in his accomplishment, with all the self-righteousness of a wife beater—which, in a sense, he is.

Style and Technique

As in many of his other stories, Alberto Moravia is concerned here with the twisted values of the Italian bourgeoisie. Giacomo, despite his pretensions to individualism, is a prisoner of his own class and a prisoner of his conception of the lower classes, to which he feels superior. The bloody sheet incident shows his determination to convince his wife that a ritual defloration has been accomplished, but it also shows that Giacomo is little different from a primitive peasant who hangs such evidence on the balcony the next morning to show off for the villagers.

Moravia tells the story, in his lean and sparse style, from the standpoint of Giacomo. In doing so, he more effectively reveals the devastation that Giacomo visits on his wife. Through his eyes, the reader sees Simona's anxiety turn into guilt and her guilt into doubt of her own sanity and thoughts of suicide. The reader observes her attempting to escape, through petulance, by conversation with Livio, and with physical resistance. All are unsuccessful. Moravia uses Giacomo to show the vapidity of the Italian middle class, especially in its tendency to view people as property. Giacomo's alienation with his wife is presented as a disease that probably will never be healed.

Part of the problem lies in humankind's inability to establish a proper relationship with the natural world. In "Bitter Honeymoon," this failure is symbolically rendered in Moravia's descriptions of nature, his use of climate to establish mood, his depiction of natural surroundings to reflect the characters' attitudes: "the odours of meadows and sea had given way to those of scorched stone and dried dung." The relationship of the story's characters to nature is most effectively dramatized in the account of the storm, which links fear and sexuality. The thunderstorm becomes a *deus ex machina*, but the release it produces is as transitory as the tempest itself; humanity is linked to nature but forever estranged.

Wm. Laird Kleine-Ahlbrandt

BLACAMÁN THE GOOD, VENDOR OF MIRACLES

Author: Gabriel García Márquez (1928-   )
Type of plot: Picaresque
Time of plot: The mid-twentieth century
Locale: The Caribbean coast of Colombia
First published: "Blacamán el bueno vendedor de milagros," 1972 (English translation, 1984)

Principal characters:
BLACAMÁN THE BAD, a sadistic huckster
BLACAMÁN THE GOOD, the narrator and disciple of Blacamán the Bad

The Story

Blacamán the Good relates how he came to know and work for Blacamán the Bad, an itinerant confidence man who, dressed in flamboyant and preposterous garb, would sell all manner of things to the unsuspecting villagers in the north Colombian province of La Guajira. In the first scene the narrator describes in grotesque detail how Blacamán the Bad feigns a poisonous snakebite in order to sell a supposedly effective antidote. The curative illusion is so convincing that, in addition to selling out his entire stock to the naïve townspeople, Blacamán the Bad manages to deceive the admiral of the United States naval fleet, anchored offshore, into purchasing the elixir as well. Most noteworthy in this first encounter with the charlatan is his incessant, eerie laugh and his self-serving, demagogic rhetoric.

Blacamán the Bad offers to adopt Blacamán the Good as his protégé, ostensibly because of "the foolish look on my face." After a flurry of wisecracks designed to impress his new master, Blacamán the Good confesses in earnest that his desire in life is to become a fortune-teller. At first, because he is an utter failure at knowing the present, much less the future, and because the two Blacamáns must flee the navy's attempts at revenge for the credulous admiral's death, they undergo considerable hardship. Later, for his role in their travails, Blacamán the Good is subjected to various forms of mental and physical torture. When Blacamán the Bad taunts the starving victim with a dead rabbit, however, Blacamán the Good loses his temper and throws the animal against a wall. To his surprise, the cadaver regains life and walks back through the air to the budding magus.

From this point on, Blacamán the Good, a real wizard rather than the sham his master was, has nothing but good fortune. He sets out on his own and plays to overflow crowds all along the coast. He becomes a successful entrepreneur, with a chain of shops that sell curios and souvenirs designed to foster his own legend. He owns a chauffer-driven car, silk shirts, topaz teeth, and lotions imported from the Orient. At the peak of his glory he declares, "What I am is an artist." When Blacamán the Bad finally reappears, pathetic and decrepit, Blacamán the Good refuses to save him from his own venomous potion. Instead, he takes revenge on his former master by burying him in his own carnival trunk and resuscitating him periodically so the old sadist can suffer for as long as the miracle worker lives: that is, forever.

Themes and Meanings

Although this fable evokes several themes of no little import, among which figure death, solitude, memory, hunger, imperialism, and revenge, none falls outside the framework or escapes the subsuming power of the motif of deception. The story ultimately is about the illusion it manifests itself to be. As a self-proclaimed artist, and in contrast to the angelically pure figure of the artist Gabriel García Márquez portrayed in "La prodigiosa tarde de Baltazar" ("Baltazar's Marvellous Afternoon"), Blacamán represents the dark or demonic side of artistic creation. He is a miniature version of Melquiades, the gypsy sage who foreordains the fate of the Buendia clan in *Cien anos de soledad* (1967; *One Hundred Years of Solitude*, 1970), the masterpiece generally recognized as most responsible for García Márquez's receiving the Nobel Prize in Literature in 1982. The only thing "good" about the character so named (and naming, or rather misnaming, is an important component in elaborating a fiction)—what distinguishes him from his mentor and antagonistic namesake—is his self-revelation as a creator of simulacra. In other respects, he is every bit as rancorous, hypocritical, and sadistic as Blacamán the Bad. There is a point, in fact, where they undergo a peripeteia and reverse roles by repeating each other's gestures in only slightly altered form. Whereas the Bad laughs ceaselessly at the outset, it is the Good who enjoys the last laugh in the end. The suffering inflicted on the Good in the early going is reflected in the eternal anguish to which the Bad is ultimately condemned, and the claims of philanthropic motives amid real putrefaction of the one are emphatically reiterated in the other. "Blacamán the Good, Vendor of Miracles" is an imaginative and morbid reflection on the falsification inherent in baroque art in general and writing in particular.

The chief deception perpetrated in the story is on the reader, represented by the defunct American admiral who perishes for credulously "swallowing" the illusion whole. The reader is tempted to do the same because Blacamán, who introduces himself as "the Good" and recounts numerous hoaxes carried out by his supposedly more perverse counterpart, sets the reader up, so to speak, to be favorably disposed toward the accusing voice. Whereas Blacamán the Bad's antics are termed "incredible," Blacamán the Good claims that his tale "has nothing to do with invention." Once the reader's trust is gained, the narrator proceeds to incorporate truly unbelievable elements (he claims to remember things that happened more than a century ago as if they were last Sunday and eventually reveals himself as everlasting, for example) with cunning casualness. Once the reader realizes the essential continuity between the two Blacamáns (or that they are merely aspects of the same dissimulating entity), it becomes plain that all the preceding has the ontological status of a mirage. If the story is disingenuous, however, its telling is undeniably authentic. Therein lies the truth value of this adroit narrative sleight of hand.

The figure of Blacamán harkens back to the Spanish *picaro*, a young rogue who portrayed himself as living on the margins of society, avoiding conventional work, and postponing starvation by serving a series of masters. The picaresque novel, whose prototype is the anonymous autobiographical narrative *Lazarillo de Tormes* (1553), placed a concave mirror before the nether strata of a rapidly changing society in the Spanish Renaissance and Baroque periods. The results were often shocking exposés of conditions and practices, which the *picaro* condemned and, quite significantly, emulated. In the graphic depiction of a grotesque reality, García Márquez is remarkably faithful to the picaresque tradition, but there is more. Blacamán the Good charges the United States Navy with the wanton annihilation of Native Colombians, Africans, Chinese, and Hindus in seeking retribution for the death of their leader. However, his parting gesture is an act of vengeance perhaps more severe in its cruelty. American military and cultural hegemony is one of the author's most ardently repeated themes—in *El otoño del patriarca* (1975; *The Autumn of the Patriarch*, 1975) the despotic leader has to sell the Caribbean Sea to the Americans in order to dissolve the nation's onerous foreign debt. In an act of admirable artistic integrity, however, García Márquez shows that no one, not even a surrogate author such as Blacamán the Good, is above reproach.

Style and Technique

As is the case with master and slave, Blacamán the Good and Blacamán the Bad are doubles. They are contrary facets, ultimately undistinguishable, of the same malicious process or phenomenon ("malicia" in Spanish means, among other things, "duplicity"): art. Their lack of a discrete personal identity is reinforced technically in the story by the use of a "floating" point of view. The voice of Blacamán the Bad is embedded in the narration of Blacamán the Good, with no quotation marks to set them apart, as in the following passage:

> From the first Sunday I saw him he reminded me of a bullring mule, . . . except that at that time he wasn't trying to sell any of that Indian mess but was asking someone to bring him a real snake so that he could demonstrate on his own flesh an antidote he had invented, *the only infallible one, ladies and gentlemen, for the bites of serpents, tarantulas, and centipedes plus all manner of poisonous mammals* [italics, to signify the voice of Blacamán the Bad, not in the original].

There is thus not one "point" from which the narration originates but a field in which it circulates. Blacamán the Bad's voice is within Blacamán the Good's, just as the opportunism and rancor of the one informs the other. In addition, the hyperbolic rhetoric of the sideshow barker, a style that runs through all of "Los funerales de la Mama Grande" ("Big Mama's Funeral") and which Blacamán the Good adopts when he assumes the mantle of vendor of miracles, sustains the tension between appearance and reality.

The last device worth noting is the multiple use of memory. Memory, of course, is the key to all narration of events in the past. Special attention is drawn to the act of re-membering in the story when the narrator claims to recall a scene from more than a century previous as clearly as if it had happened the week before. As the anecdote de-velops, memory becomes essential to the characters' survival, for when they are alone and starving, they use nostalgia as a means of fooling death. As a businessperson, Blacamán the Good panders to the tourists' memories ("souvenirs" in French). More-over, the desired effect of the narrator's vengeful coup depends on memory, for Blacamán the Bad's sentence is to live interred forever and to remember why. It is, fi-nally, Blacamán the Good's memory of his evil double's discomfiting recollections that makes his revenge so sweet.

Jonathan Tittler

THE BLACK CAT

Author: Edgar Allan Poe (1809-1849)
Type of plot: Psychological
Time of plot: The mid-nineteenth century
Locale: An unnamed American city
First published: 1843

> *Principal characters:*
> THE NARRATOR, an educated man and animal lover turned
>   alcoholic, ailurophobe, and murderer
> HIS WIFE, sensitive and silent-suffering
> PLUTO, the couple's first pet black cat
> A SECOND BLACK CAT, one-eyed, which is adopted by the couple

The Story

   Told in the first person by an unreliable narrator (a term designating one who either consciously or unconsciously distorts the truth), the story can be seen to be divided into two parts, each of which builds toward a climactic physical catastrophe: in the first part, the narrator's mutilation and later murder of a favorite pet, as well as a fire that destroys all he and his wife own; in the second part, the narrator's ax murder of his wife, followed by his arrest and death sentence.

   Opening with both suspense and mystery in his revelation that he wants to "unburden" his soul because he will die the next day, the narrator gives details (with unwitting ironic ramifications) of his early love for animals and marriage to a woman of the same sentiments, who presents him with many pets. Among these is his favorite, a black cat, whose name, Pluto (Greek god of the underworld), foreshadows the narrator's descent into the murky regions of alcoholism, self-deception, and violence.

   When he does later succumb to alcoholism, the narrator shortly thereafter begins maltreating his wife and pets, which gives a double meaning to his term for drinking, "Fiend Intemperance," referring not only to alcohol abuse but also to intemperate transgression of rational thought and behavior. Eventually the narrator maltreats "even Pluto" (which implies that the cat was valued more than his wife, whom he has maltreated earlier). One night, presumably out of frustration, he seizes the cat, which has been avoiding him. When it bites him, the narrator says he became "possessed" by a "demon" and with his pocket knife cut out one of the cat's eyes. At first grieved and then irritated by the consequences of his action, the narrator says that he was then "overthrown" by "the spirit of PERVERSENESS" (author's capitalization), Edgar Allan Poe's definition of which anticipates by a half century psychologist Sigmund Freud's concepts of the id (unconscious desires to do all things, even wrongs, for pleasure's sake) and the death wish (the impulse within all for self-destruction). The "spirit of PERVERSENESS" causes the narrator, even while weeping, to hang Pluto in a neighboring garden. That night a fire destroys his house and all his worldly wealth, and the next day the narrator discovers on the only wall that remains standing the raised gigantic image on its surface of a hanged cat.

His alcoholism continuing, the narrator one night at a disreputable tavern discovers another black cat, which he befriends and adopts (by implication making a substitution out of guilt and remorse), as does his wife. For this double (a frequent motif in Poe's works), however, the narrator rapidly develops a loathing. First, it has only one eye, which reminds him of his crimes against Pluto. Second, it is too friendly—an ironic inversion of the common complaint that cats are too aloof, as the narrator complained about Pluto. Third, it has a white patch on its breast that to the guilty narrator's imagination looks more and more like a gallows, which points both backward to his hanging of Pluto and, unknown to him, forward to his hanging for the murder of his wife.

One day, with his wife on an errand into the cellar of their decrepit old house, the narrator, infuriated when he is almost tripped on the stairs by the cat, starts to kill it with an ax, is stopped by his wife, and then instead kills her with the ax. With insane calmness and ratiocination, the narrator concocts and implements a plan of concealing the corpse in a cellar wall. Meanwhile, the cat, which has tormented his dreams, has vanished, allowing him to sleep—despite his wife's murder. Inquiries are made about his missing wife, however, and on the fourth day after the murder, the police come for a thorough search. As they are about to leave the cellar, the narrator, apparently with taunting bravado but really with unconscious guilt that seeks to delay them so he may be arrested and punished, remarks to them on the solidity of the house's walls, rapping with a cane the very spot of the concealed tomb. When a horrible scream is emitted from the wall, the police break down the bricks, discover the corpse with the black cat howling on its head, and arrest the criminal. Rationalizing to the end, the narrator blames the cat for his misdeeds and capture: "the hideous beast whose craft had seduced me into murder, and whose informing voice had consigned me to the hangman."

Themes and Meanings

The story has many themes, most of them relating to human psychology and several in the form of contraries: reason versus the irrational; human being versus animal; self-knowledge versus self-deception; sanity versus madness; love versus hate; good versus evil; the power of obsession and guilt; and the sources or motives of crime. As in many of his works, Poe is interested in the borderline between opposites and how it may be crossed.

Despite the narrator's explicit claim of sanity in the story's first paragraph, he immediately shows himself self-deceived by terming his story "a series of mere household events." Further, by the end of the first paragraph the narrator has circled to a contradictory position by expressing his hope for a calmer, more logical, and "less excitable" mind than his own to make sense of the narrative. A favorite adjective of his for pets, "sagacious," which he uses early in the story for both dogs and his cat Pluto, thus ironically indicates the wisdom he himself needs both to see life clearly and not to give in to the irrationality of drinking or violent behavior. What should distinguish man from beast—this is, the faculty of reason—the narrator too frequently abandons, a weakness expressed in the animal metaphor of his "rabid desire to say something easily" to the police searchers.

His early reference to admiring the "unselfish and self-sacrificing love" of animals reveals the narrator's blindness; ironically, his scornful words, "the paltry friendship and gossamer fidelity of mere *Man*" (author's italics), apply to himself. The narrator later reveals that his dipsomania is self-indulgent and self-loving because he "grew . . . regardless of the feelings of others" and dimly perceived that he had lost the "humanity of feeling" (compassion) that his wife retained.

Sheer emphasis or proportion in the story—the great number of words he spends on the cats contrasted with the brevity of his remarks about the maltreatment and murder of his wife—indicates the deficiency in both the narrator's insight and his feelings. He cannot see that guilt causes him to forestall mentioning his greatest misdeed until the story's end, while his feeling for his wife was too weak to prevent his murdering her. The narrator cannot see that his killing her is not a mere deflection from his murderous purpose, but its true aim, whose motives are laid down in the sixth, sixteenth, eighteenth, and twenty-second paragraphs of the story. Mutely representing goodness, she has been a constant irritant to him, one on whom he can vent all of his pent-up feelings in one blow.

Style and Technique

Besides the narrator's ironic self-contradiction or unwitting irony, Poe's other most pervasive technique in the story is symbolism. Symbols of perception include the narrator's particular mutilation of Pluto, for like his pet, the narrator is half-blind, not only in the past, in the story he relates, but also in the present, when he still cannot understand what it all means. In the past he was half-blinded by drink, and in both the past and present by guilt, rationalizing, or unwillingness to see unpleasant things. For example, though he claims to have been "half stupefied" when he first became aware of the second black cat, only a consuming if unacknowledged sense of guilt can explain his asserted failure to notice that it was one-eyed until after it was home, despite his prior continued petting of it in the tavern and detailed notice of its markings. He wanted an exact substitute, with the same injury, in order to punish himself. The words "half'" "equivocal," and "blindly," which the narrator applies to himself at various times, reveal his defective vision.

Symbols of rationality and its defeat can be found in the narrator's horrible act of burying the ax in his wife's "brain"—a word that emphasizes thinking more than the word "skull" would. In this act, the narrator has in effect extinguished his own rationality, as well as its chief human representative in his sphere. Further, when the brick wall is broken down, the black cat is found perched on the corpse's head, one more indication of the narrator's guilt (recalling the site of the wound) and its cause.

Among the symbols of "humanity of feeling" is the second cat's marking. It has, in the narrator's phrasing, "a large, although indefinite splotch of white, covering nearly the whole region of the breast." Moreover, the cat has, the narrator says, a habit of "fastening its long claws in my dress" to "clamber, in this manner, to my breast." Finally, the cat will not let him sleep; he awakens with it on his chest: "its vast weight [was] . . . incumbent on my *heart!*" (Poe's italics). The repeated references to "bosom" "breast," and especially "heart" point to the narrator's fatal deficiency of love and compassion.

Finally, several strands of symbols help express the conflict between good and evil. The very scene of the crime, a cellar, recalls the suggestive name of the narrator's first black cat and represents the narrator's descent into the darkness of irrationality, the forces of the unconscious mind, and evil. Comparable imagery of spirited darkness can be found in the narrator's recollection that, prior to the murder, "the darkest and most evil thoughts" had become habitual to him; in like manner, he refers to his wife's murder as "my dark deed." The interrelation between consciousness and conscience is suggested by the narrator's keeping his wife's corpse in this dark underworld, after walling her off—analogues of psychological repression.

Finally, the cat's howl in response to the narrator's rapping of the wall is described in symbolic terms: It begins as a muffled cry, "like the sobbing of a child," but quickly swells into a "continuous scream . . . such as might have arisen only out of hell, conjointly from the throats of the damned in their agony and of the demons that exult in the damnation." In capsule form, this utterance describes the whole of the narrator's life—and death.

Norman Prinsky

BLACK IS MY FAVORITE COLOR

Author: Bernard Malamud (1914-1986)
Type of plot: Psychological
Time of plot: The late 1950's
Locale: New York City
First published: 1963

> *Principal characters:*
> NATHAN LIME, the narrator and protagonist, a forty-four-year-old Jewish liquor merchant in Harlem
> ORNITA HARRIS, his estranged girlfriend, an African American widow
> CHARITY QUIETNESS, his black cleaning woman
> BUSTER WILSON, an African American neighbor boy during Nat's childhood

The Story

Nat Lime, a Jewish liquor dealer in Harlem, is searching for understanding, trying to explain his attraction to African Americans. He begins his monologue by describing his cleaning woman, the kind but puzzling Charity Quietness. He addresses an imaginary audience from his Brooklyn three-room apartment, where he has lived alone since his mother died. On his day off from his liquor store, he eats lunch in his kitchen while his black maid eats in the bathroom.

Although Nat jokes about this absurdity, he is hurt by Charity's refusal to join him and says that the rejection is her choice. He has offered to let her eat in the kitchen alone, but she prefers lunching in the bathroom. On an earlier occasion she accepted his offer but could not finish her meal. For nearly two years now she has eaten alone in the bathroom. Anticipating his audience's objections to this point, Nat says, "If there's a ghetto, I'm the one that's in it." As a Jew he has a historical right to define the ghetto, even though his joke implies a more contemporary definition of the word: the urban areas containing large concentrations of minorities.

With Charity, as with the other black people, Nat's attempt to develop an individual relationship fails, leading him to consider contemporary racial issues. His characteristic response to anything is to analyze it, and he tries to place his personal experiences within a larger context. In his defense, he offers two illustrations of his "fate with colored people." The first is the memory of his attempt to befriend Buster, a twelve-year-old black boy whose neighborhood bordered Nat's in prewar Brooklyn. Both were poor. Nat's father, a garment worker, died when Nat was only thirteen, and his mother sold paper bags on the street until she was stricken with cancer. At ten Nat was obsessed with the differences between his and Buster's neighborhoods, and he fantasized about them.

His clumsy attempts at closeness led only to one visit to the black family's home. This was Nat's introduction to a worse poverty than his, and he found it repellant. Buster rejected Nat's friendship, leaving Nat puzzled and feeling guilty about having stolen money from his mother to buy movie tickets for Buster and himself. After receiving many gifts, Buster ended their encounters by surprising Nat with a punch in the mouth. Buster's accompanying personal and racial slurs bewildered Nat, who had felt a kinship with him. Asking what made him deserve such treatment, Nat received no answer. Even at forty-four, Nat does not accept the idea that gifts might be considered bribes instead of tokens of friendship. He tries to make a joke about his own ignorance of Buster's evident dislike of movies.

Aside from his late mother, Ornita Harris, a black woman, is the only love of Nat's life. At first, Ornita ignores him when he picks up her glove on the street. Later, when she buys liquor at his store, he recognizes her and gives her a discount. She is cautious about his overtures, being skeptical of "white men trying to do me favors." After Ornita becomes a regular customer who receives discounts, she eventually goes out with Nat.

As Nat describes their romance, obstacles to interracial relationships and his complex attitude toward black people dominate his story. This Jewish merchant who operates a liquor store in Harlem with "colored clerks" wants to see himself merely as a man trying to romance a woman. Ornita, however, is constantly aware of society's barriers as she falls in love. After their dates, she insists on taking taxis home, but when a taxi strike forces them to ride the subway and then to walk home, they are assaulted and robbed by three black youths as a kind of punishment. Nat's attempted explanation of his respect for black people only makes matters worse.

Eventually Nat's interest in Ornita moves from curiosity to genuine love. His marriage proposal, however, forces her to leave without saying good-bye. When her brother reveals her departure without plans to return, Nat is struck nearly senseless. As he painfully makes his way home, he tries to help a blind black man cross the street and is overpowered by a neighborhood woman who misunderstands his motives. Once again Nat opens himself to physical and psychological pain.

Themes and Meanings

A product of its time, Bernard Malamud's story poses a universal question. He published it between the time of the Montgomery, Alabama, bus boycott of 1955 and the passing of the federal Civil Rights Act in 1964. It thus appeared during America's transition from Jim Crow laws to the legal assault on racial discrimination. Although New York was then considered racially free, or at least indifferent, prejudice was evident in daily behavior throughout the nation and reflected traditional attitudes. By allowing Nat to tell his story, Malamud forces readers to confront the ambiguities and complexities influencing personal relationships in modern American life. Racial stereotypes still exist in these characters' minds. Even Nat, who sincerely believes he is not prejudiced, reveals ingrained attitudes through his language and his unintended condescension toward African Americans.

In order to highlight the lack of understanding in racial matters, Malamud holds a mirror up to urban society so that it can face a harsh reality. Stereotypes and fears remain operative although individuals seek to eradicate them. Nat, for example, is unaware that as a Jewish liquor dealer located in Harlem he represents the kind of exploitation that blacks feel powerless to combat. In their automatic response to Nat, the black youths damage their community and reinforce stereotypes. Only Ornita is willing to risk a personal relationship, and even she is eventually defeated.

The title "Black Is My Favorite Color" becomes especially poignant by the end of the story. The protagonist's fixation on blackness illustrates a much-discussed Jewish identification with African Americans and their shared experience of persecution. Although Nat does not seem interested in Jewish observances, he is reminded of his ethnicity in brutal ways. Can he move beyond this condition in order to search for the good? The story ends with such a display of Nat's naïveté that the reader sees that his self-image is still intact. Readers are left with the question of whether Nat will conform to suit society or society will adapt to the reality of his search for human unity.

Thus, Malamud leaves the reader with an enduring human question: Is there a place in society for a man who continues optimistically to search for truth? Or is society correct in judging such a man as stubborn and unwilling to face facts?

Style and Technique

The story is the monologue of a first-person narrator, related in a conversational style with some humor. Nat intentionally tells the reader everything he knows in a tone that varies from self-deprecating and joking to defensive, passionate, or matter of fact. He is unaware, however, of how much he unintentionally reveals about himself and of how certain of his weaknesses dominate, placing his good intentions in the background.

As a convincing and largely credible narrator, Nat describes in realistic detail the New York that visitors expect and fear—a city in which youths rob liquor stores, innocent people are mugged, landlords squeeze money out of their ghetto tenants, and altruism is suspect. The focus is on the black ghetto, seen by an outsider, a Jew who is himself similarly stereotyped by the larger society.

The naïve, even unrealistic suggestion of color in the title becomes a metaphor for the racial identification that dominates the story's images. Just as blackness in a literal sense hinders vision and therefore calls for contrast, contrast between black people and white people becomes Malamud's technique for connecting plot with theme. Most of the story's episodes build around contrasting views generated by racial differences; in one way or another, each episode represents a larger societal issue. Images of blood parallel those of blackness and are equally powerful in conveying the philosophical issue undergirding the story: Nat's growing awareness of "one human color . . . the color of blood."

With these techniques, an apparently rambling personal reminiscence is transformed into a skillfully controlled journey toward a universal human truth.

Emma Coburn Norris

THE BLACK MADONNA

Author: Muriel Spark (1918-   )
Type of plot: Social realism
Time of plot: The 1960's
Locale: Whitney Clay, a fictitious English town
First published: 1967

>   *Principal characters:*
>   LOU PARKER, a housewife with no children
>   RAYMOND PARKER, her husband
>   ELIZABETH, her widowed sister
>   TINA, her friend
>   OXFORD ST. JOHN and
>   HENRY PIERCE, two black Jamaicans who befriend the Parkers

The Story

A Madonna figure carved from bog oak is placed in the Church of the Sacred Heart. Its black composition and angular lines make it an object of attention as well as worship in the growing English town of Whitney Clay.

Lou Parker and her husband Raymond are an apparently happily married—though childless—couple who live comfortably in their Whitney Clay apartment. They have cultivated their tastes in an aristocratic manner that they feel sets them apart from their middle-class acquaintances. As Roman Catholics, they are troubled about their lack of offspring, but they are active church members and participate in several guilds and confraternities with fellow members and friends.

Lou prides herself on cultivating aristocratic sensibilities, but the narrator regards her not as snobbish but only "sensible." When Raymond's automobile factory hires some Jamaican workers, the couple befriend two of them, Oxford St. John and Henry Pierce. The Parkers delight in their "equal" friendship with the black men and even take Henry with them on a family vacation to London, where they visit Lou's impoverished widowed sister. Lou, Raymond, and Henry are appalled at the conditions in which Lou's sister and her eight children live. However, when Henry attempts to compare the "slum mentality" of Lou's sister Elizabeth with folks in Jamaica, Lou is offended and insists that no comparisons can be made. After all, Lou thinks to herself, Elizabeth is white. Moreover, Elizabeth is not completely destitute because Lou faithfully sends her sister a pound each week.

Lou's enthusiasm for her friendship with the two Jamaicans soon wanes. Oxford seems too common and Henry too coarse. Meanwhile, the reputation of the Black Madonna in the local church increases. The Parkers learn that penitents who approach the unusual icon have their prayers answered and are granted requests. In particular, childless couples have in some cases been blessed with children. Eventually the

Parkers experience the power of the Madonna. After Lou prays to be rid of Oxford, the Jamaican announces his plans to move to Manchester. Lou's prayers for Henry's welfare are also granted. Buoyed by the apparent efficacy of petitions to the Black Madonna, Lou asks Raymond to join her in prayer for a child. After fifteen years of marriage, however, Raymond is no longer anxious for parenthood and suspects that Lou is more interested in testing the Madonna than in gaining a family. Lou wins him over by arguing that God will not give them a child if they are not "meant to have one."

Lou's eventual pregnancy attests the effectiveness of the couple's prayers to the Madonna—until their daughter is born. The baby is black, so they reject it. Perhaps, the narrator suggests, it is risky for one to get what she prays for.

Themes and Meanings

Muriel Spark delights in exposing the foibles of human nature. In "The Black Madonna" she employs elements of her own Roman Catholic faith to reveal the hypocrisy of Lou Parker and her husband. Although Raymond and Lou view themselves as "progressive" and open-minded in accepting Oxford and Henry as their equals, Spark uncovers their prejudices. The Parkers lack true Christian charity at all levels. Lou, it appears, merely practices acts of benevolence and prayer for selfish ends, such as using her friendship with the Jamaicans to prove to others how accepting she is of those who are "different." She uses the weekly pound that she sends to her poor sister to make herself feel charitable. Finally, she attempts to use her prayers to the Black Madonna to provide what she thinks she wants. In each case Spark unmasks the self-centered motive behind Lou's outwardly unselfish behavior.

The rejection of the infant at the close of the story gives weight to Spark's theme. The reader understands the embarrassment the Parkers must feel. Their friendship with the black men creates suspicion in everyone's mind, including Raymond's. Did Oxford or Henry father the child? Lou's insistent denials of impropriety offer no remedy for her shock and embarrassment. Consequently, the couple's shame is magnified when Lou's sister Elizabeth confirms that their cousins also had dark skins—a fact suggesting there is black blood in Lou's ancestry. The child symbolizes the Parkers' humiliation; it is impossible for them to see it as God's answer to their prayers. Their rejection of the baby amplifies the shallowness of their religious faith.

The linkages between "The Black Madonna" and Spark's own Christian world view are evident. Lou's priest tells her that as a Christian she must accept suffering, but Lou replies that she cannot be expected to "go against [her] nature." Therefore she resists personal sacrifice and renounces the child instead. Unlike the Virgin Mary, Lou is unwilling to rear a child whose origins are suspect or whose life may bring suffering and humiliation as did Christ's. In contrast to the Madonna, Lou is an unholy mother; unwilling to suffer, refusing to sacrifice, she rejects the gift for which she prayed.

Style and Technique

Neither cluttered nor verbose, Spark's prose emphasizes dialogue and action. Spark often employs a detached tone in her fiction that creates a distance between the reader and her characters. Such distance makes it possible for the reader to evaluate the words and deeds of the protagonists without feeling sympathy for them. In "The Black Madonna," the narrator adopts a satiric tone, for example, insisting that Lou is not a "snob"; however, Lou's behavior clearly reveals otherwise. Similarly, Raymond's disowning of the child is revealed through his actions. He smashes the cot he has made for the infant and insists that blood tests be performed to rule out the possibility that another man is the baby's father.

Spark assembles her short-story plots carefully; accordingly she employs a series of parallels in the structure of "The Black Madonna." First she emphasizes the contrast of the exterior and the interior, reinforcing the discrepancy between the characters' religious practices and their deeds. The Black Madonna is a "new" statue carved from "old" bog oak. In the same way Whitney Clay is expanding from its old village limits to a sprawling new industrial town. From these exteriors, Spark moves to a description of the Parkers' apartment in the new part of town. The couple's exterior seems attractive as well. However, the life the Parkers have carved for themselves contains nothing new. Their Roman Catholic beliefs have not given them new natures. On the contrary, they harbor old prejudices and ignorance. Even Lou's "common" friend Tina insists that if the child were hers, she would "never part with her." Tina's genuine response contrasts with Lou's self-deception and moral imbalance.

The story is framed with parallel references to the Madonna and the child. It begins by describing the statue and closes with the rejection of the Parkers' child. After the child is born, the Madonna is no longer mentioned. Both figures are the objects of attention. Penitents and admirers come to view the statue, and in the same way, nurses in the hospital gather continually around the black child while ignoring the cries of the white infants. The baby is described as "perfect," "lovely," and "beautiful."

In addition, Spark's use of names adds to the ironic humor of her tale. Lou selects Thomas and Mary as possible names for her unborn child. After the baby's birth, Elizabeth tells her that their mutual cousins Tommy and Mary were dark skinned with "nigro" hair. Thus, Lou inadvertently chooses the same names for her child as those used by throwbacks to her black ancestry. When Lou decides that Mary is too common for a first name and selects "Dawn," Raymond complains that Dawn is not a Christian name but lets Lou have her way. Ironically the child Dawn Mary lives up to her name by shedding light on the Parkers' inability to love.

Spark's short fiction combines elements of humor and drama in plots that reflect moral truth. "The Black Madonna" demonstrates the danger of self-deception and Spark's distaste for hypocrisy. The Madonna's power to answer prayers can be viewed as an opportunity to extend either revenge or redemption to the Parkers. Spark's characters thus reside in realms that are simultaneously natural and supernatural, and both forces are at work in the plot to bring knowledge or enlightenment to characters and readers alike.

Paula M. Miller

THE BLACK PRINCE

Author: Shirley Ann Grau (1929-   )
Type of plot: Fantasy
Time of plot: Probably the mid-twentieth century
Locale: The American South
First published: 1953

Principal characters:
STANLEY ALBERT THOMPSON, the Black Prince of the story, a
mysterious, folklorish hero with supernatural powers
ALBERTA LACEY, a young black girl loved by Stanley
MAGGIE MARY EVANS, a young black girl who loves Stanley
WILLIE, a black bar owner who loves Alberta and hates Stanley

The Story

The emotions are so simple, primitive, and stark in this story that one realizes immediately that this tale is Shirley Ann Grau's attempt to create a legendary fantasy. The opening situates the story not only in the poorest part of the smallest and worst county in the state but also in a fairy-tale realm where the cows are wild and unmilked and the winters are short and cold. The characters, drawn simply and directly, also suggest the two-dimensional personages of a folktale romance. Alberta first appears walking down a country road proclaiming her superiority to the birds, and Stanley Albert Thompson appears out of nowhere, calling to her like some rare bird himself, claiming that he came straight out of the morning and that he saw her name in the fire.

Stanley Albert is the central figure in the story; his designation as the Black Prince, coupled with the quotation from Isaiah at the beginning of the story—"How art thou fallen from heaven, O Lucifer, son of the morning"—suggests that he is the Prince of Darkness. He is not so much an embodiment of pure evil, however, as he is the personification of the rebel, the outcast, the mysterious, powerful figure who arrives out of nowhere. As soon as he arrives in the small community (which does not even have a name on the map), he establishes his superiority by winning fights at the central gathering place, Willie's Bar. In these fights, in which razors, bottles, and knives are used, Stanley Albert gets a reputation that earns for him the fear and hatred of the men and the admiration and love of the women.

Stanley Albert's supernatural aura is established by his inexhaustible supply of silver coins—coins that he can shuffle through the air the way that other men shuffle cards and that never seem to run out, although Stanley Albert apparently does no work to earn the money. Primarily what Stanley Albert does is stir things up. Because the men are afraid to fight him, they begin to fight one another and thus rekindle a feud that has lain dormant for several years. All this action as a result of Stanley Albert's arrival seems quite aimless, for the Black Prince has no ostensible purpose either in being in the small crossroads or in creating such turbulent activity. The only event toward which the story seems to aim is Stanley Albert's finally gaining the girl for whom he has been waiting nearly all winter—the girl he met in the beginning of the story, Alberta.

Stanley Albert's wooing of Alberta (whose similarity of name is surely not coincidental) primarily consists of singing songs to her in which he promises to give her an apron full of gold if she will only let her hair hang low. Indeed, although he does not give her gold, he manifests his supernatural power by picking off gobs of wax from the candles in his house and flipping them to Alberta, making them turn into silver coins as they flash through the air. Their courtship is marked by obsessive passion and fraught with tension as the feud rages about them and as Willie (who loves Alberta) and Maggie Mary (who loves Stanley Albert) are filled with jealousy.

The story reaches its supernaturally tinged climax when Willie uses several silver coins that he has received from Stanley Albert to make four silver bullets, with which he shoots the Black Prince. Stanley Albert and Alberta disappear, to become legendary figures who continue to haunt the area, becoming the cause of evil acts and general bad luck, such as Willie's death and weevils getting in the cotton. Children still hear the jingle of silver in Stanley Albert's pocket and the women whisper together about the legendary couple whenever there is a miscarriage or a stillbirth.

Themes and Meanings

"The Black Prince," published originally under the title "The Sound of Silver," was Grau's first story to be published in a professional literary journal. When the collection of stories *The Black Prince, and Other Stories* appeared in 1955, it made quite an impression on both critics and the general public, selling out its first printing in two weeks. The title story of the collection, as is typical of many of Grau's short stories, hovers uneasily between mythic legend and simplistic melodrama. Thus, it is not easy to determine whether it is a serious experiment with archetypes of universal primitive experience, or whether it is simply a commercial exploitation of stereotypes of the American black experience. The story certainly depends on enough clichés about black life to be uncomfortable reading for readers in a post-civil rights era. The black characters in the story are driven by no other emotions than sexual desire and physical violence. The men drink, cut off ears with razors, and pursue women. The women get pregnant, have abortions, and continue to pursue the men.

Stanley Albert Thompson seems to embody the classic black male wish fulfillment, at least as seen from a white point of view. Although he never works, he has enough money to buy fancy clothes, sport an expensive watch and ring, drink, and attract women. He has a mysterious sexual aura that immediately intimidates and alienates the men, even as it acts as an aphrodisiac for the women. Regardless of the title's suggestion that he is Lucifer, he is less a demoniac figure than he is the embodiment of a man who, in the vernacular, is a "real devil."

Still, although the story makes use of unpalatable stereotypes about black life and values, it seems probable that Grau intended it to be a classically simple exploration of the most primitive human emotions, a kind of legendary folktale that embodies archetypes of love and lust, hate and violence. In some respects, the story is similar to the work of such southern women writers as Flannery O'Connor, Carson McCullers, and Eudora Welty, for it takes place less in a real world and time than in a season of dreams in which the ordinary is transformed into the mysterious and mythical. However, this similarity is less real than apparent.

One convinced of the seriousness and value of the story might argue that its theme focuses on elemental human emotions as basic as the song "Frankie and Johnnie," but as old as the nature of story itself. For those somewhat more skeptical, the story can be seen as simply an exploitation of the clichés of black life that tells nothing valuable about either the sociology of the black experience or the psychology of love and hate.

Style and Technique

Given the folktale plot of the story, the stylized nature of its technique seems inevitable. If the events seem somewhat melodramatic and simplistic, then the language of the story is that which attempts to dignify it, for Grau tries to give the story the simple dignity of the folklore ballad or classic tale. The language is controlled and balanced; it strives to create the illusion of an oral tale even though it has the formality of a written story. In style, as well as in character and plot, the story is reminiscent of such authors as McCullers and Welty but only as a facile imitation of writers whose stories are definitely superior in both their subtlety of theme and delicacy of tone.

Grau appeared on the American literary scene in the mid-1950's amid a flurry of predictions of great things to come. However, such a simplistic story of black life as "The Black Prince" was much more likely to be acceptable to readers in the mid-1950's than any time since; the fascination with the music of black culture was beginning to manifest itself in the birth of rock and roll music (although mostly made acceptable by being recorded by white artists) and much of American society was guilty, in that age of innocence and white conservatism, of unconscious racial prejudice. These factors combined to make "The Black Prince" an easily accepted confirmation of white suspicions about black life, even as it allowed white readers the mistaken sense that they understood that life.

Charles E. May

THE BLACK QUEEN

Author: Barry Callaghan (1937-   )
Type of plot: Psychological
Time of plot: The 1970's
Locale: Toronto, Canada
First published: 1981

> *Principal characters:*
> HUGHES, a costume designer
> McCRAE, his lover of ten years

The Story

 McCrae and Hughes are a male couple who have been living together for ten years. They are fastidious men and proud of their life together in their old colonial house surrounded by a pale blue picket fence. Although their neighborhood has undergone radical change over the decade, becoming a transient area with a multicultural population, McCrae and Hughes are acutely conscious of the significance of their elegant old house and lifestyle: "It gave them an embattled sense of holding on to something important, a tattered remnant of good taste in an area of waste overrun by rootless olive-skinned children." While their Eden has fallen into a wasteland condition, they see themselves as custodians of a bygone era of culture and beauty.

 The ten-year relationship has lost much of the early eroticism of their younger years. Their lives have become highly structured by the roles each has consciously and unconsciously adopted. Hughes is a successful costume designer, and McCrae spends much of his time attending to household duties and functioning as a "wife" and homemaker. One of the characteristics that initially had attracted Hughes to Mc-Crae was the Cuban heels McCrae wore and his lacquered nails. Hughes saw his role in their relationship as a husband and protector for the more domestic McCrae.

 This formerly happy couple is not getting along these days, principally because they are becoming dissatisfied with how quickly they are aging and the toll that this process is taking on both of them, although they avoid any overt reference to their dilemma. They are alarmed over their loosening thighs, bony feet, and yellowing toenails. They silently yearn for tenderness from each other over their melancholy entrance into rueful middle age. They feel lost and depressed in their separate bedrooms; they become embarrassed when they accidentally touch each other while having their bedtime cup of tea in the kitchen, as they had done for years, using their lovely green and white Limoges cups. They cannot bear their thinning wrists and sagging chins. They joke with each other about the possibility of bringing home a beautiful young man but are keenly aware that such behavior would constitute a serious betrayal of everything they believe has differentiated them from the "vulgar" crowd. Change, more than anything else, increasingly troubles and confuses them because they are becoming aware that they have no control over it.

The one area in their life that remains invulnerable to the ravages of time is their expensive stamp collection. It has become a symbol of their ability to transcend time and to regenerate and preserve their own unique Eden, in which things do not have to change, do not fall to decline and decay. They have refused to acquire many of the new stamps because they are crude and lack the refined and delicate qualities of their older stamps. Hughes would sometimes hold a stamp up to the light with his tweezers and say, "None of this rough trade for us."

One day, as they are browsing in a stamp store in a downtown area, they each experience a major epiphany when they come across an expensive stamp of Queen Victoria in her widows' weeds. McCrae expresses a great desire to have "that little black sweetheart." When the owner of the shop smirks, Hughes suddenly insults McCrae by snorting: "You old queen, I mean why don't you just quit wearing those goddamn Cuban heels, eh? I mean why not?" He then storms out of the shop. When the owner asks McCrae what has just taken place, McCrae snarls at him and struts out.

Throughout the following week, they are deferential to each other, not wanting to ruin the Mother's Day dinner party they have each year with three other gay couples. Their dinner party has become a celebratory event that always leaves them feeling good about their committed and faithful relationship. As McCrae prepares the traditional meal of stuffed pork loin, however, he listens as the couples enter the house, hears a particularly stupid old joke coming from the dining room, and becomes deeply aware that their lives have become almost unbearably routine.

As McCrae stares at his reflection in the window over the sink, he undergoes a second threshold experience. He takes a plastic slipcase out of a drawer and removes the precious dead-letter stamp—the Black Queen—and brazenly licks it and pastes it on his forehead. McCrae then marches into the living room to serve hors d'oeuvres. Hughes is stunned as McCrae announces, "My dears, time for the crudités." As McCrae passes the tray among the guests, he winks at the unbelieving Hughes.

Themes and Meanings

The theme of this brilliantly rendered short-short story is not immediately obvious, but after a few readings it becomes clear. Time as destructive duration—J. Alfred Prufrock's old enemy—is making itself felt in the lives of these two aging homosexual men. The crisis of aging and their need to preserve the best of the past have become almost daily preoccupations for both of them, as they see themselves and their world swamped by decline and decay. Their valuable stamp collection becomes more than a mere hobby; it becomes a vivid symbol of their need to preserve the values of their youth unsullied by the degenerating effects of a mindlessly changing materialistic world. Their growing dissatisfaction with each other and an alien world seems to find temporary relief in their discovery of a rare and expensive dead-letter stamp of Queen Victoria in her widows' weeds—the Black Queen of the title.

The figure of Queen Victoria in mourning becomes an apt metaphor for their waning relationship, which has been based on their mutual attempts to preserve their youth, their almost-Victorian lifestyle, and their value system. As the Victorian era was swept away and replaced by a prevailing philistinism, so too has time and their seedy neighborhood deepened their sense of redundancy. As McCrae stares into the kitchen window, stuffing the same old roast pork and preparing the raw vegetables and homemade dip, he decides that things must change, the old musty values must somehow be replaced or renewed. By pasting the Black Queen, which he secretly bought as a gift for Hughes, in the center of his forehead, he symbolically removes it from the sacred and timeless sanctuary of their stamp album and brings it, almost sacrilegiously, into the rough-and-ready world of the present. McCrae has, symbolically, become the Black Queen by humanizing that figure and releasing it from the obligation of symbolizing the bittersweet loss of a bygone era. When he passes around the raw vegetables and announces, "My dears, time for the crudités!" he is also declaring that he and Hughes must learn to live in the here and now. The word "crudité" refers to raw vegetables but also means coarse language or offensive passages in a text. McCrae becomes the agent who rawly announces that they must face the harsh realities of the times and live in the fallen world. Humor, exemplified by satirizing the sacred icon of Queen Victoria, can redeem them from their Victorian values and lifestyles. McCrae's coquettish wink at Hughes may become the first step in the eventual acceptance of themselves as the aging "queens" they always dreaded they would become.

Style and Technique

The most impressive and effective technique that Barry Callaghan uses throughout this compact parable about growing older is the way he transforms the recurrent images of McCrae's Cuban heels, the couple's Victorian house, and Queen Victoria in her widows' weeds into deeply resonating metaphors for what the story is actually about. Their carefully tended old house becomes a symbol of their successful efforts in preserving the past in the midst of change. Callaghan's use of the stamp of the Black Queen becomes the controlling metaphor of the entire story because it symbolizes the couple's unconscious mourning for a genteel past that has disappeared; that is, a Victorian sense of refinement and manners that belonged to another time. The concluding image of McCrae "crowning" himself with the Black Queen pulls together all the images of the story into one remarkable symbol. McCrae publicly identifies himself as the Black Queen and simultaneously brings that icon into the sullied world of the present, an act that becomes a crucial reminder to his lover and the rest of the aging homosexual couples that time is unrelenting and they may as well enjoy themselves as much as they can and quit hankering after their lost youth. The raw vegetables he serves to the guests become a kind of sacramental last supper commemorating a bittersweet but belated confrontation with the raw facts of reality.

Patrick Meanor

BLACK TICKETS

Author: Jayne Anne Phillips (1952-   )
Type of plot: Psychological
Time of plot: The 1970's
Locale: A slummy neighborhood of Philadelphia and the city jail
First published: 1979

Principal characters:
THE NARRATOR, the protagonist, a drug dealer
JAMAICA DELILA, his girlfriend and drug partner
RAYMOND, their other partner in the drug operation
NEINMANN, owner of the pornography theater where they sell
    drugs

The Story

The unnamed first-person narrator/protagonist tells this story in bits and pieces from a jail cell. The central fact of the story is his obsession with his recent girlfriend, Jamaica Delila, toward whom he has ambivalent feelings. He thinks she might have "set me up . . . to do lock-up in this cadillac of castles," and he fantasizes about beating her. Even as he imagines her falling, however, he cannot help dwelling on the way her hair spreads out and her uplifted hands glow in the light. He dwells even longer on memories of their lovemaking in the bathtub, the boy's shirts and underpants she wore, and the cartoon faces she drew on their legs with lipstick.

He also remembers her in the daytime, when, high on Benzedrine, she sold tickets at the Obelisk, a run-down pornography theater. There Jamaica entertained herself by staring at the rolls of tickets and, with an ink pen, drawing lines of tickets on her thighs. She also helped keep old Neinmann, the theater's owner, in line so that she, the narrator, and Raymond could practice their drug trade on the premises: "At first it was sideline stuff, Nembies and speed balls, a little white stuff for the joy bangers who came downtown to cop." They cut the speed with powder from the crumbling tiles of the bathroom floors and sold it to "silky Main Line debs reeling in their mommys' sports cars."

Appropriately, the three drug partners developed a close fellow-feeling for the "cinematic rodents" that overran the building. The narrator also misses "reptilian Raymond," a hunchback like Quasimodo and a self-described "nice Jewish boy, doing his bit for reverse reparations" by helping Neinmann, "that old storm trooper," save money to return to Germany. For the narrator, however, the presiding goddess of the whole operation was Jamaica: "Jamaica, you thin wonder in schoolboy clothes. I could crush them all into a burlap bag full of stones and watch them sink in a sewer named for you." The narrator's qualifications for belonging to this select group include a brief Florida jail stay for statutory rape before he came to Philadelphia.

Their Obelisk operation went smoothly for months, until Raymond decided to start selling powerful amyl nitrite, "those little extras to close down the days and promote orgasmic endings." Jamaica began using the drug herself when she and the narrator made love: As he "watched the X's come up" in her eyes, she would turn into "an electric zombie, a stiff-legged gazelle shuddering in northern catatonia." Holding his amylized lover, the narrator would have a violent urge to shake the bottled-up blackness out of her, and finally one day he succumbed. Just short of shaking her to death, however, he threw down her limp body, ran to the next room, and destroyed the supply of amyl nitrite. Raymond jumped up to pound the narrator with a nightstick but put it away when Jamaica staggered in.

Raymond's protective gesture reveals the part he played in their three-way arrangement. The narrator was Jamaica's sexual partner but Raymond was her big brother. Raymond slept on the living-room couch, and, whenever Jamaica had nightmares, she would get up and go sit in the room with him. He would place her legs across his lap and touch her feet to his forehead, apparently the closest they ever came to sexual contact. The trio's relationship was potentially volatile.

Jamaica seemed in particular to need a surrogate brother because her own family life was so rotten: Her mother, a West Indian, sold her and her four sisters as prostitutes when they were growing up. Little Jamaica specialized in playing a boy's role, though her mother would never let her cut off her braids. When Jamaica shears her braids over the narrator's naked body, he believes it is a message, and indeed, that day the police pick him up with sufficient evidence to send him away for years. Even worse, the police tell him that the Obelisk burned down, with Neinmann in it. The narrator suspects Jamaica of setting him up and Raymond of torching the Obelisk, though he has no proof of either. Still, waiting in jail he makes his decision: "Tomorrow I'll sing and sell you all."

Themes and Meanings

"Black Tickets" takes a look at the drug scene from inside, from the point of view of a drug dealer. Naturally, the narrator views himself and his drug partners sympathetically, even sentimentally—as human beings who have the usual emotional needs and who even form a quasi family. Naturally, too, his point of view fluctuates somewhat when he thinks his partners have stabbed him in the back. These fluctuations combine with the objective facts (insofar as the facts can be established) to set up an ironic counterpoint in the story. The counterpoint theme reveals the drug partners to be misfits in their personal relationships much as they are in society. As human beings, they are pathetic creatures, buddies of the Obelisk rats.

They are losers in society from the beginning. Raymond grew up "cracking meters" and making other "small deals," Jamaica was a child prostitute, and the narrator is coming off a bout of statutory rape. Drug dealing is merely the next step up (or down) for them. It is hard, however, to dismiss them simply as drug dealers; in one way or another, they make a play for the reader's sympathy: The narrator has the reader's ear, Jamaica has her rotten childhood, and Raymond has his hump. Except, perhaps, for the narrator, they have been dealt "black tickets" in their lives. It is also suggested that they are only part of society's general corruption: A cross section of society flocks to the Obelisk's attractions, and even "silky Main Line debs" end up "digesting the crumbling universe of Obelisk." The drug partners are as much representatives as rejects of their society.

Still, neither their personal hardships nor society's general rottenness excuses their behavior. The narrator seems as little concerned about the victims of their drugs as he is about the burnt-up Neinmann. "Black Tickets" is one of the few stories in which going to jail is a happy ending; at least there the narrator might have a chance to "learn a new career." The confused people of "Black Tickets" are not so much loving as they are addicted to one another.

Style and Technique

Surprisingly, "Black Tickets" has humor as well as pathos, the main source of humor being the first-person point of view. The narrator's style reflects his ambivalent feelings and lack of responsibility: It combines a jaunty, reminiscing tone with street talk and rich metaphors. His ability to reel off memorable phrases—probably unusual among drug dealers—suggests that he might have been a poet. Occasionally this style is overdone, however, as when the narrator describes the many varieties of blackness that flow from Jamaica or his equally numerous "sick vomits in bathrooms of restaurants, theaters, gas stations, train depots." Most "vomits" are "sick" and it seems unnecessary to specify the places, as well as a description of the "head on the bowl," the "intimate stains of countless patrons," and so forth.

Possibly these colorful details are symbolic because the story is heavily laden with symbols that underline the sleazy lives of the characters—from the Obelisk Theater (all the world's a porno stage, so to speak) to the rats to the radiating meanings of "black tickets." By the time Jamaica's braids are mentioned, the reader might be too saturated with symbols to care. The overdone symbols, like the overdone style, show the talented young author's tendency to go to excess ("Black Tickets" is the title story of her first major collection). After reading this story, however, few people will want to rush out to buy black tickets.

Harold Branam

BLACK VENUS

Author: Angela Carter (Angela Olive Stalker, 1940-1992)
Type of plot: Fantasy
Time of plot: The mid-nineteenth century
Locale: Paris
First published: 1980

> *Principal characters:*
> DADDY (CHARLES BAUDELAIRE), a French poet
> JEANNE DUVAL, his black mistress

The Story

On an autumn afternoon, a tall, young black woman named Jeanne entertains her lover, Daddy. They are in a Parisian apartment furnished with Persian carpets and rare books. She is sad. Daddy tries to cheer her up with his fantasy about life on the tropical island where he will take her one day; however, she does not want to think about the West Indies and the old slave trade. She lights a small cigar with a discarded page of Daddy's writing and drinks rum. When he asks her to dance a slow dance that he has created for her, she strikes poses calculated to show her otherness. After they make love, they go out into the city, transformed.

Themes and Meanings

Halfway through this story, the narrator identifies Daddy as Charles Baudelaire, the author of *The Flowers of Evil* (1857), and the woman as Jeanne Duval, whom Baudelaire met in 1842 and "kept" as a mistress. After warning the reader that biographers know almost nothing of this woman, the narrator constructs an imaginary life for her. According to this story, Jeanne was born on Martinique. Her grandmother was a slave who was born on a ship from Africa and orphaned at birth. After legal slavery ended on the island, Jeanne's mother went off with white sailors, leaving Jeanne with her grandmother. When Jeanne reached womanhood, her grandmother sold her to a sailor, thereby perpetuating the slave trade. She was brought to France, where she contracted syphilis and entertained in a cheap cabaret. After attracting the attention of Baudelaire's friends with her raw sexuality, she became his mistress. After Baudelaire died of syphilis, his papers and books brought enough money to let Jeanne return to Martinique, buy a fine house, and live to a ripe old age. She also eventually died of syphilis.

In a note to this story, Angela Carter explains that several of Baudelaire's poems that are thought to be about Jeanne Duval are known as the "Black Venus" poems. Carter has absorbed these poems into the story, especially "The Jewels," which tells about the dance. Carter's "Black Venus" is thus a network of literary allusions. Nevertheless, Baudelaire fades into the background; all the story's attention goes to Jeanne.

Baudelaire is referred to by name only three times in the story, and only to situate the poet in relation to his muse. When Jeanne is said to die of the "Baudelairean" syphilis, there is the irony that she may have given him the disease, though he gave it a voice and made it a symbol of the "decadent" imagination.

Baudelaire and Jeanne are a study in contrasts. He is weak and fastidious, never going out without gloves, always afraid of mussing his clothes. Tall and strong, she enjoys her body and her sexuality. As lovers, he is slow to rouse, and she is uniquely able to arouse him. Different as they are, though, they suit each other well because both are exiles. He is out of sorts with the Age of Progress, as the nineteenth century was sometimes called; while she is far away from her sunny Caribbean childhood home and still farther from her African heritage. However, when he watches her bejeweled body, and she feels him watching, they are transported to the earthly imagination of the poets; specifically, they are transported to Cythera, the mythical island sacred to Venus, the goddess of love. When their bodies are joined in the act of love, they undergo an alchemic transformation.

Carter insists on the economics of their relationship. Jeanne thinks she is just as much a prostitute as the women who dance for any man with money. She knows that "Daddy" likes to strike a patriarchal pose, and that he fantasizes about her as a slave. He likes to reject the morality of bourgeois society by publicly flaunting his black mistress, even in the company of his white former mistresses. Perhaps he is also fulfilling the dreams of imperial France by equating what is female with what is foreign and making both the object of his pleasure. Outwardly he is exceptionally eloquent, while she is almost mute. Nevertheless they are representative of modern love. Carter suggests that "woman" as we know her is less a product of biology than of man's fantasies. She does not force the point, however; she is writing a story, not a speech.

There is a traditional irony in the story. Baudelaire, the poet, finds his themes when he looks at a silent woman. His *The Flowers of Evil* is a product of Jeanne's fantasies. Carter takes the irony further by letting the reader hear Jeanne's unspoken reflections and thus revealing to readers of Baudelaire's poems who their real author was. The final irony is that, although the poet uses his mistress as a commodity, paying her keep and demanding his due, she ultimately has a claim on his estate. His manuscripts become her ticket back to the West Indies, where she enjoys the paradisiacal surroundings that he only could imagine.

Style and Technique

Carter draws many images from Baudelaire's poetry that capture the world-weariness that Baudelaire called ennui. The albatross of Jeanne's fantasy is the same as the bird in Baudelaire's poem "The Albatross." The ship of her dreams is from his poem "The Beautiful Ship." Even the real things in his world—the cat, the hashish pipe, the autumn afternoon, the rising moon—are taken from poems. It seems that one might reconstruct his *The Flowers of Evil* from the thoughts of this one afternoon, if only one knew a little more. Carter's style is close to prose poetry when she describes the afternoon. When Daddy tells his fantasy about the tropical island, he sounds like a doting lover and a hashish smoker. When he says that she dances like a snake, she laughs because she knows how snakes look when they move; they twist and jerk their bodies because they have no feet. Baudelaire's poem "The Dancing Snake" will never be quite the same to anyone who has read this remark.

The joke may be on Baudelaire, but the eroticism is undeniable. It cannot be called pornography because it unites two willing companions; it climaxes in genuine lyricism, not in four-letter words. Readers are expected to see what arouses both lovers, and what bores them, too. They are expected to enjoy Daddy's decadence—to know his "forbidden fruit" from inside out. Then, when the style shifts to straightforward narration, readers are expected to reflect on the economic aspect of Daddy and Jeanne's relationship—economic in the literal sense of housekeeping. Readers can see what each character gives the other and receives in return. If there is anything obscene about the relationship, Carter seems to suggest, it is the society that has made them exiles, a society that treats women as "only" women, and that regards most women as slaves.

Most of these parallels emerge only from reading "Black Venus" and *The Flowers of Evil* together. The pleasure derived from reading "Black Venus" the first time comes from finding that one is reading about a famous pair of lovers. The pleasure derived from later readings is that of finding how deeply Jeanne influenced the poet, and perhaps from learning how much Carter has influenced one's understanding of Baudelaire.

There are deliberate anachronisms in the story. For example, Carter quotes from a bird book first published in 1961, to help develop the albatross lore. She compares Jeanne Duval to Josephine Baker (1906-1975), the African American woman who became the rage of Paris nightclubs between the two world wars. Baker is as important to the story as Baudelaire's mother, who gets only the briefest mention as the person legally entitled to whatever the dying poet left. A fictional man who whisks Jeanne off to Martinique gains more credibility in the story than the real person who described Jeanne as a hopeless paralytic after Baudelaire's death. Literary characters, notably Eve and the Serpent in the Bible and Helen and Mephistopheles in Johann Wolfgang von Goethe's poetical drama *Faust* (1808-1832; *The Tragedy of Faust*, 1823-1838), become more important than any of the minor characters in Jeanne's story, for they are the literary archetypes that she and the poet embody. The truth that counts, for Carter and for Carter's Baudelaire, is the truth of the imagination.

Thomas Willard

BLACKBERRY WINTER

Author: Robert Penn Warren (1905-1989)
Type of plot: Coming of age
Time of plot: 1910
Locale: Middle Tennessee
First published: 1946

> *Principal characters:*
> SETH, a nine-year-old boy
> HIS MOTHER, a self-reliant woman
> HIS FATHER, a southern farmer
> THE STRANGER, a sullen tramp
> DELLIE, the black family cook
> BIG JEBB, her elderly husband
> JEBB, their young son

The Story

"Blackberry Winter" describes one day in the life of a young boy on his parents' farm, but the story is told as a recollection by a grown man, thirty-five years later. Robert Penn Warren has said that the story grew out of two memories—that of being allowed to go barefoot in the summer when school is out and that of feeling betrayed when the promises of summer are forestalled by a sudden cold spell. After beginning with this nostalgic memory, Warren realized that for it to be a story something had to happen. Therefore, he introduced the mysterious stranger who seems, like the cold of "blackberry winter," to be wrong, out of place, incongruous.

Indeed, incongruity, or the child's discovery of a cold reality of which he was previously unaware, constitutes the plot line and structure of the story. It begins with the boy's astonishment that he is not allowed to go barefoot, even though it is June because of a fierce rainstorm and the accompanying cold weather. The adult Seth examines the significance of this disruption of his expectations by relating it to the child's perception of time, which is not something that passes and has movement, but is like a climate, like something solid and permanent. The story itself is a memory in time that retains this solidity.

The stranger who appears on the farm on this particular morning is as incomprehensible to Seth as the unseasonable cold weather. First, it is strange that he should be there at all, having come out of a swamp where no one ever goes. Seth even closes his eyes, thinking that when he opens them the man will be gone, for he seems to come from nowhere and to have no reason to be there. Seth, with the self-assurance of a child, realizes, as he does about the weather, that the man does not belong, that he "ought" to be other than as he is.

The tramp is given the job of burying dead baby chicks killed by the storm, a task he performs fastidiously and with sullen resignation. The adult Seth's comment that there is nothing that looks deader than a drowned chick is the first of several images of death and incomprehensible evil that the story introduces. When Seth goes down to the creek to watch the flood with his father, he sees a dead cow come floating down the stream, bloated and looking at first like a large piece of driftwood. When the son of a poor sharecropper wonders aloud if anyone ever ate dead cow, the more immediate implications of poor crops caused by the storm are suggested, especially when an older man says that if a man lives long enough he will eat anything.

Seth goes to the house of the family cook, Dellie, to play with her little boy, and once again is surprised by something that "ought" not to be. Dellie and her husband old Jebb have a reputation of being clean and thrifty "white folks's negroes," and Seth is surprised to see that the storm has washed trash out from under Dellie's house into the yard that she has always been proud to keep swept clean. Moreover, he cannot understand Dellie being sick and in bed, and he is shocked when she gives her son a vicious slap for making too much noise. Dellie's illness is explained to Seth by her husband as being "woman-mizry," a result of the change of life, additional realities that Seth cannot understand.

All these clashes with incongruity and the incomprehensible come to a climax when Seth returns to his house and witnesses a confrontation between his father and the tramp. After being paid a half-dollar for his half-day's work, a fair wage for 1910, the tramp utters an oath at Seth's father, who orders him off the farm. The tramp then spits at the father's feet and walks away, with Seth following him down the road. He asks the tramp where he came from and where he is going, but the only response he gets is the tramp's hurling an obscenity at him and threatening to cut his throat if he does not stop following him.

The story ends with Seth describing briefly his life since the event: the death of his father and mother, the death of Dellie, the imprisonment of little Jebb, and a meeting with old Jebb, now more than a hundred years old. The last line of the story—that he has followed the tramp all of his life—forces the reader to look back on the memory to try to determine its structure and meaning and thus understand what Seth means.

Themes and Meanings

"Blackberry Winter" has often been called one of the great stories in American literature. One of the reasons for its staying power is that it combines two of the most familiar themes in fiction: the rite of passage (the coming of age of a male youth) and the mysterious stranger (the encounter with inexplicable evil). The story is a classic initiation story in that it deals with the child's discovery of the possibility of disruption of his previously secure and predictable life. Blackberry winter is something Seth has never before encountered and thus seems to be a betrayal by nature itself. This atmosphere of betrayal and the irrational is the climate of time that the story reconstructs as remembered by the adult Seth. All the experiences he undergoes during this one day when he was nine are equally incongruous—the city tramp in the country, the flood during summer, the trash under Dellie's floor, her vicious slap—all are part of a mystery that old Jebb calls the "changes in life."

The central event that sticks in Seth's mind is the confrontation between the tramp and his father; the central image is the gob of spit lying between his father's boots with brass eyelets and leather thongs on one side and the sad and out-of-place broken black shoes of the tramp on the other. The boy follows the tramp all the rest of his life because he comes to an important realization—that the meaning of "a man" is not just that of his proud, gentlemanly father but also that of the mean and bitter human being that the tramp is. It is a recognition that has been prepared for by his sympathetic identification with the poor boy, who wonders if anyone can eat drowned cow, and by his realization, in connection with Dellie's yard, that underneath the swept-clean exterior of human life lies "mizry"and the possibility of violence born out of frustration, bad luck, and the inevitable.

The proof that Seth (a persona for Warren) has followed the tramp all of his life is not only this story, which communicates a sympathetic understanding of human reality regardless of its frequent irrational viciousness, but perhaps all of Warren's fiction, for the artist must always follow those who, like the tramp, are victims in some way— of themselves, of society, of nature, of unreasoning reality.

Style and Technique

This is a carefully controlled story, so packed with events similar in their significance that it can truly be said to be "loaded." There is nothing superfluous to the cumulative impact of Seth's confronting incongruity and coping with how to integrate the new and mysterious into his understanding of life. Because it is told from the point of view of the adult Seth recalling a memorable day, the language of the story is that of an intelligent and thoughtful adult, one trying to understand something by means of an imaginative reconstruction; in short, it is a tale told by an artist, a miniature portrait of the artist as a young man, making a discovery about the need for sympathetic understanding of other humans that is essential for the artist.

Because the story is both a description of the boy's day and a conscious effort of the adult to understand it thirty-five years later, the reader must respond to a double perspective: the uncomprehending view of the child and the probing thoughts of the adult. Thus, although the story is told primarily as simple description and narration, it also intersperses expository philosophical passages of the man attempting to understand and explain. The very fact that the story is so firmly directed toward the classic theme and structure of the rite-of-passage initiation story and the fact that it is so loaded with obvious images of death, the unexpected, the incongruous, and the mysterious, indicate that this is an artist's story, for it is told by a writer who is well aware of the tradition of the initiation story as well as the use of conventional metaphors for death and disruption. The metaphors are handled with such naturalness and confidence, however, that they seem to exist as part of a real and tangible world, even though the reader is aware that this is a highly conventional story.

Charles E. May

THE BLANK PAGE

Author: Isak Dinesen (Baroness Karen Blixen-Finecke, 1885-1962)
Type of plot: Impressionistic
Time of plot: The nineteenth century
Locale: Portugal
First published: 1957

Principal characters:
THE WRITER, who writes the story
THE STORYTELLER, who tells the story
THE LADY AND GENTLEMAN, who hear the story
THE SISTERS, who keep the bridal sheets at the Convento Velho
ROYAL PRINCESS OF PORTUGAL, who visits the convent
AN OLD SPINSTER, who visits the convent

The Story

Most stories are meant to entertain and uplift the average person, who represents the vast majority of readers. "The Blank Page," however, is a unique story conferred on chosen listeners as a rare and distinct privilege. It is unique because it illustrates the loyalty of the storyteller to the true being of the story; it illustrates the storyteller's knowledge that when words end, silence may speak a deeper truth to one who listens for it. An old storyteller, who learned the art of storytelling from her grandmother, who in turn learned it from her grandmother, tells the story to a lady and a gentleman at an ancient city gate. The writer tells the story as told by the old storyteller.

In Portugal, following an ancient tradition, whenever a princess of the royal house is married, on the morning after the wedding night the bridal sheet is displayed from a balcony by a chamberlain or a high steward, and the princess is declared to have been a virgin. The sheet is never washed or lain on again.

The sheets for the royal brides have always been provided by the Sisters of Saint Carmel at the Convento Velho. They have obtained this privilege because they grow flax and make the softest, whitest linen in the land. Their second privilege has been to have in their safekeeping the sheets from royal wedding nights. A square from the center of each sheet is cut out, framed, and decorated with a gold, coroneted plate. On it is inscribed the name of the princess whose sheet it is. The framed squares hang side by side in a row in a long gallery at the convent. In the framed canvas, people of imagination and sensibility may see signs of the zodiac, which they may use to predict the life of the married pair, or onlookers may find their own romantic ideas pictured as a rose or a sword or a heart.

Elderly princesses whose bridal sheets hang framed in the long hall come with their rich retinues on a pilgrimage to the convent. Such visits are sacred, for they are undertaken to pay homage at the altar of virginity, the acme of a virtuous life, yet they are also "secretly gay"; apparently the old princesses know some secrets that enliven their reminiscences. A very old spinster also comes. A long time ago, she had been a playmate, confidante, and maid of honor to a princess. A sister conducts her to the gallery and leaves her there by herself, respecting her wish to be alone.

The spinster is veiled in black, not unlike the storyteller herself. She nods her head, which is "skull-like," perhaps because she is very old, and she smiles and sighs in recollection as she looks at the framed sheets, remembering the omens read of her friend's life, and of the lives of other princesses, and remembering the actual events, joyful or sad, of the family and of the state, the alliances and intrigues that took place. One canvas, however, is different from all the rest, for it is blank and nameless, placed there by royal parents in full loyalty to the tradition. Such loyalty makes even the storytellers draw their veils over their faces in extreme respect.

It is in front of this spotlessly white linen more than any other that not only princesses and their old friends but also the nuns and the mother abbess herself stand in deepest contemplation. The blank page conveys something deeper to all of them. It is not limited in meaning to a pictured page. Variously and significantly to each one who thinks on it, the blank page becomes the revelation of a spiritual truth, an epiphany.

Themes and Meanings

A pure and ancient tradition, whenever preserved with integrity, may reveal to perceptive persons deeper truths than are ordinarily apprehended. Such a truth, a vision of truth, or an epiphany, is the revelation and the theme of "The Blank Page." Many continuing traditions intertwine and illustrate this view in this story. The tradition of storytelling itself is traced through a long lineage, back to a grandmother's grandmother and even back to the time when Scheherazade herself told a thousand and one tales. The continuing tradition and blessing of growing flax and making fine linen comes from the Holy Land, from the Jewish bride Achsah to Portugal, to the Carmelite sisters, the brides of Christ. The blessing pronounced on the Blessed Virgin, her Immaculate Conception, and the promise through Christ of spiritual salvation, continues to be a promise of spiritual salvation to the virginal sisters of the convent. The tradition of publicizing and preserving the evidence of virginity comes from olden days to within living memory, according to the storyteller.

The tradition of storytelling produces good stories. The tradition of flax growing produces good linen. The tradition of publicized morality brings about public recognition of that morality. The tradition of spiritual seeking brings about the promised salvation. By establishing the norm, traditions maintain their standards, but they also tend to stereotype and limit personal discovery.

Perceptive persons may and do see more than others beyond the preserved traditions, if they look for a special meaning for themselves: The crusader who brings back the seeds of the flax plant sees the possibility of growing flax in his homeland; the sisters' faith, stronger than the average Christian's, makes them commit themselves to the truth of their religious tradition as revealed to them. The canvases in the convent's gallery tell the standard stories of virginity and lend themselves to omen readings, which are no more than fallible predictions. However, the blank page makes people stop before it and ponder life, true morality, or simply the truth about the unnamed princess. It may even make people look within themselves for deeper meanings.

Traditional stories with plots and character also throw some light on life and human nature. However, the story that has no plot and no individualized characters may reveal a deeper truth. Those persons who look for a deeper meaning through their own contemplation—the lady and gentleman of the story, the old spinster who knows much about life and morality, the sisters of the convent, or the mother abbess herself—discover it in the silence beyond words. They discover it as a revealed truth, as an epiphany, on the blank page.

Style and Technique

Isak Dinesen's primary ambition, she once said, was to invent very beautiful stories. "The Blank Page" is beautifully told, as are Dinesen's other tales, but it is different from all the others; there is no plot, and there are no individualized characters. The tone and the setting are, therefore, made the substance as well as the context within which the untold story may reveal itself on the blank page. Both are conducive to the distinctly oral quality of Dinesen's writing.

Although there is no conventional plot, there are little stories linked into a context: the storyteller's strict training under her grandmother; the crusader bringing back the linseeds; the Blessed Virgin receiving the Annunciation; the public announcements of virginity; the pilgrimages of the old princesses; the coming of the old spinster; the framing of the blank canvas. All these are linked as hallmarks of traditions. In the beginning, the loyalty of the storyteller to the true being of the story is extolled, and, at the end, the dauntless loyalty to tradition of the parents who had their daughter's blank canvas framed is praised. These loyalties not only unify the narration but also create the context of the story.

Other associative and subtly connecting repetitions, such as the old, black-veiled storytellers and the old, black-veiled spinster, the Blessed Virgin, the virgin princesses, and the virgin sisters, enhance the rich cohesiveness and depth of the tale. The black-and-white tiles of the gallery of virtue are a symbolic and ironic motif: Ordinary events and everyday morality may be set down in black and white, in trite categories, but the deeper truth must be discovered personally on the blank page. The final unity and the ultimate epiphany occur paradoxically, through contrasts, by bringing opposites together. There cannot be a virgin mother, but to the devout, the mother of Christ is the Blessed Virgin. Silence cannot speak, but to the keen listener it is eloquent. The blank page conveys nothing, but to the contemplative it reveals a deep truth, not expounded by the writer or the storyteller but clearly indicating matters of sexual as well as spiritual significance, not only for temporal and spiritual brides but also for all beings in relation to their spiritual destiny. In this way, Dinesen eloquently and skillfully uses words and the absence of words to tell the story of "The Blank Page."

Sita Kapadia

BLANKETS

Author: Alex La Guma (1925-1985)
Type of plot: Social realism
Time of plot: The 1950's and 1960's
Locale: A shantytown in Cape Town, South Africa
First published: 1964

> *Principal characters:*
> CHOKER, a tough, angry black man
> HIS WOMAN FRIEND, who is estranged from the father of her baby

The Story

"Blankets" is told in the third person, interspersed with dialogue and the main character's thoughts. The main action takes place in a tiny, stifling bedroom and in the walled-in yard of one of the "box-board-and-tin shanties" of a suburban slum. Like most of Alex La Guma's short stories and novels, "Blankets" records events that deal with apartheid in South Africa.

The story begins when Choker wakes up irritated in the hot, stifling bedroom of a woman friend with whom he has just spent the night. Feeling ill and angry because of the room's oppressive heat and the unpleasant odors of the filthy blanket and sagging, smelly mattress on the old, drooping, wobbly bed, he curses irritably at everyone and everything: his sweaty, half-asleep woman friend, the wailing baby in the tin-bathtub crib who has been awakened by the "agonized sounds of the bed-spring," and the woman friend's estranged but jealous and protective lover. Tired of listening to the unrelenting "blerry noise" of the "damn kid," Choker walks out in a huff, but not before the woman warns that her estranged lover and father of her baby, who is quite displeased with Choker's visits, is likely to harm him. Dismissing her warning offhandedly and, true to his tough-man reputation, threatening to "break him in two" with his "thick, ropy, grimed hands," which he uses for "hurting rather than for working," Choker leaves the hot, humid room, scowling irritably as he heads past other equally oppressive rooms in the shanty slum to the tap outside to assuage his parched throat and cool off his face.

After Choker passes a walled-in garden, three men accost him and viciously stab him, leaving him helpless and bleeding profusely by the roadway, cursing. A crowd soon gathers, some wanting to help despite his reputation for brutality and viciousness and others wanting nothing to do with him. The helpful group prevails and carries him, under a torrent of curses, to a dusty, smelly backyard lean-to nearby to await the arrival of an ambulance. The rescuers make no bones about how much Choker deserved what happened to him even though Choker criticizes the "baskets" for doing a less than "decent job" of stabbing him. With the pain searing through his entire body, he fingers "the parched field" of a threadbare, smelly blanket someone has thrown over him. He drifts in and out of consciousness, recalling his many encounters with filthy, smelly blankets, which have come to symbolize the decay and despair of his slum life. Drifting from the blanket experience of prison to one when he was six years old, he drifts back to the blanket experience that he had in the woman's bed moments before the attack. Before the ambulance arrives, there are some light-hearted moments in the bantering of the crowd in spite of the grimness of the slum life. The ambulance finally arrives, sirens screaming like the "high-pitched metallic wailing" of the "damn kid," and bears Choker away, strapped to a stretcher and covered with a sheet as "white as cocaine" and a blanket "thick and new and warm."

Themes and Meanings

Like the majority of La Guma's short stories and novels, "Blankets" deals with the decay and despair of slum life and the squalor, isolation, disconnectedness, and loneliness of repressed people under South African apartheid. It is about hope and hopelessness, poverty, violence, entrapment, love, and hate. Like the other stories in *A Walk in the Night* (1964), "Blankets" is about "actual characters" and "actual events" observed and recorded with the precision of an eyewitness. It is also a symbolic tale that focuses on the various blankets under which Choker has been forced to sleep, all the blankets of his harried, slum-dwelling life from which there appears to be no escape.

It is ironic that Choker's discomfort and anger does not stem from the stifling feeling of his lover's hot and humid room but from his lover's "unwashed, worn blanket," a symbol of all the squalidness of his life and his feeling of being trapped. Thus, the threadbare, vermin-infested blankets of childhood and manhood represent the several levels of despair that trap him in his own misery and in his inability to react and change things. The blanket, which should function as the protective cover it is meant to be, becomes instead a smothering, stifling coverlet that gives Choker neither comfort and protection from the cold during his childhood nor the much-needed succor he seeks in his adulthood. Instead, the blanket becomes the ever-present symbol of his exposure to the inimical forces of nature and his community. Although Choker can thrust the momentary confinement of the smelly bedding from himself, he merely has to turn around moments later to encounter it in different circumstances in what appears to be unaltered, or in some cases, worse forms. Thus, the many different blankets represent the tension between the basic human rights he is denied by the apartheid system and the social responsibility of the community to meet and defeat the evil forces of the repressive racism that is responsible for the despair in the first place.

Style and Technique

Critic Ben Lindfors has stated that La Guma's works are characterized by a skillful creation of atmosphere and mood, colorful dialogue, a mixture of pathos and humor, and occasional surprise endings. La Guma is known for his ability to portray character and for his keen, reportorial eye for detail, which he conveys with poignancy and meticulousness. His main character, Choker—appropriately named to reflect both his own personal experience as a victim of poverty and oppression and a victimizer of fellow slum dwellers—is described as "a drifting hulk, an accursed ship moving through a rotting Sargasso." In other words, he is a man who must respond with brutality and viciousness in order to survive the environment of slum life. La Guma describes the sounds and smells of the slum in language that is at once sparse but graphic: The woman's bed and blankets are described as smelling of "cheap perfume, spilled powder, urine, and chicken droppings." By choosing blankets as the metaphor of entrapment, La Guma is able to convey the squalid living conditions under which disadvantaged South Africans live during apartheid.

Everything about internal and external spaces and objects is fraught with tension: the breeze is hot, the light is "slum-coloured," the baby's cry is a "high-pitched metallic wail," the bed springs make "agonized sounds," the houses are old and crammed, and the shanties are cardboard and tin, the blankets are "exhausted" and a "parched field," and the bedstead of his childhood is "narrow, cramped," and "sagging." If anything is humorous in "Blankets," it is the light-heartedness of the dialogue among the slum dwellers and the pathetic bravado Choker exhibits even as he lies helplessly on blood-soaked layers of old newspapers in a lean-to that reeks of "dust and chicken droppings."

La Guma's use of flashbacks to tie Choker's childhood experiences with blankets to his more recent adult experience with his lover's blanket gives a circular shape to the narration. It is ironic that at the end, Choker does get a "thick and new and warm" blanket, granting his adult wish for "fresh-laundered bedding," as he lies, perhaps on his last breath, in the ambulance. This may be an example of one of La Guma's surprise endings, or perhaps this is how the writer infused the element of hope in seeming hopelessness.

Pamela J. Olubunmi Smith

BLIGHT

Author: Stuart Dybek (1942-   )
Type of plot: Social realism
Time of plot: The mid-1950's through the late 1960's
Locale: Chicago
First published: 1985

> *Principal characters:*
> DAVE, the narrator
> ZIGGY ZILINSKY,
> STANLEY "PEPPER" ROSADO and
> JOEY "DEEJO" DECAMPO, his friends

The Story

This is a story of four teenage friends who come of age on the streets of southside Chicago. In a neighborhood whose streets have no names, they search for something with which to ally themselves, a place to claim as their own.

Blight is everywhere; they appropriate the word into their vocabulary so that it—the word "blight" itself—becomes the definitive influence on their world. When their neighborhood is proclaimed an Official Blight Area, they change the name of their band from the No Names to the Blighters. Baptized in the good name of blight, the Blighters know firsthand the beauty buried underneath the buildings boarded up and blackened by arson, with bulldozers waiting in the wake. Blight is a state of mind, a level of consciousness and perception, and the Blighters—Ziggy, Pepper, Deejo, and Dave—have heard "the music of viaducts"; they have been to "churches where saints winked."

A series of anecdotal digressions weaves an interrelated mosaic of visual impressions that all rise out of a shared sense of place: a Chicago that owes more to invention and the imagination than it does to the restrictions of a realistically detailed map. The narrative focus shifts from character to character, offering glimpses that range from the magically fantastic to gritty urban realism. Between two mid-century wars—Korea and Vietnam—the Blighters begin to see the world in a new light: a movement from innocence to experience. Early in the narrative, the Blighters consider the men returning from fighting in Korea as "our heroes." Eventually, the Blighters go their separate ways. Ziggy decides to become a Trappist monk and hitchhikes to the monastery down in Gethsemane, Kentucky. Pepper joins the Marines after his pregnant girlfriend, Linda Molina, moves to Texas to live with relatives. Deejo grows his beard and hair long and enjoys some local musical notoriety by recording a record that he persuades several southside bartenders to put in their jukeboxes. Dave, the narrator, eludes the military draft by hiding out in college, where he is thrust back into the past when a professor reads Percy Bysshe Shelley's "Ode to a Skylark" (1820)—a poem that begins "Hail to thee, blithe spirit"—in a way that makes "blithe spirit" sound like "blight spirit." During the spring, Dave takes the El train back to the old neighborhood, "back to blight." He finds that the neighborhood is "mostly Mexican," but the bars still have their old names. In a world in which everything is at once familiar and strange, Dave has a moment of ecstasy, "as if I'd wandered into an Official Blithe Area," as if the blight of his childhood has been mythically transformed, by memory and forgetting, into a city of bliss.

Themes and Meanings

In "Blight," Stuart Dybek explores the relationship between identity and perception. His characters see themselves in relation to how they see their world—how others tell them how to view their world. Ever "since blight had been declared we were trying . . . to determine if anything had been changed, or at least appeared different." However, in truth nothing has changed. It is the same old place, the same impersonally numbered streets of southside Chicago. The only significant difference is that the world has been given a name, a name that "sounded serious." What has defined them—though they do not yet know it—are all those "familiar things we didn't have names for": the bars and churches, drunks and junkmen who push wobbly carts up and down the streets and alleyways collecting rags and scraps of metal. Dybek beautifully transmutes the ugliness that is generally associated with urban blight into a lush, magical cityscape, in which rows of tulips "sprouted tall, more like corn than flowers." He grants his narrator the lyrical power to recall by name those images that inhabited and shaped his sense of self. He and his narrator succeed in locating a new language, a new way of naming things. They peel back the layers of blight so that rarely seen aspects of Chicago's ethnically mixed southside—a neighborhood put on the map by such gritty American realists as Nelson Algren and James T. Farrell—are revealed to readers in a new and wholly regenerative light.

Dybek's fascination with how the world is perceived is evident in the opening paragraphs of "Blight." Variations of the verb "to see" appear in thirteen of the story's first twenty-one sentences. Dybek's landlocked "coast of Chicago" is the kind of place in which reality is not always what it seems. What some might consider to be a blight zone is also a place where "people had managed to wedge in their everyday lives." In his fiction, Dybek straddles the border between appearance and reality. He brings a world that is oftentimes seen through conflicting pairs of eyes into focus. He urges his readers not only to look but also to see.

Style and Technique

Blight, Deejo's never-to-be-finished Beat novel, opens with the line, "The dawn rises like sick old men playing on the rooftops in their underwear." His second sentence, which runs twenty loose-leaf pages scribbled in ballpoint, shifts the focus away from the sick old men by describing "an epic battle between a spider and a caterpillar." As Dybek's narrator of "Blight" points out, "It seemed as though Deejo had launched into a digression before the novel had even begun." He also wants it known that it is not Deejo's "digressing that bothered us. That was how we all told stories," including Dybek himself.

Dybek's digressions are intentional—a stylistic device that serves to widen the scope of the story much as the characters themselves undergo an expansive growth of their perceptive powers as they migrate out of childhood, backward and forward through adolescence, and into the world of adults. Just as "Blight" stretches and challenges its own boundaries as a story through digression, its characters begin to step further outside—they too begin to challenge, to see a way to step out through—the confines of their world: outside the neighborhood of childhood. The anecdotal nature of this story spools the narrative line outward and sideways at the same time, as if each digression, like each character, is threatening to break out, branching off into its own territory, its own story. Dybek brings it all back together, however, with the recurring refrain: "Back to blight."

In stories, digressions are often perceived as distractions, a failure on the part of the writer to tell a story straightforwardly, from beginning to end, without breaking the reader out of what one critic calls "the fictional dream." In "Blight," Dybek employs a digressive, kaleidoscopic method of storytelling that gives the world and the story's narrative structure a jazzy, rhythmic, point-counterpoint quality that is more often found in music. "Blight" thus reads much like a song: a rarely heard B-side from a time when "rock and roll was being perfected."

Peter Markus

THE BLIND MAN

Author: D. H. Lawrence (1885-1930)
Type of plot: Psychological
Time of plot: Shortly after World War I
Locale: The English Midlands
First published: 1922

Principal characters:
MAURICE PERVIN, a farmer blinded at Flanders
ISABEL PERVIN, his wife
BERTRAM ("BERTIE") REID, Isabel's friend from childhood

The Story

Maurice Pervin, a world war veteran, has settled on a farm in the English Midlands after being blinded in combat during his second tour of army duty in Flanders. He and his wife, Isabel, have employed a tenant couple to manage the farm. Maurice discusses details of production with his manager and assists him with such tasks as attending to the domestic animals, while Isabel continues to review books for a Scottish newspaper. She is pregnant and the Pervins are both anxious about the child because their firstborn died in infancy during Maurice's initial posting in France. During the year that the Pervins have been living on the farm, a wonderful intimacy has developed between them as Isabel has devoted herself to her husband's needs, and their "connubial absorption" has effectively shut out the world beyond the farm. Isabel has joined Maurice in a private realm of solitude approximating the darkness of his existence, and she shares to some extent his "dark, palpable joy," but the absence of any contact with society has also produced a void within her, inducing a feeling of exhaustion and emptiness. When Maurice is struck with devastating depressions that cause him to question his value as a man following his loss of vision, Isabel finds it impossible to be with him in spite of her professed commitment.

At this crucial juncture in the Pervins' lives, one of Isabel's old acquaintances, Bertie Reid, a Scottish barrister, arrives for a visit. He and Isabel have shared a cerebral friendship—an instinctive understanding—since childhood, and Isabel is eager to renew their sprightly conversation and become involved with someone who is actively participating in a social flow. Reid is almost a polar opposite of Maurice, witty, quick, and ironical in contrast to Maurice's more direct, methodical manner. He is also small, thin, and wispy, whereas Maurice exudes strength and has a prepossessing physical presence. Although the two men have never gotten along, they are willing to try to establish some kind of friendship for Isabel's sake. She has a feeling that they should get on together, but many impediments prevent this.

When Reid arrives, he and Isabel immediately resume an easy familiarity that tends to exclude Maurice. Reid is both fascinated and repulsed by Maurice and his wound, and Isabel is torn between her pleasure in Reid's company and a realization that her fortress of solitude with Maurice has been invaded. Her attitude toward Reid has always been a mixture of delight at his polished, cosmopolitan style and contempt for his lack of sexuality. She knows that Reid thought of himself as neuter at the center of his being. She appreciates Reid's attempt to understand Maurice's loss but knows that he cannot understand Maurice's compensatory sensual deepening, a quality that Isabel finds inexplicably thrilling. During most of the evening, Maurice remains quiet, eventually excusing himself to attend to farm matters, but he actually seeks the relief of his own special place, the barn where he knows every turn and corner and where the animal life is exhilarating, the weather refreshing.

As the night winds on and Isabel begins to find Reid's chatter tiresome, she asks Reid to bring Maurice back from the stable. The moment that Reid steps outside, it is clear that he has left the protective sanctuary of his indoor world and entered an alien environment, the natural world of elemental forces in which Maurice thrives. Repelled by the farm animals, Reid tries to overcome his uneasiness in Maurice's presence and real conversation begins. Both men are tentative, but Maurice clearly has not had an opportunity to air his fears about being a dead weight, and correctly deduces that Reid understands Isabel well enough to assess his concerns. Encouraged by Reid's reassurance, Maurice makes a request that is essentially an attempt to extend the aura of intimacy that he shares with Isabel to include Reid. First, he asks Reid if his scar is shocking. Reid's candid reply is taken as a willingness to continue, and Maurice then asks if he may touch the barrister, the farmer's way of seeing and knowing. For Maurice, this is a gesture of love; to Reid, it is a threat of psychic annihilation. Nevertheless, "out of very philanthropy" indicating some generosity of spirit, Reid permits Maurice to grasp his head and then complies with a request to place his own hand on Maurice's disfigured eye-sockets. This is a moment of dramatic intensity that penetrates to the inner core of both men's primal selves.

When they return to the house, Maurice tells Isabel that they have become friends because he has made the kind of physical contact that is his means of expressing hot, poignant love. Isabel is pleased but befuddled because she can see that Reid has undergone a devastating experience that has destroyed his composure and left him with "one desire—to escape from this intimacy."

Themes and Meanings

Although D. H. Lawrence was an intelligent man with a solid grasp of European cultural history, he admired the instinctual wisdom of unlettered men who lived unreflective and untroubled lives in close contact with the natural world. "The Blind Man" is an exploration of two forms of male behavior, which represented for Lawrence the extreme tendencies of masculine identity. The essential difference between the men is in their response to the woman they both cherish. Without directly supporting either man's position completely, it is obvious that Lawrence is much more sympathetic to Maurice but that he does not consider Maurice a complete or fully formed individual, or condemn Reid as one without any estimable qualities.

Maurice is the embodiment of Lawrence's lifelong love for the features of the English countryside, of his belief in the possibilities of illumination through sexual intimacy, and of his fascination with a special kind of brotherhood among men. Maurice's strong contact with the earth gives him an elemental strength anchored in something fundamental, and his intelligence and oversensitive demeanor are part of his blood prescience, a form of insight not readily appreciated by conventional society. His loss of vision, however, is indicative of Lawrence's concern about a total reliance on "blood contact with the substantial world" and the devastating term "cancelled" shows both Lawrence's fear that such a man has no place in the modern world and his knowledge of the importance of his own intellectual aspirations.

Bertie Reid—whose first name echoes Lawrence's middle name, "Herbert," as a clue to Lawrence's intentions—is conceived as an attempt to confront some of the things about which Lawrence was ambivalent, just as Isabel both admires and despises him. Reid's cleverness, his facility with the etiquette of polite society, his status as a "*littérateur* of high repute," and his financial success are attributes that Lawrence envied, even as he disliked many of those who had them. Reid's almost literal obliteration at Maurice's hand and his designation as a neuter illustrate Lawrence's dismissal of a cultivation that is divorced from corporeal reality, and his reed-thin airiness is much less appealing than Maurice's earthbound mental slowness.

Isabel is appropriately feminine in the context of her era, "rich with approaching maternity" and is responsive to Maurice's earthy passion, but her artistic inclination is her most interesting facet. The men are too rigidly compartmentalized for any real merging of interests, and Isabel cannot reconcile the extremities that they represent. She is the symbolic union of their realms, responsive to Reid's cultured sensibility, slightly fearful but still excited in "the animal grossness" of Maurice's dark lair, and able to draw Maurice happily into her delicate parlor. For Lawrence, she is the fusion of mind and skin that he envisioned as the result of the application of an artistic consciousness to the natural world. His portrait of her is sympathetic because he endorses her creative aspirations and his version of her femininity. She is an early conception of the fully integrated personality that he tried to imagine in his later work.

Style and Technique

That a story written in the first quarter of the twentieth century could endure into the next century is a testament to the psychological insight and mastery of craft that Lawrence possessed. Writing at a time when the short story was still a relatively new form for serious writers, Lawrence introduced many of the motifs that are now considered essential characteristics of traditional short fiction. His ability to invest archetypal patterns of behavior with singular humanity, to evoke a world of sensual resonance through poetic language, and to shape a mood of psychological authenticity through dialogue and detailed description of settings are among the reasons his classically constructed stories retain their freshness and narrative excitement.

Leon Lewis

BLISS

Author: Katherine Mansfield (Katherine Mansfield Beauchamp, 1888-1923)
Type of plot: Psychological
Time of plot: About 1917
Locale: Probably London
First published: 1918

Principal characters:
BERTHA YOUNG, a thirty-year-old housewife
HARRY YOUNG, her husband
PEARL FULTON, a young, mysterious acquaintance
EDDIE WARREN, a young, just-published poet
MR. NORMAN KNIGHT, a theatrical producer
MRS. NORMAN KNIGHT, an interior decorator

The Story

Late one afternoon, as Bertha Young turns a corner onto her street, her body and mind suddenly feel total bliss. Only the conscious constraints of "civilization" keep her from running, dancing, and laughing.

Inside her house, she tells her housekeeper to bring her a bowl of fruit so she can decorate the table where she is to give a dinner party that night. The beauty of the fruit on the table makes her laugh almost hysterically.

Bertha runs upstairs to the nursery and begs the nurse to allow her to hold her infant daughter, Little Bertha. The nurse resentfully consents. As Bertha fondles and kisses her child, bliss again overwhelms her. The nurse returns, tells her she is wanted on the telephone, and triumphantly seizes "her Little Bertha." On the telephone, Bertha's husband, Harry, tells her that he will be home a little late. She has an urge to tell him how she feels but represses it.

Anticipating seeing Miss Pearl Fulton, a lovely, mysterious blond woman, a recent acquaintance, who is to attend the dinner party, Bertha feels bliss again, and goes to the drawing-room window and looks across the garden at a lovely pear tree in full, perfect bloom. To her, it is "a symbol of her own life": She is young; she and her husband are "really good pals"; she has a baby, no money worries, a house and garden, artistic friends, books, music, a wonderful dressmaker, a fine new cook; and a trip abroad is planned for the summer.

Mr. and Mrs. Norman Knight arrive for the dinner party; he is a would-be theatrical producer and she is an interior decorator. Eddie Warren, socially in demand as the author of a "little book of poems," arrives. In a characteristic explosion of energy, Bertha's husband arrives, and just behind him comes the alluring Pearl Fulton.

As the guests exchange witty remarks and gestures, Bertha, convinced her mood is shared by Pearl, watches for a "sign." When Pearl asks to see the garden, Bertha pulls the curtains and presents the pear tree, which now resembles Pearl. Bertha has a profound feeling of oneness with Pearl and wishes her husband, who behaves as if he dislikes Pearl, would share her feelings. Suddenly, Bertha feels another powerful emotion—sexual desire for her husband, "for the first time in her life."

The guests begin to leave. As she listens to the poet express his enthusiasm for "an incredibly beautiful line" of poetry, "Why must it always be tomato soup?" Bertha looks out into the hall, where her husband appears to be arranging a romantic rendezvous with Pearl. Bertha runs to the windows and looks out, crying "What is going to happen now?" The pear tree, however, is "as lovely as ever and as full of flower and as still."

Themes and Meanings

As an observer of human behavior, Katherine Mansfield is a psychological realist who analyzes impressionistically a single moment in her characters' lives. Bertha's moment of bliss makes her want, for a moment, to touch her husband. Later, she has a "miraculous" moment when she is certain Pearl feels what she feels. The time setting for the story is only a few hours—a moment in Bertha's life but one prefigured in her past, and one that presages her future. Bertha's moment of bliss produces another, inseparable, key moment: her "strange . . . terrifying" realization that she desires her husband.

Complex possibilities make a single interpretation of this story indefensible. An interesting possibility is to read "Bliss" solely as an expression of Bertha's moment of bliss from start to finish; from neither Bertha, from whose point of view the reader experiences the elements of the story, nor the author does the reader receive clear, literal expressions of Bertha's having negative feelings about the scene between Harry and Pearl at the end. Mansfield's intentionally ambiguous story raises many possibilities but no one to the exclusion of all others. Several questions arise. Why is Bertha "overcome, suddenly, by a feeling of bliss" on this particular day? Is it by cruel chance that on the same day she will, ironically, discover her husband's bliss with another woman? Would she have been able to sustain the feeling of bliss alone that night when, "for the first time," she desired him? Would the rushes of bliss cease tomorrow as suddenly as they had struck her today? Mansfield seems to insist that Bertha, and the reader, remain subject to the contingencies of each new day.

The reader follows Bertha's unconscious use of several psychological devices: Instead of expressing her feelings, she, as is her habit, represses them; instead of acting on her feelings, she projects them onto other people, especially Pearl; instead of authenticating her own identity, she excessively identifies with Pearl, whom she imagines is her opposite. Does bliss overwhelm her on the particular day because of her subconscious anticipation of seeing and intensely identifying with Pearl, her ideal, sensual self? The only different, new element in her life on this day is Pearl. Faulty or not (considering her discovery at the end), Bertha's perception that she has guessed Pearl's mood, instantly, exactly, is a clear example of the way she projects her own mood onto another person. That projection is most powerful as she stands close to

Pearl at the window admiring the pear tree. Having so perfectly identified with Pearl for a moment (as the pear tree's blossoms are perfect only for a moment), Bertha feels, for a moment, desire for her husband. Scrutiny of this psychological process raises the possibility that Bertha, frightened of her "terrible" desire for Harry, projects onto Pearl and Harry the natural consummation of her own feelings by misperceiving the significance of their gestures in the hall at the end of the story. Perhaps the distance between Bertha and Harry and Pearl contributes to the misconception. Bertha's perceptions and emotions throughout the evening would predispose her to project impulsively onto the scene what she believes, or only imagines, she sees.

Mansfield then shows the reader how—even in a moment, or a series of moments clustered in a brief time—faulty human perceptions generate rare, romantic emotions that, given the nature of their stimulus, may be doomed to shatter against reality in disillusionment. Feelings such as "absolute bliss," even when one willfully tries to sustain them, as Bertha does, are rare and fleeting, but, as Eddie the poet tells her just after her observation of the Harry-Pearl scene, mundane "tomato soup is dreadfully eternal." Nevertheless, such moments as Bertha's moment of bliss have their own psychological reality and intensity before external reality does its work on them, and Mansfield seems to regard those moments with awe and wonder.

Style and Technique

When a writer's meanings are intentionally ambiguous, the reader can almost always depend on the techniques used to express those meanings to be clear. As an artist, Mansfield is an impressionist; as impressionist painters offer a single image charged with emotion, she focuses on a single image, Bertha standing with Pearl communing with the pear tree, and a single emotion, bliss. The image is sharpened, the emotion is intensified, by the controlled use of two major devices: point of view and a style that evolves most naturally out of it.

The point of view is third-person, central intelligence; that is, all elements of the story are to be taken by the reader as having been filtered through Bertha's perceptions. As Bertha responds emotionally, imaginatively, and to a lesser extent intellectually, the reader receives her psychological impressions, expressed in the third person by the author in a style carefully controlled, paragraph by paragraph, to suit Bertha, on this particular day, at each instant. The reader should anticipate that Bertha's perceptions, like those of all human beings, are likely to be in error, to be flawed, or distorted, especially considering the fact that on this day a single powerful emotion is sweeping her along through the hours: bliss.

The surprise ending is one of those literary devices most often open to abuse or misinterpretation. Commercial writers use this device to stimulate a transitory thrill. The serious writer knows that a surprise ending may generate numerous misleading, distorting ambiguities. "Bliss" is an example of an unusually ambiguous story; Mansfield chose a point of view that by its nature must rely on the technical devices of context and implication to convey its meanings. Mansfield seems to intend much of the ambiguity as a device for stimulating the reader's own imagination.

When the reader comes, with Bertha, to the surprise ending, Mansfield provides a dramatic demonstration of how Bertha's perceptions have been flawed. Having chosen the point of view most effective for her purposes, Mansfield cannot tell the reader what actually happened between Harry and Pearl; she does, however, use various devices to prepare the reader's emotions, imagination, and intellect to reevaluate, retroactively (in a second reading) all of Bertha's assumptions, preconceptions, and perceptions. For readers who believe that the Harry-Pearl scene must have had a negative effect on Bertha's bliss, the surprise ending generates ambiguities that allow for several interpretations. The reader may perceive in a rush a pattern of already implied ironies. For example, Bertha is certain that Pearl shares her blissfulness, but it is with Harry that Pearl shares bliss; when Pearl, who is like the pear tree, says, "Your lovely pear tree," at the end, the irony is that Pearl is no longer lovely in Bertha's eyes.

Given her decision to filter everything through Bertha's consciousness as a way of developing a series of misperceptions, Mansfield must employ several other devices to lead the reader toward various possible, supportable interpretations of Bertha's character. It is implied, through Bertha's actions, that she is childlike, as when she forgets her key, "as usual." The theater motif also implies Bertha's childlike quality; her guests remind her of "a play by Tchekof." Mansfield uses the device of comic contrast to stress the serious elements: Tomato soup provides comic contrast to the lovely pear tree. Some readers will see Bertha's baby "in another woman's arms" as an early parallel to her husband in another woman's arms. The pear tree is the central, symbolic image of the story, charged with implications. Images of fire contrasted with cold, of clothes, and of color enhance the central image. Appropriately, in a story focusing on bliss, Mansfield's style activates all of the reader's senses.

David Madden

THE BLIZZARD

Author: Alexander Pushkin (1799-1837)
Type of plot: Coming of age
Time of plot: 1811-1816
Locale: Country estates in provincial Russia
First published: "Metel," 1831 (English translation, 1856)

> *Principal characters:*
> MARYA GAVRILOVNA, the heroine, a romantic young lady of
>   seventeen
> GAVRILA GAVRILOVITCH R——, her father, a prominent
>   landowner of the estate Nenaradova near the village of
>   Zhadrino
> PRASKOVYA PETROVNA R——, her mother
> VLADIMIR NIKOLAYEVITCH, her secret fiancé, a poor army
>   subaltern
> COLONEL BURMIN, a young Hussar, a war hero

The Story

Marya Gavrilovna, the seventeen-year-old daughter of a wealthy landowner in provincial Russia, has formed her ideas of romance by reading French romantic novels. She develops an infatuation for Vladimir Nikolayevitch, a poor army subaltern, who returns her love. Her parents consider him unacceptable for their daughter and forbid them to see each other. They continue, however, to meet in secret. When winter comes and their secret meetings become impossible, they agree to a secret wedding, planning to return later and throw themselves at her parents' feet, confident of receiving their forgiveness.

The night before her elopement, Marya writes letters to be delivered to her parents and a sentimental young girlfriend after the wedding. That night, her sleep is troubled by dreams foreboding her separation from Vladimir. The next day, she is restless and leaves the dinner table early to await the hour of her departure. In the meantime, a violent blizzard has arisen. At the appointed hour, she slips quietly from the house and goes to the end of the garden, where a sledge and Vladimir's coachman, Tereshka, await to take her to the little church in Zhadrino for the wedding.

During the day, Vladimir has arranged for a priest to officiate at the wedding and selected three witnesses. Two hours before the wedding, he sends his coachman to get Marya and leaves alone in his one-horse sledge for the twenty-minute ride to the church. Almost immediately, the blizzard begins. Unable to see through the raging, swirling storm, he loses all direction. Soon his sledge is off the road. Many times it turns over and has to be righted. As the hours pass, he grows desperate until he sees a small village and learns that he has overshot Zhadrino by a great distance. Hiring a guide, he retraces his steps and arrives at the village church just at dawn. The church is locked and empty. Alexander Pushkin adds, "And what news awaited him!"

The next morning, back at Marya's home, no one knows what has happened. Marya has burned the letters she wrote. Her maid, the priest, the witnesses, and Tereshka all keep a discreet silence about the events of the previous evening. That evening, however, Marya becomes quite ill. In her delirium, she talks confusedly about her love for Vladimir. Her parents, on consultation with neighbors, relent and send him word that they now consent to the marriage. Much to their surprise, he writes back refusing their offer and stating that his only hope is death. His wish is granted when, a short time later, he is wounded in Russia's battle against Napoleon at Borodino and dies the day Napoleon enters Moscow.

A second tragedy strikes when Marya's father dies, leaving her the sole heiress of his large estate. Surrounded by too many sad memories, Marya and her mother, Praskovya Petrovna, move to an estate in another area. Many suitors seek the hand of this beautiful, wealthy heiress, but she is faithful to the memory of Vladimir.

The war against Napoleon ends victoriously and the regiments return in showers of glory. They are the pride of Russia. The appearance of any officer in a provincial town is greeted with enthusiastic applause. A charming young Hussar, Colonel Burmin, returns to his estate near Marya's home to recuperate from a battle wound. Even though it is rumored that he has formerly been a prankster, he now appears reserved. Marya is determined to break that reserve and to see him at her feet. It seems that she is succeeding, and the neighborhood expects an imminent wedding. Burmin, however, does not propose. Finally, he decides that he must give her an explanation. He begins, "I love you passionately." She expects a declaration of love like that Saint-Preux made to Julie in Jean-Jacques Rousseau's novel and is shocked when he adds that an insuperable barrier separates them: He is already married. He continues that in 1812 he was on his way to join his regiment when a terrible blizzard arose and his driver became lost in strange country. He requested the driver to stop to ask for directions at a small wooden church that was open. Several people, asking why he was so late, rushed him into the darkened church, lit by only a few candles, to the side of a bride. In a spirit of recklessness, he allowed the priest to marry them. When he turned to kiss the bride, she cried out, "No! This is not he!" and fainted. Rushing to his sledge, he hurried away. He concludes that after so many years he has no way of finding the young lady on whom he had played such a cruel prank.

Marya seizes his hand and cries out, "So it was you? Do you not recognize me?" whereupon Burmin throws himself at her feet.

Themes and Meanings

In 1830, while Pushkin was in seclusion at Boldino, he wrote *Povesti Belkina* (1831; *The Tales of Belkin*, 1947), an experiment with a new form for him, prose narration. Actually he was breaking new ground for his nation; these five tales, of which "The Blizzard" is one, are among the first Russian short stories. Tolstoy himself credited them with having influenced his own style.

As Pushkin began writing narrative prose, he was in turn influenced by Sir Walter Scott. Like Scott, he headed his stories with suitable quotations, used fictitious narrators, and created highly romantic situations and characters. In Scott's *St. Ronan's Well* (1823), as in "The Blizzard," the heroine does not realize that she has married the wrong man until after the ceremony. Like Scott in *The Bride of Lammermoor* (1819), Pushkin uses the providential hand of nature (in both cases, a storm is used) to effect the action. The blizzard prevents Vladimir from arriving at his wedding on time and brings Burmin to the church where he thoughtlessly marries the unheeding Marya.

Pushkin, however, makes the outcome of the narrative depend also on the choices his characters make. Vladimir chooses to send his servant to bring Marya to the church rather than doing so himself. Burmin irresponsibly takes advantage of the wedding party's ignorance when they mistake him for the groom. Later, after being wounded in battle and falling in love with Marya, he matures and becomes a more serious person.

Marya also shows character growth. At the beginning of the story, she is almost a parody of the young, sentimental lady who sees life through romantic novels. Her reading has filled her head with romantic imagination, which feeds her nightmares and forms her concept of love between the sexes. She seals her letters with an emblem engraved with two flaming hearts, bursts into tears, faints easily. After Vladimir's death, she rejects all suitors, remaining faithful to his memory until Burmin, the charming Hussar, enters the scene. Then she becomes a coquette, determined to prompt him to a declaration of love even though she knows she cannot marry him. She reverts to her former concept of love, however, when she thinks that he is ready to propose to her.

Pushkin uses the community to respond to the events of the story. After Marya's illness, they use moral platitudes to justify her marriage to Vladimir, who is culturally beneath her. They rapturously welcome their victorious soldiers from the Napoleonic wars. They spread rumors of Burmin's rakish pranks and watch his courtship of Marya, certain that their marriage is imminent.

Style and Technique

Pushkin is more concerned with plot, point of view, and irony than he is with character development. To create suspense, he abruptly breaks the narrative at the climactic point when Vladimir arrives at the empty church. Not until the end of the story does the reader learn what he discovered there. The glorious return of the veterans from their defeat of Napoleon serves as the turning point; thereafter, the story moves toward an implied happy conclusion. There are, however, numerous coincidences and improbabilities that pave the way for that conclusion.

Seemingly because *The Tales of Belkin* was an experiment in prose fiction, Pushkin decided to publish it anonymously, attributing the authorship to a fictitious author, Ivan Petrovich Belkin, for whom he developed an elaborate biographical background. Scholar George Z. Patrick has pointed out a number of similarities between the "spiritual makeup" and biographical details of Pushkin and Belkin. Belkin's personality, however, is basically different from Pushkin's. Belkin is simple, artless, naïve; any flaws in the narrative can be attributed to him. Furthermore, Belkin indicates that he is merely recording narratives as told to him by someone else—in the case of "The Blizzard," a Miss K.I.T. The strong element of girlish sentimentality can be attributed to her influence. The point of view is further complicated when a character in the story, Burmin, tells of his experience during the blizzard and thus solves the mystery of that fatal night.

Pushkin's skill in ironic humor permeates the narrative. The snowstorm that keeps Vladimir and Marya apart ultimately produces her happiness; Marya's parents finally agree to her marriage to Vladimir only to find that he is no longer willing to marry her; Marya is determined to elicit a marriage proposal from a man who, unknown to her, is already her lawful husband. The final ironic twist brings the story to a happy conclusion. Marya and Vladimir believed that their happiness would be complete when, after their elopement (so they planned), they threw themselves at the feet of her parents, receiving their forgiveness and blessing. Instead, Marya realizes this happiness when Burmin at the end throws himself at her feet to ask her forgiveness for his heartless prank four years earlier. The reader surmises that she forgives him and that their felicity is complete.

James Smythe

BLOOD-BURNING MOON

Author: Jean Toomer (1894-1967)
Type of plot: Symbolist
Time of plot: The early 1920's
Locale: Rural Georgia
First published: 1923

> *Principal characters:*
> LOUISA, a black woman
> TOM BURWELL, a black man who loves her
> BOB STONE, a white man who loves her

The Story

The last of six prose pieces in the first part of the cycle of poems and stories entitled *Cane* (1923), about young black women, "Blood-Burning Moon" is the tragic story of Louisa and her two lovers, a white and a black; its action occurs in a small factory town and the surrounding sugarcane fields in rural Georgia early in the 1920's.

Louisa works in the kitchens of the Stones, a leading white family of the community, and young Bob Stone loves her; as the narrator says, "By the measure of that warm glow which came into her mind at the thought of him, he had won her." Tom Burwell, called "Big Boy" by everyone, also loves her, but because he works in the fields all day, he cannot spend as much time with Louisa as Bob Stone can. Further, even at night, when he does come to her, "Strong as he was with hands upon the ax or plow," he finds it difficult to hold her. Both men, for different reasons, have problems communicating their feelings to her. Louisa's attitude toward the pair is ambivalent; Tom's "black balanced, and pulled against, the white of Stone, when she thought of them." On the night that the action takes place, Louisa is scheduled to meet Stone in the canebrake. There is a full moon that, rising from the dusk, lights the great door of the antebellum cotton factory, an omen that the black women attempt to neutralize by means of a song: "Red nigger moon. Sinner!/ Blood-burning moon. Sinner!/ Come out that fact'ry door."

Thus, in the first part of this story Jean Toomer not only introduces the players and sets the stage for a confrontation and its consequences but also introduces three primary themes: the conflict between the races, the economy that historically is a source of the problem, and the black woman as sex object.

The second section opens at a clearing on the edge of the cane forest where men grind and boil the cane stalks while listening to Old David Georgia chatter about "the white folks, about moonshining and cotton picking, and about sweet nigger gals." When someone links Louisa with Bob Stone, Tom Burwell menacingly announces, "She's my gal," and threateningly brandishes a long knife, an action that foreshadows the pivotal confrontation to come. He then heads toward factory town, shuddering at the sight of the full moon and thinking about Louisa and Stone ("Better not be").

When he comes to Louisa's place, however, he is a different person: gentle and withdrawn, unable to speak. He grins and begins to move on, but she prompts him ("You all want me, Tom? . . . You wanted to say something?"), and he bursts forth with a confession of his love and his hopes (including having his own farm, "if ole Stone'll trust me," and "silk stockings an purple dresses" for Louisa), but he also wants reassurance: "Bob Stone likes y. Course he does. But not the way folks is awhisperin. Does he, hon?" She feigns ignorance ("I dont know what you mean, Tom") but asks what he would do if the rumors were true. "Cut him," he replies, "jes like I cut a nigger . . . already cut two." Then, hand in hand, the two walk off to make love in the canebrake.

Bob Stone, meanwhile, also is thinking of Louisa; he regrets, too, the passing of the old order, when as a white master he could have gone into the house and taken Louisa ("Direct, honest, bold") without sneaking about as he now must do. He also speculates about how his mother, sister, and friends up north would react if they knew about him and Louisa, whom he considers "lovely—in her . . . Nigger way." Unable to articulate even to himself what he means by "Nigger way," he wonders if "Nigger was something . . . to be afraid of, more?" Though he rejects the idea, it leads him to think of Tom Burwell and that "Cartwell had told him that Tom went with Louisa after she reached home," but he refuses to believe this. Stone's reaction, therefore, precisely matches Burwell's, even including a threat ("No nigger had ever been with his girl. He'd like to see one try"), and when he goes off in search of her, he hears (as Burwell does) the men at the stove talking about the trio and how the affair likely will lead to violence: "Tom Burwell's been on the gang three times fo cuttin men. . . . Young Stone ain't no quitter an I ken tell y that. Blood of th old ones in his veins."

The talk has the same effect on Stone as it has on Burwell, for he must prove the truth of the overheard characterization of him. A captive of his love for Louisa and the blacks' expectations, Stone goes to the canebrake, where he normally meets her. Because this is their regular meeting time, he assumes that she is with his rival, and he tastes blood: "Tom Burwell's blood." Trying to find the pair, he trips over a dog and starts a ruckus that stirs Burwell. They confront each other and fight; when Stone starts to lose, he takes a knife from his pocket, but Burwell cuts his throat.

The blacks who observe the struggle sneak into their houses and blow the lamps out; the white men, "like ants upon a forage," trap Burwell. They bind his wrists, drag him to the factory, pile rotting floorboards around a stake, pour kerosene on the boards, tie him to the stake, and fling torches onto the pile. As the ritualistic lynching reaches its climax, the triumphant yell of the mob echoes "against the skeleton stone walls and [sounds] like a hundred yells." Louisa, who has gone home and does not hear the cries of the lynching mob, apparently senses that something is wrong, for her eyes open slowly and she looks at the full moon, "an evil thing . . . an omen."

Themes and Meanings

"Blood-Burning Moon" brings together key thematic motifs from the earlier stories in *Cane*. Like the others, it focuses on a woman as sex object, controlled by men but at the same time exerting a powerful force over them that transcends the normal social barriers of the South at the time. The story thus addresses, too, the sexual relationship between black and white, which Toomer also examines in "Becky" (about a white woman with two black sons) and "Fern" (whose heroine, Fernie May Rosen, has a black mother and a white Jewish father). It therefore adds an extra dimension to Toomer's focus in much of the book on what he regards as a southern conspiracy to ignore the reality of miscegenation. In sum, the bigotry that pervades both blacks and whites in rural Georgia creates barriers to normal interpersonal relationships, exaggerates the tensions present in any evolving society, and ultimately results in sexual repression. Toomer presents the blacks, however, as having a firmer cultural basis than the whites do. Though they are not at all primitives in the conventional sense, the blacks who work in the fields are close to nature. In "Fern," the narrator says, "When one is on the soil of one's ancestors, most anything can come to one." The title "Blood-Burning Moon" and the folk song from whose refrain it comes emphasize this kinship and its spiritual and emotional significance. A third motif, which is important throughout *Cane*, is the economic situation—symbolized in large part by the cane of the title—in which the races are interdependent at the same time that they are rivals. In "Blood-Burning Moon," the cane is both reality and symbol in a more central way here than elsewhere in the book. It is a means of livelihood for both blacks and whites, for the decaying cotton factory is evidence that the old economic support is fading, and the smell of the cane pervades the town.

Style and Technique

Widely recognized as one of the foremost literary works of the Harlem Renaissance of the 1920's, *Cane* is a collection of stories, sketches, and poems that emerged from Toomer's experience as temporary head of a school for blacks in Georgia. The poems, which appear within the stories and between them, are in a variety of forms, though most are folk songs or ballads. As in "Blood-Burning Moon," they provide substantive reinforcement to the action and themes of the prose pieces but serve primarily to enhance the pervasive wistful and mournful tone. They also heighten the impressionistic quality of the book, for though Toomer writes about real social problems and his characters are believable, he is not only a realist. The lynching of Tom Burwell, portrayed in a deliberately ritualistic manner, thus is appropriate both stylistically and symbolically.

Because of the impressionistic style and technique of *Cane* and for other reasons, the book recalls Sherwood Anderson's *Winesburg, Ohio* (1919). For example, both books have narrators who serve as mediator between author and reader, both are collections of prose cameos, and both have characters that can be labeled "grotesques," in Toomer's case because of the lingering social and psychological effects of slavery. Finally, though its subject matter may recall the naturalist movement, the style and technique of "Blood-Burning Moon" and *Cane* as a whole link it more directly to a later period, in which myth and symbol would be dominant in American fiction.

Gerald H. Strauss

THE BLOODY CHAMBER

Author: Angela Carter (Angela Olive Stalker, 1940-1992)
Type of plot: Fantasy
Time of plot: The twentieth century
Locale: Paris and Brittany
First published: 1979

Principal characters:
THE NARRATOR, the protagonist, a gifted young pianist
THE MARQUIS, her wealthy sophisticated husband, whose first
 three wives have died
HER WIDOWED MOTHER, a brave and strong woman
JEAN-Yves, a blind piano tuner

The Story

An anonymous narrator remembers her wedding night and the events that ensued. On that night she lies in her train berth too excited to sleep, as she goes from her mother's small Paris apartment to the Breton castle of the man she has just married. Her husband sleeps in an adjoining berth; they have agreed to delay consummating the marriage until they arrive at the castle.

The narrator scarcely knows her husband, except for the facts that he is older, richer, and more experienced than she. She is only seventeen, and quite innocent, whereas the Marquis has already been married three times. She does not love him, she tells her mother; but she does want to marry him. She remembers when he took her to the opera the night before the wedding. He insisted that she wear one particular item from the trousseau he had bought—a thin white muslin shift, tied under the breast—as well as his wedding gift, a choker of rubies that resembles "an exquisitely precious slit throat." When he stared lasciviously at her, she averted her eyes until she caught sight of herself in a mirror, suddenly seeing her own body through his eyes and sensing in herself, for the first time, "a potentiality for corruption."

At dawn they arrive at his castle, which the tide cuts off from the mainland half of each day. Her husband introduces her to the sinister housekeeper, displays his other wedding presents—a piano and a portrait of St. Cecila—and leads her to a bedroom filled with mirrors, funereal lilies, and an enormous bed. There he undresses her, examines her, and fondles her until she begins to respond. Suddenly, he leaves her to explore the house on her own while he attends to some business. In the music room, she discovers that her new piano is out of tune. In the library she discovers a collection of pornography. When her husband finds her there, aghast, he leads her back to the bedroom, makes her don the choker of rubies, and deflowers her.

After their lovemaking, the telephone rings: Urgent business calls her husband to New York for six weeks. After he breaks this news to her, he gives her a huge set of keys, one for each lock in the castle, so that she may take care of things in his absence. One key, however, she must not use. He tells her that it is the key to his heart, or rather to his hell—the "dull little room" where he might sometimes go to imagine that he is not married.

After her husband leaves, the new bride tries to distract herself. She meets Jean-Yves, a blind young man hired to tune the piano. She then calls her mother and finally begins to search the castle "for evidence of [her] husband's true nature." Eventually, inevitably, she seeks out the forbidden chamber, unlocks it, and enters. There she finds the bodies of her husband's first three wives, each apparently murdered in a different way: one strangled, one hanged, and one pierced to death in the Iron Maiden. Startled, the narrator drops the key into the pool of the last wife's blood. Then she picks it up, slams the door, and flees the room. She cannot leave the castle, however, until morning, when the tide goes out and the castle is again connected with the mainland. To calm herself, she plays her piano; when the tuner creeps in to listen to the music, she finds herself telling him what has happened. Jean-Yves determines, by the sound of the sea, when it is beginning to recede. However, when she looks out the window, she sees her husband's car heading toward the castle.

She tries to wash the blood from the key but to no avail. Her husband demands the keys and finds the bloodstained one, his face displaying "a terrible, guilty joy." He presses the key to her forehead, transferring the stain there. Then he tells her to put on her white muslin shift and ruby choker and prepare for decapitation. All the servants have left, except Jean-Yves, who can provide little help. As the narrator glances desperately at the window, she sees a magnificent horsewoman riding furiously toward the castle; it is her mother. At the moment that the Marquis's sword is about to fall, her mother shoots him dead with a single bullet.

Now, the narrator tells us, she lives quietly and happily in Paris with her mother and the piano tuner. She has given away most of the Marquis's wealth, and his castle houses a school for the blind.

Themes and Meanings

A feminist revision of the folktale of Bluebeard, "The Bloody Chamber" emphasizes a woman's new awareness of female power, her own sexuality, and her responsibility for her own fate. One of the most significant changes that Angela Carter makes in the story is its ending. In most versions, Bluebeard's last bride is rescued by her brothers. The narrator of "The Bloody Chamber" is rescued, at the last possible moment, by her strong mother. The narrator apparently arouses her mother's concern when they speak on the telephone. In another sense, however, she grows more like her mother as the story progresses. When she finds herself in the bloody chamber, she remarks, "Until that moment, this spoiled child did not know she had inherited nerves and a will from [her] mother."

If the narrator discovers a new sense of women's power, she also discovers her own sexuality. From the beginning, her relationship to her husband is shaped by his sadistic voyeuristic desires and her arousal in response to them. (The imagery of the bloody key and secret chamber symbolically emphasizes the theme of sexual discovery.)

Gradually, however, she learns to distinguish between her husband's desire and her own. Indeed, instead of seeing her body—as manifested in mirrors, images, and paintings—through her husband's eyes, she inaugurates a romance with the gentle piano tuner who cannot see her at all.

The ending of Carter's story makes it clear that the narrator should accept some responsibility for her situation. The Marquis may be an ogre, but she is partly complicit in their relationship because of her avarice, vanity, and own masochistic desires. The story's disturbing last lines reveal the narrator's sense of guilt: "No paint nor powder, no matter how thick or white, can mask that red mark on my forehead; I am glad he cannot see it—not for fear of his revulsion, since I know he sees me clearly with his heart—but, because it spares my shame." The lines also suggest, ironically, that she still identifies with her physical appearance, that she still tries to change it, and that she still evaluates it in terms of how a man might see her.

Style and Technique

This story about desire and sexuality is a pleasure to read. Carter's style is sensuous, evocative, and filled with sensory descriptions, from the Marquis's skin, with its "toad-like, clammy hint of moisture," to the key to the forbidden chamber, which slides into the lock "as easily as a hot knife into butter." Such richly observed descriptions also serve to foreshadow the heroine's fate. For example, when she browses through the sumptuous leather-bound books in her husband's library, the titles stamped in gold on their spines foreshadow her own story: "The Initiation," "The Key of Mysteries," and "The Secret of Pandora's Box." She idly turns the pages of another book, a book of pornography whose sadistic and misogynistic images also prefigure her plight; one is called "Reproof of Curiosity," another "Immolation of the Wives of the Sultan." These pornographic images are especially significant because the narrator becomes acutely aware of herself as her husband sees her. The emphasis on the narrator as a visual object—comparable to an illustration out of one of her husband's books—is underscored by descriptions of her clothes, arranged on heads, hangers, and shoe trees in her dressing room, and of her body, reflected in multiple mirrors in her bedroom. Moreover, the narrator thinks of her husband's first three wives—whose bodies she later finds in the bloody chamber—as portraits in a "gallery of beautiful women." Indeed, she describes them in terms of their appearance on the stage, in an artist's engraving, and in a fashion magazine. Her husband identifies her, apparently, with the portrait of the martyred third century Saint Cecilia that he has given her, and threatens that she will experience a similar martyrdom.

By alluding to other narratives, other illustrations, and other images that repeat the experiences of the young bride, Carter reminds us that the narrator's story is in some way a repetition of the stories of the three wives who have preceded her. At the same time, her literary allusions, in particular, acknowledge that "The Bloody Chamber" is itself a witty, erotic, and subversive feminist revision of "Bluebeard."

Susan Elizabeth Sweeney

BLOW-UP

Author: Julio Cortázar (1914-1984)
Type of plot: Magical Realism
Time of plot: The 1950's
Locale: Paris
First published: "Las babas del diablo," 1958 (English translation, 1963)

> *Principal characters:*
> ROBERTO MICHEL, a Chilean-French translator and amateur
> photographer living in Paris
> A TEENAGE BOY
> A BLOND WOMAN, who attempts to seduce the teenager
> A MAN, sitting in a parked car

The Story

Roberto Michel opens his story not by telling what happened but by mulling over *how* it should be told and *why* it must be told. Once he decides that "the best thing is to put aside all decorum and tell it, "he recounts the events of his Sunday morning stroll along the Seine. His excursion is quite uneventful until, while lighting a cigarette, his eye catches an interesting scene in which a blond woman seems to be attempting to seduce a teenage boy.

With nothing better to do, Michel watches the scene carefully. As he notices the boy's nervous reactions to the woman's advances, Michel begins to imagine the particulars of the situation, details that he attempts to divine from his somewhat distant observations. Michel imagines in considerable detail the boy's background, his relationship with his friends, even his home life. He then begins to imagine the events of the morning that led the boy to this precarious situation. Now certain in his own mind of what is happening, Michel begins to derive a perverse pleasure from foreseeing the possible endings of the "cruel game," imagining both escape for the boy and conquest for the woman.

Michel notices a man in a parked car near the scene, but he is unable to establish his role in the seduction. Before the scene can disintegrate before his eyes, Michel readies his camera, still ruminating about the possible denouements of the story unfolding only a few feet away. When he finally snaps the photo, his action is noticed by both the woman and the boy. Irritated, the woman approaches Michel and demands the film. In the meantime, the boy seizes the opportunity to escape, "disappearing like a gossamer filament of angel-spit in the morning air." The mysterious man approaches from the parked car and joins the woman in demanding the film. Michel refuses to relinquish it and returns home.

Several days later, Michel develops the film and makes an enlargement of the photo of the woman and the boy. Fascinated by the shot, he tacks a poster-size blowup of it on the wall of his apartment. While working on a translation, he is mysteriously drawn to the photo. Examining it from several perspectives, he compares what is frozen in the picture with what happened immediately after it was taken. His contemplation of both the photo and the events surrounding it produces in him a self-satisfaction, for he feels that his intrusion allowed the boy the escape that the teenager so badly wanted. As Michel concludes, "In the last analysis, taking the photo had been a good act."

Magically, however, the figures in the photo begin to move and the scene develops beyond the point of Michel's intrusion, as if he and his camera had never been there. Michel sees that without his presence this time, "that which had not happened, but which was now going to happen, now was going to be fulfilled." He realizes that the woman had not been seducing the boy for her own pleasure but for that of the man in the parked car. As Michel points out, "The real boss was waiting there, smiling petulantly, already certain of the business; he was not the first to send a woman in the vanguard, to bring him the prisoners manacled in flowers." Michel painfully realizes that he cannot stop the order of events this time. He cannot interrupt the scene with another photograph, or even with a shout of warning to the boy. The figures are functioning in a time frame separate from his own, forcing him into the role of a powerless bystander.

Feeling helpless, Michel screams out and runs toward the photo. Surprisingly, the man, now out of the parked car, reacts to Michel's approach and turns to confront him. Once again, the boy seizes the opportunity afforded him by Michel's presence and escapes running. For the second time, Michel has helped the teenager, allowing him to get away, thus "returning him to his precarious paradise." Emotionally and physically exhausted, Michel breaks down in tears and makes his way to the window of his apartment. It is from this location that he narrates his story while watching the birds and the clouds pass by.

Themes and Meanings

A number of themes common to several of Julio Cortázar's stories are found in "Blow-Up." One of these is the creation of a fictionalized reality that becomes accepted as truth within the story. Michel views an isolated scene about which he has little information. He nevertheless manufactures a complex reality surrounding that scene, a fictionalized reality complete with details concerning the boy writing to his aunt in Avignon, the manner in which the young man folds his pornographic magazines, the color of the comforter on the bed in the blond's apartment, and several others. Michel establishes his own version of reality. As even he says about himself, "Michel is guilty of making literature, of indulging in fabricated unrealities."

The story also deals with Cortázar's interest in the prospect of multiple and parallel realities (either true or fictionalized). The movement of the figures in the photo contributes to the treatment of this concept in that it demonstrates a reality independent of the "main" one in which Michel and his camera are first involved. Of equal importance, however, is the duality in Michel's interpretation of the scene unfolding before him. For example, he imagines both success and failure for the seductress, thus establishing at least two separate realities, fictionalized though they both may be. By suggesting more than one possibility, more than one "truth," Cortázar, as he does in several of his works, demonstrates that "true" reality is hardly ever as simple to establish as one might logically think.

Another thematic concern of Cortázar's found in this story is the individual human being's need to tell what he knows, that to which he is privy, in an effort to cleanse himself, to rid himself of the psychological burden of his solitary knowledge. This is demonstrated in the first two pages of the story as Michel speaks of the need to tell his story, to get it out, and in doing so exorcise his soul of what he has witnessed. As he states, "Always tell it, always get rid of that tickle in the stomach that bothers you."

Style and Technique

The story is told in a somewhat complex manner. Above all, it features a self-conscious narrator who not only criticizes his own choice of words but also alternates frequently between third-person and first-person narration. The fact that Michel refers to himself in the third person is a bit disconcerting in itself. It shows, however, that he is uncomfortable associating himself with the "character" Michel who has suffered through such a psychologically painful experience. He is therefore putting distance between himself and the person who went strolling along the river with the camera. His vacillation between the two perspectives may simply demonstrate that he has not yet resigned himself fully to either position. Though certainly unorthodox, the frequent shifting from one person to the other is not a major obstacle to the reader because it is obvious that the narrator and Michel are one and the same.

Of equal interest from a technical standpoint, and certainly more disconcerting to the reader, are the narrator's frequent references, usually within parentheses, to the birds and clouds that pass by his window as he tells his story. One reason for including these references is to show the narrator's position in the present as he tells his story. The references, which interrupt the narration, also emphasize the profound effect that the experience has had on the narrator, as he is unable to maintain a steady narrative course and alternates between what happened and what he sees outside his window. The problem for the reader here is that it is virtually impossible to understand these references at the time that they are presented because Michel's physical surroundings as he narrates are not revealed until the end of the story. The disquieting effect they have on the reader is quite intentional, however, as it underscores the tenuous mental state of the narrator.

Keith H. Brower

THE BLUE CROSS

Author: G. K. Chesterton (1874-1936)
Type of plot: Mystery and detective
Time of plot: The early twentieth century
Locale: London
First published: 1911

> *Principal characters:*
> FATHER BROWN, a Roman Catholic priest and amateur sleuth
> ARISTIDE VALENTIN, chief of the Paris police
> FLAMBEAU, a notorious French thief

The Story

Aristide Valentin, the chief of the Paris police, arrives from Holland by boat at the English port of Harwich. He is pursuing an infamous thief and con man named Flambeau, to whom Parisian reporters attribute numerous mysterious and unsolved crimes committed in the French capital. Flambeau has become somewhat of a sympathetic rogue in the eyes of certain Frenchmen, and Valentin definitely wants to arrest this troublemaker, who has managed to avoid arrest by the French, Belgian, and Dutch police. Valentin's chances of catching Flambeau seem slim, however, because all he knows about the man is that he is six feet, four inches tall. Valentin certainly cannot arrest every tall man whom he encounters in England, but he is a tireless investigator. During his train journey to London, Valentin sees many short people, including a rotund Roman Catholic priest who tells him that he is carrying a valuable silver cross with blue sapphires to a eucharistic congress in London. A skeptic with no love of priests, Valentin regards this priest with contempt for revealing such information to a stranger.

After a quick visit to Scotland Yard, where he speaks with his English colleagues, Valentin formulates a plan for finding Flambeau. He decides to look for Flambeau in out-of-the-way places, believing that an escaped criminal such as Flambeau will avoid public places such as banks and railroad stations. As he eats breakfast in an Italian restaurant, he notices an odd, short clergyman who is attracting attention by putting salt in a sugar bowl and throwing soup against a wall as he leaves. The waiter who has served the priest complains about the mess. Soon after Valentin leaves the restaurant, he comes on a vegetable and fruit shop where a short priest has just switched the signs for oranges and nuts and knocked the apples from a table. The upset greengrocer tells Valentin in what direction short and tall priests have gone. When Valentin learns from a police officer that the priests have boarded a bus for Hampstead, he commandeers a police car to follow it. He believes that the tall priest is probably Flambeau and that the short one might well be the priest whom he had met on the train.

Valentin looks for anything that will tell him where Flambeau may be in Hampstead. Soon he spots a restaurant with a broken window. The restaurant's proprietor tells him that a short priest has just added ten shillings to his bill to pay for the window that he was about to smash with his umbrella. Thinking that this priest must be an escaped lunatic, the distressed proprietor tells Valentin that the two priests are headed for Hampstead Heath, where Valentin and his English colleagues soon find them.

Just before the police arrive, the two priests have a short theological discussion in which the tall priest denounces reason, while the other explains that Christianity enables us to reconcile faith and reason. The short priest, who turns out to be Father Brown, realizes that the other man's attack on reason constitutes such "bad theology" that the man cannot be a true priest. When the tall man threatens Father Brown with physical violence unless he turns over his blue cross, Brown points to the police officers hiding behind a nearby tree who then arrest Flambeau.

The story ends with Valentin admitting that Father Brown is a master detective who has behaved strangely deliberately in order to make the police follow two priests who would otherwise be inconspicuous.

Themes and Meanings

Since his death in 1936, G. K. Chesterton has remained justly famous for the five volumes of his stories in which Father Brown is an amateur sleuth. The first Father Brown story to appear in print, "The Blue Cross" illustrates Father Brown's ability to combine theological insights with intuition to solve puzzling crimes. At first glance, little distinguishes him from hundreds of other English parish priests. His drab exterior, however, hides his profound intellect from both Valentin and Flambeau, who mistake appearance for reality. Ironically, Flambeau shares with Valentin the belief that Father Brown is incapable of defending himself. Neither Valentin nor Flambeau realizes that Brown thinks intuitively and accurately and is a wise and objective judge of human behavior.

"The Blue Cross" illustrates Father Brown's ingenious ability both to save his own life and to solve a puzzling crime. Father Brown realizes that the police cannot protect citizens from criminals at all times. He must take an active role in dealing with the crime that Flambeau intends to commit. His religious superiors have entrusted Father Brown with a valuable cross that a thief should not be allowed to steal. Father Brown senses intuitively that the tall priest cannot truly be a priest because Flambeau relied on "bad theology" in affirming that Christianity was incompatible with reason. He concludes that any man who pretends to be a priest can only be up to no good. Although he does not understand at the beginning of this story exactly which crime Flambeau plans to commit, Father Brown realizes that it is not in his interest to be left alone for long with this potentially violent criminal.

Father Brown also senses intuitively that Valentin is not a totally objective detective who would go out of his way to protect Catholic priests. As Valentin and Father Brown travel together from Harwich to London, Valentin laughs at Father Brown, believing that the eucharistic congress that Father Brown will attend "had doubtless sucked out of their local stagnation many such creatures, blind and helpless, like moles disinterred." The virulence of his hatred for Catholics helps Father Brown to realize that Valentin does not care if a crucifix is stolen. Father Brown must therefore appeal to Valentin's desire to solve another crime in order to prevent physical harm to himself and the theft of the blue cross that he is carrying.

"The Blue Cross" nicely illustrates the complex motivations for human behavior. When he learns that a priest has apparently committed acts of vandalism, Valentin is delighted because he believes that sending a priest to prison will decrease public admiration for the Catholic Church, which he hates. Father Brown understands clearly that he needs police protection, but he must act in such a way that police officers will follow him without his revealing his intentions to Flambeau, whom he properly fears. It is ironic that the skeptic Valentin unintentionally serves the cause of religion. For Father Brown the arrest of Flambeau is important above all because it permits a valuable religious object to be displayed at a congress of English Catholic priests. The arrest of Flambeau does, however, also possess broader religious significance. In later Chesterton stories, Father Brown frequently visits him in prison, and Flambeau eventually converts to Catholicism. After his release from prison, Flambeau becomes a law-abiding private detective who assists Father Brown in numerous cases. There are many different levels of irony in "The Blue Cross" and in many other detective stories written by Chesterton.

Style and Technique

Reading a Chesterton detective story is an intellectually challenging experience for readers who try to solve the crimes themselves; it requires pulling together seemingly unconnected clues. Many elements in "The Blue Cross" reveal Chesterton's masterful command of paradox. At first glance, Father Brown's behavior is incomprehensible, both to the other characters and to readers. The restaurant owner whose window Father Brown smashes with an umbrella believes him to be an "escaped lunatic," and the greengrocer whose apple stand he knocks over believes him to be a "fool." However, if Chesterton's readers feel that there is a method to Father Brown's apparent madness, they must try to discover the connections among all these paradoxical actions. Gradually, readers come to realize that Father Brown's actions are essential for his own protection and to prevent the valuable blue cross from being stolen by Flambeau. It is difficult not to react intellectually to many Father Brown stories because Chesterton constantly challenges readers to discover the true explanation for many seemingly unconnected and strange clues.

"The Blue Cross" was the first of fifty Father Brown stories that Chesterton published between 1911 and 1935. Chesterton wrote in an extremely refined and witty style that still pleases and challenges readers today. His extraordinary skill in combining intuition with theological insights into human behavior remains unique in the history of detective fiction.

Edmund J. Campion

THE BLUE HOTEL

Author: Stephen Crane (1871-1900)
Type of plot: Adventure
Time of plot: The mid-1890's
Locale: Nebraska
First published: 1898

Principal characters:
PAT SCULLY, proprietor of the Blue Hotel
THE SWEDE, a visitor from New York
MR. BLANC, an easterner
BILL, a Dakota cowboy
JOHNNIE SCULLY, the proprietor's son
THE GAMBLER, a resident of Fort Romper

The Story

The light blue hue of the Palace Hotel, like the shade of a heron's legs, is a striking sight to railway passengers disembarking at Fort Romper, Nebraska. Its owner, Irishman Pat Scully, personally meets the morning and evening trains to "work his seductions" on potential customers. One wintry morning he collars three such "prisoners," a "shaky and quick-eyed" Swede from New York, a Dakota cowboy named Bill, and Mr. Blanc, a "little silent" easterner. In the hotel's small front room, the guests come on an old farmer and Scully's son Johnnie playing a card game called high-five. A conscientious host, Scully furnishes the guests with water and towels, gets Johnnie to take their baggage upstairs, and confers with his wife and daughters about the midday meal. Outside, the snow and the wind are reaching blizzard proportions.

Almost immediately, the Swede begins behaving peculiarly. Nervous and defensive, he laughingly asserts that "some of these Western communities were very dangerous." When a quarrel terminates the card game between Johnnie and the farmer, the Swede joins the table, pairing up with Mr. Blanc against Johnnie and Bill. The latter is a "board whacker," which unhinges the Swede. Whenever the cowboy played a winning card, he "whanged" it on the table, causing Johnnie to chuckle. Suddenly, the Swede says, "I suppose there have been a good many men killed in this room." Astonished, the others take issue with him. Believing his life in danger, the Swede pleads that he does not want to fight.

"Have you gone daffy?" Scully asks him while the Swede is packing upstairs: "We're goin' to have a line of ilictric street-cars in this town next spring. . . . Not to mention the four churches and the smashin' big brick school-house." Refusing to accept money for the room, Scully shows him a portrait of his deceased daughter Carrie and his elder son, who is an attorney in Lincoln. Bringing out a bottle of whiskey, he insists that the Swede take a drink.

Downstairs, the men argue about the Swede's abnormal behavior. The cowboy thinks him a phony, "some kind of a Dutchman," while Mr. Blanc figures he was frightened by Western dime-novels. Then Scully and the Swede reappear, laughing like two "roysterers from a banquet hall." When the latter is out of earshot, however, Scully confides that his strange guest thought "I was tryin' to poison 'im."

At supper the Swede behaves "like a fire-wheel," singing riotously one minute, stabbing his food menacingly the next, and all the while gazing belligerently at the others. When the meal is over, he insists on resuming high-five. Scully has just settled down to his newspaper when he hears the Swede charge Johnnie with cheating.

Despite Scully's efforts to calm things down, both adversaries insist on going outside to fight. "I can't put up with it any longer," Scully says with resignation, adding: "I've stood this damned Swede till I'm sick."

Out in the snow, the Swede bawls out that he cannot "lick you all," but Scully assures him that it will be a fair fight. As the storm wails its "long mellow cry," the two crash together "like bullocks." The easterner watches silently with a sense of foreboding tragedy, but the cowboy yells for Johnnie to "kill him! kill him! kill him!" Johnnie is no match for the bigger man, however, and ends up on the ground, bloody and humiliated. Afterward, Mrs. Scully is irate at her husband for having permitted their son to be so savagely beaten. "Shame be upon you, Patrick Scully," she cries.

As the Swede is leaving, the cowboy wants to fight him, but Scully again intervenes, even though the victor mimics Bill's cry of "kill him! kill him! kill him!" Making his way to a saloon, whose entrance is made visible by "an indomitable red light," he drinks down two glasses of whiskey in large gulps and starts bragging about his conquest. After failing to persuade the bartender to have a drink, the Swede turns to four men sitting around a table. They include two merchants, the district attorney, and a gambler, who is a family man who only fleeces ignorant farmers. When they rebuff the Swede's offer of a drink, he roughly lays his hand on the gambler, calls him a "little dude," and vows, "I'll make you." He grabs the gambler's throat and starts dragging him from his chair when the gambler stabs him with a knife. His three companions flee. Wiping off the blade with a towel, the gambler tells the bartender: "I'll be home, waiting for 'em." As the bartender goes for help, the dying Swede lies with his eyes staring vacantly at a sign atop the cash-machine that reads: "This registers the amount of your purchase."

Several months later, when the cowboy and the easterner meet, they both express sympathy for the gambler, who is serving a three-year prison sentence. The cowboy blames it all on the Swede for accusing Johnnie of cheating in a game played for fun rather than money. He was cheating, the easterner replies: "I saw him. And I refused to stand up and be a man." He concludes that they were all collaborators, that the gambler was only "the apex of a human movement." Incredulous about "this fog of mysterious theory," the cowboy blindly cries, "Well, I didn't do anythin', did I?"

Themes and Meanings

"The Blue Hotel" deals with man's vanities and illusions, which are absurd but, ironically, necessary for survival. Stephen Crane's naturalistic tale presents a view of the world as beyond comprehension and indifferent to the inconsequential matters of mankind. According to the author, people are like lice clinging to "a whirling, fire-smitten, ice-locked, disease-stricken, space-lost bulb."

Although "The Blue Hotel" is steeped in irony, Crane explores the conundrum between fate and moral choice. The story is elusive on whether human beings share moral responsibility for the consequences of their actions. The Swede's fate is tragic and of his own making, yet who is to say whether it was the whiskey, given to him by the well-intentioned Scully, which turned him into a reckless fool? On one thing Crane is clear: Life is fragile.

Whether the Swede is trapped by his fixed idea about the environment or whether it is the environment that traps him, his death comes as quickly and easily as the slicing of a melon. The motto on the cash register implies that he deserves his fate, but, ironically, the message comes too late to save him, as his eyes are already glazed over by the shadow of death.

Perhaps literary critic J. C. Levenson best summarized the story's enigmatic quality when he wrote: "Given the facts as presented, the story constructs a universe that defies every quest for certain meaning." However, this much can be said: Crane's philosophy has an existential element. Had this been merely a naturalist allegory, the author would have concluded with the Swede's death and not included the conversation between the easterner and the cowboy. Despite the chaos and moral uncertainty, Crane rejects passivity. He embraces the conceit that humankind has ethical obligations.

Style and Technique

Robert Louis Stevenson once wrote that in a good story, terrain and atmosphere should express and symbolize the characters and action. Crane follows Stevenson's injunction, as the images of the blizzard and the "screaming blue" hotel foreshadow the subsequent fistfight and stabbing. In fact, just as the blue-legged heron "declares his position" against its background, so the Swede (called a wild loony by Johnnie) has a fixed position that is antagonistic to the environment.

The blizzard symbolizes nature's harshness, the blinding rage of a hostile environment that can snuff out visibility, reducing the landscape to "a gray swampish hush." Crane writes that "the conceit of man was explained by the storm to be the very engine of life. One was a coxcomb not to die in it." The blue color of the hotel is a testimony to the owner's conceit. Scully imagines himself to be an exemplary host and entrepreneur. Rather than viewing the Blue Hotel as a tranquil haven, the Swede believes it to be a frontier outpost fraught with danger. In the end, his irrational fear becomes a self-fulfilling prophecy. Thus, a person's conceit can be an agent of death as well as an engine of life.

In some ways the three travelers parody the biblical Wise Men. Scully, who "looks curiously like a priest," tells them that guests have "sacred privileges." He provides them with (baptismal) water, shows the Swede icons (pictures of his children), and offers him (sacramental) libation. Crane even describes the stove as like an altar that hums "with godlike violence." In the end, the deluded Swede runs from the safety of the temple and meets his fate in the hellish saloon.

Crane's use of vivid colors is one of his trademarks, and literary critics have debated the meaning of the hotel's heron-blue paint as well as the saloon's beckoning red light. They obviously are contrasting focal points, beacons as well as advertising gimmicks. The tranquillity and purity of the blue seem out of place; that is its charm (and Scully's conceit). The red lamp, turning the snow the color of blood, is a warning signal that the Swede ignored. The meaning of these symbols remains mysterious, in keeping with the philosophical skepticism that runs throughout all of Crane's published writings.

James B. Lane

THE BLUSH

Author: Elizabeth Taylor (1912-1975)
Type of plot: Psychological
Time of plot: The late 1950's
Locale: A village outside of London
First published: 1958

> *Principal characters:*
> MRS. RUTH ALLEN, a middle-class, childless housewife
> MR. HUMPHREY ALLEN, her husband, a successful professional
> MRS. LACEY, her housekeeper
> MR. LACEY, her housekeeper's husband, a small, beaten-down
> man

The Story

Mrs. Ruth Allen is contemplating the disappointments of her married life. She has always longed for children and imagined raising them according to her upper-middle-class English lifestyle. However, for reasons not divulged in the story, she has remained childless.

In contrast, her housekeeper, Mrs. Lacey, complains about her own brood of three children, who appear to fall short of her expectations. However, the reader learns that she has rather neglected her children when they were little. While her children went hungry and asked for food from the villagers, Mrs. Lacey sat drinking beer in the local working-class pub, shooing them away when they approached her there. Mrs. Allen imagines both raising her own children differently and how much she would enjoy a relaxed drink in the pub frequented by Mrs. Lacey rather than her Sunday sherries consumed in the more formal atmosphere of the pub patronized by people of her social class.

With Mrs. Allen living a lonely life waiting for her husband, Humphrey, to come home after working long days in London and Mrs. Lacey going on about the troubles caused by her almost grownup children, the lives of the two women seem rather opposite. Mrs. Lacey is jealous of her employer's money, and Mrs. Allen tries hard not to resent Mrs. Lacey for what she feels are the blessings of her normal, carefree life. Looking at Mrs. Lacey's aged body, which bears the marks of a rough life, she wonders if her husband, Humphrey, would be unable to relate to her at all. Mrs. Lacey only works for Mrs. Allen in the mornings and has never met her husband.

One day, Mrs. Lacey is very late for work. She apologizes to Mrs. Allen and describes to her all the symptoms of being pregnant again, in spite of her advanced middle age. Astonished, Mrs. Allen leaves her to work in the house and walks her dog. When she returns, Mrs. Lacey has gone, leaving behind a note saying that she is too unwell for work.

Toward the evening, Mr. Lacey is a surprise visitor at Mrs. Allen's. He confronts her with some anger in his voice, begging her to stop employing his wife at night to babysit Mrs. Allen's children while she and her husband go out to party. To an utterly astonished Mrs. Allen, Mr. Lacey says that he has often wanted to confront her husband driving home Mrs. Lacey late at night, asking him to mind his own children and family and not to deprive Mr. Lacey and their children of the company and care of his wife and their mother.

Mrs. Allen agrees not to employ Mrs. Lacey anymore, definitely not at night, while she is pregnant. Awkwardly, Mr. Lacey takes his leave from Mrs. Allen. As soon as she has left her house, Mrs. Allen feels a deep blush covering her face, neck, and upper arms.

Themes and Meanings

In addition to the powerful shock at the end of the story, when Mrs. Allen must realize how completely different a life the other woman has invented for herself, Elizabeth Taylor's story features three interrelated themes: human alienation, class differences in post-World War II British society, and the disaffection of women living in this society. To her surprise, Mrs. Allen must recognize how little she really knows about Mrs. Lacey and how alienated the two women are from each other. Despite the fact that they have worked and chatted together for many years, Mrs. Allen never had an inkling of Mrs. Lacey's nightly escapades nor the fact that she is capable of using her imagination to tell such a wild story about Mrs. Allen.

This theme of human alienation is reinforced by the picture that the author paints of the married lives of the two women. Humphrey Allen is a remote presence who comes home late at night and does not seem to show much interest in the details of his wife's life. Mr. Lacey, a small, worn-out man twenty years older than his wife, does not appear to command the loving respect of his wife, so that the married couples live quite apart emotionally.

The characters' alienation from each other is powerfully reinforced by their class differences. Their different classes clearly separate and differentiate the two women from each other. Mrs. Lacey's remarkable fecundity also reflects an ironic allusion to her status as a proletarian because the word literally refers to the ample offspring born to the working classes in the times of economist Karl Marx, who popularized the idea of the proletariat. Even though her body is no longer attractive in a conventional sense, it obviously does not fail to attract the father of her fourth child.

On the other hand, Mrs. Allen's life revolves around dreams, aspirations, and limitations of the upper middle class of mid-twentieth century Great Britain. Her dreams for her children include a romp in the garden of her suburban house and contain the vision of sending off her oldest boy to that traditional British prerequisite of the middle and upper classes, the boarding school. Mrs. Allen does not rebel and contents herself with her tea at four-thirty every afternoon.

The theme of women's unhappiness with the highly gendered class society of the 1950's in England is a powerful thread unifying the story. What may contribute to the intensity of Mrs. Allen's blush is the fact that Mrs. Lacey has given her husband a picture of Mrs. Allen that completely contradicts her reality and even her dreams. Raised with the traditional expectations of a woman of her upper-middle-class standing, Mrs. Allen dreamt of finding fulfillment as a mother, wife, and homemaker. When reality fails to fulfill her expectations, she grows deeply disaffected and begins to envy Mrs. Lacey for her children and even her proletarian privilege to drink a beer in public.

Mrs. Lacey, on the other hand, refers to her children and even her marriage more as a burden than as a source of fulfillment. She is jealous of the material possessions of her employer and clearly refuses to live up to society's expectations. She transgresses by neglecting her children and cheating on her husband, breaking the taboos that would limit her life, and using her imagination to create a near-perfect alibi. The story suggests that, perhaps, Mrs. Lacey's flagrant acts of rebellion are also a source of Mrs. Allen's deep blush, who could never even think of acting in this way.

Style and Technique

Taylor's two outstanding techniques are her superb sense of irony and the subtle open-endedness of "The Blush." The story shows how each woman has exactly that which the other only dreams of having. Nevertheless, in a bitter joke, neither of the two women treasures what she has. Mrs. Lacey resents her children and her pregnancies, and Mrs. Allen fails to see much comfort in her material well-being.

By telling the short story exclusively from the point of view of Mrs. Allen, the final shock leading to her blush catches the reader as unaware as herself. Ironically, Mrs. Lacey has invented a life for her employer that, with a certain cruelty, completely contradicts the reality of Mrs. Allen's true, lonely life. She is too well-bred to march off into a pub of her own and cannot imagine using her money to pleasure herself.

Given the vividness of Mrs. Lacey's imagination, the story ends on a final, open note. Mr. Lacey is as convinced that Mr. Allen drives home Mrs. Lacey after work at night as he is of the other aspects of his wife's tall tale. Yet the reader never learns the true identity of Mrs. Lacey's lover or lovers, who may or may not be the biological father of her fourth child. This final uncertainty of the short story, coming on top of Mrs. Allen's sudden realization that she has completely misunderstood Mrs. Lacey, cleverly helps driving the blush in Mrs. Allen's astonished face.

R. C. Lutz

THE BOARDING HOUSE

Author: James Joyce (1882-1941)
Type of plot: Social realism
Time of plot: 1904
Locale: Dublin
First published: 1914

Principal characters:

> BOB DORAN, an unmarried clerk, a lodger in Mrs. Mooney's
> boardinghouse
> POLLY MOONEY, an attractive single girl, the daughter of the
> boardinghouse proprietress
> MRS. MOONEY, the owner of a shabby Dublin boardinghouse and
> Polly's mother
> JACK MOONEY, Mrs. Mooney's son, a clerk and a carouser

The Story

Mrs. Mooney, a coarse, shrewd, and determined woman, connives to marry off her daughter to one of the more responsible lodgers in her shabby, questionably respectable boardinghouse. Having given her daughter the run of the young men, Mrs. Mooney watches in silent approval as Polly seduces a meek, middle-aged clerk. As the story opens, Mrs. Mooney, having ascertained the facts of the situation from her daughter, prepares to confront the lover, Bob Doran. She is determined to make him marry the girl, under the weight of social, religious, and economic pressure. The story, told almost entirely through narrative flashbacks, recounts the collusion between mother and daughter in the entrapment of Doran. Although Doran balks inwardly against this coercion, he finds himself surrendering to the admonitions of his priest, to the middle-class conventions of Dublin life, and to his fears of scandal, of losing his job, and of reprisals by Polly's rowdy and violent brother. Despite his affection for Polly, he is repelled by her vulgarity and fears that he will be lowering himself socially by marrying her. Indeed, the narrative substantiates Doran's "notion that he was being had," while it makes clear that his capitulation is a foregone conclusion.

Because most of the story is told through exposition and flashback, very little happens in the course of the narrative, which spans only about an hour on a Sunday morning. Doran, the reluctant lover and the even more reluctant husband-to-be, is very agitated after having confessed the affair to his priest on the previous day. His anxiety increases when Polly enters, cries on his shoulder, and tells him that she has "made a clean breast of it to her mother." Feebly reassuring Polly that everything will be all right, he is summoned to an interview with Mrs. Mooney. While Mrs. Mooney has the matter out with Doran, her daughter obediently awaits the outcome of the interview, her mind filled with pleasant reminiscences of her trysts with her lover and with still more pleasant "hopes and visions of the future." At the end of the story, Mrs. Mooney, whose name recalls "money," calls Polly downstairs to inform her of the "reparation," a promise of marriage, which she has extracted from Bob Doran.

Themes and Meanings

In discussing *Dubliners* (1914), the thematically related collection of stories in which "The Boarding House" appears, James Joyce stated, "My intention was to write a chapter of the moral history of my country and I chose Dublin for the scene because that city seemed to me the centre of paralysis. I have tried to present it to the indifferent public under four of its aspects: childhood, adolescence, maturity, and public life." Viewed in these terms, "The Boarding House" does indeed comment on the "moral history" of Ireland, as evidenced by the perversion of sexuality depicted throughout the story. On the one hand, sexuality is trivialized by the meaningless promiscuity of the transients and music hall artistes who pass through Mrs. Mooney's boardinghouse. More significantly, the marriage relationship, which should be based on love and long-term sexual commitment, is effected by entrapment of the man by the woman into a sordid monetary arrangement. Accordingly, Mrs. Mooney, one of a series of monstrous, overbearing mothers who appear throughout *Dubliners*, congratulates herself that she is not like "some mothers she knew who could not get their daughters off their hands." Clearly the story demonstrates the aptness of the nickname that the lodgers have given Mrs. Mooney: They call her "the Madam." Throughout, the narrator condemns the calculation and vulgarity of Polly's seduction of Doran and pities him for his helplessness in falling into the hands of calculating women.

However, the story also notes that Doran, in his passivity and excessive cautiousness, is life-denying, himself a victim of the paralysis that pervades Irish life. Accordingly, Polly emerges, however crassly, as an embodiment of the life force, who, in Shavian terms, claims Doran as the father of her child and rescues him from deadness and sterility, in spite of himself. The great irony of "The Boarding House" is that, without the intervention of Polly Mooney, Doran, a self-proclaimed celibate, seems destined for the loveless, lonely existence of the mature protagonists of two other stories in the collection, Maria in "Clay" and Mr. Duffy in "A Painful Case." Fittingly, the only lively descriptions in this otherwise bare and austere story are of Polly, as Doran recalls her "wise innocence" in seducing him: "Her white instep shone in the opening of her furry slippers and the blood glowed warmly behind her perfumed skin. From her hands and wrists too as she lit and steadied her candle a faint perfume arose."

Style and Technique

In his own words, Joyce sought to describe the dilemmas of the inhabitants of "dear, dirty Dublin" in "a style of scrupulous meanness." He sought to give his countrymen "one good look at themselves" in a "nicely polished looking-glass," so as to take the first step toward their "spiritual liberation." Accordingly, the treatment is cool, detached, contemplative. The omniscient point of view often describes without comment the action of the story, as Mrs. Mooney would see it, and leaves all judgments to the reader: "she was an outraged mother. She had allowed him to live beneath her roof, assuming that he was a man of honour, and he had simply abused her hospitality." However, at other times, Joyce's anger and indignation show, as in his description of Polly as "a little perverse madonna" and of Mrs. Mooney: "She dealt with moral problems as a cleaver deals with meat."

The theme of paralysis is reinforced, throughout the story, by the fact that very little happens, and whatever does happen takes place offstage. Accordingly, the final scene of the story focuses on Polly daydreaming in her lover's bedroom, as her mother speaks with him downstairs, but the reader is not privy to their crucial conversation. The treatment is deliberately anticlimactic: To a character such as Bob Doran, life is what happens to him, never what he chooses or determines.

Carola M. Kaplan

BOBOK

Author: Fyodor Dostoevski (1821-1881)
Type of plot: Fantasy
Time of plot: The 1870's
Locale: St. Petersburg
First published: 1873 (English translation, 1919)

> *Principal characters:*
> IVAN IVANOVICH, the narrator and protagonist, an unsuccessful writer
> PYOTR PETROVICH KLINEVICH, a baron
> VASILY VASILEVICH PERVOEDOV, a major general
> AVDOTYA IGNATYEVNA, a lady of high society
> TARASEVICH, a seventy-year-old privy councillor
> CATICHE BESETOVA, a young girl
> PLATON NIKOLAEVICH, a philosopher, naturalist, and scientist
> SEMYON EVSEICH LEBEZYATNIKOV, a court councillor
> AN ENGINEER
> A SHOPKEEPER
> A YOUTH

The Story

The narrator, Ivan Ivanovich, is a disgruntled, unsuccessful writer who has had one novel and numerous journalistic columns rejected. He earns his living by translating from French and by writing advertisements. He is proud, resents his lack of success, and broods about his rejection. His anguished mental condition brought about by his intense feelings of inferiority leads others to regard him as insane. He himself acknowledges that something strange is happening to him. He complains of headaches and sees and hears strange visions and sounds. He is haunted by an enigmatic sound—"bobok." In order to distract himself, he attends the funeral of a distant relative, where he is treated haughtily, adding to his humiliation and resentment. After the funeral he remains in the cemetery, sits down on a tombstone, and becomes lost in reflection. He lies on a long stone shaped like a coffin and begins to hear muffled voices coming from the earth below. As he listens, he distinguishes various voices of the dead: the weighty, dignified voice of Major General Vasily Vasilevich Pervoedov; the saccharine, ingratiating voice of the court councillor Semyon Evseich Lebezyatnikov; the masculine, plebeian voice of a shopkeeper; the haughty voice of the irritable lady, Avdotya Ignatyevna; the frightened voice of a deceased youth; the lisping, peevishly imperious voice of the privy councillor, Tarasevich; the insolent, gentlemanly voice of Baron Pyotr Petrovich Klinevich; the cracked, giggling, girlish voice of the young Catiche Besetova; and the bass voice of an engineer. While listening to the conversations, Ivan realizes that the life of the dead resembles the life of the living: Lebezyatnikov accuses Pervoedov of cheating in the card game they are playing; Avdotya complains of the shopkeeper's hiccuping and accuses him of shortchanging people when he was alive; the shopkeeper accuses Avdotya of not paying her debts; Lebezyatnikov suggests to Pervoedov that they tease Avdotya to relieve their boredom; Pervoedov accuses the deceased youth's doctor of overcharging his patients; Lebezyatnikov fawns and cringes before Pervoedov and Klinevich; Klinevich, a scoundrel who, while alive, passed counterfeit money and informed on his accomplice, reveals the crimes of the debauched Tarasevich, who stole money from widows and orphans; Tarasevich lusts after Catiche; and everyone quarrels and engages in petty gossip. As the narrator continues to listen to the conversations of the deceased, the meaning of the enigmatic title of the story, "Bobok," is revealed. In response to Klinevich's query as to how it is possible that the dead can talk, Lebezyatnikov summarizes the theory of the philosopher Platon Nikolaevich, who maintains that after death, remnants of life become concentrated in the consciousness, which may last for two to six months until the decomposition of the body is complete. One of their number, Lebezyatnikov adds, one whose body has almost completely decomposed, nevertheless will occasionally utter a meaningless word or two, "Bobok, bobok"—a sign that even in him life "still flickers like an imperceptible spark." Klinevich suggests that before that vital spark of life disappears completely, they should arrange their lives differently, agreeing to be ashamed of nothing. All the deceased enthusiastically voice their assent as Klinevich urges them to live the last two months in shameless truth: "It's impossible to live on earth and not lie because living and lying are synonymous. But here, just for laughs, let's have no lying. Devil take it, after all, the grave does mean something!" Before the participants are able to bare their souls, Klinevich begins to tease General Pervoedov about his undue concern for rank and social standing even after death. The indignant Pervoedov defends rank and honor to the amusement and taunts of everyone. Amid the general pandemonium, the narrator, Ivan, inadvertently sneezes and everyone falls silent. Ivan leaves the cemetery disgusted by the pettiness and vulgarity of the dead in the midst of a holy and sanctified cemetery. He vows to return at a later date to learn more about the lives of the deceased. In the meantime, he will take his notes to a publisher in the hope that they will be printed.

Themes and Meanings

Fyodor Dostoevski was essentially a religious writer interested in spiritual and moral questions. Throughout his career he attempted to portray moral beauty in all of its perfection. Two of his major protagonists, Prince Myshkin in *Idiot* (1868; *The Idiot*, 1887) and Alyosha in *Bratya Karamazovy* (1879-1880; *The Brothers Karamazov*, 1912), have Christlike qualities. They represent Dostoevski's attempt to portray a near-perfect, moral, compassionate human being. In contrast, the characters portrayed by Dostoevski in "Bobok" represent vice, debauchery, and pettiness. They engage in fraud, gambling, and theft. This portrait of the life of the dead reflects everything that is corrupt in an immoral, imperfect world. Dostoevski portrays moral corruption with the hope of awakening the reader's spiritual consciousness. He does this by means of a most unlikely vehicle—namely, the allegedly insane narrator, Ivan, who retains a sense of moral right and outrage. Ivan's first reaction to the graveyard and corpses is disgust at the smell of the decayed bodies. It becomes apparent, however, that the stench that overwhelms him is as much moral as physical. He is dismayed by the incongruity of true grief and feigned grief mixed with considerable ribaldry; such frivolity seems profoundly out of place in a cemetery. He is equally outraged to find one of the tombstones desecrated by a sandwich that someone has left on the tombstone. He throws it onto the ground because it is not bread (something sacred) but merely a sandwich (something profane). By the end of the story, Ivan is in complete despair over the petty conversations, debauchery, and squabbling which he has witnessed among the dead: "Debauchery in such a place, debauchery of last hopes, debauchery of flabby and rotting corpses, not even sparing the last moments of consciousness! . . . And worst of all, worst of all—in such a place! No, this I cannot tolerate."

Dostoevski uses Ivan as his vehicle for affirming the importance of spiritual consciousness. By the end of the story, Ivan has rejected the debauchery he has witnessed and has condemned the desecration of hallowed ground. He has learned the meaning of the enigmatic sound "bobok," which represents the last spark of consciousness left in human beings before the final decay of their bodies. Dostoevski valued consciousness as a source of possible spiritual regeneration and hope for humankind. By describing the bizarre afterlife of his characters, he draws attention to the threat of spiritual death, challenging readers to reevaluate their own moral standards and behavior in order to understand more clearly the importance of a spiritual existence.

Style and Technique

Dostoevski may be described as a fantastic realist. He constantly blurs the distinction between the real world and the dream world, the world of the sane and the insane. Here he achieves this effect through his use of the first-person narrator, Ivan Ivanovich, who is an alienated outsider. Dostoevski creates a feeling of emotional tension by writing in a staccato-type style, employing short syntactical units in rapid succession. When Ivan's friends suspect that he may be going insane, they recognize that a change has also occurred in Ivan's style of writing. One friend remarks: "Your style is changing . . . it's choppy. You chop and chop—you interpolate a clause, and then another clause within it, and then you add still something else in parenthesis, and then you start chopping and chopping again." This quotation describes accurately the style of those parts of the story in which the reader encounters Ivan's narrative voice. The reader is presented with Ivan's seemingly random thoughts in rapid succession—a device that anticipates the use of stream of consciousness in modern fiction.

By using a first-person narrator, Dostoevski draws the reader into a more personal relationship with the main protagonist and facilitates the reader's identification with the protagonist's thoughts, questions, doubts, and fantasies. It is through Ivan's reflections that Dostoevski raises the question of the standards by which society distinguishes the boundary between the normal and the abnormal. Ivan quotes a Spanish witticism directed against the first French lunatic asylum: "They've locked up all their fools in a special house to prove they are wise people themselves." He concludes that no one can prove his own sanity by stating someone else has gone mad, thereby defending himself against the charge of madness and leaving the final judgment up to the reader. The reader cannot be certain whether Ivan is sane or not, just as he cannot be sure whether Ivan is dreaming or actually hears the voices of the dead. Before Ivan hears the voices, he states simply: "At this point I sank into oblivion." He then listens to the protracted conversations of the deceased, which continue unabated until he inadvertently interrupts them by sneezing: "And here I suddenly sneezed. This was sudden and unintentional, but the effect was remarkable: All was hushed as though in a graveyard, vanished like a dream." The sneeze interrupts both the conversations of the dead and Ivan's meditations. Ivan returns to reality and vows to record and publish what he has heard. The reader is left to determine for himself the sanity of the narrator and the significance of what the narrator has learned and revealed.

Jerome J. Rinkus

BONTSHA THE SILENT

Author: Isaac Leib Peretz (1852-1915)
Type of plot: Satire
Time of plot: The late 1800's
Locale: Eastern Europe and Heaven
First published: "Bontche Shveig," 1894 (English translation, 1899)

> *Principal characters:*
> BONTSHA THE SILENT, the protagonist, a poor laborer
> THE DEFENDING ANGEL, who recounts Bontsha's life
> THE PROSECUTING ANGEL

The Story

In this characteristically ironic tale, Isaac Leib Peretz recounts the tragic life of one of his best-known protagonists, Bontsha the Silent. By opening with Bontsha's death, Peretz projects his narrative into the realm of the folktale, as he unveils before the readers fantastic scenes of Heaven, its host, and the proceedings of the heavenly court.

In the opening phase of the story, Peretz presents a summary of Bontsha's traits and the troubled life he led. Bontsha, this insignificant man on earth, who "lived unknown, in silence, and in silence he died," is born to a poor Jewish family. He silently accepts pain from the outset when, at the age of eight days, his circumcision causes him undue bleeding and pain. Even at his Bar Mitzvah ceremony, the thirteen-year-old Bontsha remains silent, failing to deliver the traditional speech expected of young Jews entering adulthood.

Bontsha also remains silent when, as a grown-up, he uncomplainingly suffers the miseries, pain, and poverty his fate bestows on him in a world too preoccupied with itself to notice the existence of those in need in life, illness, and death. All traces of Bontsha's shadowy existence are soon lost; the ephemeral quality of his earthly life is confirmed when the wooden marker falls off his grave, to be picked up and burned.

Surprisingly, however, Bontsha's death is known by everyone in Heaven, where his reception is excitedly anticipated. Although not noted for his holiness, fame, or righteousness, the silent Bontsha is accorded the highest honors (to the consternation of some saintly residents).

Bontsha remains, in death as in life, silent. Baffled and incredulous at the honors extended to him, he is certain that this is but a dream, soon to vanish as he again awakens to his hellish existence. Perhaps, he thinks, mistaken identity is the cause of this warm outpouring, soon to be reversed as in past experiences, when the error resulted in his becoming the brunt of embarrassed anger.

Bontsha's fear becomes magnified when, finding himself standing in the magnificently bejeweled court in Paradise, he is certain that he has been mistaken for someone else who would merit standing in so rich a palace.

Bontsha's trial begins; he, like all mortals, must pass before the heavenly tribunal to be rewarded or punished for his deeds on earth. His defending angel opens the testimony by presenting specific details to illustrate Bontsha's eternal, silent suffering at the hands of others. Beginning with Bontsha's birth, the defending angel details the sad life story of this humble man; the prosecuting angel mocks the defense's testimony, but Bontsha's advocate persists, recounting how this most silent, persevering sufferer lost his mother in his early years, only to be reared by a wicked stepmother whose stinginess with food was matched only by her generosity in meting out punishment. Bontsha was finally cast out of home (and on a cold wintry night) by his own father, a drunkard, to wander aimlessly and land in prison in the big city.

Silent even then, not questioning or protesting his imprisonment or the subsequent lowly jobs at which he works after being released, Bontsha continued to go through life. Finding a more decent job as a porter, Bontsha risked life and limb as he carried heavy loads on his back through crowded, traffic-laden streets. There too, however, he remained unchanged, often begging silently with his eyes only for the meager wages due him, accepting delays, and silently tolerating outright cheating. Bontsha never, says the defending angel, would compare his lot with that of others and would always accept his lot without a murmur against man or God.

A seemingly miraculous turn of events occurred in Bontsha's life when, having rescued a wealthy Jewish passenger from catastrophe in a runaway horse-drawn carriage, he was rewarded with a job as coachman, a marriage, and a child. Before he even had a chance to pay Bontsha, however, this philanthropist mysteriously went bankrupt. Bontsha's wife, meanwhile, ran off, leaving him with her son (who, when he grew up, threw Bontsha out of his house). Through all these troubled events, continues the defending angel, Bontsha continued to accept his fate silently and submissively, without a word of protest or complaint.

The defending angel, now speaking at length without the prosecutor's interruptions, reviews the circumstances of Bontsha's death, when he was run over by the very horse-drawn carriage of his former benefactor, who, as suddenly and mysteriously as before, recovered from bankruptcy, hired a new coachman, and continued living as before. Bontsha suffered his wounds from the accident in silence, in a hospital whose doctors and nurses ignored him and did nothing to ease his pain. Even while dying, Bontsha remained silent, never uttering a word against other human beings or God.

Concluding his defense, the angel leaves Bontsha trembling in fear of what the prosecution will present from his murky past. Surprisingly, the prosecuting angel proclaims that "he was always silent—and now I too will be silent."

The judge, praising Bontsha's perseverance and silence in life, offers him any reward he wishes to choose in Paradise. Incredulously, Bontsha, now lifting his eyes, still needs the judge's repeated confirmation that it is indeed he who merits this highest of rewards. Bontsha's surprising request—in the light of all that is before him—is to have a roll and butter for breakfast every day.

The request lands like thunder, silencing and shaming the heavens. Only the prosecuting angel's loud laughter shatters the silence.

Themes and Meanings

In the character of Bontsha, Peretz has fashioned the supreme example of tolerance, passivity, and silent suffering. By his silence, Bontsha is as a mirror, reflecting the inhumanity of humanity to humanity in a modern world.

Like the biblical Job—who, as commentaries emphasize, did not complain when his fate turned bad, saying, "Shall we accept good from God, and not accept evil?" Bontsha is a little man in a big world, accepting his lot without a word against other human beings or God. Unlike Job, however, Bontsha lacks the dreams, aspirations, and passion to attain a better life. Through Bontsha's story, Peretz champions those lowly and downtrodden segments of society, targets for exploitation by a ruling class preoccupied with selfish concerns.

Writing for and about the lower class of Eastern European Jewry at the turn of the twentieth century, Peretz also adopted and adapted familiar aspects of Jewish folktales (including the tales of Hasidic Jews). Thus, for example, in this and other stories, he depends on traditional tales set in Paradise; also traditional is the depiction of the heavenly court. At the same time, in presenting the latter Peretz reveals his experiences as a lawyer. By such means, the author lends his story an aura of the folktale while also keeping the ironic barbs inherent in his modern, secularized point of view.

Style and Technique

How can the lifetime of any individual be encapsulated and dramatically presented in a brief short story? In "Bontsha the Silent," Peretz has demonstrated his skills at creating tense dramatic plot by constructing events in cyclic, repeating episodes that accomplish the desired effect of deepening the character's personality while also leaving him to represent the plight of all downtrodden people.

The first cycle constitutes the story's opening, wherein the narrative recounts—briefly and with few embellishing details—the plight and travails of the protagonist in a reverse order, moving backward from his death and returning to the circumstances of the very disappearance of his grave marker.

Peretz then shifts to ironic contrast as all in Heaven are excited at the news of Bontsha's imminent arrival. Irony is indeed the most outstanding device used by the author to lend his story the dramatic force and poignancy so necessary in a satire. Also notable is the manner in which Peretz gradually silences the prosecuting angel's objections; this permits the uninterrupted flow of the defending angel's account to envelop the reader completely.

The episode of the trial provides the occasion for the second biographical cycle, wherein the defending angel shocks the reader with more explicit details of the cruelty encountered by Bontsha during his life time. Even more so in this instance, the author expresses his strong views concerning the injustices still going on in a world proudly calling itself modern and progressive.

Stephen Katz

THE BOTTLE IMP

Author: Robert Louis Stevenson (1850-1894)
Type of plot: Fairy tale
Time of plot: The late nineteenth century
Locale: Hawaii
First published: 1893

Principal characters:
> KEAWE, a young Hawaiian sailor who is "poor, brave, and active"
> KOKUA, his wife
> LOPAKA, his friend, another Hawaiian sailor

The Story

While making a visit to San Francisco "to have a sight of the great world," Keawe, a young Hawaiian sailor, admires the opulent houses of the rich. He is particularly impressed by one house, which, while smaller than the rest, is "all finished and beautified like a toy." To his surprise, he discovers that the elderly man who lives in this beautiful house is "heavy with sorrow" and sighs constantly. The elderly man tells Keawe that his house and all his fortune came from an imp who lives in a magic bottle. The imp will grant any wish that the owner of the bottle makes, but if the owner dies before he sells the bottle, "he must burn in hell forever." The person who sells the bottle must always sell it for less than he paid for it. The elderly man tricks Keawe into buying the bottle for fifty dollars, which is all the money that Keawe has. Keawe attempts to discard the bottle or sell it for a profit, but it magically comes back to him.

When he returns to Hawaii, Keawe finds that his uncle and cousin have died, leaving him their land and a large sum of money. Resolving that he "may as well take the good along with the evil" of the bottle, Keawe has a beautiful house, called Bright House, built overlooking the ocean. His friend Lopaka persuades him to call the imp out of the bottle so that they can see what it looks like; although they are horrified at the appearance of the imp, Lopaka buys the bottle in order to enlist its power to obtain a schooner for himself.

Free of the bottle, Keawe lives in Bright House in "perpetual joy"; he could not "walk in the chambers without singing." He sees a beautiful young woman, Kokua, bathing in the sea and instantly falls in love with her. She agrees to marry him, but then Keawe discovers that he has contracted leprosy. Unwilling to marry Kokua while he has this dread disease, Keawe resolves to buy the bottle again, although "ice ran in his veins" at the thought of the evil-looking imp. He goes in search of Lopaka, and although he cannot find his friend, he succeeds in tracing the bottle, which is now in the possession of a young white man who was desperate to pay back some money that he had embezzled and paid only two cents for the bottle. It appears that anyone who buys it from him for one cent will have no opportunity to sell it for a coin of less value. Nevertheless, Keawe buys the bottle and, again resolving to "take the good along with the evil," wishes himself free of leprosy and marries Kokua.

In spite of Kokua's beauty, Keawe must "weep and groan to think upon the price that he had paid for her" because he believes that he has "no better hope but to be a cinder forever in the flames of hell." When he realizes that Kokua is blaming herself for his unhappiness, he tells her the whole story of the bottle. She tells him about a French coin, the centime, which is worth "five to the cent or thereabout," and they go to Tahiti to sell the bottle for four centimes.

When they encounter unexpected difficulty in selling the bottle, Kokua exclaims, "A love for a love, and let mine be equalled with Keawe's! A soul for a soul, and be it mine to perish!" Resolving to buy the bottle herself, she finds an old man and asks him to buy the bottle for four centimes, promising to buy it from him for three. She bravely fulfills her promise, but afterward in her imagination "all that she had heard of hell came back to her; she saw the flames blaze, and she smelled the smoke, and her flesh withered on the coals." Not realizing that his wife now owns the bottle, Keawe condemns her for not participating in his joy at being rid of it. Angry at her and feeling unacknowledged guilt over the fate of the old man who he thinks owns the bottle, he accuses Kokua of disloyalty and goes out to carouse with some friends.

One of his drinking companions is a brutal white man who has been "a boatswain of a whaler—a runaway, a digger in gold mines, a convict in prisons." The boatswain, who has a "low mind and a foul mouth," encourages Keawe to drink until he runs out of money. Returning to his house for more money, Keawe sees Kokua with the bottle and realizes her sacrifice. He slips away before Kokua sees him and resolves to become the owner of the bottle for the third time. Although his soul is "bitter with despair," he persuades the boatswain to buy the bottle for two centimes, promising to buy it from him for one. When Keawe attempts to fulfill his promise, the boatswain refuses to sell. Keawe reminds him that the owner of the bottle will go to hell, but the boatswain replies, "I reckon I'm going anyway . . . and this bottle's the best thing to go with I've struck yet." He goes away with the bottle, leaving Keawe and Kokua to the "peace of all their days in the Bright House."

Themes and Meanings

Like fairy stories and the tales from *Alf layla wa-layla* (fifteenth century; *The Arabian Nights' Entertainments*, 1706-1708) that it resembles, "The Bottle Imp" posits a clear contrast between good and evil, asserts the power of love and sacrifice in overcoming evil, and rewards its good characters with a lifetime of continuing happiness.

Keawe rather innocently entangles himself with evil because he is so deeply impressed by the opulent house in San Francisco, but once he buys the bottle—without quite realizing that he has done so—he finds it difficult to disentangle himself from its evil. The fact that his uncle and cousin die to leave him the land on which he builds his house and the coincidence that the cost of this house is exactly the sum that his uncle leaves him suggest that the evil imp in the bottle exacts a high price for his favors, but Robert Louis Stevenson does not insist on this point as the story develops.

Having relied on the imp for his house, Keawe, perhaps naturally, seeks his help in curing his leprosy, but this time an important new motive has been added: Keawe would willingly resign himself to exile in the leper colony at Molokai if it were not for his love of Kokua. The importance of love in opposition to evil is henceforth the main theme of the story.

In Tahiti, Kokua, mindful that Keawe bought the bottle the second time because of his love for her, buys the bottle herself, willing to sacrifice her own soul for Keawe. When Keawe discovers what she has done, he resolves to purchase the bottle a third time to save his wife. This time, it is important to note, he is motivated by awareness of her sacrifice rather than by delight in her beauty; his infatuation seems to have deepened into a nobler love.

Although the lovers overcome the evil of the imp, Stevenson throughout the story emphasizes the stark reality of evil. Lopaka and Keawe are figuratively "turned to stone" by the sight of the imp, and both Keawe and Kokua are cast in such despair by the prospect of an eternity in hell that they are unable to enjoy the love for which they have sacrificed themselves.

Style and Technique

As the theme of the story utilizes the clear contrast of good and evil that is characteristic of a fairy story, so are the plot devices and the style reminiscent of this genre. Keawe, motivated initially by Kokua's beauty, falls in love at first sight; after they succeed in disposing of the bottle, they live "happily ever after"—and Stevenson narrowly misses ending the story with this venerable cliche. Of the plot devices borrowed from the fairy-tale tradition, the most significant is the bottle imp himself, who can grant any wish but who nevertheless is a sinister presence. No attempt is made to explain this bottle by any rational means or to treat it as a symbol: It is simply magic.

Stevenson's descriptions deliberately emulate the lack of specificity and the unreality of a fairy story: When Keawe builds his house, "a garden bloomed about that house with every hue of flowers," and Kokua is "so fashioned, from the hair upon her head to the nails upon her toes, that none could see her without joy." The tone of the dialogue is more conventional than real: Keawe declares that in his beautiful house his wish is "to live there without care and to make merry with my friends and relatives." Studied inversions of word order ("great was their joy that night") and occasional use of exclamations such as "behold!" give the style a deliberately archaic flavor.

Erwin Hester

A BOTTLE OF MILK FOR MOTHER

Author: Nelson Algren (Nelson Ahlgren Abraham, 1909-1981)
Type of plot: Naturalistic
Time of plot: The 1930's
Locale: Chicago
First published: 1941

Principal characters:
BRUNO "LEFTY" BICEK, the protagonist, a hoodlum and boxer
CAPTAIN KOZAK, his principal interrogator
SERGEANT ADAMOVITCH, an older police officer
A NEWSPAPER REPORTER, the witness to the interrogation

The Story

"A Bottle of Milk for Mother" is an interrogation story that pits a young Polish hoodlum against an experienced, cynical police captain. From the time that he is brought into the interrogation room until he is led to his cell, Bruno struggles to maintain his composure, to use his street knowledge of law, and to avoid implicating his friend and accomplice Benkowski. Unfortunately for Bruno, while he succeeds in shielding Benkowski, his case is "well disposed of," and he is left to tell himself, "I knew I'd never get to be twenty-one anyhow."

Rather than have his men tell their story about the robbery and shooting of the drunk, Kozak insists on Bruno telling his own story. From the start, Kozak assumes Bruno's guilt, as well as Benkowski's, and Bruno is quickly reduced from denying knowledge of the drunk to explaining how the one shot must have "bounced." Kozak dismisses out of hand the "just getting a bottle of milk for Mother" explanation, and then he attacks Bruno's ego. First, Kozak breaks Bruno's valuable spring-blade knife, a symbol of his manhood, and Bruno winces "as though he himself had received the blow." Then Kozak calls Bruno "Lefty," thereby appealing to his vanity, for he is proud of his pitching prowess, but also encouraging him to talk. Just as the appeal to motherhood fails, so do his appeals to identification ("I'm just a neighborhood kid"), to political interference (he "innocently" refers to his ties to the "alderman," Kozak's brother), to ethnicity (he claims that he spoke Polish to the drunk and tried to make him a better Polish "citizen"), and even to patriotism (his gang is not the Warriors but the "Baldhead True American Social 'n Athletic Club").

As Bruno continues his story, Kozak abruptly intervenes with questions that assume Bruno's guilt. When Bruno talks about his pitching arm, Kozak interjects, "So you kept the rod in your left hand?" When Bruno inadvertently mentions that "we" saw the drunk, Kozak notes the reference and asks, "Who's 'we,' Left-hander?" When Bruno declares that he does not know Benkowski very well, Kozak catches him in the lie. By the time that Bruno finishes his rambling story about what "possessed" the

gang to shave their heads, there is no question about his guilt. After he refuses to im-
plicate Benkowski, only the sentencing remains, and he receives no mercy.

Perhaps because Benkowski has advised him, Bruno assumes that he will be able to
escape relatively unscathed. He considers acting "screwy," weighs the chances of having a conviction overturned because of the newspaperman's presence, figures that the
"bouncing bullet" will mean manslaughter instead of murder, and believes that because "this is a first offense 'n self-defense," he will receive only "one to fourteen"
years as a sentence. Kozak asks, "Who give you that idea?" He appears to know that
Bruno has been counseled, probably by Benkowski, and when Bruno again fails to cooperate, he explains that, in fact, he will not be able to "lam out" of the death penalty
for first-degree murder. Bruno's fate is sealed when Kozak asks, "What do you think
we ought to do with a man like you, Bicek?" While Bruno notices the change from the
familiar "Lefty" to the more impersonal "Bicek," he does not notice the significance
of "man." Bruno has referred to himself as a "kid" to win sympathy—and to avoid the
"adult" murder charge—and Kozak has called Bruno and his gang "boys." Although it
is true that Bruno does not want to be considered a "greenhorn sprout," he is not ready
to be treated and tried as an adult.

Bruno passes from boyhood to manhood and then to a state of nonbeing. Once
Kozak has "disposed" of his case, Bruno ceases to exist for the authorities. Kozak
studies the charge sheet "as though Bruno 'Lefty' Bicek were no longer in the room"
and looks at Bruno with "no light of recognition." Bruno implores the police officers,
"Don't look at me like I ain't nowheres," but no one listens to him. At this point,
Bruno is not a person but a "case" for Kozak; for Adamovitch, the traditionalist,
Bruno is a sinner who must be made to feel his guilt. When he sees Bruno go down on
his knees, he is satisfied that the unrepentant sinner has turned to God. Bruno, however, is only groping for his hat. The image with which the reader is left is not one of
the repentant sinner or even of a defiant young man; it is one of a man "on all fours"
like an animal, certain only of his impending death.

Themes and Meanings

"A Bottle of Milk for Mother," the winner of an O. Henry Memorial Prize, is a typical Nelson Algren story in its characters, setting, and themes. In fact, the story in revised form also appears in Algren's novel *Never Come Morning* (1942), which also
has Bruno "Lefty" Bicek as its protagonist. In both the short story and the novel,
Bruno's world is circumscribed: the Polish ghetto of Chicago in the novel, and an interrogation room in the short story. While Bruno is ambitious, he has only the illusion
of freedom. He is, in fact, a victim who cannot really "move" or escape from the fate
that his environment—ethnic, economic, political—imposes on him.

In the first sentence of the story, Algren describes the murder as Bruno's "final difficulty with the Racine Street police," and the reader learns that the outcome of the
story is never in doubt. Algren focuses not on what will happen but on Bruno's growing awareness of and resignation to his fate. Though the setting remains the same,
Bruno's options disappear one by one until his only "escape" is an imaginative one.

Algren's theme is Bruno's entrapment, "imprisonment," so to speak, before the sentence is ever pronounced. Early in the story, Bruno feels "the semicircle about him drawing closer," even though none of the police actually moves toward him. Throughout the interrogation Bruno stands immobile. When he shuffles his feet and moves to unbutton his shirt, Adamovitch stops him; his only movements are the "scuffling" of his shoes. He does move his eyes but only to "fix" them as a window to the outside world. In effect, the athletic Bruno is ironically rendered incapable of real action, and he "acts" only in a dramatic sense. When his act elicits only guffaws and derisive laughter from his "audience," he retreats into a fantasy world in which he "zigzags" his way to freedom; the fact that his escape is imagined in cinematic terms implies that Bruno cannot literally see himself escaping.

Style and Technique

Like many of the other stories from *The Neon Wilderness* (1946), "A Bottle of Milk for Mother" is essentially a "slice of life," a story that is short on external action, focusing instead on the protagonist's internal action, in this case the realization that he is incapable of acting. The title of the volume of Algren's short stories stresses the ironic incongruity between neon modernity and old-fashioned wilderness: There are no contemporary heroes. As in Algren's other works, irony abounds in this story, particularly in terms of the "lone wolf" motif (which is particularly appropriate to a "wilderness"). After Bruno mentions that he was acting on his own, practicing "lone-wolf stuff," that term is used, even exploited, by the newspaper reporter, who envisions using the term ironically to comment on Bruno's paralysis: "The Lone Wolf of Potomac Street waited miserably." Certainly there is irony at the end of the story when the penitent sinner turns out to be a criminal who is looking for his hat.

Algren uses a mixture of realism and impressionism to convey setting, characters, and theme. While he uses "realistic" dialogue, which effectively captures the street vernacular, with its bad grammar, slang, and colloquial expressions, Algren is hardly objective in his selection of details and his metaphors. Kozak is characterized by his "St. Bernard mouth," which renders him less human, and on another occasion his manner is compared to "the false friendliness of the insurance man urging a fleeced customer toward the door." The reporter is never identified by name; in fact, he is not a person but a "raccoon coat" adjusting his glasses. The images of the setting that Algren presents are equally depressing. When Bruno looks out the window, he sees a January sun "glowing sullenly," almost as if it were commenting on the actions within the room. When Bruno hears "outside" sounds, the Chicago Avenue streetcar seems to screech "as though a cat were caught beneath its back wheels." There certainly are ties between the cat and Bruno, for both face death, but there are also ties between the streetcar wheels and the proverbial "wheels of justice." When the simile is followed by the shadows "within shadows" in the cell, the reader is left with images that suggest inevitable death at the hands of a mechanistic, impersonal machine.

Thomas L. Erskine

BOULE DE SUIF

Author: Guy de Maupassant (1850-1893)
Type of plot: Social realism
Time of plot: About 1870
Locale: On the road between Rouen and the port city of Havre, France
First published: 1880 (English translation, 1903)

> *Principal characters:*
> ELIZABETH ROUSSET, "Boule de Suif," a prostitute and the
>   protagonist
> MONSIEUR AND MADAME LOISEAU, wholesale wine merchants
> CORNUDET, a dissolute man with political ambitions
> PRUSSIAN OFFICER

The Story

A coach is making its way along the icy road to Havre. Its passengers are silently eyeing one another, trying to reach the port in spite of the war-torn countryside and the advancing Prussian troops. Self-conscious of respectability, they are uncomfortable sharing a coach with "a member of the courtesan class," who is nicknamed "Boule de Suif" (ball of fat) because she is so round. The journey is long and tedious, so that when Boule de Suif takes some food from her traveling basket and good-heartedly offers to share it among the others, the passengers—begrudgingly at first and then avidly—eat and drink their fill; even the two nuns indulge with comic delicacy. Before long, they are all talking amiably about patriotism and the evil Prussians.

That night, the coach stops at an inn behind the Prussian lines and the passengers are given separate rooms. During the night, officious Monsieur Loiseau keeps his eyes to the keyhole of his door, trying to observe "the mysteries of the corridor." He sees the rogue Cornudet make advances to Boule de Suif, but she rebuffs him, insisting on maintaining her dignity in the midst of the enemy. A Prussian officer, the presiding "law" in that part of the country, has set up his headquarters in the inn and is staying in a room just down the hall. Under such circumstances, she tells Cornudet, one must keep one's self-respect.

The next morning, the passengers find the coach unharnessed and themselves detained. They learn that the Prussian officer has forbidden them to leave until Boule de Suif gives herself to him. She is shocked and angry at the proposal, and, for a while, so are the other passengers. Days pass. The Prussian waits. Soon the passengers grow impatient, and the Prussian's tactic of wearing down their shallow moral indignation begins to work. They begin to hatch their own strategy for getting Boule de Suif to capitulate. The wives talk to her of romantic self-sacrifice; the nuns, too, are enlisted, preaching to her of purity of motive. The men talk of war and glorious patriotism. Throughout lunch and dinner and into the evening hours the psychological assault on

Boule de Suif continues. Ironically, only Cornudet, the old rogue, refuses to have anything to do with the scheme.

Finally, exhausted, confused, and burdened with guilt over being the cause of the group's internment, Boule de Suif yields and gives herself to the Prussian. That night, the passengers celebrate victory. Loiseau "stands champagne all round." Only Cornudet is sullen. "You have done an infamous thing," he tells them.

Next morning, the passengers find the coach ready for their departure. Boule de Suif is the first to climb in, and at last they resume their journey. Now, however, the passengers snub Boule de Suif. They talk among themselves, showing her their disdain. Chatting amiably, they do not seem to care that in the dark corner of the coach Boule de Suif is silently weeping.

Themes and Meanings

"Boule de Suif" is primarily a study of character: an objective account of how people can be kind when it is easy to be so but selfish and mean when they must endure even the most temporary of personal privations.

The coach making its way to the port is, in effect, a ship of fools and knaves. Guy de Maupassant himself tells the reader that the passengers represent "Society," a cross section of humanity, the middle class of steady virtue, smugly riding to their destination. Boule de Suif is also part of the cross section. Of strong peasant stock, she is as easy, as free with her public virtue as her fellow passengers are sternly covetous of theirs. In fact, the power of "Boule de Suif" is achieved thematically by a contrast between the public virtue practiced by the majority and the private, personal morality that only Boule de Suif truly possesses. Publicly, the characters are solid bourgeois playing the role society expects of them, even showing their "democratic" spirit when sharing Boule de Suif's lunch. They have already condemned her, nevertheless, because, as a prostitute, Boule de Suif has publicly played her expected role as well. In the privacy of their cabal, and in their hearts, they are as corrupt as the public image they perceive to be Boule de Suif. Their plot is demoniacally brilliant, depending as it does on the cooperation of all the members of the group—society—and appealing to the various forms of public virtue, such as patriotism and self-sacrifice. "What did you expect from that kind of woman?" is their ultimate response to the success of their scheme.

Boule de Suif ironically shows herself superior to her fellow passengers. Her initial refusal to submit to Cornudet and then to the Prussian runs contrary to her public image. Her private moral principles are inviolate; though the others talk of patriotism, they spout mere platitudes and generalities. They are thus supreme hypocrites. Only Boule de Suif is honest, and she shows true courage and patriotism in standing up for her principles. Though she ultimately submits, her surrender is not for personal gain or public approval but motivated by guilt, by fear that she was hurting her companions. Her capitulation is thus of the same order as her sharing of her lunch with them—a generosity of spirit, a wholesomeness that her bourgeois companions would never understand. She sacrifices her body; they, their souls.

Style and Technique

Like many great literary works, "Boule de Suif" succeeds by in integration of method with subject matter. Though Maupassant is often classified as a naturalistic writer, that is, as an artist who records events with relentless objectivity, "Boule de Suif" is marked by subtle ironies of tone and detail that shrewdly comment on the action while seemingly only recording it. Though the authorial voice seems never to judge the characters or the action, narrating events swiftly and precisely, such basic narrative techniques as description of setting and the use of metaphor often amplify and deepen the meaning of the simple prose.

Maupassant takes great care in presenting the chaos of the French countryside during the Franco-Prussian War, delaying the introduction of the characters until the details of violence have established a tension that effectively prepares the reader for the real conflict between private and public virtue. The setting serves as a correlative to the battle that the coach party will wage against the principles of Boule de Suif. The season is winter, and the French are losing the war, just as the coach party coldly lays its trap, having already lost its virtue.

Even the metaphors support the idea of warfare. As the characters plot against Boule de Suif, Maupassant describes their machinations in terms of infantry besieging a "human citadel" which must "receive the enemy within its walls." Each agrees on the "plan of attack," and it is the women who begin, quoting ancient examples of self-sacrifice during wartime, from Judith and Holofernes to the Roman matrons and Hannibal. Moreover, the weather grows worse as the characters hatch their scheme. Each day of their detainment, the cold grows more intense, more painful, so that their assault on Boule de Suif takes place during a time of numbing cold, again paralleling their own heartlessness.

Finally, there is irony even in the song Cornudet sings at the close of the story. "The love of country is sacred," he sings. "Liberty, dear liberty, fight with her defenders." The true defenders of liberty are not the passengers and their bourgeois values but the country courtesan, Boule de Suif. Thus, Maupassant reinforces a swiftly moving, simple narrative with equally simple technical devices and rhetorical descriptions to make "Boule de Suif" a masterpiece of irony.

Edward Fiorelli

THE BOUND MAN

Author: Ilse Aichinger (1921-   )
Type of plot: Fable
Time of plot: Summer
Locale: Unspecified
First published: "Der Gefesselte," 1953 (English translation, 1955)

> *Principal characters:*
> THE BOUND MAN
> THE CIRCUS OWNER, who promotes the bound man
> THE CIRCUS OWNER'S WIFE, who cuts the cords

The Story

A man awakened by strong spring sunlight discovers that he is bound but in a loose way that makes him smile. He can move his legs a little, and his arms are bound to themselves, not to his body. Wanting to cut the cord, he finds that his knife, money, coat, and shoes are missing. There is also blood on his head.

After several attempts, he manages to stand up. Unable to walk, he hops away like a bird, and hears stifled laughter. Realizing that he might not be in a position to defend himself frightens him.

He heads for the nearest village. As evening falls, he learns how to walk in his bonds. He feels that he is in the power of the earth, which sometimes comes up toward him like a swift current. Before midnight, he lies down and sleeps.

The next morning, he goes through the intricate maneuver of picking up an empty wine bottle, intending to smash it and cut his bonds with a sharp edge. He is seen, however, by the owner of a circus, and becomes its chief attraction. The owner is delighted by the charm of his movements, which "seemed like the voluntary limitation of a high speed."

Everyone who goes to the circus goes to see the bound man. He is different from the other performers because he does not remove the cord between performances, although he can free himself if he wants to. To bathe, he jumps fully clothed into the river each morning. Because he never reveals anything of his past, and keeps to the same simple story of how he found himself bound, the villagers begin to think that perhaps the man has bound himself or that he is in league with the circus owner.

As autumn approaches, the circus owner speaks of moving south. Then one of the circus wolves escapes and causes trouble in the village. No one can catch it. As the bound man returns through the woods from watching the sunset, he is attacked by the wolf. In one movement, he hurls himself on the animal and brings it down. As though intoxicated, he feels that he has lost the superiority of free limbs that causes humans to be subjugated.

At the next performance, the hostile crowd insists that the bound man kill another wolf. The circus owner's wife, fearing for the bound man's safety, cuts his cords at a crucial moment. Feeling his blood flowing downwards, he grabs a gun from the wall of the cage and shoots the animal between the eyes.

Eluding his pursuers, he comes to the river at dawn. It seems as if snow has fallen, removing all memory.

Themes and Meanings

The main interpretive question raised by Ilse Aichinger's story concerns the nature of bonds. Written in the aftermath of World War II, the story seems to be a criticism of the direction that humankind was taking. People were distancing themselves from nature, and society was becoming preoccupied with the invention of high-powered weapons. In taking this direction, humankind was neglecting and denying the positive aspects of its basic animal nature. Something essential was missing in modern society. The bound man reverses this trend by voluntarily going back to the basics, dispensing with things commonly considered indispensable: his knife, money, coat, and shoes. He is, as it were, reborn. He has no past because his experiment is an alternative unfolding of human evolution from the very birth of humanity. What if one could go back in time and do things differently? Would it not be preferable to remain in one's natural state, in touch with the earth and the animals, one's body in perfect shape, responding to one's instincts?

The bound man felt himself in the power of the earth. He was exhilarated by the rediscovery of his physical potential and felt "that he had reached a speed at which no motorcycle could have overtaken him." Human beings were not made to ride around on machines that give a false sense of speed and power. Aichinger suggests that the ultimate experience of strength or speed stems from self-discipline and practice, from accepting human limitations and pushing against their boundaries, rather than reaching for easy and uninspired solutions. The most rewarding sensations result from developing one's potential, from the pride of self-reliance, and from accepting and adjusting to one's natural limitations. One line in the story stands out both typographically and thematically: When the bound man swoops down on the wolf like a bird, and he knows "with certainty that flying is possible only within a certain kind of bondage."

Aichinger implies that people have lost touch with nature through an overly cerebral approach to all situations. They have money, motorcycles, and guns, all artificial solutions. With her subtle sense of humor, Aichinger shows that humans are incurably intellectual. The spectators at the circus ask "about the ratio of the cord lengths to the length of his limbs." She also states that the bound man himself poses the greatest danger to his bonds, for his head and neck are too free. On dark mornings, he forgets the cords, moves against them, and might be tempted to cut them.

The greatest problem, however, is that a human is a social animal, reliant on others, and always subject to peer pressure. It is next to impossible for an individual in the late twentieth century to revert back to nature. The bound man needs the care and protection of the circus owner, who in turn must satisfy the spectators. Only children try, unsuccessfully, to emulate him. Among adults, the opinion is that he should be relieved of his bonds and be allowed to join them. The story is thus an exploration of an idyllic retreat, coupled with the recognition that it cannot be realized.

Style and Technique

Aichinger's use of landscape parallels the evolution of human beings and suggests the passage of time. When the bound man awakens at the beginning of the story, he is outside under a flowering elder bush. He feels compelled to head for the nearest village. Later, as a member of the circus, he moves from village to village, and these are located along a river. He is thus symbolically following the course of civilization.

The scene in which he is completely at one with nature, in which he kills the wolf as one animal kills another, is set in the woods. He feels "tenderness for an equal, for the erect one in the crouching one," and nature personified approves of his action: "He could feel the softness of the withered leaves stroking the back of his hand."

Once the bonds are cut he does not return to the woods but to the river. Time flows on. There is no going back. Aichinger's sadness at this realization is reflected in her use of the seasons. At the beginning of the story it is spring. The sun is getting stronger and making life outdoors possible. All summer long, the circus draws record crowds. Then autumn comes. Not only has summer run its course, so too has the popularity of the bound man. Preparing for winter, the spectators are no longer attracted by natural man. After he shoots the second wolf for them, it is winter, with ice floes on the water and snow, "which removes all memory." Humankind has entered an unhappy age of sophisticated weaponry, and seems to have forgotten what it means to be truly alive.

With the contrast in the killing of the two wolves, Aichinger draws a stark comparison between the way people once lived and twentieth century life. When the bound man kills the wolf in the woods in self-defense, there is an exhilarating feeling of fair competition between equals. When the unbound man shoots the wolf in the cage, however, there is only a feeling of disgust that such a beautiful creature should be wasted in this manner.

"The Bound Man" illustrates the paradoxical position of modern humankind. In thinking that people have thrown off all bondage, they are now less free than ever before. They are experiencing the "deadly superiority of free limbs which causes man's subjection." Their civilization is a circus. They are their own worst enemies. With all their so-called technological advances, they have lost touch with the earth.

Jean M. Snook

THE BOWMEN OF SHU

Author: Guy Davenport (1927-   )
Type of plot: War
Time of plot: 1914-1915
Locale: The World War I French-German front
First published: 1984

> *Principal characters:*
> HENRI GAUDIER-BRZESKA, a modernist sculptor who died in
>   1915
> SOPHIE, the sculptor's wife

The Story

The title of "The Bowmen of Shu" suggests a time and place far from the World War I foxholes that readers see the story's hero, Henri Gaudier-Brzeska, inhabiting. The twenty-three-year-old French sculptor, in whose work and intelligence the poet Ezra Pound discerned the signs of a twentieth century renaissance, has left his London studio for the trenches. Readers see him sleeping on mud and ice, fighting lustily, meditating on art, war, and nature, asking London correspondents about the art culture he is cut off from, and discussing labyrinths with the scholar and fellow soldier Robert de Launay. "The Bowmen of Shu" is named for a poem of the same title by Ezra Pound that Gaudier-Brzeska quotes in letters to friends in London. The poem presents the feelings of ancient Chinese warriors fighting a lingering war with a stubborn enemy. Their fight, like that of the soldiers of World War I, is a stalemate, with many battles fought but no victory. Gaudier-Brzeska savors the closeness of the centuries-old Chinese emotions to his own. The bowman who says, "Our sorrow is bitter, but we would not return to our country," Gaudier-Brzeska echoes in a letter describing the surprising stoicism he feels about his most miserable circumstances: "Whatever the suffering may be it is soon forgotten and we want the victory."

The story is a collection of images and anecdotes having to do with Gaudier-Brzeska's life before, as well as during, the war. Selections from his foxhole mail to friends are interspersed with scenes of his life before the war, as far back as his first day of school. As a child he loved to draw insects and flowers. He defied his parents' spankings with precociously stubborn and reasonable arguments. As an art student of seventeen he fell in love with Sophie, his senior by twenty-two years, whose biography, a testament of pure misery, is summarized in two pages of the story. As a sculptor, Gaudier-Brzeska showed a striking originality. He was part of the modernist movement, which included Sir Jacob Epstein, Constantin Brancusi, and Amedeo Modigliani, names whose fame, this story assures readers, Henri Gaudier-Brzeska would have surpassed had he lived. His personal manifesto on sculpture was claimed by the vorticist movement in London as the clearest statement of what they were about.

The war took him. His captain praised him for the bravery and intelligence he demonstrated to others. Bullets, bombs, and gas inhibited neither his craft ("With my knife I have carved the stock of a German rifle into a woman.") nor his theorizing: "Like the Africans I am constrained by the volume of my material, the figure to be found wholly within a section of trunk" ("the trunk" referring to the gun stock). Descended from the masons who built Chartres Cathedral, Gaudier-Brzeska watches as a cathedral burns to the ground, its lead roof melting onto the rubble. He savors the irony and pattern of his fate, trapped in the labyrinth of trenches that the anthropologist de Launay, who has made a career of studying mazes, now has the opportunity to study in actuality. The Germans constructed a real labyrinth during the war, a system of fortifications, tunnels, caves, and shelters out of which they would come to surprise the enemy. The primitiveness of war, its brutality, Gaudier-Brzeska and de Launay both see as the expression of urges people have acted out since the days of Paleolithic hunters. They stand up to it with philosophical interest and curiosity but admit its unspeakable horror, and it claims both of them. De Launay is shot through the neck, and Gaudier-Brzeska, leading a charge, is shot through the head.

Themes and Meanings

A central thread in the story is the theme of the artist's precariousness in the world, a world that in its mysterious history turns on itself and devours the riches of human culture that artists such as Gaudier-Brzeska create, or, in Gaudier-Brzeska's case, which destroys the maker himself. The story, however, is more than a tirade against stupid people who kill geniuses. As Gaudier-Brzeska recognized, art and contention have a mysterious linkage. Stone Age people filled caves with drawings of animals as a result of daily conflicts with real animals. Gaudier-Brzeska, known for his intense absorption while in the act of sculpting, found shooting at Germans similarly stimulating: "We shot at each other some quarter of an hour at a distance of 12 to 15 yards and the work was deadly. I brought down two great giants who stood against a burning heap of straw." The war paradoxically heightens his sense of life: "I have been fighting for two months and I can now gauge the intensity of life." That intensity took for Gaudier-Brzeska a vision of life persisting unabated by the stupendous destruction of modern war, which set out to blast every square foot of soil held by the enemy. Life ignored the bombardment. Gaudier-Brzeska explained in the manifesto he wrote in the trenches that the outline of the hills did not change as a result of the barrage of exploding shells. Life does not alter, but people alter and are altered. Gaudier-Brzeska's medium, stone, required the cutting, grinding, and biting of tools: "You brush away, blow away the dust the fine blade has crumbled." Arguments by art critics such as T. E. Hulme required words chosen "with booming precision and attack." A model posing for one of Gaudier-Brzeska's sculptures fights her body's inclination to relax. While sculpting, Gaudier-Brzeska pauses to watch a dogfight in the street outside his studio. His nose bleeds as he works, and the model ties a rag to his face to absorb the blood.

The story, then, posits the mystery of the artist's dealings with energy, the energy or passion stirred in him by what he sees, and the form of energy he establishes in a work of art. Unfortunately for Gaudier-Brzeska, the energy he was born to observe—the stance of a panther, the head of his friend Ezra Pound, the monumental curves of a woman—conflicted with another energy of which the poem's bowmen and Gaudier-Brzeska shared experience in wars. Gaudier-Brzeska's avid entry into conflict, whether with a spanking parent or a German soldier, is heroic. As a sculptor, he battled the stone to establish a form he carried in his head, a form of beauty. As a soldier, he kills and dies "pour la Patrie" (for the fatherland). To Sophie, his beloved, he was nasty because "you don't love me nearly so much as I love you," he said. The resistance of stone, the resistance of the enemy, the resistance of the beloved—"whatever the suffering may be it is soon forgotten and we want the victory."

Style and Technique

The author of this story, Guy Davenport, has his own term to describe his style. He calls it "assemblage." Blocks of narrative are arranged in a series with no chronological order. Each piece in the assemblage is titled, whether it is a two-page description of Gaudier-Brzeska's wife or a single line explaining the nickname ("La Rosalie") of the bayonet ("so called because we draw it red from the round guts of pig eyed Germans").

This "assemblage" style emphasizes the story's visual presence and structure. To heighten the visual even more, Davenport insets his drawings of Gaudier-Brzeska's statues, drawings, and photos of the sculptor. The subject of the story, Gaudier-Brzeska, presides even in the interstices. Gaudier-Brzeska contributed to the birth of a new style of sculpture, one that created emotion in the viewer through the abstract arrangement of planes. Sculpting the head of Ezra Pound, he explained that no natural resemblance would result: "It will look like your energy." Davenport's technique— the fragmenting of narrative, the use of real historical people as characters, the quoting of real letters (and creative transpositions of real letters)—owes much to the revolution all artistic forms underwent in the early twentieth century. As a story it is a graph of the author's peculiarly bright, visualizing mind as it confronts the subject— the sculptor Henri Gaudier-Brzeska. There are sharp twists, assimilations, sudden pictures, sharp edges of single sentences that work more like a poetic line than narrative. The art of such technique lies in striking from discontinuous surfaces the desired result of irony, contrast, or restatement. French erupts to conclude the second half of a paragraph begun in English. In one fragment, Gaudier-Brzeska's captain praises him for his bravery, and in the next, the obscure mother of the dead sculptor laments his passing. The style forces the reader to pay attention to the text in a new way. It challenges the reader to interpret, to discern, without the help of transitions, introductions, and footnotes. The result, for the attentive reader, is a sense of history much brighter than history read in textbooks. In "The Bowmen of Shu," it creates a graph of an outmoded concept: the hero.

Bruce Wiebe

BOXCAR OF CHRYSANTHEMUMS

Author: Fumiko Enchi (1905-1986)
Type of plot: Domestic realism
Time of plot: The 1960's
Locale: Karuizawa and vicinity
First published: "Kikuguruma," 1967 (English translation, 1982)

> *Principal characters:*
> I, the narrator, a woman writer
> ICHIGE MASUTOSHI, a mental defective who was once scion to a
>   wealthy family
> ICHIGE RIE, Masutoshi's wife
> KUROKAWA, a local resident whose father has told him about the
>   Ichige family
> KASHIMURA, a psychiatric intern who once hoped to marry Rie

The Story

   A middle-aged woman, much like the author, the narrator has left her summer home at Karuizawa to go to a nearby town to give a talk to a woman's group. She returns to Karuizawa on a train that is unexpectedly slow, not only stopping at every single station along the way but also making remarkably long stops.

   At one stop the narrator finally gets off the train, partly to relieve her irritation and frustration and partly to learn the cause of the delays. She finds the station attendants loading long bundles into freight cars. At the same time, she encounters a middle-aged woman accompanied by an old man who is clearly mentally deficient. The station attendants are loading bundles of cut chrysanthemums that are being shipped on the overnight train to flower markets in Tokyo. The couple has come to the station because the old man has an obsessive concern about how his flowers are handled.

   Returning to her seat on the train, the narrator learns from a local person named Kurokawa something about the odd couple she has met on the platform. He confirms that the old man is retarded and obsessed with growing chrysanthemums; he also informs the narrator that the train is going to be much slower than she had planned but that "you might as well just get used to it and consider it an elegant way to travel." He then tells the story of the couple, Ichige Masutoshi and his wife, Rie, as it was passed on to him by his father. The Ichiges had once been a wealthy family, although they have since gone bankrupt. The narrator is shocked to learn that when the family was in its heyday, they arranged for Rie, one of their servants, to be a sort of human sacrifice and to marry their retarded son. Kurokawa explains that he, too, was shocked at first, but that during the war, Rie had always shown up for volunteer work, had effectively managed the family garden, and, in short, had won everyone's respect by working hard and taking good care of her husband. Now that the Ichige family has lost its money, Rie has to work harder than ever to feed her husband. Indeed, Kurokawa's father saw Rie as supernaturally good, an embodiment of Kannon, the goddess of mercy.

Kurokawa's story reminds the narrator of yet an earlier occasion when she had heard something about the Ichige family. Many years earlier, while writing a play about a mental patient, the narrator had gotten to know some psychiatric interns from whom she learned another aspect of the Ichige family history. Because their retarded son had excessive sexual drives, the family chose to marry him to one of the maids who could look after all of his physical needs, although they had taken the precaution of having the son sterilized before he was married. At the same time, the family hired interns from the school of psychiatry to take turns standing by each night in a room next to the bedroom of the newlyweds so that they could intervene if the son turned violent. Again, censure is aimed at Rie: How could anyone agree to such a marriage, no matter how much she was being paid? Blame is also heaped on the Ichige family for doing this. Years later, however, one of the former interns, now Dr. Kashimura, confessed to the narrator that he had fallen in love with Rie and had asked her to marry him, but she had refused, saying that she loved her husband.

At last the narrator arrives home at Karuizawa, far later than she had expected. She is still troubled about Rie and her motives for living with her retarded husband. The narrator finds Rie's devotion to be absurd; her final observation, however, is that she has reached an age when she can accept the motives and behavior of others even when their actions seem beyond comprehension.

Themes and Meanings

In this work, as in many of her stories and novels, the author explores the situation of women in the modern world. Here, she puzzles over the motives and feelings that have led Rie to devote herself to an older and mentally deficient man who has been abusive to her. In her own mind the narrator finds Rie's choice absurd, yet each time the narrator comes to this conclusion, there is a redeeming consideration. When Kurokawa tells his father's story, both the narrator and Kurokawa are appalled at Rie's fate, yet Kurokawa then goes on to depict Rie as a model wife who has won the respect of all the local people. Similarly, when the narrator recalls the experience of the psychiatric interns, she is disbelieving that anyone would put herself into such a physically and emotionally outrageous position. At precisely this point, the reader learns that Dr. Kashimura asked Rie to marry him and she refused, so one knows that she was not desperately seeking some means of escape. She has chosen to live this way and makes herself an example of virtuous behavior; she truly becomes transfigured into the goddess of mercy, as Kurokawa's father saw her. In the end, the reader is left with the narrator to ponder Rie's fate and the manner in which she has chosen to come to terms with it. Just as the narrator has to resign herself to taking a slow train and chooses to see it as a luxurious way to travel with all those fresh chrysanthemums, so too, perhaps, has Rie accepted her fate and transformed it into a life of virtue and beauty.

Style and Technique

In this complex narrative, the author presents her story as a series of stories, each laid out as a mystery that leads to a further mystery, and finally to a fuller understanding of Rie but not to a solution to the mystery. The first mystery is why the train is so slow and what the odd bundles being loaded at every station are. This leads to the encounter with the Ichiges and to Kurokawa telling the story his father had told him. This, in turn, leads deeper to the author's recollection of the mysterious duty performed nightly by the interns. Finally, the reader comes to Kashimura's confession of love; the narrator adds that he died in the war.

In terms of imagery, the reader is first presented with Ichige's favorite flower, Shiratama, which means "White Jewel." The reader does not actually see the flower at first but is only told of its mysterious and elusive fragrance. When the author gets off the train at Karuizawa, she sees for the first time the full, white moon in the cloudless sky and associates its transcendent beauty with Rie. Finally, the story closes on a more subdued and earthly note as the narrator associates Rie's middle-aged face with the modest, white chrysanthemum, an expression of restrained beauty.

Stephen W. Kohl

BOY IN THE SUMMER SUN

Author: Mark Schorer (1908-1977)
Type of plot: Psychological
Time of plot: The 1930's
Locale: A farm in the rural United States
First published: 1937

Principal characters:
WILL, the boy of the title, a college dropout and lover
RACHEL HARLEY, a college student and the object of Will's
attention
MAX GAREY, a college professor and the second suitor of Rachel
MRS. HARLEY, Rachel's mother

The Story

After dropping out of college during his third year, Will has taken a job in an accounting office in the city. He visits longtime sweetheart Rachel, who is still a student. Rachel is now vaguely enamored with Professor Max Garey, one of her English teachers, who happens to visit her at the farm while Will is there. The three lie in the sun near a farm lake. When Max reads poetry to Rachel, Will grows angry and takes a walk. The couple break up as an immediate consequence.

Themes and Meanings

The story contains several tensions and conflicts, including the expected competition between Max and Will for Rachel's love. This rivalry, though important, is secondary to the tensions experienced by Max and Rachel in their relationship as lovers. Also evident are conflicts relating to being in school and not being in school, having a future and not having one, differences between the country and the city, between biological love and spiritual fulfillment, and between youth and age. For both Rachel and Will, the breakup occurs with the utmost passivity. They accept their differences and move on, each parting in the interests of the other and denial of self, for the matter of peace and inevitability, given the differing directions their lives have taken.

The tale here is not so much one of a broken love relation caused by a "triangle" or by lives that have taken opposite courses; rather, the story is about the manner and necessity of disintegration of a relationship in which the two characters do love each other in both deed and fact. The story's primary revelation is that their parting is necessary because they love each other. They do not agree to separate because of the obstacles worked on them by circumstances, nor is the second suitor, Max, a serious contender for Rachel's love.

The story has no surprises; the inevitability of the couple's separation is made clear by the tone and atmosphere from its opening paragraph. There is an overwhelming recognition that parting is the only way each of them can survive, that their love can survive only if they are not together. Just as it is understood that their love will not grow, it is clear that it will not be destroyed.

Mark Schorer makes explicit his most important theme in the final section of the story. Will realizes that "Maybe living is really a lot of little dyings." Accordingly, the dissolution of the relationship is not only made complete but is poignantly put into perspective in the overall scheme of human behavior and value. The characters must get on with life—which means they must stoically accept a permanent separation. They also realize that such events will happen to them again—that life itself is a series of partings that must be accepted.

This realization is accomplished after Will acknowledges that "We were both in love with much more than each other." In the manner of youth, each defined love as something far more important than the feelings (as deep and real and emotional as these are) for the other. All meaning in life for them became bound in the experience of the relationship such that their love has taken a life of its own. This third entity is what they mutually agree to kill off in themselves. The author reveals this as an act of maturity and heroism on their behalf, a decision that may leave them with something better, more lasting, and more meaningful than a youthful idealism doomed to failure. Rather, they now can retain respect for one another and for themselves; they are hurt but at peace.

With this realization, other items must also be voided from their collective life as they reassume their individual identities. Rachel will remain in the country on the farm, while Will must return to the city. Similarly, Rachel will remain in school under the influence of professors such as Max Garey, and Will will not return to them or to their way of thinking. Schorer also emphasizes a difference in their spiritual ages; until the end of the story, Rachel appears to be older than Will; these descriptions are reversed when Will comes to understand that living is a matter of "a lot of little dyings."

Will learns another lesson from his experience with Rachel. She acknowledges that she truly loves him, but at the same time she is honest enough to admit that she loves Max Garey more. For the moment this is true, but it is clearly only a matter of time— and probably sooner rather than later—until her relationship with Max ends as well.

In the meantime, each character is left only with human activity. They leave the lake, go back up the slope to the Harley home—to the lights and sounds of voices. They return to movement and understanding, and they help each other do so, even though their farewells have already been said and they have functionally dismissed one another from their immediate and future lives. Will, as the "boy" in the summer sun, has learned that mature people must accept having others walking in and out of their lives. That he is now left alone is not as important as the fact that he is prepared to be left alone in the future, time after time—to live through a series of "little dyings" until he finally reaches physical death.

Style and Technique

Schorer tells this story entirely in a straightforward manner. There are few surprises, no startling character revelations, no unexpected twists of the plot, and no deep symbols on which the meaning rests. The action moves slowly through the summer afternoon, carried forward primarily by dialogue, description, and details. Every aspect of the story is deceptively simple because nothing much seems to be happening. In fact, little is happening, except to Will, who is learning a great lesson of how to get on in life, as well as what love is all about. What he learns is that it is all a matter of coming to an end and that one must be prepared to live through life by experiencing and accepting a series of returns to what he calls "aloneness." His effort in life is to get through these relationships—to exit from them—"somewhat less empty, less deadly calm."

Schorer's message is directly connected to his style of writing. The repetition of short, simple sentences (most of the story is dialogue between Will and Rachel) reveals and accents the thoughts and feelings of the two main characters. Their simple thoughts about love are expressed in simple sentences using only basic vocabulary. To reinforce this technique, the author's third-person omniscient voice replicates it. That is, the characters both speak and are spoken of in the same manner and toward the same effect. The emptiness and calmness of Will's existence at the end of the story are described in language that not merely reflects but enhances the emptiness and calmness of life.

Another effect of this simplicity in syntax and vocabulary is that the two lovers are depicted not as children—but as childlike. They foolishly believe that their feelings are complex, that they know things about each other and about love that others have not known or experienced before. Their conversation, however, proves them to be not unique but mundane. The tone of their talk and of the story itself exhibits the banality and blandness of real life in the modern world, a place where love is not and cannot be accomplished—but can only be lived through until arrival at its newest, most recent, advent of death.

Carl Singleton

THE BOY WHO DREW CATS

Author: Lafcadio Hearn (1850-1904)
Type of plot: Fable
Time of plot: The seventh to eighteenth centuries
Locale: Rural Japan
First published: 1898

> *Principal characters:*
> THE BOY, a young temple acolyte
> THE OLD PRIEST, his teacher and master

The Story

The protagonist, the youngest son of poor, hardworking farmers, lives in a country village of old Japan. Because he is small, weak, and bright, his parents send him to the village priest to be trained for the priesthood. The boy learns well and pleases his master in almost all ways, but he persists in one act of disobedience—drawing cats whenever he can. Although warned to stop, he continues, as if possessed by a spirit, to draw cats in every color, pose, and mood.

The boy's disobedience causes the old priest to send him away with the advice to stop trying to become a priest but instead become an artist. The priest cautions the boy to avoid large places at night and keep to the small. Puzzled by the strange warning, the boy reluctantly leaves his temple home and walks to the next village, where there is a large temple at which he hopes to continue his religious training.

He arrives at the temple at night, only to find it deserted and covered with thick layers of dust and cobwebs. He does not know the temple has been abandoned because a bloodthirsty goblin now lives there. Earlier, soldiers entered the temple at night to kill the goblin but did not survive the attempt. The unsuspecting boy sits quietly and waits for temple priests to appear. He notices large, white screens, wonderful surfaces for drawing cats, and soon has drawing ink and brushes ready. He unhesitatingly draws cats, not stopping until he is too tired to continue. Sleepily he remembers the old priest's warning as he lies down, so he crawls into a small cabinet and pulls the door closed before he sleeps.

Hours later, the boy wakes to sounds of horrible screaming and fighting. He cowers silently while the fight rages, and only ventures out after daylight streams into the room. He finds a floor wet with blood and, lying dead, a monster goblin-rat the size of a cow. Scanning the temple, he notices the wet, blood-red mouths of the cats he has drawn on the screens. Suddenly he understands the priest's advice, and realizes that his cats have destroyed the goblin in the vicious fight he has overheard. The boy later becomes a famous artist, whose pictures of cats can still be seen in Japan.

Themes and Meanings

In this fable, the fate of the boy illustrates the mysterious power of nature to save or destroy human life. This young artist has devoted himself to cats, and in drawing them, he wholeheartedly worships the genius, or spirit, of cats within himself. This natural genius guides him on his path to becoming a famous artist. First it sends him from his obscure temple home in the unknown village, and later it saves his life when a ravenous spirit, the enormous rat-goblin, seeks to attack and destroy him. The soldiers who earlier entered the temple at night to slay the goblin and did not survive the attempt illustrate the danger of facing life's difficulties without a powerful natural ally, such as the cat genius of the young boy, to protect and fight for oneself.

This traditional Japanese fable expresses themes central to the ancient Shinto religion of Japan. "The Way of the Gods," Shinto is a nature-based system of beliefs, according to which the world is guided by nature gods, composed of the powers of nature, and the enduring spirits of dead ancestors, who acquire supernatural powers after death. These ghosts continue to exist with supernatural power in the world, influencing the lives of their descendants and other nearby humans. Together, these spiritual forces influence natural events, such as rain, tides, harvest, birth, and death, for evil or good.

The Shinto gods and spirits protect and care for those humans who pay homage to their ancestors and the ancient powers of nature through prayers and offerings of food, music, dance, and other gifts. In Hearn's story, the cat spirits protect and save the life of their devoted boy artist, just as other satisfied benign gods and spirits look after their faithful worshipers. In contrast, those neglected gods and spirits who receive no prayers and offerings become vengeful. Like the murderous rat-goblin, these forgotten ones attack and devour those who failed to remember them.

The old priest, wise in spiritual matters, recognizes the boy's real devotion to drawing cats as his way of pleasing the gods. So he advises the boy to give up the study of religion and follow his true path. His warning to avoid large places and keep to small suggests that he knows about the crisis the boy will face on his way to becoming a great artist.

Another element of the story, the cats drawn on the white temple screens, suggests the way Shinto gods interface with the human world. The boy's drawings, executed with skill and devotion, become a medium of spiritual power: In the dark night, they come alive to attack and kill the goblin. Later these cat drawings show evidence of their magical power in the marks of wet blood remaining on their mouths. In this vivid image of sketched black-and-white cats with mouths dripping in red blood, the reader perceives Shinto's mystical interplay between nature's supernatural powers and human action.

Style and Technique

Lafcadio Hearn has described his style as simplicity, and he worked to touch readers with simple words. He hoped that his writing style would reveal meaning as a glass transmits light. His subjects were often the favorite folktales and legends of common people, which he told in a brief and direct way to capture their mood and meaning without adding extra elements. The story reveals this direct style in a passage describing the boy: "He was very clever, cleverer than all his brothers and sisters; but he was quite weak and small, and people said he could never grow very big." Such description reminds readers of a childhood time when they heard folktales remembered and told by elders during quiet evenings or read and reread in favorite childhood books. A childlike mood of honesty and directness is echoed in the simple, direct writing style.

Another childlike element captured in Hearn's writing style is fantastic, vivid imagery. Consider the scene of death the boy finds in the morning: "The first thing he saw was that all the floor of the temple was covered with blood. And then he saw, lying dead in the middle of it, an enormous, monstrous rat—a goblin-rat—bigger than a cow!" This impossibly large rat surrounded by a huge pool of blood on the temple floor invites readers to suspend their knowledge of actual rats and enter a lurid world of horrible possibilities. The scene vividly portrays the dangerous situation the boy unwittingly entered.

The same fantastic kind of imagery ends the story. "Suddenly the boy observed that the mouths of all the cats he had drawn the night before, were red and wet with blood." The realm of the two-dimensional cats and the magical world of goblins have intersected in conflict, leaving evidence of victory as well as defeat. Invisible goblins bleed, and paper-and-ink cats bite with weapon-sharp teeth.

While the naïve simplicity of style and vividness of fantastic imagery lead readers to see the story events in a childlike way, Hearn includes narrative details that give the story a realistic tone. An example is the fact that after priests prudently abandoned the haunted temple, the goblin made a light shine in the temple to tempt weary travelers to rest there. A light shining at the window is a signal quickly recognized and understood by weary travelers everywhere. In another instance of realism, the story ends with a comment that the boy's cat drawings can still be seen by travelers in Japan, adding a note of seeming historical evidence to the fantastic tale. These realistic details offer a comforting flavor of the familiar, everyday world to the eerie story.

Hearn's storytelling style evokes a mood in which the reader sees and understands the world as children do. It also evokes a feeling for a more ancient mythical time, when humans lived in an exciting primitive world populated by giants, dragons, and warrior heroes.

Patricia H. Fulbright

BOYS AND GIRLS

Author: Alice Munro (1931-   )
Type of plot: Coming of age
Time of plot: World War II
Locale: Southwestern Ontario, Canada
First published: 1968

> *Principal characters:*
> THE NARRATOR, an unnamed eleven-year-old girl
> LAIRD, her younger brother
> MOTHER, a homemaker
> FATHER, a fox breeder
> HENRY, the family's hired man

The Story

The narrator, an eleven-year-old girl living on a fox-breeding farm with her parents and younger brother, details the work of the farm: the killing, skinning, and preparation of the silver foxes; their feeding and watering; and the killing of horses to get meat to feed the foxes. All this work is a normal and everyday part of life to the narrator, who takes great pride in helping her father with the outdoor chores. She blushes with pleasure when her father introduces her as his "hired man" but dreads the dreary and monotonous work inside the house. She is apprehensive about her mother's plans for her when she grows older and must take on more traditional female roles. Though she loves her mother, she also sees her as an "enemy" who is plotting to take her away from more important pursuits. The girl also tries hard to avoid her grandmother, who constantly nags her to behave in more ladylike ways.

During the winter the family keeps two horses until they must be killed for meat for the foxes. Mack is an old and indifferent horse; Flora is a high-stepping and nervous mare. The girl has never seen a horse killed before, and curiosity compels her and her brother to watch their father shoot Mack. Though she tries to shrug off Mack's death as inevitable, she worries about its effect on Laird. She also feels ashamed, wary, and restrained around her father for the first time.

Other things are changing. Laird is now big and strong enough to match his sister in a fight. The narrator starts wondering if she will be pretty when she grows up; she tries to fix up her side of the room that she shares with Laird to make it more adult; she feels increasingly distant from both Laird and her father but is still not entirely allied with her mother. In the past she fantasized about being a hero or a rescuer; now she daydreams about being rescued.

The story climaxes when the narrator realizes that Flora will be shot the next day. She is playing with Laird in the field when Flora breaks away from her father and Henry, and tries to escape toward the lane. After her father shouts to her to run and shut the gate, she reaches the gate in time to prevent Flora from getting away. When Flora runs toward her, however, she opens the gate as wide as she can. As Laird and the men go out in a truck to catch Flora, the girl puzzles over why she has disobeyed her father and sees that she is no longer "on his side."

When the men return after shooting and skinning Flora, Laird announces that his sister is responsible for the horse's escape. When told that his daughter is crying, the father says that "she's only a girl." The words both forgive the girl and push her aside.

Themes and Meanings

Alice Munro has often written about the seemingly unbridgeable gap that separates men and women. In "Boys and Girls," this gap is examined in the small world of a farm. Because the narrator is female, she is expected to behave in a subdued and frivolous way, to be devoted to domestic chores, and to ally with her mother against "male" pursuits such as farming, shooting, and heroism. The girl rebels against these stereotypes. Initially, she identifies more readily with her father than with her mother, noting that her father's work seems important and interesting while her mother's is depressing. Her mother says that she feels she does not have a daughter at all and looks forward to the day that Laird can be a "real help" to her husband. When that day arrives, her daughter will be expected to work indoors.

Several of Munro's stories examine the pain and necessity of children "choosing sides." Here the daughter is proud that her father appreciates her hard work, but she is ambivalent about the violence and callousness that is necessary to please him. At first, it seems that Munro intends the girl's guilty reaction and feelings of horror at Flora's death to be stereotypical "feminine" responses, just as her brother's casual acceptance is a "masculine" reaction. Munro suggests, however, that these expectations are arbitrary and hurtful to both genders. At first Laird is shocked by Mack's shooting; later he comes to regard the killings as a sort of male bonding, and he deliberately distances himself from the situation. His sister sees that her rebellion (opening the gate) is useless and only causes her to lose her father's trust, but it is impossible for her to ignore her conscience.

A girl, the narrator realizes, is something that she must become; her gender forces a whole complex of behaviors on her. She resists by working with her father, by slamming doors, by asking questions, and by staging elaborate daydreams in which she is the hero. Munro suggests that this resistance is eroded partly through social expectations and partly through the girl's reluctant complicity: She is torn between wanting her father's respect and trust and her growing awareness of the subtle cruelty in his job. She also grows apart from Laird; their final separation occurs when Laird tells their father she has allowed Flora to escape. Laird's betrayal makes her realize that she is no longer a part of the "outside" world of the farm, chores, and violence; however, she is not yet comfortable with her mother's world. At the end of the story she acknowledges that maybe she is "only a girl," but she is unsure whether this label is liberating or enslaving.

Style and Technique

Munro writes stories about everyday people and ordinary events that trigger flashes of insight. Here the narrator is unnamed, possibly because her identity is determined so fully by her gender. Interestingly, her brother's name, Laird (a Scottish word for "lord"), also reveals his status in a sexist society. Other small details reveal Munro's vision of the splits between men and women, nature and civilization, and wealth and poverty. The "heroic" calendars on the wall depict noble savages exploited by whites, Henry sings a racist song, and wealthy women who are far away will wear the furs that are bought with the deaths of the foxes and horses.

Munro's tone is ironic and deliberately deflationary. At first her narrator has grand dreams of action, heroism, and acclaim, but later the daydreams show her as a passive beneficiary of someone else's heroism. These differing fantasy roles show the strict split between the genders. Similarly, the repetition of the phrase "only a girl" shows how society puts an imaginative and energetic girl firmly in her place. The story's coming-of-age theme uses several traditional symbols. The horses, representing the freedom and independence with which the girl identifies, are callously killed; the "inside" domestic world is stifling, while the "outside" world of nature is harsh.

The girl tells her own story but leaves many events to the interpretation of the reader. She begins by telling about her hatred of housework and her happiness in helping her father but interrupts this with an aside: "I have forgotten to say what the horses were fed." This technique shows the girl's ambivalence about her father's work; omitting this important detail allows her to relate the story about the killing of Mack. The point of view is that of an adult looking back on her youth, attempting now to understand events whose meaning eluded her at the time. She attempts to analyze the reasons for her behavior but admits that she cannot understand why, for example, she disobeyed her father—only that it seemed her only real choice at that time.

As with many Canadian writers, Munro's use of setting is crucial. The world of the farm mirrors the exploitative world outside. Like Flora, the foxes are beautiful, wild, and ultimately helpless against their fate. Like the girl, the animals rebel against their "use" by the civilized world, but it is impossible to escape. The father's change in attitude to his daughter from "my new hired man" to "only a girl" signals his acceptance of her secondary status in his world. Like his daughter, the father has also chosen sides.

Michelle Jones

BRAINS

Author: Gottfried Benn (1886-1956)
Type of plot: Psychological
Time of plot: 1914
Locale: Germany
First published: "Gehirne," 1915 (English translation, 1972)

> *Principal character:*
> RÖNNE, a young physician who loses touch with reality

The Story

A young doctor named Rönne is riding a train in southern Germany, on his way north to stand in for a clinic doctor who is going away on holiday. For the past two years, Rönne has worked in pathology. After having two thousand bodies pass through his hands, he feels strangely exhausted.

As he rides the train, he notes such sights as scarlet fields that seem to be on fire with poppies and houses that appear to be propped up by roses. He thinks to himself that he should buy a notebook and pencil with which to record things before they pass out of sight. He cannot remember when things stopped sticking in his mind.

At the hospital precinct, Rönne sees only hospital employees and patients. His mood is solemn as he discusses professional matters with nurses, to whom he leaves such matters as fixing lamps and starting motors. As he works with patients, Rönne becomes both preoccupied with his hands and somehow detached from them. He deals with patients' lungs or fingers but never with whole persons. As Rönne becomes preoccupied with his thoughts, he finds it increasingly difficult to separate the relevant from the irrelevant. All around him, space seems to surge off into infinity. Often he twists his hands and looks at them.

Once a nurse sees Rönne smelling his hands and manipulating them oddly, as though squeezing open a large, soft fruit. One day a large animal is slaughtered in the hospital as Rönne happens to come along. As its head is split open, Rönne takes its brain in his hands and forces it apart. The nurse recognizes his gesture as identical to that which she earlier saw him perform.

Gradually, Rönne becomes irregular in his duties. When he is asked to contribute his opinion, he goes to pieces. In search of mental rest, he walks in the gardens. There he feels the upsurge of life in the earth; however, it stops short of entering him. He retreats to his room, where he locks the door and lies stiffly on his back, allowing the earth to bear him gently and smoothly through the ether and past the stars.

Eventually the doctor in charge of the clinic is recalled. He is kind to Rönne, who tries to explain his obsession with his hands. After having held thousands of "them in these hands of mine . . . some soft, some hard, all ready to dissolve," he is now holding his "own" in his hands and cannot stop probing into the limits of its possibilities. What are brains all about, he asks. Weary, he seeks release. He wishes to be borne aloft by wings into the midday sun.

Themes and Meanings

"Brains" is the first of Gottfried Benn's five stories about Rönne. Together these stories portray the disintegration of the character's ego, whose foundations were built on fragile intellectual constructs, and his gradual return to health as he permits himself to experience emotional and intuitive interactions with the world he inhabits. This story has strong autobiographical roots in Benn's own disastrous personal experience in psychiatry—which was his first career choice. After losing the ability to concentrate on individual cases, he—like Rönne—was dismissed.

The central theme of "Brains" is the eternal dichotomy of human intellect and emotion: in biblical terms, the fallen state of humanity. Benn was not alone in the early twentieth century in stressing the inherent antinomy in human nature. Following a long trend in German philosophy, the novelist Thomas Mann dealt extensively with the conflict between the Dionysian impulse in human beings, which is characterized by the acquisition of creative, imaginative power, and the critical, rational power embodied by the Apollonian impulse.

Another way of representing this dichotomy in mythology and religion is through the use of the right hand and the left hand, with the right hand representing the intellect and science, and the left hand representing intuition, emotion, the arts, and deep spiritual insight. It was not until the late 1960's that modern science validated this duality with the "split brain" theory. Intuitively, Benn has availed himself of this symbolism in "Brains." In the most dramatic gesture, which occurs almost exactly in the middle of the story, Rönne splits open an animal brain, which seconds earlier was alive. This is the repeated motion of his hands witnessed by a nurse, a motion that symbolizes his ongoing preoccupation with the nature and possibilities of the brain. After having seen brains in all sizes and conditions, he knows that they consist of twelve chemical substances, but substances that "combined without awaiting his command and that would separate again without consulting him." Science is inadequate to probe the essence of human nature. Disregarding a nurse who loves him and who could be thought of as embodying one road through and beyond his mental breakdown, Rönne in this first story feels primarily intellectual frustration.

Benn's use of hand symbolism is extraordinarily subtle and accurate. Near the beginning of the story, Rönne looks at his right hand and muses that the "power of Life is so great . . . this hand will never be able to undermine it." The right hand represents science and the intellect. Rönne is taking the wrong approach to the fundamental questions of life. He repeats his mistake later in the story, when he taps a finger of his right hand against one on his left hand "and there was a lung underneath." The right hand is pushing down the left, science is pushing down intuition, and the result is singularly prosaic.

Rönne's urge to rationalize, indeed the weight given to intellectual fragmentation of the world into reducible discrete components by the mechanistic worldview of the late nineteenth century, is at the heart of his malaise, and the intellectual malaise of the first decades of the twentieth century. Rönne has fragmented his world to the point that he can make only the most infantile observations.

However, his situation, even in this first story, is not entirely hopeless. There is no recognized schizophrenia that does not resemble states that other cultures regard as holy or curative. In addition to showing that Rönne is on the wrong track, Benn points the way back to health. Not only do right and left represent the intellectual and emotional respectively, so do north and south, an ancient metaphysical construct brilliantly employed by Thomas Mann in his story "Tonio Kröger" (1903), with which Benn was undoubtedly familiar. It is suggestive that "Brains" begins with Rönne "on his way north" while still attempting to apprehend his world entirely through the intellect. At the end of "Brains" Rönne longs to fall into ruins "of the south." The word "south" alone introduces the concept so important for Benn that means not only gardens, summer, and the "upsurge of life in the earth," but also South Sea islands, the simplicity of a previous, more primitive existence, indeed, the Garden of Eden before the fall. However, one knows from Genesis that reentry is barred by two angels with flaming swords. The price of reentry is the dissolution of the personality. Rönne, at the end of "Brains," seems prepared to make that sacrifice.

Style and Technique

"Brains" is an exemplary piece of expressionist prose. As in expressionist painting, in which connections to reality may be tenuous and colors subjective, the emphasis in expressionist literature is not on the external world but on inner reality. Few authors are better able to conduct readers convincingly through the enigmas of the human mind than Benn. He not only studied psychiatry but also personally experienced the terrifying dissolution of the self portrayed in "Brains." His story is a case history that apprehends the experience as well as the symptoms. It focuses on experience and its manifestations; its more poetic passages have the ring of immediate experience about them. "Brains" is a masterful and rare exploration of the spontaneous collapse of the ego and a regression to the first questions of life: Who and what am I?

To illustrate the tenuousness of Rönne's grasp on his present time and place, Benn uses the stylistic technique he calls montage: The last few lines consist of fragmentary and disjointed associative remarks. Paradoxically, while reflecting Rönne's loss of more ordered thought patterns, this stylistic technique enables him, by dispensing with complete syntax, vastly to expand the range of his imagery, to transcend and trivialize his own immediate time and surroundings as he concentrates in an ecstatic rush of association on a wealth of feelings and sensations, on exactly what is needed to counterbalance his overly cerebral and narrow approach to existence. "Brains" may, in fact, be seen as a microcosm of Benn's work, of his cosmic overview and transcendent, at times humorous, response to daily events, which are indeed dated. He deals with fundamental truths.

Jean M. Snook

THE BRIDE COMES TO YELLOW SKY

Author: Stephen Crane (1871-1900)
Type of plot: Parody
Time of plot: About 1900
Locale: Yellow Sky, Texas
First published: 1898

Principal characters:
JACK POTTER, the marshal in Yellow Sky
HIS WIFE
SCRATCHY WILSON, the last surviving member of a gang of
    outlaws
A "DRUMMER" (SALESPERSON) FROM THE EAST

The Story
"The Bride Comes to Yellow Sky" concerns the efforts of a town marshal bringing his new bride to the "frontier" town of Yellow Sky, Texas, at a time when the Old West is being slowly but inevitably civilized. At the climax of the story, the stereotypical and seemingly inevitable gunfight, a staple feature of Westerns, is averted, and the reader senses that all such gunplay is a thing of the past, that in fact Stephen Crane is describing the "end of an era."

Crane's four-part story concerns human beings' interaction with their environment. (Jack's wife is not an individualized person with a name; she is important only because she represents marriage as a civilized institution.) In part 1, Crane describes the progress of the "great Pullman" train across Texas. With its luxurious appointments ("the dazzling fittings of the coach"), the train is a foreign country to the newlyweds, whom Crane portrays as self-conscious aliens: Jack's hands "perform" in a "most conscious fashion," and his bride is "embarrassed" by her puff sleeves. The couple are so self-conscious and intimidated by their surroundings that the black porter "bullies" them, regards them with "an amused and superior grin," and generally "oppresses" them, treatment that they also receive from the black waiter, who "patronizes them." As the train nears Yellow Sky, Jack becomes "commensurately restless," primarily because he knows that he has committed an "extraordinary crime" by going "headlong over all the social hedges" and ignoring his "duty to his friends," members of an "innocent and unsuspecting community." Marshals in frontier towns apparently do not marry because they need to be free of domestic entanglements. Because Jack and his bride sense their "mutual guilt," they "slink" away from the train station and walk rapidly to his home, a "safe citadel" from which Jack can later emerge to make his peace with the community.

While Jack and his bride make their way to his house, Crane cuts to the Weary Gentleman saloon, where six men, including the Eastern "drummer," sit drinking at the bar. While the drummer tells a story, another man appears at the door to announce that

Scratchy Wilson is drunk and "has turned loose with both hands." The remainder of part 2 is exposition: The "innocent" drummer, whom Crane describes as a "foreigner," is told that there will be some shooting, that Scratchy and Jack are old adversaries, and that Scratchy is "the last one of the old gang that used to hang out along the river here."

Scratchy makes his appearance in part 3, which completes the preparation for the "show down," the anticipated gunfight of part 4. Scratchy issues unanswered challenges, shoots at a dog, and then approaches the saloon, where he demands a drink. When he is ignored, he uses the saloon door for target practice and then, remembering his traditional opponent, goes to Jack's house and howls challenges and epithets at the empty house.

In part 4, Jack and his bride encounter Scratchy near Jack's house. Scratchy gets the "drop" on Jack, accuses him of trying to sneak up on him, and warns him about trying to draw his gun. When Jack tells him that he has no gun, Scratchy is "livid" and tells him, "Don't take me for no kid." Jack answers that he is not lying, but Scratchy presses him for a reason, suggesting that perhaps he has been to "Sunday-school." Jack's response is to Scratchy almost as unlikely: "I'm married." Unable to deal with "this foreign condition," Scratchy supposes that "it's all off now" and walks away.

Themes and Meanings

Crane's frontier setting is essential to his theme, which concerns the conflict between the East and West and the passing of an era. While Yellow Sky is located in western Texas, it is accessible by train, which acts as a "vehicle" to bring Eastern civilization to the West. In fact, Yellow Sky has already been civilized, despite the anachronistic presence of Scratchy Wilson, who seems determined to preserve the "good old days." Unfortunately, Scratchy's clothes reveal the extent to which even he has been "Easternized": He wears a "maroon-coloured flannel shirt" made by "some Jewish women on the East Side of New York," and his red-topped boots have gilded imprints beloved by "little sledding boys on the hillsides of New England."

At the end of the story Crane writes of Scratchy, "In the presence of this foreign condition he was a simple child of the earlier plains," thereby indicating that Scratchy is a "holdover," a man with ties to the Old West, but also that he is a "simple child." In the story Crane depicts Scratchy not as a mature adult but as a child-man, an adult who refuses to "grow up." His boots are related to children, and he "plays" with the town, which is described as a "toy for him." When Jack tells him that he has no gun, Scratchy is concerned that he not be taken "for no kid," and Jack himself seems to understand the importance of being treated as an adult for he assures Scratchy, "I ain't takin' you for no kid." In fact, the confrontation between Jack and Scratchy resembles the "show downs" between young boys who cannot back down but who have to assert their own lack of fear while simultaneously not provoking their opponent. In taking a bride, Jack has broken with the traditions of the Old West and also become a civilized man, one who has truly "put away childish things."

Just as marriage is a foreign condition to Scratchy, the last vestiges of the Old West are "foreign" to the drummer, who has apparently ignored the possibility that men like

Scratchy might still exist. The drummer is "innocent" of the implications of Scratchy's drinking, and his questions reveal not only his fear but also his astonishment that someone might be killed in this "civilized" town. The townspeople strike the appropriate balance, however, for they accept Scratchy's behavior as a remnant of the past, a worn-out ritual prompted by alcohol. Jack, who "goes out and fights Scratchy when he gets on one of these tears," is a part of this *High Noon* drama. By the end of the story, however, Jack has assumed a different role in a new ritual.

Style and Technique

Although Jack believes that he is guilty of a crime and has been a traitor to the community, he takes himself, as do many Crane protagonists, much too seriously. His perceptions of himself and his situation are not shared by the other characters or by Crane's readers. The saloon conversation indicates that Jack is useful in containing Scratchy, but it does not reflect Jack's "centrality" in the community. (In fact, Jack's decision to marry must have followed his subconscious awareness that it was "safe" to marry.)

The gap between perception and reality is apparent on the train: "To the minds of the pair, their surroundings reflected the glory of their marriage." The passengers and the black porter are not impressed, however, for they see the bride's "under-class countenance," her "shy and clumsy coquetry," and the groom's self-consciousness and lack of sophistication. To Jack, his house is his "citadel" and his marriage is his new "estate." The mock-heroic style is epitomized in the bride's reaction to the meeting with Scratchy: "She was a slave to hideous rites, gazing at the apparitional snake." Crane elevates the meeting of Jack and his bride with Scratchy to myth: The "apparitional snake," the satanic force that introduces evil into the new Edenic estate, is the drunken Scratchy Wilson; Jack and his bride are the innocent Adam and Eve; the "rite" is the fall from grace. Surely, nothing could be further from reality.

In Crane's fiction, insignificant human beings perceive themselves to be the center of the universe, but the universe seems indifferent to their posturings and pretensions. Scratchy, who had thought of his "ancient antagonist" ("ancient" is also mock-heroic), goes to Jack's house. There he chants "Apache scalp music" and howls challenges, but Crane writes that the house "regarded him as might a great stone god." The man's (and humanity's) presumption is such that he believes he can disturb the "immobility of a house."

Part of the incongruity between human being's illusions and reality is reflected in the death imagery that pervades the story. Crane describes Jack "as one announcing death" and compares his mouth to a "grave for his tongue"; as Scratchy walks the streets, the stillness forms the "arch of a tomb over him." Through the use of such figurative language, Crane builds his story to its anticlimactic scene. As Scratchy walks away, dragging his feet and making "funnel-shaped tracks," the new era arrives: "Yellow Sky," "the hour of daylight," as Crane defines it, replaces the twilight of the Old West.

Thomas L. Erskine

THE BRIDEGROOM

Author: Ha Jin (1956-   )
Type of plot: Domestic realism
Time of plot: 1976
Locale: Muji, China
First published: 1999

> *Principal characters:*
> OLD CHENG, the chief of security at a sewing factory
> BEINA, his twenty-three-year-old daughter, a bride
> HUANG BAOWEN, his daughter's husband and coworker
> LONG FUHAI, a nurse at the sanatorium to which Baowen is sent

The Story

From the day that handsome Huang Baowen proposes to Beina, his homely co-worker at a sewing factory in northeastern China, Old Cheng, Beina's adoptive father and the chief of security at the factory, begins to dread the failure of their marriage. However, when the couple marry after a short engagement, the old man begins to hope for the best. Eight months later, however, Beina is not yet pregnant, and Cheng fears the young man will lose interest in an apparently barren wife whose puffy face reminds even her own father of a blowfish. Consequently, when Beina rushes into Cheng's office to report Baowen's overnight absence, Cheng thinks his fears have been realized and starts to worry in earnest.

The reason for Baowen's disappearance becomes clear when Cheng receives a call from Maio, the chief of public security of Muji, informing him that Baowen has been arrested for indecent activity. Cheng goes downtown to the public security office, where he learns that the young man has been detained on a charge of homosexuality. He does not know how serious the charge is, and Maio explains that homosexuality is a crime if intercourse has occurred and a social disease if it has not. Cheng is greatly relieved when Baowen tells him he did not act on his desires the previous night. Cheng pleads Baowen's case before the factory manager and the Communist Party secretary, citing insanity as the young man's defense. The men agree to support Baowen. The secretary is especially eager to keep the young man out of jail. The factory manager offers mitigating stories, comparing Baowen's conduct to the behavior of emperors in the Han Dynasty.

Cheng goes to Beina's apartment to deliver the bad news that her husband is a homosexual and the good news that he is insane and has a good chance for leniency. As he visits, Cheng looks around the room and is impressed by the decor, attributing its charm to Baowen's good taste and fastidiousness. When her father asks, Beina confirms that her marriage to Baowen has not been consummated. When he expresses his sympathy, she says she does not mind because her husband has explained that he must refrain from lovemaking while practicing martial arts. Cheng does not contradict her statement, allowing his daughter to keep her fantasy while thinking her a fool.

Baowen is sent to a sanatorium, where he is to be treated for homosexuality. When Cheng visits him, he learns that his son-in-law is being treated with an electric bath. Curious about the young man's anatomy, Cheng asks Dr. Mai, the attending physician, if he can view the bath and receives permission to do so. While Cheng waits in the treatment room for Baowen to enter, he meets Long Fuhai, the male nurse who is to supervise the bath. Long assures Cheng that his son-in-law is getting the mildest shock treatment available because he is such a good patient. When Baowen enters the room, he is wearing shorts, so Cheng sees only a bulge in his pants. The size of the bulge convinces Cheng that Baowen is a real man, not a hermaphrodite or eunuch as rumored at the factory. During the electric bath, he watches the young man squirm and grow increasingly agitated. With stoic determination, or erotic pleasure, Baowen endures piercing electrical sensations. Nurse Long wipes sweat from Baowen's brow, and Cheng's heart fills with pity for his son-in-law.

Two weeks before New Years' Day, Cheng takes Beina to visit Baowen. While the couple chat happily, he delivers presents to Dr. Mai, who, in confidence, tells him that homosexuality is not a disease that can be cured by electric treatments or any other method but rather an orientation that is present from birth.

As the New Year draws closer, Beina begins cooking for the holidays. In the midst of her preparations, Cheng goes to her apartment and sees that she has turned the place into a mess. Beina talks about the possibility of her husband's coming home for the holidays, but Cheng does not encourage her hopes. He realizes that if Dr. Mai's assessment is correct, there is no future for the marriage.

While Cheng ponders what to do, Chief Maio calls to inform him that Baowen is being sent to prison because he had sex with a man at the sanatorium. This time, the evidence is incontrovertible. Nurse Long, scared by the possibility that someone saw him and Baowen together, has confessed that he was Baowen's sexual partner. However, because Long successfully argued that he was seduced by Baowen, he received probation, while Baowen was sentenced to two years in prison.

After Cheng reports this information to Beina, he asks her to divorce Baowen. When she refuses, Cheng, who cannot bear further humiliation, says that if she stays married to a criminal, he does not want to see her again.

Themes and Meanings

If Cheng tried to keep Beina and Baowen together simply because he was afraid that his daughter might suffer, the reader might consider his obsession understandable and perhaps even comical. However, even a cursory reading of the story reveals that his anxiety is not only personal but has deep social and political roots.

Because Cheng has built his life on appearances, he sees Beina's marriage as related to his own standing in society. In the public eye, he would have failed as a father if his daughter remained single. However, Beina is not a pretty girl, and her appearance is a source of deep personal discomfort to Cheng. This embarrassment and ill ease manifest themselves in his constant, private criticism of the way his daughter looks and the anger he shows toward beautiful women who, unaware of Baowen's sexual orientation, have tried to lure him away from Beina.

In the homogenized world in which Cheng lives, not only ugliness but also all individual differences, homosexuality included, stand out as undesirable and evoke dread and anxiety in people loyal to the government. To fit in, Cheng must constantly seek ways to reconcile human rights abuses inherent in the system to his tacitly held sense of morality. For Cheng, the conflicts cannot be easily resolved and, as a result, his life becomes an emotional roller coaster. That Cheng, a fearful conformist, is chief of security at the sewing plant is the ultimate irony on which the story turns.

The story is set in 1976, shortly after the death of China's Chairman Mao Zedong and the arrest of his wife, Jiang Qing, for her role in the Cultural Revolution (1966-1976). The old regime is crumbling, and Cheng, a product of the repressive government, will soon become an anachronism. Ha Jin uses contrasting imagery to depict the shift from a staid, agrarian society to a liberal, industrialized new world order. For example, Cheng bicycles across the countryside, overtaking a horse cart loaded with sheaves of wheat, and rides seamlessly into a city filled with new buildings and straight cement paths. Jin depicts smokestacks, larch woods, and heavy fluffy snow as well as brick buildings, asphalt roads, and power lines.

Style and Technique

Although Jin's writing style is mainly straightforward and unadorned, he focuses metaphorically on sparrows twice in the story to show the ill effects of social homogenization on the individual. First, after Baowen has been arrested, Jin allows Cheng to interrupt his train of thought to meditate on a sparrow, the most common of birds. Cheng imagines that a single renegade sparrow, having a complete set of organs like the others, can disrupt the order of its entire society, just as a political dissenter can disrupt human society. Thinking along this line allows Cheng to prepare himself to accept the full measure of the law, whatever the offense warrants, applied to Baowen.

Second, Jin evokes sparrows to acknowledge the awful price an individual pays for having an unusual, perhaps handicapping, trait. Right after the doctor tells Cheng that Baowen has a congenital orientation, not a curable disease, Cheng looks out a window and sees a flock of birds in flight. He notices one flying out front with food in its mouth and the others seeming to give chase. Soon Cheng spots a loner trailing well behind the masses, and as he studies the lone bird, he notices a yellow string tied to its leg. Cheng realizes that with such a visible handicap, it will never catch up. By extension, the reader gets Jin's larger point: Regardless of social designs that are meant to keep people in formation, class stratification is inevitable. For, as in the universe of sparrows, in the universe of humankind, there will always be someone who will outfly the masses and become a leader and someone who will lag behind and become an outcast.

Sarah Smith Ducksworth

THE BRIDGE

Author: Pamela Painter (1941-   )
Type of plot: Psychological
Time of plot: The 1980's
Locale: Cambridge, Massachusetts
First published: 1985

Principal characters:
AN UNNAMED WOMAN, with a bag of groceries
AN UNNAMED WOMAN, with a baby or a bunch of flowers

The Story

As a woman on her way home with a bag of groceries crosses a bridge, she sees a younger woman ahead of her cradling a bundle. The bundle might contain flowers or a baby; the first woman cannot tell which. She thinks that if she catches up with the woman and finds that it is a baby that she is carrying, she might smile at the baby, admire its hair or nose, and ask how old it is. Or she might say, "What lovely flowers," although she believes that this remark will not lead to much conversation.

As the first woman thinks about all this, the young woman stops and leans over the edge of the bridge as if something in the water has caught her eye. The protagonist stops also, sets down her groceries, and peers down to learn what it is the young woman sees in the water below. Just as she looks back up, "in a graceful curve as of a ballet gesture," the young woman throws the bundle over the side of the bridge. The protagonist tries to guess the weight of the package—does it contain a spray of flowers or a helpless infant? She cannot tell which. She tries to scream but cannot, realizing immediately that whether it is a baby or flowers will make no difference, as she will not tear off her jacket and scarf and leap into the river. As she looks down, she still cannot tell if what she sees is a flower or a baby's bonnet, or if it is paper from around flowers or a baby's blanket.

Finally, the protagonist runs up to the young woman and asks what she has thrown off the bridge; however, the young woman acts as if she does not know what she is talking about, or as if her act is insignificant. She merely says, "I think it is going to rain again. It's ruined everything I planned." After the young woman walks away, the protagonist sets down her own grocery bag, "as if it contains bottles, quarts of heavy rich milk." She then takes a cantaloupe out of her bag, palms it as if it were a basketball and heaves it into the river. As the story ends, "she tries to remember the soft plop of entry, and failing that, listens for a cry."

Themes and Meanings

The protagonist's witnessing of the other woman's throwing of an object off the bridge is the single event in this story. It hardly seems enough to justify a complete story, even one as short as this. However, it is not the event that supplies the story's central interest, as bizarre as that event may be; rather, it is the protagonist's reaction to what she sees or thinks that she sees. Her reaction seems more than just that of the horrified response of a bystander witnessing a possible tragedy. Her feeling that a baby may have been thrown into the river seems somehow personal; when she confronts the young woman, she feels a "new emptiness" and half believes that something has died for her. This is thus a story in which the motivation of the protagonist who observes the action is more important than that of the young woman who is at the center of the action. The real mystery of the story is thus not what is in the bundle that the young woman throws but why the protagonist reacts as she does.

What makes "The Bridge" challenging is that in spite of the dramatic event at its center, it does not, at first glance, appear to be a story that communicates any strong thematic significance. Like the woman in the story, readers are inclined to ask what happened. Moreover, as readers expect a story to have some thematic meaning, they ask what it all means. Finally, as human beings interested in other human beings, they ask what can we know about these characters. The reader's central interest is with the protagonist; the young woman who throws the bundle off the bridge is simply a catalyst whose behavior helps to reveal something about the protagonist, for it is her stake in the action that seems most important in this story.

"The Bridge" begins with a common human inclination to watch a stranger and idly invent a story about that person. When people do this, the stories that they make up are usually reflections of their own need. What can we know about the protagonist's needs in this story? One knows little about her beyond the fact that she has a husband, as she wonders what she will tell him about the young woman on the bridge. Moreover, the fact that her groceries contain only two lamb chops suggests that she and her husband live alone. The fact that she wonders how much a baby weighs suggests that she has never had children of her own. Although she thinks that the bundle contains flowers, she is more inclined to suspect that it contains a baby.

Drawing on these details and their implications, the reader might assume that the protagonist suspects that the young woman has thrown a baby off the bridge because that action is an objectification of her own childlessness. When she runs up to the woman, she experiences a feeling of emptiness objectified by the fact that she sets down the grocery bag because it feels heavy, as if it contains quarts of heavy rich milk—an image suggesting the fullness of the maternal characteristics that she herself lacks. Finally, her act of heaving the cantaloupe off the bridge as she mimics the woman's throwing off the imagined baby is an image of her own loneliness. It objectifies her own lack of what she thinks would fulfill her.

Style and Technique

As has been typical of most short fiction since Anton Chekhov first developed modern techniques, "The Bridge" communicates its meaning by simple description and implication rather than by exposition, by allegorizing, or by overt metaphor. The method of communicating meaning in the story is covert rather than overt, and readers must make their best guesses about its significance, drawing on the few details that the writer provides. What communicates meaning in "The Bridge" is not the time-bound cause-and-effect sequence of its events but rather the implications the reader can derive from the details clustered about the protagonist. The image of the flowers floating on the water, for example, suggests the death of something, even as the image of the floating object resembling a baby's cap suggests the bleakness of the woman's emptiness.

Although subtle and covert, many details in the story imply that the protagonist longs for a child, does not have one, and sees the action on the bridge as an objectification of her own loss. The details of the story do not lead the reader to identify with or condemn the young woman but rather to feel the protagonist's emptiness and lack of identity. For example, when she runs up to the young woman, she looks back down the bridge to determine just how far away she was, but she cannot find a point to identify her place along the railing of the bridge.

The protagonist's relation to the central action of the story is not a simple one. Although the protagonist identifies with the young woman when she first sees her, making a comparison between the way they are dressed, this does not mean that the protagonist may have killed her own baby, or that she identifies with anyone who kills a baby; rather, it suggests that the action that she witnesses is a dramatic objectification of her longing and loss. Her projection of her own assumptions onto the young woman and her invention of a story about a baby being thrown off a bridge create a hallucinatory, dreamlike effect. The reader does not feel that the story takes place in the real world so much as in a metaphor of the protagonist's situation. The final scene, when she picks up the cantaloupe and, like a catapult, heaves it into the river, is a poignant image of the human effort to cope with an event by projecting it outside the self and acting it out. It is an attempt to gain some control over the despair of loss and helplessness by acting out a metaphoric objectification of that loss. As the protagonist tries to remember the soft plop of entry, she listens for a cry that she will never hear.

Charles E. May

THE BRIDGE OF DREAMS

Author: Jun'ichirō Tanizaki (1886-1965)
Type of plot: Psychological
Time of plot: The 1920's
Locale: Kyoto
First published: "Yume no ukihashi," 1959 (English translation, 1963)

> *Principal characters:*
> OTOKUNI TADASU, the narrator and son of a well-to-do family
> TSUNEKO, his stepmother, who takes his mother's place and name
> HIS FATHER, a reclusive patron of the arts
> CHINU, his mother
> SAWAKO, his wife

The Story

Tadasu is a young man who loses his mother at age five. When his father remarries three years later, the boy is encouraged to rekindle his Oedipal relationship with his young new stepmother. He is both obsessed and guilt-ridden about his attraction to her, so he tries to understand his feelings in the form of a confessional memoir, which he writes years later.

Tadasu's memories of his real mother are those of a young child: her bosom and the feminine smell of hair oil. She suckles her son, as many Japanese mothers do, longer than Western mothers, and this forms a close erotic attachment. They live a quiet, secluded, and comfortable life in a traditional Japanese house called "Heron's Nest" with a large garden in the suburbs of Kyoto. (Virtually the entire story takes place in this tranquil villa.) His father seldom ventures out to his bank, enjoying the garden and its pond, concentrating his attention on his wife Chinu.

This domestic tranquillity is shattered when Chinu dies suddenly from an infected womb early in a pregnancy. The family mourns her loss for nearly a year. Then Tadasu's father brings home a young woman who plays the koto for them. She gradually becomes a presence in the household, so Tadasu is not surprised when his father announces his intention of marrying her. Only much later does he learn that his stepmother was apprenticed as a geisha at age eleven and bought by a cotton merchant at age fifteen; they divorced when she was eighteen, and two years later she married Tadasu's father. Tadasu never discovered how they met.

Tadasu suspects in his memoir that his father wanted the new wife to look and act like his lost mother, and in fact Tadasu has difficulty recalling where one left off and the other began because the two women resembled each other so much. One evening his new mother calls him into her room and cuddles him as his mother had, opening her kimono and letting him play with her breasts. He sucks her nipples, but of course there is no milk. Tadasu finds it more and more difficult to remember his real mother's face and voice, or the touch and smell of her body, as he substitutes his new mother.

Years later, when Tadasu is about nineteen, his stepmother unexpectedly becomes pregnant. His father becomes morose as he remembers his first wife's death, although the baby is born without incident. When he returns from school one day two weeks after his brother's birth, however, Tadasu is shocked to discover that he has been sent out to the countryside for adoption. Neither parent seems bereaved, and they explain that Tadasu is the only child they need. Upset, Tadasu tries to find his baby brother but gives up and becomes resigned to the situation.

A few days later, there is an incident that haunts Tadasu for years to come. His stepmother is lactating, but with no child to suckle, she uses a milking device to relieve the swelling. Tadasu accidentally comes across her in their garden pavilion. Now nearly a man, he is embarrassed at her nakedness but impulsively accepts her offer to taste her milk, nursing for half an hour, then running off guilt-ridden. He is disturbed by his actions and tries to understand why she put herself into such a position. He thinks his father may have encouraged it to draw the two closer together, however shameful their actions might be. Despite his guilt, he later is drawn back to her.

Tadasu soon discovers that his father is suffering from a terminal illness, tuberculosis of the kidneys. His stepmother devotes herself to his care as the disease steadily disables him. Before he dies, his father plans a marriage for Tadasu with the daughter of their gardener, a most unsuitable arrangement in the eyes of their relatives, who suspect that Tadasu and his stepmother have committed incest. They also suspect that his father wants the marriage to cover up this situation.

Soon after his father dies, Sawako, the gardener's daughter, begins paying regular visits to Tadasu and his stepmother, and a three-way relationship forms. Eventually the marriage takes place but without enthusiasm on Tadasu's part. During and after his honeymoon, he makes sure his new wife does not become pregnant. The three seem to settle into a quiet life in the small world of the Heron's Nest, but it is shattered by the sudden and suspicious death of Tadasu's stepmother.

One evening when his new wife is massaging Tsuneko's legs, a centipede crawls on her drowsy form and bites her. She dies of shock a few hours later. Tadasu is horrified by this sudden turn of events. He harbors unexpressed feelings that his wife may have deliberately placed the poisonous insect in her mother-in-law's bed, feelings that have motivated him to write his memoir. His unconfirmed suspicions and lack of love for Sawako lead to an expensive divorce and the sale of the Heron's Nest. He seeks out his young brother, who reminds him of his dead stepmother, and there the memoir ends, the two living together in 1931.

Themes and Meanings

The title of this story, "The Bridge of Dreams," is the same as that of the last chapter of the eleventh century Japanese classic, *The Tale of Genji*. The bridge is life itself, linking memories of dead loved ones with the living. In this story, a young boy becomes so confused about the identities of his real mother and his father's second wife that the two women merge into one nurturing figure.

Jun'ichirō Tanizaki's writing has two particular traits: It focuses on the mystery of women and is steeped in the classical literature of Japan. Both are evident in "The Bridge of Dreams." The theme of the dimly remembered mother and the deliberate attempt of Tadasu's father to substitute Tsuneko for her suggests a search for an idealized, if erotic, relationship. Tadasu seems less an active agent than a passive observer of his life. This life is determined by women; first his mother, then her substitute, Tsuneko.

There is a dark undercurrent throughout the memoir, as though it were written as a catharsis for the guilt he feels for his relationship with Tsuneko. The late weaning at age four—although in Japan this is not as uncommon as in the West—is followed by his being drawn into a childlike role with his new mother. However, the man-child is aware of the sexuality that has been aroused after Tsuneko bears his brother.

Readers learn that the relatives and neighbors had long suspected an incestuous affair, possibly even with his father's encouragement, but one cannot tell for sure from evidence in the story. One is left with an uneasy suspicion that perhaps all is not revealed. This suspicion is heightened by Tadasu's admission: "I do not allow myself the slightest falsehood or distortion. But there are limits even to telling the truth; there is a line one ought not to cross." Tanizaki thus leaves readers with the unstated, the possibility that there are even darker secrets at which they can only guess.

Style and Technique

Modern Japanese fiction frequently has taken the form of the "I-novel," an often intimate first-person narrative with a strong confessional tendency. Tanizaki follows this technique by utilizing a memoir that is not directed at any audience, nor is it intended to be read until after Tadasu's death. This gives the whole story an authenticity and intimacy that allows readers to see a character's innermost thoughts in an almost voyeuristic way. The use of a memoir—other Japanese authors have used long letters—creates this authenticity. One follows Tadasu's personal thoughts with almost embarrassing clarity, but at the same time one sees the other characters only through his eyes. Their motives are therefore as obscure to readers as they are to Tadasu.

The story, like all of Tanizaki's work, is heavily laden with literary and cultural references. As in Japanese poetry, he evokes the seasons with allusions to insects or the color of trees or blossoms. For example, Tadasu knows that his shocking encounter with his stepmother was in late spring because the silk tree his grandfather had planted was in blossom. He begins massaging his stepmother when the crape myrtle is beginning to bloom and the plantain is ripening. The passing of time is marked by these familiar references from traditional Japanese literature.

Poetry, calligraphy, and other arts provide a rich background for this psychological study, giving the story a classical quality that provides a context for its eroticism. The Heron's Nest, itself a reference to *The Tale of Genji*, is a quiet eddy of Japanese culture, protected from the rapid changes of the world beyond the walls of the garden.

Richard Rice

BRIDGING

Author: Max Apple (1941-   )
Type of plot: Domestic realism
Time of plot: 1973
Locale: Houston, Texas
First published: 1984

> *Principal characters:*
> DADDY, the narrator
> JESSICA, his nine-year-old daughter
> KAY RANDALL, a thirty-three-year-old Girl Scout leader
> SHARON, Jessica's psychiatrist
> MRS. CLARK, the narrator's den mother when he was a Cub Scout
> JOHN CLARK, her son

The Story

Today is the first whole day that the narrator has left his daughter, Jessica, alone since his wife died from a complicated neurologic disease eight months earlier. His housekeeper, Juana, is taking care of Jessica while he attends a Girl Scout meeting. Jessica is an avid baseball fan, and she and her father have season tickets to the Houston Astros. Her conversations with her father are often about famous players, their batting averages, and their relative greatness. Tonight Jessica must watch the Astros game on television, a fact that upsets the family routine greatly.

The narrator has volunteered to assist the Girl Scout leader, Kay Randall, because he wants to encourage Jessica to reach out to others her age. So far, however, she has resisted joining the scouts. To demonstrate to her the importance of sticking to one's commitments, the narrator is leaving her home tonight as he takes twenty-two young girls on a field trip to east Texas to collect wildflowers.

During this trip his mind wanders and he recalls various events—from earlier today, from a week or so earlier, and from his own childhood. He remembers his conversations with Jessica over the past two months; he encouraged her to give scouting a try, but her response was that Kay Randall and the scouts can never replace her lost mother. He recalls, as well, his own Cub Scout experience, when he was Jessica's age. His den mother, Mrs. Clark, was so large that she could not sit in normal chairs—she had to use couches. When she walked upstairs she filled them completely. Her son, John, was stocky. Although ten-year-olds generally find such people humorous, the scouts looked on Mrs. Clark and her son with a certain respect because they carried themselves with a certain dignity. Also, they had a difficult life because Mr. Clark had been killed in the Korean War.

The narrator also thinks about his recent conversations with Jessica's psychiatrist, whom she sees twice weekly. The doctor diagnoses the girl as suffering from separation anxiety and congratulates the father for being able to express his anger. However, she hopes that both Jessica and her father will be able to trust the world again, despite their recent loss. The father recalls an interview with his daughter's school principal a few weeks earlier, when Jessica was reprimanded for listening to a baseball game in class instead of participating in the lesson.

During the scout field trip, the narrator is surprised to realize that he is actually enjoying himself. He learns from Kay Randall that she has separated from her husband because he only had time for his work; she adds that although she is lonely, her life is all right. When he returns home from the field trip, his daughter tearfully greets him. He hugs her, but in his heart recognizes that this is only the first of many times that he will have to leave her on her own.

Themes and Meanings

The title of Max Apple's story suggests its theme, which is played out on a number of levels. The reader first sees it in the motion that Kay Randall makes to explain how Brownies become Girl Scouts: She holds her hands out from her chest with her fingertips on each other. It takes a full year for little girls to go through this "bridging" process of moving to the more mature level of scouting. It is, therefore, not something that one can rush. Significantly, as the Brownies imitate Miss Randall's motion, so too does the narrator—thereby suggesting that he also must do a certain amount of bridging as the story progresses.

Jessica's difficulty in moving beyond the trauma of her mother's death is, however, the most obvious bridging on which the narrator focuses. How, he wonders, can he get his daughter to break out of her shell and socialize with others her own age? He understands that she prefers to stay home and watch television because she is afraid of losing anyone else or of being hurt herself, but he knows that life demands that people find ways to move past tragedies and dependence on their parents and that they assert their independence and self-confidence.

Jessica still seems unprepared to bridge with her peers. She instead lives vicariously through baseball. One wonders if Jessica used the language of baseball equally obsessively when her mother was alive and if it is now her surest way to maintain a close relationship with her father. If so, this, too, is a sort of bridge. This may explain why Jessica turns her attention to another sport, basketball, at the close of the story: Because baseball no longer keeps her father with her, she must find another bridge.

Her father, of course, has his own difficulties following the loss of his wife. He notes that life is throwing curves and fastballs at him and his daughter and that they feel like they are standing blindfolded at home plate. He seems to be trying to fill the role of both parents. On the one hand, he finds himself the only male in the female world of Girl Scouting; on the other hand, he tries awkwardly to get to know other women. He recognizes a kindred spirit in Kay Randall but ultimately decides that he cannot bridge in any meaningful way with her because all they really have in common is sadness and the Girl Scouts.

Most pointedly, the narrator suffers through the trial of finding a way both to protect his daughter and to prepare her adequately for a world in which people die. He recalls John Clark, the Cub Scout who had to mature without having a father around, and wonders if Jessica's schoolmates feel the same way about her that he once felt about John, namely, that John had a certain seriousness about life that they all admired. He knows, however, that the death of John's father could at least be portrayed as heroic and therefore meaningful. By contrast, the death of Jessica's mother was incomprehensible—a sudden attack from nowhere. He ultimately draws the heartbreaking conclusion to which all parents must come: that he can be a scout for his daughter, but he cannot make the actual journey for her.

Style and Technique

Apple typically incorporates famous people into his stories and often uses games as metaphors for American society. In this story he manages to do both by employing baseball and some of its most famous players. The story takes place on the day that Houston Astro star Nolan Ryan became the all-time major league strikeout king. This coincidence also implicitly reminds Jessica and her father that in order for someone to become a strikeout king, many other people must strike out. Life is like that, and we must roll with the punches. The narrator is also setting an important example for his daughter, reminding her that while watching games is fine, being a player is even better—even if more dangerous.

Jessica's language is worth noting, as well. She uses baseball jargon in a way that is traditionally associated with boys. Meanwhile, her father is echoing the language of the Girl Scout leader. There is a kind of role reversal implied in the game that Apple plays here, and that serves his theme well. The narrator, after all, mentions several times that he thinks his daughter understands life better than he does. In the face of the real dangers out there, her fear is quite legitimate.

However, this is also Apple's way of parodying cultural clichés, reminding the reader in a gentle way that the games that define social roles in the United States do not ultimately get us through serious crises, which are anything but games. No one is keeping score, he seems to imply, and it is difficult to figure out what the rules are. As with most of Apple's fiction, the story has both a bittersweet tone that recognizes life's inscrutable challenges, and a quietly optimistic sense that whatever answers there are can be found in the ordinary lives of ordinary people.

John C. Hawley

THE BRIGADIER AND THE GOLF WIDOW

Author: John Cheever (1912-1982)
Type of plot: Social realism
Time of plot: The late 1950's
Locale: A New York City suburb
First published: 1964

> *Principal characters:*
> CHARLIE PASTERN, a businessperson
> MRS. PASTERN, his wife
> MRS. FLANNAGAN, his mistress

The Story

Charlie Pastern lives in a suburb of New York City and spends much of his time at the country club playing golf. He earns the nickname "brigadier" by carrying on in the locker room about America's enemies, insisting that the only way to deal with them is to drop nuclear bombs on them. Because he spends so little time at home, his wife is the "golf widow" in the title of the story. The marked difference in their personalities is initially dramatized by their attitudes toward the bomb shelter that Charlie Pastern has had constructed under their yard. Charlie is warlike and expects Armageddon, while his wife does her best to maintain appearances, decorating the ugly lump that the bomb shelter makes in the yard with a birdbath and plaster figures. She is also subtly irritable, pointing out the flaws in her neighbors' possessions to make up for the lack of fulfillment that she feels as a wife and mother—a failure that she does not consider her own fault. While her husband, Charlie, is plump and aggressive, she is gaunt and oblique.

Mrs. Pastern, like her neighbors, is active in collecting donations for medical research. Each of these suburban housewives concentrates on a given illness. Mrs. Pastern's charity is hepatitis. One autumn day, she goes around the neighborhood collecting for her charity. She covers all of her route except for two families. One of them is the Flannagan family, and while his wife is preparing dinner, Charlie Pastern, to escape the boredom of his house and the lingering boredom of his day in general, agrees to collect the remaining donations.

The fact that he does not know the Flannagans does not stop him from accepting Mrs. Flannagan's invitation for a drink in her house. Explaining that her husband has been away on business for six weeks, she proceeds to seduce Charlie, which is not difficult—he has been cheating on his wife for some time.

Charlie and Mrs. Flannagan have an affair. They meet in secret several times in New York City. Charlie succumbs to her wheedling and buys her gifts—perfume, a peignoir, a silk umbrella—which he can ill afford. Because of bad investments, his finances are in disarray. After several meetings, Mrs. Flannagan stands Charlie up.

When he phones her, she says that she wants to end the affair, but when he confronts her in person, she agrees to continue it if he gives her the key to his bomb shelter, which he does.

Meanwhile Mrs. Pastern is visited by her minister, Mr. Ludgate, and her bishop. What little sense of comfort she has left is all but shattered when it becomes clear that the bishop, apparently a heavy drinker, has come only to see the bomb shelter. He seems more interested in his own and his congregation's physical survival in the event of a nuclear attack than in the life after death. After the bishop leaves, the final blow to Mrs. Pastern's composure is delivered by Beatrice, the maid who comes to clean the Pastern's house twice a week. On the phone, Beatrice informs Mrs. Pastern that her husband has given Mrs. Flannagan the key to the bomb shelter.

Drunk on the remainder of the batch of martinis that she had made for the bishop, Mrs. Pastern corners her husband when he comes home that night. Long debased by their loveless marriage and Charlie's infidelities, she tells him what she knows about the key. Charlie drives immediately to the Flannagan house, where he finds Mrs. Flannagan's newest lover hiding naked in a bathroom. Having threatened to kill her (which is in character with his melodramatic hostility against the enemies of America), Charlie goes back home, where his wife accuses him of acting the way he does because he wants the world to be destroyed along with himself. She knows that he is all but bankrupt, that he cannot pay for the bomb shelter, and that far from standing for survival, he is committed to destruction.

Though the Pasterns remain married, they lose everything. Charlie ends up in jail for failure to pay his bills, the house is sold, the children leave college, and Mrs. Pastern lives on welfare with her son in the Bronx. Mrs. Flannagan is last seen divorced and penniless, and when she makes a visit to the bomb shelter one snowy afternoon, she is turned away by the new owners of the Pastern's house.

Themes and Meanings

Cheever's story is about social pretense and about how his middle-class characters maintain it. On the surface, Charlie Pastern, the protagonist, wants others to think of him as a strong man who is successful in life and honest about his feelings. This is why he belongs to the country club and harangues his golf cronies with his political conservatism, and why he makes no secret about his bomb shelter, which is not only an eyesore but also a blatant symbol of his patriotism and his commitment to free enterprise—as opposed, one assumes, to communism. However, underneath Charlie's veneer of strength and patriotic hostility lies the truth, which turns his outward demeanor into a pretense. He has, in fact, squandered everything by which spiritual and worldly success is measured in the suburban milieu that he inhabits: fidelity and money. He is habitually unfaithful to his wife—and would be, the story suggests, to Mrs. Flannagan were their affair to last long enough. He has wasted the money that his mother left him and has critically overextended his credit. He is not, in short, a preserver of values but a destroyer of them, victimizing in the process his wife, his children, and himself. The intelligence to which he pretends as a successful member of

his suburban community is no more than stupidity. He fails to make smart investments, relies on gambling to recoup his losses, and entrusts his well-being to a woman
(Mrs. Flannagan) who is too selfish to further it.

Charlie's wife is also interested in being well thought of by her neighbors. She tries
to hide the harsh reality of the bomb shelter and of her empty life with Charlie, but she
is less able than Charlie to conceal her real condition. Her wasted looks and contempt
for her neighbors' tastes suggest her unhappiness. Her attempt to decorate the bomb
shelter is futile; the garden ornaments that she uses for this purpose are ugly and
cheap. Like Charlie's, her pretensions arise from desperation; unlike Charlie's,
though, her desperation is not self-imposed, so it is easier to sympathize with her. Indeed, she has a kind of courage that her husband lacks, for the truth about him does not
drive her from their marriage, just as the truth about the bishop does not cause her to
break from Christianity—or so it seems.

Mrs. Flannagan is as much a deceiver as Charlie or his wife. It becomes clear that
she, like Charlie, has had many affairs, though she insists to him that he is her first ex-
tramarital lover. She seems to be naïve and childlike, but this is only a ploy that she
uses to seduce men and to get them to buy gifts for her. In Charlie's case, she pretends
to break up with him so she can get him to give her the key to his bomb shelter, and
when he storms into her house after finding out that she has not kept her possession of
the key a secret, she pretends that she is not entertaining another lover.

The story's social insight is that people who define their lives in the context of a
community will go to great lengths to hide their failures, and the story's moral is that
these failures—moral in nature—can be neither hidden nor made up for by pretense.
Dishonesty compounds such failures, as the story demonstrates when Charlie Pastern,
his wife, and Mrs. Flannagan are forced to leave the community by their own actions
(Mrs. Flannagan's infidelity leads to divorce, Charlie's imprudence to bankruptcy,
and Mrs. Pastern's pride to shame), thus compromising the very survival that Charlie
with his bomb shelter and Mrs. Flannagan with the key to it are so anxious about.

Style and Technique

The story is told from the vantage of a narrator who owns property adjoining the
Pastern's property; the narrator learns the ultimate fate of the Pasterns and Mrs.
Flannagan from a letter that his mother sends him. This narrative device suggests that
the story is a form of gossip, but it also underscores the story's authority, for the narrator himself is a member of the community that the story anatomizes.

Beyond this, Cheever uses the image of the bomb shelter to focus the social meaning of the story. In itself, the shelter stands for survival selfishly conceived. For Charlie Pastern, the bishop, and Mrs. Flannagan, it represents their personal survival at the
expense of the survival of others and of those values that make a living community
meaningful. As such, it represents failure: Charlie cannot pay for it and loses it to the
new owners of his house, and Mrs. Flannagan cannot use her key to it in the end.

Mark McCloskey

BRIGHT AND MORNING STAR

Author: Richard Wright (1908-1960)
Type of plot: Social realism
Time of plot: The 1930's
Locale: Near Memphis, Tennessee
First published: 1938

Principal characters:
JOHNNY-BOY, a communist activist
SUE, his mother
SUG, his brother
REVA, a woman in love with Johnny-Boy
BOOKER, a man who joins the Communist Party to betray it

The Story

In the first of the story's six sections, Sue, an elderly and dignified black woman, recalls her burdensome life and efforts to survive the death of her husband and the births of her sons, Sug and Johnny-Boy. Both sons believe in the promise of the Communist Party to end strife between the races and economic classes. Sug, however, is imprisoned for his party activities, and Johnny-Boy, like many Richard Wright characters, is fleeing from white people who seek to identify Communist Party members in order to destroy both them and the party. Sue and Reva, a white woman in love with Johnny-Boy, share a well-founded concern for Johnny-Boy's safety.

In the next section, Johnny-Boy explains to his mother that he is committed to communism for economic, not racial reasons, noting that black people cannot fight rich bosses alone and that only by working with white party members can they attain economic equality. Sue believes that Johnny-Boy is blinded by his idealism, but her maternal love does not allow her to prevent his attending a party meeting, even though Reva has warned her that the sheriff and other white men plan to raid the meeting.

In the third section the sheriff arrives to determine the whereabouts of Johnny-Boy and the meeting. He brutally beats Sue, but she will not tell him anything. Angered by her defiance, the sheriff knocks her unconscious. Sue's pride, her ability to maintain her secret, and her pronouncement that she has the strength to remain silent are her nearly fatal undoing.

In the fourth section, Sue, her son, and the black race are betrayed when a white man named Booker arrives, ostensibly to warn those planning to attend the Communist Party meeting of the sheriff's intention. In his manipulation of Sue in her weakened state, Richard Wright's Booker does indeed reveal his Judas-like qualities. When he leaves, Sue fears she has revealed her secret to the wrong person.

Sue's fears are confirmed in the next section, in which Reva reappears and warns Sue not to trust Booker. The warning comes too late, so Sue decides to take action.

She arms herself with a gun and her conviction that she will go to the spot where she believes the sheriff is waiting for her son and the other Communist Party members.

In the final section of the story, the battle lines are drawn clearly: black versus white, the powerless versus the powerful, and Sue and her son versus the sheriff and his conspirators. After Sue sees the sheriff break her son's kneecaps and his ear drums because he will not reveal the names of his comrades, she sees Booker, the man for whom she is really waiting. She shoots Booker, thereby killing the man whose betrayal has destroyed her son, his dreams, and her own. Sue, in turn, is killed by the white posse, her blood adding to the drama of the final battlefield scene.

Themes and Meanings

"Bright and Morning Star" is the fifth and last story in Wright's collection *Uncle Tom's Children* (1940), whose title is an obvious allusion to Harriet Beecher Stowe's antislavery novel *Uncle Tom's Cabin* (1851-1852). If, as President Abraham Lincoln suggested, Stowe's novel started the Civil War, then Wright's story continues the saga of war, specifically the war between blacks and whites. Divided into six sections, the story uses communism as the racial battleground.

If Sue's murder were the end of the story, "Bright and Morning Star" might be viewed as a tragic tale of the powerful destroying the powerless. This, however, is not the final note in this last story in *Uncle Tom's Children*. On the contrary, Sue dies victorious, finally realizing that what she had viewed as the "white mountain" of the race that had persecuted her was now toppled through her action. She lies on the ground, in her last moments of life, without struggling; she is at peace, experiencing an intensity of life in her last moments. She realizes that the white men may think that they have killed her, but in reality, she has actually relinquished her life before they could take it from her, thus controlling her own destiny. When her lips move soundlessly, mouthing the words "yuh didnt git yuh didnt yuh didnt," Sue becomes one with her bright and morning star.

The theme of betrayal is at the heart of "Bright and Morning Star," a story whose title suggests hopes and dreams and aspirations—all of which are destroyed by both human and ideological means. In the first case—that of human betrayal—the obvious culprit in this story is Booker, the white turncoat who joins the Communist Party to identify its members, thereby ingratiating himself with the sheriff and elevating himself in the southern community in which he resides. Booker's name is clearly an allusion to Booker T. Washington, whom Wright and others have viewed as a black man whose accommodation to white precepts betrayed his own race. Wright's Judas-like Booker accomplishes his plan of betrayal, only to be shot by the woman who most symbolizes the values and humanity that he denies.

Perhaps more subtle than this human betrayal, however, is the ideological betrayal of the Communist Party. Johnny-Boy explains to his mother that the party will connect blacks and whites, destroying economic distinctions so that blacks can obtain equality and justice by working alongside more privileged whites. Just as Wright demonstrates the naïveté of that dream in *Native Son*, his autobiographical novel published the same year as *Uncle Tom's Children*, and in his autobiography *Black Boy* (1945), so he suggests in "Bright and Morning Star" the destructive idealism inherent in the Communist Party. Betrayed by that idealism, both Johnny-Boy and his mother are victims of a Judas that is not merely one person—Booker—but actually a deceptive vision that blacks and whites can be united by the ideological tenets of communism.

Style and Technique

Consistent with a major theme of the story—Booker's Judas-like betrayal of Sue and her son—a major technique to communicate this theme is Wright's use of religious imagery. This imagery is obviously demonstrated in the title of the story, which is a reference to a spiritual that Sue remembers from her childhood: "Hes the Lily of the Valley, the Bright n Mawnin Star/ Hes the Fairest of Ten Thousan t ma soul." This musical context is reinforced by frequent references to traditional black Christianity. Repeated throughout the story, these references speak to the role of religion in Sue's life as a stable, reassuring belief that the toil and struggle and burdens of life on this earth—a painful life for Sue, to be sure—will be replaced by a resurrection such as was experienced by the Jesus in whom she deeply believes. This is her vision.

Sue's vision, however, is replaced by another vision, one that she views as "a new and terrible vision." The vision of Christianity is replaced by the vision of communism, and Wright's imagery dramatically underscores that replacement: "The wrongs and sufferings of black men had taken the place of Him nailed to the Cross; the meager beginnings of the party had become another Resurrection." This new and terrible vision might have been a source for a new and terrible world order, one in which justice and equality and humanity rule. Instead it is betrayed by Booker and the sheriff and those others who, like the biblical Judas, are more concerned with their security than others' survival. In this battle, the bright and morning star shines over a battlefield in which both the betrayer and the betrayed are destroyed.

Marjorie Smelstor

BROKEBACK MOUNTAIN

Author: E. Annie Proulx (1935-   )
Type of plot: Realism, regional
Time of plot: The 1960's to 1980's
Locale: Wyoming
First published: 1997

> *Principal characters:*
> JACK TWIST, a cowboy
> ENNIS DEL MAR, a cowboy

The Story

Jack Twist and Ennis del Mar are in their late teens when they are hired to tend sheep above the tree line on Brokeback Mountain in Wyoming during the summer of 1963. When the temperature drops in the evening, Ennis wakes Jack up with his teeth chattering, and Jack invites him into his bedroll. The two men have sex and continue to have sex through the rest of the summer, although they never talk about it except when Ennis declares, "I'm not no queer," and Jack agrees, saying it is a one-shot deal and not anyone else's business.

When the two men separate at the end of the summer, Ennis feels so bad that he stops on the side of the road and vomits. In December, Ennis marries Alma Beers, to whom he has been engaged; she is pregnant by mid-January.

Four years later, Ennis gets a letter from Jack saying he is coming through and wants to buy Ennis a beer. When they meet, they grab each other and kiss each other on the mouth so hard that they draw blood. By this time, Ennis has two daughters, and Jack is married with a son. Jack and Ennis go off to a motel, and both men are astonished at the power of their feelings for each other. However, both are frightened about these feelings, realizing that they must do something about it, for if they act that way in the wrong place they will be dead.

Jack, who has been a rodeo performer, thinks he and Ennis should get themselves a little ranch and live together, but Ennis says he does not want to be one of those old guys who live together until someone takes a tire iron to them. However, both men realize that their feelings for each other are serious and not merely sexual.

Ennis goes on a fishing trip with Jack once or twice a year, and Ennis and Alma begin to grow apart, for she has seen the two men embrace. She divorces him, and Ennis goes back to ranch work. The two men continue to see each other, but they reach a point at which Ennis cannot see Jack as much as Jack would like. Jack tells Ennis they could have had a good life together, but all they really have is the memory of Brokeback Mountain. Jack tells Ennis he does not know how to quit him.

Several months later, Ennis sends a postcard to Jack, which is returned, stamped "Deceased." He calls Jack's wife, Laureen, who tells him it was an accident, that when

Jack was pumping up a flat tire, it blew out and knocked the tire rim into his face, causing him to bleed to death. Ennis thinks to himself that somebody got him with a tire iron after all. Laureen tells him that Jack wanted his ashes scattered on Brokeback Mountain, and Ennis goes to Jack's parents' house and offers to fulfill that wish. However, Jack's father refuses, saying he is going to bury the ashes in the family plot. The story ends with Ennis dreaming about Jack as he first saw him as a young man on Brokeback Mountain.

Themes and Meanings

"Brokeback Mountain" is not so much a story about homosexuality as it is a love story that happens to involve two males. Conventional stories about sexual relations between men are either about men identified as homosexuals or men, such as prisoners, who have no other available partners. However, "Brokeback Mountain" does not fit either of these categories. Both Ennis and Jack insist that they are not homosexual, and neither of them have sex with other men. Moreover, although they first have sex while alone on the mountain, they continue to have sex over the years even though both get married. The two men seem to genuinely love each other, both craving that time on Brokeback Mountain when their embrace satisfied "some shared and sexless hunger."

E. Annie Proulx takes a creative chance here because many readers may try to simplify the story by classifying Jack and Ennis as homosexuals, or latent homosexuals or even bisexual—both meaningless terms. However, such an easy classification will not serve here. When Jack and Ennis deny their homosexuality, they mean it. The fact of the matter is that Jack and Ennis love each other—with tenderness, passion, and concern—and people who love each other in this way—regardless of their gender—desire to be physically close.

One of the most poignant and revealing moments in the story occurs in May, 1983, when, out on the range, the two men hold each other, talk about their children, and have sex. The sexuality is no more important than their domestic conversation; it merely seems a natural part of their love for each other.

This is not to say that the story ignores the social taboos against the relationship the men have. Both of them are scared, for they know—especially in the male-dominated cowboy society in which they live—that if their sexual relationship is discovered, they may be killed. Ennis recalls when he was a boy that an old man was beaten to death with a tire iron for his homosexuality. He wonders if the feeling they have for each other happens to other people, and Jack says that it does not happen in Wyoming.

However, this barrier to their being open about their relationship serves less as a means to deal with the social issue of intolerance toward homosexuality than as a typical literary impediment that gives famous love stories their tragic inevitability, such as the feud between the families of Romeo and Juliet. Moreover, at the end of the story when Jack is killed, there is no real evidence that he was murdered by homophobes. Ennis only suspects this when he learns from Jack's father that Jack had made plans with another man to come up and build a place and help run the ranch. The story ends not with a message about the social intolerance of homosexuality but rather with a poignant image of Ennis creating a simple memorial to Jack with a postcard picture of Brokeback Mountain and two old shirts the men wore when they spent their first summer together.

Style and Technique

The technical challenge Proulx faces in "Brokeback Mountain" is how to write a love story involving two men without falling into the clichés and conventions of a homosexual story. She achieves this by creating a fablelike style for the story, with little or no attention paid to its realistic social context. Instead, the story focuses on the passionate love affair between Jack and Ennis against a stark landscape. Proulx focuses almost entirely on the encounters between the two men as mysterious passionate couplings and tender concerned sharing. The other characters in the story—the wives of both men and the parents of Jack—serve only minor supplemental roles. Proulx does not create an explicit social opposition to the relationship, complete with specific enemies whom Jack and Ennis must fear. All she need do is suggest, by the fears of the two men, that they live in a homophobic society, in which there is a constant danger of discovery and disaster.

Another challenge Proulx faces in this story is how to handle the descriptions of the sexuality between the two men, for even though sexual desire is not the sole source of their relationship, it is a passionate and powerful force for them that they do not understand. Their first encounter Proulx treats as a natural event, describing the act explicitly and straightforwardly. By developing the relationship of the two men over a period of some twenty years, She also suggests that it is not merely the sexuality that holds them together but something more emotional and lasting. She achieves this by focusing not only on the sexuality but also on the domestic relationship between the two men, their mutual concern for each other.

By refusing to make judgments and by treating the relationship of the two men with dignity and respect, Proulx succeeds in making the reader believe in this love affair between two men without classifying it narrowly as a homosexual story.

Charles E. May

THE BROTHER

Author: Robert Coover (1932-   )
Type of plot: Parody
Time of plot: The time of the biblical Flood
Locale: Probably the Middle East
First published: 1969

> *Principal characters:*
> THE NARRATOR, an unnamed man who appears to be Noah's
>   brother
> HIS WIFE
> HIS OLDER BROTHER, also unnamed but probably the biblical
>   Noah
> HIS BROTHER'S WIFE

The Story

The narrator contemplates the most recent of his elder brother's "buggy ideas": building a boat—a rather large boat, in a field far from any water. Although he is skeptical, as are his and his brother's wives, he does what he always has done for his sibling. He helps and humors him, though he also wonders how his simple-minded brother has managed to learn so much about boat building. Devoting more and more time to helping his brother, the narrator guiltily neglects both his own farm and his pregnant wife. She, however, manages to sow enough seed to ensure their survival during the coming year if it rains sufficiently. After the boat is completed, the brother takes up residence on board, much to his wife's disgust and the narrator and his wife's amusement. Then rain begins to fall. Initially the rain gives the young couple a reason to stay indoors together, but as it floods their fields and ruins their crops, the narrator's wife wonders despairingly whether they should have wasted their time building a boat themselves. When the downpour turns into deluge, the narrator goes to his brother to seek temporary refuge for himself, his wife, and his unborn child, but he is silently rebuffed. Fighting the rising waters, he reaches the relative safety of a nearby hill, from which he sees the boat sailing into the distance and his own house nearly covered.

As the story ends, the narrator—after a futile attempt to save his wife—is back on the hill again. He calculates that he may have a day left if the rain continues. Unable to see his brother's boat, he wonders how his brother knew the rain was coming. He concludes that "it's not hard to see who's crazy here I can't see my house no more just left my wife inside where I found her I couldn't hardly stand to look at her the way she was."

Themes and Meanings

"The Brother" appears among the "Seven Exemplary Fictions" section of Robert Coover's first collection, *Pricksongs & Descants* (1969). Dedicated to Miguel de Cervantes, the author of *El ingenioso hidalgo don Quixote de la Mancha* (1605, 1615; *The History of the Valorous and Wittie Knight-Errant, Don Quixote of the Mancha*, 1612-1620; better known as *Don Quixote de la Mancha*), Coover's gathering of early works resembles in effect—although not necessarily in original intention—Cervantes's own *Novelas ejemplares* (1613). Written as exercises in various narrative styles, the latter's "exemplary fictions" do more than entertain the reader and enable the writer to become adept in various narrative forms and styles. As Coover explains in his own "Prologue," they "struggle against the unconscious mythic residue in human life" in order to expose "adolescent thought modes and exhausted art forms." Just as Cervantes struggled against outmoded medieval ways of thinking and writing, Coover, no less comically and self-consciously, struggles against the "mythic residue" of that more modern age that Cervantes himself helped usher in. More specifically, Coover "struggles against" two of the most powerful modern "myths." One involves the primacy of rational thinking, the other the primacy of the individual artist and the prizing of his or her originality (the modern equivalent of the divine inspiration that sanctions Noah's building his ark).

The struggle is evident in the terms that Coover uses to describe his work. "The Brother" is not so much a short story as a "pricksong," or a "descant" (terms for what is essentially the same musical form), and a "fiction"—something man-made and therefore every bit as artificial as a musical composition. Coover's comically combative stance is even more noticeable in his choice of the Noah legend from Genesis as his base text. Coover's ironic retelling of the familiar Judeo-Christian myth of Noah and the Flood undermines the authority of the original in several ways. Most obviously, it presents the Noah figure as considerably less than the "just man and perfect" commended in Genesis. No less important, it gives eloquent if somewhat idiosyncratic voice to a character whom the biblical account prefers to silence: one of Noah's numerous and nameless, but here entirely sympathetic and memorable, siblings. This is the narrator, the younger brother, whose entreaties fail to move Noah. In questioning and thus undermining the biblical justification both for the Flood and for Noah's deliverance, Coover also subverts the larger dominant Judeo-Christian mythology. However, even as he does so, he manages to persuade the reader of the power and pleasure of myth as myth, as fiction. Unlike realistic fiction, which offers a window through which the reader can view the world, "The Brother" offers an art of self-consciously wrought artifice. In it, the medium (fiction, language) is more real than the "world" that medium seems to represent. Thus, Coover's story struggles not only against the power of established myths, such as that of Noah and the Ark, but against the power of established literary forms such as literary realism as well. Literary realism—the dominant literary mode of the past few centuries—assumes that art imitates life. "The Brother" suggests something quite different: that art imitates art.

Style and Technique

The first of *Pricksongs & Descants*'s two epigraphs provides a useful introduction to the narrative technique of Coover's collection in general and to "The Brother" in particular. It is, "He thrusts, she heaves," from John Cleland's semipornographic novel, *Fanny Hill* (1748-1749). This epigraph calls the reader's attention to the story's sexual dimension, one that Coover highlights by translating the perfunctory "begats" of his biblical source into an emotional and sexual bond connecting the narrator and his pregnant wife. Less obviously but no less importantly, the epigraph underscores two other stylistic relationships found in "The Brother." These are the ones between old-fashioned narrative drive and new-fangled narrative experimentation on the one hand and between the original story of Noah and the Flood and Coover's variation on this mythic theme on the other. Indeed, it is Coover's ability to combine entertaining narrative and narrative theory that unifies his collection's twenty fictions despite obvious and rather considerable differences in their subject matter and style.

Coover takes considerable pains to make the lives of his story's protagonist and his wife both sympathetic and "real." Not only does he endow them with a depth of feeling; he provides them with the very existence that the biblical story denies them. Against the "thrust" of this realistic, or mock-realistic, surface, however, Coover posits the "heave" of narrative technique. One of the most important and noticeable ways in which he focuses the reader's attention on manner over matter (or manner as matter) is by rendering the entire 2,900-word story in the form of a single uninterrupted and largely unpunctuated sentence. There are no periods, semicolons, or even commas, only quotation and question marks and a sprinkling of hyphens and dashes. The technique is certainly unusual but not at all original. In much the same way that Coover borrows the story's ostensible subject matter from the Old Testament, he borrows his "sentence structure" from Molly Bloom's famous soliloquy at the end of James Joyce's *Ulysses* (1922).

Other narrative techniques serve Coover's thematic purposes equally well. He develops his story cumulatively rather than causally (thus the frequent use of the connective "and"). He narrates the entire story in the present tense (a technique that ultimately adds a blackly humorous touch in light of the narrator's final predicament). Coover also chooses not to name his characters (in effect reducing them to their narrative functions—such as brother, husband, wife, or child—while parodying the parabolic quality of so many Bible stories). Coover also literalizes clichés, such as "would I help him for God's sake," and introduces other forms of dramatic irony for equally comic effect (as in the narrator and his wife's wishing for rain and getting a deluge). Finally, Coover's retelling the Noah story in a contemporary and decidedly colloquial idiom, and from a Huck Finn-like vernacular perspective, adds yet another comically jarring note and thus further undermines the seriousness as well as the explanatory power of the biblical version.

Robert A. Morace

THE BUCK STOPS HERE

Author: Stuart M. Kaminsky (1934-   )
Type of plot: Mystery and detective
Time of plot: 1957
Locale: Independence, Missouri
First published: 1989

Principal characters:
> HARRY S. TRUMAN, the former president of the United States
> LIEUTENANT PEVSNER, an Army Intelligence officer
> CARL GADES, a professional assassin
> KOSTER and
> FRANKLIN, Secret Service agents assigned to protect Truman

The Story

Lieutenant Pevsner of Army Intelligence rushes overnight from Washington, D.C., to the Truman Library in Independence, Missouri, because word has been received that Carl Gades plans to kill former president Harry Truman the next day. Truman had refused to pardon the man's only brother, Arthur, who recently died in prison after serving ten years for trying to blow up a plane.

Pevsner is assigned to this case because he is considered a "hawk," one whose photographic memory allows him to see and then recall every detail of a scene. While on another army assignment, Pevsner saw Gades three years earlier and he remembers many details about the man—including the unusual shape of his left ear, his blue eyes, and even the freckles on his wrist. Nevertheless, Pevsner doubts if he can recognize Gades, who is known as a master of disguise. No one in the Secret Service, however, has ever seen Gades.

Pevsner is exhausted when he arrives in Missouri, but he has no time to spare because it is expected that the attempt on Truman's life will occur at 3:00 P.M. that same day—one month, to the minute, after Gades's brother died. Pevsner studies the layout of the library and the people who are working there. It is being used by Truman, though the final stages of construction are still taking place. Characteristically, Pevsner notes small details about each of the clerical staff, painters, and people who make deliveries—even Koster and Franklin, the two armed Secret Service men assigned to guard Truman. He especially notices how similar these agents are in height, facial appearance—including their brown eyes—and the gray suits that they wear.

Pevsner questions the former president, who is surprisingly unconcerned and refuses to alter his schedule. After showing Pevsner around his office, a replica of the Oval Office of the White House, Truman invites Pevsner to lunch. Afterward, Pevsner is so tired that he takes a brief nap under a tree. Suddenly, however, he is startled awake. His powers of observation have forced themselves into his subconscious, and he realizes how Gades has disguised himself. The last time that Pevsner saw Franklin, he noticed that the man's eyes were blue, not brown. He rushes to Truman's office, where he finds the door is locked. Through a window, he sees that Gades is holding Truman prisoner, apparently waiting for the exact minute of his brother's death to kill him.

From Koster, Pevsner verifies that "Franklin" has been assigned only recently to Independence. It is now obvious that Gades somehow disposed of the real Franklin and substituted himself. He has probably removed the contact lenses that made his eyes appear brown because of an eye irritation. When Pevsner and Koster break down the office door, Gades points his gun at them before they can act. Meanwhile, Truman sits, calmly facing death, even taunting his would-be murderer. Suddenly, with the cane that he carried on his famous walks, Truman strikes his assailant's gun hand, breaking his wrist. The would-be assassin is then quickly disarmed and captured. When Pevsner compliments Truman on his quick action, the former president merely smiles and points to the famous sign on his desk: THE BUCK STOPS HERE.

Themes and Meanings

A little-recognized fact about most of Stuart M. Kaminsky's mystery novels is that they are also historical fiction. "The Buck Stops Here" is deliberately set in the past. Also, it must be recognized that the story is primarily escape literature. Although some crime fiction deals with larger issues of morality and character, Kaminsky has not done this in depth here.

Although Pevsner is the narrator of this story and its ostensible protagonist, it is Truman who is the hero. The contrast between the two is made clear, even though Kaminsky leaves readers to draw the proper conclusions. Pevsner is the intellectual and the observer of life. Indeed, the only talent that he possesses, so far as we are informed, is his unusual ability to retain what he has seen. Although a young man, he is so fatigued by his travel that he literally sleeps on the job, a situation that confines him to a relatively passive role until the conclusion.

On the other hand, this story can be read as Kaminsky's paean to Truman, as it emphasizes the former president's considerable strengths, including his intelligence and belief in the dignity of his former office. It is Truman who emerges as the decisive man of action and resolves the stalemate. As Pevsner and Koster, an armed Secret Service man, are immobilized by the gun trained on them, Truman risks his own life and disarms a dangerous professional killer.

Style and Technique

Kaminsky employs few stylistic flourishes, rarely using metaphors or other forms of word imagery, instead devoting the story's limited space to straightforward narration in order to build suspense. As in Frederick Forsyth's novel *The Day of the Jackal* (1971), about a real plot to assassinate French president Charles de Gaulle, Kaminsky's potential victim is a real person, so there can be no doubt about whether the targeted victim will be killed. Nevertheless, there is considerable uncertainty about how the potential assassination will be thwarted and whether the would-be assassin will escape.

Although Pevsner is essentially faceless, and even partly nameless, Kaminsky allows the reader to identify with him as a first-person narrator with an urgent assignment. He places Pevsner firmly in a tradition that has become especially important in detective fiction since the 1970's: His protagonist is an essentially ordinary man, possessing neither the enormous intellect nor the eccentricity of a Sherlock Holmes.

Unlike some historical fiction, "The Buck Stops Here" is remarkably free of anachronisms. Only a reference to "a Marcello Mastroianni hat" fails to ring true, as it predates the Italian film actor's general recognition in the United States. On the other hand, Kaminsky does not attempt to superimpose 1980's political attitudes on 1957. There are references to the Central Intelligence Agency and Federal Bureau of Investigation but no criticism, as both organizations were generally held in high public regard during the 1950's. Moreover, it was clearly not the author's intent to reevaluate Truman's controversial political decisions. Instead, Truman appears in a fictional, "private" matter.

Although it is not clear until the story nears its end who Gades is in disguise, Kaminsky does not use all the elements of the classic detective story. He provides few clues, and alibis are not a factor. He assembles a relatively large cast of potential suspects but says little about each of them. However, the one legitimate clue to the identity of Gades is subtly but openly placed in the story: Before Pevsner takes his nap, he mentions that Franklin's eyes are blue, even though he does not consciously realize it until later. Kaminsky thus adopts one of the devices of the traditional puzzle by playing fair with his readers, allowing them, if they are sufficiently alert, to spot this clue before Pevsner does. Ultimately, however, his story is a thriller, requiring physical activity for its resolution following a brief period of considerable suspense. Thus, Kaminsky has effectively combined two subgenres of crime fiction.

Marvin Lachman

THE BUNCHGRASS EDGE OF THE WORLD

Author: E. Annie Proulx (1935-   )
Type of plot: Domestic realism, regional
Time of plot: The 1980's
Locale: Rural Wyoming
First published: 1999

> *Principal characters:*
> OTTALINE TOUHEY, a member of a ranching family
> OLD RED, her ninety-six-year-old grandfather
> ALADDIN, her father
> WAUNETA, her mother
> FLYBY AMENDINGER, a cattle buyer's son whom she marries

The Story

The story opens by establishing the heritage of the Touhey family. Old Red, the ninety-six-year-old patriarch, along with his Vietnam War veteran son Aladdin and family, raise sheep and cattle in the arid bunchgrass region of northwestern prairie land in Wyoming. Grandson Tyler and granddaughter Shan, siblings of Ottaline, leave their home, proving themselves to be unreliable ranch workers. In contrast, Ottaline has little choice but to stay home and join her father as the primary workforce on the ranch. The narration suggests her numerous skills for working the place, but the loneliness of her existence becomes more pronounced as time goes by. References to her weight problem accentuate her isolation. She endures insults from her mother and serves as an often unappreciated laborer for her father. Her connection to the world outside the ranch is limited to listening to vulgar conversations on the police scanner. Her interior life diminishes to the point that she converses with a junked tractor.

As the story moves toward resolution, Ottaline is required by her father to show the cattle to a buyer because of her father's illness. In an ironic turn, the cattle buyer's son, Flyby, unexpectedly shows up in his father's place. He recognizes Ottaline's knowledge of cattle, confesses his own loneliness, and decides to marry her. Shortly thereafter, Aladdin wrecks his airplane and dies. Old Red understands then that Ottaline will take her father's place and manage the ranch. Her existence will continue to be defined within the parameters she has always known.

Themes and Meanings

"The Bunchgrass Edge of the World" is told in a third-person narrative voice that describes the principal character, Ottaline, in the austere context of three generations of a ranching family. The story displays both the external and internal conflicts of Ottaline. Her struggles with loneliness, obesity, identity, and coming to terms with the limitations of her place in the world eventually lead her to hold conversations with a dilapidated tractor. In the end, she marries the son of a cattle buyer and, on the eventual death of her father, is designated to become ranch manager.

Landscape is routinely a significant element in E. Annie Proulx's stories. Her method is to portray the landscape in accurate detail so that the characters can become pronounced within the landscape. Landscape is almost a force of character for this author. It has a defining quality that accompanies the sparse dialogue of the characters. It has an omnipresent austerity that refuses to be molded to the wishes of the characters but rather bends them into submission. In this story, the landscape works to intensify the loneliness of Ottaline. She becomes an isolated being in a desert void of conversation. The limitations of her existence are physically reinforced by the place in which she was born and seems destined to live. She is forbidden to drive to town or ride to town, and she can only imagine the world to which her sister has escaped. Her brother is a wanderer who rejects the daily claims a ranch makes on its people. The landscape functions like a powerful voice, having its own consciousness, that constantly reminds Ottaline that her choices are few if any and that, like her father and grandfather, her life is to be in disparate communion with a stark place that diminishes human interaction and significance.

The story is about loneliness. Implicitly readers see the loneliness of Aladdin and Wauneta and each of the children, but the force of loneliness is displayed most powerfully in the life of Ottaline. She turns to a police scanner to hear about life outside of the ranch. She has a few meaningless sexual encounters with a hired cowboy, but he is soon out of the picture, leaving Ottaline to converse with a tractor. This dialogue suggests the intense pathos of Ottaline, but ironically, it also seems to eventually empower her, as if she has found a being equally dysfunctional. Their conversations reveal the existential barrenness that Ottaline battles, but they seem to have some cathartic effect also since she determines to reconstruct the tractor.

The rebuilding of the tractor is Ottaline's idea, one that overcomes her father's pessimism. The process of rebuilding takes on sexual overtones, as if Ottaline is the male penetrator of the female tractor. The rebuilding of the machine, which her father sees as useless, seems to correlate with Ottaline finding an inner strength to endure what she fears. It suggests a coming to terms with herself in her environment. The author presents this event with sexual comments that seem to reinforce the theme of questioning traditional male and female roles within this society. Ottaline identifies closely with her father and proves herself to be as capable a hand as any man. Though she voices her fear, she in fact fulfills the assumed masculine role, thereby replacing her mother's negative authority. The story seems to suggest that presupposed gender roles are essentially meaningless in the presented context. Ottaline wants to marry, and in the end does, but the marriage is not a celebration of male dominance over the female, nor is it overly romantic in the best sense of that word. The resolution of the story is indefinite; it is uncertain whether or not the marriage to Flyby and the continuation of the ranching heritage is suspect or validated in an ironic way. Only time will tell, but clearly the tone of the resolution suggests that the place will continue to define the people.

The passing of time is another important theme in the story. At the beginning, readers realize that Old Red, an archetypal Western character, lives in the story only as an emblem of history. Of his six children, only Aladdin has not abandoned the ranching way of life. This diminishing continues with the children of Aladdin. His son and one of his two daughters leave the ranch to find their lives in other contexts. In the end, only Ottaline has a future in this heritage. So the story suggests a passing way of life. Fewer and fewer families ranch in the late twentieth century, and fewer of their children continue in their parents' path. Because Ottaline is the inheritor of her father's and grandfather's lineage, the story also recognizes that the passing of the birthright from one generation to the next is now not routinely a male enterprise.

Style and Technique

Proulx uses a number of stylistic devices to carry her plot. Perhaps the most obvious is the personification of the tractor that engages in dialogues with Ottaline. This innovative approach significantly underscores the theme of loneliness so prevalent in the story. The rebuilding of the tractor also symbolically suggests the salvaging of Ottaline's otherwise expendable person.

Another symbol that Proulx employs is bunchgrass. The native grass demarcates the place of the story (the perennial wheatgrass grows in the northwest prairies), adding realistic detail to the evident landscape theme. It defines the parameters of the ranch, but it also functions beyond these concerns to represent Wauneta's world that ends when Ottaline and Flyby marry.

Most of the action of the story is internal conflict that a third-person narrator describes. The description, however, is presented in sparse, terse language that stylistically matches the sparse landscape of the bunchgrass world. The limited dialogue effectively betrays the insensitivity of Ottaline's family and reveals the inadequacies and fears Ottaline has. The narration and dialogue is presented in an abbreviated laconic manner that correlates to a realistic Western context.

A remarkable amount of information is provided in a relatively small amount of space. There is much distinct characterization for a short story; the sum effect is to foil Ottaline and to define her in a context of limitations and loneliness.

The use of a Western landscape with a modern ranching setting suggests an antipastoral of the American West in which romantic idealism is superfluous and the internal questioning of the meaning of human existence is pronounced.

Kenneth Hada

THE BURNING HOUSE

Author: Ann Beattie (1947-   )
Type of plot: Psychological
Time of plot: The 1970's
Locale: Fairfield County, Connecticut
First published: 1979

Principal characters:
AMY WAYNE, the mother of a young son
FRANK WAYNE, her husband, an accountant
JOHNNY, her lover
J. D., Frank's former college professor
TUCKER, the owner of a New York City art gallery
FREDDY FOX, Frank's gay half brother

The Story

Amy hosts a group of her husband's friends who are visiting for the weekend. She is the only woman in the house, but Frank's homosexual half brother, Freddy Fox, is her confidante and likes to help her in the kitchen. Freddy is already high on marijuana, however, and begins to flick ashes into the sauce that Amy is making. In the next room, her husband Frank, who does the books for Tucker's art gallery in Soho, listens to jazz and rock music and to Tucker's gossipy stories about artists and performers. Tucker seems to have picked up most of his stories in gay bars in Greenwich Village; Freddy suggests to Amy that there is a homosexual motive in Tucker's choice of artists to show in his gallery. Much to his annoyance, Freddy himself becomes a topic of conversation; he has failed to finish college and now drifts from one anonymous sexual relationship to another. After dinner, Amy catches Freddy up on a secret that they share, namely that she knows that Frank is having an affair with a woman named Natalie. When Amy's young son Mark, who is on an overnight visit with a neighboring child, wants to come home, Amy senses that her child's anxiety is a reaction to Frank's affair, which has made him cold and unavailable.

While Amy washes the dinner dishes, J. D., who was once Frank's college adviser, appears at the kitchen window wearing a goat mask, frightening Amy into dropping a glass and cutting herself. J. D., who has lost his way, found the mask in a Goodwill bin. His late arrival for dinner adds to the offbeat and disorderly atmosphere. Having abandoned teaching in despair after his wife and son were killed in an automobile accident, J. D. is constantly on the move; he plans to fly to Paris the next day. While J. D. helps Amy treat her badly cut finger, Amy's lover, Johnny, telephones. J. D.—who introduced them—is aware of the affair, but Amy is worried that her husband will overhear, so she pretends that Johnny is someone else. Johnny, who is also cheating on his spouse, pretends to be calling to check the weather in Key West. The brief conversation with Johnny causes Amy's sense of disorientation to grow. She begins to feel she is out of touch with the true identities of the people around her. Beneath the surface charm and insouciance of her husband's friends, she begins to see them as vulnerable, lost boys. Although J. D. appears to be off on a jaunt to Paris, Amy knows that his life is really on hold; she sees that Freddy's use of marijuana is less recreational than desperate; and she knows that Tucker is a needy and lonely man. In spite of these insights, Amy does not feel close to these men—she feels as if they are merely photographs of people, rather than people themselves; her life feels unreal to her.

Before they retire for the night, Frank says something about storms in Key West that leaves Amy unclear as to how much he knows about her relationship with Johnny. Unable to sleep, she asks Frank to make some kind of decision about their future together. Is he staying or going? Frank tells Amy that she should not blame herself for what has gone wrong, and that although she is surrounded by men, she does not really understand them. Men, he says, are like little boys who think that they are going to the stars. Like the cartoon characters Spider Man, Buck Rogers, or Superman, men, he says, are always psychologically up in the sky, looking down on earth. In a very real sense, he tells her, "I'm already gone." He is telling her that he will never take his place in her household as an adult male; even worse, he has abandoned her emotionally.

Themes and Meanings

The main theme of this story is conveyed by its title. There is not a literal burning house anywhere in the narrative; the image of the burning house is a metaphor for Amy's marriage. It is J. D. who, late in the story, alludes to the story's title when he jokingly refers to that "wicked fairy tale crap," which decrees that if you do something you know to be wrong, "your heart will break, your house will burn." In this context, Amy's house is burning. While she and her husband seem to be enjoying an amusing weekend with their arty friends, in reality their marriage is falling apart. Beneath the conviviality is a sense of hellish despair. Their guests are on the road to perdition as well. They represent the "peace and freedom" generation of the 1960's that has lost its way, drifting aimlessly and lovelessly through unstructured, empty lives. The characterization of men as a series of make-believe or cartoon characters, combined with their use of drugs and alcohol, indicates not only a delayed maturity but a loss of common humanity. The image of the goat mask, which suggests Dionysian celebration, also indicates a tragic metamorphosis in the character of the men around Amy.

The title also suggests the heavy use of marijuana cigarettes in the story. The golden age of the 1960's, an era of youthful romanticism that first empowered the postwar baby boomers, has in this story ended in a circle of drug-dazed lost souls who seem to float through a field of unstable and provisional relationships. They have neither meaningful work nor happy personal lives, and their dreams of love and liberation have ended in neurosis and even nihilism.

Although Amy's house is burning metaphorically, she maintains an overly calm and unaffected persona. Like Alice in Wonderland, Amy seems at first to be a remote and dispassionate observer of the madness around her, but the reader comes to understand that although she has erected an invisible wall, or a mask of glass, between herself and the others, she is in fact deeply hurt. Her cut finger becomes an image of a deeper, emotional wound. At the end of the story, when Frank gives her a list of nice things to think about in order to help her sleep (such as flowers or a shooting star), his last rather malicious suggestion is that she imagine she has been given a chance to do her life over again—an image revealing that Amy knows she has lost. In contrast to the antic behavior of the men around her, prancing in goat masks, telling funny stories, getting high, Amy seems to be sunk in a depression. She seems emotionally paralyzed and unable to decide whether to leave her husband, although she desperately wants to do so. Instead, she is overwhelmed with feelings of regret and failure. The underlying sense of emptiness and isolation, even of existential nothingness, has left her in a helpless, drifting condition. It is as if nothing that she does will make any difference or even speak to the abandonment and despair that she feels she must endure.

Style and Technique

Ann Beattie writes in a minimalist style, but in contrast to other minimalists, her characters are more economically and culturally privileged. She uses various telling details, such as references to the college campus, Paris vacations, the art of Mark Rothko, or the music of John Coltrane or Lou Reed, to indicate that her characters belong to an upscale bohemian cultural world. Although her characters inhabit an elite cultural and economic circle, her way of describing them is low-key, even flat. Her first-person point of view is drained of color and feeling through the use of an uninflected voice reminiscent of Ernest Hemingway's "hard-boiled" style. This colorless, cool, detached voice sometimes becomes a vehicle for deadpan humor, but more often it suggests a numbed or despairing sensibility.

Like other minimalists, Beattie deploys plot sparingly. "The Burning House" links together a series of almost pointless episodes that do not build to a conventional turning point or conclusion. One senses that at the end of this weekend, nothing has happened. This lack of consequence is communicated by a deliberately plotless structure and a deliberately monotonous, banal tone of voice.

Margaret Boe Birns

THE BURROW

Author: Franz Kafka (1883-1924)
Type of plot: Character study
Time of plot: Unspecified
Locale: A burrow in a forest
First published: "Der Bau," 1931 (English translation, 1946)

Principal character:
AN ANONYMOUS BURROWING ANIMAL

The Story

"The Burrow" opens with the successful completion of the burrow and the narrator claiming that he is no longer afraid, then immediately stating his fear that someone could inadvertently discover the opening of the burrow and "destroy everything for good." Though at the zenith of his life, he cannot be tranquil, even in his burrow's strongest, innermost chamber, for some unknown, unnamed enemy may be burrowing toward him. The narrator has the advantage of knowing all the burrow's passages and each of its more than fifty rooms; he is, however, growing old. Not only do real, external enemies frighten him; so do legendary creatures of the inner earth, in whom he firmly believes. Still, the burrow is peaceful, and hunting the "small fry" that venture through it gives him a constant, if modest, food supply.

The narrator boasts particularly of his Castle Keep, the burrow's chief cell, into the construction of which he has literally poured his life's blood, pounding its walls with his forehead to harden them. In the Keep he has placed all of his food stores, the extent of which he now gloatingly contemplates. On the other hand, he sometimes fears that storing all of his food in one place may be disastrously wrong. At such times, he panics and feverishly redistributes it to several chambers, randomly. Then, reflecting on the problems with the scheme—and the cost to his conceit when he can no longer see all of his stores together—he puts them back in the Castle Keep, wishing now that he had planned and constructed several of them when he was younger. At times, the tempting smells of the stockpiled food overwhelm him: Gorging sessions ensue, followed by renewed guilt and recrimination.

Such lapses always lead to a review of the burrow's entire plan, and his gluttony necessitates his leaving the burrow to restock it. As he approaches the elaborate labyrinth just inside the entrance, he feels both pride in this theoretically brilliant tour de force and fear that it could not sustain a serious attack. In any case, it is too late now to think seriously of constructing another, absolutely impregnable labyrinth; that would take a giant's strength, of which he can only dream.

Exiting through the moss-covered trapdoor, he momentarily appreciates the freedoms of life outside: the better (if more difficult) hunting, the sense of bodily strength. However, he can never venture too far from the burrow; indeed, the thought of its presence sustains him. Even watching the entrance for days and nights on end reaffirms his sense of its safety: He has yet to see anyone investigating the front door. Admittedly, he has had to flee at the scent of any serious enemy, so he cannot be sure of their ignorance of or attitude toward the burrow. This very reflection on its safety inevitably leads him to consider its perils. He even briefly toys with the idea of going back to his pre-burrow existence, "one indiscriminate succession of perils," but perils whose universality kept him from focusing on any particular one—as he now must do.

The fear of reentering the burrow also paralyzes him for days: An enemy might see him enter and, unobserved, follow him down the hole and attack. He thinks, if only he had someone, a "trusty confederate," to stand guard. However, then the advantage of the burrow, its secrecy, would be lost, for the trustee would need to know of it, perhaps even to see inside, perhaps even to share it. Also, the narrator would be obliged to rely on the trustee, even though he could not supervise his ally. It is best after all, he concludes, not to complain that he is alone and has nobody to trust.

The narrator daydreams of a two-entrance burrow, which would allow him to watch one entrance unobserved while peeping from the other. The dream, however, shames him. Is not the burrow more than enough already, a place still and empty where he can be so at home as even to accept death calmly? Finally, worn out by the internal turmoil, he creeps exhaustedly back inside and tries to sleep.

Being back in the burrow, however, reawakens his zeal for inspecting and improving on it, tired from his hunting, wandering, watching, and fretting though he may be. His new supply of flesh must be stored in the Castle Keep, the few small defects in the fortress repaired, and all the other rooms and passages visited and inspected. Still, the joy of being back home makes the work seem like play: He goes contentedly about it until overcome by sleep.

He wakes to an almost inaudible whistling noise. At first, he attributes it to the small fry's having burrowed a new channel somewhere, a passage that has intersected an older one and produced the bothersome sound. He sets off to find and repair the noise's source. As the search continues, however, the noise seems more pervasive, more troubling, more distinct and uniform wherever he is. Perhaps there are two noises. The whistling is audible even in the Castle Keep, where the insolent small fry apparently have penetrated, drawn by the smell of his hoard. Why has he not heard them before, though? Perhaps the intruder is a new, unknown animal—or a swarm of them. Alternating between feigned nonchalance and desperate agitation, the narrator determines to find the truth, whatever the labor and the consequence. He conceives and abandons various schemes, attempts to ignore the noise, eats and pretends it was never there, busies himself repairing the walls.

However, as he does so the noise seems subtly louder and closer. Fearful, distracted, he wanders about the burrow, finding himself eventually at the entrance. Outside, all seems tranquil, as it used to be in the burrow, which is now "plunged into the melee of the world and all its perils." He pauses between the surface and below, his conviction growing that a single, large beast is approaching his home, burrowing at furious speed and sending reverberations great distances through the ground. The whistling must come from the beast's pointed muzzle; it works with constant fresh-ness and vigor, never veering from its object.

Cursing himself that he has not been constantly prepared for such a foe, longing for the "petty dangers" of the past, wondering why he has not defended the burrow more elaborately against such a danger as the present one, the narrator now thinks back to an earlier, similar peril. Then, at the beginning of his work, he had heard another bur-rower approach, then move away. Perhaps that burrower is returning, though the nar-rator remains as unprepared as before. In fact, his situation is worse: He now has an elaborate burrow to defend, yet he is no longer the vigorous young apprentice who might successfully do so but an "old architect." Even death seems preferable to this new life, filled with uncertainty and ceaseless anxiety.

At last, the narrator retreats to the Castle Keep, there to munch on the flesh of his stores and wonder about the approaching beast. Is it merely wandering, or is it digging its own burrow? Does the beast know about him? If so, how, because his own digging has been so quiet, his own movement so discreet? The narrative—apparently unfin-ished, the ending lost or destroyed—closes abruptly, leaving the narrator isolated, fearful, with none of his questions answered, and the noise continuing unabated.

Themes and Meanings

Because "The Burrow" is a long and finally inconclusive fragment, it is difficult to establish with certainty Franz Kafka's thematic intent. (One version of its creation as-serts that the narrator ultimately meets and defeats the unknown animal, an ending that seems at variance tonally with the rest of the story.) Readers aware that this was one of Kafka's last stories tend to view the narrator as a mask for the author himself. In this view, the burrow is a metaphor for either Kafka's body—being besieged by vari-ous internal ailments as well as by Death, the unknown "outside" him—or the body of Kafka's work—the structure of puzzles he has set for readers who wish to attack the heart of Kafka's meaning, to know him.

At any rate, the story clearly deals with fear of the outside world, perhaps even paranoia, and the results of that fear. The central figure, like those in Kafka's more fin-ished and better-known stories "Die Verwandlung" ("Metamorphosis") and "Ein Landartzt" ("The Country Doctor") is isolated from his usual sources of security. A nightmare existence ensues, with no miraculous awakening or reversal. In the most general reading, the narrator's condition resembles that of humanity itself, feverishly toiling to achieve security and happiness but inevitably condemned to death. The nar-rator, like Albert Camus's Sisyphus, has only his work; unlike that existentialist hero, however, he cannot be imagined happy or even, within his limits, free. Instead, he is trapped in a prison of his own making, his paranoia (perhaps justified by the facts of his existence) continuing and intensifying as his end draws near.

Style and Technique

Because Kafka strictly limits the story's point of view to that of the narrator, his mode of expression becomes the most important stylistic consideration. Here Kafka, like his narrator, constructs a labyrinthine tour de force. The style might be termed "manic obsessive": Throughout the story, the narrator circles over and over the same concerns, expressing by turns his pride in his elaborate construction and his fear that it will not protect him. The ideas double back on one another, sometimes within the same sentence, rendering concrete the narrator's mental turmoil, as do the frequent questions, unanswered and perhaps unanswerable. The style perfectly fits the narrator's psyche and situation, its shifting tone reflecting his constantly changing outlook and state of mind.

As the narrative develops, Kafka—facing his own imminent death—gradually modulates the narrator's tone. Near the story's end, he even declares, "I have reached the stage where I no longer wish to have certainty." The narrator despairs of concocting and carrying out any new defense plan or even reaching an understanding of his enemy; at the end, his only hope is that he will somehow be spared by the other beast's ignorance of him. Even as he tries to convince himself that the other beast may not have heard him, the fragment concludes, "Yet all remained unchanged," leaving him hopeless as the beast draws near.

David E. Robinson

BUT AT THE STROKE OF MIDNIGHT

Author: Sylvia Townsend Warner (1893-1978)
Type of plot: Psychological
Time of plot: The late 1960's
Locale: London and its environs
First published: 1971

Principal characters:
> MRS. LUCY RIDPATH, a housewife, married for twenty-five years
> ASTON RIDPATH, her husband, a "born bachelor"
> VERE, Aston's sister, a "successful widow"
> MRS. BARKER, the charwoman

The Story

One ordinary Saturday, Mrs. Lucy Ridpath, from all appearances a typical routine-oriented housewife, leaves her home without informing her husband or anyone where she is going. Her husband Aston feels guilty that because of an "unlucky moment of inattention," he failed to listen or attend to her, part of his practice of taking her for granted. His sister Vere advises him to call the police; otherwise, he might be suspected of murder.

Taking on the identity of Aurelia Lefanu, Lucy's cousin, whose flightiness and adventurous personality "exert a powerful intoxicating influence on her," Lucy sells her wedding ring and visits the Tate Gallery, where she meets a man working for an art publishing firm. He takes her home, marveling at her aplomb and uncalculating frankness. He plans to take her to Provence, to save her from the lunatic asylum from which he suspects she escaped, but she disappears as he is trying to secure her passport.

Lucy as Aurelia spends her time as an anonymous rider on the London buses. She sleeps in the King's Cross Station waiting room and then finally gets Lancelot Fogg, a clergyman she meets at a funeral in Highgate Cemetery, to tell her where she can find a middle-aged hostel. The clergyman is awed at meeting a "spiritual woman" who strikes him as "exceedingly tranquil and trustful."

Lucy's stay with Miss Larke of St. Hilda's Guesthouse leads to her projecting her Lucy-self onto a tomcat, allowing her to continue as Aurelia. "Since her adoption of Lucy [the cat], she had become so unshakably Aurelia that she could contemplate being Lucy, too, so far as being Lucy would further Aurelia's designs." She then sends two letters to Aston demanding fifty pounds, one promising to return and the other promising to stay away. This equivocal or ambiguous message accurately conveys the schizoid state of Aurelia-Lucy. Aston replies with chagrin because he does not want to live with Lucy again; he prefers a "manly solitude," so he sends her four five-pound notes; Vere also replies, asking Lucy to stay away and enclosing one hundred pounds.

On a train, Lucy meets George Bastable, a builder and plumber, who rents for her a bungalow where his "young lady," now dead, once lived. Lucy spends the summer in an immunizing happiness, oblivious of past and future, living "with carefree economy" and enjoying Mr. Bastable's gifts of food. Her blackmail money spent, she begins to paint for vacationers in caravans, earning enough by the end of September to tide her over to Christmas. She busies herself gathering fuel for winter, with Lucy her cat acting as orderly timekeeper.

One foggy night, the cat comes home, dragging himself, head smashed in and jaw dangling, obviously hit by a car. His death triggers a shattering trauma and revelation: It was Aurelia's death that brought about Lucy's possession by the departed cousin. This "agony of dislocation" brings back to life Mrs. Lucy Ridpath. Amid the torrential rain, with floodwaters overwhelming the place, Lucy goes out to bury the cat, only to be swept away and killed by the roaring tumult of water.

Themes and Meanings

One of Sylvia Townsend Warner's recurring themes is the incalculable nature of human personality. Lucy Ridpath symbolizes the "nova," the aborted or inchoate possibilities in everyone. More a possessed psyche than an eccentric, Lucy stands as a pathetic but sharp indictment of the selfish insensitivity of men, a critique of hypocritical society dominated by prudence and calculating pettiness, where money dictates the terms of freedom and happiness.

When Lucy's ego is taken over by the spirit of the dead Aurelia Lefanu (the name evokes the mysterious and supernatural tales of the nineteenth century Irish writer Joseph Sheridan Le Fanu), an alternative life opens up for her. Losing her memory, she assumes a persona that functions as an empty signifier whose meaning can be filled by anyone. Thus she symbolizes spirituality to Fogg, an art object to the man she calls "Ithamore," and a surrogate sweetheart to Mr. Bastable. Oblivious of any class constraints, she delights in "a total lack of obligation," which she associates with the compline ritual.

Lucy definitively becomes Aurelia when she is able to project her old self onto the cat that she rescues, nurses, and adopts as Lucy. The theory underlying this is that identity can be fixed only with reference to another. However, Aurelia herself is a fluid sign. The fair or carnival where Lucy finds the cat, lost and abandoned, signifies fantasy, games, free play. All of her repressed energies are released in the care and attention she gives to the cat; when he dies, she succumbs to an agonizing trauma: The beloved Aurelia, overtaken by death, restores to a particular body the social or public mask of Lucy Ridpath. Lucy is able to overcome the fixity of Aurelia's death by negating her own existence as Lucy Ridpath. What will she do with Lucy (the cat) dead? Her death in the storm indicates that she can no longer return to life in normal bourgeois society.

In retrospect, Lucy's ordinary life is precisely the death from which she has been trying to escape. She is alive only as Aurelia Lefanu.

Lucy's wanderings as Aurelia may also be interpreted as an allegory of the power of art's influence on "real" life. When Lucy disappears, Aston has to refer to William Wordsworth's Lucy to find out why. Lucy herself moves in a realm of fantasy constituted by Christopher Marlowe (the allusion to *Doctor Faustus*, 1604, suggests that her masquerade cannot escape the measure of conventional time), the picture postcard of southern France with "a pale landscape full of cemetery trees," Claude Monet, and Giorgio Vasari's *Le vite de pit! eccelenti architettori, pittori, e scultori italiani* (1550; *Lives of the Most Eminent Painters, Sculptors, and Architects*, 1850-1855). Her imitation of a practical lesson from Vasari confirms the parasitism of reality on the imagination. However, this faculty of making believe, the narrator hints, cannot long survive in a world suspicious of anything irrational or pleasurable. Lucy (as Aurelia) has to depend on the money given to her by her husband and sister-in-law, a bribe for her to maintain her disappearance. She has to submit to the demands of commissioned painting, art for sale. In effect, one can say that Lucy dies not from the violence of the flood but from the sterile, mechanical, and alienating life of middle-class society.

Style and Technique

Warner has been praised for her astringent style, for her elegance and precision in portraying eccentrics, for her ironic but "compassionate wit." This story demonstrates all these features, but it is the satire on social types such as Aston, Vere, Fogg, and Miss Larke that enables the weird behavior of Lucy to command the reader's amused and sympathetic attention.

The plot follows a chronological sequence. The initial scene depicting Lucy as the predictable housewife is followed by a quick succession of scenes showing her various possibilities: as an art object for the anonymous "Ithamore," model of piety for Fogg, harmless eccentric for Miss Larke, and memento of his vanished "nova" for Bastable. Aurelia is Lucy's "nova": the realized Other. The narrative manages to blend the fancifulness of Aurelia with the prudent tactfulness of Lucy in the plotted drifting she goes through.

The most hilarious spoof on bourgeois mores is found in Lucy's weighing of alternatives (the two letters) as she combs out the fleas in the cat "to a new rhythm of 'he loves me, he loves me not.'" The two letters condense the inescapable subordination of ethics to money and social class. The folly of the middle-class doting on the charm of the past is exposed in the exchange between the two ladies who boarded the train at Peckover Junction. Warner also ridicules the sentimental Victorian moralizing of landscapes when Lucy wonders if the tomcat's "tastes ran to the romantic, if high mountains were to him a feeling." In these moments, one feels that Lucy performs an antirealistic or countermimetic function: Like Aurelia and other artists, the authorial voice also speaks through her. Lucy's character determines the logic of the plot in its "improbable probability."

An element of semigothic melodrama intrudes when the tomcat is described in all of his gory, dying convulsions one November evening. The texture of the narrative also thickens, shifting the point of view away from Lucy's psyche to the outside, where nature accumulates its chaotic, indifferent force. The last two epithets used to fix Lucy's struggling form in the exploding landscape are "tricked and impatient," compressing the senses of fatality and of irrepressible vitality in one image. Having begun in the unperturbed kitchen of Lucy Ridpath, where bourgeois decorum concealed seething passions, the reader ends with this final scene of wild, open destructiveness that destroys public boundaries and wipes out private enclosures.

Lucy's last few months spent in happy seclusion in the remote countryside, where for the first time she is able to paint "from life" to express herself creatively and be appreciated even though for money, constitute a fable of the fulfilled life. Its disruption by the cat's unannounced departure, analogous to Lucy's own act of separating herself from her home and her past, and its mauling by a machine, qualifies that fable of solitude and suggests that community or solidarity (whose emblem is the caravan) cannot be rejected without fatal consequences. Real life and fiction interact together. To suppress either term leads to the schizoid experience of Lucy as Aurelia because each depends on the other. The companionship of Lucy the tomcat and Aurelia may be construed as the figure for the precarious interdependence of the real and the imagined, of prudence and desire: "He was happy enough out of her sight," the narrator says of the cat Lucy, "but he liked to have her within his."

E. San Juan, Jr.

BUTCHER BIRD

Author: Wallace Stegner (1909-1993)
Type of plot: Social realism
Time of plot: World War II era
Locale: Saskatchewan, Canada
First published: 1941

> *Principal characters:*
> THE BOY, less than twelve years of age
> HIS FATHER
> HIS MOTHER
> MR. GARFIELD, an elderly English neighbor

The Story

The events of "Butcher Bird" take place during a single afternoon. A family sets out to visit their new neighbors, Mr. and Mrs. Garfield. Mr. Garfield is an Englishman, whose talk of scientific farming methods and making the desert bloom has reached the family. The father clearly has no desire to visit them, but the mother wants to be neighborly, so they go.

The mother's and boy's experiences during this visit are vastly different from the father's. For the mother and her son, the Garfields' home is a place of wonder, beauty, and discovery. There is a rug in the house, there is music, and outside, in this barren country, are trees that Mr. Garfield has been trying to grow from cuttings taken down at Old-Man-on-His-Back, a nearby spot where a creek comes out of the hills. To the father, however, the Garfield home represents everything that he is not, so he is scarcely able to behave pleasantly.

The visit gets off to a bad start because the father is determined not to like Mr. Garfield. When Mrs. Garfield serves lemonade without ice, the father's face reveals his contempt and disdain; he has just spent two weeks digging an icehouse in order to have ice-cold water and beer during the hot season.

Mr. Garfield then shows the boy his gramophone. As the delighted boy inspects this curious machine, his father sharply commands him to keep his hands off; Mr. Garfield, kindly insisting that the boy cannot harm the gramophone, undermines the father's authority. Soon the father is moodily looking out the window, and tension grows in the room. Realizing this, Mr. Garfield gropes somewhat helplessly for something to say, some way of reconnecting with his guests. He turns to the boy, asking him questions about his life on his family farm and what he does with his days. When the talk turns to hunting, Mr. Garfield leaves the room for a moment and returns with a .22-caliber gun, which he offers to the excited boy. Mr. Garfield looks to the boy's mother for permission; the boy looks to his father, who nods his approval. The gift is given conditionally, however: Mr. Garfield makes the boy promise to shoot only at predators, not at birds or prairie dogs. What about butcher birds, the boy asks. The boy's mother explains to her host that butcher birds, also called shrikes, kill all sorts of things just for the fun of it and then hang their victims on the post or barbed wire of a fence. Mr. Garfield's response is significant: "Shoot all the shrikes you see. A thing that kills for the fun of it." Leaving the sentence unfinished, he shakes his head, and his voice gets solemn.

As soon as the family drives away from the Garfields' farm, the father roars his laughter at Garfield's pacifism, his trees, and his gentleness, as he scorns and ridicules the man. His scorn turns to incredulity when he realizes that his wife likes this neighbor, and then to rage when he senses that his wife's attitude toward Garfield is a judgment against him. They argue, their anger escalating, each determined to have the last word. The boy is on the porch with both his parents, the father helping him clean the gun, which has been neglected. A final, calculated comment from the mother fuels the dying argument and the father's dwindling anger. Enraged, he takes aim at a sparrow scratching for bugs in the yard. His wife warns him not to shoot the helpless bird; the boy yells, "No." Still the father, quietly mimicking Mr. Garfield, pulls the trigger. Drawn to the dead bird, the boy picks it up, getting blood on his fingers, and asks his mother what he should do with it. Likening the father to the butcher birds, the mother tells the boy to leave the sparrow there, that his father will want to hang it on the fence.

Themes and Meanings

Wallace Stegner's story takes its meaning from two themes that unfold simultaneously. One is a delineation of the character of the father and the effects that an ungenerous, hard land has had on his spirit and personality. The other is the story of a young boy's rite of passage into a more complex world in which his father loses stature and authority in his eyes. The gift of the gun is a pivotal moment in this story. Although the father is the one in the story who represents killing, it is Mr. Garfield who gives the gun—the implement of death—to the son. Now that taking life is no longer the exclusive domain of the father, it gains a new dimension: It must be done thoughtfully. When Mr. Garfield gives the gun conditionally, making the boy promise to kill only cruel and bloodthirsty animals, the boy's sense of responsibility changes dramatically. He now has two mentors; his father is no longer the absolute authority, so he must weigh ethical questions within a more complex system of thought and feeling.

These two interdependent themes take on greater significance in the historical context of the story's creation. Originally published in January, 1941, "Butcher Bird" speaks directly to the contemporary debate over the war in Europe and the question of whether the United States should become involved. The story speaks to painful, difficult decisions about whether to kill, whom to kill, and—if they exist—the justifications for killing. The boy, as well as the reader, is caught between the values represented by the father and Mr. Garfield. By the end of the story, the father has revealed himself to be hotheaded, to kill out of anger and a need for control, and to do so indiscriminately. Mr. Garfield introduces a more pacifist position; his conditional gift of the gun forces these questions to the surface.

Style and Technique

Stegner was an exceptionally economical writer, communicating much with few, telling details. For example, the information that the father has spent two weeks digging an icehouse so that he can have cold beer and ice water during the summer suggests that he is a hard worker who focuses on satisfying his desires. When this detail is contrasted with his adamant refusal to spend even a small part of his afternoon to drive his wife to Old-Man-on-His-Back so that she can cut willow slips, the icehouse takes on new meaning, exposing the father's selfishness, his domination and control of his family, and his ability to thwart his wife's desires.

Stegner's use of perspective in this story also contributes beautifully to his creation of the father's "butcher bird" personality. The story is told by an unidentified third-person narrator, whose perspective and sympathy lie with the boy. The first few paragraphs demonstrate that the weather strongly influences—almost determines—the mood of the father, a wheat farmer, and the father's mood dictates the actions of the boy and his mother—whether they will have to walk and talk quietly through the house so as not to aggravate the father's already foul temper. The experience of living on the farm, with this particular father, is related as the boy's experience. We see all excursions as adventures for the boy. The detail of the soft gingersnaps is a boy's, not an adult's, weather barometer. As the argument between the parents intensifies, Stegner offers a series of details by which the boy marks the progress of a familiar pattern. He marks his father's snorts and taunting, his mother's persistence, trying to concentrate on his gun and close out the sound of his parents' battle. As children so often are, the boy is desperate to do or say something to intervene and make the situation better.

Stegner artfully places the boy between the characters of the father on the one hand and his mother and Mr. Garfield on the other; the boy is also caught between the positions that these two opposing parties represent. By making the boy the point of perspective, Stegner maximizes the emotional impact on the reader. Sympathizing with the boy, the reader also is placed in the uncomfortable position between the father and the mother, between killing and nurturing, between hard-earned survival in an inhospitable land and the luxuries of music and flowers.

Julie Thompson

BY THE WATERS OF BABYLON

Author: Stephen Vincent Benét (1898-1943)
Type of plot: Science fiction
Time of plot: The future
Locale: New York area
First published: 1937

Principal characters:
THE NARRATOR, the son of a priest
HIS FATHER, a priest who encourages his son's search for
knowledge but values traditional taboos

The Story

The Forest People compete with the Hill People, who have slightly more advanced skills in spinning wool, hunting, and using metals. The priests of the Hill People have not forgotten the old writings and have some knowledge of healing—such as how to stop bleeding. Bound by superstition and taboos based on experience, tribe members are forbidden to go east, cross the great river, enter the Dead Places, or touch metal not purified by priests. These strictures have been in force throughout tribal memory. In addition, the people fear spirits and demons and have an ancestral memory of a "Great Burning."

A young member of the Hill People, the narrator has studied for the priesthood under his father. He has learned chants, spells, and medical secrets, and has made dangerous journeys searching for metal in spirit houses. Now he has come of age and has reached the time of initiation and spirit journey. He undergoes purification rites, answers questions about his dreams, and tells his father about the vision that he sees in the smoke of the fire. His vision is of a gigantic Dead Place in its time of glory; although his father fears that his son's strong dream will eat him up, he sends his son on the journey of discovery required as the final initiation into the priesthood. After fasting, the young man awaits a sign. After he sees an eagle flying east and kills a panther by shooting a single arrow through its eye while it attacks a white fawn, he is convinced that he is right to break tribal taboos and journey to the Dead Place.

He travels east for eight days, following a "god-road" that time and the forests have reduced to great blocks of stone. He is driven by his thirst for knowledge and his desire to regain the secrets of a lost civilization whose forest-encroached ruins hold clues to the past and signs for the future. As he travels he observes that the causes of the taboos ("burning" ground, strange fogs) have disappeared, so he bravely crosses the forbidden river and enters "the Place of the Gods."

Wild cats and packs of wild dogs roam the ancient city, and pigeons fly overhead. There are subterranean tunnels and huge temples, food in enchanted boxes and jars, strong bottled drinks, bronze doors without handles, high-rise dwellings with inexplicable machinery, lovely paintings, and books. The young would-be priest gazes over the ruins—with their broken bridges and tumbling towers—and envisions the city at the moment that it died: huge, restless, destroyed by fire from the skies from weapons of unimagined horror, followed by a poisonous mist that left the ground burning for aeons. When he sees a "dead god" sitting by a window looking out on the ruined city, he realizes that the "god" is only a man and that despite its wonders, this city, New York, was once a city of men like himself. He longs for the knowledge they possessed and is sure of his ability to use that knowledge more wisely than they. As a new priest he will help his people make a new beginning, recapturing lost knowledge from the broken city in order to build again.

Themes and Meanings

Originally titled "The Place of the Gods," this Stephen Vincent Benét story initially seems to be set in an unspecified, early period of American Indian history. It is, however, actually a prophetic warning of dread future possibilities. Although modern people's almost magical powers have allowed them to harness electricity and nuclear power, build subways and elevators, drive cars, fly planes, and create washers and driers, electric stoves, and refrigerators, Benét warns that people must still learn to control the savages in themselves that lead to war and annihilation.

The forbidden river of the story, with its "bitter waters," is the Hudson River ("Oudis-sun"); the "god-roads" are complex highway systems; the door with no handles is an elevator entrance; "UBTREAS" is the "Subtreasury"; the statue of "ASHING" is of George Washington, and the other great men are Abraham Lincoln, Moses, and, ironically, Biltmore (reflecting the grandeur of the Biltmore Hotel); the "chariots" of the vision are cars and trucks; the magic torches are electric lights; the falling fire that causes the "Great Burning" and the poisonous mist is from a super bomb, and the resultant fallout causes radiation poisoning. This past civilization is thus present-day civilization; present-day people are the dead whose secrets the Hill People seek.

Writing two years before World War II began, with a sure sense of the destructiveness of World War I and a fear of the new technological might that would be unleashed in a second world war, Benét envisions the possibility of people bombing themselves back to the Stone Age. Before the fire-bombing of Dresden or the nuclear bombing of Hiroshima and Nagasaki, Benét looked into the human heart and read there the strange mixture of positive and negative that could compel human destruction: a thirst for knowledge, experimentation, advancement, and control of natural forces coupled by ignorance, internecine conflict, and a willingness to use power before its disastrous potential is fully understood. His young narrator is proud of his own tribe's superiority to the Forest People; he enjoys outwitting them and makes fun of their food ("grubs") and their inability to detect his stealthy movements; he is a capable hunter with an instinct for the kill. In other words, the seeds of competition and of conflict, of racism and of blood sports are present, ready to grow alongside the narrator's growing technical knowledge.

The title heightens the poignant ironies: "By the Waters of Babylon" takes the reader back to the origins of Western civilization, to the Tigris and Euphrates and a magnificent ancient culture savagely destroyed, then later rebuilt. The title suggests that this pattern of two steps forward, three steps back, is an ancient one, endlessly repeated. The narrator's references to "chariots" reinforces that connection with Babylon. The title also recalls the haranguing warnings of Old Testament prophets. The human race, as personified in the enthusiastic neophyte priest, is forever a sorcerer's apprentice—who knows just enough for self-injury, while failing to learn from history. History is cyclical. Great nations rise and fall. Just as mighty Babylon fell, forever losing its secrets and greatness, so, too, might New York fall. In each beginning are the seeds that will produce an ending. This story is prophetic about nuclear and human destructiveness, and seems more possible today than it did when first published, eight years before the first nuclear bomb was exploded.

Style and Technique

A major part of what makes Benét's story compelling, its language captures the dignity, simplicity, and repetition of oral tradition. For the Hill People, the ancient writings are sacred, and religion is bound up with translation and interpretation. The narrator, a "Noble Savage," speaks in simple sentences. His repetition echoes oral chants or storytelling: "It is forbidden to go east. It is forbidden. . . . It is forbidden. . . . this is most strictly forbidden." His simple imagery derives from nature: "like the buzzing of bees," "cold as a frog," "knees like water," knowledge that is "a squirrel's heap of winter nuts." "Fire" and "burning" images equate the narrator's desire for knowledge with both the Promethean gift of fire and knowledge and the destroyed city. At the beginning of his journey the narrator feels as "naked as a new-hatched bird" and his father warns him that "Truth is a hard deer to hunt." By its end he looks forward to when he will become chief priest and vows that then "we shall go beyond the great river" for "we must build again." That final phrase contains the ultimate irony: the human race's eternal desire to progress contains within it the arrogance, pride, and ambition that guarantee future disaster.

Gina Macdonald

THE CAMBERWELL BEAUTY

Author: V. S. Pritchett (1900-1997)
Type of plot: Satire
Time of plot: Possibly the 1950's
Locale: London
First published: 1974

> *Principal characters:*
> THE NARRATOR, an unnamed young man, probably in his twenties at the time of the story
> AUGUST, an antique dealer and petty criminal
> MRS. PRICE, August's mistress and Isabel's aunt
> PLINY, an antique dealer, tall, thin, with large ears, fiftyish
> ISABEL, a fourteen year old who marries Pliny in her early twenties

The Story

"The Camberwell Beauty" is told by a narrator looking back on his years in the antique trade and those years just following, when he was intimate with all the dealers in southern England. He first became involved with August, Pliny, and the other figures in this tale when he began searching for a rare piece of Staffordshire porcelain for one of his customers. In the process, he met Mrs. Price and her niece Isabel. Some time later, shortly after the death of Pliny's aged mother, he accidentally meets August, Mrs. Price, and other dealers in a Salisbury pub. They repeat the rumors that Pliny used to lock his mother in her room to prevent her giving away his merchandise and that one night a month he visits his mistress in Brixton. This precipitates an outburst by Mrs. Price against August, during which she accuses him of trying to seduce Isabel.

On a visit to Pliny's shop, the narrator again runs into August, Mrs. Price, and Isabel. He is fascinated to see the girl write her name, or rather part of it, ISAB, in the dust on an antique table. Later, he reflects that it is sad to see a young girl grow up in the eccentric world of antique dealers. During the following year, the narrator's business fails, and he is forced to quit and take a job as a real estate agent. He remains sufficiently in touch, however, to hear that August has been sentenced to two years in prison for receiving stolen goods and that Isabel has run away. Passing Pliny's shop one day, he stops for a visit but finds the store locked. Oddly, he hears what sounds like drumming and the sound of a bugle. Eventually, the rumor reaches him that Pliny has married, and when again he stops in at his shop, he is surprised to find Isabel there, although she refuses to let him come in. His curiosity now piqued, he makes several visits, eventually learning that Isabel is Pliny's wife. Back in his own flat, he realizes that, like an antique dealer with a secret passion, he now desires Isabel above all things.

Over the next several months, the narrator watches for an opportunity to visit Isabel, and when he does find a chance, he again hears the drum and bugle. Isabel reluctantly reveals that when her husband is gone she dresses in a helmet, bangs on a drum, and blows a bugle to frighten away potential thieves. Feigning interest in buying something, the narrator picks out a Dresden figurine that he knows is expensive and asks if he may buy it; Isabel, pretending to an expertise she does not have, sells it for only thirty shillings. After this, the narrator returns many times, but Isabel refuses him entry.

Finally, just when the narrator thinks he is free of Isabel's spell, he sees Pliny in a pub with his former mistress and hurries to the shop to see Isabel. When he offers to return the figurine, she lets him in, and he confesses his love. She rejects him, however, saying that Pliny loves her, because unlike August, he does not come to her room, though at night he undresses her and admires her like some rare object. The narrator objects that this is not love, but Isabel remains loyal to her husband. Pliny returns unexpectedly and attacks the narrator, who easily defends himself but loses all chance to win Isabel. He leaves them and walks into the night, where people look odd under the sodium street lamps.

Themes and Meanings

"The Camberwell Beauty" is a subtle and complex study of human nature through the eccentric people of the London antique trade. They are a tragicomic group, a subculture with strange mores and dubious lusts, like August's passion for ivory figures and Pliny's for Caughley ware. This is, as the narrator says, no atmosphere in which to rear a young girl, particularly in view of the abnormal sexual neuroses that flourish among these people. August's advances on young Isabel border on the incestuous, and Pliny's relationship with his mistress and his solemn promise to his mother to give up sex are indicative of the slightly twisted mentality that reigns in the group as a whole.

In comparison with the others, the narrator appears normal. At one point, he catches Isabel looking at him with unusual intensity—not because he is unusual but precisely because he is not. What is not certain, however, is whether his love for Isabel is any less possessive than Pliny's bizarre connoisseurship, which reduces Isabel to a delicate object of art, for the narrator himself compares his obsession with her to the desire of a collector to own some rare and beautiful thing. Nevertheless, whatever the narrator's motives may be, the story takes readers beyond the strange world of antique dealing and collecting to a wider social arena, suggesting that these people and their passions are metaphors for a materialistic society in which sex is but one more commodity and people merely objects to be manipulated.

Style and Technique

V. S. Pritchett is the master of a prose style and narrative technique that are both daringly original and yet apparently traditional. All the stylistic devices and narrative techniques in this social satire have been used many times before, but Pritchett's ability to select and manipulate detail and to catch the nuances of speech and gesture lift his stories above the ordinary and invest them with a significance beyond the trivialities of their characters and events. In "The Camberwell Beauty," he paints an absolutely convincing picture of antique shops and people by weaving together bits of arcane jargon with acute descriptions of objects and people. Enveloping these unusual characters is an atmosphere of claustrophobia and suspicion worthy of a suspense thriller. Critics have frequently called his characters eccentrics, and in this instance the term is apt, but because Pritchett is so convincingly accurate in the details of their speech, habits, and mannerisms, they are never caricatures. To read a Pritchett story is to enter a fictional world in which every word, every detail, carries its full weight of meaning.

Dean Baldwin

A CANARY FOR ONE

Author: Ernest Hemingway (1899-1961)
Type of plot: Psychological
Time of plot: The 1920's
Locale: A train en route to Paris
First published: 1927

Principal characters:

THE WOMAN, a rich American from upstate New York

THE NARRATOR AND HIS WIFE, Americans in their late twenties

The Story

Three unnamed Americans—a middle-aged woman and a younger couple—travel together on an overnight train to Paris. The older woman fears that the speed of modern transit will produce wrecks; she does most of the talking. Although she does not mention her absent husband, who apparently is home with their daughter, she continually asserts that only American men make "good husbands" for American women. Her main concern is for the marriage of her own daughter. Two years earlier, while the family was vacationing at Vevey, Switzerland, her daughter had fallen madly in love with a Swiss gentleman of good family and prospects, and the two had wanted to marry. The mother, however, refusing to let her daughter marry a foreigner, had forced her family to depart for the United States. Now, she tells the American couple, her daughter is still devastated by the affair; to cheer her despondent daughter, the mother has purchased a caged, singing canary.

Only the wife of the young couple participates in the conversation, giving only vague or ambiguous responses, particularly to the question of "good" American husbands. Only once does she extend the conversation by asking directly if the daughter has recovered from her lost love. She also volunteers the information that she and her husband once honeymooned one fall in Vevey; they had lived in Paris for several years before "the Great European War" forced them out. They are now returning to Paris for the first time since the war.

The young husband, who speaks aloud only once, seems satisfied to be isolated from the women's conversation. Almost incidentally the reader discovers that he is the first-person narrator of the story, for he steadfastly looks out the train windows during the journey. He reports in such a flat, unemotional tone that the reader almost forgets that he is a character in the story until the last sentence of the story. Only as the train is pulling into Paris does he wonder whether even trivial points of existence have remained the same after the war. As the train enters the station, he finally reveals the truth of his condition and the point of the story: He and his wife have returned to Paris, the city of light and love, to begin their divorce.

Themes and Meanings

As in his condemnation of the unnatural male-female relationships encouraged by the war and by postwar society in *The Sun Also Rises* (1926) and *A Farewell to Arms* (1929), Ernest Hemingway, in this very short story, questions the prevailing lack of stability and morality of that era, seeing the destruction of love and marriage as a part of the overall malaise of Western civilization. The American woman's pride, materialism, and narrow-minded prejudices against foreigners recall American greed and isolation following World War I, as do her fears, especially of speed. She wants the world to revert to the slower pace of the past. She is not only deaf but also blind to the real emotional problems in her home and in her train compartment.

The younger couple, on the other hand, have also become isolationists: They have survived the war only to become victims of emotional warfare, which has destroyed their love and marriage. Revealing their emotional state indirectly, they do not even attempt to communicate with each other. They know that the past cannot be regained, that nothing can ever be counted on for stability again for either of them, that simply being American cannot protect them in a rapidly changing world that has abandoned the old mores and verities. When marriages are wrecked, each survivor can depend only on himself.

"A Canary for One" can be grouped with other Hemingway short stories of this same period, all emphasizing the fragility of marriage in the postwar world, where values lost their meaning and the individual lost the hope of harmony. "Cat in the Rain," "Hills Like White Elephants," "Out of Season," and "Mr. and Mrs. Elliot" fall into this category.

Style and Technique

More than fifty years after their publication, Hemingway's short stories still strike the reader as highly experimental. The action and conflicts are usually internal rather than external. The traditional conclusion is abbreviated or eliminated; all authorial intrusion, by which past authors told their readers how to respond, is stripped away. Hemingway instead depends on highly stylized dialogue and carefully selected, realistic detail to produce the correct response to the story. His clean, pure line, his economy and exactness of diction, his rhythms and repetitions are here perfectly matched to the self-effacing, tightly controlled objectivity of his first-person narrator. It is only after the final sentence that the reader realizes that the story must be reassessed as an ironic tour de force. The narrator's seeming disinterest in the conversation on marriage is really a protective device to keep his emotions under control. The reader sees, however, those images on which the narrator's mind dwells. Through the train window, he notes a burning farmhouse with many spectators merely watching. He sees the fortifications around Paris, still barren from the recently ended war. He focuses on the remnants of a train wreck—splintered, sagging rail cars pulled off the main line. Each image that catches his attention is, in fact, a metaphor for the state of his marriage. Even his strange, repetitious comparisons reflect his emotional state: He is stupefied, not fully alert—unkempt and unready to face life.

Finally, Hemingway calls attention to the modernism of his story by deliberately creating ironic parallels with Henry James's famous *Daisy Miller* (1878). The references to Vevey, Switzerland, and the Trois Couronnes Hotel are unmistakable, for that is where James's story begins. The marriage tale that the American mother relates is a variation of Daisy Miller's disastrous courtship. Like Daisy, the American woman's daughter is from upstate New York. As in James's story, the father is at home, working. The daughter's courtship is a variation on the courtship of Daisy Miller. However, the traditional values and morality that sustained the world of Henry James have disappeared in the postwar world that Hemingway has inherited. Here nothing—not marriage or train schedules—can be counted on to be the same after the war. Nor is the form of the short story the same. The authorial presence, the drawn-out plot line, and the laborious, well-mannered sentence have all disappeared. In a challenge match, Hemingway has taken on James to show that the art of fiction has been just as radically altered by the war as have the lives of his characters.

Ann E. Reynolds

A CAP FOR STEVE

Author: Morley Callaghan (1903-1990)
Type of plot: Domestic realism
Time of plot: 1952
Locale: An unspecified city in North America
First published: 1952

> *Principal characters:*
> DAVE DIAMOND, a carpenter's assistant
> ANNA, his wife
> STEVE, their twelve-year-old son
> MR. HUDSON, a lawyer
> MR. HUDSON'S SON

The Story

Twelve-year-old Steve Diamond loves baseball. Although his family is poor, he spends nearly every leisure moment playing or watching the game rather than working to supplement the family's meager income. Steve's obsession with the game is a constant source of perplexity and irritation to Dave Diamond, Steve's father, who is a carpenter's assistant. Anna Diamond, Steve's mother, does not understand her son's fascination with the sport either but is tolerant of it. When a major league team comes to town to play an exhibition game, Dave reluctantly agrees to take Steve if Steve will promise to help with some carpentry work. Steve agrees, and they go off to the stadium. Dave is unable to share his son's enthusiasm for the game and is appalled by Steve's extensive knowledge of professional teams and players. He feels that the time spent following professional baseball is time wasted. Steve feels isolated and chilled by his father's sullen disapproval.

As they are leaving the park after the game, Steve joins a throng of young autograph seekers swarming around the players, but he is too shy to get close enough to ask for a signature. Then one of the stars of the game breaks away from the crowd and strides toward the dugout. His cap falls off at Steve's feet, and Steve picks it up. He looks at the player in "an awed trance." The player, responding to the worship and appeal in Steve's eyes, tells him to keep it. Dave and Steve hurry home with the news.

In the following days, Steve is seldom without the cap on his head even though it is too big for him. Inevitably, Steve's parents tire of all the fuss that Steve and his friends make about the cap. One night, Steve is very late coming home from the park where he usually plays baseball. When he finally arrives, he desolately explains that he has been searching for the cap, which must have been stolen. Dave is furious with Steve because he does not understand how the boy could lose something that is so important to him. Steve explains that he was not careless, that he put the cap in his back pocket because it kept falling off when he ran the bases. Someone, he believes, must have taken it from there. Dave remains uncompromisingly bitter about the situation, suggesting to Steve that he lost the cap only because he did not have a right appreciation of its value. Night after night, Steve returns to the park, looking for his cap.

A few weeks later, Steve and his father are passing an ice-cream parlor when Steve spots his cap on the head of a big boy just coming out. Steve snatches it off and challenges the boy. Dave separates them and confirms the fact that it is Steve's cap. The boy coolly tells them that he bought it from another boy at the park. Moreover, his father, he warns them, is a lawyer. Dave agrees to see the boy's father in order to resolve the issue.

The boy lives in a comparatively wealthy part of the city, and when they arrive at the house, Dave is awed by it. Dave and Steve wait outside while the boy goes in to prepare his father for the meeting. The lawyer comes to the door, introduces himself as Mr. Hudson, and invites them in. Mr. Hudson is tall, well-dressed, and self-assured. He treats Dave and Steve with elaborate politeness. Dave feels shabby and confused in the man's presence but is determined to recover what belongs to his son.

Mr. Hudson asks for the details of the situation and confirms his son's story. He assures Dave, however, that legally the cap belongs to Steve; he also asserts that legally the Diamonds are required to reimburse his son for the money that he paid for it if they want it back from him. Dave contends that this is unfair but asks the amount. When he hears that it was two dollars, he is shocked and worried. Two dollars is more than he can afford, as Mr. Hudson shrewdly realizes.

Nevertheless, Dave agrees to pay, and Steve is delighted. Mr. Hudson, on the other hand, is quite surprised and disappointed. He tells Dave that his boy has grown fond of the cap and that he (Mr. Hudson) would be willing to pay five dollars to keep it. Dave nervously refuses but is not sure he is doing the right thing, because five dollars would mean so much to his family. Mr. Hudson raises the offer again, and again, finally pressing twenty dollars into Dave's hands. Twenty dollars for a cap seems impossible to refuse, but even now he turns to his son for a sign of agreement or disagreement. The boy smiles, expecting his father once again to reject the money, but Dave interprets his smile as a sign of triumph at exacting so much for so little. He accepts the money. Steve is stunned.

When they leave the Hudson's house, Steve is sullen and refuses to walk with his father. Dave tries to explain that he sold the cap because he felt sure that Steve understood and accepted the necessity. He says that Steve is being unfair, but he really means that the situation is unfair: Mr. Hudson could afford to offer far more than Dave could afford to refuse. They arrive home, and Anna Diamond tries to comfort each of them. Steve goes to bed unreconciled with his father.

Finally, Dave goes in to talk with his son. He apologizes for not understanding the importance of the cap to him, and he admits that he might have known it had he tried to share Steve's interests and aspirations. He tells his son that he is proud of him and wants to take some active part in his life. Steve responds to him with a gesture of love. He touches Dave's arm and indicates that the cap was a small price to pay for "his father's admiration and approval."

Themes and Meanings

One of the enduring themes in fiction is the importance of money and its effect on human relationships, a theme that Morley Callaghan explores in this story. Both Mr. Hudson and Dave Diamond seek to make their sons happy; both have some claim to the cap. However, in the world that Callaghan depicts, honest poverty is no match for money and class. It seems a foregone conclusion that Dave will relinquish the cap. He is intimidated by Mr. Hudson's dress and manner, disoriented by the lawyer's increasingly extravagant offers, and trapped by his own poverty. There is, as Callaghan makes clear, an important connection between economic and psychological independence.

If the story ended with Dave's defeat, one might describe it as a grim, naturalistic fable about the survival of the fattest. However, it expands to embrace another, more important theme—the relationship between fathers and sons. Mr. Hudson, it is true, offers so much money for the cap that he secures it for his own son. It clearly gives him satisfaction to do this. Presumably, his son is happy to have the cap and proud of his father's display of economic power. For them the ownership of the cap remains strictly an economic issue.

Dave, however, comes to see the cap as more than simply a prize to be contested. He eventually realizes that for his own son the cap was a link to a larger, more significant world, and perhaps a pledge of future glory. Because Dave finally recognizes the importance of the cap to Steve, he begins to respond to the boy's aspirations and enthusiasms. He and his son lose possession of the cap, but it nevertheless provides them with the opportunity for an intimacy that is beyond price.

Style and Technique

The story covers a few weeks in the life of a poor family, during which a boy acquires and then loses a cap that has tremendous value to him. Only a few scenes from this period are dramatized, and they are presented in chronological order. Description is kept to essentials, and dialogue carries the story forward. The narrative voice is third person and largely objective, though occasionally revealing Dave's observations and thoughts. In general, the prose has a cinematic quality. As the story unfolds, it seems immediate, dramatic, and realistic.

In the story, the cap is not symbolic in the ordinary sense, yet some characters invest it with significance beyond its functional and market value. Hence, Callaghan is able to maintain his focus on the external world while calling attention to the existence of other, more important human realities. Also, Callaghan uses the cap as a way of structuring his story. When it is first acquired, it becomes a source of conflict between Dave and Steve; when its ownership is contested, it provides a measure of the distance and difference between the cost of something and its ultimate worth; finally, when it is relinquished, it allows the strong current of natural affection between father and son to be expressed.

Michael J. Larsen

542

CAR CRASH WHILE HITCHHIKING

Author: Denis Johnson (1949-   )
Type of plot: Psychological
Time of plot: The 1980's
Locale: A highway in Missouri
First published: 1990

> *Principal characters:*
> THE NARRATOR, a young man who is hitchhiking
> A SALESPERSON, who gives him a ride
> JANICE, the wife of a man killed in a car accident

The Story

"Car Crash While Hitchhiking" is the first story in *Jesus' Son* (1992), an interrelated collection of short stories that traces the progress of a young man from drug addiction to recovery. Told in the first person by a seemingly clairvoyant narrator who claims that he can perceive future events, the story jumps around in time. The bulk of the story is devoted to a description of an automobile accident and its aftermath.

In chronological order, the events of the story are as follows. The hitchhiking narrator is picked up by a Cherokee, a salesperson, and a college student and consumes large amounts of alcohol and drugs with them. The married salesperson, who is on his way to meet his girlfriend, first picks up the narrator in Texas. The salesperson shares his amphetamines and whiskey with the narrator and rhapsodizes about his capacity to feel love for everyone in his life but then leaves the narrator in Kansas City. A student gives the narrator a ride to the city limits and offers him hashish. Overcome by the quantity of drugs he has taken, the narrator falls asleep in a puddle beside a highway.

Eventually a family—a man and his wife, Janice, and their baby—gives the narrator a ride, and he falls asleep. The family's car is struck by another car, the driver of which apparently has fallen asleep at the wheel. Sprayed with blood and carrying the baby, the narrator seeks help from a reluctant truck driver. He observes that the driver of the other car in the collision is hanging upside down and snoring, still asleep. The police force the narrator to go to the hospital, where he sees hospital personnel telling Janice that her husband died in the accident.

The narration shifts to several years in the future when the narrator is admitted to a hospital for medical treatment of his substance abuse. A nurse injects him with vitamins, and while hallucinating that he is in a pastoral setting, the narrator denies that he can help anyone, including the reader. It appears that the narrator's experience with drugs will persist for some time.

Themes and Meanings

In the tradition of the French Symbolist poets Charles Baudelaire and Arthur Rimbaud, who believed that the creative writer should experiment with drugs to produce visionary texts, Denis Johnson's story is less concerned with developing a conventional linear plot than with illuminating a certain state of mind for the purposes of exploring philosophical and religious questions. Under the influence of drugs and alcohol, the narrator maintains that during the thunderstorm he can distinctly identify every drop of rain, even going so far as to recognize each droplet by name. This mystical hyperawareness is partially a delusional effect of the drugs he has taken, but at the same time, it brings into the story the hypothetical possibility of complete omniscience. In Western culture, this perspective has usually been allocated to the Judeo-Christian God. However, the story implies that, if this God exists, he takes no position whatsoever in the face of violent chaos and suffering.

Despite the narrator's clairvoyant powers, the story suggests that human experience is random and bereft of benevolent transcendental meaning. Humanity's being caught in inescapable solipsism further complicates the condition of human absurdity. Contemplating the sleeping driver hanging from his wrecked car, the narrator maintains that the fundamental sadness of human life is not death itself as much as the fact that the dying man cannot communicate what he is dreaming to the narrator; likewise, the narrator cannot share his sense of phenomenal reality with the other man.

Johnson borrows from the ancient conceit that life is a journey, but the story is not traditionally allegorical because allegory usually posits a stable mode of allegorical meaning to which the textual details refer. The story nowhere indicates the possibility of a mode of being or symbolic system that is not rooted in human transience. Nonetheless, the story relies on the journey analogy to offer that, if life is a journey, it is a journey filled with madness, carnage, and inexplicable grief.

Although the narrator is not an artist or about to embark on a conventional quest, his extraordinary receptiveness to events has the quality of artistic perception and visionary intensity. The narrator concentrates on mundane details such as light spreading from beneath a door into a hallway, describing them with an astonishing and memorable acuity. This propensity for paying attention to the drama he witnesses becomes the most powerful when the narrator listens to the wife as she howls in pain when she is informed of her husband's death. Detached from the situation, the narrator recognizes a sublime purity in Janice's cry; more important, he is grateful that he has heard it because it makes him feel astonishingly alive. That the narrator self-consciously desires to experience something of this magnitude again demonstrates his lust for both extreme situations and exhilarating knowledge, however ugly the circumstances may be.

Although Johnson does not directly allude to Walter Pater, the English prose writer and theorist, the latter's aestheticism usefully illuminates the story. Pater recommended that if people wished to live fully, they should be acutely sensitive to every detail and sensation of their lives. In effect, Pater believed that to live intensely is to make one's life a work of art, an attitude that parallels the narrator's approach to experience. Overall, the story's nihilistic outlook grants a view of a universe in which events are not so much determined by human agency as by the ungraspable movement of time and chance.

Style and Technique

"Car Crash While Hitchhiking" owes a debt to the minimalist style often favored by late twentieth century short-story writers such as Frederick Barthelme and Raymond Carver in that the story's events are presented sparsely, the narrator concentrating primarily on surface detail and offering very little information about the characters' lives preceding the dramatic situation. Unlike most minimalist texts, however, Johnson's story accentuates an idiosyncratic and deeply personalized narratorial voice. The first-person narration in this story is openly discursive. The narrator comments on the potential philosophical significance of events and clearly identifies his subjective response to them, often pointing to metaphysical questions that seem to arise from within a given situation.

In its effort to render both the sensation of intoxication and the absurdity of human life, the story offers strikingly original images derived from ordinary experience and changes them into something unfamiliar. For example, by juxtaposing the familiar action of a baby feeling its cheeks with scenes of terrible violence and the narrator's hallucinogenic point of view, the story transforms the domestic image from an everyday occurrence into something strange and provocative. Although babies are part of daily reality, Johnson's decision to show a baby exploring its body subtly demonstrates human isolation: Adults have forgotten what it means to live in the world as babies do. That the baby is ignorant of the complex and brutal universe into which it has been born and will most likely have no recollection of the horrific events of that night in the rain serves as a microcosm of the story's thematic concerns. Further, the baby's innocence is all the more poignant because the rest of the characters exist in a kind of blamelessness; throughout the story, no one intentionally wishes to cause harm and indeed most have actively chosen compassion. However, these virtues do not matter; awful suffering takes place regardless of the characters' moral sensibility.

This style of compressing thematic elements within textual detail occurs throughout the story; however, the narrator's pastoral vision at the story's end would seem to be at odds with the story's overall bleakness. The somewhat utopian images of nature offered in this vision, though, are undercut by the narrator's open address to readers that he cannot be expected to help them. "Car Crash While Hitchhiking" thus makes powerful use of irony, both as a rhetorical strategy and mode of being. Describing a dreadful series of events, the narrator offers an interpretation of them that depends as much on what is implied in the story as what is clearly spoken.

Michael Trussler

THE CARDINAL'S FIRST TALE

Author: Isak Dinesen (Baroness Karen Blixen-Finecke, 1885-1962)
Type of plot: Fable
Time of plot: The eighteenth century
Locale: Italy
First published: "Kardinalens tredie Historie," 1957 (English translation, 1957)

Principal characters:
>CARDINAL SALVIATI, the frame narrator
>THE LADY IN BLACK, a woman whom he counsels
>PRINCESS BENEDETTA, his mother
>PRINCE POMPILIO, his father
>ERCOLE, their one-eyed first son
>ATANASIO, their older twin son, named by his father and destined
> for the church
>DIONYSIO, their younger twin son, named by his mother and
> destined for the worldly arts

The Story

When a lady in black asks Cardinal Salviati, "Who are you?" he replies not with a straight answer but with a story. The cardinal's mother, Benedetta, was married at fifteen to Prince Pompilio, a nobleman of forty-five. She bore him a son, as expected, but the boy was weak and physically deformed. Pompilio then took his young wife to the country, following the advice that she would benefit from being away from the temptations of city life. In their country villa Princess Benedetta matured and experienced a discovery of self. She transformed from a traditionally submissive wife to a woman of self-awareness. Her change grew out of her love for singing, which surpassed even her prior love for literature. In singing she found a language all her own.

The climax of her self-transformation occurred during a trip to Venice to see Pietro Trapassi Metastasio's opera *Achilles in Scyros* (1736), whose music awakened her entire sense of identity. Within a few hours, every particle of her nature underwent a change, and she triumphantly became her whole self. Her awakening was realized in her spiritual communion with the *castrato* Marelli when their momentary gaze into each other's eyes united them, bestowing manhood on him and imparting passion to her—a mentally virginal woman. Afterward, Benedetta was impregnated by her husband, but she knew the spiritual father of her child to be the *castrato*.

Benedetta and her husband then disagreed about how to rear their unborn child. The prince was determined that if the child were a boy, he should be a pillar of the church, and that he should be named Atanasio, after the church leader Athanasius. Benedetta was determined that any son she bore should become an artist of the world and be named Dionysio, after the "God of inspired ecstacy."

Benedetta eventually bore identical twins, resolving the conflict. Only six weeks later, however, a tragic fire took the life of one of them. The sole means of differentiating the twins was a blue ribbon that Dionysio wore round his neck; it was burned away, so the prince declared the surviving baby to be Atanasio. Benedetta did not contest his decision but secretly called the child Pyrrha—the name given to Achilles by his mother in *Achilles in Scyros*, believing him to be Dionysio.

Atanasio excelled at both ecclesiastical classics and secular skills and eventually was ordained into the priesthood. The first son, Ercole, died soon afterward, leaving Atanasio his parents' sole heir. Following the deaths of Pompilio and Benedetta— which complete the story—Atanasio became both an earthly and a heavenly prince.

Returning to the frame story, the cardinal and the lady in black discuss the nature of character and the value of the story. The cardinal explains the distinction between story and the newly popular—at the time—form of narrative, the novel. He argues that the novel is a valuable but human-contrived form focusing on character, and the story is a divine art in which all elements, including character, unite to form a whole.

Themes and Meanings

The world that Isak Dinesen describes through God's voice in "The Cardinal's First Tale"—diverse elements uniting into a divine whole—explains both her understanding of identity and her argument for the value of the story itself. The question of identity, which the lady in black poses to the cardinal, rightly begins the story, for it introduces the narrative impulse and establishes the foundation for Dinesen's defense of her own art form. "Who are you?" is answered with a story of the cardinal's parents, his own conception, and his childhood. The birth of identity is introduced early on, even prior to the internal story, when the lady in black distinguishes between the cardinal's having "created" her and his having shown her the self that already existed, the self created by God. This distinction is important because it emphasizes the self as part of divine creation, not as formed by humanity. Here she also describes her self as a uniting of "fragments . . . into a whole." Her life is not simplified—in fact, she sees it as a *furioso*—but its elements are "in harmony."

The lady's metaphorical reference to music heightens the connection to Benedetta's "birth" of selfhood at the opera; the princess merges with the music and "triumphantly [becomes] her whole self." Most important, this birth, "the pangs of which [are] sweet beyond words," not only "needed" but also "made use of, every particle of her being." All facets of an individual, even those that might seem contradictory, are not only necessary but will combine to establish one's whole identity.

The symbolic force of this idea is developed in the child Atanasio. Atanasio and Dionysio are opposites—constructed by their parents as such, one destined for the church, the other for artistic ecstasy. When one child dies, the surviving son is forced to adopt both his father's and his mother's vision of his identity. This is literally true because his father believes him to be Atanasio and his mother secretly believes him to be Dionysio. However, merging the seemingly conflicting personalities of the priest and the artist is not difficult: The child Atanasio excels at both ecclesiastical and secular studies and skills, and the adult Atanasio, the cardinal, declares vehemently that, though these two halves of him exist, they are not incompatible, not even always distinguishable. As a servant of God, the cardinal accepts that God has created a world "with all things necessary to the purpose in it" and that his childhood history and present personality are but one example of this.

Under this concept of "all things necessary," story, the genre, becomes glorified. Characters who are sympathetic, knowable, and appealing are what the writers of novels attempt, but in focusing on character, novelists sacrifice the story; novels, according to the cardinal and Dinesen herself, are a consciously constructed "human art" wherein events occur merely to facilitate character development. The defense of the story delivered through the voice of the cardinal is founded in Dinesen's belief that character is only one element of the story—all elements of which must be present and work together to create the whole. The cardinal charges that "*sans* story the human race would perish," and, indeed, the story as a genre matches perfectly the description of the world as described by God: "a sublime world, with all things necessary to the purpose in it, and none left out."

Style and Technique

Reflecting the sublime world presented within her story, Dinesen creates through her style a world of grandeur elevated from the mundane. "The Cardinal's First Tale" is delivered with a controlled formality of language that separates the reader from the authorial presence, emphasizing the distance between the imagination of her story and daily life. Similarly, though Dinesen's characters may be intriguingly individualized through detailed traits—for example, the development of the princess through her unique passion and convergence with music—their speech is indistinct, revealing them to be extensions of the authorial voice. These techniques punctuate the artificiality of the story, validating it as story instead of an attempt to portray reality.

The structure, like the style, is not merely complementary to the intended meaning but a vital element in the formation of that meaning: Form as part of content asserts the concept that the unity of all parts will effect the whole. Narrative framing is a device that further develops her story's central idea. The external and internal stories are so tightly interwoven that neither can be seen as a facilitator of the other; for example, the large theme of self-realization through the unifying of seemingly disparate parts is initially presented by the lady in black in the frame, intensifies in the story of Benedetta's individual growth, is dramatically symbolized by the twins who become one, continues in the discussion of the dualistic yet harmonious personalities of priest and artist, and culminates in the comparison of God's creation of the world to the nature of the genre story. The interconnections establish a fluidity that demands a reading that is holistic rather than fragmented, which melds the frame and internal story. The very process through which the reader experiences Dinesen's narrative is integral to the revelation of this story's message and, indeed, the nature of all stories.

Tiffany Elizabeth Thraves

CAREFUL

Author: Raymond Carver (1938-1988)
Type of plot: Domestic realism
Time of plot: The 1970's
Locale: An unnamed city
First published: 1983

> *Principal characters:*
> LLOYD, who is separated from his wife and trying to overcome a drinking problem
> INEZ, his estranged wife
> MRS. MATTHEWS, his landlady

The Story

Lloyd and Inez have recently gone through what Inez calls "an assessment." The outcome of this assessment is that they decide to separate. As the story opens, Lloyd has recently moved into a two-room and bath attic apartment in Mrs. Matthews's house. The ceilings in the apartment are low and slanting, so much so that Lloyd has to stoop to look out the windows and has to be careful not to hit his head when he gets out of bed.

The reader first meets Lloyd as he enters the building in which he lives, carrying his groceries—some lunch meat and three bottles of Andre champagne. As he passes Mrs. Matthews's door, he looks in and sees that she is lying on the floor. He thinks that she might have collapsed, but her television set is on, and he does not venture to find out whether she is all right. She moves slightly, so he knows that she is not dead.

Lloyd's cooking facilities are minimal: A single unit contains his two-burner stove and a tiny refrigerator. Sometimes he makes himself instant coffee on the stove, but he is more likely to have a breakfast of crumb doughnuts and champagne. He switched to champagne in an attempt to wean himself away from hard liquor, but now he is drinking three or four bottles of champagne a day.

On the day of the story's action, Inez, Lloyd's estranged wife, comes unannounced to see him. Because he does not have a telephone, she has not been able to forewarn him of her visit. When she arrives at eleven o'clock in the morning, Lloyd is sitting in the apartment, not yet dressed, banging his head with his fist. His right ear passage has become blocked with wax, which he is trying to dislodge. The blockage makes all sounds seem distorted. When Lloyd talks, he hears himself talking like someone in a barrel, and his balance is affected as well.

Inez has come to talk with him about the details of their separation, some of them having to do with money. It soon becomes evident, however, that little can be accomplished until Lloyd's ear is fixed, so Inez immediately leaps into the role of mother-nurse. Lloyd recalls that one of his schoolteachers, who was like a nurse, years ago had warned her students not to put anything smaller than their elbows in their ears, and he tells Inez of this warning. She responds, "Well, your nurse was never faced with this exact problem," and she proceeds to search for a hairpin or some other implement to stick into Lloyd's ear to dislodge the wax.

Finally, after an abortive attempt to work with a small nail file wrapped in tissue, Inez goes to ask the landlady to borrow some oil, which she heats and pours into Lloyd's ear, warning him to keep his head positioned so that the oil will not run out for at least ten minutes. While Inez is downstairs borrowing the oil, which quite significantly turns out to be baby oil, Lloyd slips into the bathroom and finishes off the bottle of champagne that he stashed there when he heard Inez arriving a few minutes earlier. Lying as he must to keep the oil in his ear, Lloyd sees everything around him from an odd perspective. All the objects in his vision seem at the far end of the room.

Finally, the oil works, and the wax is dislodged. However, too much time has passed for Inez to talk with Lloyd about whatever it was that originally brought her to his apartment. She has other commitments to keep. Lloyd asks her where she has to go, and she replies vaguely, "I'm late for something." When she gets downstairs, Lloyd hears her talking with Mrs. Matthews, who asks her to leave her telephone number in case Lloyd should need her. Inez says that she hopes he will not, but she gives Mrs. Matthews the number. Lloyd hears her drive away in their car.

Lloyd pours some champagne into the glass in which Inez had put the baby oil. Although he has rinsed the glass out, he notices that some oil is floating on top of the champagne. He throws the champagne down the sink, gets the champagne bottle, and drinks from it.

Themes and Meanings

In "Careful," Raymond Carver focuses on the details of a specific, small situation, giving little information about such matters as locale, the year of the action, or the occupations of the participants, except for Mrs. Matthews, who is Lloyd's landlady.

Carver is concerned in this story with the theme of regression to infantilism. Because the story is not set in a definite locale or in a definite time frame, the focus is on the tawdry apartment to which Lloyd has moved and on the two major characters in the story. Readers learn that the ceilings of the apartment seem to close in on Lloyd, that he does not have a telephone, that the furnished apartment has minimal housekeeping facilities, including a broken-down television, which he plays all day and all night, keeping the volume turned down. One gets the feeling that the apartment is a sort of womb into which Lloyd has retreated.

When his ear becomes clogged with wax, Lloyd has difficulty hearing, and his visit with his wife recalls the silent television images that usually inhabit the apartment with Lloyd. If Lloyd has a job, that information is not revealed. Because he is sitting home alone at eleven o'clock in the morning, one would assume that he is not employed.

Lloyd thinks back to his old teacher who warned children about putting things in their ears. The word "careful" occurs six times in the story (once as "carefully") and recalls what mothers and primary school teachers often say to children: "Be careful, dear." It is interesting that the word is used only once before Inez arrives on the scene. She immediately falls into the mothering role, and Lloyd regresses noticeably. He wants sympathy, and his blocked ear is the vehicle for his attaining it. Inez suggests that Wesson oil and Q-tips would be appropriate props for her in her mothering-nursing role. Lloyd has nothing like this in the apartment, so Inez must see whether she can borrow what she needs from the landlady.

It is significant that Inez must settle for baby oil, which she heats and, after it has cooled a little, pours into Lloyd's ear. When she leaves, and Lloyd overhears her talking with Mrs. Matthews, one is reminded of how a mother visiting school might talk in hushed tones to her child's teacher outside the classroom door.

As the story ends, Lloyd is alone in his womblike dwelling, and he is drinking his champagne from the bottle, just as a baby drinks its milk from a bottle. Inez has twice told him that she cannot linger because she is "late for something." She feels no obligation to explain anything to Lloyd, for whom she feels pity rather than love at this point; metaphorically, perhaps, her words suggest that she has, because of him, missed out on life but that something lies ahead for her despite her late start.

Style and Technique

Carver has the ability to take a commonplace event and imbue it with considerable meaning. His style is characterized by tight control and calculated understatement. He allows details to move in on the reader, who, for example, is told little about Lloyd's economic situation but who comes immediately to understand that the man is faced with economic problems. Carver achieves this end in small, subtle ways.

First the reader is told that Lloyd is buying Andre champagne, which is one of the cheaper brands. Lloyd does not have a telephone. He does not have to pay for the electricity in this small, furnished apartment on the top floor, so he leaves the television on all day and all night. The implication is that if he had to pay the electric bill, he would be more conserving. Inez tells Lloyd that she has come to talk with him about necessary things including money, but she utters the word only once and apparently does not feel pressed to pursue the matter immediately.

In contrast to Lloyd's obvious poverty, Inez is carrying a new canvas handbag with bright flowers stitched on it, and she is dressed well. Inez is looking ahead; Lloyd is retreating from life. Carver shows that because of the separation, Lloyd does not even have a doctor to go to now. Also he has lost the car, as is evident when "he heard her start their car and drive away."

By placing the story in Lloyd's dank quarters, Carver heightens the contrast between Lloyd and Inez. Lloyd is still in his robe and is disheveled when Inez gets there. She is a well-groomed spot of brightness on an otherwise drab foreground. Lloyd is in the process of falling apart. Inez appears to be on the brink of finding a new life for herself.

R. Baird Shuman

THE CARIBOO CAFÉ

Author: Helena María Viramontes (1954-   )
Type of plot: Social realism
Time of plot: The 1980's
Locale: An American city and El Salvador
First published: 1985

>   *Principal characters:*
>   SONYA, the young daughter of a Latino immigrant to the United
>   States
>   MACKY, her brother
>   THE COOK, the owner of the Cariboo Café
>   JOJO, the cook's son
>   NELL, the cook's former wife
>   PAULIE, a café patron
>   A WASHERWOMAN, from El Salvador
>   GERALDO, the washerwoman's young son

The Story

   In the first of the story's three parts, a young girl named Sonya has lost the key to her father's apartment that she usually keeps on a string around her neck. Her father works by day while she goes to school, and her brother Macky is tended by Mrs. Avila. Today Sonya has brought Macky home from Mrs. Avila's house; she arrives at the apartment before she realizes that her key is missing. Street smart but young, she tries to guide her brother back through the ghetto area where they live to Mrs. Avila's house but quickly becomes disoriented.

   As they walk, Sonya observes various human examples of homelessness, poverty, and vice. She sees a man and innocently thinks he might be the father of a classmate at her school (because both schoolmate and man are African American). She considers approaching the man for help, when he is suddenly stopped, searched, and taken away by the police. Her father has taught her to fear the police—who work in league with immigration officials—so witnessing this incident confirms to Sonya that what he says about the authorities is accurate. She seizes her brother by the hand and they run into the unfamiliar warehouse district of the city. Tired and frightened as darkness falls, they head toward the lights of a café that Sonya spots in the distance.

   The second part of the story is narrated by the owner of the Cariboo Café, who is in the process of rationalizing some of his recent actions and ruminating about his life. Something has recently happened in his café that makes patrons avoid it and that makes the man scrub stains off its floor. He tries to be fair to the odd assortment of people who enter his place, including the disabled and those down on their luck. He is especially kind to a man named Paulie, who has a drug or mental problem (which may stem from his experience in the Vietnam War), because something about him reminds the man of his own son, JoJo, who was killed in Vietnam. The café owner's level-headed wife, Nell, has left him, and he misses her. One day, he recalls, a disheveled Latina woman ordered food for two children sitting with her in a booth. The younger child (whom he thinks of as Short Order) reminded him of JoJo as a little boy. The boy's sister appeared distrustful. After they left, the owner saw a television news bulletin about two missing children and recognized the boy as the one in his café.

The next day immigration agents raid a nearby factory and some workers run into the café to hide. Although the owner recognizes them as regular customers, he gestures toward their hiding place when the agents enter, and they are taken away in handcuffs. Shaken by this incident, he is further distressed to see the woman from the day before return with the two children.

The final section of the story is the first-person narrative of an unnamed El Salvadoran woman whose five-and-a-half-year-old son, Geraldo, was taken off the streets by army officials and never seen again. Along with other women whose children disappeared, she went to the authorities at the "detainers" (where bodies of people accused of helping the Contras were collected) trying to find her son. Crippled by her grief and the sadism that she encountered while seeking information about her son, she finally gave up hope of regaining her life in El Salvador. With the help of her nephew Tavo, she crossed the border into the United States from Juarez, Mexico.

While working as a housecleaner, the woman one day sees a boy in the street whom she believes to be Geraldo; he is with a girl. The woman takes both children to eat at a café, where the cook is kind to the boy, and then takes them home, where she bathes the boy lovingly and sings to him, tucking him into the bed. She dreams of taking him home and having their old lives of harmony restored. The next day she returns to the café with the children.

At this point the stories of the bereft mother and café owner converge. When the owner sees the children, he calls the police. After they arrive, the point of view shifts from the owner to the woman, who desperately tries to stop the police from taking the boy—whom she believes to be her own Geraldo—away from her. As the owner cowers behind the counter, the woman clings to the boy and fights a police officer holding a gun with all her might; in him she sees personified the officials with whom she dealt at home, and she vows to herself not to allow these uniformed men to take her beloved son from her again.

Themes and Meanings

"The Cariboo Café" is a story of the terrible psychic wounds wrought by political repression and displacement. Two of its primary themes are the randomness of terror at the hands of powerful authorities and the banality of evil. Readers see the latter in the young guard with whom the mother pleads in El Salvador and in the hazy thoughts that lie behind the café owner's actions. For Helena María Viramontes's Latino characters, the world is a dangerous place. Racism is insidious: The café owner sees himself as a relatively good and generous man, but he feels no loyalty or connection to the Spanish-speaking workers who frequent his café. He can thus turn them in to the police without thinking and does not clearly understand the discomfort he feels as they are taken away.

In using two different settings for her story, Viramontes draws parallels between the kinds of repression experienced in the United States and in El Salvador. In Central America her characters are subjected to a reign of terror instigated by a totalitarian and corrupt military regime. In the United States undocumented Spanish-speaking residents live in poverty and in fear of relocation or reprisal from police acting in conjunction with immigration officials. Viramontes explores the terrible emotional consequences of such forms of repression and the intensity of the urban environment of poverty. The horror, loss, and bewilderment that her characters experience sharply contrast with their simple desire to live a decent life unencumbered by fear.

Style and Technique

In its sensitive treatment of the themes of social marginality and alienation, "The Cariboo Café" recalls the work of Carson McCullers. Viramontes uses narrative and characterization techniques similar to those of McCullers's novel *The Heart Is a Lonely Hunter* (1940). These include revolving points of view, the presentation of overlapping personal realities, and the use of projection as a device. In "The Cariboo Café" both the woman and the café owner project an identity onto the figure of the inarticulate little boy that is based on their own deprivations and inner needs—much as McCullers's characters do with the deaf mute at the center of her novel.

Using a nonlinear structure to great effect, Viramontes creates a kind of kaleidoscope of human pain and longing in which many details go unmentioned and from which the reader must sort out meaning. She tells events out of sequence and from multiple standpoints, ending the story in the midst of conflict, without revealing exactly what happens to the children and the woman. The story first jumps between the different characters' consciousness, revealing their inner motivations, choices, and perceptions, and then brings them together in a tragic web of misunderstanding that apparently leads to the El Salvadoran woman's being shot by the police. Although Viramontes never makes it explicit, one suspects when the story ends that what the café owner had to scrub off the floor was the distraught mother's blood.

In the Cariboo Café's neon sign all the lights are burnt out except those forming what the characters read as the double "zeroes." The place that gives the story its title is thus the site of negation. It is a point of encounter for people whose lives are deemed worthless by others—lives that seem to add up to nothing when measured by fate.

In bringing her protagonists together at the café, Viramontes makes essential use of irony. Privy to the inner thoughts of the characters, the reader knows that there are commonalities between the café owner who has lost his son and wife and the mother who has lost her child, but each character's true reality remains unknown to the other. Instead, they face each other as if over an abyss, and the harm, trauma, and loss that has brought each of them there adds up to fatal consequences.

Barbara J. Bair

THE CASK OF AMONTILLADO

Author: Edgar Allan Poe (1809-1849)
Type of plot: Horror
Time of plot: Unspecified
Locale: Italy
First published: 1846

Principal characters:
MONTRESOR, the narrator, an Italian nobleman
FORTUNATO, a connoisseur of wine

The Story

Told in the first person by an Italian aristocrat, "The Cask of Amontillado" engages the reader by making him or her a confidant to Montresor's macabre tale of revenge. The victim is Fortunato, who, the narrator claims, gave him a thousand injuries that he endured patiently, but when Fortunato dared insult him, he vowed revenge. It must be a perfect revenge, one in which Fortunato will know fully what is happening to him and in which Montresor will be forever undetected. To accomplish it, Montresor waits until carnival season, a time of "supreme madness," when Fortunato, already half-drunk and costumed as a jester, is particularly vulnerable. Montresor then informs him that he has purchased a pipe of Amontillado wine but is not sure he has gotten the genuine article. He should, he says, have consulted Fortunato, who prides himself on being an expert on wine, adding that because Fortunato is engaged, he will go instead to Luchesi. Knowing his victim's vanity, Montresor baits him by saying that some fools argue that Luchesi's taste is as fine as Fortunato's. The latter is hooked, and Montresor conducts him to his empty palazzo and leads him down into the family cat-acombs, all the while plying him with drink. Through underground corridors with piles of skeletons alternating with wine casks, Montresor leads Fortunato, whose jester's bells jingle grotesquely in the funereal atmosphere. In the deepest crypt there is a small recess, and there Montresor chains Fortunato to a pair of iron staples and then begins to lay a wall of stone and mortar, with which he buries his enemy alive. While he does so, he relishes the mental torment of his victim, whom he then leaves alone in the dark, waiting in terror for his death.

Themes and Meanings

Edgar Allan Poe himself seems to have had a morbid fear of premature burial; it is a theme he dealt with repeatedly in such stories as "The Premature Burial," "The Fall of the House of Usher," "Berenice," "Ligeia," and "Morella," all of which reverberate with a claustrophobic terror. He also turned again to walling up a victim in "The Black Cat." The fear was that the buried person would still be conscious, aware of the enveloping horror.

"The Cask of Amontillado" belongs to the Romantic movement in art; it is part of the Romantic subgenre of the gothic, a tale of horror with the gothic paraphernalia of dungeons, catacombs, and cadavers. At his best, though, Poe transcends the genre. As he observed, his horror was not of Germany (meaning gothicism) but of the soul. To the extent that this is true, Poe was a pioneer in writing psychological fiction, often of extremely neurotic, if not abnormal, personalities. He also was an early advocate of art for art's sake; unlike his contemporary, Nathaniel Hawthorne, he did not write moral allegories. In "The Cask of Amontillado," the murderer gets away with his crime. Whatever meaning the tale offers lies in the portrait of Montresor, contained in his own words. D. H. Lawrence, in *Studies in Classic American Literature* (1923), says that Montresor is devoured by the lust of hate, which destroys his soul just as he destroys Fortunato. By this token, Montresor resembles Hawthorne's unpardonable sinners, who suffer from an intellectual pride and monomania that destroys their humanity. His revenge echoes (whether consciously or not) a passage from Thomas Nashe's Renaissance novel *The Unfortunate Traveller* (1594):

> Nothing so long of memorie as a dog, these Italians are old dogs, and will carrie an injurie a whole age in memorie: I have heard of a boxe on the eare that hath been revenged thirtie yeare after. The Neopolitane carrieth the bloodiest mind, and is the most secret fleering murdrer: whereupon it is growen to a common proverbe, Ile give him the Neopolitan shrug, when one intends to play the villaine, and make no boast of it.

Style and Technique

James Russell Lowell, in his satiric poem *A Fable for Critics* (1848), called Poe's work three-fifths genius and two-fifths fudge. In the genius-fudge ratio, "The Cask of Amontillado" ranks high on the genius side. A brief, concise story, it fulfills Poe's literary theory that every detail and word in a tale or poem should contribute to the intended effect. Here, there are only two characters, and though Montresor insists on his patience in devising an appropriate and satisfying revenge, the story moves quickly and relentlessly to its climax. In contrast to the verbosity found in the works of Sir Walter Scott and James Fenimore Cooper, Poe's story, only about four pages long, has not a wasted word. Poe grips readers and plunges them right in with the opening sentence, "The thousand injuries of Fortunato I had borne as I best could, but when he ventured upon insult I vowed revenge." Readers learn almost nothing about the background of the characters; one is told nothing about their age, their families, their wives and children, if any, or their appearance. One is not even told when and where the story takes place, though the name Fortunato and references to a palazzo indicate Italy. From the last sentence, stating that Fortunato's bones have moldered in the tomb for half a century, one can deduce that they were young men at the time of the tale, which could occur no later than the end of the eighteenth century. As for character, Montresor tells readers that Fortunato was to be respected and even feared, that his only weak point was his pride in being a connoisseur of wine. This pride in such a trivial matter becomes grotesquely disproportionate and leads him into the trap.

Critics have complained that all of Poe's characters sound alike, that Poe has only one voice, but in "The Cask of Amontillado" the narrative voice—learned, passionate but cold, ironic—fits perfectly the character of the avenger. Like Shakespeare's Iago and Richard III, Montresor takes the reader into his confidence, assuming he or she will approve not only of his revenge but also of the clever and grotesque manner of it, and share his gloating satisfaction. The sensitive reader will also identify with Fortunato, however, and share his fear of the charnel-like catacombs and his horror of being walled up alive, to die slowly in the dark of starvation or suffocation among the skeletons of Montresor's ancestors.

The reader should realize, as Montresor does not, that despite his cleverness and irony, Montresor is an inhuman monster and something of a madman. Montresor's tone throughout is jocose. Repeatedly, he baits Fortunato (whose name is ironic in light of his ghastly fate) by playing on his vanity, suggesting that Luchesi can judge the wine as well, pretending to be his concerned friend, giving his enemy chance after chance to escape. The vaults are too damp, Fortunato has a cough, his health is precious, and they should turn back. With foreknowledge, Montresor observes that Fortunato will not die of a cough and drinks to his long life. Montresor interprets his family's coat of arms—signifying, he says, that no one injures him with impunity, a warning that Fortunato has ignored. When Fortunato makes a secret gesture and asks if Montresor is a mason, the latter produces a trowel, which he will use to wall up his enemy. Thus, Montresor plays cat and mouse with his victim. After chaining his enemy, he implores him to return, then says he must render him "all the little attention in my power," and proceeds to the masonry. Clearly, he savors every moment of his murderous revenge. When Fortunato begins to scream, Montresor reveals his own madness. Unsheathing his rapier, he thrusts about with it and then responds by echoing and surpassing the cries of his victim. At the end, he returns to his jocose tone, observing that his heart grew sick on account of "the dampness of the catacombs," and concluding, fifty years later, "In pace requiescat": "May he rest in peace."

Robert E. Morsberger

THE CATBIRD SEAT

Author: James Thurber (1894-1961)
Type of plot: Wit and humor
Time of plot: 1942
Locale: New York City
First published: 1942

Principal characters:
ERWIN MARTIN, the department head at F & S
ULGINE BARROWS, the new special adviser to the president of
F & S
MR. FITWEILER, the "F" and elderly president of F & S

The Story

"The Catbird Seat" is the story of Erwin Martin's calculated destruction of the vulgar, ruthless Ulgine Barrows, who has made life at F & S miserable since her appearance two years before the story begins. The tale might almost be called a revenge comedy, and it is even more amusing because Mr. Martin's very dullness enables him to succeed. The story begins with an uncharacteristic action by Mr. Martin. He does not smoke; yet he is surreptitiously buying a pack of cigarettes. The purchase is part of his plan to kill Mrs. Ulgine Barrows, a plan that he has worked out during the preceding week.

Mr. Martin has no qualms about his action. Since charming the elderly Mr. Fitweiler at a party and persuading him to make her his all-powerful adviser, Mrs. Barrows has fired some employees and caused the resignations of others. As she has moved from department to department, she has changed systems and, Mr. Martin believes, is threatening the very existence of the firm, while Mr. Fitweiler, besotted, applauds. Although he is consistently annoyed by her southern expressions, evidently picked up from a baseball announcer, such as "sitting in the catbird seat," that is, in a perfect situation, Mr. Martin has not thought that she deserved death until her appearance in the filing department, which he heads. When she suggests that his filing cabinets were not necessary, Ulgine Barrows signs her own death warrant. Mr. Martin's purchase of a brand of cigarettes that she does not smoke is only one element in a thoughtful plan.

At a time of day when the streets are relatively deserted, Mr. Martin goes to the apartment of Mrs. Barrows. She is surprised to see him, puzzled when he refuses to remove his gloves, and amused when Mr. Martin, who is known never to drink, accepts a scotch. As he looks about for a weapon, Mr. Martin realizes that the murder he had planned is simply too difficult. Another idea comes to him, however: He can eliminate Mrs. Barrows by destroying her credibility.

When Mrs. Barrows returns with his drink, Mr. Martin smokes, drinks, announces that he takes heroin regularly, and suggests that he intends to kill Mr. Fitweiler. Commenting that he is in the "catbird seat," he leaves, goes home unseen, and goes to sleep.

At the office the next morning, Mrs. Barrows reports the incident to Mr. Fitweiler. Faced with Mr. Martin's usual propriety, Mr. Fitweiler can only assume that Mrs. Barrows has developed delusions. After consultation with his psychiatrist, Mr. Fitweiler has concluded that she must be fired. Furious, Mrs. Barrows screams at Mr. Martin, voicing her suspicions that he may have planned the whole situation. Still screaming, she is removed from the office. Accepting Mr. Fitweiler's apology, Mr. Martin permits himself a faster pace in the hall, but back in his department, he resumes his usual propriety and returns to his files.

Themes and Meanings

The well-known James Thurber drawings of women in the act of seducing, menacing, attacking, or intimidating men are matched in his short stories by accounts of the ongoing war between the sexes. Armed with sex appeal, defiant illogic, physical strength, and their institution of marriage, Thurber's women seem to have the odds on their side. When a man as meek as Walter Mitty or Erwin Martin must deal with a female antagonist, only his imagination can bring him the victory.

In the battle recounted in "The Catbird Seat," each side uses characteristic weapons. Mrs. Ulgine Barrows has gained her job initially by strength and sex appeal. At a party, she rescued the elderly Mr. Fitweiler from a large drunk and then charmed him into offering her the job. Once committed to her, he gives her complete control; he is completely at her mercy, playing Samson to her Delilah.

Initially, Mr. Martin intended to destroy Mrs. Barrows by brute force, hoping to avoid suspicion by such detective-story devices as the use of gloves, the choice of a weapon from the victim's own apartment, and the deceptive clue of the partially smoked cigarette. He realizes, however, that violence is not his best weapon; indeed, that he cannot win in a game where the hefty Mrs. Barrows is at her best. It is his imagination, a talent that fortunately has remained hidden, which can defeat her. Therefore, like Walter Mitty, he becomes another person, but he reveals that personality only to Mrs. Barrows, who is therefore trapped into a seeming lie that can only be interpreted as madness. The silent self-control that makes Mr. Martin a good file clerk ensures his victory, for he is too disciplined ever to tell anyone what he has done, ever to reveal his secret self.

Although Thurber, like George Bernard Shaw, suggests that women are the stronger sex, it is clear that men can sometimes triumph if only they use the weapons that have always been available to the oppressed: craftiness, imagination, and the ability to keep a secret. Armed only with these, Mr. Martin has attained his victory.

Style and Technique

The comic irony that is so important an element in Thurber's stories is effected in "The Catbird Seat" by the technique of limited omniscience. From the beginning to the end of the story, Thurber reveals the thoughts only of his Mr. Martin. However, the impression that Mr. Martin makes on others is clearly revealed through objective comments, such as the fact that the cigarette clerk did not look at him, and by comments recalled by Mr. Martin, such as those of Mr. Fitweiler and of the late Sam Schlosser. With the judgment of the outside world thus established, Thurber can produce his comic effect by letting the reader in on the secret. Only the reader shares Mr. Martin's carefully dissembled anger; only the reader follows the formulation of his plot; and only the reader anticipates and then experiences the final scene, in which no one will believe Mrs. Barrows, even though she is telling the truth.

Because the character of Mr. Martin is so important, both in the plot line and in the total comic effect, Thurber establishes his spinsterish fussiness, his bureaucratic orderliness, by the use of numerous details. He plans to eliminate Mrs. Barrows as if she were an error. He tries and convicts her in a mental courtroom, while he is drinking his milk. He shines his glasses and sharpens pencils while he waits to murder her.

The other characters are seen through Mr. Martin's eyes. Mrs. Barrows "romped . . . like a circus horse," "was constantly shouting," "demanded," "brayed," and "bawled." To the quiet Mr. Martin, her bouncy noisiness is clearly distasteful. Similarly, when Mr. Fitweiler is forced to speak to Mr. Martin about the woman's allegations, Mr. Martin notices that he is "pale and nervous," that he plays with his glasses—in other words, that his employer has less control over the situation than Martin has.

It is a final refinement of Thurber's comedy that Martin does not reveal the fact of his control. Thus, he expresses regret that his employer must fire Mrs. Barrows, and after Mr. Fitweiler's apology for the loud attacks of Mrs. Barrows, Martin agrees to forget the incident. At the end of the story, Mr. Martin is in "the catbird seat," and only the reader, who has been admitted to his thoughts as well as having watched his actions, is party to his triumph against the odds.

Rosemary M. Canfield Reisman

CATHEDRAL

Author: Raymond Carver (1938-1988)
Type of plot: Domestic realism
Time of plot: About 1980
Locale: New England
First published: 1981

> *Principal characters:*
> THE NARRATOR, a shy but sensitive blue-collar worker
> HIS WIFE, who once worked for Robert as a reader and secretary
> ROBERT, their overnight guest, a blind man in his late forties

The Story

A blind man named Robert is coming to have dinner and stay overnight. The narrator's wife worked for him for one summer about ten years earlier. The two became friends and have continued to correspond by using cassette tapes. The narrator, who lacks social graces, is apprehensive about having to entertain Robert. He does not know what he should do or say. Jealous of the former relationship between his wife and Robert, he is suspicious. He knows that his wife has told Robert about him and has probably complained about his faults. This makes him feel guilty, insecure, and somewhat hostile toward both his wife and Robert.

The blind man proves to be such an outgoing, amiable person that one can understand why he made such a strong impression on the narrator's wife that she has corresponded with him for years. Despite the narrator's conversational blunders, the two men get along well; they drink together and smoke marijuana together after dinner. Under the influence of the drugs, the narrator lets down his guard with Robert.

Robert's handicap has compensations: It has made him compassionate, tolerant, and open-minded. Being dependent on others has made him trusting, and this trust leads him to reveal intimacies that he might otherwise not share. As the evening progresses and the narrator's wife falls asleep on the sofa, he and his guest grow closer. Finally he finds himself describing a documentary about cathedrals being shown on the television screen. Robert admits that he has no idea what a cathedral looks like, although he knows they required hundreds of people and decades to build. He persuades his host to sketch a cathedral while he holds the hand moving the pen. Through this spiritual contact with the blind man, the narrator discovers unsuspected artistic gifts.

The narrator sheds his inhibitions and sketches an elaborate cathedral with spires, buttresses, massive doorways, gargoyles, and a throng of worshippers. It is a unique and memorable experience that forms the story's climax. The narrator not only shares his vision with the blind Robert, but he simultaneously shares Robert's inner vision. At the same time, both share the spiritual vision of men who lived centuries earlier and collaborated to build the beautiful, mystery-laden Gothic cathedrals of Europe.

Themes and Meanings

Raymond Carver wrote mostly about the joys and sorrows of politically powerless and socially insignificant working-class people. In this respect he resembled John Steinbeck, whose best-known work is the Depression-era novel *The Grapes of Wrath* (1939). Carver differed from Steinbeck, however, in having no political agenda. Steinbeck was a socialist for most of his life, believing that the lives of the masses could be improved by government and by substituting faith in socialism for faith in God. Carver was apolitical in his writings but seems to have had a working-class distrust of politicians and people who did not work with their hands.

Like many contemporary minimalist writers of his era, Carver displays a nihilistic view of life. His favorite theme in his stories and poetry is alienation or anomie. The latter is the feeling that many people have of being only half alive, of being on a treadmill or in a rat race, of being trapped in meaningless jobs, of not being able to love and not being able to relate to others—perhaps especially of not being able to see any higher meaning to life.

After shedding his inhibitions through liquor and marijuana, and feeling somewhat invisible in the presence of his sightless house guest, the narrator confesses that he does not believe in religion or anything else. "Sometimes it's hard," he says, "You know what I'm saying?" Robert replies: "Sure, I do." Although the narrator knows that cathedrals are products of a great religious faith that existed during the Middle Ages, he confesses that "cathedrals don't mean anything special to me."

The cathedral that the narrator and Robert draw on the side of a shopping bag might be seen as symbolizing the vestiges of religious faith in the Western world. It is significant that the men copy a cathedral seen through the modern medium of television, because science and technology have been particularly responsible in undermining traditional religious faith since the Middle Ages.

The joint artistic creation of these late twentieth century men represents their pathetic wish for a spiritual life that is an unavoidable part of their humanity. These hapless strangers—one a man who hates his job, drinks too much, has no friends, and seems on the verge of divorce, the other a blind widower, a former Amway distributor with a bleak future—come together momentarily because of their common yearning for a more fulfilling and spiritually more meaningful life. The epiphany described in this story is of the smallest possible kind—a sort of "mini-epiphany" appropriate to a minimalistic story. The narrator concludes with the ambiguous understatement of an inarticulate man: "It's really something."

Style and Technique

Carver is generally considered the leading writer of the school of fiction called minimalism, which—as its name implies—eliminates all but the most important details. Minimalists are noted for using simple language and focusing on factual statements, implying rather than attempting to explain precisely what is going on inside their characters. The reader of a minimalist story is forced to make inferences from what the characters do and say. For example, it can be inferred that the narrator of

"Cathedral" and his wife are not getting along well and might be on the verge of divorce. Indeed, the most striking thing about "Cathedral" is its simplicity of language. This type of narration from the viewpoint of a simple, uneducated man creates an impression of truthfulness, as the narrator seems too naïve to be dishonest or evasive.

Characteristically, Carver neither names nor describes the two principal characters and does not even reveal where the story takes place. Like other minimalist fiction writers, such as Ann Beattie, Carver deletes every word that he possibly can and even deletes punctuation marks whenever possible. The effect of minimalism is to engage one's imagination, forcing the reader to make guesses and assumptions and thereby participate in the creative process.

In "Cathedral," as in many of his other stories, Carver uses a narrator who is a faux naïf, like the narrators of Mark Twain's *Adventures of Huckleberry Finn* (1884) and J. D. Salinger's *The Catcher in the Rye* (1951). Such "naïve" narrators supposedly do not understand the full import of what they are telling. This narrative device enhances verisimilitude, characterizes and creates sympathy for the narrator, and provides a basis for humor. The typical point of stories involving faux naïf narrator-protagonists is that they experience events that teach them something about life or about themselves, thereby making them less naïve. In identifying with the narrator, the reader vicariously experiences the learning event and feels changed by the story.

Minimalist short-story writers often write about seemingly trivial domestic incidents and tend to avoid what James Joyce called "epiphanies"—sudden intuitive perceptions of a higher spiritual meaning to life. Minimalists have been attacked as having nothing to say because they do not offer solutions to the existential problems they dramatize in their stories. In a typical Carver story, little changes; his endings might be called "mini-epiphanies." This is characteristic of minimalists, who usually display a nihilistic outlook and do not believe there are answers to life's larger questions. Carver's "downbeat" endings tend to leave the reader depressed or perplexed—and this is the intention. Carver tried to capture the feelings of alienation and frustration that are so much a part of modern life.

Carver has been credited with single-handedly reviving interest in the short story, a genre that had been perfected by American authors beginning with Nathaniel Hawthorne and Edgar Allan Poe but had been rapidly declining in popularity and social influence with the advent of television after World War II. Some readers dislike Carver's stories because they seem depressing or pointless. Others appreciate them because they are so truthful. He writes about working-class folk who lead lives of quiet desperation, are chronically in debt, and often overdrink. He tells bitter truths but has an indestructible sense of humor that always shines through. It is impossible to appreciate "Cathedral" without being aware of its offbeat humor, such as in the narrator's offer to take the blind man bowling and his wife's reaction to that bizarre suggestion. The subtle humor spicing this poignant story is typically Carveresque.

Bill Delaney

THE CELEBRATED JUMPING FROG OF
CALAVERAS COUNTY

Author: Mark Twain (Samuel Langhorne Clemens, 1835-1910)
Type of plot: Tall tale
Time of plot: 1850
Locale: Northern California
First published: 1865

Principal characters:

AN UNNAMED NARRATOR
SIMON WHEELER, a current resident of Angel's Camp
JIM SMILEY, a former resident of Angel's Camp

The Story

The narrator, urged by a friend from the East, decides to call on Simon Wheeler, a good-natured and garrulous old fellow who resides at Angel's Camp, a northern California mining settlement. His errand is to inquire about a certain Reverend Leonidas W. Smiley, but he, the narrator, is already half persuaded that Leonidas W. Smiley never existed. Asking about him will only result in releasing a torrent of Simon Wheeler's boring reminiscences about Jim Smiley.

Simon Wheeler, a genial man, fat and bald-headed, wears a look of perpetual simplicity and tranquillity. As the narrator suspects, Wheeler cannot place Leonidas W. Smiley, but he does recall the presence of a fellow by the name of Jim Smiley who, some years previously, had been an Angel's Camp inhabitant. Wheeler's tone never changes, his voice never wavers from a pattern of earnestness and sincerity as he launches into his tale. He never registers anything but the utmost respect and admiration for the two heroes whose adventures he relates.

Jim Smiley, according to Simon Wheeler, was "always betting on anything that turned up." He would lay odds on either side of a bet, and if he could not find a taker for the other side, he would simply change sides. He bet on horse races, dog fights, and chicken fights. If he had had the opportunity, he would have bet on how long a straddle bug's flight was between one destination and another—then he would have followed the bug all the way to Mexico, if he had needed to, in order to win a bet. Smiley would bet on anything.

Smiley loved to employ animals in his betting schemes. He had a mare, an old nag really, but he used to win money on her, for all that she was slow and prey to myriad diseases such as asthma, distemper, and consumption. He also had a bull-pup, named Andrew Jackson, that he had taught to fight using a most peculiar strategy. Andrew Jackson always went for his opponent's hind legs, and, holding these in a vise-like grip, could hold on for a year. Smiley always won money on that pup until he came up against a dog whose hind legs had been sawed off with a circular saw.

One day Smiley caught a frog and took him home, swearing that all a frog needed was a good education—he stayed home for three months educating him. Daniel Webster was the creature's name, and Jim trained him so well that all he would have to do was yell, "Flies, Dan'l, flies," and the frog would leap off counters, displaying amazing feats of skill to startled onlookers. A modest frog, too, Daniel Webster was not given to airs despite his great gift of agility. So naturally Jim Smiley began to bet on him, and he would take on all comers. He was exceedingly proud of his frog, convinced that Daniel was the finest example of the species to be found.

Once a stranger to Angel's Camp saw Jim's frog and inquired as to what he was good for. Jim eagerly explained that Daniel Webster could outjump any frog in Calaveras County. "I don't see no p'ints about that frog that's any better'n any other frog," the stranger observed. However, he sportingly declared that he would bet with Smiley, if only he had a frog himself. Jim took that bet, and a sum of forty dollars was wagered. Then Smiley willingly went off to the swamp to look for another frog. In his absence, the stranger pried open Daniel Webster's mouth and filled him full of quail shot. When Smiley returned with another frog, both contestants were placed on the ground, and each was given a push from behind by his respective human. The new frog hopped off immediately, but Daniel Webster remained behind, as if bolted to the ground. The stranger collected his forty dollars and readily departed.

Smiley was dumbfounded by this turn of events and picked up the frog. Feeling his radically increased weight, he turned the animal upside down and Daniel Webster belched out a double handful of shot. Smiley set out after the stranger, but he never caught him.

At this point the narrator interrupts Wheeler's tale, assuring him that further information about Jim Smiley would shed no light on the activities of Leonidas W. Smiley. Lacking the desire to hear anything further relating to Jim Smiley, he leaves.

Themes and Meanings

To load a frog with shot so that it cannot engage in a jumping match is amusing. Beyond the obvious laugh, however, the slyness with which the defeat of the champion frog is managed seems to be an indication of Mark Twain's interest in championing frontier common sense. It is not really an endorsement of cheating or deception in a malicious sense. The narrator's casual reference to an Eastern friend is followed by an indulgently superior description of Simon Wheeler. Wheeler's winning gentleness and simplicity are of primary importance to the author. This disparity establishes Twain's dislike of the affectations and hypocrisy of the East, a dislike he readily contrasts with the informality and openness of the West. If the similarities of dramatic situation at the outset of the tale seem to indicate a familiar story line—the country stooge bested by the polished urbanite—the story upsets these calculations. The narrator, as things turn out, is not as clever as he sees himself. Assuming that he is more sophisticated than the man he meets, the encounter teaches him just the reverse—it is he, not Simon Wheeler, who is simple. The innocence of Simon Wheeler's expression is a mask that he assumes to deceive the outsider by seeming to fulfill all his preconceived notions of Western simplemindedness.

Simon Wheeler's tall tale also endorses democracy by making fun of superior feelings. Gazing at Daniel Webster, the stranger is unable to see anything that makes him innately superior to any other frog in creation. The subsequent triumph of the underfrog over the highly touted excellence of Daniel Webster comically vindicates the stranger's radical democracy. The lesson here is that it does not pay to be too proud or too haughty in the egalitarian West.

Twain is not merely embellishing a well-known theme. Though not immune to the sentiments of cynicism and skepticism, Twain was imbued with the frontier spirit of openness and sincerity characteristic of the West. By poking fun at hidebound tradition, manifested through the narrator's arrogant and polite speech, he ridicules Eastern customs and manners. In creating these three "simple" characters, Simon Wheeler, Jim Smiley, and the stranger, all of whom are superior to the narrator, Mark Twain places his humorist's stamp of legitimacy on the American West.

Style and Technique

In this highly significant humorous experiment, the author incorporates the traditional form of the tall tale into a story of his own creation. He produces a sort of literary tug-of-war between town and country, provincialism and urbanity. In appropriating this apocryphal frog story for his own purposes, Twain makes numerous changes in its composition. First and foremost, he embellishes the anecdote with a frame, in which he presents the narrator, Mark Twain, who in turn explains his encounter with Simon Wheeler in the mining settlement at Angel's Camp.

The names of the bulldog, Andrew Jackson, and the frog, Daniel Webster, may suggest that Twain was merely indulging in topical political satire. In fact, however, his intention was to mock politicians and lawmakers as a species—an activity in which he gleefully engaged throughout his literary career. Simon Wheeler's tall tale does not attempt to size up recent history. Its content is purely Western in feeling and, as such, is generous in its ready acceptance of the exaggerated and the absurd. In this story, it is the vernacular, not the traditional style of polite speech, that emerges triumphant. The city slicker narrator receives, not teaches, the lesson.

This is not merely the repetition of an oft-told tall tale, redesigned and decked out in a new guise. From the beginning it is made clear that there is no Leonidas W Smiley, especially no Reverend Leonidas W Smiley, and that his existence is mere pretense in order to hear Simon Wheeler elucidate on the past experiences of Jim Smiley. Simon Wheeler's calculated ramblings admirably provide a platform for Twain's subtle and not-so-subtle humor. His literary greatness, in part, emanates from a perpetual malicious shrewdness that he frequently chooses to cloak under an assumed simplicity. His innocence is always pure sham, and the fact that he openly shares this secret with the reader is part of the fun.

Rhona E. Zaid

THE CELESTIAL OMNIBUS

Author: E. M. Forster (1879-1970)
Type of plot: Allegory
Time of plot: The early twentieth century
Locale: "Surbiton," a suburban town outside London
First published: 1911

> *Principal characters:*
>> THE BOY, the protagonist, who is enthusiastic and instinctive in his pursuit of knowledge
>>
>> HIS FATHER AND MOTHER, typical middle-class parents with pretensions to culture
>>
>> MR. BONS, a churchwarden, a candidate for county council, a benefactor of the free library, the head of the literary society, and a pseudointellectual

The Story

E. M. Forster has filled this modern fantasy with wordplay and hidden allusions that allow it to function as an allegory on literary snobbery. The unnamed protagonist, a boy, has begun to discover the joy of literature; untutored, he plunges ahead uncritically and appreciates the popular and the classical with equal enthusiasm. He is, however, spiritually imprisoned in his parents' suburban home in "Surbiton," Agathox Lodge, appropriately a corruption of *agathos*, the Greek word for "good."

The adults who surround the boy merely stifle his curiosity. For example, when he naïvely asks the meaning of the sign that points toward a blind alley but reads "To Heaven," his flustered mother answers that it had been placed there by "naughty young men." She elaborates, though she still does not answer, by adding that one of them wrote verse and was expelled from the university, an oblique reference to Percy Bysshe Shelley. Mr. Bons ("snob" spelled backward), a family friend and frequent guest, wants the adults to know that he has caught the reference, though he does not tell the boy what he wants to know. The boy innocently admits that he has never heard of Shelley, and Mr. Bons is aghast ("no Shelley in the house?"). There are "at least" two Shelleys in the house—not, however, collections of Shelley's poems but rather framed prints, both of which were wedding presents. (Mr. Bons has seven Shelleys.)

Surbiton at sunset has, for the boy, the beauty of an Alpine valley. He is filled with vague stirrings "for something just a little different," and he finds it in a cryptic paper posted on the wall of "the alley to heaven." Shelley had his skylark; the boy has a celestial omnibus, which leaves for Heaven twice daily from that very alley opposite his home.

The boy's journey is a Wagnerian spectacular straight out of *Der Ring des Nibe-*

lungen (1852). The driver (the essayist Sir Thomas Browne) heads upward through lightning and thunder, which synthesize to create a rainbow bridge to Heaven. Color and sound become one for the boy. Sir Thomas Browne and the boy pass the gulf between the real and ideal and hear the song of the Rhinemaidens. The boy does not recognize the music as being from *Das Rheingold* (1852). He knows only that it is very beautiful. His journey is an adventure into the world of literature and art, naïvely but genuinely appreciated. It is also a determined striking out against the boredom and oppression of Agathox Lodge and Surbiton. When he returns home, his father punishes the boy for the disappearance with a sound, middle-class caning and by forcing him to memorize poetry. With typical ignorance, he assigns John Keats's sonnet "To Homer" in praise of the blind poet's ability to see the enchanted world described in the *Odyssey* (c. 725 B.C.E., English translation, 1614). Forster does not explicitly identify the poem, though he has the boy quote its first line: "Standing aloof in great ignorance." The boy's father applies the words to his son; the reader realizes that they more fittingly apply to those such as the father, who would punish joyful discovery and naïve enthusiasm.

Mr. Bons is present at the recitation and perversely curious at the boy's sudden knowledge of literary lore. He determines to "cure" the boy by accompanying him the next evening on his search for the omnibus. Indeed they find it, though the driver this time is not the freethinker Sir Thomas Browne but someone identified explicitly only as "Dan." That the driver is Dante is clear from the emended *Inferno* quotation that is placed above the door of the coach: "*Lasciate ogni baldanza voi che entrate*" ("Abandon all self-importance, you who enter here"). Mr. Bons explains in a voice that "sounded as if he was in church" that "*baldanza*" is obviously a mistake, that it should read "*speranza*" ("hope"). The reader, however, knows that with Mr. Bons in the omnibus, "*baldanza*" is undoubtedly more appropriate.

Mr. Bons corrects the boy's literary errors during the journey. It is wrong for him to prefer Sir Thomas to Dante, Mrs. Gamp (a Charles Dickens character) to Homer, Tom Jones (the protagonist of the Henry Fielding novel) to William Shakespeare. He also lectures the boy on how to behave toward literary immortals. The boy, though he resolves to become "self-conscious, reticent, and prim," cannot resist meeting Achilles, who raises him on his shield. Mr. Bons is frightened out of his wits and wants to return; the boy would remain with Achilles forever.

Great books are the means, not the end, as Dante tells Mr. Bons, who wants to return to his vellum-bound copies of Dante's *La divina commedia* (c. 1320; *The Divine Comedy*, 1802) and his comfortable, secondhand knowledge rather than pursue this actual experience. Mr. Bons tries to escape and return to the world, but he falls through a moonlit rock, no doubt because he does not believe that it exists. The postscript "quotation" from the *Surbiton Times* reporting the discovery of Mr. Bons's mutilated body near "Bermondsey Gas-Works" provides a fittingly ironic death for a "windbag." Because Mr. Bons held both return tickets, the boy is presumably still enjoying life among the immortals.

Themes and Meanings

"The Celestial Omnibus" is one of Forster's earliest works. Though fantasy, it is also one of his most personal. His Cambridge years (1897-1901), which coincided with the end of Queen Victoria's reign, were his period of intellectual awakening. The dons and fellows included Goldsworthy Lowes Dickinson, Roger Fry, G. E. Moore, Bertrand Russell, and Alfred North Whitehead. His fellow undergraduates were John Maynard Keynes, Sir Desmond MacCarthy, Lytton Strachey, and Leonard Woolf. For Dickinson and for his student Forster, Shelley became a "Daedalus," providing the most suitable literary "wings" to escape convention yet never to forget humanity. This credo would ultimately draw Forster to the Bloomsbury group.

Shelley's skylark becomes an omnibus in Forster's story, the vehicle that introduces the boy to a veritable pantheon of great authors, both classical and popular. Significantly, this pantheon is available "to everyone," though only those with an unaffected appreciation of art survive the journey to this literary Valhalla. Finally, the story's theme of self-discovery is as clear as that of Sir James Barrie's play *Peter Pan* (1904) or Lewis Carroll's Alice stories.

Style and Technique

Forster adds wordplay to symbol in "The Celestial Omnibus." Mr. Bons, for example, represents apparent good (bon) only; he is actually pure snob, as his name spelled backward indicates. His poetry is an ornament to be worn, something to be quoted, corrected, or criticized rather than a faith to be held or a trust to be kept. He demands that Dante return him to the world because he has "honoured . . . quoted . . . and bound" him, but Dante replies that he (his works) are the means, not the end. Mr. Bons's death is mere poetic justice.

Though Marxist critics have savaged this story as an escapist response to bourgeois oppression, Forster intended no political implications at the time he wrote it. The socially conscious Forster would emerge in *A Passage to India* (1924) and in the prewar political essays, but "The Celestial Omnibus" is an intelligently written fantasy, filled with the scholarly enthusiasms of a bright young man who has recently come down from Cambridge.

Robert J. Forman

A CHAIN OF LOVE

Author: Reynolds Price (1933-   )
Type of plot: Social realism
Time of plot: The 1950's or 1960's
Locale: Afton, North Carolina, a small town near the border between North Carolina
and Virginia; Raleigh, North Carolina
First published: 1963

Principal characters:
ROSACOKE MUSTIAN, a teenage girl from Afton, North Carolina
HORATIO "RATO" MUSTIAN and
MILO MUSTIAN, her brothers
SISSIE MUSTIAN, Milo's wife
BABY SISTER, Rosacoke's six-year-old sister
MAMA MUSTIAN, Rosacoke's mother
PAPA, Rosacoke's grandfather, Mama's father-in-law
WESLEY BEAVERS, Rosacoke's boyfriend
MR. LEDWELL, a dying hospital patient

The Story

The chain of love to which the title of this story alludes represents the closeness of the Mustian family, three generations of whom live in Afton, North Carolina, on the Virginia-North Carolina border. Papa, a widower, has just celebrated his birthday with appropriate family festivities. The next day he falls sick, and Dr. Sledge decides that he must be hospitalized in Raleigh, an hour's drive away. As is customary among rural southern families, all the kinfolk go to Raleigh for Papa's hospitalization.

Mama, Rosacoke's mother and the widow of Papa's son, cannot stay in Raleigh, as would be expected of her, because she is in charge of Children's Day at the Baptist Church. She must see that responsibility through. She accompanies Papa to Raleigh, bringing with her half a gallon of custard she has made to leave with him. When Papa enters the hospital, he is offered a large corner room for twelve dollars a day, but he decides there is "no use trying the good will of the Blue Cross Hospital Insurance so he took a ten-dollar room standing empty across the hall."

Mama promises to come back on Sunday, after the Children's Day festivities are over, and stay with him until he can go home. Meanwhile, she leaves her daughter Rosacoke and her son Rato to look after Papa for several days.

Rosacoke often goes into the still vacant corner room across the hall to look out the window during her vigil with Papa. From the room she can see a statue of Jesus, head down, hands spread by his sides. The statue is bare-chested and a cloth is draped over its right shoulder. Rosacoke cannot see its face, but she remembers it as a kindly countenance from having seen it when they came into the hospital.

After two days, someone checks into the corner room, a man, later revealed to be Mr. Ledwell. He looks healthy and is able to walk in under his own power, accompanied by his wife and son. Meanwhile, Papa can find out little from the doctors about his own condition, and he tells them little except that he wants to die at home.

The first day Mr. Ledwell is in his room, Rosacoke mistakes his son, who is sitting in the hall, for her boyfriend, Wesley Beavers, and embarrasses herself by saying something inane to the youth, who reacts gracefully. Before long, Rosacoke learns from Snowball, a hospital attendant, that Mr. Ledwell is to undergo surgery for lung cancer and that one lung will have to be removed. The prognosis is bleak.

The next morning, Mr. Ledwell is operated on and at first seems to be doing quite well, but after a few hours, his condition deteriorates and his doctor is called in the middle of the night to come in and use emergency measures to save his life. Mr. Ledwell is resuscitated, and Rosacoke decides that she should go in to visit him and his family and to offer to help them if she can.

She does not want to go in without taking anything for Mr. Ledwell, so she sends a card to her mother asking her to bring some altheas with her when she comes on Sunday to visit Papa. Rosacoke is nervous about visiting Mr. Ledwell but feels it is her duty to do so because he has lived in Raleigh only six months, having moved there from Baltimore, and he has no friends to visit him.

On Sunday, Mama brings the altheas, not knowing what Rosacoke intends to do with them. The whole family has come to spend the day with Papa, whose room, in sharp contrast to Mr. Ledwell's, is filled with people. When things have settled down, Rosacoke puts on some makeup, wraps the altheas, ties a note to them, and knocks softly on the high oak door of Mr. Ledwell's room. There is no answer. She pushes the door gently. The room is dark except for some candies she sees burning. When her eyes adjust, Rosacoke sees that Mr. Ledwell's son is standing at the head of the bed. An old man in black, presumably a priest, is conducting some sort of rite that is foreign to Rosacoke. She suspects that she should not be there, but as she turns to leave, the son sees her and almost smiles. She watches as the dying man is anointed, not knowing the meaning of Extreme Unction but realizing what this sort of service must mean. She leaves her flowers on the chair and goes back to Papa's room to say good-bye before her brother Milo comes by to pick her up and take her home to Afton.

Before Rosacoke goes home, Rato reveals that Mr. Ledwell has died and suggests that they leave the door open a crack so that they can see his body being removed. Rosacoke absolutely rejects this suggestion, and Rato leaves the room, slamming the door behind him.

Themes and Meanings

"A Chain of Love" is a gentle story whose characters are the same people Reynolds Price wrote about in his novels *A Long and Happy Life* (1962) and *A Generous Man* (1966). Essentially, the story is about continuity from generation to generation, about family ties and family closeness. The Mustian family gathers to help Papa through an illness that could be his final one. They are with him as much as they can be.

The Ledwells are quite shadowy people compared with the Mustians, as the reader sees them from Rosacoke's vantage point. She observes them from the shadows. They are unaware that she is observing them, and they never really come to know the sympathy she feels for them. From her standpoint, they are lonely and alienated because they are living as newly arrived strangers in a place where family ties are paramount.

Price never reveals the Ledwells or anyone else in the story from any point of view other than Rosacoke's, and he successfully works within the limitations of this point of view. Rosacoke's innocence and naïveté color everything in the story, and soften the realities substantially. The reader is shown that not all the relatives in Papa's sickroom have Rosacoke's innocence. Milo is planning to duck out of the sick man's room to take his wife to a Chinese dinner and movie. He wears a necktie that lights up in the dark to read, "Kiss Me in the Dark!" Rosacoke, in her innocence, is learning to deal with death, which she has experienced before, but which she is now experiencing for the first time as a somewhat mature person.

Price has Rosacoke ponder questions relating to death. Mr. Ledwell was said to have been clinically dead but his doctor revived him. Rosacoke remembers the time the Phelps boy fell off the dam at Fleming's Mill and almost drowned. He, like Mr. Ledwell, was dead until they revived him. Rosacoke wonders if people who go through that experience know what lies on the other side. She suspects the Phelps boy knows, but he will not tell, saying that what he found out when he was dead for half an hour is between him and Jesus.

Style and Technique

Price has not only managed to capture expertly the speech patterns of people from Warren County, North Carolina, but has also managed to capture in all of its detail the rich fabric of family life in that part of the country. "A Chain of Love" exudes authenticity. If its title is a bit ironic—chains do, after all, bind—the irony is softened because the love is genuine. If the love is also a bit cloying, it seems a small price to pay for the security it offers. The story's dialogue, both overt and internal, is rambling and discursive. It is filled with details, not all of them pertinent. Nevertheless, it is just these qualities that make the dialogue totally believable to anyone who has experienced the part of the country about which Price is writing.

Price presents his characters with considerable skill. In this story, the reader sees almost nothing of Milo's wife, Sissie, yet every word that is spent on her serves to build an unforgettable image of a woman who feels outside the family, who is frustrated at not being accepted more fully, and who is forced into doing things that she does not want to do because the family decrees it. Milo is caught in the middle and tries to humor Sissie. Price stays in total control of his characters by remaining always within the limitations imposed by the point of view he has selected. He provides no information that is not available within his chosen viewpoint. His ability to keep his focus accurate and consistent is noteworthy.

R. Baird Shuman

CHANGE

Author: Larry Woiwode (1941-   )
Type of plot: Domestic realism
Time of plot: 1979
Locale: Chicago
First published: 1980

> *Principal characters:*
> THE HUSBAND
> HIS WIFE
> THEIR EIGHT-YEAR-OLD DAUGHTER
> THEIR INFANT SON
> BOB AND BETTY, their neighbors
> "THE BOYS" of Bob and Betty

The Story

Through recall, Larry Woiwode engages in a discursive examination of two households, particularly the home of the narrator, for a period of about six months, from April to fall.

A glowing doorknob, with its paint and grime removed in the spring, is a reminder to the narrator of the time and energy expended on it before it began to shine "like a miniature burnished sun." With the door swung against the left end of the table at which he is now sitting and "walling" him in "somewhat on one open side," the knob still shines "above the edge" of his vision in the room in a ramshackle apartment house.

It is fall now, and the narrator is at work on transcribing notes that—or so he believes at times—will be an "indisputable proof of the existence of God." These notes range over a thirteen-year period during which he has had "different opinions or interpretations of their meaning during different recastings of them." He especially desires to leave the events, not of his making, free of "subjective coloring." This new work is a "stock-taking interim."

Now "walled-in" at the table, the narrator begins to recall the effects of bolts of lightning striking twice at the apartment house. Following the first bolt, he recalls, he simply sat at the table, feeling guilty about not being able to get at the work he set for himself. Picking up a glossy magazine, he read an article on guerrilla warfare in Palestine. The account of the violence and of bystanders being injured by bombs merely sharpened the guilt he does not wish to examine.

The next bolt came within a matter of months; a week or two later, he saw a troubling cartoon in the same glossy magazine: "a pair of angels on a cloud, looking over its edge, one of them with a bunch of jagged cartoon thunderbolts under an arm, and had a caption that went something like 'Get him again!'" The bolts meant external change, at least for the "upper limbs" of the oak tree in his yard.

In the time covered by these recollections, the narrator's wife gave birth to their first son "right there in the apartment house." Soon, the baby son changes from an "indrawn center of internal listening" to a freer human being, grasping and grabbing at objects. Then, he begins to laugh, freely and heartily, especially when he plays "games" with his parents and eight-year-old sister. What is particularly thrilling is the happy occasion when the family is together in the same room and his mother lifts him up to the mirror, in which he sees the various angles from which he can view the family. When the sister gives the child a playful scare, he bursts out in such laughter that the father is amazed, unable to believe that a child of his can laugh with such "seizure of freedom."

The daughter, too, can shriek with hilarity, particularly at the father and the baby having one of "their talks," but she can change from apparent happiness to what seems to be jealousy as she silently observes in a detached manner her little brother as though each were in an "isolated room."

The work and play of most members of the household mount. The mother moves from chore to chore every hour of the day. The daughter is transformed when she pretends to be an adult, replacing her own clothes with the clothing of her mother and father. The parents know that there will be another change: Someday they will be abandoned, just as the clothes are: "seldom picked up, left lying where they have been discarded." There is yet another change that come with these foreshadowings of adolescence: At times there is a "pained evasiveness" about the daughter that causes the narrator to think of "the boys" next door.

These three boys are reminders of "the unendingness of violence." Whether they throw eggs or tomatoes at their neighbors' windows or dirt at their daughter, set the walls of the garage on fire, or beat up one another, one of their chief characteristics is violence. The father of the boys is "a huge, unsmiling man" with a flattop; conjecturing that the man saw action in Korea, the narrator pauses in his musings to wonder how many of the men he passes on the street have been trained to kill.

The narrator's family closes itself in and keeps to itself. They study with a pastor, attend a Reformed and Presbyterian chapel, make public confession of Christ, and have their son baptized. They pray, in general, for the other family, but they also begin to ignore it.

One night, the disturbed mother of the boys phones her neighbors and urges the narrator to check on "what those kids are up to" down in his basement. The phone call is an implicit admission that the boys are out of control; it is also, more fundamentally, a cry for help, to which the narrator does not respond. The woman's husband leaves her soon after, only to return a "few nights later"—at the request of a social worker and the police—"to settle some matters." While he is there, Betty, the distressed woman, attempts to cut her wrists.

Another change comes. The mother is in a hospital under psychiatric care; the father comes back to live with the boys. The narrator tries to visit the woman, but only family can see her. He gives the boys a copy of the Gospel of John to give her, and intends to mention "the gift of Christ and the grace of God" but is unable to follow his intentions. Finally, the boys move away, and a bulldozer levels the old house next door, bringing yet another change. A parking lot begins to take shape.

It is now cool again. The thermostat needs adjusting, but the narrator desires no change in his position in order to make the adjustment. After all, he must not move until "a certain amount of work is fixed" in his files "for good."

The doorknob still glows, mirroring the narrator. He sees as he looks up at it "a meditative kingbolt," and he asks the question: "Which side do you open a door from if the door's never really closed, but more a wall that holds you inward?" The season has changed from spring to fall, and there are no fingerprints on the glowing knob.

Themes and Meanings

"Change" is a complex, penetrating vision of the complicated modern human being who hardly knows his own identity. The modern man in "Change" can participate to some extent in the joyous discoveries of his family, especially the baby boy who soon rises "from that indrawn center of internal listening" and lives and laughs without inhibitions. The narrator walls himself in and finds difficulty in knowing who he is and what he is to do.

Amid all the changes about him, he observes others busy with their own lives, apparently having found their exact niche, but he is unable to establish his place. Others work with purpose; he always intends to do something. What to do with his work, his faith, and his relation to others are problems for the narrator—this modern human being.

Modern human beings see the hopeful and positive; they also see the painful and negative, but what they are to be or to do in the midst of a confused world is almost impossible to know.

Perhaps there is also an expressed concern for the artist in this short story. What must the artist do in a world in which there is violence on all levels? How can he do his work as an artist in such circumstances? Does the artist have a responsibility to fulfill to a disturbed and violent world in ways other than through his writing?

Style and Technique

Woiwode's style captures the flow of human thought as it merges past and present and, at the same time, captures the perplexity of modern humanity. The involuted sentences combined with the steady unraveling of the story relentlessly pull the reader into the writer's world. The musings and realities fuse in a way that disallows any neat allegorical pattern or any easily determined point. Woiwode's style, however, is never obscure; it is clear and direct. His images express his intensely personal and ambiguous response to a world that is equally ambiguous. The style makes real the intangible inner life of a sensitive human being by capturing the nuances, intricacies, and complexities of humankind's inner existence. Indeed, Woiwode's style demands neither more nor less than what every excellent writer deserves: complete concentration.

E. Beatrice Batson

CHARLES

Author: Shirley Jackson (1919-1965)
Type of plot: Domestic realism
Time of plot: The mid-twentieth century
Locale: Bennington, Vermont
First published: 1948

Principal characters:
LAURIE HYMAN, a kindergarten student
THE NARRATOR, her mother
HER FATHER

The Story

The narrator tells the story of Laurie's first month at kindergarten. Laurie comes home each day to report on the doings of a fellow student, Charles, who behaves in an extraordinary manner. For the first two weeks, Charles is spanked or otherwise punished almost daily for being "fresh," for hitting or kicking the teachers, for injuring fellow students, and for a host of proscribed activities. Charles proves so interesting to the kindergarten class that whenever he is punished, all the students watch him; whenever he stays after school, all the students stay with him.

As a result of this behavior, Charles becomes an institution at the Hyman house. Whenever anyone does anything bad, inconsiderate, or clumsy, he or she is compared to Charles. During the third week, however, Charles undergoes a conversion. For several days, he becomes a model student, the teacher's helper. Reports of this transformation astonish the Hyman household. Then, Charles seems to return to normal, first persuading a girl to say a terrible word twice, for which her mouth is washed out with soap. The next day, Charles himself says the word several times and receives several washings.

When the day of the monthly Parent Teacher Association meeting arrives, Laurie's mother is anxious to go and to meet the mother of the remarkable Charles. At the meeting, she learns from Laurie's teacher not only that Laurie has had some difficulty adjusting to kindergarten, but also that there is no student named Charles in her class.

Themes and Meanings

After "The Lottery," "Charles" may be Shirley Jackson's best-known short story and is often anthologized for young readers. The story's appeal seems to derive more from the irony of its surprise ending and from its humor than from any very significant thematic content. One interesting thematic aspect of the tale, however, emerges from considering the significance of Laurie's creation and characterization of Charles.

The narrator reflects, as she sends Laurie off to his first day at kindergarten, that in his change of dress from corduroy overalls with bibs to blue jeans and a belt, he has been transformed from an innocent tot into "a swaggering character who forgot to stop at the corner and wave goodbye to me." One can see Laurie as beginning the discovery of his identity. At school, he tries various modes of self-construction and self-assertion. Although his stories about Charles protect him from parental wrath, they also reveal that he naturally conceives of his self as a fictional construct over which he has considerable power. The Charles he creates is also a person who can create himself, who can be extremely "bad" one day and extremely "good" the next, as he chooses.

Part of the interest of this thematic aspect of the tale is that an interest in how the self is constructed pervades Jackson's fiction, and is often near the thematic center in her horror novels and stories.

Style and Technique

"Charles" is a short sketch, originally published in *Mademoiselle* and eventually incorporated into Jackson's fictionalized memoirs of family life in Bennington, Vermont, *Life Among the Savages* (1953).

In *Shirley Jackson* (1975), Lenemaja Friedman points out that when the real Laurie Hyman went to kindergarten, there actually was a boy there who performed several of the exploits that the fictional Laurie attributes to the fictional Charles. Altering this fact enhances the dramatic and thematic effects of "Charles." The surprise discovery that Charles is Laurie's fiction produces irony, the realization that all along the story has been meaning something other than what it has been saying. What it has been meaning becomes more interesting as well, for depths of complexity become visible in the child's character. One result is a kind of wonder at the fiction-making powers that all people possess.

Terry Heller

CHARLOTTE

Author: Tony Earley (1961-   )
Type of plot: Realism
Time of plot: The early 1990's
Locale: Charlotte, North Carolina
First published: 1993

> *Principal characters:*
> THE NARRATOR, a manager at P. J. O'Mulligan's bar and grill
> STARLA, his girlfriend
> LORD POETRY,
> BOB NOXIOUS, and
> ROCKIN' ROBBIE FRAZIER, professional wrestlers
> DARLING DONNIS, Lord Poetry's sweetheart

The Story

"Charlotte" is told in the first person by an unnamed narrator who interweaves the story of a contest of strength and wills between two professional wrestlers for the affection of a woman with his own attempts to win an acknowledgment of the power and even existence of love from his girlfriend, Starla. At the same time, he ponders the nature of the city of Charlotte, North Carolina, itself. He begins by describing how Charlotte has changed. Once a city ruled by its allegiance to professional wrestling, the city is now obsessed with its new professional basketball team, the Hornets. Instead of seeing men in tight pants with giant biceps, strange haircuts, snakeskin boots, and thick gold chains, the city's residents see tall graceful men who seem alien to them. Frannie Belk, owner of the Southeastern Wrestling Alliance, has sold the franchise to cable television magnate Ted Turner, and the wrestlers have relocated to Atlanta, Georgia.

At various times throughout his story, the narrator digresses to focus on the character of the city of Charlotte; everyone who now lives in Charlotte, he says, was originally from somewhere else. They have all flocked to the big city to remake their lives over into something wonderful, something sublime, but they all inevitably meet with disappointment. Rather than the city of dreams, as the narrator points out, Charlotte is a city that once housed a crooked television evangelist who fleeced his flock out of millions of dollars. Somehow, the people of Charlotte have lost sight of the things in life that truly matter and make the mistake of buying into the false glitter of the skyline of Charlotte and the decorations of bars like P. J. O'Mulligan's.

Against this canvas, the narrator, a manager at P. J. O'Mulligan's, tells the story of his love for Starla. He has tried constantly to make her acknowledge the fact that she loves him, but she does so only grudgingly and only after harsh and almost violent bouts of sex. She tells him over and over that all they have together and all that truly exists between men and women is sex; love in itself is mythical, nonexistent, a ruse intended to keep lovers from sleeping around. She tells the narrator that he should be satisfied with their sexual relationship, yet he wants more.

Juxtaposed against the story of the narrator and Starla is the recounting of the battle between professional wrestlers Lord Poetry and Bob Noxious for the affections of the so-called sweetheart of the wrestling alliance, Darling Donnis. Lord Poetry is aligned with the forces of "good" in the wrestling world and has often been almost defeated by the "evil" Bob Noxious's misdeeds in the ring, as when he struck Lord Poetry with a folding chair while the referee's back was turned. Although Darling Donnis seems to love Lord Poetry in her heart, she is fascinated on a different level by Bob Noxious's animal physicality. In several of their earlier battles, Noxious knocked Lord Poetry down and started flexing his pectoral muscles, the quivering of his chest almost hypnotizing Darling Donnis. Each time this happened, Lord Poetry's ally Rockin' Robbie Frazier brought Lord Poetry's book of poetry to him; each time, the wrestler read a poem that swayed Darling Donnis's heart and brought her back to him.

Lord Poetry and Bob Noxious have one last showdown in the wrestling alliance's finale before the wrestlers are to be relocated. A few days before the fight, while visiting P. J. O'Mulligan's, Lord Poetry shares a poem he has memorized, part of "Adam's Curse" (1902) by Irish poet William Butler Yeats. The poem at least partly hints at the futility of love, a sentiment shared in a less wistful sense a few days later by Starla as she roots and screams for Bob Noxious to destroy Lord Poetry and all for which he hopes to stand. The wrestlers grapple, each grasping the other man's throat; finally at an impasse, Bob Noxious breaks free and again begins to make his pectoral muscles quiver for Darling Donnis. As before, Rockin' Robbie Frazier comes to Lord Poetry's aid with the book of poems. Lord Poetry tries to break the spell over Donnis by reading a William Shakespeare sonnet and is even aided by the announcer, Big Bill Boscoe, but to no avail. Bob Noxious takes Darling Donnis by the shoulders, claiming her for his own, as Starla takes her seat in triumph.

Themes and Meanings

"Charlotte" is a deceptively complex story, weaving several themes together so seamlessly that they seem to be various parts of the same tapestry. The narrator makes clear from the start of the story that the wrestlers are not just a flashy form of *nouveau* aristocracy: With their exotic names, strange powers, and alliances with the forces of good or evil, they are a kind of pantheon of mythological gods to the people of Charlotte. Just as the travails of Olympic gods such as Zeus, Apollo, Hera, Aphrodite, and Athena once served to reflect the internal struggles of mortals in ancient Greece, the modern gods of the Southeastern Wrestling Alliance—the Hidden Pagans, Paolo the Peruvian, the Sheik of the East and his Harem of Three, as well as Lord Poetry and Bob Noxious—play out moral conflicts for their followers.

On one level, the story states clearly that Lord Poetry and his allies represent "good" just as Bob Noxious and his allies represent "evil." At the same time, good and evil as such are broadly construed in the story. The dichotomy between good and evil in "Charlotte" represents, also, the dichotomy between the soul and the body, the spiritual, angelic side of humans as opposed to the physical, bestial part of humans. Correspondingly, love is aligned with good, from the narrator's perspective, just as lust is aligned with evil.

For the narrator, this struggle also incorporates the distinction between what is true, important, and lasting in life versus what is ephemeral, fleeting, transitory, and artificial. To the narrator, lust is temporary, and love is eternal. Starla's refusal to commit her soul as well as her body to the narrator signifies to him that their relationship is fated to be short-lived. Bob Noxious's triumph over Lord Poetry is the triumph of lust over love and further symbolizes Starla's win over the narrator; she will not have to commit to anything beyond a certain revelry in her physical relationship.

Similarly, all the newcomers who look for happiness in Charlotte are fooling themselves about what is really important, just as they are fooled by the false Tiffany lampshades, replicated soda and beer signs, and plastic ferns at P. J. O'Mulligan's. The failure of love, truth, and good in general are indicated at the very beginning of the story by the fact that the wrestlers have left and have been replaced by a National Basketball Association team; the battle between good and evil has become such a foregone conclusion that it does not even need to be fought anymore.

Style and Technique

"Charlotte" makes use of a complicated plan of organization; the story begins with an examination of present-day Charlotte, then leaps back to the time when the wrestlers still lived in Charlotte. Within the retrospection that makes up most of the story, the narrator moves back and forth from discussion of the wrestling scene in Charlotte in general to the specific events of the final battle, all the while discussing the nature of the city as well as his relationship with Starla.

One of the more interesting approaches taken by the story is that the narrator never questions the truthfulness or validity of the combat between professional wrestlers. Although most professional wrestlers call themselves "entertainers" as much as they do "athletes," the artifice of the "sport" is never truly examined. At the same time, the narrator does point out that the referee never seems to notice when a combatant cheats in some way such as wielding a folding chair. He never follows this thread to its logical conclusion, however, and for the narrator's purposes, Lord Poetry and Bob Noxious truly are arch-rivals in pitched combat over Darling Donnis.

"Charlotte" demonstrates the literary style common to many of the stories in *Here We Are in Paradise* (1994), Tony Earley's debut collection of short fiction. The narrative introduces a fairly absurd or comic situation—in this case, a battle for true love being fought by professional wrestlers, including one who reads and recites poetry—and uses it as a metaphor to render a poignant, heartfelt discussion on some aspect of the human experience. He juxtaposes lyrical descriptions with observations of eccentricities. Earley's style later gravitates to a sparser, simpler style of prose, as exhibited in his novel *Jim the Boy* (2000).

Scott Yarbrough

THE CHASER

Author: John Collier (1901-1980)
Type of plot: Horror
Time of plot: About 1940
Locale: New York City
First published: 1951

> *Principal characters:*
> ALAN AUSTEN, a young man who is very much in love
> AN OLD MAN, a dealer in magical potions

The Story

Alan Austen, a young man who is passionately in love with a young woman who is indifferent to him, comes to the establishment of a mysterious old man who deals in magic potions. Austen has been told that he can buy a potion that will make the object of his affections fall madly in love with him. The old man shows little interest in the financial profit to be gained from selling Alan a love potion. Instead, he devotes most of his sales talk to recommending a potion that he calls a spot remover or a life cleaner, a powerful poison that is undetectable in an autopsy. Without ever saying so directly, the old man is suggesting that the time will inevitably come when Alan will want to murder the woman whom he now loves so desperately.

The potent poison costs five thousand dollars for a single teaspoonful, and the love potion costs just one dollar. Alan cannot believe his good fortune. He seeks the old man's assurance that the love potion will be effective. The old man ruefully assures him that it will make the woman fall so completely in love that she will cling to Alan and make him her sole interest in life.

After their marriage, the young woman will want to know everything that Alan is thinking, everything that he has done when he was away from her, and everything that he intends to do when he leaves again. She will demand all his attention. She will be insanely jealous. The reader gradually gets the picture of a suffocating relationship that would drive anyone to distraction, even to thoughts of murder. This is not the picture that Alan visualizes, however, because he is held so tightly in the grip of passion that he can think of no greater happiness than to be in the company of his loved one perpetually.

Alan finally purchases the vial of love potion for one dollar. The old man assures him that he only deals in such potions to establish customer relations. People who want love potions are invariably young and have little money. Later in life, when they are more affluent, they will come back to him to buy his real moneymaker, the tasteless, undetectable poison that will rid them of the hated, clinging, sexually unappealing, aging spouse.

Alan seizes the vial, thanks the old man enthusiastically, and says, "Good-bye." The old man replies, *"Au revoir,"* a French phrase that might be translated into English as, "I'll be seeing you."

Themes and Meanings

John Collier's message in "The Chaser" is clear, although he never states it in words: Love is only a temporary illusion. People fall in love and believe it will last forever. While they are in the grip of this illusion, they will do anything to obtain possession of the loved one. Once the illusion has dissipated and grim reality has intruded, the former ardent lover realizes that he or she has tied himself or herself for life to a stranger who may be totally incompatible, and who does not fulfill all the wonderful expectations the illusion of love initially created. At that point the lover has two choices: either to remain in a loveless relationship and live a life of pretense or to find some means of obtaining freedom.

In "The Chaser," the old man emphasizes the fact that the young man's loved one will cling to him so tenaciously that he may have to use drastic means to free himself from her clutches. She will make herself disagreeable by demanding all his time and attention. Because the price of the love potion is so cheap and the price of the chaser, the vial of undetectable poison, so exorbitant, Collier implies that it is easy to fall in love and to get married, but very difficult to extricate oneself from such a legally, socially, and morally binding relationship after discovering that marriage is often monotonous, expensive, overly demanding, and sexually unsatisfying.

Collier was cynical about human beings in general and wrote several stories in which a husband kills his wife. A good example is his "De Mortuis" (1951), in which an unworldly middle-aged man, who finds out that the beautiful young woman he married is notorious as the town slut, decides to murder her and bury her body in the basement. Many of Collier's short stories deal with human wickedness. He exposes both his male and female characters as being greedy, selfish, dishonest, immoral, and sadistic. In fact, it might be said that Collier's dominant theme was human depravity. His misanthropy and pessimism would have prevented him from becoming a popular writer if he had not had the wisdom to leaven his stories with humor.

Collier resembles Ambrose Bierce, whose *The Devil's Dictionary* (1906) cynically defines marriage as "The state or condition of a community consisting of a master, a mistress and two slaves, making in all, two," and love as "A temporary insanity curable by marriage or the removal of the patient from the influences under which he incurred the disorder." Collier would certainly have agreed with these definitions, as well as with most of the other definitions in Bierce's bitterly cynical book. Like Bierce, Collier made his grim philosophy palatable to the average reader by sprinkling his stories with humor, a humor that was often based on the contrast between fact and fantasy, between expectation and outcome, between illusion and reality. Like most humorists, he had a great deal of melancholy in his temperament. His humor is laughter in the dark.

Style and Technique

In this exceptionally short work, Collier uses a strictly objective technique. He briefly describes the two characters and the setting in the opening paragraphs, then lets his characters tell the story almost entirely through their dialogue. This technique is perfect for the author's purposes, because he wants his message to dawn on the reader without his having to spell it out. It is interesting to observe how Collier displays his technical virtuosity by suggesting the debilitating effects of long years of married life while respecting the classic Aristotelian unities of time, place, and action.

The entire story unfolds in only a few minutes and is confined to a simple setting. It contains only two characters, and these two are sharply contrasted so that it is easy to visualize both and to imagine how their voices sound. One is young, the other old. One is idealistic, the other realistic. The young man is governed by his passions; the old man has been disillusioned by long years of living and is governed by the cold light of reason. The young man is interested in love; the old man is only interested in money. The young man has his whole life ahead of him but acts as if he is pressed for time; the old man obviously is at the end of his life but acts as if he has all the time in the world.

Collier often wrote unrealistic stories with realistic settings. He was noted for putting his genii, jinns, sibyls, demons, and ghosts in contemporary Manhattan and London apartments. The old man in "The Chaser" is a mystical character who belongs in a medieval folktale. What is he doing in twentieth century New York? Characteristically, Collier does not bother to explain how this sorcerer ended up here. Collier did not expect most of his stories to be taken seriously. This paradoxical element contributed to the quixotic humor to be found in most of his fiction.

Collier's style is light, witty, whimsical, playful. He plays with literary conventions, and his fiction is full of literary allusions, hints of connoisseurship, sophisticated dialogue, and French words and phrases. He invariably sounds cultured, worldly, and well educated. He was born in England and had the tastes and values of an English country gentleman. He often has been compared to writers such as Noël Coward, P. G. Wodehouse, and W. Somerset Maugham, all of whom wrote about upper-class people who were far more interested in manners and money than morals. The world they wrote about was at its zenith in the first quarter of the twentieth century. The Great Depression and World War II had a sobering effect on the tastes of American and European readers, and Collier, along with many other sophisticated writers, experienced a sharp decline in popularity as a result.

Bill Delaney

CHEAP IN AUGUST

Author: Graham Greene (1904-1991)
Type of plot: Wit and humor
Time of plot: The 1960's
Locale: Kingston, Jamaica
First published: 1967

> *Principal characters:*
> MARY WATSON, the protagonist, in Jamaica on an inexpensive
> month's holiday
> HENRY HICKSLAUGHTER, in his seventies, who picks up Mary
> Watson

The Story

Mary Watson, an Englishwoman married to an American university professor who is in Europe to complete a study of the eighteenth century poet James Thomson, decides to take an inexpensive month's holiday in Jamaica during the off-season. She has written her husband that an old friend from England has insisted that she accompany her on the holiday, but she has in fact gone off alone. The off-season rates explain the story's title on its simplest level.

In the first days of her holiday, yearning for a brief affair to give her life a fillip before she enters her forties, Mary is put off by the oversized St. Louis matrons who, in hair rollers and Bermuda shorts, attempt to befriend her. As she sits and dines alone on red snapper and tomatoes, she begins to review her marriage and her life as a Connecticut faculty wife. At thirty-nine she feels ready for an affair, in part as a refuge from the staleness of her marriage to a kindly although pedantic husband who is as faithful to his scholarship as he is to her, in part as a refuge from the tedium of a university community. In the off-season, however, there are few eligible men, and Mary, alone, moves into an assessment of her sexual, social, and, although she does not know this, spiritual roles.

She knows that she is by no means unhappy with either her marriage or her position—the marriage has, the reader infers, produced no children—yet she yearns for an experience that will provide her life with a restorative perspective. She hopes, too, that her husband will have such an experience, but she is fairly certain from the tenor of his daily letters to her that no such adventure is possible for him.

One morning, while sunning by the hotel pool, she observes a bald, fat man in his seventies who introduces himself to her as Henry Hickslaughter. She is amused by his "pick-up," then intrigued by his disappointed look; she glimpses a tousled child within his gross form. She is pleased when he tells her that he has been observing her for several days, and she learns that their rooms are only a few doors apart. They share a table at dinner, and Hickslaughter invites Mary to have drinks with him in his room. She begins to understand that he, too, is taking advantage of the off-season rates and is further intrigued by his old-pirate demeanor.

Ostensibly looking for a maid to give her a carafe of ice water, Mary goes into Hickslaughter's room, where she has very recently seen the maid. She reads a vaguely threatening letter that Hickslaughter has written to his brother asking for money. Hickslaughter finds her in his room, asks her to have drinks with him that evening, and she agrees. She returns later to find that he has been crying. Years ago she had seen her husband cry when his volume of essays had been refused by a university press. "I'm afraid of dying, with nobody around, in the dark," Hickslaughter says to her. Moved by his fear, his loneliness, his attempt to stave off the unknown, his failure at life, Mary spends the night with the frightened old man whom she almost loves. Later, when she remembers the affair, she wonders what they had in common, except for the fact that they shared a cheap Jamaican holiday.

Themes and Meanings

Very little happens by way of action in "Cheap in August": A woman has a brief affair with a fat, old, and lonely man. However, the texture of a human life is revealed in all of its complexities, of fear and loneliness, of courage and compassion, of truth and beauty. It is the subtext of the tale that reveals its essential truth—that connection with others is what gives life whatever meaning it possesses.

In his introduction to his *Collected Stories* (1972), Graham Greene explains that the notion for the story came to him in Kingston, Jamaica, in August of 1963. He included it in his collection entitled *May We Borrow Your Husband? and Other Comedies of the Sexual Life* (1967): "I sat over my red snapper and tomatoes watching the monstrous Bermuda shorts worn by fat parties from St. Louis, and wondered, as my character did, what possible pick-up [sic] were possible in this out-of-season hotel." Mary Watson's emotion of tenderness for the gross old man who picks her up fulfills her need for human connection, as she does his. Felt emotion is infinitely more conducive to meaning than action described or spoken dialogue. Perhaps the ultimate meaning of the story can be discovered in the word "cheap," which etymologically once meant "trade" or "bargain." Mary Watson and Henry Hickslaughter do strike a bargain, one that confirms their humanity as it staves off, for a brief moment, the certainty of death. The pun on the surname of Henry Hickslaughter becomes equally significant.

Style and Technique

If sadness is the overarching tone of "Cheap in August," then the farcical coming together of two seemingly mismatched people undercuts the sadness to give the tale its bittersweet quality. What the story does best, by means of subtle authorial suggestions, is to reveal the reality of pain behind a comic facade. That Greene has included the story in his collection of comedies dealing with sexual experience indicates that the grotesqueness of an old man still yearning for sex and the romantic sentimentalism of a woman seeking confirmation of her attractiveness are to be seen as one more turn in the comic ronde that life presents to the careful onlooker. The presence of the narrator is felt strongly in the story's subtext as he directs his reader to an awareness of how simple emotion can overwhelm one and dignify life. The story achieves, as a result, a tragicomic resonance that links it to the stories and dramas of Anton Chekhov. What the reader feels as he reads through the events of the narrative is what William Wordsworth called "the still, sad music of humanity."

Mary and Hickslaughter's affair is ultimately life enhancing as it comments on the temporality of life through the spiritual quality of a compassionate experience; it provides the reader with an insight into what it means to verify one's humanity through the sexual act.

A. A. DeVitis

CHECK!

Author: Sławomir Mrożek (1930-   )
Type of plot: Fable
Time of plot: Around the 1960's
Locale: Courtyard of an old palace, presumably in Poland
First published: "Szach," 1962 (English translation, 1968)

Principal characters:
>THE NARRATOR, an unemployed man who substitutes for a piece
>in a game of living chess
>THE REGULAR WHITE BISHOP, his ill friend
>THE WHITE KNIGHT, a chess piece who gives advice
>THE BLACK ROOK, the jingoist who wants to win

The Story

Two friends who have in the past worked together at trivial jobs meet on a day when a storm threatens. Complaining about his various physical ailments that will worsen if he is caught in a storm, the man who has been working regularly as a piece in living chess games asks the narrator to substitute for him. He describes the life-sized chess game as a public spectacle in which people dressed as pieces move about on a great outdoor board controlled by players sitting on elevated platforms. He regards it as a relatively easy way to make money—so long as the weather cooperates, which it rarely does. The people serving as chess pieces are not volunteer chess aficionados—who tend to quit when they dislike how the game is going—but disinterested people who are paid for doing a job. The narrator's friend has worked his way up to playing the white Bishop, for which he gets more money and does more work than the pawns. The narrator agrees to fill in for his friend when the latter assures him that the chess match is just the private sport of two old men and that the white Knight will give him practical advice.

When the narrator arrives at the courtyard, he is put off by its ominous and gloomy atmosphere, the pathetic tattered shoes that the chess pieces are wearing beneath their monstrous papier-mâché cardboard costumes, and by the threats of a black Rook. Nevertheless, he locates the white Knight, who shows him how to dress, how to smoke and eat surreptitiously, and how to exploit the stratified system.

It does not take the new Bishop long to realize that the two old chess players controlling the game are incompetent. The Knight confirms his fears that the game has neither rhyme nor reason, telling him that the two senile players sometimes even leave the pieces out overnight. After the Bishop has been moved about randomly for some time, it begins to rain and gradually intensifies. During the long intervals between moves, the Knight warns the Bishop about the cruel, heavily booted black Rook, who will do anything to win.

Eventually the white Bishop can endure the tedious game no longer. Not caring whether white wins or loses, but keeping out of the black Rook's way, he decides to cheat so that a King can be checkmated. Although he captures the drunk black Bishop and two pawns, he discovers that the balance of the game has not changed. Someone on the other side must be cheating as well: It is the black Rook, who is now openly kicking white pieces. The Knight sees what is happening but cannot help the Bishop for fear of jeopardizing his own job and leaves after being captured by the Rook.

When only the two Kings, the black Rook, and the white Bishop are left, cheating is no longer possible. The Bishop tries to reason with the Rook that because the game is obviously a draw, they should all go home, but the Rook refuses to listen. Fearing that the Rook will injure the white King, the Bishop stealthily steers the sleepy old man off the board, with angry cries of "Check!" rising over the storm. When they near the gate, the Rook closes in on them, but inspired by fear, the Bishop takes off their cardboard costumes, throws them as far as possible, and hides. As the Rook repeatedly stabs the sodden costumes, the Bishop and the King walk out of the courtyard.

Themes and Meanings

None of the characters in Sławomir Mrożek's allegory have real names, yet their positions on the giant chessboard provide clues to what their lives may mean. The narrator, who substitutes as the white Bishop, is a basically decent man, trying to eke out a living at a series of insignificant jobs. Like his hypochondriac friend, he is only a human who must live, so he hopes for as pleasant a job as possible even though he is at the mercy of changing circumstances. Human chess pieces who care about the game do not last long; only the regulars who work for pay survive long. Their workplace, like chess, is not an egalitarian structure. With time and effort, some can rise in status, even if their lack of intrinsic value is betrayed by the vulgarity of their papier-mâché costumes and the shabbiness of their footwear. Even more important, might makes right in this society. The black Rook is reincarnated in all levels of society, from schoolyard bullies to totalitarian rulers. Nameless individuals can survive in such settings but rarely with their dignity intact, as seen by the demeaning tricks they must perform just to eat and smoke. Even the dignity that might come from helping fellow humans is corrupted by a system that encourages its playing pieces merely to go along. The Knight sympathizes with the Bishop's plans but does not want to jeopardize his job. In the end, the Bishop outwits the evil Rook; spurred by fear and cunning, he escapes from the game. He earns his dignity by initiative alone.

On the cosmic rather than the political scale, the chess game takes place in a closed universe under the control of a God who is worse than absent; he is incompetent. The senile chess players cannot even see the logical plays, much less the beneficial ones. They might be seen as representing a dualism of equally balanced good and evil, but that seems unlikely in a chess game in which there is no inherent rightness to one side or the other. Rather, together the players symbolize a world in which any deity that may exist is neither good nor powerful. Because God is evil and weak, humans must figure out how to survive on their own, at odds with him as well as the world. Neither rationality nor altruism is an effective guide to living in this gloomy courtyard of a universe in which "clever architecture had joined space to enclosure." With physical and moral freedom only an illusion, humanity is trapped by an absurd cosmic chaos. Decent people cannot count on the "happy accident" of chance. In this world in which the absence of good creates a vacuum, cruel rooks can rush in to take control. The reader must even question the ultimate fate of the escapees. Perhaps on a political level, fear and cleverness can create an escape route, but cosmically, what lies outside the chess game? The weather and the jobs are just as bad out there; prior to joining the game, the substitute had been demeaned by showing the theater spectators his boil. There is no place that protects human freedom and dignity.

Style and Technique

Mrożek is primarily known as a playwright in Poland's post-World War II avant-garde tradition, but throughout his literary career he has produced numerous short stories and cartoon collections. "Check!" is a prime example of his typically allegorical approach to literature in which, as his biographer remarked, his "characters are symbolic representation while situations illustrate theses."

On a strictly literal level, "Check!" makes sense. The narrative has a clear beginning, middle, and end. Mrożek's plain verbal style reinforces the simplicity of his plot. The words themselves make inherent sense at the surface level. The reader knows what is happening—because the words reveal it in reportorial fashion—when the Bishop is recruited, when he dresses, receives instructions, tries to cheat and outwit the Rook, and when he and the King make their escape.

Though simple, Mrożek's language is also vivid and visual. For example, in describing the chess pieces the narrator says: "Only their feet, protruding from under the fantastic dress, remained normal, shod in a variety of old shoes. Above them necks and heads of horses, their teeth bared, each tooth the size of a tile, the severe-looking, geometric and crenelated Rooks, and saucer-like ruffs of the bishops." It is this juxtaposition of "reality" and grotesque images that, as Martin Esslin, writing about the Theater of the Absurd, claims, allowed East European playwrights to produce something of significance without being censored. Additionally, the characters in "Check!" as in Mrożek's other short stories collected for *The Ugupu Bird* (1968), are anonymous. Each chess piece is an Everyman trapped in a dangerous closed society, and by extension, Everyman trapped in the modern world.

The absurdity arises, therefore, from the situations that Mrożek describes so visually. The event reported is not the puzzle. "What does this mean?" is instead the puzzle. The ordinariness of the language highlights the seriousness of the fable's "moral." The elements of the logical plot, anonymous characters, and matter-of-fact tone combine to produce both a biting satire and tragic fable about the human condition in a world where people would have been better off if God had been dead because he is doing such a dreadful job of running the universe. If only life were a chess game!

Barbara J. Hampton

THE CHEMIST'S WIFE

Author: Anton Chekhov (1860-1904)
Type of plot: Realism
Time of plot: The nineteenth century
Locale: A small town in Russia
First published: "Aptekarsha," 1886 (English translation, 1916)

> *Principal characters:*
> TCHERNOMORDIK, a chemist in the town of B——
> MME TCHERNOMORDIK, the chemist's wife
> OBTYOSOV, a thin officer
> THE DOCTOR, another officer, "the big one"

The Story

"The Chemist's Wife" is told in the third person through the consciousness of the title character. The main action of the story occurs within the mind and the emotions of the chemist's wife, who progresses from sleeplessness and boredom to the realization that she is truly unhappy. As in so many Anton Chekhov stories, there is very little external action; the action that is attempted is thwarted.

The story begins late at night, near dawn, in a little Russian town. The chemist is snoring contentedly, in a sleep so deep that nothing could awaken him, certainly not the restlessness of his young wife. Mme Tchernomordik cannot sleep; she does not know why. She feels close to tears; she does not know why.

Just at daybreak two officers appear, talking casually as they pass the chemist's shop. Mme Tchernomordik hears them speculating as to whether she loves her husband and imagining how she looks in bed. On impulse, Obtyosov suggests that they ring the chemist's bell and make a purchase; perhaps, he says, they will see the wife.

Now the mood of the chemist's wife changes. She puts on a dress and hurries to admit the officers, who buy some lozenges. During brief conversation, Mme Tchernomordik keeps her eyes on the slender, rosy Obtyosov. Attempting to prolong the slight adventure, the doctor orders soda, and Obtyosov thinks of seltzer-water. When the doctor asks for red wine to go into the seltzer-water, the men have an excuse to sit down at the counter, and the little flirtation progresses. Soon the chemist's wife is quite happy, and she even drinks some of the wine. At last the doctor suggests that the men return to camp. As Obtyosov pays the reckoning, he once again mentions the fact that the chemist is asleep.

When the officers leave, Mme Tchernomordik watches them walk a little distance, then stop and whisper. Obtyosov returns and rings the bell. This time, however, the chemist answers the door and sells the lozenges. Again, the chemist's wife watches; Obtyosov throws away the package of lozenges, the doctor joins him, and the two men then walk away. Angrily, Mme Tchernomordik tells her husband that she is unhappy and bursts into tears. He merely asks her to put away fourpence that he left on the counter and falls asleep again.

Themes and Meanings

Like many of Chekhov's stories, "The Chemist's Wife" deals with loneliness. Even the title is appropriate; Mme Tchernomordik has no name, either to her husband or to the officers who flirt with her. She is simply an appendage of the chemist. When Obtyosov returns to the shop, perhaps on a dare, he hopes to steal a few words, a kiss, perhaps something more, if the husband remains asleep. However, to him it is only a casual adventure, the stuff of military boasts. Seeing the older, ugly man to whom the pretty, young woman is married, he and the doctor have sensed an opportunity. Their approach to her, however, is purely a matter of whim and chance. They happen to be passing the shop after a party; they think of her. Her husband is asleep, and she answers the door. While they are with her, the conversation rambles, leading to no certain conclusion. Only Obtyosov's repeated comment that the chemist is asleep suggests the possibility of seduction. However, even his return is marked by irresolution; he and the doctor whisper at length before Obtyosov turns back toward the chemist's shop; on reaching the shop, the officer hesitates, passing back and forth in front of the door before finally ringing the bell. When by chance the chemist wakens and answers the summons, Obtyosov is easily defeated. When he throws away the lozenges he has been forced to purchase, he is throwing away the whim, the passing fancy for the chemist's wife. It really does not matter much to Obtyosov, nor, indeed, would have a brief relationship with her; that would have been quite as easy to discard.

To Tchernomordik, also, the young woman is unimportant. Early in the story, when she looks at him asleep, she thinks that nothing could waken him, not even an embrace. Suggestive though the officers' hints may be, the dreams of the chemist are only of business. Although Tchernomordik's dreams should not convict him of indifference toward his wife, his conduct when she announces her unhappiness and bursts into tears must do so, for he simply ignores her, worrying only about a few pennies that have been left on the counter. At the end of the story, his sleep is symbolic, for he is oblivious of the needs of his wife. When he goes to sleep, he discards her as clearly as Obtyosov did when he threw away the lozenges.

If both Obtyosov and Tchernomordik find it easy to turn away from the chemist's wife, however, she cannot discard the possibilities of a fuller life so easily. There is a depth to her emotions that neither man possesses. Her very unhappiness suggests her sensitivity, for she does not know what she lacks. Nor does she know what she wants, unlike Obtyosov, who wants a trivial adventure, and unlike Tchernomordik, who wants to make money and to sleep. While the officers stumble along unseeing in the dawn, the chemist's wife is responding to the flaming sun and to the red moon, which symbolize passion and adventure to her. Later, while the officers are flirting uncertainly, her emotions are violent. When she watches them whispering before Obtyosov returns, it is as if her fate is being decided, she thinks, again feeling intensely. At the end of the story, when nothing has happened, her tears are not casual but well up from a real agony in her heart.

The tragedy of the chemist's wife is not only that she is viewed merely as an object of desire or of convenience, as someone to flirt with or to put money in the till, but also that the men whose attention she seeks could never give her what she deserves. Thus her own sensitivity and her capacity for a passionate response to life have doomed her to loneliness.

Style and Technique

In Chekhov's play *Tri Sestry* (1901; *The Three Sisters*, 1920), the title characters dream of going to Moscow. At the end of the play, no one has gone to Moscow, and it is clear that no one ever will. Typically, in Chekhov's works, human beings dream, but the dreams are negated by life. In depicting life as a situation in which very little happens, Chekhov considered himself a realistic writer, in contrast to the melodramatic style of much nineteenth century literature. However, if, as in "The Chemist's Wife," very little external action occurs, in Chekhov's stories and plays there is much internal action. In revealing the emotional reactions of his characters to the slight external events, Chekhov deliberately avoided seeming to be involved, believing that his own detachment would actually produce more sympathy for characters such as the unhappy chemist's wife than would the typical nineteenth century authorial commentary.

Chekhov also differed from other realists, choosing merely to suggest setting rather than describing it in full detail. Thus, at the beginning of "The Chemist's Wife," four short sentences establish the stillness of the night, and the detail that makes it sharpest for readers is probably the brief mention of a dog's bark in the distance. The unlovely chemist is described snoring, with a flea on his nose; the officers are introduced with the sound of spurs. All the details are realistic, but they are sparse.

Finally, Chekhov typically used a small detail or a minor action at the end of a story to suggest a revelation that had come to a character or to forecast future action. At the end of "The Chemist's Wife," Mme Tchernomordik realizes not only that she is truly unhappy but also that no one is aware of the fact. As if to prove her point, the chemist asks her to see to his money and promptly falls asleep. There Chekhov stops the story. The chemist's wife has come to understand her own misery; the chemist is indifferent. It is suggested that Mme Tchernomordik's future will be no different from the moments that Chekhov has just described. Typically, she will not get to a metaphoric Moscow.

Rosemary M. Canfield Reisman

CHICKAMAUGA

Author: Ambrose Bierce (1842-1914?)
Type of plot: Psychological
Time of plot: The American Civil War
Locale: The Battle of Chickamauga
First published: 1891

> *Principal characters:*
> AN UNNAMED BOY, who is six years old
> CONFEDERATE SOLDIERS, who have suffered a defeat

The Story

There is actually only one character in this story—the six-year-old boy who wanders away from his home and gets lost in the forest—and even he is not individualized but rather is presented simply as "the child." When he encounters defeated soldiers in retreat from the Civil War battle of Chickamauga, his response to them is one only of childish curiosity. Although the soldiers are grotesquely wounded, maimed, and bleeding, the boy sees them as circus animals and clowns, and instead of being horrified, as the reader is, he is delighted at having someone with whom to play. He uses his toy sword to lead the men back whence he has come, leaving many of them dying in a river as he makes his way home. When he reaches his home, he discovers that it is burning and his mother is dead, her brains blown out by an artillery shell. The story ends with the boy making inarticulate cries—"a startling, soulless, unholy sound, the language of a devil." The reader's final shocking realization is that the child is a deaf-mute.

This climactic discovery "explains" the most striking aspect of the story—the disengaged and almost autistic response that the boy makes to the horrors of war. It is the gap between the boy's indifferent response and the reader's shock that gives the story the powerful impact that it has. Ambrose Bierce's most basic purpose here is to create an antiwar story; he does this by setting up a tension between an innocent, childish response to reality and an ironic adult one. The story begins with the narrator explaining that the boy is the son of a planter who had once been a soldier. As a result of the father's teaching the boy about war through books and pictures, the "warrior-fire" survives in the boy. In his play, he sees himself as the son of a heroic race, and he chases imaginary foes, putting all to death with his toy sword.

Thus, when the boy encounters the retreating soldiers, they become part of his play, creeping like babes instead of men through the forest. He has seen his father's slaves crawl on their hands and knees, playing horses with him; thus he crawls on the back of one of the dying men to ride him similarly. He laughs as he watches what to him is a merry spectacle and is as unaware as the men are of "the dramatic contrast between his laughter and their own ghastly gravity." Even when he returns to his burning home, he still reacts to the devastation as if it were merely spectacle, and he dances with glee around the fire, collecting more fuel to throw on the blaze. Only when he recognizes some of the buildings with "oddly familiar appearances, as if he had dreamed of them," does the plantation seem to swing around as if on a pivot, and he then realizes that it is his own home.

The fact that the boy is a deaf-mute emphasizes his childish fantasy world, detached from external reality, and makes more plausible the primary device of contrasting the child's view of war as a game with the adult's view of it as a horrifying actuality. It enables the author to set up a strange, dreamlike effect as the reader sees the events primarily from the boy's point of view. Even at the end of the story, the boy's inarticulate cries suggest a horrifying realization that goes beyond the ability of any language to express fully.

Themes and Meanings

The antiwar theme of Bierce's story depends on the basic tensions between the child world and the adult world and between fantasy and reality. The boy's fantasy world of playing at war is his only reality; consequently, when he encounters the genuine, external reality of war it seems curiously fantastic to him; thus he is able to integrate it effortlessly into his fantasy play world. Bierce develops the story on the ironic realization that the adult view of war often springs from childlike views in which men glorify battle in a heroic and fantasy image, only to find out too late that the reality of war is horror and death. This is a common antiwar convention, used in other Civil War stories, often in terms of the southern gallantry of noble knights who then confront the gritty and horrifying reality of battle. It was also a common device in World War I stories, in which young American men go off to fight the honorable battle and save the Old World only to confront the horrors of the muddy trenches of Europe. The primary communicators of this fantasy image of war in Bierce's story are books and pictures that glorify war, for the boy has been taught "postures of aggression and defense" by the "engraver's art." Thus when he encounters the actuality of war, the boy responds to it as he has to the fantasy pictures that he has seen and the world of play-reality that he has known.

Style and Technique

As is typical of many Bierce stories, style and technique are practically everything in "Chickamauga." Although he wrote during a period of American literature characterized by realistic depictions of external reality, Bierce maintained his allegiance to Romanticism. Often compared with the originator of the American short story, Edgar Allan Poe, Bierce focuses not so much on external reality as he does on the strange, dreamlike world that lies somewhere between fantasy and reality. Thus, the genius of his stories lies not in their theme, which is often fairly obvious, but in the delicate and tightly controlled way that Bierce tells the story, creating a playfully nightmarish world that involves the reader emotionally.

Perhaps the most interesting aspect of "Chickamauga" —the technique that creates its unforgettable effect—is Bierce's handling of point of view and tone. On the one hand, the story depends on Bierce's developing the perspective of the child, in which the reader is made to see the maimed and bleeding soldiers as circus clowns and child-like playmates for the boy. However, this point of view is balanced by that of an adult narrator, who counterpoints the boy's childish view, sometimes in a developed back-ground exposition, sometimes in a flat declarative statement. For example, when the boy seems to see some strange animals that he does not recognize crawling through the forest, the narrator simply says, "They were men." When the boy sees men lying in the water as if without heads, the narrator simply says, "They were drowned."

This narrator is not named in the story but is presented as a disembodied presence who not only sees what the boy sees but also sees the boy and draws conclusions about the boy's responses. The boy's mind is as inaccessible to the narrator as it is to the reader. This technique enables the reader to respond dually, both to the boy's point of view and to the adult narrator. As the narrator says about the scene witnessed by the boy, "not all of this did the child note; it is what would have been noted by an elder ob-server." Indeed, it is the elder observer who establishes the ironic tone at the beginning of the story that mocks the "warrior-fire," the heroic race, and the notion of a spirit of battle in the boy that make him born to "war and dominion as a heritage."

It is indeed the subtle tension between this adult point of view and the childish per-ception of the boy that creates the story's impact and reflects its theme. At one point in the story, when the boy goes to sleep and (because of his deafness) sleeps through the battle that rages nearby, the adult narrator says that he was as "heedless of the gran-deur of the struggle as the dead who had died to make the glory." Because of this struc-tural counterpoint, the narrator has no need to make any more explicit comment on the action. The juxtaposition of the two perspectives creates a tragic irony of war as some-thing more than a heroic and childish game, even as it makes the reader see how war, in order to persist, depends on precisely such a childish point of view. The boy is inno-cent in his playful point of view, but at the same time the playful point of view is what is responsible for the death of the men who surround the child.

Like many of Bierce's other stories, "Chickamauga" is meant to shock, to catch the reader up in a nightmarish reality. Also like many of his other stories, it is an artistic tour de force of romantic short fictional style. Bierce holds the reader suspended be-tween reality and fantasy until the final grotesque realization, which retrospectively illumines the story's restrained, ironic control.

Charles E. May

MASTERPLOTS II

SHORT STORY SERIES
REVISED EDITION

TITLE INDEX

TITLE INDEX

TITLE INDEX